BAGEHOT'S HISTORICAL ESSAYS

BAGEHOT'S
HISTORICAL ESSAYS

EDITED, WITH AN INTRODUCTION BY
Norman St. John-Stevas

NEW YORK UNIVERSITY PRESS
1966

This book was first published in 1965 by
Doubleday Anchor Books.

TABLE OF CONTENTS

INTRODUCTION

Walter Bagehot (1826–77)

Walter Bagehot, banker, economist, political thinker, critic, and man of letters, was Victorian England's most versatile genius. He was born at Langport, a small Somerset town on the river Parret on February 3, 1826. His father, Thomas Watson Bagehot, was a partner in Stuckey's bank, set up at Langport in 1772, which later became one of the country's first joint-stock banks. His mother, Edith Stuckey, was a niece of the Samuel Stuckey who originally founded the bank. Bagehot's relationship with his parents was extremely happy in childhood and remained so throughout his life. His happiness was marred only by the fits of insanity to which his mother was subject, "the dark realities" to which he sometimes refers cryptically in his essays, and which made him at times fear for his own mental stability. This secret sorrow tempered Bagehot's natural buoyancy, and he developed a vein of deep reserve. "Every trouble in life," he remarked later, "is a joke compared to madness."

Both his parents were religious, but they were divided by a difference of creed. A Socinian streak had emerged in the Bagehot family during the eighteenth century, and although it had been overlaid by subsequent orthodoxy, Thomas Bagehot had reverted to nonconformity and become a Unitarian. His wife, on the other hand, had been brought up in the Church of England and remained loyal to her childhood faith. Bagehot himself was always a religious man, "a thorough transcendentalist," as his friend Hutton called him, but the eclectic doctrinal atmosphere of his home, together with his own detached intelligence, prevented him from becoming a dogmatist.

Bagehot's father was determined that his son should enjoy the sound and liberal education which he himself had been denied, and after a period as a day boy at Langport Gram-

mar School, Walter was sent to Bristol College, where he
proved a brilliant student, and thanks to his mother's connections in the city was able to enter the learned circle led
by Dr. Carpenter, Dr. Addington Symonds, and Mr. Estlin,
which flourished in Clifton at the time. In 1842, when
he was sixteen, he went up to University College, London.
Oxford and Cambridge were ruled out because of the religious tests to which his father objected. It was no great
loss, since University College was a far more lively place than
the still unreformed ancient universities with their torpid
colleges, "hotels without bells," as Bagehot was later to describe them.

Bagehot's academic career was distinguished. A first class
in classics was followed by another first in philosophy and
the gold medal for intellectual and moral philosophy. His
period at University College was also remarkable for the close
friendships he formed with Richard Holt Hutton, later editor of the *Spectator*, Timothy Smith Osler, and William Roscoe, whose literary essays have recently been favourably re-
appraised. In November 1847, he published his first article,
in the *Prospective Review*, a review of Bailey's *Festus*, and
this was followed by essays on "The Currency Monopoly"
and "John Stuart Mill" in 1848. Bagehot was called to the
Bar but did not find it satisfactory, and in 1851, a prey to depression and anxiety and uncertain about his future, he left
London for Paris. He had timed his visit well, for in December Louis Napoleon's *coup d'état* provided ample distraction for his over-burdened mind.

From Paris he wrote seven brilliant letters for publication in the *Inquirer*, a Unitarian journal, which outraged
readers by eulogising the Catholic Church, defending Louis
Napoleon's use of force, attacking the freedom of the French
Press, and maintaining that the country was totally unfitted
for parliamentary government. "They were light and airy,"
wrote R. H. Hutton, "and even flippant, on a very grave subject. They made nothing of the Prince's perjury; and they
took impertinent liberties with all the dearest prepossessions
of the readers of the *Inquirer* and assumed their sympathy
just where Bagehot knew they would be most revolted by his
opinions." Whatever their effect on readers, they proved a
therapy for Bagehot, and he returned to England in 1852
refreshed and invigorated, resolved to leave the Bar and enter
the family bank.

Bagehot was much influenced in his choice of banking by the prospect it offered him of leisure to write, although he never thought of becoming a professional writer. During the fifties he published some of his best essays on Hartley Coleridge, Shakespeare, and Bishop Butler in the *Prospective Review*, and when it failed, in the *National*. The *National Review* was founded by Bagehot and Hutton, and they edited it jointly. In its pages appeared Bagehot's essays on Gibbon, Brougham, Peel, and Gladstone and critical assessments of Milton, Scott, Cowper, Dickens, and Thackeray, as well as articles on religion and economics. In 1864 the *National* went out of existence.

In 1857 Bagehot became friendly with James Wilson, founder and proprietor of *The Economist*, and began to contribute to the paper. In the same year he became engaged to Wilson's eldest daughter, Eliza, whom he married in 1858. Bagehot's fame slowly increased. His collected essays were published in 1858 under the forbidding title, *Estimates of Some Englishmen and Scotchmen*, but partly because of this did not attract much attention at the time. In 1859, however, he became a celebrity, thanks to his article on Parliamentary Reform, published in the *National Review*, in which he advocated a moderate reform of the franchise to give greater weight to the *growing* as opposed to the *stationary* part of the country. So much praise was lavished on the article (reproduced later in this volume) that in February Bagehot brought it out as a pamphlet, and it aroused even greater interest. In March, James Wilson gave a dinner in his honour which was attended amongst others by Lord Grey, Lord Granville, Robert Lowe, George Cornewall Lewis, and Thackeray. "It will really be fine collection of public animals," wrote Bagehot to his wife.

In August 1859, James Wilson was appointed Chancellor of the Indian Exchequer, and, expecting to be away for five years, he appointed Bagehot to act as director of *The Economist*, retaining Hutton as editor for the period of the visit, but in August 1860, Wilson contracted dysentery in India and died. Bagehot was then appointed permanent director of *The Economist* and in 1861 Hutton resigned the editorship which Bagehot took on as well. The change was more nominal than real since Bagehot had been virtually acting as editor. From 1859 to 1877 he contributed two articles every week to *The Economist* on current affairs. Through his

editorship of the paper he became one of the most influential
financial journalists in London, constantly consulted by Gladstone and other ministers, "a kind of supplementary Chancellor of the Exchequer" as Woodrow Wilson has described
him.

The year 1865 saw the Banks Notes Issue Bill being modified in accordance with Bagehot's advice, and in the same
year he was invited to Paris to give evidence before the committee set up to inquire into the principles governing mone-
tary circulation and credit. The year was also memorable for
the appearance of the first part of what was later to become
his most famous work, *The English Constitution*. The first
part was published in the first issue of the *Fortnightly Review*, the whole being spread out over eighteen months, and
in 1867 it was published in book form. *Physics and Politics*,
an application of modified Darwinian doctrines to politics
and the growth of societies, was published in similar manner,
the first part appearing in the *Fortnightly* on November 1,
1867, and the whole coming out in book form in 1872.

In middle life Bagehot made a number of attempts to enter Parliament, but they were not successful. In 1860 he allowed his name to go forward as candidate for London University, but he was not adopted. Five years later he agreed
to allow his name to go forward for Manchester, but again
was unsuccessful. His electoral career is tersely disposed of
in his wife's diary. "Walter spoke at a meeting in the Town
Hall at Manchester but was badly received and gave up standing." Bagehot wrote to a friend: "I had a letter from Mr
Gladstone recommending me, but it was of no use. They
said: 'If he is so celebrated, why does not not Finsbury elect
him.'" On Bagehot's third attempt he did become a candidate and contested the Bridgwater division of Somerset in
1866 as a Liberal, but was defeated by 301 votes to 294.
Bribery had been rampant, and Bridgwater was later disfranchised. In 1867 Hutton made another attempt to secure
Bagehot the London University seat, but once again he was
rejected and the seat went to Robert Lowe. After this Bagehot gave up the idea of entering Parliament.

Failure to get into Parliament meant that Bagehot could
concentrate on his writing. In 1873 he published *Lombard
Street*, a study of the London money market that has become
a classic. During 1875 and 1876 he was busily engaged in
economic and financial affairs. In July 1875 he was invited

to give evidence before the committee on banks of issue and through this formed a close friendship with Sir Stafford Northcote. He began work on a study of the English economy which was planned to run into three volumes but was never completed. A first instalment appeared in the *Fortnightly* in early 1876 under the title "The Postulates of English Political Economy." The second volume was to be made up of biographies of eminent economists, but only a few of these, including Adam Smith, Malthus, and Ricardo, were written. After his death, these and other essays, together with some articles in note form, were pieced together by Richard Hutton and Sir Robert Giffen, who had been Bagehot's assistant on *The Economist*, and published as *Economic Studies*. During 1876 he also wrote a series of seventeen articles on the depreciation of silver which was reprinted as a pamphlet. His last article in the *Fortnightly*, "Lord Althorp and the Reform Act of 1832," was published in November 1876. His last practical contribution to economics was made early in 1877, when he was consulted by Sir Stafford Northcote, who was perplexed by the fall in public support for Exchequer Bills at a time when the government was in need of money, owing to an expensive programme of educational and sanitary reform. Bagehot promptly invented the Treasury Bills, which have been in use ever since.

The winter of 1876–77 was passed in a new house in Queen's Gate Place in London where he worked on his *Economic Studies*, and in March Bagehot contracted a chill. Realising perhaps that death was near, he made the journey to his father's house at Herd's Hill Somerset, where he had been born. By March 23 he was gravely ill and the doctor diagnosed congestion of the lung. Bagehot amused himself by reading *Rob Roy*, but as the day passed he grew weaker and died peacefully as the sun was setting. He is buried in the churchyard at Langport overlooking the valley of the river Parret and the Somerset country that he loved. When the news of his death became known, appreciations and tributes from his friends and leading contemporaries flowed into Herd's Hill. "I should never have known how great a man Walter was," remarked his father, "had I not survived him."

The appeal of Bagehot, both as a man and as a writer, is irresistible. He combined a mind of extraordinary keenness and subtlety with a nature dominated by deep and passionate feeling. In this he was akin to Newman, of whom he was

a life-long admirer. Intellectual detachment stamps all his
work, yet from his youth he was immersed in the world of
affairs both as a banker and as an editor. Aware of the limitations of both the business and social worlds, he never had the
narrow-mindedness to despise them. Business, he always
maintained, was much more enjoyable than pleasure, because
it commanded the whole, and not part, of man. Society always appealed to him and he appreciated with zest "the
grand *shine* on the surface of life." For this he commended
Béranger and Horace: "Both enjoy the roll of wheels; both
love the glitter of the carriages: neither is angry at the sun."
He had little sympathy with the Victorian cult of ceaseless
activity, but no thinker has been more convinced of the value
of activity as a basis for the life of the mind. The theme of
the educative efficacy of affairs recurs throughout his works.
"The exclusive devotion to books tires," he writes in his essay
on Macaulay. "We require to love and hate, to act and live."
He ridiculed Carlyle's dictum that the "true University of
this day is a collection of books" as being true "if you wish to
form a bookworm but not else." The uniqueness of Bagehot
as a man and his distinction as a writer can both be traced to
this capacity to bridge the gulf between the practical and intellectual worlds, so that the opposing impulses in his character made for unity rather than for division. What was peculiarly his own, as G. M. Young has noted, was the perfect
management of all his energy and resources.

Bagehot's character—its freshness and originality—is reflected in his style. "You receive stimulation from him,"
wrote Woodrow Wilson, "and a certain feeling of elation.
There is a fresh air stirring in all his utterances that is unspeakably refreshing." There is only one way to experience
the truth of this and that is to read Bagehot for oneself. He
is not a writer who lends himself to commentary. He is a
writer to be read. His style has all the merits of good conversation: it is vivid, discursive, and witty. Those who knew him
witness that as a conversationalist he was even more brilliant
than as a writer.

"He was," recalled Lord Bryce, "some of us used to think
far back in the seventies, the most interesting man in London
to meet, so bright and stimulating was his conversation. It
was always conversation, never declamation or lecturing. He
could listen as well as talk." Talk with Bagehot, remarked
William Roscoe, was "like riding a horse with a perfect

mouth." Fragments of his conversation have come down to us. On one occasion while strolling round a friend's estate he remarked: "Ah, you've got the church in the grounds. It's well the tenants shouldn't be *quite* sure that the landlord's power stops with this world." On another he told someone that when in low spirits it cheered him to go down to the bank and dabble his hand in a heap of sovereigns. Helen Gladstone, who met him in the sixties, recalls that he told her "he knew what a nut felt like when it was going to be cracked, as he once got his head caught between a cart-shed and a lamp post." It was Bagehot who, during a lecture on literature to the Langport Literary and Scientific Institution, told his audience to make it a rule to read the whole of *The Times* every day, including the advertisements. Then, he assured them, they would know "what the world was really about." Again, it was Bagehot who in a flash of animation invented the word "padding." I had the good fortune some years ago to meet Mr. Guy Barrington, Bagehot's nephew, when he was eighty-nine. The one thing he could remember about his uncle was an incident at breakfast when he was aged eight or nine. He had difficulty in opening his egg, and Bagehot encouraged him to greater efforts, saying, "Go on, Guy. Hit it hard on the head. It has no friends."

Bagehot brought to his writing every kind of equipment save that of the professional literary critic or the trained historian. By education a classicist and philosopher, he supplemented this formal training by voracious reading until the end of his life. Such a reader, as he himself points out in his essay on Bishop Butler, "is apt when he comes to write, to exhibit his reading in casual references and careless innuendoes, which run out insensibly from the fullness of his literary memory." This gives a richness to his style. As banker and editor he knew men and the world of law, politics, and commerce. He used this knowledge to illustrate and give body to his historical and literary judgments. "The reason why so few good books are written," he says caustically in his essay on Shakespeare, "is that so few people that can write know anything. In general an author has always lived in a room, has read books, has cultivated science, is acquainted with the style and sentiments of the best authors, but he is out of the way of employing his own eyes and ears. He has nothing to hear and nothing to see. His life is a vacuum." Southey's life typified for Bagehot the bloodless existence of the literary

man. "He wrote poetry (as if anybody could) before breakfast: he read during breakfast."

Bagehot's style is remarkable for its wealth of epigram,
which seems to have risen spontaneously in his mind. Queen
Anne was "one of the smallest people ever set in a great
place"; George III "a consecrated obstruction"; Swift, "a detective in a dean's wig"; Palmerston was "not a common man
but a common man might have been cut out of him." Gladstone had "the soul of a martyr with the intellect of an advocate." Brougham had a quality which ordinary men called
"devil." He had a "glare" in his eye. "If he were a horse nobody would buy him; with that eye, no one would answer
for his temper." He had the faculty of easy anger—"like an
Englishman on the Continent, he is ready to blow up anyone." Sydney Smith was "an after-dinner writer." Hartley
Coleridge "was not like the Duke of Wellington—To the
Duke of Wellington a coat was a coat." John Newton, who
took the unfortunate William Cowper in hand, "was one of
those men who seem intended to make excellence disagreeable. He was a converting engine." Macaulay regarded "existing men as painful prerequisites of great grandchildren."

Bagehot expressed his surprise that Bishop Butler should
ever have achieved a mitre: "In general we observe that
those become most eminent in the sheepfold who partake
most eminently of the qualities of the wolf." On broader
themes his touch was as sure: "The defect of *Paradise Lost*
is that, after all, it is founded on a *political* transaction."
Milton has "made God argue." As to the battle between Sa-
tan and our first parents: "It is as if any army should invest a
cottage." Elsewhere he reflects that the French treat "deduction as a game, induction as a grievance," while the English can think only in terms of committees: "we are born with
a belief in a green cloth, clean pens, and twelve men with
grey hair. In topics of belief the ultimate standard is the
jury."

Bagehot, as some of his contemporaries saw him, and as
we see him through his political and historical essays in particular, was a sardonic, no-nonsense, experienced man of the
world. But there was Bagehot's other self, closer to the "dark
realities" of life, which, perhaps for that reason, he sheered
away from in later life: the passionate, mystical Bagehot,
known only to his wife and possibly to a few of his intimate
friends, whom we know chiefly by tantalising glimpses in his

literary essays. "We see but one aspect of our neighbour," writes Bagehot, "as we see but one side of the moon: in either case there is also a dark half which is unknown to us. We all come down to dinner, but each has a room to himself."

Bagehot, the mystic, is not to be found in his political, historical, and economic writings, which reflect Bagehot the man of the world. But, mercifully, Bagehot the wit is not excluded. His *English Constitution* is not only interesting and readable but diverting. Other writers may have written more learnedly on the English Constitution, but no one else has succeeded in making it amusing. Yet Bagehot's political and historical writings are very much more than *jeux d'esprit*. *The English Constitution* is a sustained and masterly observation of how the British political system actually works, full of brilliant insights into contemporary political life, many of which remain applicable today.

The English Constitution deals with legal and political facts, but Bagehot always connected them with the social and psychological realities that they reflect. The same is true of his more ambitious work, *Physics and Politics*, "that golden little book," as William James called it, in which Bagehot sets out to trace the laws governing the rise and decline of human societies. Until it was written, as Alastair Buchan has pointed out, it was still possible "to consider political institutions in moral terms without reference to the level of political consciousness and cohesion of the societies for whom they were intended." "The cake of custom," wearisomely accumulated, Bagehot stresses, is society's earliest treasure, but to advance, a breakaway has to be made, and in this ability to adapt, Bagehot finds the difference between progressive and stagnant societies.

Physics and Politics indicates one base of Bagehot's conservatism, his consciousness of the achievement and advance that any form of society represents. Another was his sense of reality. "Germans deny it," he writes in his essay on Gibbon, "but in every country common opinions are very common. Everywhere, there exists the comfortable mass; quiet, sagacious, short-sighted—such as the Jews whom Rabshakeh tempted by their vine and their fig-tree, such as the English with their snug dining-room and after-dinner nap, domestic happiness and Bullo coal; sensible, solid men, without stretching irritable reason, but with a placid, supine instinct;

without originality and without folly; judicious in their dealings, respected in the world; wanting little, sacrificing nothing;
good tempered people in a word, caring for nothing until
they are themselves hurt." This "commonness" or "stupidity,"
as he calls it in his *Letters on the French Coup d'État*, is an
indispensable prerequisite for political stability. The coarse
English nature has it, but the French does not.

Bagehot was also directed towards conservatism by the distrust of precipitate action, which he learned from his friend
Clough and which was confirmed by his sense of history.
Furthermore, deep in his character lay a vein of cynicism.
The cynic's merit, as Leslie Stephen says, is to see facts, and
those who see facts tend to be conservative. Not that there
was anything "Eldonine" about Bagehot's conservatism. He
did not make an idol out of the status quo. In fact he favoured individual reforms and all his life was an official
Liberal. Yet he had no sympathy with reforming enthusiasms.
"I hate these Liberal enthusiasts," he is recorded as saying to
Lord Morley. "I feel like saying, 'Go home sir and take a dose
of salts and see if it won't wash it all out of you.'"

Bagehot had no sympathy with the masses of men, and his
conservatism sprang in part from lack of compassion. From
time to time one gets a glimpse of his harshness in his essays.
"Ugly men are and ought to be ashamed of their existence,"
he says in his essay on Milton. He praises Scott's sympathetic treatment of the poor in his novels but adds: "The requirements of the case present an unusual difficulty to artistic delineation: a good deal of the character of the poor is
an unfit topic for continuous art, and yet we wish to have in
our books a life-like exhibition of the whole of that character.
Mean manners and mean vices are unfit for prolonged delineation: the everyday pressure of narrow necessities is too
petty a pain and too anxious a reality to be dwelt on." No
one who felt strongly about the poor could write like that.
One cannot imagine Dickens making such a remark, and it
is significant that Bagehot disliked Dickens' political creed,
despising him as an exponent of "sentimental radicalism."
Bagehot saw as clearly as Dickens the sufferings, the failures,
and the miseries of the poor, but he accepted them as inevitable. "The difficulty in truth," he says in his essay on
Cowper, "is in the existence of the world. It is the fact, that
by the constitution of society the bold, the vigorous, and the
buoyant, rise and rule; and that the weak, the shrinking, and

the timid, fall and serve." Yet there was still another side to Bagehot's conservatism, more agreeable than this doctrine of the survival of the fittest—the conservatism of the cavalier. It drew him to Scott. It was based on reverence, and love, and contentment, rather than on fear. "The essence of Toryism," Bagehot once wrote, "is enjoyment."

Presenting a selection of Bagehot's writings is peculiarly difficult in that while he ranged over a vast field, literary, political, historical, and economic, there is a wide degree of overlap, and the essays refuse to be fitted into a neat and tidy classification. Bagehot's first editor, Richard Hutton, divided the essays into literary and biographical, but it was not a happy division, many of the so-called literary essays being in fact biographical in character. A better division, although it can be faulted, is into literary and historical, with two further divisions of political and economic. The present selection excludes *The English Constitution* and *Physics and Politics* as well as a great number of political essays. None of the economic essays has been included. The majority of the essays present statesmen of the eighteenth and nineteenth centuries. Bagehot had, of course, no direct experience of the eighteenth century, but unlike so many of his contemporaries he viewed the period with sympathetic interest. The nineteenth-century portraits have a more immediate interest since they give a contemporary assessment of the virtues and defects of their subjects, and many of them were known to Bagehot personally. Bagehot's views on the reform issue, which dominated English mid-nineteenth-century domestic politics, are given in his essay *Parliamentary Reform*, published in 1859; his views on the United States and the American Constitution, in the essay entitled *The American Constitution at the Present Crisis*, written in 1861 at the beginning of the Civil War. Finally Bagehot's views on Napoleon III and France are given in his *Letters on the French Coup d'État*, and in subsequent essays.

The first essay in this volume, entitled "Bolingbroke as a Statesman," admirably illustrates Bagehot's historical method. Bagehot was primarily interested in the character of those he wrote about, which in part explains why his essays still retain their interest, and this one is a brilliant example of connecting the character of the man with his success and failure in politics.

"We see in Bolingbroke's case," he writes, "that a life of

brilliant license is really compatible with a life of brilliant
statesmanship; that license itself may even be thought to
quicken the imagination for oratorical efforts; that an intellect similarly aroused may, at exciting conjectures, perceive
possibilities which are hidden from duller men; that the favourite of society will be able to use his companionship with
men and his power over women so much as to aid his strokes
of policy; but, on the other hand that these secondary aids
and occasional advantages are purchased by the total sacrifice of a primary necessity; that a life of great excitement is
incompatible with the calm circumspection and the sound
estimate of probability essential to great affairs; that though
the excited hero may perceive distant things which others
overlook, he will overlook near things that others see; that
though he may be stimulated to great speeches which others
would not; that he will attract enmities but not confidence;
that he will not observe how few and plain are the alternatives of common business, and how little even genius can enlarge them; that his prosperity will be a wild dream of unattainable possibilities, and his adversity a long regret that
those possibilities have departed. At any rate, such was Bolingbroke's career."

Poor Bolingbroke! After that paragraph one feels that there
is nothing more to be said about him.

Bagehot also wrote of William Pitt and found the secret of
his greatness in his combination of high administrative gifts
with the commanding temperament of a great dictator. According to Bagehot, representative government gives an opportunity and a career to two kinds of statesmen, dictators
and administrators, and it was Pitt's good fortune to combine
some of the best qualities of both, although Bagehot is careful to point out that he did not possess a creative intellect.
He did, however, have a gift rare among politicians, which
Bagehot fully appreciated: a developed sense of humour.

Bagehot's first portrait of a nineteenth-century statesman
was his study of Brougham, and it is brilliantly etched.
Brougham's genius was to be a successful agitator, and the
first part of his career was crowned with high success since
his gifts admirably suited the times. Reform dominated the
English political scene after the long years of Tory reaction
against the French Revolution and Napoleon, and Brougham
was in his element. "In later life," writes Bagehot, "his natural gifts were not so suited to his circumstances. There was

something unfitting—so it was thought and so perhaps it was
—in making a great agitator Lord Chancellor; it seemed like
making a field preacher Archbishop of Canterbury." In dealing with Brougham's appointment as Lord Chancellor, Bagehot's impish humour is seen at its best. "He was too mobile;
you could not fancy him droning. He had attacked Lord Eldon during many years, of course; but did he know law? He
was a most active person; would he sit *still* upon the woolsack? Of his inattention to his profession men circulated idle
tales. 'Pity he hadn't known a little law, and then he would
have known a little of everything', was the remark of one
who certainly knows only one thing. A more circumstantial
person recounted that when Brougham had been a pupil of
Sir Nicholas Tindal, in the Temple, an uncle of his, having
high hopes of his ability, asked the latter: 'I hope my nephew
is giving himself up, soul and body to his profession' 'I do
not know anything', replied the distinct special-pleader, 'as
to his *soul*, but his body is very seldom in my chambers.'
. . . Mr Brougham was a hero; Lord Brougham was 'a
necessity.' It was like Disraeli being Chancellor of the Exchequer."

In Sir Robert Peel, Bagehot found a graver subject for
study. For Bagehot, Peel was the ideal of a constitutional
statesman, "a man of common opinions and uncommon abilities." Bagehot divides Peel's career into two halves, for the
first of which he was the nominee of the nobility, the general manager who carried out the wishes of the directors of
the firm. In the second part, Peel became the representative
of the new dynasty, the middle class, with whom he wholly
identified himself. Peel, as Bagehot clearly saw, was not a
great thinker, but he "became what nature designed, a great
agent." Bagehot's epitome of Peel is as devastating in its way
as his summing up of Bolingbroke:

"If we picture in our minds a nature at once active and
facile, easily acquiring its opinions from without, not easily
devising them from within, a large placid adaptive intellect,
devoid of irritable intense originality, prone to forget the
ideas of yesterday, inclined to accept the ideas of today—if
we imagine a man so formed cast early into absorbing, exhausting industry of detail, with work enough to fill up a
life, with action of itself enough to render speculation almost
impossible—placed too in a position unsuited to abstract
thought, of which the conventions and rules require that a

man should feign other men's thoughts, should impugn his own opinions—we shall begin to imagine a conscientious man destitute of convictions on the occupations of his life—to comprehend the character of Sir Robert Peel."

Such a man was ideally suited to represent the middle classes, whose political instinct and contribution to social stability Bagehot fully appreciated, but whose limited outlook Bagehot could not resist mocking. As he writes of them in his essay on Peel: "Original theories give trouble; besides a grave man on the coal exchange does not desire to be an apostle of novelties amongst the contemporaneous dealers in fuel; he wants to be provided with remarks he can make on the topics of the day which will not be known *not* to be his; that are not too profound; which he can fancy the paper only reminded him of."

This passage, as do so many others that the reader will find in the following essays, illustrates Bagehot's ironical sense of humour. There was nothing Swiftian or savage about Bagehot's irony, nothing cruel. He was an extraordinarily tolerant man, amused by but not contemptuous of the men of business surrounding him who thought they understood what the world was really about. He describes his own attitude exactly in his essay on Shakespeare when he writes: "It is within the limits of what may be called malevolent sense, to take extreme and habitual pleasure in remarking the foolish opinions, the narrow notions, and fallacious deductions which seem to cling to the pompous and prosperous man of business." His irony was always tempered by his sense of fun as this passage from his essay on Browning shows: "From a defect, partly of subject, and partly of style, many of Mr Browning's works make a demand upon the reader's zeal and sense of duty to which the nature of most readers is unequal. They have on the turf the convenient expression 'staying power;' some horses can hold on and others cannot. But hardly any reader not of especial and peculiar nature can hold on through such composition. There is not enough 'staying power' in human nature."

Bagehot called the ludicrous "the imagination of common life." His own antithetical sense of humour had a metaphysical foundation. "A universe," he writes, "in which Dignity No. I conversed decorously with Dignity No. II on topics befitting their state would be perhaps a levée of great intellects and a tea-table of enormous thoughts; but it would want the best charm of this earth—the medley of great things and little, of things mundane and things celestial, things low and things awful, of things eternal and things half a minute." This sense of the contrast between the nature of the human mind and its employments was at the root of Bagehot's humour. "How," he asks, "can a soul be a merchant? What relation to an immortal being have the price of linseed, the fall of butter, the tare on tallow, or the brokerage on hemp? Can an undying creature debit *petty expenses* and charge for *carriage paid?* . . . The soul ties its shoes; the mind washes its hands in a basin. All is incongruous."

Not even Bagehot could find much that was humorous in Gladstone's character, and his essay on the grand old man, written when he was in mid-career, lacks the brilliance and sprightliness of most of his other essays. Bagehot knew Gladstone, they discussed financial matters, and Bagehot seemed a little nervous when he wrote his assessment of him in 1860. "We believe," his essay opens a little defensively, "that Quarterly essayists have a peculiar mission in relation to the characters of public men. We believe it is their duty to be personal." Bagehot proceeded to be critically personal but not offensively so, and Gladstone was not offended. Years later he wrote to Bagehot's wife: "I remember feeling, and I still feel, how true the article on myself is in the parts least favourable to my vanity." Gladstone's financial genius was clear by the time of Bagehot's first essay. His first great budget of 1853 had established his reputation, and Bagehot fully appreciated this aspect of his greatness, but he was still unsure whether he would make a great national leader. Gladstone was an enigma: "Who can tell whether he will be the greatest orator of a great administration; whether he will rule the House of Commons; whether he will be, as his gifts at first sight mark him out to be, our greatest statesman? or whether, below the gangway, he will utter unintelligible discourses; will aid in destroying many ministries and share in none; will pour forth during many hopeless years a bitter, a splendid, and a vituperative eloquence?"

Bagehot analysed Gladstone's intellectual inconsistency sharply but fairly and traced it back to his first "Oxford" creed, which he formulated in his work on the relationship between Church and State and then had to modify in order not to be cut off from the dominant intellectual and political movements of his times. He was forced to expend great in-

tellectual energy in presenting to the world (and himself)
as a development what was in fact a total repudiation. He
needed, as Bagehot saw, a settled and plain creed, an overruling principle, but Oxford had prevented him from having
one. Accordingly Bagehot concluded that Gladstone was a
man who could not impose his creed on his time: "he must
learn the creed *of* his time." Bagehot was afraid that Gladstone might learn the wrong creed. "A statesman who will
hereafter learn what our real public opinion is, will not have
to regard loud agitators, but to disregard them; will not have
to yield to a loud voice, but to listen for a still small voice;
will have to seek for the opinion which is treasured in secret
rather than for that which is noised abroad. If Mr Gladstone
will accept the conditions of his age; if he will guide himself
by the mature, settled, and cultured reflection of his time,
and not by its loud and noisy organs; if he will look for
that which is thought, rather than for that which is said—he
may leave a great name, be useful to his country, may
steady and balance his own mind. But if not, not."

For Gladstone's programme of moderate and constructive
reform Bagehot had both sympathy and admiration. Gladstone's first ministry with its impressive record of reform in
Ireland, education, the Civil Service, and the Army, earned
his approval. Bagehot's commendation of the ministry when
it finally came to an end in 1874 was warm. Gladstone's
espousal of the cause of democracy was, on the other hand,
not approved by Bagehot. In 1865 Gladstone had enunciated
his doctrine that "every man who is not presumably incapacitated by some consideration of unfitness or of political
danger is morally entitled to come within the pale of the
constitution" and this and the subsequent abortive Liberal
legislative attempts at reform paved the way for the Disraeli
Reform Act of 1867, which Bagehot detested.

Gladstone's gift for oratory—and the didactic and contentious impulses that lay behind it—was fully appreciated by
Bagehot. "He longs to pour forth his own belief; he cannot
rest till he has contradicted everyone else." Bagehot was also
quick to see the significance of Gladstone's speech at Greenwich in 1871, when he addressed a mass meeting of 25,000
constituents, speaking for nearly two hours, bareheaded in
the rain. It marked, wrote Bagehot, a new era in English politics: "the coming of a time when it will be one of the most
important qualifications of a Prime Minister to exert a di-

rect control over the masses—when the ability to reach them, not as his views may be filtered through an intermediate class of political teachers and writers, but *directly* by the vitality of his own mind, will give a vast advantage in the political race to any statesman." Bagehot did not care for this development, but he grasped its importance. What Bagehot did not foresee was Gladstone's conversion to the principle of Home Rule; had he done so his disapproval would have been profound.

Bagehot's assessments of Gladstone may have been astringent, but they were never unfair; the same cannot be said of his judgments of Disraeli. Where Disraeli was concerned, Bagehot's detachment, in other respects so conspicuous, deserted him. In part this was the dislike of a Liberal for a Conservative, of an insider for an outsider (although Bagehot professed his admiration for the way Disraeli had risen through his own talents); but Bagehot's feelings went deeper. He had a profound distrust of Disraeli's character: he thought him an adventurer with no profound convictions, lacking the gravity and seriousness that Bagehot often mocked, but that he thought essential to a British statesman. For Bagehot Disraeli was always a litterateur who had strayed into politics; his success stemmed from "his very unusual capacity for *applying* a literary genius, in itself limited, to the practical purposes of daily life." Bagehot was convinced that Disraeli had little capacity for sustained hard work: "if you ask such a man to regulate the stupendous business of Parliament—to arrange, and if possible effect, the most complex *agenda* that ever was in the world—failure is inevitable. It is like entering a light hack for a ploughing match."

Bagehot was intrigued by what he called "the great Asian mystery" of how a man like Disraeli could have become the leader of a party of squires and landowners. He found the key in Disraeli's ability to articulate the feelings of his speechless followers. In Bagehot's day the Tory party was still dominated by the landed interest and drew a great part of its strength from the counties. To be a county member required a residential qualification, and this ensured that the squirearchy would be represented by members of its own class. This was Disraeli's opportunity, and he took it. Bagehot ironically appraised the utility of having a party leader who shared few of his followers' prejudices. "It has been Mr Disraeli's misfortune throughout his main political career to lead a party of very strong prejudices and principles, without feeling himself any cordial sympathy with either the one or the other. No doubt that is precisely the fact which has enabled him on most great emergencies to be of use to his party. His completely external intelligence has been to them what the elephant driver's—the mahout's—is to the elephant, comparatively insignificant as a force, but so familiar with all the habits of the creature which his sagacity has to guide, and so entirely, if it only knew, at its mercy, that all his acuteness is displayed in contriving to turn the creature's habits and instinct to his own end, profit and advantage,—which, however, cannot be done without also carefully preserving the creature itself from great dangers, and guarding it against the violence of its own passions. In this way Mr Disraeli has necessarily been of great use to the Tory party."

Bagehot, who was almost obsessed with the "tone" of political discussion, was alienated from Disraeli by his showiness, his "false melodramatic taste." This prevented him from seeing the substructure of principle that underlay Disraeli's policies. He never for a moment suspected the hold that Disraeli would exercise on the imagination of later generations of Tory thinkers and leaders; he grossly underestimated his influence on his own times. "He had," wrote Bagehot, "no influence with the country. Such a vast power over Englishmen as has been possessed by Lord Palmerston and by Mr Gladstone was out of his way altogether. Between Mr Disraeli and common Englishmen there was too broad a gulf—too great a difference. He was simply unintelligible to them. 'Ten miles from London,' to use the old phrase, there is scarcely any real conception of him."

Disraeli's ambitious foreign policy did not commend itself to Bagehot: *The Economist* was suspicious of the purchase of the Suez Canal shares in 1876 and quick to expose the risk of foreign entanglements that the investment involved. Imperialism was no less unwelcome, and Bagehot wrote a crabby article when the Queen became Empress of India in 1876. His full fury, however, was reserved for the Reform Act of 1867, which greatly extended the suffrage and for which Disraeli was principally responsible. Bagehot had no doubt about Disraeli's expedient motives: "Mr Disraeli all along wished to go down very low, to beat the Whigs—if possible the Radicals too—by basing the support of the Conservative party upon a lower class than those which they

could influence. For this end he induced his party to surrender their creed and their policy; he altered what his followers had to say, even more than the Constitution under
which they are going to live." The only points Bagehot admitted in Disraeli's favour were that he was skillful at managing Parliament and distributing the offices in his administration. The "Dizzy" affectionately held in reverence by the
nation and fascinating to posterity escaped him.

Bagehot castigated the Reform Act of 1867 as "mischievous
and monstrous." He feared that middle-class hegemony would
be destroyed and the way opened for political domination by
a largely illiterate working class. Bagehot's views on democracy were closely akin to those of Robert Lowe, and he reacted to its arrival with the same prophetic pessimism. To
Bagehot the idea that the ignorant should govern the instructed was irrational and unacceptable. Fitness to govern
was not a quality found equally in every individual, and
Bagehot passionately believed in the political virtues of the
middle class of his day. He saw the need to counter ultra-
democratic theory, and in his pamphlet of 1859 on parliamentary reform formulated a law of relative rights of partici-
pation in government, which he hoped would do it. In fact,
the pamphlet was only a stick to stop a flood but it has considerable interest as one of the last attempts by a first-class
intellect to justify the mid-Victorian status quo before advancing egalitarianism carried everything before it.

"A savage chief," wrote Bagehot, "may be capable of
governing a savage tribe; he may have the right of governing
it, for he may be the sole person capable of so doing; but he
would have no right to govern England. We must look likewise to the competitors for the sovereignty. Whatever may be
your capacity for rule, you have no right to obtain the opportunity of exercising it by dethroning a person who is *more*
capable. You are wronging the community if you do; for you
are depriving it of a better government than that which you
can give to it. You are wronging also the ruler you supersede; for you are depriving him of the exercise of his faculties. Two wrongs are thus committed from a fancied idea
that abstract capacity gives a right to rule irrespective of
comparative relations. The true principle is that every person
has a right to 'so much political power as he can exercise
without impeding any other person who would fitly exercise
more.' "

Every section and class of the community should be represented in Parliament, but not in proportion to its numerical strength, for this would inevitably result in domination by the working class.[1] Free government succeeded in England only because England was a "deferential" nation. By "deferential" Bagehot meant that the lower orders were content that the predominant, although not the exclusive, power in the state should rest with the higher classes, to whom the actual government of the country was entrusted. "Where no one knows, or cares for, or respects any one else," he wrote in *The English Constitution*, "all must rank equal; no one's opinion can be more potent than that of another. But, as has been explained, a deferential nation has a structure of its own. Certain persons are by common consent agreed to be wiser than others, and their opinion is by consent to rank for much more than its numerical value. We may in these happy nations weigh votes as well as count them, though in less favoured countries we can count only."

Bagehot set his face against democracy and articulated the fears of many members of the middle class of his time. The great interest and approval aroused by Lowe's speeches and Bagehot's pamphlet show how deeply the middle class feared democracy. Yet Bagehot was no Eldon and favoured moderate parliamentary reform. He approved of the Reform Act of 1832, which had transferred power from certain special classes to "the general aggregate of fairly instructed men," but saw that by mid-century changes in the 1832 settlement were necessary. The distribution of seats was out of date, giving

[1] W. M. McGovern in his study "Social Darwinists and their Allies," which appeared in *From Luther to Hitler*, published in Boston in 1941, presents Bagehot as a thinker who anticipated Fascist ideology on the corporate state. Like Bagehot, Fascist theorists put forward ideas to constitute legislatures on the basis of interests, but they pushed these ideas to extremes that Bagehot never approached. One example of Bagehot's modification of the concept of a legislature of interests must suffice. It was published in an article in *The Economist* on July 22, 1865, when Oxford had rejected Mr. Gladstone. "There ought," he wrote, "to be some special constituencies in Parliament for every such special type of thought—some for the shipowner, some for the manufacturer, some for the landlord, some for the clergy; but there ought to be a vastly greater number of constituencies of no aberrant type, no eccentric idiosyncrasy, which simply represent the common voice of educated men, which must hear what the commissioned advocates of classes allege, weigh their arguments, estimate their often conflicting assertions and in the last resort decide."

too much weight to the landed interest and not enough to the new expanding industrial parts of the country. Since 1832 a new industrial kingdom had been created in the North, centred round Manchester, of which the constitution took no account. To increase the representation of the North would not only accord with sound political theory but would also diminish the agitation for democracy. "In every age and every country," wrote Bagehot, "a class which has not as much power as it thinks it ought to have snatches at the notion that all classes ought to have equal power. . . . We cannot fail to observe that the new business wealth of the present day (of which Mr Bright is the orator and mouthpiece) has a tendency to democracy for the same reason. Such a symptom in the body politic is an indication of danger. So energetic a class as the creators of Manchester need to be conciliated; their active intelligence has rights which assuredly will make it heard. The great political want of our day is a *capitalist* conservatism."

Bagehot went on to recommend certain franchise reforms. Proportional representation, which resulted in weak government, was rejected in favour of a limited extension of the franchise. What should be the qualification for its exercise? An intelligence qualification had much to recommend it, but it could not be established by any visible criterion. A franchise criterion, Bagehot maintained, must be evident and conspicuous, and difficult to manufacture for political purposes. In practice this meant adoption of a property qualification. "Property," said Bagehot, "is, indeed, a very imperfect test of intelligence; but it is some test. If it has been inherited, it guarantees education; if acquired, it guarantees ability. . . . Property has not only a certain connection with general intelligence, but it has a peculiar connection with *political* intelligence. It is a great guide to a good judgment to have much to lose by a bad judgment." Accordingly, Bagehot suggested that the rate-paying franchise should be extended to all towns with a population over 75,000, which would effectively increase the representation of the working classes without allowing them to dominate the House of Commons. The landed preponderance would be to some extent reduced, and it could be cut down further by abolishing the smaller boroughs.[2]

[2] Bagehot thought that the suffrage should be extended to women and that they should be admitted to university degrees. "The frivolity of women is one of the greatest causes of vice and frivolity in men.

Events were moving too swiftly and strongly for Bagehot, and his scheme never became anything more than an academic exercise. Once Disraeli had taken his "leap in the dark" in 1867, establishment of complete democracy became not a matter of principle but of time. Bagehot's forecast of the effects of the Reform Act was gloomy. He doubted whether the newly enfranchised class would long remain deferential. In the first edition of *The English Constitution*, he stated his view that the adoption of democratic theory would make the parliamentary system unworkable, since members would be drawn from the lowest urban and agricultural class. "Each class would speak a language of its own; each would be unintelligible to the other; and the only thriving class would be the immoral representatives, who were chosen by corrupt machination, and who would probably get a good profit on the capital they laid out in that corruption."[3]

Once the Reform Act had been passed Bagehot gave up the role of Cassandra and made more constructive criticisms. He realised that the administration of the Act would be as important as its substantive provisions. The effects of the first Reform Act had not been fully felt for thirty years because it was worked by Lord Melbourne, Lord John Russell, Lord Derby, Lord Palmerston and Sir Robert Peel, all statesmen of the pre-reform era. Thus he declared, in his introduction to the 1872 edition of *The English Constitution*, a great responsibility rested on the new generation of statesmen. They should avoid raising issues which would bind the poor together as a class, should not make them think that some new law could ensure their comfort, or that the government possessed some inexhaustible fund from which all their wants could be supplied. "If the first work of the poor voters is to try to create a *poor man's paradise,* as poor men

---

If we can but have a generation of women somewhat less dull, and somewhat less inclined to devote themselves to silly occupations, we hope that not only their children but their husbands and brothers will be the gainers." "The Women's Degrees." *The Economist*, May 23, 1874.

[3] In the country districts Bagehot feared that the effect of lowering the franchise would be to increase the influence of the squirearchy over an illiterate constituency. In the boroughs it would lead to the dominance of the artisan. Instead of having a House of Commons dominated by like-minded people, it would be dominated by clashing prejudices.

are apt to fancy that paradise, and as they are apt to think they can create it, the great political trial now beginning will simply fail. The wide gift of the elective franchise will be a great calamity to the whole nation, and to those who gain it as great a calamity as any. . . . In plain English, what I fear is that both our political parties will bid for the support of the working man; that both of them will promise to do as he likes if he will only tell them what it is; that, as he now holds the casting vote in our affairs, both parties will beg and pray him to give that vote to them. I can conceive of nothing more corrupting or worse for a set of poor ignorant people than that two combinations of well taught and rich men should constantly offer to defer that decision, and compete for the office of executing it. Vox populi will be Vox diaboli if worked in that manner."

Although the tone of political discussion has in some ways been lowered since Bagehot wrote, his gloomy prognostications have not been fulfilled.[4] Why? Bagehot himself gave the answer in an essay he wrote in 1848. "If power," he wrote, "be given to a miserable democracy, that democracy will endeavour above all things not to be miserable. This it will attempt by whatever schemes are congenial to minds and consciences, corrupted by ages of hereditary ignorance and hereditary suffering. And woe to those who, under such a Government propound plans for the benefit of their rulers; *Saevi proximis ingruunt.* The favourite theorist of yesterday is punished to-day because the Millennium is not yet come. Such is the lesson which the annals of Europe in the year 1848 teach to the English statesmen. The only effective security against the rule of an ignorant, miserable and vicious democracy, is to take care that the democracy shall be educated, and comfortable, and moral. Now is the time for scheming, deliberating and acting. To tell a mob how their condition may be improved is talking hydrostatics to the ocean. Science is of use now because she may be heard and

---

[4] Bagehot set great store by the tone of public discussion. "No defect really eats away so soon the political ability of a nation. A vulgar tone of discussion disgusts cultivated minds with the subject of politics; they will not apply themselves to master a topic which, besides its natural difficulties is encumbered with disgusting phrases, low arguments and the undisguised language of coarse selfishness." (*Parliamentary Reform*)

understood. If she be not heard before the democracy come, when it is come her voice will be drowned in the uproar."[5]

He expanded this theme in his address to the electors of London University nearly twenty years later, in 1867, when he was attempting (unsuccessfully) to become the parliamentary candidate. "The very name of our University of itself suggests the greatest and most urgent of our tasks. Thirty years ago we founded a University for an excluded class; now we have to frame, upon the very same principles, an education which will suit the whole nation. Our University has shown upon what principles a sound and sensible culture can be given to young men sincerely bred in different religious creeds, without sacrificing either the faith to the culture or the culture to the faith. For myself, I believe that the experiment is capable of indefinite development. The sudden extension of the franchise is one of those facts 'of the first magnitude' which are never long resisted. After the first Reform Act the cry was, 'Register! Register! Register!' The cry should now be, 'Educate! Educate! Educate!' The State will have to intervene far more widely than is as yet thought ere the problem of wide education in a mixed society is solved, and before the principles of our University are developed to their proper limit."

Apart from education Bagehot saw that the other great contemporary need to make democracy tolerable was the spread of "comfort," or in today's jargon, the improvement of the standard of living. In pursuing this aim traditional fears of a strong executive would have to be abandoned. "The English State is but another name for the English people, and to be afraid of it, is to be alarmed at ourselves. From countless causes the age of great cities requires a strong government. The due extension of the functions of the State in superintending the health and in lessening the vice and misery of our large towns must receive speedy attention from a Parliament in which most of the inhabitants of those towns are for the first time directly represented." Bagehot saw what had to be done, but he was sceptical as to whether it could be done in time. In fact, education and comfort have been diffused extraordinarily rapidly in England, and English democracy has thus been built on stable foundations.

When Bagehot was writing the only other major country

[5] "The Principles of Political Economy," *The Prospective Review*.

apart from Britain governed by "discussion" was the United States of America. Like so many mid-Victorian cultivated Englishmen, he had a distorted and rather grim picture of American society. He had never been to the United States and, as far as I can make out, never especially wanted to; he relied on writers such as Tocqueville and Dickens as sources for American life and manners. One reason why Bagehot is such a brilliant delineator of the nineteenth-century political scene in England is that he never failed to connect political and social realities. He looked at the social facts and drew political conclusions. When writing about the United States he did just the opposite, passing judgments on American society from a study of American political institutions. He never had the opportunity of "looking closely and for himself," as Hutton put it, at the working of American political life, and his work preceded that of Bryce, so that despite some brilliant *aperçus* into the American character and political genius, his judgments on American politics are less reliable than those on the working of the English constitution. This partial blindness to American virtues also affected his conclusions about democracy, which would not have been so pessimistic had he been more familar with the realities of American life and not misled by the vulgar tone of American politics.

Bagehot first passed judgment at length on American institutions in his long essay "The American Constitution at the Present Crisis," published in the *National Review* for October 1861, shortly after the outbreak of the American Civil War. He returned to the theme in *The English Constitution*, which makes many references to the American form of government and is in effect a comparative study of the cabinet and presidential systems, with conclusions highly favourable to English government. Bagehot was staking a claim for the adoption of the English rather than the American system in the free states of the future.

He saw the American Constitution as an unhappy compromise between the federal and state systems of government, which might be adequate in favourable circumstances, but which would fail under strain from inherent defect. "It is," he wrote, "essentially a collection of *imperia in imperio*. It rather displays than conceals the grave disadvantages which have made that name so very unpopular. Each State is a subordinate Republic, and yet the entire Union is but a single

Republic. Each State is in some sense a centre of disunion. Each State attracts to itself a share of political attachment, has separate interests, real or supposed, has a separate set of public men anxious to increase its importance—upon which their own depends,—anxious to weaken the power of the United Government, by which theirs is overshadowed. At every critical period the sinister influence of the *imperium in imperio* will be felt; at every such period the cry of each subordinate aggregate will be, 'Our interests are threatened, our authority diminished, our rights attacked.'"

Bagehot detested American democracy, and this antipathy prejudiced him against a country that had been rash enough to entrust ultimate political power not to the enlightened middle classes, but to the uneducated lower orders. The only sufficient safeguard against the tyranny of the lower classes was to place the predominant, although not the exclusive, power in the state in the hands of the higher classes. "The framers of the American Constitution chose a very different expedient. They placed the predominant power in the hands of the numerical majority of the population and hoped to restrain and balance it by paper checks and constitutional stratagems. At the present time, almost every one of their ingenious devices has aggravated the calamities of their descendants." The chief effect of the paper checks, he held, was to make government too rigid. "You have got a congress elected for a fixed period," he wrote in *The English Constitution,* "going out perhaps by fixed instalments which cannot be accelerated or retarded—you have a President chosen for a fixed period, and immovable during that period: all the arrangements are for *stated* times. There is no *elastic* element, everything is rigid, specified, dated." He feared that a deadlock would occur, either between the President and Congress, or between the House of Representatives and the Senate; and, if this happened, no machinery existed to resolve the dispute. Bagehot failed to foresee that the growth in the powers and prestige of the presidency would to a considerable extent overcome the difficulty.

He was severely critical of the machinery by which the President was chosen. "The plan was," he writes in *The English Constitution,* "that the citizens at large should vote for the statesman they liked best. But no one does anything of the sort. They vote for the ticket made by the *caucus* and the caucus is a sort of representative meeting which sits voting and voting till they have cut out all the known men against whom much is to be said, and agreed on some unknown man against whom there is nothing known, and therefore nothing to be alleged." The President, Bagehot concluded, is not the choice of the nation but of the "wirepullers."

"What worse mode," he asked, "of electing a ruler could by possibility have been selected? If the wit of man had been set to devise a system specially calculated to bring to the head of affairs an incompetent man at a pressing crisis, it could not have devised one more fit: probably it would not have devised one as fit. It almost secures the rejection of tried and trained genius, and almost insures the selection of untrained and unknown mediocrity." In fact, the effect of the caucus has not been as disastrous as this, and the spread of the direct primary has to some extent reduced its power. The electoral college was dismissed by Bagehot as a mere sham, and it has certainly not achieved the end for which Washington and Hamilton hoped; instead of being a body of intelligent men, using their own judgment in selecting a President, the members have become delegates, an inevitable development. As for the vice-presidency, instead of being a post filled by the "second wisest man" in the state, Bagehot stressed it had become a sinecure. If the President died in office, "government by an unknown quantity" resulted. Bagehot grudgingly admitted that some vice-presidents have made outstanding Presidents, and that Lincoln had redeeming qualities but added hastily, "success in a lottery is no argument for lotteries."

Bagehot was also highly critical of the doctrine of the separation of powers, which, he maintained, degraded the legislature. "Count Cavour well knew and thoroughly showed," he wrote in "The American Constitution at the Present Crisis," "how far the power of a parliamentary premier, supported by a willing and confiding parliament, is superior to all other political powers, whether in despotic government or in free. The American Constitution, however, expressly prohibits the possibility of such a position. It enacts that "no person holding any office under the United States shall be a member of either House during his continuance in office." In consequence the position of a great parliamentary member who is responsible more or less for the due performance of his own administrative functions, and also of all lesser ones, is in America an illegal one. If a politician has executive authority, he cannot enter Parliament; if he is in Parliament, he cannot possess executive authority. No man of great talents and high ambition has therefore under the Constitution of the United States a proper sphere for those talents or a suitable vista for that ambition."

He returned to this theme in *The English Constitution*. "Unless a member of the legislature be sure of something more than speech, unless he is incited by the hope of action, and chastened by the chance of responsibility, a first-rate man will not care to take the place, and will not do much if he takes it. To belong to a debating society adhering to an executive (and this is no inapt description of a congress under a Presidential Constitution) is not an object to stir a noble ambition and is a position to encourage idleness." Bagehot was right about the House of Representatives, which is more a collection of local delegates, but he underestimated the prestige of the Senate. Unlike the lower House, which has to seek re-election every two years, it is a semi-permanent body, only one third of its members having to go to the polls every second year.

Bagehot also thought that the separation of powers lowered the quality of the executive, claiming that its "intrinsic quality" was impaired. Cabinet offices, he thought, tended to be given to favourites. This is by no means true, and Presidential freedom of choice in choosing a cabinet is not an unmitigated evil, for it enables the President to draw on able men not associated with public life and obtain their services for the nation.[6]

One of Bagehot's earliest tasks as director and then editor of *The Economist*, a post to which he was appointed in 1861, was to comment on and assess the American Civil War. Throughout its progress the paper remained reasonably objective and well informed. Bagehot saw the faults and shortcomings of both sides. He disliked the arrogance and boastfulness of the North, the fruits of its democracy, but was also highly critical of the institution of slavery as it was found in the South. He was not doctrinaire in his condemnation of slavery but thought it could only give rise to evils in a com-

---

[6] These arguments greatly impressed Woodrow Wilson, a lifelong admirer of Bagehot, when at Princeton, and at that time he wrote an article arguing for the introduction of cabinet government into the U.S. See "Committee or Cabinet Government?" *Overland Monthly*, January 1884, pages 17–33. He later abandoned the idea.

mercial society.[7] Bagehot was against any extension of slavery but also against its precipitate abolition, and Lincoln's declaration of emancipation in October 1862 was strongly criticised by *The Economist*. Bagehot never viewed the Civil War as an anti-slavery crusade, seeing it much more as a clash of societies and cultures of which slavery was one symbol. In this *The Economist* was in marked contrast to its contemporary, the *Spectator*, which under Hutton was consistently pro-North and looked upon the Civil War as a simple attempt to end slavery by the North which was being resisted by the South.

Bagehot thought the South had a right to secede and would be successful in implementing it, since it had no need to conquer but only to resist. The North, he thought, would eventually grow tired of the war and recognise natural facts. Reabsorption of the South in the Union against its will was an impossibility: it would merely constitute an enclave disposed to sedition and sabotage. Britain, he maintained, should remain neutral, not recognising the South as a separate state, at any rate until it had established *de facto* independence beyond all reasonable doubt. Recognition as a belligerent was another matter and met with his approval. Many of Bagehot's subscribers had cotton interests, but he did not let this influence his judgment when considering the Northern blockade, which he consistently maintained should be respected. When, however, the Trent incident took place in November 1861, and the Confederate envoys were seized from a British ship by Northern sailors, *The Economist's* reaction was sharp and unequivocal. Unless they were released, war would inevitably and rightly follow. When the release and apology came, *The Economist* counselled acceptance and moderation.

Like other English editors Bagehot underestimated Lincoln and was highly critical of his lack of education and political

[7] Bagehot expressed his views on slavery some years earlier in a letter to Richard Hutton dated January 1853. "I can imagine," he wrote, "many cases in which Slavery is good, for a population, but none or not many in which traders can be trusted to be slaveowners. It may answer in rural villages, where they only supply their own demand and where the notion of the slaves being capital is extremely secondary, but never in a mercantile community where that notion is the main one and the notion of moral and personal dependence extremely faint."

and diplomatic training and experience. Only after Lincoln's assassination were amends made. "It is not merely that a great man has passed away, but he has disappeared at the very time when his special greatness seemed almost essential to the world, when his death would work the widest conceivable evil, when the chance of replacing him, even partially approached nearest to zero, and he has been removed in the very way which almost alone among causes of death could have doubled the political injury entailed by the decease itself. . . . We do not know in history such an example of the growth of a ruler in wisdom as was exhibited by Mr Lincoln. Power and responsibility visibly widened his mind and elevated his character. Difficulties, instead of irritating him as they do most men, only increased his reliance on patience; opposition instead of ulcerating, only made him more tolerant and determined. The very style of his public papers altered, till the very man who had written in an official despatch about 'Uncle Sam's web feet,' drew up his final inaugural in a style which exhorted from critics so hostile as the *Saturday Reviewers*, a burst of involuntary admiration."[8]

Apart from the United States the other great nation to engage Bagehot's consistent interest was France. From the time of his first visit to Paris in 1851 Bagehot was fascinated by Louis Napoleon and considered him intrinsically more interesting than his famous uncle Napoleon I. He watched him closely throughout his career with what his sister-in-law, Mrs. Russell Barrington, called "a strange, almost personal interest." He followed him from triumph through adversity to his death at suburban Chislehurst in January 1873. His early admiration faded and he grew more critical, but in the end his assessment was by no means entirely unfavourable and certainly sympathetic. It was a misfortune that they never met.

Bagehot, as has been noted, was an eyewitness of the *coup d'état* of 1851 and in contrast to most educated Englishmen of the time passed favourable judgment. In England the feeling against Napoleon was intense, and Palmerston was forced to relinquish the premiership because of his premature public approval of the new régime. Bagehot's letters to the *Inquirer* favoured and justified Napoleon, and this public

[8] *The Economist*, April 29, 1865.

assessment was reflected in his private correspondence. "I wish for the President decidedly myself as against M. Thiers and his set in the Parliamentary World," he wrote to his mother in a letter of December 7, 1851, "even I can't believe in a Government of barristers and newspaper editors, and also as against the Red party who, though not insincere, are too abstruse and theoretical for a plain man. It is easy to see what they would abolish, but horribly hard to say what they would *leave*, and what they would *find*. I am in short what they call here a réactionnair, and I think I am with the majority—a healthy habit for a young man to contract."

The letters on the *coup d'état*, which are reproduced later in this volume, remain among the most brilliant essays to have come from Bagehot's pen: for a young man of twenty-five they were astonishing. They contain many seeds of Bagehot's later thought, including the connecting of political with social facts and the importance he attached to national character. "I fear you will laugh," he wrote in his second letter, "when I tell you what I conceive to be about the most essential mental quality for a free people, whose liberty is to be progressive, permanent and on a large scale: it is much *stupidity*." By this he did not mean mere impenetrability to ideas, but a certain sane common sense, distrustful of extreme theoretical conclusions and unwilling to apply them as solutions of practical problems. The obstinacy of stupidity was nature's safeguard against the restlessness of genius. The English were liberally endowed with this quality and the French had very little. In both cases this quality or the lack of it was an essential ingredient of the national character, and of all circumstances affecting political problems he selected national character as "by far and out of all question the most important." The dull, bovine English character was ideally suited to parliamentary government, and Bagehot contrasted it in this respect with that of the mercurial French. The essence of the French character was "a certain mobility; that is, as it has been defined, a certain 'excessive sensibility to *present* impressions', which is sometimes *levity*,—for it issues in a postponement of seemingly fixed principles to a momentary temptation or to a transient whim; sometimes *impatience*, as leading to an exaggerated sense of existing evils; often *excitement*—a total absorption in existing emotion; oftener *inconsistency*—the sacrifice of old habits to present

emergencies; and yet other unfavourable qualities." Such a
character could support only a small degree of civil liberty
and needed a strong executive to keep its worst excesses in
check. The French as a people did not care for parliamentary
government; their passion was not for constitutions but for
"gain and glory."

The first need of any society, Bagehot laid down, was government, a point he developed later in *Physics and Politics*,
and this was, given the French character, pre-eminently true
of France. "You will not be misled," he wrote in the first
letter, "by any high flown speculations about liberty or equality. You will, I imagine, concede to me that the first duty of
a Government is to ensure the security of that industry which
is the condition of social life and civilised cultivation; that
especially in so excitable a country as France it is necessary
that the dangerous classes should be saved from the strong
temptation of long idleness; and that no danger could be
more formidable than six months' beggary among the revolutionary 'ouvriers', immediately preceding the exact period
fixed by European as well as French opinion for an apprehended convulsion. It is from this state of things, whether
by fair means or foul, that Louis Napoleon has delivered
France." And it was for this reason that Bagehot praised him.
True, he curbed the press, but the press exercised a far
greater influence in France than in England and encouraged
the factiousness that was ruining the country. True also that
the means he employed were, to say the least, dubious, but
the situation in France was desperate, and contemporary
English experience could offer no parallel.

With the passage of time Bagehot grew less enraptured with
Napoleon. He saw that his character meant trouble for
England and for Europe. "He is," he wrote in 1863, "essentially *restless*. He has a busy mind rather than a prompt and
active will. He broods much; and he broods in silence and in
darkness. He is ever full of schemes and projects, which from
time to time he throws out to disturb and dismay Europe.
Occasionally he puts them forth in a tentative form, and
when they have only reached the nebulous and floating stage
in his brain. At other times he waits till he has matured them.
It is the *incalculable* nature of his restlessness that renders
it so peculiarly pernicious. He is for ever breaking out in a
fresh place. You never know what he will do or say next.
You only know that he will not be long quiet. He is, and will

always be as long as he lives the volcanic and *rémuant* element in the cauldron of European politics."[9]

Under his leadership France counted for more in Europe than at any time (the reign of Napoleon I apart) since the days of Louis XIV, but she was not so much "influential" as "disturbing." The judgment was shrewd and today could be applied with equal justice to the effect of the foreign policy of General de Gaulle. Strangely enough for so sharp an observer, Bagehot failed to see the dangers of Napoleon's Mexican adventure, which in fact he mildly commended but which turned out to be a fatal turning point in the fortunes of the régime.

Bagehot was full of admiration for the economic progress made by France under Napoleonic rule. He commended Napoleon for the steps taken towards free trade and saw that France could have been moved in this direction only by a strong ruler. He also admired the subtlety of his intellect and the fact that his policies were based on principles and on thought. Napoleon was a despot, but a despot with a difference, quite different from his feudal and legitimist predecessors. "The old monarchies claim the obedience of the people upon grounds of duty. They say they have consecrated claims to the loyalty of mankind. They appeal to conscience, and even to religion. But Louis Napoleon is a Benthamite despot. He is for the 'greatest happiness of the greatest number.' He says, 'I am where I am, because I know better than any one else what is good for the French people, and they know that I know better.' He is not the Lord's anointed; he is the people's agent."[10] Napoleon was "the crowned democrat" or the "democratic despot" embodying not constitutional principles but the spirit of 1789.

Bagehot clearly perceived the deficiencies of Napoleon's rule and its intrinsic weakness. Napoleon ruled over the middle classes, in defiance of the educated classes and with the support of the lower classes. When a crisis came he would be unable to free himself from domination by the most unthinking section of his subjects. The Empire was estopped by its structure from educating the nation: it could not form public opinion since the speaking minority was alienated. Another grave defect was its openness to corruption, which was, in fact, even more extensive than Bagehot sus-

[9] *The Economist*, November 28, 1863.
[10] *The Economist*, March 4, 1865.

pected. Above all, everything depended on the life of one
man: "First *catch* your despot," observed Bagehot in a memorable phrase. Personal rule protected property but ruined
credit since no one knew how long it would last. "The present
Government," concluded Bagehot, "avowedly depends, is ostentatiously concentrated, in the existing Caesar. Its existence depends on the permanent occupation of the Tuileries
by an extraordinary man. The democratic despot—the representative despot—must have the sagacity to divine the people's will and the sagacity to execute it. What is the likelihood
that these will be hereditary? Can they be expected in the
next heirs, a child for Emperor, and a woman for a Regent?
The present happiness of France is happiness on a short life
lease; it may end with the life of a man who is not young,
who has not spared himself, who has always thought, who has
always *lived*."[11] Bagehot's view of the Empire five years before it crumbled was succinctly expressed in an *Economist*
article of 1865: "It is an admirable Government for present
and coarse purposes, but a detestable Government for future
and refined purposes."[12]

To the liberal empire Bagehot was sympathetic but detached and a little sceptical of its likelihood of success; yet
it was infinitely preferable to the only alternative, a socialist
republic, and through *The Economist* Bagehot advised
French liberals to accept the shadow of empire if they could
obtain the substance of freedom. Whether the liberal empire
could have worked long term will never be known; its life was
cut short by the Franco-Prussian War and the disaster of
Sedan. Bagehot, like most contemporaries, held France responsible for the war and knew nothing of Bismarck's per-
fidy. Napoleon, he thought, had abandoned all his statescraft
and staked everything on a gambler's throw. The sudden
collapse of the empire took Bagehot by surprise, but he was
able to explain it. Caesarism contained within itself the seeds
of its own decay: it was "the abuse of the confidence reposed
by the most ignorant in a great name to hold at bay the reasoned arguments of men who both know the popular wish
and also are sufficiently educated to discuss the best means
of gratifying those wishes. A virtually irresponsible power
obtained by one man from the vague preference of the masses
for a particular name,—that is Caesarism, and that is a system

11 *The Economist*, March 4, 1865.
12 Ibid.

which has undoubtedly undergone a sudden and frightful collapse such as none but the very worst hereditary monarchies of Europe have sustained."[13]

The collapse was no accident; it came from the nature of the system itself: "the absence of all intermediate links of moral responsibility and co-operation, which such a system necessarily leaves between the throne and the people. It is the very object of the plebiscite to give the Emperor an authority which reduces all intermediate Powers to comparative insignificance if they come into collision with his own. Consequently everything must depend on him, and if he be not practically omniscient there is no substantial check at all on the creatures whom he sets up to execute his will. This has evidently been the ruin of the great military power of France."[14] This intrinsic defect was made worse by Napoleon's inability to pick talented ministers, partly, Bagehot thought, because of his innate self-distrust, which made him jealous of a capacity greater than his own.

At the time he wrote this article Bagehot did not know how ravaged by disease Napoleon was, a factor he was able to take into account when he wrote his obituary in *The Economist* for January 11, 1873; but it did not radically alter his assessment. His admiration for Napoleon was still there, and he praised his perception of the power of the principle of nationalities, his desire for an alliance with England, and his moderate policy towards the papacy. He even speculated that the liberal empire had a fair chance of survival. Napoleon was not a great administrator, or especially farsighted, but he was the most *"insighted"* of the modern statesmen of France. "To declare him a great man," concluded Bagehot, "may be impossible in the face of his failures, but to declare him a small one is ridiculous. Small men dying in exile do not leave wide gaps in the European political horizon."

After the collapse of the empire Bagehot observed curiously the revival of imperialism in France and assessed the chances of the young Napoleon with a cool and unsentimental eye. Yet the bases of his thought on French politics remained unchanged, and in two articles written in *The Economist* in the summer of 1874 the wheel came full circle. The judgments in the articles are substantially identical to those he

[13] *The Economist*, August 20, 1870.
[14] Ibid.

had passed as an exuberant young man in Paris nearly a quarter of a century before. "There is something to a Frenchman," he wrote, "dearer than free thought, much dearer than parliamentary Government, dearer even than successful foreign policy, and that is *fixity*. He wants to be sure that he will have the same Government to-morrow as to-day, next month as this month, next year as this year. He lives in the constant presence of a revolutionary force; he is always imagining an outbreak of it; he has heard of the terrors of '93, and has seen the losses of the Commune; above all things he desires a sufficient and incessant force which is able to prevent revolutions and make them impossible."[15]

In the second article, cumbrously but revealingly entitled "Why an English Liberal may look without disapproval on the progress of Imperialism in France," the echoes of 1851 are even clearer, although the tone is sober. An ordinary Frenchman, he wrote, regards parliamentary government as more unstable than any other. The French are "naturally excitable, uncontrollable, and sensitive to risk; they have been so used to political misfortune that they now are scared at any shadow. There are generally two simultaneous but contrary excitements; one of the revolutionist, who wants to revive the *Commune*: the other of the peasant or the shopkeeper who fears the Commune. And the passion of each tends to intensify the passion of the other. These frenzies—for on both sides they are often little better—work on the most inflammable and least stoical of national characters. There is no soil so unsuitable to Parliamentary Government."[16] There was nothing inconsistent, Bagehot concluded, with a firm allegiance to parliamentary government, where parliamentary government is possible and looking on the "rapid revival of Imperialism in France without dismay and even with satisfaction."

Yet there was to be no Napoleonic restoration. In 1879 Bonapartist hopes perished forever when the young and gallant Prince Imperial fell under African spears in an obscure kraal in Zululand. Bagehot himself had already been dead two years. We have had to wait until our own time to see his judgments on France vindicated.

[15] "The Prospects of Bonapartism in France," *The Economist*, May 30, 1874.
[16] *The Economist*, June 6, 1874.

BOLINGBROKE AS A STATESMAN[1]*

(1863)

Henry St. John, first Viscount Bolingbroke, was born at Battersea in 1678, the only son of Sir Henry St. John and Lady Mary Rich. The elder St. John held the manors of Battersea and Wandsworth. The son was educated at Eton and, it is said, at Christ Church, Oxford, but there is no record of this. In 1701 he became M.P. for the borough of Wootton-Bassett, supporting Harley and the Tory party. He was appointed to prepare and bring in a bill for the security of Protestant succession to the throne. From 1704–8 he was Secretary for War; in 1710 he became Secretary of State, and in 1710 was M.P. for Berkshire. He was created Viscount Bolingbroke in 1712. Bolingbroke went to France in 1712 to make the final arrangements for peace after the French war, and again he took charge of peace negotiations in 1713 when the Treaty of Utrecht was signed. On the accession of George I, Bolingbroke was dismissed from office. In 1714 a motion for his impeachment was carried, a bill of attainder passed, and his name erased from the role of peers. He fled to France and became Secretary of State to James the Pretender. He left the Pretender's service in 1716 and for a while lived in France until in 1723 he was pardoned and returned to England. He joined Walpole's party but became estranged from him because Walpole opposed an act permitting Bolingbroke to inherit and acquire real estate. Bolingbroke retired to France where he wrote essays upon history in the form of letters to friends, and upon political subjects. Bolingbroke died at Battersea in 1751.

---

[1] *The Life of Henry St. John*, Viscount Bolingbroke, Secretary of State in the reign of Queen Anne. By Thomas Macknight, author of the *History of the Life and Times of Edmund Burke*.

* This essay was first published in the *National Review* for April 1863, Volume XVI, pages 389–426.

Who now reads Bolingbroke? was asked sixty years ago. Who
knows anything about him? we may ask now. Professed students of our history or of our literature may have special
knowledge; but out of the general mass of educated men,
how many could give an intelligible account of his career?
How many could describe even vaguely his character as a
statesman? Our grandfathers and their fathers quarrelled for
two generations as to the Peace of Utrecht, but only an odd
person here and there could now give an account of its provisions. The most cultivated lady would not mind asking
"The Peace of Utrecht! yes—what was that?" Whether Mr St
John was right to make that peace; whether Queen Anne was
right to create him a peer for making it; whether the Whigs
were right in impeaching him for making it—the mass of men
must have forgotten. So is history *un*made. Even now, the
dust of forgetfulness is falling over the Congress of Vienna
and the Peace of Paris; we are forgetting the last great pacification as we have wholly forgotten the pacification before
that; in another fifty years "Vienna" will be as "Utrecht,"
and Wellington no more than Marlborough.

In the meantime, however, Mr Macknight has done well
to collect for those who wish to know them the principal
events of Bolingbroke's career. There was no tolerable outline
of them before, and in some respects this is a good one. Mr
Macknight's style is clear, though often ponderous; his remarks are sensible, and he has the great merit of not being
imposed on by great names and traditional reputations. The
defect of the book is, that he takes too literary a view of politics and politicians; that he has not looked closely and for
himself at real political life; that he therefore misses the
guiding traits which show what in Queen Anne's time was so
like our present politics, and what so wholly unlike. We shall
venture in the course of this article to supply some general
outline of the controversies that were to be then decided, and
of the political forces which decided them; for unless these
are distinctly imagined, a reader of the present day cannot
comprehend why such a man as Bolingbroke was at one
moment the most conspicuous and influential of English
statesmen, and then for years an exile and a wanderer.

We must own, however, that it is not the intrinsic interest
even of events once so very important as the war of the
Grand Alliance and the Peace of Utrecht which tempts us to
write this article. It is the interest of Bolingbroke's own

character. He tried a great experiment. There lurks about the fancies of many men and women an imaginary conception of an ideal statesman, resembling the character of which Alcibiades has been the recognised type for centuries. There is a sort of intellectual luxury in the idea which fascinates the human mind. We like to fancy a young man, in the first vigour of body and in the first vigour of mind, who is full of bounding enjoyment, who is fond of irregular luxury, who is the favourite of society, who excels all rivals at masculine feats, who gains the love of women by a magic attraction; but who is also a powerful statesman, who regulates great events, who settles great measures, who guides a great nation. We seem to outstep the *mœnia mundi*, the recognised limits of human nature, when we conceive a man in the pride of youth to have dominion over the pursuits of age, to rule both the light things of women and the grave things of men. Human imagination so much loves to surpass human power, that we shall never be able to extirpate the conception. But we may examine the approximations to it in life. We see in Bolingbroke's case that a life of brilliant license is really compatible with a life of brilliant statesmanship; that license itself may even be thought to quicken the imagination for oratorical efforts; that an intellect similarly aroused may, at exciting conjectures, perceive possibilities which are hidden from duller men; that the favourite of society will be able to use his companionship with men and his power over women so as much to aid his strokes of policy; but, on the other hand, that these secondary aids and occasional advantages are purchased by the total sacrifice of a primary necessity; that a life of great excitement is incompatible with the calm circumspection and the sound estimate of probability essential to great affairs; that though the excited hero may perceive distant things which others overlook, he will overlook near things that others see; that though he may be stimulated to great speeches which others could not make, he will also be irritated to petty speeches which others would not; that he will attract enmities, but not confidence; that he will not observe how few and plain are the alternatives of common business, and how little even genius can enlarge them; that his prosperity will be a wild dream of unattainable possibilities, and his adversity a long regret that those possibilities have departed. At any rate, such was Bolingbroke's career. We have better evidence about him than about any similar statesman, for the events in which he was concerned were large, and he has given us a narrative of them from his own hand. A summary retrospect of his career will not be worthless, if it show what sudden brilliancy and what incurable ruin such a life as his, with such a genius as his, was calculated to ensure.

Bolingbroke's father was a type of his generation. He was a rake of the Restoration. Charles II is the only king of England who had both the social qualities which fitted him to be the head of society, and the immoral qualities which fitted him to corrupt society. His easy talk, his good anecdotes, his happy manners, his conversancy with various life, made Whitehall the "best club" of that time. What sort of life he encouraged men to lead there we all know. Bolingbroke's father learned of him all the evil which he could learn. It was not singular that he committed excesses of dissipation, but it was rather singular that he committed what was thought to be a murder. He stabbed a man in a drunken broil, and, if Burnet can be trusted, only escaped from the gallows by a great bribe. He dawdled on at the coffeehouses far into George II's time, a monument of extinct profligacy, and a spectacle and a wonder to a graver generation.

Bolingbroke's mother was a daughter of the Earl of Warwick; but she died early, and his father married again, so that we hear very little about her. If the silence of his biographers may be trusted as evidence, she exercised but little influence upon his infancy or upon his life.

The most influential preceptors of Bolingbroke's boyhood were his grandfather and grandmother, who also were not unusual characters in their generation. The former was a serious and moderate Royalist, the latter was a serious but moderate Puritan. Bolingbroke's father apparently did not much like keeping house: it must have interfered with his pleasures, and marred the life of coffee-houses. The whole direction of Bolingbroke's mind was given to his grave grandfather and grandmother. In after-times, when he was a prominent Tory and a professed High-Churchman, satirists used to say that he was brought up among "Dissenters". And it is probable that his grandmother, who was the daughter of the celebrated Oliver St. John, the great parliamentary lawyer and chief justice, was far from being in opinion what a high Anglican divine would term a "Churchwoman". Bolingbroke himself used to relate terrible stories of having been compelled to read the sermons of Puritan divines. But, as far as our slight information goes, he did not suffer more than in any moderately "serious" family of our own time. All serious families were then thought to have a little taint of Dissent, and Bolingbroke was probably very sensitive to the partial dulness of a semipuritanical religion.

At any rate, we have no doubt it was said (and that his elder relatives much grieved at it) that "the boy was gone wrong, like his father". When he came out into the world he astonished his associates by his license. He had been at Eton and Oxford; but he had not learned, what is often learned there, a decorum in profligacy. To what precise enormities his license extended is immaterial, and cannot now be known. Goldsmith had talked to an old gentleman who related that Bolingbroke and his companions, in a drunken frolic, ran "naked through the park". But this is hardly credible; and probably Goldsmith's informant was one of the many old people who believe that the more wonderful the stories they tell, the more wonderful they themselves become. But at any rate his outrages attracted censure. He did not, like his father, belong to his generation. The age of King William tolerated much that we tolerate no longer, but it was not like the first years of Charles II. There was no longer a headlong recoil from Puritan strictness, and the Crown was on the side of at least apparent morality. As is usual in England, grave decorum and obvious morals had a substantial influence, and against these Bolingbroke offended.

He wrote poetry too, and the sort of poetry can only be appreciated by reading Locke's celebrated warning against that art, and the connections which it occasions. Bolingbroke's verses are addressed to a Clara A., an orange-girl, who pretended to sell that fruit near the Court of Requests, but who really had other objects. She was a lady of what may be called mutable connections; and the object of Bolingbroke's verses is to induce her to give them up and adhere to him only. He says:—

> "No, Clara, no; that person and that mind
> Were formed by Nature, and by Heaven designed
> For nobler ends: to these return, though late;
> Return to these, and so avert thy fate.
> Think, Clara, think; nor will that thought be vain;

Thy slave, thy Harry, doom'd to drag his chain
Of love ill-treated and abused, that he
From more inglorious chains might rescue thee:
Thy drooping health restored by his fond care,
Once more thy beauty its full lustre wear;
Moved by his love, by his example taught,
Soon shall thy soul, once more with virtue fraught,
With kind and generous truth thy bosom warm,
And thy fair mind, like thy fair person, charm,
To virtue thus and to thyself restored,
By all admired, by one alone adored,
Be to thy Harry ever kind and true,
And live for him who more than dies for you."

One would like to know what the orange-girl thought of all this; but it would seem he was lavish of money as well as of verses.

At twenty-two he married. We do not know much about his money matters; and, as his father and grandfather were both alive, his means could not have been at all large, especially as his expenses had been great. But his wife had certainly a considerable fortune. She was descended from a clothier called Jack of Newbury, who had made a fortune several generations before, and was one of the co-heiresses of Sir Henry Winchescomb, who had large property. What sort of person she was does not very clearly appear. But it does appear that the match was an unhappy one. He said she had a bad temper, with what truth we cannot ascertain now; and she said he was a bad husband, which was unquestionably true. He had been a rake before marriage, and did not cease afterwards. He could drink more wine than any one in London, and continued that habit too. A kind of connection was kept up between them for many years, but it was a dubious and unhappy connection. We may suppose, however, that when he was a great statesman she derived some glory, if little happiness, from him; and he certainly received a large income from her property during very many years.

At the age of twenty-eight Bolingbroke entered the House of Commons. Before that time he had done nothing to prove himself a man of great ability. At school and college he had done well, and had laid up perhaps a greater store of classical knowledge than those around him knew of. When abroad for a year or so, he had learned to speak French unusually well and unusually easily. But since he had been of age and in the world, his vices had been great, and he had not done much to compensate for them. Probably his boon companions considered him very clever; but then sober men rated very low the judgment of those companions. His skill in writing poetry had not been greater than most people's, and his choice of subjects had been worse. Until now he had had no opportunity of showing great talents, and much opportunity of showing considerable vices.

In the House of Commons it was otherwise. His handsome person, long descent, and aristocratic mien set off a very remarkable eloquence, which seems to have been very ready even at the first. Years afterwards he was the model to whom Lord Chesterfield pointed in all the arts of manner and expression. "Lord Bolingbroke," he tells us, "without the least trouble, talked all day long full as elegantly as he wrote. He adorned whatever subject he either spoke or wrote upon by the most splendid eloquence; not a studied and laboured eloquence, but by such a flowing happiness of diction which (from care perhaps at first) was become so habitual to him, that even his most familiar conversations, if taken down in writing, would have borne the press without the least correction either as to method or style." "He had the most elegant politeness and good-breeding which ever any courtier or man of the world was blessed with."

Nor did he neglect matter in the pursuit of manner. In later life he wrote some characters of the two great orators of antiquity, which showed how acutely he had studied them. He turned aside from the commonplace topics, from their language and their manner, to comment on their acquaintance with all the topics of their time, and on the practical questions. No one can read those delineations without perceiving that the writer is speaking of an art which he has himself practised. Those who knew how little studious Bolingbroke's habits were, appear to have been surprised at the information he displayed. But his excitable life rather promoted than forbade brief crises of keen study. His parts were quick, his language vague, though imposing, and he could always talk very happily on subjects of which he only knew a very little.

The time was favourable to a great orator. The Tory party was exactly in the state in which it has been in our own time. It had many votes and no tongue. Our county system tends to prevent our county magnates from ruling England. Strin-

gent limitations are laid down which narrow the electoral
choice, and tend to exclude available talent. It is wise and
natural that the landed interest should choose to be represented by landed gentlemen; a community of nature between
it and its representatives is desirable and inevitable. But our
counties are more exacting than this: each county requires
that the member shall have land within the county, and as in
each the number of candidates thus limited is but small, unsuitable ones must be chosen. We have left off expecting eloquence from a county member. Grave files 'of speechless men
have always represented the land of England. In Queen
Anne's time too, as in our own time, a lingering prejudice
haunted rural minds, and inclined them to prefer stupid magnates who shared it to clever ones who were emancipated
from it. Bolingbroke, like Mr Disraeli, found the Tory party
in a state of dumb power; like him, too, he became its spokesman and obtained its power.

Bolingbroke came into Parliament just at the end of King
William's reign, and was at once forced into contact with the
two subjects which were to occupy almost exclusively his active life. The reign of King William, which was about to end,
and that of Queen Anne, which was just about to begin,
were filled by two of the greatest topics which can occupy a
period. The first of these was a question of dynasty. Our
revolution has been called the "minimum of a revolution,"[2]
and in the eyes of a political philosopher so it is. It altered
but little in the substance of our institutions and in our positive law. But to common people, when it happened, the
change was great. Even now the detail of our parliamentary
system is not much understood by the poorer part of the public, and they care for it but little; the Queen and her family,
and the Prince of Wales and the Princess Alexandra, mainly
interest them. The person of the sovereign embodies to them
constitution, law, power. But our revolution changed the sovereign. The only political name and idea known to rural hamlets were taken away, and another name and idea were substituted in their stead. Jacobites went about saying that there
was one king whom God had made, and another king whom
Parliament had made. At this moment, though the dogma
of hereditary right has been confuted for ages, though it has
been laughed at for ages, though Parliaments have con-

[2] Sir G. C. Lewis.

demned it, though divines have been impeached for preaching it, though it is a misdemeanour to maintain it, the tenet still lives in ordinary minds. In Somersetshire and half the quiet counties the inhabitants would say that Queen Victoria ruled by the right of birth and the grace of God, and not by virtue of an Act of Parliament. They still think that she has a divine right to the crown, and not a right by statute only. If the old creed of the Jacobites is still so powerful, what must have been its force in Queen Anne's time? That generation had seen the change from "God's king" to "man's king," and very many of them did not like it. Shrewd men said that England was prosperous under the revolutionary government; common sense said that an ill-born king who governed well was better than a well-born king who governed ill; Whigs said that England was free after the revolution, and would have been enslaved but for the revolution; yet on the simple superstition of many natural minds the force of these arguments was lost. They admitted the advantage of liberty and of prosperity, but they would not renounce "the Lord's anointed for a mess of pottage". Happily this political feeling was counteracted by a religious feeling. The hatred to Popery supported the successful and rebellious king, who was a Protestant, against the unsuccessful and legitimate king, who was a Papist. But the strength so obtained was precarious; it might cease at any time. The "Pretender" might change his religion, and reports were continually circulated that he had done so, or was to do so. The existing dynasty could not be strong when its best support in the most natural minds was the continued profession of one religion by a person who had very strong motives to profess another.

The question of dynasty was the prominent question in Bolingbroke's age; such a question must always be the first where it exists. The question, who shall be king, can never be secondary. But it had a formidable rival. All through King William's and all through Queen Anne's time, the English mind was occupied with almost the only question which could compete with the question who should be King of England— the question whether there ought or ought not to be war with France. Frequent battles, daily hopes of battles, daily arguments whether there should be battles or not, kept even the greatest domestic question out of our thoughts.

On both these subjects Bolingbroke was compelled to critical action in his first Parliament. The question of dynasty was in a very odd and very English state of complexity. It might have been thought to be a question of bare alternatives, and to have been susceptible of no compromise. *Either* Parliament had no power to choose a sovereign upon grounds of expediency, or it might choose any sovereign who was expedient. If King James might be expelled at all, it could only be because he was a bad king, and in order to put in a better king. On principle, Parliament was either powerless or omnipotent. But this clear decisive logic has never suited Englishmen. As for King William, indeed, no one could say he was any sort of king except a parliamentary king, but his heir was the Princess Anne. "Surely, it was thought, she and her children had *some* divine right—a little, if not much? She had no right by birth certainly, for her father and her brother came before her; she was not the nearest heir, but she was the nearest Protestant heir; she was not the eldest son of the last king, but she was his eldest daughter that was living." These facts do not seem to be very material to us now, but at the time they were critically material. Half the population probably believed that it would be right—not merely expedient, but right in some high mystic sense—to obey Anne and her children. They were not only ready, but were anxious, to take her for the root of a new dynasty. But the Fates seemed capriciously determined to defeat their wishes. Anne had thirteen children, and all the thirteen died. At the death of the Duke of Gloucester, who was the last of them, some further settlement was necessary, and what it should be was decided in Bolingbroke's first Parliament.

On this subject he ought to have been a Whig of the Whigs. His writings are full of such expressions as the "chimera of prerogative"; "the slavish principles of passive obedience and non-resistance which had skulked" in old books till the reign of James I. And he has stated the Whig conception of the revolution as well as any one, if not better. "If," he says, "a divine, indefeasible, hereditary right to govern a community be once acknowledged; a right independent of the community, and which vests in every successive prince immediately on the death of his predecessor, and previously to any engagement taken on his part towards the people; if the people once acknowledge themselves bound to such princes by the ties of passive obedience and non-resistance, by an allegiance unconditional, and not reciprocal to protection; if a kind of oral law, or mysterious cabbala, which pharisees of the black gown and the long robe are always at hand to report and interpret as a prince desires, be once added, like a supplemental code, to the known laws of the land: then, I say, such princes have the power, if not the right, given them of commencing tyrants; and princes who have the power, are prone to think that they have the right. Such was the state of king and people before the revolution." He could have no horror of Popery, for he regarded all the historical forms of Christianity with an impartial scepticism; he probably thought it more gentlemanly than Presbyterianism, and not more absurd than Anglicanism. He ought to have been ready to obey whatever king was most eligible upon grounds of rational expediency.

The proposal of the Whigs, too, was as moderate as it was possible for it to be. As public opinion required, they selected the next Protestant heir. They passed over all the children of James II, who were Catholics, the descendants of Henrietta, daughter of Charles I, who were Catholics, the elder descendants of Elizabeth, the daughter of James I, who were Catholics, and found the Princess Sophia, a younger daughter of Elizabeth, who was a very clever and accomplished lady, and who, if she had any religion, was a Protestant. All the reasonable and prudent part of the nation was in favour of this scheme. The Whigs were of course in favour of it, for it was their scheme. Harley, at the head of the moderate Tories, strenuously supported it. But it was not popular with the unthinking masses, and perhaps could not be. Half or more than half the believers in divine right were ready, as we have explained, to pay obedience to Queen Anne as a sort of consecrated queen; she was at any rate a princess born of a real king and queen in real England; we had always been used to her. But a search in Germany for the sort of Protestants we were likely to find there was not pleasant to the mass of Englishmen; and of the strong-minded old lady who had been discovered nothing whatever was commonly known. After all, too, there was no certainty that in future we should be obeying the nearest Protestant heir. We were passing over several Catholic families; and if hereafter any one of them were to become a Protestant—according to *principle*, or what was called such, we must obey him as our king.

Though the choice of the Hanoverian family as heirs to the Crown was prudent, wise, and statesmanlike, there was no strong popular sentiment on which it was firmly based,

and no neat popular phrase by which it could in argument
be precisely supported. In a word, unthinking people of the
common sort did not much like the House of Hanover, and
a mass of ill-defined prejudice accumulated against it. Of this
prejudice Bolingbroke made himself the organ. He did not
share it or try to share it. But, finding a large and speechless
party, he thought he could become at once politically important by saying for them that which they could not say for
themselves. The scheme was successful. He became at once
important in Parliament, because he was the eloquent spokesman of many inaudible persons.

In foreign policy, Bolingbroke's tactics were the same. The
aggression of France was the natural terror of lovers of liberty at that time. Louis XIV was as ready to use his power
without scruple against free nations as Napoleon; and his
power, though not equal to that of Napoleon at his zenith,
was greater than that of Napoleon at most times, and than
that of any other French sovereign at any time. The King of
Spain, too, was about to die; it was to be feared that he
would name as his heir Philip, the grandson of Louis; and
few doubted but that Louis, notwithstanding an express renunciation of all such claims by treaty, would permit his
grandson to accept the throne. Nor was the Spain of 1700
merely the Spain of our time. She was much more powerful.
She possessed the "California of that age, a vast empire in
South America, producing gold and silver, which were then
thought to be magically potent substances, for the whole
civilised world. She possessed, too, Sicily, and Naples, and
Milan, and Belgium; and the popular imagination, which
ever clings to decaying grandeur, still believed that Spain itself was a nation of great power—was still able, as in former
generations, to obtain ascendency in Europe. The *terror*, for
such it was, of liberal politicians then was, that that vast inheritance would practically fall into the dominion of Louis
XIV—that it would belong to a Bourbon prince brought up
under his eye, and slavishly in subjection to him. The Whigs
contended that this calamity should be prevented, if possible,
by an amicable partition of Spain, by giving France as little
as possible, and that little in places as little important as
possible. If no such amicable arrangement were possible, they
said, it must be prevented by a war. The Tories did not like
war, did not like partition treaties. They did not love France,
but they were not anxious to oppose France. In that age we

were uneducated in foreign policy; the mass of men had no distinct conception of continental transactions, nor was reason reinforced very distinctly by antipathy. We hated France, it is true, but we hated Holland also; she was our rival in commerce and our enemy—sometimes our successful enemy—in naval warfare; and to vanquish the French by the aid of the Dutch did not greatly gratify our animosity. The anti-revolutionary part of the nation did not care for liberty, for that was the code of the Whigs and the basis of the revolution. In a word, though there was little distinct or rational opinion opposed to a war with France, there was much indistinct and crude prejudice. Of this too Bolingbroke became the organ.

In the later part of his life he did not attempt to defend his first notion of foreign policy. He says: "I have sometimes considered, in reflecting on these passages, what I should have done if I had sat in Parliament at that time; and have been forced to own myself that I should have voted for disbanding the army then, as I voted in the following Parliament for censuring the partition treaties. I am forced to own this, because I remember how imperfect my notions were of the situation of Europe in that extraordinary crisis, and how much I saw the true interest of my own country in a half light. But, my lords, I own it with some shame, because in truth nothing could be more absurd than the conduct we held. What! because we had not reduced the power of France by the war, nor excluded the house of Bourbon from the Spanish succession, nor compounded with her upon it by the peace; and because the House of Austria had not helped herself, nor put it into our power to help her with more advantage and better prospect of success—were we to leave that whole succession open to the invasions of France, and to suffer even the contingency to subsist of seeing those monarchies united? What! because it was become extravagant, after the trials so lately made, to think ourselves any longer engaged by treaty, or obliged by good policy, to put the House of Austria in possession of the whole Spanish monarchy, and to defend her in this possession by force of arms, were we to leave the whole at the mercy of France? If we were not to do so, if we were not to do one of the three things that I said above remained to be done, and if the Emperor put it out of our power to do another of them with advantage; were we to put it still more out of our power, and to wait unarmed for the death of the King of Spain? In fine, if we had not the prospect of disputing with France, so successfully as we might have had it, the Spanish succession whenever it should be open; were we not only to show, by disarming, that we would not dispute it at all, but to censure likewise the second of the three things mentioned above, and which King William put in practice, the compounding with France, to prevent if possible a war, in which we were averse to engage?" The truth doubtless is, that Bolingbroke never believed, or much believed these absurdities. As he was the spokesman of the Tories, he advocated, and was compelled to advocate, the vague notions which they not unnaturally held, and these were prejudices imbibed by habit, not opinions elaborated by effort.

That his mode of advocacy was very skilful, we may easily believe. His speeches have perished, but their merit may be conjectured. He is in his writings a great master of *specious* statement. Accessory arguments and subordinate facts seem of themselves to fall precisely where they should fall. He has the knack of never *making* a case; the case always seems made for him; he seems to be giving it its most suitable expression, but to be doing no more. In the greater part of his writings which were written late in life, except when he defends the Peace of Utrecht, he had no tenet to defend in which he took a keen interest. He had not the habits suitable to abstract thought, nor the genius for it. He is apt, therefore, to embody meagre thoughts in excellent words, to develop long arguments from sparse facts. He had a pleasure in writing, and he had little to say. But when his passions were eager, when his interest was vivid, when the very dissipation of his life quickened his excitability, when the topic of discussion was critically important to himself—we may well believe his advocacy to have been effective. He could ever say what he pleased, and in early life he had much to say which he well knew and for which he much cared.

A blunder of Louis' for several years simplified English politics. At the death of James II he acknowledged his son, the "Pretender," as King of England; and he could have done him no greater harm. The English people were not very sure of abstract rights, but they were very sure of practical applications. Whether they had a right to choose a king for themselves might be doubtful, but it was clear that the King of France had no such right. Whoever might be our king, it certainly should not be his *protégé*. War with France became popular. The King of Spain was dead; as was feared, he had left the vast inheritance of Spain to Louis' grandson, and war with France became expedient. It was declared accordingly.

The death of William simplified politics still further. Bolingbroke himself may explain this. "The alliances," he tells us, "were concluded, the quotas were settled, and the season for taking the field approached, when King William died. The event could not fail to occasion some consternation on one side, and to give some hopes on the other; for, notwithstanding the ill success with which he made war generally, he was looked upon as the sole centre of union that could keep together the great confederacy then forming; and how much the French feared from his life had appeared a few years before, in the extravagant and indecent joy they expressed on a false report of his death. A short time showed how vain the fears of some, and the hopes of others, were. By his death, the Duke of Marlborough was raised to the head of the army, and indeed of the confederacy; where he, a new, a private man, a subject, acquired by merit and by management a more deciding influence than high birth, confirmed authority, and even the crown of Great Britain, had given to King William. Not only all the parts of that vast machine, the grand alliance, were kept more compact and entire, but a more rapid and vigorous motion was given to the whole; and, instead of languishing or disastrous campaigns, we saw every scene of the war full of action. All those wherein he appeared, and many of those wherein he was not then an actor—but abettor, however, of their action—were crowned with the most triumphant success. I take with pleasure this opportunity of doing justice to that great man, whose faults I knew, whose virtues I admired, and whose memory, as the greatest general and as the greatest minister that our country or perhaps any other has produced, I honour." The war absorbed England for several years. For the first time in our history we were the centre of a great confederacy, and our general was the victorious leader, in great battles, of miscellaneous armies. It was then that we first acquired that great name as a military people, which, notwithstanding our small numbers and small armies, we have since supported, and that a great foresight, a minute diligence, and a splendid courage in modern war, were first combined in an English-

man. Marlborough was in one respect more fortunate than
Wellington. Napoleon must always be the first military figure
of his generation; but throughout the last century the whole
Continent talked of the wars of Marlborough, for he was the
most fascinating as well as the most successful general in
them.

During the first eight years of Marlborough's wars, the
English nation was nearly united. A war always unites a people; the objector to it becomes a kind of traitor to his country; he seems to be a favourer of the enemy, even though he
is not. Not only Harley, a moderate Tory, but Bolingbroke,
an extreme Tory, took office in the war ministry. It is true
there was no dereliction of party principle in their doing so,
either as such principle was then understood, or as it is understood now. Marlborough himself had never been a Whig;
and Godolphin, the head of the Treasury and first minister
for the home administration, had ever been a Tory. But
though plain party ties might not be violated by a Tory support of Marlborough's wars, a sort of sentiment was violated.
The war was a Whig war, and could only be carried on by
Whig support. Ere long Godolphin and Marlborough were
compelled to give the Whigs a large share in the actual administration. The ministry became a composite one. Though
many Tories remained in it, yet its essence and its spirit were
Whig. It was carrying on the sort of war which one party in
the State had extolled for years, and which the antagonist
party had deprecated for years. It has been called after its
cause. It has been called the Whig Ministry of Godolphin
and Marlborough, the two leading Tories of the age.

The place which Bolingbroke accepted was that of Secretary at War, which brought him into contact with the best
business of the time, with that sort of business upon which
most depended. As far as appears, he did it well, and the
official experience he then acquired must have been inestimable to him afterwards. There is much which no statesman can in truth know, and much more which he will not
be thought to know, unless he has gone through a certain
necessary official education, and learn to use certain conven-
tional official expressions. This sort of knowledge Bolingbroke
now acquired. But it was not by success or failure in office
desk-work that the movements of his life were to be regulated.

The Whigs naturally did not quite like the subordinate
position which they occupied in a ministry which was carry-

ing out a Whig policy. They thought it hard that Tories should be paid for Whig measures; that the glory of delivering Europe should be given, not to Whigs, who had striven to deliver her, but to Tories, who would have liked not to deliver her. Their support was necessary to Godolphin and to Marlborough, and they gradually raised the price of that support. Early in 1708 most of the remaining Tories were turned out, and Bolingbroke among them. Except the two chiefs, Godolphin and Marlborough, the ministry became a Whig ministry almost exclusively.

That Bolingbroke did not like to be turned out is probable; but he professed to like it. He sought refuge in retirement; he professed to study philosophy, and passed much of his time in the country, and in reading. Such professions from a man of great ambition and lax life were ridiculed. A friend suggested that he should write this motto over his favourite rural retreat:—

"From business and the noisy world retired,
   Nor vexed by love, nor by ambition fired,
   Gently I wait the call of Charon's boat,
   Still drinking like a fish, and amorous like a goat."[3]

And Swift says he could hardly bear the jest, for he was a man rather sensitive to ridicule. And though satirists might laugh at his meditations and his studies, and though he permitted them to derange very little his pleasure or his vices, there is no doubt but that they were real, and that they were valuable. Doubtless, too, though he was only twenty-eight, he was a little tired of subordinate office. His disposition was very impatient, and his sense of personal dignity very considerable. Even so patient a pattern of routine diligence as Sir Robert Peel rejoiced as a young man to be for a year or so out of office. His mind, he acknowledged, widened, and his capacity to think for himself improved. If Peel, who was made to toil in the furrow, felt this, Bolingbroke, who was made to exult in the desert, might well feel it. During three years he really read much and thought much.

But a great change was at hand. The war with France was still successful and still popular, but it might be doubted if it was still necessary. We had weakened France so much, that it might be questionable if she wanted weakening more. Our victories had destroyed her prestige, and the results of these

[3] Swift's *Journal to Stella*.

victories had weakened her vigour. Sensible men began to inquire what was to be the time, what the occasion, and what
the terms of peace.

The ministry, indeed, appeared to be firm, but it was firm
in appearance only. The conditions of ministerial continuance
differed in that age in a most material respect from the present conditions. Now, the House of Commons, in almost all
cases, prescribes imperatively not only what measures shall
be taken, but what men shall take them: it chooses both
policy and ministers. In Queen Anne's time Parliament had
acquired an almost complete ascendency in policy; it could
fix precisely whether there should be war or no war, peace
or no peace; it had acquired a perfect control upon legislation,
and a nearly perfect control upon internal administration.
But it had no choice, or but little in the selection of persons.
What was to be done Parliament settled, but *who* was to do
it the queen settled.

Queen Anne had done so at her accession. Though she
was engaged in a Whig war, she removed the Whig ministers
whom she found in office. She appointed as supreme general-
issimo over the war abroad, and real prime minister over
matters of state at home, the Duke of Marlborough, not because of his discretion or his acquaintance with business, or
his military genius, but because his wife was her early friend
and her special favourite. As the Duke of Wellington justly
observed, the Duke of Marlborough *was* the English Government; he was not liable to be thwarted, or misconstrued, or
neglected; his operations in Flanders were never cramped by
the home Government, as the operations of the Duke of
Wellington in Spain were cramped. He appointed the lord
high treasurer Godolphin; he placed the Treasury, then even
more than now the supreme internal office, in Godolphin's
hands, because he was connected with him by domestic ties,
because they had long acted together, because he had great
confidence in his financial ability. The Duke of Marlborough
was not only great because of his wife, but absolutely because
of his wife.

By a kind of compensation the source of his power was
the cause also of his downfall. The Queen and the duchess
quarrelled, as was natural. The duchess was virulent and ob-
trusive, and the Queen was sensitive and sullen. The Queen
had a strong sense of personal dignity, which the duchess
used to outrage. The duchess, who was clever, thought the

Queen a fool, and scarcely forbore to look and say so. From early habit the friendship lasted much longer than could have been thought likely, but it could not last for ever. As it was breaking up, a small force produced a large effect. The Queen, Swift says, had not a "stock of amity" for more than one person at a time: she commonly cared but little for anybody save one; but she required one. The duchess had placed at court a poor relative of her own, a Miss Hill, whom both she and the Queen regarded as a petty dependent, a *real* maid, who would be useful and lie on the floor when peeresses and young ladies of quality were useless and went to bed. As she was humble and artful, she acquired influence; she was never in the way and never out of the way. She was always pleasant to the Queen, and the duchess was commonly unpleasant. The consequence was certain. The abject new favourite soon supplanted the querulous old favourite.

A very curious man took advantage of this. Wits and satirists have been fond of describing Robert Harley, but perhaps they have not described him very well. They have made a heap of incongruities of him. They have told us that, being bred a Puritan, and retaining till his death much of the Puritan phraseology, he yet became the favourite leader of High Churchmen and Tories; that being a muddle-headed dawdler, he gained a great reputation for the transaction of business; that having an incapacity for intelligible speech, he became an influential orator in Parliament; that being a puzzle-headed man, of less than average ability, and less than average activity, he long ruled a great party, for years ruled the court, and was at last Prime Minister of England.

It is very natural that brilliant and vehement men should depreciate Harley, for he had nothing which they possess, but had everything which they commonly do not possess. He was by nature a moderate man. In that age they called such a man a trimmer, but they called him ill. Such a man does not consciously shift or purposely trim his course. He firmly believes that he is substantially consistent. "I do not wish in this House," he would say in our age, "to be a party to any extreme course. Mr Gladstone brings forward a great many things which I cannot understand; I assure you he does. There is more in that bill of his about tobacco than he thinks; I am confident there is. Money is a serious thing, a *very* serious thing. And I am sorry to say Mr Disraeli commits the party very much. He avows sentiments which are injudi-

cious. I cannot go along with him nor can Sir John. He was
not taught the Catechism; I know he was not. There is a want
in him of sound and sober religion—and Sir John agrees with
me—which would keep him from distressing the clergy, who
are very important. Great orators are very well; but, as I said,
how is the revenue? And the point is, not to be led away and
to be moderate, and not to go to an extreme. As soon as it
seems *very* clear, then I begin to doubt. I have been many
years in Parliament, and *that* is my experience." We may
laugh at such speeches, but there have been plenty of them
in every English Parliament. A great English divine has been
described as always leaving out the principle upon which his
arguments rested; even if it was stated to him, he regarded
it as far-fetched and extravagant. Any politician who has this
temper of mind will always have many followers; and he may
be nearly sure that all great measures will be passed more
nearly as he wishes them to be passed than as great orators
wish. Harley had this temper, and he enjoyed its results. He
always had a certain influence over moderate Whigs when he
was a Tory, and over moderate Tories when he was a Whig.
Nine-tenths of mankind are more afraid of violence than of
anything else; and inconsistent moderation is always popular,
because of all qualities it is most opposite to violence—most
likely to preserve the present safe existence.

Harley's moderation, which was influential because it was
unaffected, was assisted by two powers which brilliant people
despise, because in general they do not share them. Harley
excelled in the forms of business. There is distinct evidence
that official persons preferred his management of the Treasury to that of Lord Godolphin, who preceded him, or Sir R.
Walpole, who succeeded him. In real judgment and substantial knowledge of affairs, there was doubtless no comparison.
Godolphin was the best financier of his generation; and Walpole was the best not only of his own but of many which
came after him. But the ultimate issue of business is not the
part of it which most impresses the officials of a department.
They understand how business is conducted better than what
comes of it. The statesman who gives them no trouble—who
coincides with that which they recommend—who thinks of
the things which they think of, is more satisfactory to his
mere subordinates than a real ruler, who has plans which
others do not share, and whose mind is occupied by large

considerations, which only a few can appreciate, and only experience can test. In his own time, both with the Tory party and with moderate Whigs, Harley's reputation as a man of business was a means of influence which, on the same scene and in our own day, could hardly be surpassed.

But it was surpassed in his own day. In personal questions, as we have explained, the Parliament in Queen Anne's time was only a subordinate power; the court was the principal and the determining power. Now the faculty of business is but secondary in all courts; the faculty of intrigue is the main source of real influence. To be able to manage men, to know with whom to be silent, to know with whom to say how much, to be able to drop casual observations, to have a sense of that which others mean, though they do not say— to be aware what Lady A is in secret planning, though she says the very opposite—to know that Lord B has no influence, though he seems most potent—to know that little C is a wire-puller, and can get you anything, though he looks mean and though no one knows; in a word, to understand, to feel, to be unable to help feeling, the *by-play* of life, is the principal necessity for success in courts. It is the instinct of management which is not to be shown even in conversation, far less in writing or speculation, but yet which rules all small societies. Harley possessed it, and the obscure but potent talents of business also; and we need seek no farther explanation why he was one of the most successful men in his own time.

Harley was some sort of relative to Miss Hill (or Mrs Masham, for she married), the rising favourite of Queen Anne's time. He was the favourite leader of all moderate Tories; and, on the whole, though not without grumblings from extreme men, the most important leader of the Tory party. He had been turned out when Bolingbroke was turned out, and he wished to return. The fly was brought to the spider. Mrs Masham, the new favourite, asked Harley what counsel she should give the Queen. He said, "Turn out the Whigs"; and meant "Bring *me* in".

The Queen was inert, for that was her nature; and the evident popularity and the glorious success of the Whig war naturally staggered her. But the Whigs made an error. The High-Church and semi-High-Church party had enormous power in the nation; they had always advocated non-resistance before the revolution, and though they had taken the oaths

to King William's Government, they did not like to think
that they were supporting a Government which was conspicuously rebellious, which began in resistance to legitimate authority. Of course, the fact was so. King William invaded
England with Dutch troops, and was joined by English rebels; but the divine right of princes, and the duty of unconditional obedience, retained much influence over most of the
clergy and over many of the laity. If the Whigs had been
wise, they would have offended this powerful sentiment as
little as possible. High Churchmen were certainly powerful,
but were necessarily inert; they had no distinct course to recommend; they *would* have done much, but they *could* do
nothing. They had assented to the existing Government, and
though their assent might be unwilling and ungracious, the
existing Government should have let them alone. The Whigs
adopted the reverse course. A foolish parson expressed with
unusual folly the sentiments of the great majority of his order. The Commons, at the instigation of the Whigs, actually
impeached him at the bar of the Lords. In their folly they
used against a pious and innocuous fool the extreme remedy
which the constitution provides for the final punishment of
impious and dangerous traitors. The country was in a ferment; the Tory party were active; the moderate classes were
alarmed; the clergy were incensed; the Whigs became unpopular.

Harley seized the opportunity. He persuaded Mrs Masham
to persuade the Queen that now was the moment to gratify
her new antipathy to her old favourite; that now she should
punish the Duchess of Marlborough; that now she should dismiss the Whig ministry. She did so. He came in himself, and
made Bolingbroke a secretary of state, and the first member
in the House of Commons.

It has been said, and is very likely, that Harley would have
preferred to retain in office the quiet and moderate Whigs,
and not to bring in Bolingbroke, an extreme and unquiet
Tory. The Whig party, however, was compact, and held together; it must be expelled as a whole, or retained as a whole.
If it had been wholly retained, Harley could not have come
in, and he was therefore obliged to ally himself with the aggravated Tories and with Bolingbroke, who had made himself their mouthpiece. It only completes the mingled character of Bolingbroke to repeat the legend of the time, that
his acceptance of office was heard with gladness, not only in

grave manor-houses, and by severe High Churchmen, but in more unmentionable places and by more questionable persons. Some ladies of much beauty and little virtue, so runs the legend, were heard to say, "Bolingbroke is minister. He has six thousand guineas a year. Six thousand guineas, and all for us." The auspices of such a ministry were not good.

The public aspect of affairs was, however, in the most critical particular very favourable. While the French War lasted, indeed, the new ministry must be perplexed. They must either retain the Duke of Marlborough as general-in-chief, which was not pleasant, as he was the chief of the party opposed to them, and since probably Mrs Masham did not wish it; or they must dismiss the duke in the midst of victory, and find a new general, who might be defeated. But this painful alternative was temporary only. The English nation had been sated with sieges and victories, and more than sated with taxes and with debt; it was disposed to peace. The new ministry came therefore into the enjoyment of a great inheritance, the greatest that has ever fallen to a new ministry. France had been so reduced by Marlborough's victories that she was ready to consent to a peace which a few years before she would have thought most shameful, which a few years before we should have thought most honourable. The new ministry were to make that peace.

The preliminary difficulty soon assumed its worst shape. It became necessary to dismiss the Duke of Marlborough; and, as might be expected, the Duke of Ormond, who succeeded him, was much less successful. There was happily no great defeat, but there were minor disasters, which were magnified by the contrast with past glories. We had been used to a great exploit every year, and we were now asked to be thankful for not being defeated very much. The contrast was painful, and the necessity of making peace became greater than ever.

Up to this time Bolingbroke had been the most successful politician of his age, and almost of any age, in England. He had, it is true, no influence at court. Queen Anne distrusted him; she liked decorous men of regulated life. But, though little over thirty, he was the leader of the House of Commons; the first orator there; the second minister in the Cabinet; the favourite minister of the most ardent section of his party—a section just strengthened by an election. The fame of his oratory filled London, and the fame of his genius filled

the country. Mr Pitt excepted, no Englishman had risen so
high and so rapidly under our Parliamentary system. It was
at this crisis that his eager nature and his life of excitement
began to prepare his downfall, as they had prepared his rise.

The official management of the foreign negotiations was in
the hands of Bolingbroke. Lord Dartmouth, the other secretary of state, could speak no French, and Harley, the Prime
Minister, could speak but little; but Bolingbroke spoke it
well. Harley, too, had no directing ability. He had the defects of the late Lord Aberdeen: he was moderate and useful and judicious. But he could not upon the spur of the
moment strike out a distinct policy. Other statesmen must
create before he could decide on their creations. Bolingbroke
was to devise how a peace should be made.

A plain and strong-headed statesman—such a statesman as
Walpole or as Palmerston—would have had little difficulty.
France was most anxious to make peace, and it mattered but
little for England or for Europe what were the precise conditions of it. There are occasions when a war itself does its own
work, and does it better than any pacification. The Crimean
War was an instance of this. That war thoroughly destroyed
the prestige of Russia and the pernicious predominance of
Russia. At the end of it, what were to be the conditions of
peace was almost immaterial. The wars of Marlborough had
done their work also. We had gone to war to prevent the acquisition of overbearing power by Louis XIV. If a grandson
who was devoted to him had succeeded to Spain and the
Spanish empire while France was unexhausted, he would
have been a despot in Europe; he would have been terrible
to us as Napoleon was terrible. But nine years of continuous
defeat had exhausted France, and Louis XIV was now a vanquished and decayed old man. At his death the crown of
France would pass to Louis XV, who was an infant; it was not
much to be feared that the policy of France and the policy
of Spain would be dangerously connected because their kings
were second cousins. Possibly, indeed, Louis XV might die,
and the King of Spain might come to the throne of France.
But this was a remote and contingent danger; it would have
been unwise in our ancestors to lavish blood and spend
treasure because a prince might have died young who really
lived to be extremely old. The true object of the war had
been accomplished by the war itself, and the substantial task
of making a peace was therefore very easy.

The accessories of the task, too, it would seem, were easy also. As we had been victorious in a first-rate war, it was right that we should be dignified in the final pacification. It was right that we should be ready, that we should even be anxious to make peace; but, at any rate, France, who was vanquished, ought to seem equally anxious. Since, in part, the war was a war to reduce her influence over the European imagination, the manner of making peace was at least as material as the terms of it. We were principal members of a great league, and we had stirred up a part of Spain to resist the French King of Spain. We were bound to keep clear faith with our allies, and bound not to desert brave provinces who had relied principally on our protection.

Bolingbroke was too eager to perceive these plain considerations. He sent a man to Paris to ask for peace; and the French minister was so astounded that he would hardly believe the man. He owned afterwards that, when he was asked the preliminary question, "Do you want a peace?" it seemed to him like asking a lingering invalid whether he wanted to recover. He could hardly bring himself to believe that Bolingbroke's messenger was duly authorised.

The previous life of that messenger certainly was not such as to gain him credit. He was a French abbé named Gaultier, who had been a French spy, and perhaps still was so, in England. He was an acute, plausible person, very fat, and not very respectable, and altogether as unlikely a person to be sent from a victorious nation to a defeated nation as could be imagined.

Nevertheless, the Abbé Gaultier was so sent. He said to Torcy, the French minister, "Do you want a peace? I bring you the means of treating independently of the Dutch, who are unworthy of his Majesty's kindness and the honour he has done them in addressing himself to them so many times to restore peace to Europe." In an ordinary alliance, such a clandestine reconciliation with the enemy, and such a secret desertion of allies, would have been plainly dishonest. There would have been little to say for it, and very few would have been willing to say that little. But the Grand Alliance was not an ordinary one. Its acute framers had perceived the difficulty of their task. They had foreseen the difficulty of retaining in firm cohesion a miscellaneous league of scattered States. They had adopted the best expedient at their disposal: they had prohibited the very commencement of exclusive negotiation by individual States. Their words are as clear as words can be. They are these: "Neutri partium fas sit, Bello semel suscepto, de Pace cum Hoste tractare nisi conjunctim et communicatis conciliis cum altera Parte". These words expressly forbid such secret missions as those of Gaultier, and were inserted expressly to forbid them.

The separate treaty with Holland was even more express: it said that "no negotiation shall be set on foot by one of the allies without the concurrence of the other; and that each ally shall continually, and from time to time, impart to the other everything which passes in the said negotiation". And yet it was especially from Holland that Bolingbroke was anxious, by every secret disguise, and every diplomatic artifice, to conceal his negotiation. He hoped, by a separate and secret peace, to obtain commercial advantages for the English, in which the Dutch should have no share.

Even after the first mission of Gaultier had terminated, there was an intricate series of secret negotiations, in which he and Prior were employed for us, and Mesnager for the French. Prior expressly required on our behalf "that the secret should be inviolably kept till allowed by both parties to be divulged"; and the French minister wrote to Bolingbroke: "It wholly depends upon the secrecy and good use you will make of the entire confidence he testifies to the Queen of Great Britain; and the King of France extols the firmness of the Queen, and sees with great pleasure the new marks of resolution she shows". It was impossible to desert our allies more absolutely or more dishonourably. It was impossible to violate an express treaty more audaciously or more corruptly.

Nor was the secret negotiation a mere crime; it was also a miserable blunder. Diplomacy could hardly commit a greater. There was a splendid, a nearly unexampled power of compelling France to make a good peace. There was a great coalition against her, which had always been victorious under Eugene and Marlborough; which had obtained such successes as no Englishman had imagined; which had reduced France to a pitch of shame, degradation, and weakness, that surprised her most sanguine enemies, and depressed her most sanguine friends. So long as the coalition was compact, the coalition was all-powerful. But by the mere act of commencing a separate negotiation, Bolingbroke dissolved the coalition. There could be no mutual trust after that. The principal member of the league deserted the league, and its bond was immediately

disunited. We all know what would have been the consequences if England had acted thus in the great war. Suppose Lords Grey and Grenville had come in before the campaign of 1814; suppose that they had sent a secret emissary
to Napoleon; suppose that they had offered a separate peace
without Spain, or Austria, or Russia. We know that Napoleon would again have been a principal potentate in Europe, for the coalition which alone could extirpate him would
have been dissolved.

The truth of these remarks is written on the very face of
the Treaty of Utrecht, and is obvious in every part of the negotiation of it. A few months before Louis had been willing
to abandon Spain and to abandon his grandson. He had said:
"If you can take Spain from him, take it; I will not help
him". But the allies were not content. They required that
Louis should compel his grandson to resign, and this he considered dishonourable. But at Utrecht it was not even proposed that Philip should abandon Spain; that the House of
Bourbon should possess Spain was a conceded and admitted
principle. We had dissolved the European confederacy, and
we could not hope to attain its objects.

Nor was the desertion of the other powers combined with
us in the Grand Alliance our only desertion, or our worst. All
these powers were States of some magnitude, and some were
States of great magnitude. They would be able to go on as
they had always gone on—to shift for themselves, as they had
always shifted. But we also deserted others who were not so
independent. We had incited the Catalans in the north-east
of Spain to resist the French King of Spain; we had promised
them in express terms our support and aid; for a long time
we had given them that aid. But at the Peace of Utrecht we
deserted them. The Catalans made a brave resistance, but a
small province could do nothing against a great nation. The
Catalans were soon overcome, and deprived of all their liberties. Throughout Europe, and doubtless throughout England
also, there were many murmurs against our policy. We had
encouraged a brave people to rebel; we had even threatened
them if they did not rebel; and when they did rebel, we
deserted them. If, at present, France and England were to
incite the Poles to rebel against Russia, they hardly *could* desert them: the public opinion of the world is now so powerful; in Queen Anne's time public opinion could only mur-

mur, but it did murmur. The Peace of Utrecht, men said, was a base crime as well as a gross blunder.

But why, it will be asked, did Bolingbroke commit so gross a blunder? What reasons could have rendered it plausible to him? The principal answer is the principal key to his character. With many splendid gifts, he was exceedingly defective in cool and plain judgment. He failed where in all ages such men as Alcibiades have failed. Whether by nature he was much gifted with judgment we cannot tell; the probability is that he was about as well gifted as other men. But his life was such as to render a cool judgment impossible. "His fine imagination," says Lord Chesterfield, "was often heated and exhausted with his body in celebrating and almost deifying the prostitute of the night; and his convivial joys were pushed to all the extravagancy of frantic bacchanals." Swift tells graphic stories of his drinking till his associates could drink no longer and his being left at three in the morning calling for "t'other flask". Many men lead gross lives and keep cool heads, but such are not men of Bolingbroke's temperament. A man like Walpole, or a man like Louis Napoleon, is protected by an unsensitive nature from intellectual destruction. But such a man as Bolingbroke, whose nature is warm and whose imagination is excitable, imbibes the eager poison into the very heart of his mind. Such is our protection against the possibilities of an Alcibiades. No one who has not a vivid imagination can succeed in such a career; and any man of vivid imagination that career would burn away and destroy. Cold men may be wild in life and not wild in mind. But warm and eager men, fit to be the favourites of society, and fit to be great orators, will be erratic not only in conduct but in judgment. They will see men "like trees walking".

Bolingbroke's excitement did not prevent his working. He laboured many hours and wrote many letters. He often complains of the number of hours he has been at his desk, and of the labours which were thrown upon him. But his work probably only excited him the more; for a time *vires acquirit eundo* is the law of such wild strength. In the course of the negotiations he went to Paris, became the idol of society there, and used his social advantages efficiently for political purposes. To dazzle people more, he learned, or pretended to learn, the Spanish language, to read such diplomatic documents as were written in it. But such minor excellences could not mend the incurable badness of a peace commenced by a surrender of the best we had to surrender, by a dissolution of our alliance. A plain strong-headed man would have left alone the accessory advantages, and succeeded in the main point. Without Spanish and without French, Walpole would have made a good peace; Bolingbroke could not do so with both.

Bolingbroke, too, had a scheme, as imaginative and excited men will have. He knew that in relinquishing Spain to the House of Bourbon, he was giving the opponents of peace a great argumentative advantage. The mass of mankind, who judge by visible symbols, considered that a peace by which the king whom we had opposed should reign in Spain, and by which the king whom we had proposed did not reign there, was a gross failure. In sound argument, it was probably right for us to concede. As we have explained, the war had accomplished its own work; France was excessively weakened, and there was little fear of present danger from her. If, by a possible death, the crown of France should fall to the King of Spain, it would be time enough then to prevent the same person from reigning in the two kingdoms. The Treaty of Utrecht provides that the same prince shall not reign in both; and, if necessary, we could go to war to enforce the treaty. The Bourbon king was popular in Spain, and was preferred by the Spaniards to any one else. It would have been hard to dislodge him. But Bolingbroke did not like to rely on these plain arguments. He hoped to make the peace popular by an appeal to our commercial jealousy, by gaining mercantile advantages for ourselves which our rivals the Dutch did not share. He obtained for us the celebrated Assiento contract, giving us the right of carrying negro slaves to the West Indies, and also certain privileges which would have given our manufacturers great advantage in the French markets. He hoped this commercial bribe would silence the national conscience—that it would induce us to forget our treachery to our allies, our desertion of the Catalans, and the establishment of the House of Bourbon in Spain. He hoped it would make the peace popular.

He was disappointed. The reception of that peace by the nation, and especially by the Tory party, was very like the reception of Mr Disraeli's great Budget of 1852. A great secret had been long paraded of something which was to please everybody: it was divulged, and it pleased nobody. Bol-

ingbroke may himself describe the effect that his work produced on the more moderate portion of his party:—

"The whimsical or the Hanover Tories continued zealous
in appearance with us till the peace was signed. I saw no
people so eager for the conclusion of it. Some of them
were in such haste, that they thought any peace preferable
to the least delay, and omitted no instances to quicken
their friends who were actors in it. As soon as the treaties
were perfected and laid before Parliament, the scheme of
these gentlemen began to disclose itself entirely. Their love
of the peace, like other passions, cooled by enjoyment.
They grew nice about the construction of the articles,
could come up to no direct approbation, and, being let into
the secret of what was to happen, would not preclude
themselves from the glorious advantage of rising on the
ruins of their friends and of their party."

Nothing could be more natural than their conduct. The
moderate Tory party, and most sensible men, wished for a
satisfactory peace made in a satisfactory manner: they wished
for dignity in diplomacy, and desirable results. They were disappointed. After a war which every one was proud of, we
concluded a peace which nobody was proud of, in a manner
that every one was ashamed of.

The commercial treaties on which Bolingbroke relied, so
far from helping him, were a hindrance to him. The right of
taking slaves to the West Indies was indeed popular: the day
for anti-slavery scruples had not commenced. But, in return
for the privileges which the French gave to our manufacturers, we had given many privileges to them. We had established an approximation to free-trade, and every one was
aghast. The English producer clamoured for protection, and
he has seldom clamoured in vain. The commercial treaties
required the consent of Parliament, and were rejected. If Bolingbroke had been a free-trader upon principle, his convictions might have consoled him. But he professed to know
nothing of commerce, and did know nothing. His books are
full of nonsense on such topics: he hated the City because
they were Whigs, and he hated the Dutch because he had
deserted them; and these were his cardinal sentiments on
mercantile affairs. He speaks of "matters, such as that of

commerce, which the negotiators of the Peace of Utrecht could not be supposed to understand". Certainly he did not understand them. He only directed his subordinates to get out of the French as much for ourselves, and as little for the Dutch, as possible.

"Instead of gathering strength" (says Bolingbroke), "either as a ministry or as a party, we grew weaker every day. The peace had been judged with reason to be the only solid foundation whereupon we could erect a Tory system; and yet when it was made, we found ourselves at a full stand. Nay, the very work, which ought to have been the basis of our strength, was in part demolished before our eyes and we were stoned with the ruins of it."

In our time he would have been really stoned. The fierce warlike disposition of the English people would not have endured such dishonour. We may doubt if it would have endured any peace. It certainly would not have endured the best peace, unless it were made with dignity and with honesty. We should have been wildly elated by Marlborough's victories, and little in a mood to bear shame and to be guilty of desertion. The English people has been much the same for centuries. In country manor-houses, where a son had been killed for the cause which was sacrificed—in alehouses, where men were used to hear of glorious victories—in large towns, where the wrongs of injured races like the Catalans were understood—through a whole nation, which has ever been proud, brave, and honourable, a mean peace, effected by desertion, must have been abhorred. It was merely endured because it was made, and because in those days, when communication was slow, public opinion, as in America now, did not distinctly form itself till the crisis for action was over. But though for the moment endured, it was long abhorred. For very many years half our political talk was coloured by it. It was to the Tories what the coalition between Lord North and Fox was to the Whigs, a principal operating cause in excluding them from office during fifty years.

And, what for the time was worse, the Tory ministry of the moment was disunited. "Whilst this was doing," says Bolingbroke, "Harley looked on, as if he had not been a party to all which had passed; broke now and then a jest, which savoured of the Inns of Court, and the bad company in which he had been bred; and on those occasions where his station obliged him to speak of business, was absolutely unintelligible". In reality Harley disliked his position. He had always been a moderate man, respected by moderate men; he had the reputation of a man of care and judgment, and he had thriven by that reputation. On a sudden he became a party to disreputable peace, at which even moderate Whigs were frantic, for which even moderate Tories could not vote. That the negotiations had commenced by artifice and deceit did not horrify him much, for he was a man much given to stratagem. But he knew also that the negotiation had ended in conspicuous meanness and unpopular concessions; he felt that his reputation for judgment was weakened. All shrewd observers knew that there would soon be disunion between Harley, the old head of the moderate Tories, and Bolingbroke, the present head of the extreme Tories. Swift, who was a very shrewd observer, and who was close at hand, knew that there was already disunion.

Before the treaties had been discussed by, and the commercial part of them rejected in, the House of Commons, Bolingbroke made another error. He left the House of Commons. Harley had been created Earl of Oxford, and he could not endure to be inferior to him. There was much delay in conferring the peerage, and he was very angry at it. He was, Oxford says, "in the utmost rage against the Treasurer, Lady Masham, and without sparing the greatest," and made "outrageous speeches". A wise friend would have observed to him that no greater kindness could have been done him than to refuse him a peerage altogether. The great but gradual revolution which was consummated in the time of Walpole was then beginning to be apparent. Before Queen Anne's time our most conspicuous statesmen had been, during the most important part of their lives, members of the House of Lords; since Queen Anne's time they have at similar periods been usually members of the House of Commons. There are several causes for this, but the principal is one on which Bolingbroke has often commented. From time immemorial the Commons have been the guardians of the public purse; and whenever the public purse was to be touched, they have always been the first body in the State. But before the revolution they were seldom wanted. They granted the king, at the commencement of his reign, an estimated revenue, which was supposed to be adequate to the estimated expenditure in time of peace. As our wealth was rapidly increasing, it was often more than sufficient. In time of war the House of Commons must be applied to; new money was needful for new expenses; but the ordinary expenditure went on every year without their being consulted or required. The expense of William's wars and Queen Anne's wars made a great change: taxation became larger than it had ever been, though very small as it seems to us now. Since that time the estimated revenue which the Crown yearly enjoyed, without additional Parliamentary aid, has scarcely ever been adequate to the estimated expenditure. There has yearly been a Budget, and yearly a recourse to the House of Commons. The position of a minister in the House of Commons has therefore greatly risen. Nine years out of ten the nation could at present dispense with a House of Lords—though a useful, it is an auxiliary power; but every year we want a House of Commons, for it has to grant funds of primary necessity. The minister who can manage the Commons, and extract from them the necessary moneys, has then become our most necessary minister.

The change was just beginning; for Walpole, Bolingbroke's schoolfellow and Parliamentary rival, ruled his generation by his Parliamentary and financial abilities. But Bolingbroke was too eager and impetuous to foresee the action of this powerful but obscure cause. The tradition had been, that the peers were superior to the Commons, and he adhered to this tradition. He was angry till he obtained his peerage.

Nor was he satisfied when he did obtain it. He was made a viscount only, and Harley had been made an earl. He could not bear to be inferior to him in anything, especially as there was an extinct earldom in his own family. He was vexed, angry, and dissatisfied. Once he went out of town, and would attend to no business for days. He was angry too with the press. The Peace of Utrecht was attacked and assailed, and it was his peace. It is true that Bolingbroke should have been able to bear literary comments, even when rather bitter. He was himself through life an unscrupulous writer, using the press without reluctance and without cessation. He was then employing Swift, the most bitter writer of libels, both political and personal, that can be conceived. He lived with Swift in intimacy, and printed his libels. He gave him political information and ideas, and praised him when he used them so as most to hurt his adversaries. He ought to have been able to bear anything, yet he could bear nothing. He prosecuted many more persons than it was usual to prosecute then, and far more than have been prosecuted since. He thought, with a continental wit, that "a press is free when Government newspapers are licentious". He thought that everything should be said for him, and that nothing should be said against him. The copyists of Alcibiades are commonly irritable, for neither their nature nor their habits teach them forbearance.

But neither Bolingbroke's disunion with his principal colleague, nor the attacks of the press, were his greatest danger. He was in the worst political position which can be imagined. As we have explained, the principal question of the age was a question of dynasty: after the peace with France it was the sole great question; it is in the nature of a topic so absorbing to swallow up every subject of minor interest. There were only two solutions of the problem possible. The law prescribed one, and a sort of superstition prescribed another. The Act of Settlement said that the House of Hanover was to succeed Queen Anne; the doctrine of non-resistance said that the Pretender was to succeed her. The Jacobites adhered to the doctrine of non-resistance. The Whigs adhered to the Act of Parliament. Both these parties had a definite solution of the principal topic of the hour. But between these fluctuated the great mass of the Tory party, who did not like the House of Hanover because it had no hereditary right, who did not like the Pretender because he was a Roman Catholic. This party objected to both possible solutions; they lived in the vague hope that the Pretender might turn Protestant—that some unforeseen circumstance would intervene—that Queen Anne would last their time. For persons in a private station such a state of mind was very possible and very natural. But it was of this very party that Bolingbroke was the spokesman and the leader, and he was a minister. He could not well remain without a distinct policy. Queen Anne, though not old, was often ill. She was suspected to be, and we now know she was, very near her death. He must make a choice.

Yet which king was Bolingbroke to choose? If he chose the House of Hanover, he himself ought not to be minister. This was the Whig candidate, this was the candidate whom his party disliked—at whom they murmured—whom they declined to support. A Tory ministry which should bring in the House of Hanover was like a Derbyite ministry that should propose free trade or reform of Parliament. It was a ministry which tried to maintain its existence by denying its party tenets. Probably in those times a Tory ministry could not have done what we have seen them do in our own time. Party spirit ran much stronger in Queen Anne's time than in ours. The political contentions of London were like the contests at a borough election now. At three o'clock on the polling day it is very difficult to change your politics and keep your character. So it was in London then. A fierce strife raged. Whig society and Tory society were separated like two hostile camps, and a deserter from one to the other was sure of contemptuous hatred from those he left, and of contemptuous patronage from those to whom he came. Bolingbroke could not do even once that which Mr Disraeli has done twice.

Bolingbroke's enemies have been very anxious to fix on him a formed design to bring in the Pretender. He would doubtless have been very glad to do so, if he could have formed a coherent scheme. But he could not. Oxford was far too moderate and timid a man to break the law, or to plan to break it. He had himself supported the Act of Settlement. He knew that the Hanoverian succession, though not popular to the imagination of any class, was acceptable to the reason of the most thinking class. He knew that the aristocracy, the large towns, and all the cultivated part of the community, were in favour of it. He knew that, as the aristocratic classes had the command of the House of Lords, of the small boroughs, and of very many counties, as the great towns were of themselves favourable, the House of Hanover was sure of a majority in Parliament. He knew that the general vulgar, and especially the rural vulgar, who were favourable to the House of Stuart, though numerically strong, were but weak in Parliamentary representation. He was probably a party to some covert intrigues, for intrigue was intrinsically agreeable to him; but, in reality, he was too timid to abandon the plain and legal course for a tortuous and illegal one. Bolingbroke had, on the other hand, a constitutional predilection for violent courses, and no particular objection to an illegal course. If he could have turned out Oxford—if he could have carried his party with him, he would certainly have contrived some scheme for proclaiming the Pretender at Queen Anne's death. But even he was not mad enough to commit himself to a definite plan before he knew that he should have the power to execute it. In the meantime "Tom Harley," the prime minister's brother, exactly expressed the position of the ministry. "We ought," he said, "to be better or worse with Hanover than we are." The case, as men saw it then, was simple. The Queen was daily approaching the grave. The ministry in power were uncertain what to do in the event of her death. They had "no settled intention" of breaking the law, Bolingbroke tells us; but he does not venture to contend that they had a settled intention of obeying it. They were drifting to a crisis without a plan.

Now was Bolingbroke comfortable while the Queen lived. She herself did not like him. A smaller person has never been placed by the caprices of fate amid great affairs than the "good Queen Anne". She had not, Swift says, "a sufficient stock of amity" for more than one person at a time; she was always choosing a favourite upon whom to concentrate her affections exclusively. Her comprehension was as limited as her affections. She seriously objected, it is said, to one minister for appearing before her in a tie-wig instead of a full-bottom; and even if this anecdote has been exaggerated by continual narration, it expresses the sort of objections which ruled her mind and determined her conduct. She had a strong objection to all license; decorum was a sort of morality to her, as to most great ladies; she would have been much puzzled to fix where manners ended and where morals began. Bolingbroke was license personified; and therefore she distrusted and disliked him. She did not altogether approve, either, of the Peace of Utrecht. She probably did not understand the details, but she evidently understood that it was a "perplexing matter," and "not the sort of thing to which she had been accustomed under Lord Marlborough". The original strength of the Tory ministry had been in the Queen's predilection for Miss Hill, afterwards Lady Masham; Harley ruled Miss Hill, and Miss Hill ruled the Queen. But the Queen was not quite sure about Miss Hill. One of her tastes was a taste for aristocracy; and she was half ashamed of having taken a great liking to a waiting-maid who had been' placed about her. She had an old predilection also for the Duchess of Somerset, by birth the last of the Percies, whose husband was a Whig. Swift was never easy as to the effect of this friendship. He said, "the Duchess of Somerset is a proud woman, but I will pull her down"; so he libelled her, which did not make her more propitious to him or his masters.

There was always a danger that the ex-waiting-maid, on whom all depended, should be discarded, as the Duchess of Marlborough had been discarded; that the Duchess of Somerset might become prime favourite in her stead; that the policy of the Government, and all the persons of our rulers, should be again changed by the inexplicable caprice of a quiet old lady.

And Bolingbroke had another difficulty. The distrust of him was not confined to Queen Anne. It extended through his party, and was an inevitable result of his peculiar position. He was an eloquent man without prejudices, speaking the prejudices of men who could not speak. But the speechless client and the eloquent advocate differ in nature so much that they can never much like or well understand each other. The Tory party knew that when Bolingbroke expressed their favourite conviction, he did not himself believe a word of what he was saying. And they could not tell what he did believe. And, being for the most part regular men of middle life from the agricultural counties, they did not much like to trust as their leader a young man of loose life about town. After the Peace of Utrecht especially, he could not tell what they would think, and they could not tell what he would do. They could never have anticipated his doing anything so mean as that, and he could never understand what disgrace there was in so obvious a diplomatic stratagem as breach of faith. In our own time, it is easy to vex Tories. You have only to ask, "What is Dizzy's next move?" Such short words would not have suited our formal ancestors. But many a courteous Whig, doubtless, asked many a Tory, "What is to be my Lord Bolingbroke's next fine stroke of policy?" and the Tory could not have known what to say. So long as Oxford was at the head of affairs common men felt that there was still something ordinary about the Government. But if Bolingbroke were to become sole minister, or chief minister, we should be subjected to the bold schemes of undiluted genius.

In this difficult position Bolingbroke showed great ability. He could not, indeed, remove its irremovable defects. He could not declare for the House of Hanover; and he could not declare for the House of Stuart. He could not remove the dislike which a dull Queen, and a dull party, felt for a brilliant man. But what could be done he did. He showed great Parliamentary ability, and was ever ready with wonderful eloquence. He pleased his party by a Schism Bill, agreeable to

High Churchmen, and disagreeable to Dissenters. He obtained the favour of the waiting-maid, if he could not obtain that of the Queen, her mistress. Miss Hill (or Lady Masham, as she now was) was a sort of relation of Oxford's; and this had first brought them together. For a long time the union was firm; he gave her much counsel and some money, and she gave him much power. But Oxford had a conscience, or vestiges of a conscience, in the use of public money. He was not ready to give Miss Hill, or Miss Hill's brother, all that they wanted. Swift puts it that he was too careful of the public interest for the corruption of the time; or, as we should put it, he would not bribe without limit against the public interest out of the public treasury. But Bolingbroke had no scruples; he bid higher; he gave Miss Hill and "Jack Hill" all he could, and promised that they should have more if they would make him first minister and maintain him as such. He himself may tell the result: "The Earl of Oxford was removed on Tuesday; the Queen died on Sunday. What a world is this, and how our fortune banters us!" Such was the close of three years of intrigue. He had bribed the waiting-maid just when the mistress was no more.

Nor at the moment was this the worst. The Queen's distrust of Bolingbroke had lasted till her death. The white staff—the "magic wand," as Bolingbroke calls it, long disused in English politics, but then the symbol of the lord high treasurer and of the prime minister—had been taken from Oxford, but it had not been given to any one. Bolingbroke could not gain it for himself. It was arranged that the Treasury should be put into commission, as it had been in King William's time, and as it always now is. Bolingbroke was to continue secretary of state, and be in fact principal minister; yet he was not to have the indefinite power of the lord treasurer—the mystic power of the white staff. But on her deathbed Queen Anne felt that Bolingbroke could not be trusted even so far. She was dying, and knew that she was dying. She doubtless felt that it was her duty to place the administration in the hands of some one who would obey the law on her death. She did not like the family of Hanover; she had the most keen repugnance to the presence of any of them in England during her life. She could not endure to see her successor close at hand, and it probably never struck her as a matter of duty to save the country from a possible convulsion of civil war. She was a very little-minded woman, but at the same time she was a decorous woman, and a well-meaning woman. She would not have planned or dared or wished to break the law which she had passed. As death was coming upon her, she knew that the practical premiership of Bolingbroke would endanger the security of the Act of Settlement. Of all statesmen he was least likely to obey it, and therefore most unfit to be prime minister when it was of critical importance to obey it. Obscurely, perhaps, but effectually, Queen Anne felt this. She gave the white staff to Shrewsbury; and Bolingbroke's three days of premiership were at an end.

Probably Bolingbroke felt the disaster the more that he was obliged to seem to assent to it. Shrewsbury had been acting as confidential adviser to the Queen for some time, to Bolingbroke's dismay. He knew, he said, how he stood with Oxford—that was open war; but how he stood with Shrewsbury, he did not know. As soon as the Queen was despaired of, the privy council was summoned, and by ordinary rule only those summoned should attend; a ministry thus secures a privy council of chosen friends. But at this meeting two Whig dukes, the Duke of Somerset and the Duke of Argyle, attended, though not summoned, and by their influence the council was induced to ask the Queen to make Shrewsbury high treasurer; and Bolingbroke was obliged to assent. Neither in the nation, nor at the court, had he substantial influence or effectual power.

He had in truth no alternative. A frantic bishop, Atterbury, bishop of Rochester, wanted him to proclaim the Pretender. But Bolingbroke, though a hot-headed statesman, had a notion of law and a perception of obvious consequences. He was not a hot-headed divine: he knew that by law George I must be proclaimed at once; he knew that Shrewsbury, who wielded the white staff, which every one would obey, would at once proclaim George I. He knew that he could not himself command the obedience of a watchman. All the force of government had at once passed from him, and he acquiesced in the new order of things. He assisted at the proclamation of George I.

The law had indicated the steps which should be taken in case of the Queen's death, and before her successor could be brought over from Germany. A document was produced by the Hanoverian minister, naming Lords Justices, who were to administer the government until the arrival of George I. Of

these Lords Justices, Bolingbroke, of course, was not one.
They were all sound Whigs, and steady friends to the House
of Hanover. As Bolingbroke had for four years been wielding
the force of government so as to give pain to them, they immediately began to exercise it so as to give pain to him. They
appointed Addison as their secretary; desired all documents
to be addressed to him; and, though Bolingbroke was still in
high office, and had at the last moment been real prime
minister, they kept him waiting at their door with studied
circumstances of indignity, which were much remarked on
then, and which much tried his philosophy.

It would, however, have well been for Bolingbroke if mere
indignities like these had been all which was in store for him,
or all which he deserved. When Parliament met, zealous
Whigs naturally began to murmur a good deal as to the past.
Bolingbroke had ruled them hardly during his reign. His
ministry had removed Marlborough from his appointments;
his ministry had expelled Walpole from the House of Commons. Walpole would most likely have said that the Whig
"innings" had arrived, and that the actions of their predecessors must be scrutinised. Bolingbroke for a time affected to
fear nothing. Oxford went to and fro in London, and Bolingbroke followed his example. All at once he changed his policy.
He appeared at the theatre in state, and took pains while
there to attract attention; went home, changed his dress, and
fled to France.

In truth, he was thoroughly frightened. He declared that
"his blood was," he understood, "to have been the cement of
a new alliance," between the moderate Tories and the Whigs.
Some have traced this notion to the hints of Marlborough,
but it was most likely due as much to Bolingbroke's own conscience. He knew well that the secret negotiations prior to
the Peace of Utrecht would not bear even fair scrutiny. He
knew that they were now to be subjected to hostile scrutiny.
Even from impartial judges he could only expect condemnation, and his case would now be tried by his enemies. His
life, indeed, was in no danger. Neither the nation, nor the
party opposed to him, were inclined to bloodshed; but he felt
he was in danger of something. His guilty conscience magnified the possibilities of punishment; to escape them, he did
exactly what was worst for his reputation. Though it was as
much as pleading guilty, he fled.

He was attainted as a traitor in his absence, and there may

be legal doubt as to whether the attainder was deserved. That a minister who advises his sovereign to violate a treaty, and who violates it accordingly, is worthy of severe punishment, will be admitted by every one; and that Bolingbroke had done this is beyond question or dispute. But this offence does not amount to high treason, and the details of an incidental transaction as to the town of Tournay had to be pressed into the service; and it required much stretching to make these amount even to a constructive treason. But whatever might be the legal correctness or the incorrectness of the precise punishment inflicted on Bolingbroke is scarcely material now. He well deserved a bill of "Pains and Penalties"; and whether he was or was not visited with the very penalty that was most suitable, does not matter much.

On Bolingbroke's arrival in France, he looked about him for awhile. He was at once solicited by the emissaries of the Pretender, but he deliberated for some time, and it would have been wiser for him to have deliberated longer. He well knew that, though there was much latent Jacobite sentiment in England, there was no good material for a Jacobite rebellion. Many squires and rectors and peasants would have been glad to see the legitimate king restored; but their zeal was not very active; it belonged to the region of traditional sentiment and vague prejudice, rather than to that of practical and vigorous life. The House of Hanover had the force of the Government and the *sense* of the country in its favour. It was in possession, and Bolingbroke was aware that the Jacobites could not expel it from possession. He knew all this well, but his passions were too strong for his judgment; from excitability, restlessness, and rage, he joined the Pretender. He could not help being busy, and hoped, or half-hoped, to be revenged on his enemies.

He could not, however, long agree with his new associates. The descent from actual office to imaginary office was too sudden; to many men it was pleasing to be secretary of state to a mock king, but it was very painful to one who had just been secretary to a real queen. His contempt, too, for the Irish associates of the Pretender was unbounded. He saw that they were hot-headed and ignorant men—who knew nothing of the country which they hoped to rule—whom that country would not endure for a day. He knew that the Roman Catholics in England were a small and unpopular body, and their aid more dangerous than their enmity. The genuine Jacobites distrusted him also. He said that they were untrustworthy because they were fools, and they said that he was untrustworthy because he was a traitor. This could not last; after a brief interval, he left the Pretender and his Court: they began to slander him, and he began to speak much evil of them.

With his secession from the Jacobites Bolingbroke's active career ends. He was afterwards only an aspirant for a career. He was, after several years, permitted to return to England, and to enjoy his estate, though he was an attainted traitor; but the attainder was not reversed, and while it was in force he could not take his seat in the House of Lords, or hold any office whatever. He wrote much against Walpole, but he did not turn out Walpole. On one occasion he was much mortified because Pulteney and the practical opponents of Walpole said that the support of his name rather weakened than strengthened them. He gave in a long memorial of suggestions to George I; but the king said they were "bagatelles". He then fancied that he should become minister because of the support of Lady Suffolk, George II's mistress; but Lady Suffolk had no influence, and Queen Caroline, who had predominant influence, supported Walpole. He then hoped to be minister under the Prince of Wales, George II's son, and wrote a treatise on a "Patriot King" for that Prince's use. But George II outlived his son; and he was saved the mortification of seeing how little that small prince would have carried out his great ideas. Though he survived Queen Anne more than thirty years, he never after her death attained to a day's power in England. Three years of eager unwise power, and thirty-five of sickly longing and impotent regret—such, or something like it, will ever be in this cold modern world the fate of an Alcibiades.

WILLIAM PITT[1]*

(1861)

William Pitt was born in 1759 at Hayes, Kent, the second son of William Pitt, first earl of Chatham, and of Hester Grenville. He was educated at Pembroke College, Cambridge, and was called to the Bar at Lincoln's Inn in 1780. He became M.P. for Appledore in 1871. He became Chancellor of the Exchequer under Shelburne upon Rockingham's death in 1782, and when Shelburne was overthrown by the coalition of North and Fox and the ministry dismissed in 1783, Pitt was made Prime Minister in December of that year, at the age of twenty-five. He had great difficulty in forming a ministry, and was then often defeated in Parliament, but he refused to dissolve Parliament until he was sure that public feeling was on his side. He won an overwhelming majority at the general election of 1784. He now took measures to reduce the national debt and made great reductions in customs duties. Pitt was disturbed by the spread of republican ideas in England following the outbreak of the French Revolution, and this coloured his attitude to the French demand for the opening of the Scheldt, which led to war with France in 1793. Pitt sought to oppose France by a series of European coalitions which were not successful and which imposed a heavy burden of taxation on the country. However, after the end of the war on the Continent in 1797, a second series of alliances drove the French back to the Rhine.

At the outbreak of the Irish rebellion of 1798, Pitt renewed the suspension of the Habeas Corpus Act and passed other coercive measures. The Irish Parliament was united to that of Great Britain in 1800. Pitt sought to complete his Irish policy by introducing a measure of Catholic emancipation, but found George III so obdurate in opposing him that Pitt resigned in 1801. He agreed to support Addington's administration but gradually came into opposition to it and re-entered office in 1804

---

[1] Life of the Right Honourable William Pitt. By Earl Stanhope, author of the History of England from the Peace of Utrecht.

* This essay was first published in the National Review for July 1861, Volume XIII, pages 197–228.

on Addington's resignation, though without the support of most
of his former allies among the Whigs. He formed a third coali-
tion with Russia, Austria, and Sweden, which brought about a
war with Spain. The battle of Austerlitz sundered the coalition
he built up, and the news of it contributed to his death. Pitt
died at Putney in 1806.

Lord Stanhope's Life of Mr Pitt has both the excellences
and the defects which we should expect from him, and
neither of them are what we expect in a great historical writer
of the present age. Even simple readers are becoming aware
that historical investigations, which used to be a sombre and
respectable calling, is now an audacious pursuit. Paradoxes
are very bold and very numerous. Many of the recognised
"good people" in history have become bad, and all the very
bad people have become rather good. We have palliations
of Tiberius, eulogies on Henry VIII, devotional exercises to
Cromwell, and fulsome adulation of Julius Cæsar and of the
first Napoleon. The philosophy of history is more alarming
still. One school sees in it but a gradual development of
atheistic belief, another threatens to resolve it all into "the
three simple agencies, starch, fibrin, and albumen". But in
these exploits of audacious ingenuity and specious learning
Lord Stanhope has taken no part. He is not anxious to be
original. He travels, if possible, in the worn track of previous
historians; he tells a plain tale in an easy plain way; he shrinks
from wonderful novelties; with the cautious scepticism of
true common sense, he is always glad to find that the conclusions at which he arrives coincide with those of former inquirers. His style is characteristic of his matter. He narrates
with a gentle sense and languid accuracy, very different from
the stimulating rhetoric and exciting brilliancy of his more
renowned contemporaries.

In the present case Lord Stanhope has been very fortunate
both in his subject and his materials. Mr Pitt has never had
even a decent biographer, though the peculiarities of his career are singularly inviting to literary ambition. His life had
much of the solid usefulness of modern times, and not a little
also of the romance of old times. He was skilled in economical
reform, but retained some of the majesty of old-world eloquence. He was as keen in small figures as a rising politician
now; yet he was a despotic Premier at an age when, in these

times, a politician could barely aspire to be an Under-Secretary. It is not wonderful that Lord Stanhope should have been attracted to a subject which is so interesting in itself, and which lies so precisely in the direction of his previous studies. From his high standing and his personal connections, he has been able to add much to our minuter knowledge. He has obtained from various quarters many valuable letters which have not been published before. There is a whole series from George III to Mr Pitt, and a scarcely less curious series from Mr Pitt to his mother. We need not add that Lord Stanhope has digested his important materials with great care; that he has made of them almost as much as could be made; that he has a warm admiration and a delicate respect for the great statesman of whom he is writing. His nearest approach to an ungentle feeling is a quiet dislike to the great Whig families.

Mr Pitt is an example of one of the modes in which the popular imagination is, even in historical times, frequently and easily misled. Mankind judge of a great statesman principally by the most marked and memorable passage in his career. By chance we lately had the honour to travel with a gentleman who said, that Sir Robert Peel was the "leader of the Whigs"; and though historical evidence will always prevent common opinion from becoming so absurd as this, it is undeniable that, in the popular fancy of young men, Sir Robert Peel is the Liberal minister who repealed the corn-laws and carried Catholic emancipation. The world is forgetting that he was once the favourite leader of the old Tory party—the steady opponent of Mr Canning, and the steady adherent of Lord Sidmouth and Lord Eldon. We remember his great reforms, of which we daily feel the benefit; we forget that, during a complete political generation, he was the most plausible supporter of ancient prejudices, and the most decent advocate of inveterate abuses. Mr Pitt's fate has been very similar, but far less fortunate. The event in his life most deeply implanted in the popular memory is his resistance to the French Revolution; it is this which has made him the object of affection to extreme Tories, and of suspicion and distrust to reasonable Liberals. Yet no rash inference was ever more unfounded and false. It can be proved that, in all the other parts of Mr Pitt's life, the natural tendency of his favourite plan was uniformly Liberal; that, at the time of the French Revolution itself, he only did what the immense majority of the English people, even of the cultivated English people, deliberately desired; that he did it anxiously, with many misgivings, and in opposition to his natural inclinations; that it is very dubious whether, in the temper of the French nation and the temper of the English nation, a war between them could by possibility have been avoided at that juncture; that, in his administration and under his auspices, the spirit of legislative improvement which characterises modern times may almost be said to begin; that he was the first English minister who discussed political questions with the cultivated thoughtfulness and considerate discretion which seem to characterise us now; that, in political instruction, he was immeasurably superior to Fox, and that in the practical application of just principles to ordinary events, he was equally superior to Burke.

There are two kinds of statesmen to whom, at different times, representative government gives an opportunity and a career—dictators and administrators. There are certain men who are called in conjunctures of great danger to save the State. When national peril was imminent, all nations have felt it needful to select the best man who could be found— for better, for worse; to put unlimited trust in him; to allow him to do whatever he wished, and to leave undone whatever he did not approve of. The qualities which are necessary for a dictator are two—a commanding character and an original intellect. All other qualities are secondary. Regular industry, a conciliatory disposition, a power of logical exposition, and argumentative discussion, which are necessary to a Parliamentary statesman in ordinary times, are not essential to the selected dictator of a particular juncture. If he have force of character to overawe men into trusting him, and originality of intellect sufficient to enable him to cope with the pressing, terrible, and critical events with which he is selected to cope, it is enough. Every subordinate shortcoming, every incidental defect, will be pardoned. "Save us!" is the cry of the moment; and, in the confident hope of safety, any deficiency will be overlooked, and any frailty pardoned.

The genius requisite for a great administrator is not so imposing, but it is, perhaps, equally rare, and needs a more peculiar combination of qualities. Ordinary administrators are very common: every-day life requires and produces every-day persons. But a really great administrator thinks not only of the day but of the morrow; does not only what he must but what he wants; is eager to extirpate every abuse, and on the watch for every improvement; is on a level with the highest political thought of his time, and persuades his age to be ruled according to it—to permit him to embody it in policy and in laws. Administration in this large sense includes legislation, for it is concerned with the far-seeing regulation of future conduct, as well as with the limited management of the present. Great dictators are doubtless rare in political history; but they are not more so than great administrators, such as we have just defined them. It is not easy to manage any age; it is not easy to be on a level with the highest thought of any age; but to manage that age according to that highest thought is among the most arduous tasks of the world. The intellectual character of a dictator is noble but simple; that of a great administrator and legislator is also complex.

The exact description of Mr Pitt is, that he had in the most complete perfection the faculties of a great administrator, and that he added to it the commanding temperament, though not the creative intellect, of a great dictator. He was tried by long and prosperous years, which exercised to the utmost his peculiar faculties, which enabled him to effect brilliant triumphs of policy and of legislation: he was tried likewise by a terrible crisis, with which he had not the originality entirely to cope, which he did not understand as we understand it now, but in which he showed a hardihood of resolution and a consistency of action which captivated the English people, and which impressed the whole world.

A very slight survey of Mr Pitt's career is all we have room for here; indeed, it is not easy within the compass of an article to make any survey, however slight; but we hope at least to show that peculiar training, peculiar opportunity, and peculiar ability, combined to make him what he was.

It may seem silly to observe that Mr Pitt was the son of his father, and yet there is no doubt that it was a critical circumstance in the formation of his character. When he was born, as Lord Macaulay has described, his father's name was the most celebrated in the whole civilised world; every post brought the news of some victory or some great stroke of policy, and his imagination dwelt upon the realities before him. "I am glad I am not the eldest son," he said. "I should like to speak in the House of Commons, like papa." And there are other sayings indicating an early ambition and an early consciousness of power. There is nothing extraordinary in this. Most boys are conceited; most boys have a wonderful belief in their own power. "At sixteen," says Mr Disraeli, "every one believes he is the most peculiar man who ever lived." And there is certainly no difficulty in imagining Mr Disraeli thinking so. The difficulty is, not to entertain this proud belief, but to keep it; not to have these lofty visions, but to hold them. Manhood comes, and with it come the plain facts of the world. There is no illusion in them; they have a distinct teaching. "The world," they say definitely, "does not believe in you. You fancy you have a call to a great career, but no one else even imagines that you fancy it. You do not dare to say it out loud." Before the fear of ridicule and the touch of reality, the illusions of youth pass away, and with them goes all intellectual courage. We have no longer the hardihood, we have scarcely the wish to form our own creed, to think our own thoughts, to act upon our own belief; we try to be sensible, and we end in being ordinary; we fear to be eccentric, and we end in being commonplace. It is from this fate that the son of a commanding Prime Minister is at any rate preserved; the world thinks about him; the world alludes to him. He can speak "in the grand style," and he will not be laughed at, or not much. When we wonder at the indomitable resolution and the inflexible self-reliance which Mr Pitt through life displayed, we may lessen our wonder by remembering that he never endured the bitter ignominy of youth; that his self-confidence was never disheartened by being "an unknown man"; that he early received from fortune the inestimable permission *to be himself*.

The education of Mr Pitt was as favourable to the development of his peculiar powers as his position. The public education of England has very great merits, and is well fitted for the cultivation of the average Englishman; but one at least of the qualities which fit it for training ordinary men unfit it for training an extraordinary man. Its greatest value to the mass of those who are brought up in it, is its influence in diminishing their self-confidence. They are early brought into a little but rough world, which effects on a small scale what the real world will afterwards effect still more thoroughly on a large one. It teaches boys who are no better than other boys, that they are no better than other boys; that the advantages of one are compensated by the advantages of others; that the world is a miscellaneous and motley medley, in which it is not easy to conquer, and over which it is impossible to rule. But it is not desirable that a young man in Pitt's position should learn this lesson. If you are to train a man to be Prime Minister at five and twenty, you must not dishearten his self-confidence, though it be overweening; you must not tame his energy, though it seem presumptuous. Ordinary men should and must be taught to fear the face of the world; they are to be guided by its laws and regulated by its manners; the one exceptional man, who is in his first youth to rule the world, must be trained not to fear it, but despise it.

The legitimate food of a self-relying nature is early solitude, and the most stimulating solitude is solitude in the midst of society. Mr Pitt's education was of this kind entirely. He was educated at home during his whole boyhood. He was sent to Cambridge at a most unusually early age. He lived there almost wholly with Mr Pretyman, his tutor. "While Mr Pitt was undergraduate," writes that gentleman, "he never omitted attending chapel morning and evening, or dining in the public hall, except when prevented by indisposition. Nor did he pass a single evening out of the college walls; indeed, most of his time was spent with me. During his whole residence at the university," Mr Pretyman continues, "I never knew him spend an idle day, nor did he ever fail to attend me at the appointed hour." He did not make any friends, scarcely any social acquaintances till he had taken his degree. He passed very much of his time, his tutor tells us, in very severe study, and very much of it, as we may easily believe, in the most absorbing of early pleasures—the monotonous excitement of ambitious anticipation. On an inferior man, this sort of youth could have had but one effect—it must have made him a prig. But it had not that effect on Pitt. It contributed to make him a shy, haughty, and inaccessible man. Such he emerged from Cambridge, and such he continued through life to be; but he was preserved from the characteristic degradation of well-intentioned and erudite youth by two great counteracting influences,—a strong sense of humour and a genuine interest in great subjects. His sense of fun was, indeed, disguised from the vulgar by a rigid mask of grave dignity; but in private it was his strongest characteristic. "Don't tell me," he is said to have remarked, "of a man's being able to talk sense; every one can talk sense; can he talk nonsense?" And Mr Wilberforce, the most cheerful of human beings, who had seen the most amusing society of his generation, always declared that Pitt's wit was the best which he had ever known. And it was likely to be; humour gains much by constant suppression, and at no time of life was Pitt ever wanting in dexterous words. No man who really cares for great things, and who sees the laughable side of little things, ever becomes a "prig".

While at Cambridge Pitt likewise paid, as his tutor tells us, great attention to what are now, in popular estimation, the characteristic studies of the place. His attainments in mathematics were probably not much like the elaborate and exact knowledge which the higher wranglers now yearly carry away from the university; but they were considerable for his time, and they comprehended the most instructive part of the subject, the first principles; a vague hope, too, is expressed that he may read Newton's *Principia* "after some summer circuit," which, as we may easily suppose, was not realised.

Though the tutor's information is not very exact, we may accept his general testimony that Pitt was a good mathematician, according to the academic standing of that day. There is, indeed, strong corroborative evidence of the fact in Mr Pitt's financial speeches. It is not easy to draw out the evidence in writing, and it would be very tiresome to read the evidence if it were drawn out; but a skilful observer of the contrast between educated and uneducated language will find in Pitt many traces of mathematical studies. Raw argument and common-sense correctness come by nature, but only a preliminary education can give the final edge to accuracy in statement, and the last nicety to polished and penetrating discussion. In later life, the facile use of financial rhetoric was as familiar to Mr Pitt as to Mr Gladstone.

His classical studies were pursued upon a plan suggested by his father, which was certainly well adapted for the particular case, though it would not be good for mankind in general. A sufficient experience proves that no one can be taught any language thoroughly and accurately except by composition in it; and Mr Pitt had apparently never practised any sort of composition in Greek or Latin, whether verse or prose. But, for the purpose of disciplining a student in *his own* language, the reverse practice of translating from the classical languages is the best single expedient which has ever been made use of. And to this Mr Pitt was trained by his father from early boyhood. He was taught to read off the classics into the best English he could find, never inserting a word with which he was not satisfied, but waiting till he found one with which he *was* satisfied. By constant practice he became so ready that he never stopped at all; the right word always presented itself immediately. When he was asked in later life, how he had acquired the mellifluous abundance of appropriate language with which he amazed and charmed the House of Commons, it was to this suggestion of his father that he at once imputed it.

To the probably unconscious influence of the same instructor we may ascribe his early interest in Parliamentary conflict. We have before quoted the naïve expression of his boyish desire to be in the House of Commons. There is a still more curious story of him in very early youth. It is said, "He was introduced, on the steps of the throne in the House of Lords, to Mr Fox, who was his senior by ten years, and already in the fulness of his fame. Fox used afterwards to relate that, as the discussion proceeded, Pitt repeatedly turned to him, and said, 'But surely, Mr Fox, that might be met thus'; or, 'Yes, but he lays himself open to retort'. What the particular criticisms were, Fox had forgotten; but he said that he was much struck at the time by the precocity of a lad who through the whole sitting was thinking only how all the speeches on both sides could be answered."

Nor were his political studies confined to the studious cultivation of oratorical language, or to a thorough acquisition of the art of argumentative fence: he attended also to the *substance* of political science. He was the first great English statesman who read, understood, and valued *The Wealth of Nations*. Fox had "no great opinion of *those* reasonings"; and the doctrines of free trade, though present, like all great political ideas, to the overflowing mind of Burke, were, like all his ideas, at the daily mercy of his eager passions and his intense and vivid imagination. Mr Pitt, as it would seem, while still at college, acquired and arranged them with the collected consistency which was the characteristic of his mind. So thorough a training in the superficial accomplishments, the peculiar associations, and the abstract studies of political life, has not perhaps fallen to the lot of any other English statesman.

Nor was the political opportunity of Mr Pitt at all inferior to his political training. The history of the first twenty years

of the reign of George III is a history of his struggles with the
aristocratic proprietors of parliamentary boroughs. Neither
the extension of the power of the Crown, nor the maintenance of the political ascendency of the Whig families, was
very popular with the nation at large; the popular element in
the Constitution was for the most part neutral in the conflict; it reserved the greater part of its influence for objects
more interesting to itself; but between the two parties, between the Crown and the great borough proprietors, the strife
was eager, intense, and unremitting.

As the present writer has elsewhere explained, the situation
in which a constitutional king was placed under the old system of an unreformed Parliament was more than an energetic man could endure. According to the theory of that
Government, the patronage of the Crown was to be used to
purchase votes in Parliament, and to maintain a Parliamentary majority by constant bargains with borough proprietors.

"But who is to use the patronage? The theory assumes
that it is to be used by the minister of the day. According
to it, the head of the party which is predominant in Parliament is to employ the patronage of the Crown for the
purpose of confirming that predominance. But suppose
that the Crown chooses to object to this; suppose that the
king for the time being should say, 'This patronage is mine;
the places in question are places in my service; the pensions in question are pensions from me. I will myself have
at least some share in the influence that is acquired by the
conferring of those pensions and the distribution of those
places.' George III actually did say this. He was a king in
one respect among a thousand; he was willing to do the
work of a Secretary of the Treasury; his letters for very
many years are filled with the petty details of patronage;
he directed who should have what, and stipulated who
should not have anything. This interference of the king
must evidently in theory, and did certainly in fact, destroy
the efficiency of the alleged expedient. Very much of the
patronage of the Crown went, not to the adherents of the
prime minister, because they were his adherents, but to the
king's friends, because they were his friends. Many writers
have been very severe on George III for taking the course
which he did take, and have frequently repeated the well-
known maxims, which show that what he did was a de-

viation from the Constitution. Very likely it was; but what is the use of a Constitution which takes no account of the ordinary motives of human nature? It was inevitable that an ambitious king, who had industry enough to act as he did, would so act. Let us consider his position. He was invested with authority which was apparently great. He was surrounded by noblemen and gentlemen who passed their life in paying him homage, and in professing perhaps excessive doctrines of loyal obedience to him. When the Duke of Devonshire, or the Duke of Bedford, or the Duke of Newcastle, approached the royal closet, they implied by words and manner that he had immeasurably more power than they had. In fact, it was expected that he should have immeasurably less. It was expected that, though these noblemen daily acknowledged that he was their superior, he should constantly act as if he were their inferior. The prime minister was in reality appointed by them, and it was extold him; that he should assent to measures on which he pected that the king should do what the prime minister was not consulted; that he should make peace when Mr Grenville said peace was right; that he should make war whenever Mr Grenville said war was right; that he should allow the offices of his household and the dignities of his court to be used as a means for the support of cabinets whose members he disliked, and whose policy he disapproved of. It is evident that no man who was not imbecile would be content with such a position. It is not difficult to bear to be without power, it is not very difficult to bear to have only the mockery of power; but it is unbearable to have real power, and to be told that you must content yourself with the mockery of it; it is unendurable to have in your hands an effectual instrument of substantial influence, and also to act day by day as a pageant, without any influence whatever. Human nature has never endured this, and we may be quite sure that it never will endure it. It is a fundamental error in the 'esoteric theory' of the Tory party, that it assumed the king and the prime minister to be always of the same mind, while they often were of different minds."[2]

By a series of stratagems George III at last obtained, in

[2] *Essays on Parliamentary Reform*, p. 154. By Walter Bagehot. Kegan Paul, Trench & Co., 1883.

the person of Lord North, a minister who combined a sufficient amount of Parliamentary support with an unlimited devotion to the royal pleasure. He was a minister of great ability, great Parliamentary tact, unbounded good humour, and no firmness. He yielded everything to the intense, eager, petty incisiveness of his sovereign. The king was the true minister for all purposes of policy and business. Lord North was only the talking minister of the present French Assemblies, who is bound to explain and to defend measures which he did not suggest, and about which he was not consulted.

It is difficult to say how long Lord North's Government might not have continued, if it had not been for the military calamities of the American War. That war had been very popular at its commencement, and continued popular as long as it was likely to be successful: it became unpopular as soon as it was likely to fail. The merchants began to murmur at the stoppage of trade. The country gentlemen began to murmur at the oppressive burden of war-taxes. The nation began to reconsider its opinion as to the justice of the quarrel, as soon as it appeared that our military efforts would probably be disastrous. Lord North shared in these feelings; he did not believe the war would succeed; no longer hoped it would succeed; no longer thought that there was any motive for continuing to carry it on, but for several years he did continue to carry it on. The will of George III was a very efficient force on every one just about him, and his personal ascendency over many men intellectually far his superiors is a curious example of the immense influence of a distinct judgment and inflexible decision, with fair abilities and indefatigable industry, and placed in a close contact with great men and great affairs.

At length, in March, 1782, the calamitous issue of the American War became too evident, and Lord North resigned. Lord Holland gives us a curious history of the mode in which he announced to the House that he was no longer Prime Minister.

"I have heard my uncle Fitzpatrick give a very diverting account of the scene that passed in the House of Commons on the day of Lord North's resignation, which happened to be a remarkably cold day, with a fall of snow. A motion of Lord Surrey's for the dismissal of ministers, stood for that day, and the Whigs were anxious that it should come on before the resignation of Lord North was officially announced, that his removal from office might be more manifestly and formally the act of the House of Commons. He and Lord Surrey rose at the same instant. After much clamour, disorder, and some insignificant speeches on order, Mr Fox, with great quickness and address, moved, as the most regular method of extricating the House from its embarrassment, 'That Lord Surrey be now heard'. But Lord North, with yet more admirable presence of mind, mixed with pleasantry, rose immediately and said, 'I rise to speak to that motion'; and, as his reason for opposing it, stated his resignation and the dissolution of the Ministry. The House, satisfied, became impatient, and after some ineffectual efforts of speakers on both sides to procure a hearing, an adjournment took place. Snow was falling and the night tremendous. All the members' carriages were dismissed, and Mrs Bennet's room at the door was crowded. But Lord North's carriage was waiting. He put into it one or two of his friends, whom he had invited to go home with him; and turning to the crowd, chiefly composed of his bitter enemies, in the midst of their triumph, exclaimed, in this hour of defeat and supposed mortification, with admirable good humour and pleasantry, 'I have my carriage. You see, gentlemen, the advantage of being in the secret. Good-night.'"

Such acquiescent *bonhomie* is admirable, no doubt; but easy good-nature is no virtue for a man of action, least of all for a practical politician in critical times. It was Lord North's "happy temper" which first made him the mean slave of George III, which afterwards induced him to ally himself with the most virulent assailants of that monarch, and, at a preceding period, of himself.

When Lord North resigned, it was natural that the leaders of the Opposition should come at once into predominant power; but a ministerial crisis in the early part of George III's reign was never permitted to proceed in what is now fixed as the constitutional etiquette. The King always interfered with it. On this occasion, the only political party who could take office was that which, under the judicious guidance of Lord Rockingham, and supported by the unequalled oratory of Fox and Burke, had consistently opposed the American War. But the leaders of this party were personally disliked by George III. Lord Rockingham he had once before called "one of the most insignificant noblemen in my service". Mr Fox, from a curious combination of causes, he hated. Accordingly, though it was necessary for him to treat with Lord Rockingham and his friends, he did not treat with them directly. He employed as an intermediate agent Lord Shelburne, the father of the present Marquis of Lansdowne, a politician whom it is not difficult to describe, but whom it is difficult really to understand. Policemen tell us that there is such a character as a "reputed thief," who has never been convicted of any particular act of thievery. Lord Shelburne was precisely that character in political life; every one always said he was dishonest, but no particular act of dishonesty has ever been brought home to him. It is not for us now to discuss the dubious peculiarities of so singular a character. But it will be admitted, that it was a most unfortunate one for conducting the delicate personal negotiations inevitable on the formation of a Cabinet, and that it specially unfitted the person believed to possess it to be a good go-between a king who hated the Opposition and an Opposition who distrusted the King. The inevitable result followed: every member of the incoming party was displeased with the King; every one disbelieved the assertions of Lord Shelburne; every one distrusted the solidity of a ministry constructed in a manner so anomalous. A ministry, however, was constructed, of which Lord Shelburne and Lord Rockingham were both members; and both, Mr Fox said, intended to be Prime Ministers.

Lord Rockingham must evidently have been a man of very fine and delicate judgment. He could not speak in the House of Lords, and his letters are rather awkwardly expressed; but those who compare the history of the Whig party for some years before his death with the history of that party for some years after it, and those who compare the career of Burke for the same two periods, will perceive that both over the turbulence of the great party and the turbulence of the great orator the same almost invisible discretion exercised a guiding and restraining control. After Lord Rockingham's death, both the Whig party and Mr Burke committed great errors and fell into lamentable excesses, which were entirely unlike anything which happened while he was yet alive. If he had been permitted to exercise a composing influence, it is possible that the ministry we have described might have lasted; but, unfortunately, within three months after its formation he fell ill and died. Mr Fox, who had just been quarrelling with Lord Shelburne, refused to serve under him and sent in his resignation; and his example was followed by Burke, and by most of the followers of Lord Rockingham.

Lord Shelburne, however, still intended to be Prime Minister. The King was in his favour. The Whigs had no great aristocratic leader. The Duke of Portland, who was put forward as such, had no powers of speech and but feeble powers of thought. There was no difference of political opinion which need have separated any Whig from Shelburne. He was therefore justified in hoping that if he persevered, he might rally round him in no long time the greater portion of the Whig party, notwithstanding the secession of its present leaders. He doubtless hoped also, by taking advantage of the various influences of the Crown, to attach to himself very many of the followers of Lord North, who were the old adherents of the Crown. But these were anticipations only. For the moment he was more completely separated from the Parliamentary ability of his age than any minister has since been. He came into office in opposition to Lord North and one great party; he remained in office in opposition to Fox and Burke, the leaders of the other great party. The trained leaders of the old Ministry and the trained leaders of the old Opposition were both opposed to him. If he decided to remain Prime Minister, it was necessary for him to take some bold step. He did so. He made Mr Pitt Chancellor of the Exchequer and the leader of the House of Commons, though he was but twenty-three.

Such singular good fortune has never happened to any English statesman since Parliamentary government in this country has been consolidated into its present form, and it is very unlikely that anything like it can ever happen again. Perhaps no man of twenty-three could get through the quantity of work that is now required to fill the two offices of Finance Minister and leader of the House of Commons. In Pitt's time the Chancellor of the Exchequer (he himself tells us) needed no private secretary; he had no business requiring any. The leader of the House of Commons did not even require one-tenth part of the ready available miscellaneous information which he must now have at his command, and most of which cannot be learned from any books. To fill the offices which Mr Pitt filled at twenty-three, it would in this age be necessary that a man should have a trained faculty of transacting business rapidly, which no man of twenty-three can have; and that he should have also a varied knowledge of half a hundred subjects, which no college can teach, and which no book of reference will ever contain. Mr Pitt, however, met with no difficulty. Though the finances of the country had been disordered by the American war, and though the Ministry was daily assailed by the dexterous good-humour of Lord North and the vehement invectives of Fox and Burke, "the boy," as they called him, was successful in his Budget, and successful in his management of the House of Commons. It soon, however, became evident that Lord Shelburne's Ministry could not stand long. There were three parties in the House, and a coalition of any two was sufficient to outnumber any one. According to a calculation preserved in a letter from Gibbon, everything depended on the decision of Mr Fox. If he returned to the Government, it would be strong; if he allied himself with Lord North, it must fail. He did ally himself with Lord North, and Lord Shelburne resigned.

The coalition between Fox and Lord North is not defended even by Lord John Russell, who defends almost every act in the political life of his great hero. Indeed, it was not likely that he would defend it; for to it we owe the almost unbroken subjection of the Whigs, and the almost unbroken reign of the Tories, for five and twenty years.

No political alliance in English history has been more unpopular than this coalition. For once the King and the people were on the same side, and that side the right side. During by far the greater part of his reign the wishes of George III were either opposed to the wishes of his people; or the wishes of the two, though identical, were pernicious. During the first part of his reign his attempts to increase the royal influence were generally unpopular; during the latter part, he and his people were both favourable to the American War and to the French War, with what result history shows. But at the period at which we are speaking, both the prominent prejudices of the King, and the deepest feelings of the people were offended by the same event. The Coalition deeply annoyed the King. It was hateful to him that his favourite, Lord North, who had been his confidential minister for years, who was enriched with the marks of his bounty and good-will, who was the leader of many politicians, always biassed in favour of the Crown, and always anxious to support its influence, if they could, should after all ally himself with Mr Fox, who had opposed the Crown for years; who had called its latent influence "an infernal spirit"; who was the leader of the party opposed to the American War, and therefore, in the King's view, of the party which had advocated treason and abetted the disruption of the empire; who, worse than all, was the companion and encourager of the Prince of Wales in every species of dissipation; who introduced him to haunts and countenanced him in habits which made the very heart of an economical and decorous monarch horrified and angry: who at that very moment was endeavouring to make "capital," as we should now say, out of the political prospects and present influence of his profligate associate. George III used to call the "Coalition Ministry" his son's ministry; and he could not embody his detestation of it in terms more expressive, to those who knew their meaning. On the other hand, the people were not unnaturally offended also. The Coalition brought into very clear prominence the most characteristic weakness of our unreformed Constitution. Though it professed to be, and really was, a popular Constitution, the people could not be induced to believe that they had much concern in it. The members chosen by popular election were a minority; those nominated by aristocratic and indirect influence were a majority. Accordingly, most men believed, or were prone to believe, that the struggles in Parliament were faction-fights for place and power; that the interest of the nation had little to do with them, or nothing; that they were contests for political power, and for the rich pecuniary rewards which influential office then conferred. The Coalition seemed to prove that this was so even to demonstration. If there ever had been a *bonâ fide*, and not a simulated, struggle in Parliament, it was the struggle between Fox and Lord North. They had opposed one another for years; Fox had heaped on Lord North every term of invective, opprobrium, and contempt; Lord North had said everything which a good-natured and passive man *could* say in reply. They had taken different sides both on the obvious question which had been the dividing and critical one of the last few years, and on the latent question which was the real one underlying the greater part of the controversies of the age and giving to them most of their importance. Lord North was the great Parliamentary advocate of the American War; Fox was its most celebrated and effective opponent. Lord North was the most decent

agent, and the most successful co-operator, whom George III
had yet found in his incessant policy of maintaining and augmenting the power of the Crown. Fox was known to be opposed to that policy with all his mind, soul, and strength;
he was known to have heaped upon that policy every bitter
term of contempt, opprobrium, and execration which the
English language contains; he was known to have incurred
the bitter hatred of George III by so doing. With these facts
before them, what could the nation infer when they saw these
two statesmen combine for the evident purpose of obtaining
immediate office? They could only say what they did. They
said at once that the Coalition must be dishonest if the previous opposition had been real, and that the coalescing statesmen were utterly untrustworthy if that opposition had been
simulated.

The Government of the Coalition was not, however, destined to be durable. George III was a dangerous man to drive
to extremity. Though without great creative ability, he had
dexterous powers of political management, cultivated by long
habit and experience; he had an eager obstinacy allied to the
obstinacy of insanity; it was not safe to try him too far. The
Coalition Government, however, tried him as far as it was
possible. They framed an India Bill, giving the patronage of
India to commissioners, to be from time to time nominated
by Parliament, to be irremovable by the Crown, the first of
whom were to be nominated by themselves. The King was
enraged at a scheme so injurious to his secret influence. He
considered that it was a scheme for enabling Mr Fox to buy
votes in Parliament. Lord Fitzwilliam, his intimate political
friend, was to be at the head of the new Board; and it was
expected, perhaps intended, that the Board should be an independent instrument of Parliamentary power at the service
of the aristocratic Whigs, and in daily opposition to the influence of the Crown—to that personal influence which George
III had all his life been hoarding and acquiring. The people
were almost as much enraged at the scheme as the King himself. They thought that the politicians who had just formed
a corrupt coalition to obtain office were now providing a corrupt expedient for retaining that office. "Being dishonest
themselves," it was said, "they are providing themselves with
the means of purchasing the votes of others who are dishonest
likewise." The exact value of these accusations we have not
space to estimate now; something might certainly be said in

extenuation, if it were needful, but at the time the popular feeling was powerfully excited by them; they were expressed by Pitt with marvellous force and marvellous variety, and re-echoed through the nation.

The Parliamentary influence of the Coalition Government, which was supported by the greater part of the borough pro-prietors, both Whig and Tory, was, however, sufficient to carry their India Bill through the House of Commons by ma-jorities which would now be considered very large. It reached the House of Lords, and would have passed that House too, if George III had not taken one of the most curious steps in our constitutional history. He wrote on a card: "His Majesty al-lowed Earl Temple to say that whoever voted for the India Bill was not only not his friend, but would be considered by him as an enemy; and if these words were not strong enough, Earl Temple might use whatever words he might deem stronger and more to the purpose".

Such was the influence of the Crown, such was especially the personal influence which George III had acquired by steady industry and incessant attention to the personalities of politics, that the fate of the India Bill in the Lords very soon became dubious. "The bishops wavered;" the staunchest fol-lowers of Lord North especially, being high Tories, became uncertain; and in the end the Bill was rejected by a majority of ninety-five over seventy-six.

Nor did the King's active influence stop here. The Coali-tion Ministry did not resign; although their principal measure had been rejected in the Lords, they kept their places; they induced the House of Commons to resolve that it was a breach of the privilege of Parliament to attempt to influence votes in either House by announcing "any opinion or pre-tended opinion of his Majesty". The Ministry was passive in its place; but George III was never deterred by minor diffi-culties. He sent his commands at midnight to Mr Fox and Lord North to deliver up the seals of office, and to send them by their under-secretaries, as he must decline to see them in person. By this Parliamentary *coup d'état* he broke up an ad-ministration which, though unpopular in the country, was supported by the "great owners" of Parliamentary influence and an overwhelming majority in the House of Commons.

But who was to come in? That the King could turn out the old Ministry was very clear, for he had done so; but that he could form a Ministry that could last in such circumstances

seemed unlikely; that he could form any Ministry at all was
not evident. Political expectation was very eager. As soon as
the House met on the day after the midnight dismissal, a
new writ was moved for the borough of Appleby, "in the
room of the Right Honourable William Pitt, who, since his
election, has accepted the office of first Lord of the Treasury
and Chancellor of the Exchequer". The announcement was
received with laughter, for it seemed unlikely that an ambitious boy (such was the speech of the time) should be able
to carry on the government, and to lead the House of Commons in the face of an adverse majority, in direct opposition
to the most experienced statesmen, the most practised debaters, and the most skilful manœuvrers of his age.

Mr Pitt was only twenty-five, and he had no one to rely
on. Mr Dundas was a useful subordinate and an efficient man
of business, but he was not a great statesman or a great orator,
and he *was* a Scotch adventurer. In the Lords, Mr Pitt was
confident of the support of Lord Temple, who had effected
the defeat of the India Bill by use of the King's name; but
Lord Temple wanted to be paid. He had great borough connections, which gave him permanent claims on every Government; he had just turned out the old Government, which
gave him a peculiar claim upon the favour of the new. He
asked for a dukedom, and was refused. The King thought he
had asked too much, and perhaps believed that it would be
most dangerous at that critical moment to give the highest
of honorary rewards to the principal agent in an alarming act
of royal influence. At any rate, the application was declined,
and Lord Temple resigned. Mr Pitt was thus left almost
alone. His Cabinet consisted but of seven persons, and he
himself was the only member of the House of Commons
among those seven.

Everybody expected that Parliament would be immediately
dissolved. As Mr Pitt was evidently in a minority in the House
of Commons which then existed, it was confidently believed
that he would at once see whether he would not have a majority in a new House of Commons. He was too wary, however, to do so. In that age, public opinion formed itself slowly
and declared itself slowly. The nation, as far as it had an
opinion, was in favour of the new administration; but in many
parts of the country there was no opinion. Delay was in favour of the side which had the advantage in telling argument;
and so strong were the objections of reasonable and moderate

men to the coalition between Fox and Lord North—so entirely was their India Bill interpreted by the help of that connection, and regarded in its relation to it—that every day's discussion made converts. The members for close boroughs, and for counties in which individual interest predominated, were, it is true, a majority in the House of Commons, and they adhered for the most part to the Coalition. But the strength so obtained was always weak at a trying crisis. The same influences acted on the borough proprietors which acted upon others, and they never liked to be opposed to the national will when it was distinctly declared. Nor had the extreme partisans of either party ever liked the coalition of the two parties. The warmest Whigs were alienated from Fox, and the strongest Tories were alienated from Lord North. The majority of Fox began to waver, and the minority of Pitt began to augment. Every division showed a tendency in the same direction. Pitt maintained the struggle with dauntless courage and unbounded dialectical dexterity, against all the orators in the House of Commons. The event began to be doubtful. In the unreformed Parliament no more was necessary. A large section of every part was attached to it by the hope of patronage; it had been bought by promises of that patronage. As the present writer has elsewhere explained, the strength so obtained was unstable.

"It especially failed at the moment at which it was especially wanted. A majority in Parliament which is united by a sincere opinion, and is combined to carry out that opinion, is in some sense secure. As long as that opinion is unchanged, it will remain; it can only be destroyed by weakening the conviction which binds it together. A majority which is obtained by the employment of patronage is very different; it is combined mainly by *an expectation*. Sir Robert Walpole, the great master in the art of dispensing patronage, defined gratitude as an anticipation of future favours; he meant that the majority which maintained his administration was collected, not by recollection, but by hope; they thought not so much of favours which were past as of favours which were to come. At a critical moment this bond of union was ordinarily weak."[3]

[3] *Essays on Parliamentary Reform*, p. 157. By Walter Bagehot. Kegan Paul, Trench & Co., 1883.

As soon as it seemed likely that Mr Pitt would be victorious,
the selfish part of the followers of the Coalition—a very large
part—began to go over to Mr Pitt. The last motion of Mr
Fox was carried by a majority of *one*.

Mr Pitt then saw that his time had come; he dissolved
Parliament, and his triumph was complete. The popular feeling was overwhelming. It prevailed even in the strongholds
of the Whig aristocracy. "Thus in Norfolk," says Lord Stanhope, "the late member had been Mr Coke, lord of the vast
domains of Holkham, a gentleman who, according to his own
opinion, as stated in his address to the county, had played
'a distinguished part' in opposing the American War. But
notwithstanding his alleged claims of distinction, and his
much more certain claims of property, Mr Coke found it
necessary to decline the contest." But of all the contests of
this period, the most important in that point of view was for
the county of York. That great county, not yet at election
times severed into Ridings, had been under the sway of the
Whig Houses. Bolton Abbey, Castle Howard, and Wentworth
Park had claimed the right to dictate at the hustings. It was
not till 1780 that the spirit of the country rose. "Hitherto"
—so in that year spoke Sir George Savile—"I have been elected
in Lord Rockingham's dining-room. Now I am returned by
my constituents." And in 1784 the spirit of the country rose
higher still. In 1784 the independent freeholders of Yorkshire
boldly confronted the great houses, and insisted on returning,
in conjunction with the heir of Duncombe Park, a banker's
son, of few years and of scarcely tried abilities, though destined to a high place in his country's annals—Mr Wilberforce.
With the help of the country gentlemen, they raised the vast
sum of £18,662 for the expense of the election; and so great
was their show of numbers and of resolution, that the candidates upon the other side did not venture to stand a contest.
Wilberforce was also returned at the head of the poll by his
former constituents at Hull. "I can never congratulate you
enough on such glorious success," wrote the Prime Minister
to his young friend. One hundred and sixty followers of Mr
Fox lost their seats, and were called "Fox's martyrs". The
majority for Pitt in the new Parliament was complete, overwhelming, and enthusiastic.

The constitutional aspect of the events of 1784 has been
much discussed, and well merits discussion. It is certain that
George III did much that was, according to the good notions

now fixedly established, thoroughly unconstitutional; it is certain that scarcely any one will, upon any constitutional doctrines, new or old, defend the "card" displayed by Lord Temple. But, if we had room to argue the subject, we think it might be shown that it would have been inexpedient to apply, in the year 1784, the strict constitutional maxims on which we should act in the year 1861; that the beneficial relations, and that the inevitable relations of the Parliament and the Crown, were different then from what they are now; that, under such an aristocratic Legislature as the unreformed Parliament principally was, it was needful that the Crown should sometimes intervene, when the opinion of Parliament was opposed to the opinion of the people; that, in times when public opinion was formed but slowly, it was advisable that the Crown should do so, not by an instant dissolution of the House of Commons, as we should now exact, but by a deferred dissolution, which would enable the thinking part of the community to reflect, and give the whole country, far and near, time to form a real judgment.

But, at present, we have to deal with the events of 1784, not in their relation to the Constitution of England, but in their relation to the life of Mr Pitt. They were the completion of his opportunity. But a short time previously the political isolation of Lord Shelburne had made him Chancellor of the Exchequer at a boyish age; the isolation of George III now made him Prime Minister while still very young. The first good fortune would have been a marvel in the life of any other man, but was nothing to the marvel of the second. By a strange course of great incidents, he was in the most commanding position which an English subject has ever occupied since Parliamentary government was thoroughly established in the country. The victory was so complete, that the mercenaries of the enemy had deserted to his standard. The Crown was necessarily on his side, for he alone stood between George III and the hated Coalition, which he had discarded and insulted; the people were on his side, from a hatred of the official corruption of which they considered his opponents to be the representatives and the embodiments, from a firm belief in his true integrity, from a proud admiration of his single-handed courage and audacious self-reliance. He had the power to do what he would.

Nor was this all. The opportunity was not only a great opportunity, but was an opportunity in the hands of a *young man*. Half of our greatest statesmen would have been wholly unprepared for it. When Lord Palmerston was in office in the spring of 1857 with a large majority, a shrewd observer, now no longer among us, said, "Well, it is a large majority; but what is he to do with it?" He did not know himself; by paltry errors and frivolous haughtiness he frittered it away immediately. An old man of the world has no great objects, no telling enthusiasm, no large proposals, no noble reforms; his advice is that of the old banker, "Live, sir, from day to day, and don't trouble yourself!" Years of acquiescing in proposals as to which he has not been consulted, of voting for measures which he did not frame, and in the wisdom of which he often did not believe, of arguing for proposals from half of which he dissents—usually de-intellectualise a Parliamentary statesman before he comes to half his power. From all this Pitt was exempt. He came to great power with a fresh mind. And not only so; he came into power with the cultivated thought of a new generation. Too many of us scarcely remember how young a man he was. He was born in 1759, and might have well been in the vigour of life in 1830. Lord Sidmouth, his contemporary, did not die till after 1840; he was younger than his cousin, Mr Thomas Grenville, who long represented in London society the traditions of the past, and who died in 1846. He governed men of the generation before him. Alone among English statesmen, while yet a youth he was governing middle-aged men. He had the power of applying the eager thought of five and twenty, of making it rule over the petty knowledge and trained acquiescence of five and fifty. Alone as yet, and alone perhaps for ever in our Parliamentary history, while his own mind was still original, while his own spirit was still unbroken, he was able to impose an absolute yoke on acquiescent spirits whom the world had broken for him.

We have expended so much space on a delineation of the peculiar opportunities which Mr Pitt enjoyed, that we must be very concise in showing how he used them. Three subjects then needed the attention of a great statesman, though none of them were so pressing as to force themselves on the attention of a little statesman. These were, our economical and financial legislation, the imperfection of our Parliamentary representation, and the unhappy condition of Ireland. Pitt dealt with all three.

Our economical legislation was partly in an uncared-for

state, and partly in an ill-cared-for state. Our customs laws
were a chaos of confusion. Innumerable Acts of Parliament
had been passed on temporary occasions and for temporary
purposes; blunders had been discovered in them; other Acts
were passed to amend those blunders; those other Acts contained other blunders; new corrective legislation was required,
and here too there were errors, omissions, and imperfections.
And in so far as our economical legislation was based upon a
theory, that theory was a very mistaken one; it was the theory of Protection. The first duty of the English Legislature,
it was believed, was to develop English industry and to injure
foreign industry. Our manufactures, it was thought, could be
made better by Acts of Parliament; the manufactures of our
rivals, it was believed, could be made worse. The industry
of the nation worked in a complicated network of fetters and
bonds.

Mr Pitt applied himself vigorously to this chaos. He
brought in a series of resolutions consolidating our customs
laws, of which the inevitable complexity may be estimated
by their number. They amounted to 133, and the number
of Acts of Parliament which they restrained or completed was
much greater. He attempted, and successfully, to apply the
principles of Free Trade, the principles which he was the first
of English statesmen to learn from Adam Smith, to the actual
commerce of the country, and to the part of our commerce
which afforded the greatest temptations to a philosophic
statesman, and presented the greatest accumulation of irritable and stupid prejudice. France and England were near one
another, but had no trade with one another; no such trade, at
least, as two countries so different in soil, in climate, and in
natural aptitude, ought to have. So far from either nation
much wishing to trade with the other, neither wished to depend on the other for anything. The national dignity was
supposed to be compromised by buying from an ancient rival.
Mr Pitt, however, framed a treaty which, if its consequences
had not been swept away with so much else, both good and
evil, in the European storm of the French Revolution, would
have been quoted as the true commencement of Free Trade
legislation; would have been referred to as we now refer to the
tentative reforms of Huskisson, and to the earlier Budgets of
Sir Robert Peel. So little was the subject then understood,
even by those most likely to understand it, that both Fox and
Burke opposed the treaty with virulence and vehemence; de-

claring that France was our natural enemy, and that it was unworthy of any one who pretended to be a statesman to create a "peddling traffic," and maintain "huckstering" relations with her.

The financial reputation of Pitt has greatly suffered from the absurd praise which was once lavished on the worst part of it. The dread of national ruin from the augmentation of the National Debt was a sort of nightmare in that age; the evil was apparent, and the counteracting force was not seen. No one perceived that English industry was yearly growing with an accelerating rapidity; no one foresaw that in a few years it would be aided by a hundred wonderful inventions— by the innumerable results of applied science; no one comprehended that the national estate was augmenting far faster than the national burden. The popular mind was apprehensive, and wished to see some remedy applied to what seemed to be an evident and dangerous evil. Mr Pitt sympathised with the general apprehension, and created the well-known *Sinking Fund.* He proposed to apply annually a certain fixed sum to the payment of the debt, which was in itself excellent; but he omitted to provide real money to be so paid. The only source out of which debt can be defrayed, as every one now understands, is a surplus revenue; out of an empty exchequer no claims can ever be liquidated by possibility: an excess of income over outlay is a prerequisite of a true repayment. Mr Pitt, however, not only did not see this, but persuaded a whole generation that it was not so. He proposed to borrow the money to pay off the debt, and fancied that he thus diminished it. He had framed a puzzle in compound interest, which deceived himself, and every one who was entrusted with the national finances, for very many years.

The exposure of this financial juggle, for though not intended to be so, such in fact it was, has reacted very unfavourably upon Mr Pitt's deserved fame. It was so long said "that he was a great financier *because* he invented the Sinking Fund," that it came at last to be believed that he could not be a great financier inasmuch as he had invented it. So much merit had been claimed for something bad, that no search was made for anything good. But an accurate study of these times will prove that Pitt was really one of the greatest financiers in our history, that he repaired the great disorders of the American War, that he restored a surplus revenue, that he understood the true principles of taxation, that he even knew that the best way to increase a revenue from the consumption of the masses is to lower the rate of duty and develop their consuming power.

The subject of Parliamentary reform is the one with which, in Mr Pitt's early days, the public most connected his name, and is also that with which we are now least apt to connect it. We have so long and so often heard him treated as the great Conservative minister, that we can hardly realise to ourselves that he was an unsparing and ardent reformer. Yet such is the indisputable fact. He proposed the abolition of the worst of the rotten boroughs fifty years before Lord Grey accomplished it. The period was a favourable one for reform. The failure of the American War had left behind it a bitter irritation and an anxious self-reproach. Why had we, with our great wealth, our great valour, our long experience, failed in what seemed a trivial enterprise? Why had we been put to shame in the face of Europe? Why had we been forced to humble ourselves in the face of Europe? Why had we been compelled to make an ignominious peace? Why had we, one of the greatest of civilised States, failed to conquer a raw and unknown colony? The popular answer was that our arms had been unsuccessful because our Government was corrupt. The practical working of our unreformed Constitution has been tersely described as the barter of patronage for power; the Parliamentary majorities of that age were kept by an incessant commerce between the proprietors of seats who sold and the Secretary of the Treasury who bought. In the present day refined arguments are often brought forward to justify or to palliate the system of government. But whatever may be the abstract worth of those arguments, their practical worth is not great. They will never convince the mass of men; they will never satisfy the unsophisticated instinct of ordinary men; they will not remove their natural distrust of what they believe to be unpatriotic selfishness; they will not lessen their conscientious repugnance to that which they call corruption. After the disasters of the American War, this feeling was very strong and very diffused. An unpopular tree was judged of by unpopular fruits; our calamities were evident, and our corruption was conspicuous. A most distinct association of the two was formed in the popular mind. Of this Mr Pitt took advantage. If the strong counteracting influence of the French Revolution had not changed the national opinion, he would unquestionably have amended our Parliamentary representa-

tion. Even after the French Revolution he never changed his
own opinion; he considered that the time was not favourable
for what we now call organic changes; and he judged wisely,
for the mass of the nation was wildly and frantically Conservative; but he did not abandon his early principles: he
never became a "Pittite".

The state of Ireland was a more pressing difficulty than
our financial confusion, our economical errors, or our Parliamentary corruption. It had an independent Legislature, which
might at any time take a dangerously different view of national interests, of the expediency of a peace, or the expediency of a war, from the English Parliament. That Legislature was a Protestant Legislature in the midst of a Catholic
people; it was the Legislature of a small and hated minority
in the midst of an excitable, tumultuous, oppressed people.
The mass of the Irish Catholics believed that the mass of the
property, which belonged in fact to the Protestants, was in
strict right theirs; they believed that they were the true owners of the soil, and that the Protestants were intruders; they
believed that they had a right to govern the country, and that
the Protestants were usurpers; they believed that the Church
which the State supported was a heretic Church; that the
Church which the State did not support was the true Church
—the only true Church in Christendom. In every parish the
distinction between Protestant and Catholic was periodically
ruled by the most critical of tests—the pecuniary test. The
collection of the tithe in detail over the country, from the
Catholic population for the Protestant Church, was the source
of chronic confusion and incessant bloodshed. Mr Pitt proposed to remedy all these evils in turn, and effectually. He
proposed to remedy the most immediate and pressing cause
of trouble throughout the country by changing—as has since
been done—the periodical extortion of the Irish tithe from
the hostile farmer into an equivalent payment by a rent-
charge, which could be easily collected and could give rise
to no disgraceful scenes. He proposed to put the Catholic
majority and the Protestant minority upon a perfect equality
so far as civil rights were concerned. He was desirous that
Catholics should be eligible to all offices, and be electors for
all offices. He was ready likewise to destroy the prevalent
religious agitation at its very root, by paying the ministers
of the Church of the poor as well as the ministers of the
Church of the rich. He proposed at once to remedy the na-

tional danger of having two Parliaments, and to remove the incredible corruption of the old Irish Parliament, by uniting the three kingdoms in a single representative system, of which the Parliament should sit in England. He framed, in a word, a scheme which would have cured the internal divisions of Ireland, which would have united her effectually to the Empire without impairing her real liberty.

Of these great reforms he was only permitted to carry a few into execution. His power, as we have described it, was great when his reign commenced, and very great it continued to be for very many years; but the time became unfavourable for all forward-looking statesmanship—for everything which could be called innovation. The French Revolution and the French War destroyed for many years our national taste for political improvement. But, notwithstanding these calamities, Pitt achieved some part of all his cherished schemes save one.

No opportunity would have enabled Pitt to effect these great reforms, no peculiar situation would have suggested them to him, if he had not had certain more than ordinary tendencies and abilities—the tendencies and abilities of a great administrator. Contrary to what might at first sight be supposed, using the word "administrator" in its most enlarged sense—in the sense in which we used it at the commencement of this article—the first qualification of the highest administrator is, that he should think of something which he need not think of—of something which is not the pressing difficulty of the hour. For inferior men no rule could be so dangerous. Ambitious mediocrity is dangerous mediocrity; ordinary men find what they must do amply enough for them to do; the exacting difficulty of the hour, which will not be stayed, which must be met, absorbs their whole time and all their energies. But the ideal administrator has time, has mind—for that is the difficulty—for something more; he can do what he must, and he will do what he wishes. This is Mr Pitt's peculiarity among the great English statesmen of the eighteenth century. As a rule, the spirit of Sir Robert Walpole ruled over all these statesmen. They respected his favourite maxim, *quieta non movere;* to deal shrewdly and adroitly with what must be dealt with; to leave alone whatever might be left alone; to accumulate every possible resource against the inevitable difficulties of the present moment, and never to think or dream or treat of what was

not inevitable;—these were then, as always, the justifiable aims
of commonplace men. They did *their* possible; they did
all that they could with their strength and their faculties in
their day and generation. The philosophy of the time, with
its definite problems and its unaspiring tendencies, encouraged them; it made them unalive to the higher possibilities they were forgetting, to the higher duties they were
half-consciously, half-unconsciously passing over. It was with
reference to this oblivious neglect of the future, this short-
sighted absorption in the present, that Dr Arnold called this
century the "misused trial-time of modern Europe". It is the
distinctive characteristic of Pitt that, having a great opportunity, having power such as no Parliamentary statesman
has ever had, having in his mind a fresh stock of youthful
thought such as no similar statesman has ever possessed—he
applied *that* power steadily and perseveringly to embody that
thought. To persons who think but slightly, this may seem
only a very slight merit. The first remark of many a commonplace man would be, "If I had great power, I would carry
out my own ideas". A modern Socrates, if there were such a
person, would answer, "But, my good friend, what are your
ideas?" When explained to an exact and scrutinising ques-
tioner, still more when confronted with the awful facts—the
inevitable necessities of the real world—these "ideas" would
melt away; after a little while the commonplace person, who
was at first so proud of them, would cease to believe that he
ever entertained them; he would say, "Men of *business* do
not indulge in those speculations". The characteristic merit
of Pitt is, that in the midst of harassing details, in the
midst of obvious cares, in the face of most keen, most able,
and most stimulated opposition, he applied his whole power
to the accomplishment of great but practicable schemes.

The marvel, or at any rate the merit, is greater. Pitt was
by no means an excited visionary. He had by no means one
of those minds upon which great ideas fasten as a fanaticism.
There was among his contemporaries a great man, who was
in the highest gifts of abstract genius, in the best acquisitions
of political culture, far superior to him. But in the mind of
Burke great ideas were a supernatural burden, a superincum-
bent inspiration. He saw a great truth, and he saw nothing
else. At all times with the intense irritability of genius, in
later years with the extreme one-sidedness of insanity, he
was content, in season and out of season, with the great vi-

sions which had been revealed to him, with the great lessons which he had to teach, and which he could but very rarely induce any one to hear. But Pitt's mind was an absolute contrast to this. He had an extreme discretion, tested at the most trying conjunctures. In 1784, when he had no power, when there was a hostile majority in the House of Commons, when he had no sure majority in the House of Lords, when the support of the King, which he undeniably had, was an undeniable difficulty;—for he did not intend to be a second Lord North; he did not intend to be a servitor of the Palace; he would not have stooped to carry out measures which he disapproved of; he would not have been willing to enunciate measures as to which he had not been consulted;—at this very moment, with most of the constitutional powers against him, with the very greatest greatly against him, with no useful part of it truly for him—he never made a false step; he guided the most feeble administration of modern times so ably and so dexterously that in a· few months it became the strongest. A mind with so delicate a tact as this is entitled to some merit for adhering to distant principles. It is those who understand the present that feel the temptation of the present; it is those who comprehend the hour that feel the truly arduous, though upon paper it may seem the petty, difficulty of thinking beyond the hour. It is no merit in those who cannot have the present to attempt to act for posterity. There is nothing else left to them; they have no other occupation open to them. But it is a great merit in those who can have what is plain, apparent, and immediate, to think of the unseen, unasking, impalpable future.

It is this singular discretion which is Mr Pitt's peculiar merit, because he belongs to the class of statesmen who are most apt to be defective in that discretion. He was an oratorical statesman; and an oratorical statesman means, *ex vi termini*, an excitable statesman. His art consists in the power of giving successfully in a more than ordinary manner the true feelings and sentiments of ordinary men; not their superficial notions, nor their coarser sentiments, for with these any inferior man may deal, but their most intimate nature, that which in their highest moments is most truly themselves. How is the exercise of this art to be reconciled with terrestrial discretion? Is the preacher to come down from his pedestal? is he who can deal worthily with great thoughts to be asked also to deal fittingly with small details? is it possible

that the same mind which can touch the hearts of all men
can also be alive to the petty interests of itself? is the microscopic power to be added to the telescopic power? is the
capacity for careful management to be added to the power
of creating unbounded enthusiasm? Yet this is the perpetual difficulty of Parliamentary statesmen. A dry man can do
the necessary business; an excitable man can give to the popular House of Parliament the necessary excitement. Mr Pitt
was able, with surpassing ability and surpassing ease, to do
both; scarcely any one else has been so.

This great Parliamentary position he owed to a combination of Parliamentary abilities, of which only one or two can
be, within our necessary limits, distinctly specified, but one
or two of which are very prominent.

First, his singular oratorical power. He was, Lord Macaulay
tells us, "at once the one man who could explain a Budget
without notes, and who could speak that most unmeaningly
evasive of human compositions, a Queen's Speech, off hand".
He had the eloquence of business both in its expressive and
its inexpressive forms, and he had likewise the eloquence of
character; that is, he had the singular power, which not half
a dozen men in a generation possess, of imparting to a large
audience the exact copy of the feelings, the exact impress of
the determination, with which they are themselves possessed. On a matter of figures, "Pitt said so," was enough;
on a question of legislative improvement, an apathetic Parliament caught some interest from his example; in the deepest
moments of national despair, an anxious nation could show
some remains of their characteristic courage, from his bold
audacity, and unwearied, inflexible, and augmenting determination.

No man could have achieved this without a sanguine temperament, and accordingly good observers pronounced Mr
Pitt the most sanguine man they had ever known. In no
stage of national despondency, in no epoch of national despair, was his capacity of hope, one of the important capacities for great men in anxious affairs, ever shaken. At the
crisis of his early life, Lord Temple's resignation, which
seemed the last possible addition to the coalition of difficulties under which he was labouring, is said to have deprived
him of sleep; but nothing else ever did so after his power
attained its maturity, and while his body retained its strength.

Over the House of Commons, too, his anxious love of

detail had an influence which will not surprise those who know how sensitive that critical assembly is to every sort of genuineness, and how keenly watchful it is for every kind of falsity. The labour bestowed on his reform of the Customs Acts, on his Indian measures, on his financial proposals from year to year, is matter of history; no one can look with an instructed eye at these measures without instantly being conscious of it. In addition to his other great powers, Mr Pitt added the rare one of an intense capacity for work, in an age when that capacity was rarer than it is now, and in a Parliament where the element of dandies and idlers was far more dominant than it has since become.

Nor would this enumeration of Pitt's great Parliamentary qualities be complete—it would want, perhaps, the most striking and obvious characteristic—if we omitted to mention Pitt's well-managed shyness and his surpassing pride.

In all descriptions of Pitt's appearance in the House of Commons, a certain aloofness fills an odd space. He is a "thing apart," different somehow from other members. Fox was the exact opposite. He was a good fellow; he rolled into the House, fat, good-humoured, and popular. Pitt was spare, dignified, and reserved. When he entered the House, he walked to the place of the Premier, without looking to the right or to the left, and he sat at the same place. He was ready to discuss important business with all proper persons, upon all necessary occasions; but he was not ready to discuss business unnecessarily with any one, nor did he discuss anything but business with any save a very few intimate friends, with whom his reserve at once vanished, and his wit and humour at once expanded, and his genuine interests in all really great subjects was at once displayed. In a popular assembly this sort of reserve rightly manipulated is a power. It is analogous to the manner which the accomplished author of *Eöthen* recommends in dealing with Orientals: "it excites terror and inspires respect". A recent book of memoirs illustrates it. During Addington's administration, a certain rather obscure "Mr G." was made a privy councillor; and the question was raised in Pitt's presence as to the mode in which he could have obtained that honour. Some one said, "I suppose he was always talking to the Premier, and bothering him". Mr Pitt quietly observed, "In *my* time I would much rather have made him a privy councillor *than have spoken to him*". It is easy to conceive the mental exhaustion which this

well-managed reserve spared him, the number of trivial conversations which it economised, the number of imperfect
ambitions which it quelled before they were uttered. An
ordinary man could not of course make use of it. But Pitt at
the earliest period imparted to the House of Commons the
two most important convictions for a member in his position:
he convinced them that he would not be the King's creature, and that he desired no pecuniary profit for himself. As
he despised royal favour and despised real money, the House
of Commons thought he might well despise *them*.

We have left ourselves no room to speak of Mr Pitt's
policy at the time of the French Revolution. It would require an essay of considerable length to do it substantial justice. But we may observe, that the crisis which that Revolution presented to an English statesman was one rather for a
great dictator than for a great administrator. The English
people were at first in general pleased with the commencement of the French Revolution. "*Anglo-manie*," it seemed,
had been prevalent on the Continent; the English Constitution, it was hoped, would be transplanted; the fundamental
principles of the English Revolution it was, at any rate,
hoped, would be imitated. The essay of Burke by its arguments, the progress of events by an evident experience, proved
that such would not be the history. What was to come was
uncertain. There was no precedent on the English file; the
English people did not know what they ought to think;
they were ready to submit to any one who would think for
them. The only point upon which their opinion was decided
was, that the French Revolution was very dangerous; that it
had produced awful results in France; that it was no model
for imitation for sober men in a sober country. They were
ready to concede anything to a statesman who allowed this,
who acted on this, who embodied this in appropriate action.

Mr Pitt saw little further than the rest of the nation;
what the French Revolution was he did not understand; what
forces it would develop he did not foresee; what sort of opposition it would require he did not apprehend. He was, indeed, on one point much in advance of his contemporaries.
The instinct of uncultivated persons is always towards an
intemperate interference with anything of which they do not
approve. A most worthy police-magistrate in our own time
said, that "he intended to put down *suicide*". The English
people, in the very same spirit of uncultured benevolence,

wished to "put down the French Revolution". They were irritated at its excess; they were alarmed at its example; they conceived that such impiety should be punished for the past and prohibited for the future. Mr Pitt's natural instinct, however, was certainly in an entirely opposite direction. He was by inclination and by temperament opposed to all war; he was very humane, and all war is inhumane; he was a great financier, and all war is opposed to well-regulated finance. He postponed a French war as long as he could; he consented to it with reluctance, and continued it from necessity.

Of the great powers which the sudden excitement of democratic revolution would stimulate in a nation seemingly exhausted, Mr Pitt knew no more than those who were around him. Burke said that, as a military power, France was "blotted from the map of Europe"; and though Pitt, with characteristic discretion, did not advance any sentiment which would be so extreme, or any phrase which would adhere so fixedly to every one's memory, it is undeniable that he did not anticipate the martial power which the new France, as by magic, displayed; that he fancied she would be an effete country; that he fancied he was making war with certain scanty vestiges of the *ancien régime*, instead of contending against the renewed, excited, and intensified energies of a united people. He did not know that, for temporary purposes, a revolutionary government was the most powerful of all governments; for it does not care for the future, and has the entire legacy of the past. He forgot that it was possible, that from a brief period of tumultuous disorder, there might issue a military despotism more compact, more disciplined, and more overpowering than any which had preceded it, or any which has followed it.

But, as we have said, the conclusion of a prolonged article is no place for discussing the precise nature of Mr Pitt's anti-revolutionary policy. Undoubtedly, he did not comprehend the Revolution in France; as Lord Macaulay has explained, with his habitual power, he over-rated the danger of a revolution in this country; he entirely over-estimated the power of the democratic assailants, and he entirely underestimated the force of the conservative, maintaining, restraining, and, if need were, reactionary, influence. He saw his enemy;—he did not see his allies. But it is not given to many men to conquer such difficulties; it is not given to the greatest of administrators to apprehend entirely new phenomena. A highly imaginative statesman, a man of great moments and great visions, a greater Lord Chatham, might have done so, but the educated sense and equable dexterity of Mr Pitt failed. All that he could do he did. He burnt the memory of his own name into the Continental mind. After sixty years, the French people still half believe that it was the gold of Pitt which caused many of their misfortunes; after half a century it is still certain that it was Pitt's indomitable spirit and Pitt's hopeful temper which was the soul of every Continental coalition, and the animating life of every anti-revolutionary movement. He showed most distinctly how potent is the influence of a commanding character just when he most exhibited the characteristic limitation of even the best administrative intellect.

ADAM SMITH AS A PERSON*

(1876)

Adam Smith was born at Kirkcaldy in 1723, the only child of Adam Smith, writer to the signet (the Scots equivalent of a barrister), and Margaret Douglas. He was educated at the burgh school in Kirkcaldy, at Glasgow University, and at Balliol College, Oxford. In 1751 he was elected to the chair of logic at Glasgow, and in 1752 transferred to the chair of moral philosophy, lecturing on theology, ethics, jurisprudence, and political institutions. The fame of his lectures brought him a tutorship to the duke of Buccleuch, and during his travels with the duke he met Hume, Turgot, and others in Paris, and Voltaire at Geneva. In 1767 he settled in Kirkcaldy on a pension from the duke of Buccleuch. Smith's great work The Wealth of Nations, *which initiated the study of political economy as a separate science, was published in 1776. Adam Smith died in Edinburgh in 1790.*

Of Adam Smith's Political Economy almost an infinite quantity has been said, but very little has been said as to Adam Smith himself. And yet not only was he one of the most curious of human beings, but his books can hardly be understood without having some notion of what manner of man he was. There certainly are economical treatises that go straight on, and that might have been written by a calculating machine. But *The Wealth of Nations* is not one of these. Any one who would explain what is in it, and what is not in it, must apply the "historical method," and state what was the experience of its author and how he worked up that experience. Perhaps, therefore, now that there is a sort of centenary of Adam Smith, it may not be amiss to give a slight sketch of him and of his life, and especially of the peculiar points

* This essay was first published in the *Fortnightly Review* for July 1, 1876, Volume XX [N.S.], pages 18–42.

in them that led him to write the book which still in its effects, even more than in its theory, occupies mankind.

The founder of the science of business was one of the most
unbusinesslike of mankind. He was an awkward Scotch professor, apparently choked with books and absorbed in abstrac-
tions. He was never engaged in any sort of trade, and would
probably never have made sixpence by any if he had been.
His absence of mind was amazing. On one occasion, having
to sign his name to an official document, he produced not
his own signature, but an elaborate imitation of the signature
of the person who signed before him; on another, a sentinel
on duty having saluted him in military fashion, he astounded
and offended the man by acknowledging it with a copy—a
very clumsy copy, no doubt—of the same gestures. And
Lord Brougham preserves other similar traditions. "It is related," he says, "by old people in Edinburgh that while he
moved through the Fishmarket in his accustomed attitude—
that is with his hands behind his back, and his head in the
air—a female of the trade exclaimed, taking him for an idiot
broken loose, "Hech, sirs, to see the like o' him to be aboot.
And yet he is weel eneugh put on" (dressed). It was often so
too in society. Once, during a dinner at Dalkeith, he broke
out into a lecture on some politics of the day, and was bestowing a variety of severe epithets on a statesman, when he
suddenly perceived the nearest relative of the politician he
was criticising, sitting opposite, and stopped; but he was
heard to go on muttering, "Deil care, Deil care, it's all true".
And these are only specimens of a crowd of anecdotes.

The wonder that such a man should have composed *The
Wealth of Nations*, which shows so profound a knowledge of
the real occupations of mankind, is enhanced by the mode in
which it was written. It was not the exclusive product of a
lifelong study, such as an absent man might, while in seeming abstraction, be really making of the affairs of the world.
On the contrary, it was in the mind of its author only one of
many books, or rather a single part of a great book, which
he intended to write. A vast scheme floated before him,
much like the dream of the late Mr Buckle as to a History
of Civilisation, and he spent his life accordingly, in studying
the origin and progress of the sciences, the laws, the politics,
and all the other aids and forces which have raised man from
the savage to the civilised state. The plan of Adam Smith
was indeed more comprehensive even than this. He wanted

to trace not only the progress of the race, but also of the individual; he wanted to show how each man being born (as he thought) with few faculties, came to attain to many and great faculties. He wanted to answer the question, how did man—race or individual—come to be what he is? These immense dreams are among the commonest phenomena of literary history; and, as a rule, the vaster the intention, the less the result. The musings of the author are too miscellaneous, his studies too scattered, his attempts too incoherent, for him to think out anything valuable, or to produce anything connected. But in Adam Smith's case the very contrary is true; he produced an enduring particular result in consequence of a comprehensive and diffused ambition. He discovered the laws of wealth in looking for "the natural progress of opulence"; and he investigated the progress of opulence as part of the growth and progress of all things.

The best way to get a distinct notion of Adam Smith's scheme is to look at the other works which he published besides *The Wealth of Nations*. The greatest, and the one which made his original reputation, was *The Theory of Moral Sentiments*, in which he builds up the whole moral nature of man out of a single primitive emotion—sympathy; and in which he gives a history of ethical philosophy besides. With this are commonly bound up *Some Considerations concerning the first Formation of Languages*, which discuss how "two savages who had never been taught to speak, but had been bred up remote from the society of man, would naturally begin their converse". Then there is a very curious *History of Astronomy*, left imperfect; and another fragment on the *History of Ancient Physics*, which is a kind of sequel to that part of the *History of Astronomy* which relates to the ancient astronomy; then a similar essay on *Ancient Logic and Metaphysics*; then another on the nature and development of the Fine—or, as he calls them, *The Imitative Arts—Painting, Poetry, and Music*, in which was meant to have been included a history of the Theatre—all forming part, his executors tell us, "of a plan he had once formed for giving a connected history of the liberal and elegant arts". And he destroyed before his death the remains of the book, *Lectures on Justice*, "in which," we are told by a student who heard them, "he followed Montesquieu in endeavouring to trace the gradual progress of jurisprudence, both public and private, from the rudest to the most refined ages, and to point out the effects

of those arts which contribute to subsistence and to the accumulation of property in producing correspondent alterations in law and government"; or, as he himself announces it
at the conclusion of *The Moral Sentiments,* "another discourse" in which he designs "to endeavour to give an account
of the general principles of law and government, and of the
different revolutions they have undergone in the different
ages and periods of society, not only in what concerns justice,
but in what concerns police, revenue, and arms, and whatever else is the subject of law". Scarcely any philosopher has
imagined a vaster dream.

Undoubtedly it is a great literary marvel that so huge a
scheme, on so many abstract subjects, should have produced
anything valuable, and still more so that it should have produced what has been for a whole century a fundamental book
on trade and money—at first sight, the least fit for a secluded
man to treat at all, and which, if he did treat of them, would
seem more than any other to require from him an absorbed
and exclusive attention. A little study of the life of Adam
Smith, however, in some degree lessens the wonder; because
it shows how in the course of his universal studies he came to
meet with this particular train of thought, and how he came
to be able to pursue it effectually.

Adam Smith was born early in the first half of the eighteenth century, at Kirkcaldy in Scotland, on 5th June, 1713.
His father died before he was born; but his mother, who is
said to have been a woman of unusual energy and ability,
lived to be very old, and to see her son at the height of his
reputation as a philosopher. He was educated at school in
the usual Scotch way, and at the University of Glasgow; and
at both he is said, doubtless truly, to have shown an unusual
facility of acquisition, and an unusual interest in books and
study. As we should also expect, a very strong memory, which
he retained till the last, showed itself very early. Nothing,
however, is known with precision as to the amount of knowledge he acquired in Scotland, nor as to his place among his
contemporaries. The examination system, which nowadays in
England discriminates both so accurately, has in Scotland
never been equally developed, and in Adam Smith's time had
never been heard of there at all.

His exceptional training begins at the next stage. There is
at the University of Glasgow a certain endowment called the
Snell exhibition, after the name of its founder, which en-

ables the students selected for it to study for some years at the University of Oxford. Of these exhibitioners Adam Smith became one, and as such studied at Oxford for as many as seven years. As might be expected, he gave the worst account of the state of the university at that time. In the sketch of the history of education which forms so odd an episode in *The Wealth of Nations,* he shows perpetually that he thought the system which he had seen at Oxford exceedingly bad, and its government excessively corrupt. "If," he says, "the authority to which a teacher is subject resides in the body corporate of the college or university of which he is himself a member, and in which the greater part of the other members are, like himself, persons who either are or ought to be teachers, they are likely to make a common cause, to be all very indulgent to one another, and every man to consent that his neighbour may neglect his duty, provided he is himself allowed to neglect his own. In the University of Oxford the greater part of the public professors have for these many years given up altogether even the pretence of teaching." And he adds, "In England, the public schools are much less corrupted than the universities. In the schools, the youths are taught, or at least may be taught, Greek and Latin. That is everything which the masters pretend to teach, or which it is expected they should teach. In the universities, the youth neither are taught, nor can always find the means of being taught, the sciences which it is the business of these incorporated bodies to teach." And he retained through life a fixed belief that endowments for education tended only to the "ease" of the teacher, and not to the advantage of the learner. But though he says he had the means of learning little at Oxford, he certainly, in fact, learnt much. "Greek," as Sydney Smith says, "never crossed the Tweed in any force"; but Adam Smith incessantly shows a real familiarity with Greek books and a sound accumulation of Greek learning. Very likely his erudition would not bear much comparison with what is now carried away from Balliol. If we compare him with a more recent Snell exhibitioner, Sir William Hamilton, we shall see that Greek teaching has enormously advanced in the time between them; but, on the other hand, if we compare Adam Smith with Scotch philosophers of purely Scotch education, say with Reid or Hume, we cannot help seeing that his acquaintance with Greek things belongs, both in quantity and in quality, to an order altogether superior to theirs.

For the vast works which Adam Smith contemplated, a sound knowledge of Greek was, as he must have felt, far more necessary than any other kind of knowledge. The beginnings of nine-tenths of all philosophy are to be found there, and the rudiments of many other things. But for the purpose of the great task which he actually performed, Adam Smith learned at Oxford something much more valuable than Greek. He acquired there a kind of knowledge and sympathy with England, in which the other eminent Scotchmen —especially literary Scotchmen—of his time were often very deficient. At that time the recollection of the old rivalry between the two countries had by no means died away; there was still a separate Scotch philosophy, and a separate literature; and when it happened, as it perpetually did, that Scotch writers were not thought so much of in England as they thought they ought to be, they were apt to impute their discredit to English prejudice, and to appeal to France and Paris to correct the error. Half Hume's mind, or more than half, was distorted by his hatred of England and his love of France. He often could not speak of English things with tolerable temper, and he always viewed French ones with extravagant admiration. Whether Adam Smith altogether liked this country may perhaps be doubted—Englishmen then hated Scotchmen so much—but he had no kind of antagonism to her, and quite understood that in most economical respects she was then exceedingly superior to France. And this exceptional sympathy and knowledge we may fairly ascribe to a long and pleasant residence in England. For his great work no qualification was more necessary; *The Wealth of Nations* would have been utterly spoiled if he had tried (as Hume incessantly would have tried) to show that, in industrial respects, England might not be better than France, or at any rate was not so very much better.

The Snell foundation at Oxford has often been an avenue to the English Church, and it seems to have been intended that Adam Smith should use it as such. The only anecdote which remains of his college life may be a clue to his reasons for not doing so. He is said to have been found by his tutor in the act of reading Hume's *Philosophical Essays*, then lately published, and to have been reproved for it. And it is certain that any one who at all sympathised with Hume's teaching in that book would have felt exceedingly little sympathy with the formularies of the Church of England, even as they were understood in the very Broad Church of that age. At any rate, for some reason or other, Adam Smith disappointed the wishes of his friends, gave up all idea of entering the Church of England, and returned to Scotland without fixed outlook or employment. He resided, we are told, two years with his mother, studying no doubt, but earning nothing, and visibly employed in nothing. In England such a career would probably have ended in his writing for the booksellers, a fate of which he speaks in *The Wealth of Nations* with contempt. But in Scotland there was a much better opening for philosophers. The Scotch universities had then, as now, several professorships very fairly paid, and very fairly distributed. The educated world in Scotland was probably stronger a century ago than it ever was before or since. The Union with England had removed the aristocracy of birth which overshadowed it before, and commerce had not yet created the aristocracy of wealth which overshadows it now. Philosophical merit had therefore then in Scotland an excellent chance of being far better rewarded than it usually is in the world. There were educated people who cared for philosophy, and these people had prizes to give away. One of those prizes Adam Smith soon obtained. He read lectures, we are told, under the patronage of Lord Kames, an eminent lawyer, who wrote books on philosophy that are still quoted, and who was no doubt deeply interested in Adam Smith's plans of books on the origin and growth of all arts and sciences, as these were the topics which he himself studied and handled. Contrary to what might have been expected, these lectures were very successful. Though silent and awkward in social life, Adam Smith possessed in considerable perfection the peculiarly Scotch gift of abstract oratory. Even in common conversation, when once moved he expounded his favourite ideas very admirably. As a teacher in public he did even better: he wrote almost nothing, and though at the beginning of a lecture he often hesitated, we are told, and seemed "not sufficiently possessed of the subject," yet in a minute or two he became fluent, and poured out an interesting series of animated arguments. Commonly, indeed, the silent man, whose brain is loaded with unexpressed ideas, is more likely to be a successful public speaker than the brilliant talker who daily exhausts himself in sharp sayings. Adam Smith acquired

great reputation as a lecturer, and in consequence obtained
two of the best prizes then given to philosophers in Scotland
—first the professorship of logic, and then that of moral
philosophy, in the University of Glasgow.

The rules, or at any rate the practice, of the Scotch universities, seem at that time to have allowed a professor in either
of these chairs great latitude in the choice of his subject.
Adam Smith during his first year lectured on rhetoric and
belles lettres "instead of on logic," and in the chair of moral
philosophy he expounded, besides the theory of duty, a great
scheme of social evolution. The beginnings of *The Wealth of
Nations* made part of the course, but only as a fragment of
the immense design of showing the origin and development
of cultivation and law; or, as we may perhaps put it, not in-
appropriately, of saying how, from being a savage, man rose
to be a Scotchman. This course of lectures seems to have been
specially successful. So high, we are told, was his reputation
as a professor, "that a multitude of students from a great
distance resorted to the university merely upon his account.
Those branches of science which he taught became fashionable" in the city, "and his opinions were the chief topics of
discussion in clubs and literary societies. Even the small
peculiarities of his pronunciation and manner of speaking became frequently the objects of imitation." This is the partial
recollection of an attached pupil in distant years;—it may be
over-coloured a little—but even after a fair abatement it is certainly the record of a great temporary triumph and local
success.

That the greater part of the lectures can have been of
much intrinsic merit it is not now easy to believe. An historical account "of the general principles of law and government, and of the different revolutions which they have undergone in the different ages and periods of society," would be
too great a task for a great scholar of the ripest years and
with all the accumulated materials of the present time, and
it was altogether beyond the strength of a young man a century ago;—not to say that he combined it with an account of
the origin of the moral faculties, a theory of *belles lettres*,
and other matters. The delivery of that part of the course
which was concerned with wealth and revenue may have
been useful to him, because it compelled him to bring his
ideas on those subjects into a distinct form. Otherwise, being
a bookish man, he might have been too absorbed in bookish

matters, and neglected what can only be taught by life for that which is already to be learned from literature. But at the time this was only a minor merit;—the main design of the lectures was only an impossible aim at an unbounded task.

So complex, however, is life, that this Scotch professorship, though in a superficial view wasteful, and likely to exhaust and hurt his mind by demanding the constant efflux of inferior matter, was, nevertheless, on the whole, exceedingly useful. It not only induced him to study as a part of his vast scheme the particular phenomena of wealth, but it gave him an excellent opportunity of seeing those phenomena and of learning how to explain them. It was situated at Glasgow; and Glasgow, though a petty place in comparison with its present magnitude, was nevertheless a considerable mercantile place according to the notions of those times. The Union with England had opened to it the trade with our West Indian colonies, as well as with the rest of the English empire, and it had in consequence grown rapidly and made large profits. That its size was small, as we should think now, was to a learner rather an aid than a disadvantage. A small commerce is more easily seen than an immense one; that of Liverpool or London is now so vast that it terrifies more than excites the imagination. And a small commerce, if varied, has almost as much to teach as a large one; the elements are the same though the figures are smaller, and the less the figures the easier are they to combine. An inspection of Liverpool now would not teach much more than an inspection of Glasgow a hundred years ago, and the lessons of modern Liverpool would be much more difficult to learn. But the mere sight of the phenomena of Glasgow commerce was but a small part of the advantage to Adam Smith of a residence at Glasgow. The most characteristic and most valuable tenets of Adam Smith are, when examined, by no means of a very abstract and recondite sort. We are, indeed, in this generation not fully able to appreciate the difficulty of arriving at them. We have been bred up upon them; our disposition is more to wonder how any one could help seeing them, than to appreciate the effort of discovering them. Experience shows that many of them—the doctrine of Free Trade for example—are very uncongenial to the untaught human mind. On political economy the English-speaking race is undoubtedly the best instructed part of mankind; and, nevertheless, in the United States and in every English-speaking colony,

Protection is the firm creed of the ruling classes, and Free
Trade is but a heresy. We must not fancy that any of the
main doctrines of Adam Smith were very easily arrived at by
him because they seem very obvious to us. But, on the other
hand, although such doctrines as his are too opposed to many
interests and to many first impressions to establish themselves
easily as a dominant creed, they are quite within the reach
and quite congenial to the taste of an intelligent dissenting
minority. There was a whole race of mercantile Free Traders
long before Adam Smith was born; in his time the doctrine
was in the air; it was not accepted or established;—on the contrary, it was a tenet against which a respectable parent would
probably caution his son;—still it was known as a tempting
heresy, and one against which a warning was needed. In Glasgow there were doubtless many heretics. Probably in consequence of the firm belief in a rigid theology, and of the incessant discussion of its technical tenets, there has long been,
and there is still, in the South of Scotland, a strong tendency
to abstract argument quite unknown in England. Englishmen
have been sometimes laughing at it, and sometimes gravely
criticising it for several generations: Mr Buckle wrote half a
volume on it: Sydney Smith alleged that he heard a Scotch
girl answer in a quadrille, "But, my lord, as to what ye were
saying as to love in the *aib*stract," and so on. Yet, in spite
both of ridicule and argument, the passion for doctrine is
still strong in southern Scotland, and it will take many years
more to root it out. At Glasgow in Adam Smith's time it
had no doubt very great influence; a certain number of hard-
headed merchants were believers in Free Trade and kindred
tenets. One of these is still by chance known to us. Dr
Carlyle, whom Mr Gladstone not unhappily described as a
"gentleman clergyman" of the Church of Scotland, tells us of
a certain Provost Cochrane, to whom Adam Smith always
acknowledged his obligations, and who was the founder and
leading member of a club "in which the express design was
to inquire into the nature and principles of trade in all its
branches, and to communicate their knowledge on that subject to each other". From this club Adam Smith not only
learned much which he would never have found in any book,
but also in part perhaps acquired the influential and so to
say practical way of explaining things which so much distinguishes *The Wealth of Nations*. Mr Mill says he learned
from his intercourse with East India directors the habit of

looking for, and the art of discovering, "the mode of putting a thought which gives it easiest admittance into minds not prepared for it by habit!" and Adam Smith probably gained something of this sort by living with the Glasgow merchants, for no other book written by a learned professor shows anything like the same power of expressing and illustrating arguments in a way likely to influence minds like theirs. And it is mainly by his systematic cultivation of this borderland between theory and practice that Adam Smith attained his pre-eminent place and influence.

But this usefulness of his Scotch professorship was only in the distant future. It was something for posterity to detect, but it could not have been known at the time. The only pages of his professorial work which Adam Smith then gave to the public were his lectures on Moral Philosophy, in what an Englishman would consider its more legitimate sense. These formed the once celebrated *Theory of Moral Sentiments,* which, though we should now think them rather pompous, were then much praised and much read. For a great part, indeed, of Adam Smith's life they constituted his main title to reputation. *The Wealth of Nations* was not published till seventeen years later; he wrote nothing else of any importance in the interval, and it is now curious to find that when *The Wealth of Nations* was published, many good judges thought it not so good as *The Theory of Moral Sentiments,* and that the author himself was by no means certain they were not right.

The Theory of Moral Sentiments was, indeed, for many years, exceedingly praised. One sect of philosophers praised it, as it seems to me, because they were glad of a celebrated ally, and another because they were glad of a celebrated opponent: the first said, "See that so great an authority as Adam Smith concurs with us"; and the second replied, "But see how very weak his arguments are; if so able an arguer as Adam Smith can say so little for your doctrines, how destitute of argumentative grounds those doctrines must be". Several works in the history of philosophy have had a similar fate. But a mere student of philosophy who cares for no sect, and wants only to know the truth, will nowadays, I think, find little to interest him in this celebrated book. In Adam Smith's mind, as I have said before, it was part of a whole; he wanted to begin with the origin of the faculties of each man, and then build up that man—just as he wished to arrive at the origin of human society, and then build up society. His *Theory of Moral Sentiments* builds them all out of one source, sympathy, and in this way he has obtained praise from friends and enemies. His friends are the school of "moral sense" thinkers, because he is on their side, and believes in a special moral faculty, which he laboriously constructs from sympathy; his enemies are the Utilitarian school, who believe in no such special faculty, and who set themselves to show that his labour has been in vain, and that no such faculty has been so built up. One party says the book is good to gain authority for the conclusion, and the other that you may gain credit by refuting its arguments. For unquestionably its arguments *are* very weak, and attractive to refutation. If the intuitive school had had no better grounds than these, the Utilitarians would have vanquished them ages since. There is a fundamental difficulty in founding morals on sympathy; an obvious confusion of two familiar sentiments. We often sympathise where we cannot approve, and approve where we cannot sympathise. The special vice of party spirit is that it effaces the distinction between the two; we sympathise with our party, till we approve its actions. There is a story of a Radical wit in the last century who was standing for Parliament, and his opponent, of course a Tory, objected that he was always *against* the king whether right or wrong, upon which the wit retorted that on his own showing the Tory was exposed to equal objection, since he was always *for* the king whether right or wrong. And so it will always be. Even the wisest party men more or less sympathise with the errors of their own side; they would be powerless if they did not do so; they would gain no influence if they were not of like passions with those near them. Adam Smith could not help being aware of this obvious objection; he was far too able a reasoner to elaborate a theory without foreseeing what would be said against it. But the way in which he tries to meet the objection only shows that the objection is invincible. He sets up a supplementary theory—a little epicycle—that the sympathy which is to test good morals must be the sympathy of an "impartial spectator". But, then, who is to watch the watchman? Who is to say when the spectator is impartial, and when he is not? If he sympathises with one side, the other will always say that he is partial. As a moralist, the supposed spectator must warmly approve good actions and warmly disapprove bad actions; as an impartial person, he must never do either the one or the other. He is a fiction of inconsistent halves; if he sympathises he is not impartial, and if he is impartial he does not sympathise. The radical vice of the theory is shown by its requiring this accessory invention of a being both hot and cold, because the essence of the theory is to identify the passion which loves with the sentiment which approves.

But although we may now believe *The Theory of Moral Sentiments* to be of inconsiderable philosophical value, and though it would at first sight seem very little likely to contribute to the production of *The Wealth of Nations,* yet it was, in fact, in a curious way most useful to it. The education of young noblemen has always been a difficulty in the world, and many schemes have been invented to meet it. In Scotland, a hundred years ago, the most fashionable way was to send them to travel in Europe, and to send with them some scholar of repute to look after their morals and to superintend their general education. The guardians of the great border nobleman, the Duke of Buccleuch, were in want of such a tutor to take him such a tour, and it seems to have struck them that Adam Smith was the very person adapted for the purpose. To all appearance an odder selection could hardly have been made. Adam Smith was, as we have seen, the most absent-minded of men, an awkward Scotch professor, and he was utterly unacquainted with the Continent. He had never crossed the English Channel in his life, and if he had been left to himself would probably never have done so. But one of the guardians was Charles Townshend, who had married the young duke's mother. He was not much unlike Mr Disraeli in character, and had great influence at that time. He read *The Theory of Moral Sentiments,* and Hume writes to Adam Smith: "Charles Townshend, who passes for the cleverest fellow in England, is so taken with the performance, that he said to Oswald he would put the duke under the author's care and would make it worth his while to accept of that charge. As soon as I heard this, I called on him twice with a view of talking with him about the matter, and of convincing him of the propriety of sending that young nobleman to Glasgow; for I could not hope that he could offer you any terms which would tempt you to renounce your professorship. But I missed him. Mr Townshend passes for being a little uncertain in his resolutions, so perhaps you need not build much on this sally." Mr Townshend was, however, this time in earnest, and the offer was made to Adam Smith. In our time there would have been an insuperable difficulty. He was a professor of great repute, they were asking him to give up a life-professorship that yielded a considerable income, and they would have hardly been able to offer him anything equally permanent. But in the eighteenth century there was a way of facilitating such arrangements that we do not now possess. The family of Buccleuch had great political influence, and Charles Townshend, the duke's step-father, at times possessed more; and accordingly the guardians of the young duke agreed that they should pay Adam Smith £200 a year till they should get him an equal office of profit under the Crown. A person apparently more unfit for the public service could not easily have been found; but in that age of sinecures and pensions it was probably never expected that he should perform any service;—an arrangement more characteristic of the old world, and more unlike our present world, could hardly have been made. The friends of the young duke might, not unnaturally, have had some fears about it; but, in fact, for his interests, it turned out very well. Long afterwards, when Adam Smith was dead, the duke wrote: "In October, 1766, we returned to London, after having spent near three years together without the slightest disagreement or coolness; on my part with every advantage that could be expected from the society of such a man. We continued to live in friendship till the hour of his death; and I shall always remain with the impression of having lost a friend whom I loved and respected, not only for his great talents, but for every private virtue." Very few of Charles Townshend's caprices were as successful. Through life there was about Adam Smith a sort of lumbering *bonhomie* which amused and endeared him to those around him.

To Adam Smith the result was even better. If it had not been for this odd consequence of *The Theory of Moral Sentiments*, he might have passed all his life in Scotland, delivering similar lectures and clothing very questionable theories in rather pompous words. He said in after-life that there was no better way of compelling a man to master a science than by setting him to teach it. And this may be true of the definite sciences. But nothing can be conceived worse for a man of inventive originality, than to set him to roam over huge subjects like law, morals, politics, and civilisation, particularly at a time when few good data for sound theories on such subjects are at hand for him to use. In such a position the cleverer the man, the worse are likely to be the consequences: the wider his curiosity and the more fertile his mind, the surer he is to pour out a series of gigantic conjectures of little use to himself or to any one. A one-eyed man with a taste for one subject, even at this disadvantage, may produce something good. The limitation of his mind may save him from being destroyed by his position; but a man of large interests will fail utterly. As Adam Smith had peculiarly wide interests, and as he was the very reverse of a one-eyed man, he was in special danger; and the mere removal from his professorship was to him a gain of the first magnitude. It was of cardinal importance to him to be delivered from the production of incessant words and to be brought into contact with facts and the world. And as it turned out, the caprice of Charles Townshend had a singular further felicity. It not only brought him into contact with facts and the world; but with the most suitable sort of facts, and, for his purpose, the best part of the world.

The greater part of his three years abroad was naturally spent in France. France was then by far the greatest country on the Continent. Germany was divided and had not yet risen; Spain had fallen; Italy was of little account. In one respect, indeed, France was relatively greater than even at the time of her greatest elevation, the time of the first Napoleon. The political power of the first empire was almost unbounded, but it had no intellectual power; under it Paris had ceased to be an important focus of thought and literature. The vehement rule which created the soldiers also stamped out the ideas. But under the mild government of the old *régime*, Paris was the principal centre of European authorship. The deficiency of the old *régime* in eminent soldiers and statesmen only added to the eminence of its literary men. Paris was then queen of two worlds: of that of politics by a tradition from the past, and of literature by a force and life vigorously evidenced in the present. France therefore thus attracted the main attention of all travellers who cared for the existing life of the time; Adam Smith and his pupil spent the greater part of their stay abroad there. And as a preparation for writing *The Wealth of Nations* he could nowhere else have been placed so well. Macaulay says that "ancient abuses and new theories" flourished together in France just before the meeting of the States-General in greater vigour than they had been seen to be combined before or since. And the description is quite as true economically as politically; on all economical matters the France of that time was a sort of museum stocked with the most important errors.

By nature then, as now, France was fitted to be a great agricultural country, a great producer and exporter of corn and wine; but her legislators for several generations had endeavoured to counteract the aim of nature, and had tried to make her a manufacturing country and an exporter of her manufactures. Like most persons in those times, they had been prodigiously impressed by the high position which the maritime powers, as they were then called (the comparatively little powers of England and Holland), were able to take in the politics of Europe. They saw that this influence came from wealth, that this wealth was made in trade and manufacture, and therefore they determined that France should not be behindhand, but should have as much trade and manufacture as possible. Accordingly, they imposed prohibitive or deterring duties on the importation of foreign manufactures; they gave bounties to the corresponding home manufactures. They tried, in opposition to the home-keeping bent of the French character, to found colonies abroad. These colonies were, according to the maxim then everywhere received, to be markets for the trade and nurseries for the commerce of the mother country;—they were mostly forbidden to manufacture for themselves, and were compelled to import all the manufactures and luxuries they required from Europe exclusively in French ships. Meanwhile, at home, agriculture was neglected. There was not even a free passage for goods from one part of the country to another. As Adam Smith himself describes it:—

"In France, the different revenue laws which exist in the different provinces require a multitude of revenue officers to surround, not only the frontiers of the kingdom, but those of almost each particular province, in order either to prevent the importation of certain goods or to subject it to the payment of certain duties, to the no small interruption of the interior commerce of the country. Some provinces are allowed to compound for the gabelle or salt-tax. Others are exempted from it altogether. Some provinces are exempted from the exclusive sale of tobacco, which the farmers-general enjoy through the greater part of the kingdom. The *Aides*, which correspond to the excise in England, are very different in different provinces. Some provinces are exempted from them, and pay a composition or equivalent. In those in which they take place and are in farm, there are many local duties which do not extend beyond a particular town or district. The *Traites*, which correspond to our customs, divide the kingdom into three great parts: first, the provinces subject to the tariff of 1664, which are called the provinces of the five great farms, and under which are comprehended Picardy, Normandy, and the greater part of the interior provinces of the kingdom; secondly, the provinces subject to the tariff of 1667, which are called the provinces reckoned foreign, and under which are comprehended the greater part of the frontier provinces; and, thirdly, those provinces which are said to be treated as foreign, or which because they are allowed a free commerce with foreign countries are in their commerce with the other provinces of France subjected to the same duties as other foreign countries. These are Alsace, the three Bishoprics of Metz, Toul and Verdun, and the three cities of Dunkirk, Bayonne, and Marseilles. Both in the provinces of the five great farms (called so on account of an ancient division of the duties of customs into five great branches, each of which was originally the subject of a particular farm, though they are now all united into one), and in those which are said to be reckoned foreign, there are many local duties which do not extend beyond a particular town or district. There are some such even in the provinces which are said to be treated as foreign, particularly in the city of Marseilles. It is unnecessary to observe how much both the restraints upon the interior commerce of the country and the number of the revenue officers must be multiplied, in order to guard the frontiers of those different provinces and districts which are subject to such different systems of taxation."

And there were numerous attendant errors, such as generally accompany a great Protective legislation, but which need not be specified in detail.

In consequence, the people were exceedingly miserable. The system of taxation was often enough by itself to cause great misery. "In the provinces," says Adam Smith, "where the personal *taille* on the farm is imposed, the farmer is afraid to have a good team of horses or oxen, but endeavours to cultivate with the meanest and most wretched instruments of husbandry that he can." The numerous imposts on the land due from the peasantry to the nobles had the same effect even then—most of the country was practically held in a kind of double ownership; the peasant cultivator had usually, by habit if not by law, a fixed hold upon the soil, but he was subject in the cultivation of it to innumerable exactions of varying kinds, which the lord could change pretty much as he chose. "In France," continues Adam Smith, so oddly contrary to everything which we should say now, "the inferior ranks of the people must suffer patiently the usage which their superiors choose to inflict on them." The country in Europe where there is now, perhaps, the most of social equality was then the one in which there was, perhaps, the least.

And side by side with this museum of economical errors there was a most vigorous political economy which exposed them. The doctrines of Free Trade had been before several times suggested by isolated thinkers, but by far the most powerful combined school of philosophers who incessantly inculcated them were the French *Économistes*. They delighted in proving that the whole structure of the French laws upon industry was utterly wrong; that prohibitions ought not to be imposed on the import of foreign manufactures; that bounties ought not to be given to native ones; that the exportation of corn ought to be free; that the whole country ought to be a fiscal unit; that there should be no duty between any province; and so on in other cases. No one could state the abstract doctrines on which they rested everything more clearly. "Acheter, c'est vendre," said Quesnay, the founder of the school, "vendre, c'est acheter." You cannot better express the doctrine of modern political economy that "trade is barter". "Do not attempt," Quesnay continues, "to fix the price of your products, goods, or services; they will escape your rules. Competition alone can regulate prices with equity; it alone restricts them to a moderation which varies little; it alone attracts with certainty provisions where they are wanted or labour where it is required." "That which we call dearness is the only remedy of dearness: dearness causes plenty." Any quantity of sensible remarks to this effect might be disinterred from these writers. They were not always equally wise.

As the prime maxim of the ruling policy was to encourage commerce and neglect agriculture, this sect set up a doctrine

that agriculture was the only source of wealth, and that trade
and commerce contributed nothing to it. The labour of ar-
tificers and merchants was sterile; that of agriculturists was
alone truly productive. The way in which they arrived at this
strange idea was, if I understand it, something like this: they
took the whole agricultural produce of a country, worth say
£5,000,000 as it stood in the hands of the farmer, and applied it thus:—

First, as we should say, in repayment of capi-
    tal spent in wages, etc.   £3,000,000
Secondly, in payment of profit by way of hire
    of capital, say, or as subsistence to himself   500,000
                                    Total outlay   £3,500,000

But that outlay of £3,500,000 has produced a value of
£5,000,000; there is therefore an overplus over and above
the outlay of £1,500,000; and this overplus, or *produit net*
as the *Économistes* call it, goes to the landlord for rent, as
we should call it. But no other employment yields any similar
produit net. A cotton spinner only replaces his own capital,
and obtains his profit on it; like the farmer (as they said),
he pays the outlay, and he gains a profit or subsistence for
himself. But he does no more. There is no extra overplus in
farming; no balance, after paying wages and hiring capital;
nothing to go to any landlord. In the same way commerce is,
according to this system, transfer only—the expense of distribution is paid; the necessary number of capitalists and of
labourers is maintained, but that is all; there is nothing beyond the wages and beyond the profit. In agriculture only is
there a third element—a *produit net*.

From this doctrine the *Économistes* drew two inferences
—one very agreeable to agriculturists, the other very disagreeable; but both exactly opposite to the practice of their government. *First*, they said, as agriculture was the exclusive source
of all wealth, it was absurd to depress it or neglect it, or to
encourage commerce or manufacture in place of it. They had
no toleration for the system of finance and commercial legislation which they saw around them, of which the one object
was to make France a trading and manufacturing country,
when nature meant it to be an agricultural one. *Secondly*,
they inferred that most, if not all, the existing taxes in France
were wrong in principle. "If," they argued, "agriculture is the

only source of wealth, and if, as we know, wealth only can
pay taxes, then all taxes should be imposed on agriculture."
They reasoned: "In manufactures there is only a necessary
hire of labour, and a similar hire of capital, at a cost which
cannot be diminished; there is in them no available surplus
for taxation. If you attempt to impose taxes on them, and if
in name you make them pay such taxes, they will charge
higher for their necessary work. They will in a roundabout way
throw the burden of those taxes on agriculture. The *produit
net* of the latter is the one real purse of the State; no other
pursuit can truly pay anything, for it has no purse. And therefore," they summed up, "all taxes, save a single one on the
produit net, were absurd. They only attempted to make those
pay who could not pay; to extract money from fancied funds,
in which there was no money." All the then existing taxes in
France, therefore, they proposed to abolish, and to replace
them by a single tax on agriculture only.

As this system was so opposed to the practice of the Government, one would have expected that it should have been
discountenanced, if not persecuted, by the Government. But,
in fact, it was rather favoured by it. Quesnay, the founder of
the system, had a place at Court, and was under the special
protection of the king's mistress, who was then the king's
Government. M. de Lavergne has quoted a graphic description of him. "Quesnay," writes Marmontel, "well lodged in a
small *appartement* in the *entresol* of Madame de Pompadour, only occupied himself from morning till night with
political and agricultural economy. He believed that he had
reduced the system to calculation, and to axioms of irresistible evidence; and as he was collecting a school, he gave himself the trouble to explain to me his new doctrine, in order
to make me one of his proselytes. I applied all my force of
comprehension to understand those truths which he told me
were self-evident; but I found in them only vagueness and
obscurity. To make him believe that I understood that which
I really did not understand was beyond my power; but I lis-
tened with patient docility, and left him the hope that in the
end he would enlighten me and make me believe his doctrine.
I did more; I applauded his work, which I really thought very
useful, for he tried to recommend agriculture in a country
where it was too much disdained, and to turn many excellent
understandings towards the study of it. While political storms
were forming and dissolving above the *entresol* of Quesnay,

he perfected his calculations and his axioms of rural economy, as tranquil and as indifferent to the movements of the Court, as if he had been a hundred leagues off. Below, in the *salon* of Madame de Pompadour, they deliberated on peace or war —on the choice of generals—on the recall of Ministers; while we in the *entresol* were reasoning on agriculture, calculating the *produit net*, or sometimes were dining gaily with Diderot, d'Alembert, Duclos, Helvetius, Turgot, Buffon; and Madame de Pompadour, not being able to induce this troop of philosophers to come down to her *salon*, came herself to see them at table and to chat with them." An opposition philosophy has rarely been so petted and well treated. Much as the reign of Louis XVI differed in most respects from that of Louis XV, it was like it in this patronage of the *Économistes*. Turgot was made Minister of Finance to reform France by applying their doctrines.

The reason of this favour to the *Économistes* from the Government was, that on the question in which the Government took far the most interest the *Économistes* were on its side. The daily want of the French Government was more power; though nominally a despotism, it was feeble in reality. But the *Économistes* were above all things anxious for a very strong Government; they held to the maxim, everything *for* the people—nothing *by* them; they had a horror of checks and counterpoises and resistances; they wished to do everything by the *fiat* of the sovereign. They had, in fact, the natural wish of eager speculators, to have an irresistible despotism behind them and supporting them; and with the simplicity which marks so much of the political speculation of the eighteenth century, but which now seems so childlike, they never seemed to think how they were to get their despot, or how they were to ensure that he should be on their side. The painful experience of a hundred years has taught us that influential despotisms are not easy to make, and that good ones are still less so. But in their own time nothing could be more advantageous to the *Économistes* than to have an eager zeal for a perfect despotism; in consequence they were patronised by the greatest existing authority, instead of being discountenanced by it.

This account of the *Économistes* may seem to a reader who looks at Adam Smith exclusively by the light of modern political economy to be too long for their relation to him. But he would not have thought so himself. He so well knew how much his mind had been affected by them and by their teaching, that he at one time thought of dedicating *The Wealth of Nations* to Quesnay, their founder; and though he relinquished that intention, he always speaks of him with the gravest respect. If, indeed, we consider what Glasgow is now, still more what it must have been a hundred years ago, we shall comprehend the degree to which this French experience—this sight of a country so managed, and with such a political economy—must have excited the mind of Adam Smith. It was the passage from a world where there was no *spectacle* to one in which there was the best which the world has ever seen, and simultaneously the passage from the most Scotch of ideas to others the most un-Scotch. A feeble head would have been upset in the transit, but Adam Smith kept his.

From France he went home to Scotland, and stayed quietly with his mother at his native town of Kirkcaldy for a whole ten years. He lived on the annuity from the Duke of Buccleuch, and occupied himself in study only. What he was studying, if we considered *The Wealth of Nations* as a book of political economy only, we might be somewhat puzzled to say. But the contents of that book are, as has been said, most miscellaneous, and in its author's mind it was but a fragment of an immensely larger whole. Much more than ten years' study would have been necessary for the entire book which he contemplated.

At last, in 1776, *The Wealth of Nations* was published, and was, on the whole, well received. Dr Carlyle, indeed, preserves an impression that, in point of style, it was inferior to *The Theory of Moral Sentiments*. But all competent readers were agreed as to the great value of the substance. And almost everybody will probably now think, in spite of Dr Carlyle, that the style is very much better than that of the *Moral Sentiments*. There is about the latter a certain showiness and an "air of the professor trying to be fascinating," which are not very agreeable; and, after all, there is a ponderous weight in the words which seems to bear down the rather flimsy matter. But the style of *The Wealth of Nations* is entirely plain and manly. The author had, in the interval, seen at least a little of the living world and of society, and had learnt that the greatest mistake is the trying to be more agreeable than you can be, and that the surest way to spoil an important book is to try to attract the attention of, to "write down" to, a class of readers too low to take a serious interest in the subject. A really great style, indeed, Adam Smith's certainly is not. Lord Mansfield is said to have told Boswell that he did not feel, in reading either Hume or Adam Smith, that he was reading English at all; and it was very natural that it should be so. English was not the mother tongue of either. Adam Smith had, no doubt, spoken somewhat broad Scotch for the first fourteen or fifteen years of his life; probably he never spoke anything that could quite be called English till he went to Oxford. And nothing so much hampers the free use of the pen in any language as the incessant remembrance of a kindred but different one; you are never sure the idioms nature prompts are those of the tongue you would speak, or of the tongue you would reject. Hume and Adam Smith exemplify the difficulty in opposite ways. Hume is always idiomatic, but his idioms are constantly wrong; many of his best passages are, on that account, curiously grating and puzzling; you feel that they are very like what an Englishman would say, but yet that, after all, somehow or other, they are what he never would say;—there is a minute seasoning of imperceptible difference which distracts your attention, and which you are for ever stopping to analyse. Adam Smith's habit was very different. His style is not colloquial in the least. He adheres to the heavy "book" English which he had found in the works of others, and was sure that he could repeat in his own. And in that sort of style he has eminent merit. No one ever has to read him twice to gather his meaning; no one can bring much valid objection to his way of expressing that meaning; there is even a sort of appropriateness, though often a clumsy sort, in his way of saying it. But the style has no intrinsic happiness; no one would read it for its own sake; the words do not cleave to the meaning, so that you cannot think of them without it, or of it without them. This is only given to those who write in the speech of their childhood, and only to the very few of those—the five or six in every generation—who have from nature the best grace, who think by inborn feeling in words at once charming and accurate.

Of *The Wealth of Nations* as an economic treatise, I have nothing to say now; but it is not useless to say that it is a very amusing book about old times. As it is dropping out of immediate use from change of times, it is well to observe that this very change brings it a new sort of interest of its own.

There are few books from which there may be gathered more curious particulars of the old world. I cull at random almost that "a broad wheel waggon, attended by two men, and drawn by eight horses," then "in about six weeks'" time carried and brought trade between London and Edinburgh;—that in Adam Smith's opinion, if there were such an effectual demand for grain as would require a million tons of shipping to import it, the "navy of England," the mercantile navy of course, would not be sufficient for it;—that "Holland was the great emporium of European goods"; that she was, in proportion to the land and the number of inhabitants, by far the richest country in Europe; that she had the greatest share of the ocean-carrying trade; that her citizens possessed £40,-000,000 in the French and English funds;—that in Sheffield no master cutler can have more than one apprentice, by a by-law of the corporation, and in Norfolk and Norwich no weaver more than two;—that, if Adam Smith's eyes served him right, "the common people in Scotland, who are fed with oatmeal, are in general neither so strong nor so handsome as the same class of people in England, who are fed with wheaten bread," and that they do not look or work as well; that—and this is odder still—"the porters and coal-heavers in London, and those unfortunate women who live by prostitution—the strongest men and the most beautiful women, perhaps, in the British dominions—are from the lowest rank of people in Ireland, and fed with the potato";—that £1000 share in India stock "gave a share not in the plunder, but in the appointment of the plunderers of India";—that "the expense of the establishment of Massachusetts Bay, before the commencement of the late disturbances," that is, the American War, "used to be about £18,000 a year, and that of New York, £4500";—that all the civil establishments in America did not at the same date cost £67,000 a year;—that "in consequence of the monopoly of the American colonial market," the commerce of England, "instead of running in a great number of small channels, has been taught to run principally in one great channel";—that "the territorial acquisitions of the East India Company, the undoubted right of the Crown," "might be rendered another source of revenue more abundant, perhaps, than all" others from which much addition could be expected;—that Great Britain is, perhaps, since "the world began, the only State which has extended its empire" "without augmenting the area of its resources";—that, and this is the final sentence of the book, "if any of the provinces of the British empire cannot be made to contribute towards the support of the whole empire, it is surely time that Great Britain should free herself from the expense of defending those provinces in time of war, and of supporting any part of their civil or military establishments in time of peace, and endeavour to accommodate her future views and designs to the real mediocrity of her circumstances". A strange passage, considering all that has happened since, and all the provinces which we have since taken. No one can justly estimate *The Wealth of Nations* who thinks of it as a book of mere political economy, such as Quesnay had then written, or as Ricardo afterwards wrote. It is really full both of the most various kinds of facts and of thoughts often as curious on the most various kinds of subjects.

The effect of the publication of *The Wealth of Nations* on the fortunes of its author was very remarkable. It gave the Duke of Buccleuch the power of relieving himself of his annuity, by performing the equivalent clause in the bargain; he obtained for Adam Smith a commissionership of customs for Scotland—an appointment of which we do not know the precise income, but which was clearly, according to the notions of those times, a very good one indeed. A person less fitted to fill it could not indeed easily have been found. Adam Smith had, as we have seen, never been used to pecuniary business of any kind; he had never even taken part in any sort of action out of such business; he was an absent and meditative student. It was indeed during his tenure of this office that, as I have said, he startled a subordinate, who asked for his signature, by imitating the signature of the last commissioner, instead of giving his own—of course in pure absence of mind. He was no doubt better acquainted with the theory of taxation than any other man of his time; he could have given a Minister in the capital better advice than any one else as to what taxes he should, or should not, impose. But a commissioner of customs, in a provincial city, has nothing to do with the imposition of taxes, or with giving advice about them. His business simply is to see that those which already exist are regularly collected and methodically transmitted, which involves an infinity of transactions requiring a trained man of detail. But a man of detail Adam Smith certainly was not—at least, of detail in business. Nature had probably not well fitted him for it, and his mode of life had completed the

result, and utterly unfitted him. The appointment that was
given him was one in which the great abilities which he possessed were useless, and in which much smaller ones, which he
had not, would have been of extreme value.

But in another respect this appointment has been more
blamed than I think is just. However small may be the value
of Adam Smith's work at the custom-house, the effect of performing it and the time which it occupied prevented him
from writing anything more. And it has been thought that
posterity has in consequence suffered much. But I own that I
doubt this exceedingly. Adam Smith had no doubt made a
vast accumulation of miscellaneous materials for his great design. But these materials were probably of very second-rate
value. Neither for the history of law, nor of science, nor of
art, had the preliminary work been finished, which is necessary before such a mind as Adam Smith's can usefully be
applied to them. Before the theorising philosopher must come
the accurate historian. To write the history either of law or
science or art is enough for the life of any single man: neither
have as yet been written with the least approach to completeness. The best of the fragments on these subjects, which
we now have, did not exist in Adam Smith's time. There
was, therefore, but little use in his thinking or writing at
large about them. If he had set down for us some account of
his residence in France, and the society which he saw there,
posterity would have been most grateful to him. But this he
had no idea of doing; and nobody would now much care for a
series of elaborate theories, founded upon facts insufficiently
collected.

Adam Smith lived for fourteen years after the publication
of *The Wealth of Nations;* but he wrote nothing, and scarcely
studied anything. The duties of his office, though of an easy
and routine character, which would probably have enabled a
man bred to business to spend much of his time and almost
all his mind on other things, were, we are told, enough "to
waste his spirits and dissipate his attention". And not unnaturally, for those who have ever been used to give all their
days to literary work, rarely seem able to do that work when
they are even in a slight degree struck and knocked against
the world; only those who have scarcely ever known what it
is to have unbroken calm are able to accomplish much without that calm. During these years Adam Smith's life passed
easily and pleasantly in the Edinburgh society of that time—

a very suitable one, for it was one to which professors and lawyers gave the tone, and of which intellectual exertion was the life and being. Adam Smith was, it is true, no easy talker —was full neither of ready replies nor of prepared replies. He rather liked to listen, but if he talked—and traps it is said were laid to make him do so—he could expound admirably on the subjects which he knew, and also (which is quite as characteristic of the man as we see him in his works) could run up rapid theories on such data as occurred to him, when, as Dugald Stewart tells us in his dignified dialect, "he gave a loose to his genius upon the very few branches of knowledge of which he only possessed the outlines".

He died calmly and quietly, leaving directions about his manuscripts and such other literary things, and saying, in a melancholy way, "I meant to have done more". The sort of fame which *The Wealth of Nations* has obtained, and its special influence, did not begin in his lifetime, and he had no notion of it. Nor would he perhaps have quite appreciated it, if he had. His mind was full of his great scheme of the origin and history of all cultivation. As happens to so many men, though scarcely ever on so great a scale, aiming at one sort of reputation, he attained another. To use Lord Bacon's perpetual illustration, like Saul, he "went in search of his father's asses, and he found a kingdom".

Adam Smith has been said to belong to the Macaulay type of Scotchmen, and the saying has been thought a paradox, particularly by those who, having misread Macaulay, think him a showy rhetorician, and not having at all read Adam Smith, think of him as a dry and dull political economist. But the saying is true, nevertheless. Macaulay is anything but a mere rhetorical writer—there is a very hard kernel of business in him; and Adam Smith is not dry at all—the objection to him is that he is not enough so, and that the real truth in several parts of his subject cannot be made so interesting as his mode of treatment implies. And there is this fundamental likeness between Macaulay and Adam Smith, that they can both describe practical matters in such a way as to fasten them on the imagination, and not only get what they say read, but get it remembered and make it part of the substance of the reader's mind ever afterwards. Abstract theorists may say that such a style as that of Adam Smith is not suitable to an abstract science; but then Adam Smith has carried political economy far beyond the bounds of those who

care for abstract science, or who understand exactly what it
means. He has popularised it in the only sense in which it
can be popularised without being spoiled; that is, he has put
certain broad conclusions into the minds of hard-headed men,
which are all which they need know, and all which they for
the most part will ever care for, and he has put those conclusions there ineradicably. This, too, is what Macaulay does
for us in history, at least what he does best; he engraves indelibly the main outlines and the rough common sense of
the matter. Other more refining, and perhaps in some respects
more delicate, minds may add the nicer details, and explain
those wavering, flickering, inconstant facts of human nature
which are either above common sense or below it. Both these
great Scotchmen excelled in the "osteology of their subject,"
a term invented by Dr Chalmers, a third great Scotchman
who excelled in it himself; perhaps, indeed, it is an idiosyncrasy of their race.

Like many other great Scotchmen—Macaulay is one of
them—Adam Smith was so much repelled by the dominant
Calvinism in which he was born, that he never voluntarily
wrote of religious subjects, nor, as far as we know, spoke of
them. Nothing, indeed, can repel a man more from such
things than what Macaulay called the "bray of Exeter Hall".
What can be worse for people than to hear in their youth
arguments, alike clamorous and endless, founded on ignorant
interpretations of inconclusive words? As soon as they come
to years of discretion, all instructed persons cease to take part
in such discussions, and often say nothing at all on the great
problems of human life and destiny. Sometimes the effect
goes farther; those subjected to this training become not only
silent but careless. There is nothing like Calvinism for gener-
ating indifference. The saying goes that Scotchmen are those
who believe most or least; and it is most natural that it should
be so, for they have been so hurt and pestered with religious
stimulants, that it is natural they should find total absti-
nence from them both pleasant and healthy. How far this indifference went in Adam Smith's case we do not exactly
know; but there is reason to think it extended to all religion.
On the contrary, there are many traces of the complacent
optimism of the eighteenth century—a doctrine the more
agreeable to him perhaps, because it is the exact opposite of
Calvinism—and one which was very popular in an easy-
going age, though the storms and calamities of a later time

dispelled it, and have made it seem to us thin and unreal. The only occasion when Adam Smith ever came near to theological discussion was in a letter on Hume's death, in which he said that Hume, one of his oldest friends, was the best man he had ever known—praise which perhaps was scarcely meant to be taken too literally, but which naturally caused a great storm. The obvious thing to say about it is, that it does not indicate any very lofty moral standard, for there certainly was no sublime excellence in Hume, who, as Carlyle long ago said, "all his life through did not so much morally live, as critically investigate". But though the bigots of his time misunderstood him, Adam Smith did not by so saying mean to identify himself with irreligion or even with scepticism.

Adam Smith's life, however, was not like Macaulay's—"a life without a lady". There are vestiges of an early love affair, though but vague ones. Dugald Stewart, an estimable man in his way, but one of the most detestable of biographers, for he seems always thinking much more of his own words than of the facts he has to relate, says: "In the early part of Mr Smith's life, it is well known to his friends that he was for several years attached to a young lady of great beauty and accomplishment". But he does not tell us who she was, and "has not been able to learn" "how far his addresses were favourably received," or, in fact, anything about the matter. It seems, however, that the lady died unmarried, and in that case the unsentimental French novelists say that the gentleman is not often continuously in earnest, for that "a lady cannot be always saying No!" But whether such was the case with Adam Smith or not, we cannot tell. He was a lonely bookish man, but that may tell both ways. The books may be opposed to the lady, but the solitude will preserve her remembrance.

If Adam Smith did abandon sentiment and devote himself to study, he has at least the excuse of having succeeded. Scarcely any writer's work has had so much visible fruit. He has, at least, annexed his name to a great practical movement which is still in progress through the world. Free Trade has become in the popular mind almost as much his subject as the war of Troy was Homer's: only curious inquirers think of teachers before the one any more than of poets before the other. If all the speeches made at our Anti-Corn-Law League were examined, I doubt if any reference could be found to

any preceding writer, though the name of Adam Smith was
always on men's lips. And in other countries it was the same.
Smith-ism is a name of reproach with all who reject such
doctrines, and of respect with those who believe them; no
other name is used equally or comparably by either. So long
as the doctrines of Protection exist—and they seem likely to
do so, as human interests are what they are and human nature
is what it is—Adam Smith will always be quoted as the great
authority on Anti-Protectionism—as the man who first told
the world the truth so that the world could learn and believe
it.

And besides this great practical movement, Adam Smith
started a great theoretical one also. On one side his teaching
created Mr Cobden and Mr Bright, on another it rendered
possible Ricardo and Mr Mill. He is the founder of that
analysis of the "great commerce" which in England we now
call political economy, and which, dry, imperfect, and unfinished as it is, will be thought by posterity one of the most
valuable and peculiar creations of English thought. As far as
accuracy goes, Ricardo no doubt began this science; but his
whole train of thought was suggested by Adam Smith, and he
could not have written without him. So much theory and so
much practice have really perhaps never sprung from a single
mind.

Fortunate in many things, Adam Smith was above all
things fortunate in his age. Commerce had become far larger,
far more striking, far more world-wide than it ever was before, and it needed an effectual explainer. A vigorous Scotchman, with the hard-headedness and the abstraction of his
country, trained in England and familiar with France, was
the species of man best fitted to explain it; and such a man
was Adam Smith.

LORD BROUGHAM[1]*

(1857)

Henry Peter Brougham, Baron Brougham and Vaux, born in
Edinburgh in 1778, was the eldest son of Henry Brougham
and Eleanor Syme. He was educated at Edinburgh High School
and at Edinburgh University. Brougham passed advocate in
1800, and went on the southern circuit. In 1802 Brougham,
Jeffrey and Sydney Smith founded the Edinburgh Review, to the
first issue of which Brougham contributed three articles. He became a member of Lincoln's Inn in 1803 and supported himself
largely by writing for the Edinburgh Review. His earlier articles
had been scientific; he now wrote on political and economic subjects with the intention of adopting a political career. He was
called to the Bar in 1808 and went on the northern circuit,
but he had small success in the courts until he had made his
mark in politics. In 1810 he became M.P. for Camelford, and
for Winchelsea in 1815. Brougham had already won Wilberforce's good opinion by his sympathy with the anti-slavery movement; only a few months after he had entered Parliament
Brougham moved an address on slavery to the crown. He drew
attention in Parliament to the need for retrenchment and a
sound commercial policy, and to the importance of popular
education. When she became Queen, the Princess of Wales,
who constantly consulted Brougham, appointed him her attorney-general, and he defended her during her trial in 1820.
Brougham urged the government to resist the dictation of the
Holy Alliance in Europe in 1824, pointing out the iniquity of
the French invasion of Spain and the tyranny of the Austrians
in Italy. In the same year Brougham proposed the vote of censure on the government of Demerara, which was a milestone in
the history of abolition.

When Canning succeeded Lord Liverpool in 1827, Brougham

---

[1] Works of Henry Lord Brougham, F.R.S., Member of the National Institute of France and the Royal Academy of Naples. London: Griffin.

* This essay was first published in the National Review for July
1857, Volume V, pages 164–96.

*left the opposition benches and joined the ministerial side. In
1828 Brougham brought in a scheme of reform which enormously
improved the system of common-law procedure. Upon Wellington's accession in 1828, Brougham returned to the opposition,
though he vigorously upheld Wellington and Peel in their efforts
to secure Catholic emancipation. Brougham became M.P. for
Knaresborough and for Yorkshire in 1830, and in the same year
he was elevated to the peerage and became Lord Chancellor.
He effected great legal reforms, especially in the court of chancery; he substituted the judicial committee of the privy council
for the court of delegates, and he instituted the central criminal
court. Brougham lost office at the dismissal of Melbourne's government in 1834; after the re-establishment of Melbourne's
ministry in 1835 Brougham virtually led the opposition in the
House of Lords until he gradually withdrew from politics altogether.*

*Brougham's interest in popular education was very practical.
He published in 1825* Observations on the Education of the
People, *a plan for the publication of cheap and useful works,
which was carried out by the Society for the Diffusion of Useful
Knowledge, of which he formed the first committee. Brougham
also helped to found London University in 1828. He took a leading part in education debates in the Commons and brought forward several bills for developing the educational system.*

Brougham died at Cannes in 1868.

It was a bold, perhaps a rash idea, to collect the writings of
Henry Brougham. They were written at such distant dates;
their subjects are so various; they are often so wedged into the
circumstances of an age—that they scarcely look natural in a
series of volumes. Some men, doubtless, by a strong grasp of
intellect, have compacted together subjects as various; the
finger-marks of a few are on all human knowledge; others,
by a rare illuminative power, have lit up as many with a light
that seems peculiar to themselves. *Franciscus Baconus sic
cogitavit* may well illustrate an *opera omnia*. But Lord
Brougham has neither power; his restless genius has no claim
to the still, illuminating imagination; his many-handed, apprehensive intelligence is scarcely able to fuse and concentrate. Variety is his taste, and versatility his power. His career has not been quiet. For many years rushing among the
details of an age, he has written as he ran. There are not many
undertakings bolder than to collect the works of such a life
and such a man.

The edition itself seems a good one. The volumes are convenient in size, well printed, and fairly arranged. The various writings it contains have been revised, but not over-revised, by their author. It is not, however, of the collection that we wish to speak. We would endeavour, so far as a few hasty pages may serve, to delineate the career and character of the writer. The attempt is among the most difficult. He is still among us; we have not the materials, possibly not the impartiality, of posterity. Nor have we the familiar knowledge of contemporaries; the time when Lord Brougham exerted his greatest faculties is beyond the political memory of younger men. There are no sufficient books on the events of a quarter of a century ago, we have only traditions; and this must be our excuse if we fall, or seem to fall, into error and confusion.

The years immediately succeeding the great peace were years of sullenness and difficulty. The idea of the war had passed away; the thrill and excitement of the great struggle were no longer felt. We had maintained, with the greatest potentate of modern times, a successful contest for existence. We had our existence, but we had no more; our victory had been great, but it had no fruits. By the aid of pertinacity and capital, we had vanquished genius and valour; but no visible increase of European influence followed. Napoleon said that Wellington had made peace as if he had been defeated. We had delivered the continent; such was our natural idea: but the continent went its own way. There was nothing in its state to please the everyday Englishman. There were kings and emperors; "which was very well for foreigners, they had always been like that; but it was not many kings could pay ten per cent income tax". Absolutism, as such, cannot be popular in a free country. The Holy Alliance, which made a religion of despotism, was scarcely to be reconciled with the British constitution. Altogether we had vanquished Napoleon, but we had no pleasure in what came after him. The cause which agitated our hearts was gone; there was no longer a noise of victories in the air; continental affairs were dead, despotic, dull; we scarcely liked to think that we had made them so; with weary dissatisfaction we turned to our own condition.

This was profoundly unsatisfactory. Trade was depressed; agriculture ruinous; the working class singularly disaffected. During the war, our manufacturing industry had grown most rapidly; there was a not unnatural expectation that, after a general peace, the rate of increase would be accelerated. The whole continent, it was considered, would be opened to us; Milan and Berlin decrees no longer excluded us; Napoleon did not now interpose between "the nation of shopkeepers" and its customers; now he was at St Helena, surely those customers would buy? It was half forgotten that they could not. The drain of capital for the war had been, at times, heavily felt in England; there had been years of poverty and discredit; still our industry had gone on, our workshops had not stopped. We had never known what it was to be the seat of war, as well as a power at war. We had never known our burdens enormously increased, just when our industry was utterly stopped; disarranged as trading credit sometimes was, it had not been destroyed. No conscription had drained us of our most efficient consumers. The continent, south and north, had, though not everywhere alike, suffered all these evils; its populations were poor, harassed, depressed. They could not buy our manufactures, for they had no money. The large preparations for a continental export lay on hand; our traders were angry and displeased. Nor was content to be found in the agricultural districts. During the war, the British farmer had inevitably a monopoly of this market; at the approach of peace, his natural antipathy to foreign corn influenced the legislator. The Home Secretary of the time had taken into consideration whether 76s. or 80s. was such a remunerating price as the agriculturist should obtain, and a corn law had passed accordingly. But no law could give the farmer famine prices, when there was scarcity here and plenty abroad. There were riots at the passing of the "Bread-tax," as it was; in 1813, the price of corn was 120s.; the rural mind was sullen in 1816, when it sunk to 57s. The protection given, though unpopular with the poor, did not satisfy the farmer.

The lower orders in the manufacturing districts were, of necessity, in great distress. The depression of trade produced its inevitable results of closed mills and scanty employment. Wages, when they could be obtained, were very low. The artisan population was then new to the vicissitudes of industry: how far they are, even now, instructed in the laws of trade, recent prosperity will hardly let us judge; but, at that time, they had no doubt that it was the fault of the State, and if not of particular statesmen, then of the essential institutions, that they were in want. They believed the Government ought to regulate their remuneration, and make it suf-

ficient. During some straitened years of the war the name of
"Luddites" became known. They had principally shown their
discontent by breaking certain machines, which they fancied
deprived them of work. After the peace, the records of the
time are full of "Spencean Philanthropists," "Hampden
Clubs," and similar associations, all desiring a great reform
—some of mere politics, others of the law of property and all
social economy. Large meetings were everywhere held, something like those of the year 1839: a general insurrection,
doubtless a wild dream of a few hot-brained dreamers, was
fancied to have been really planned. The name "Radical"
came to be associated with this discontent. The spirit which,
in after years, clamoured distinctly for the five points of the
Charter, made itself heard in mutterings and threatenings.

Nor were the capitalists, who had created the new wealth,
socially more at ease. Many of them, as large employers of
labour, had a taste for Toryism; the rule of the people to
them meant the rule of their workpeople. Some of the wealth-
iest and most skilful became associated with the aristocracy,
but it was vain with the majority to attempt it. Between
them and the possessors of hereditary wealth there was fixed
a great gulf; the contrast of habits, speech, manners, was too
wide. The two might coincide in particular opinions; they
might agree to support the same institutions; they might set
forth, in a Conservative creed, the same form of sound
words: but, though the abstract conclusions were identical,
the mode of holding them—to borrow a subtlety of Father
Newman's—was exceedingly different. The refined, discriminating, timorous immobility of the aristocracy was distinct
from the coarse, dogmatic, keep-downishness of the manufacturer. Yet more marked was the contrast, when the oppo-
side tendencies of temperament had produced, as they soon
could not but do, a diversity of opinion. The case was not
quite new in England. Mr Burke spoke of the tendency of
the first East Indians to Jacobinism. They could not, he said,
bear that their present importance should have no proportion
to their recently acquired riches. No extravagant fortunes
have, in this century, been made by Englishmen in India;
but Lancashire has been a California. Families have been
created there, whose names we all know, which we think of
when we mention wealth; some of which are now, by lapse of
time, passing into the hereditary caste of recognised opulence.
This, however, has been a work of time; and, before it oc-

curred, there was no such intermediate class between the new
wealth and the old. "It takes," it is said that Sir Robert Peel
observed, "three generations to make a gentleman." In the
meantime, there was an inevitable misunderstanding; the
new cloth was too coarse for the old. Besides this, many actual institutions offended the eyes of the middle class. The
state of the law was opposed both to their prejudices and interests: that you could only recover your debts by spending
more than the debt, was hard; and the injury was aggravated,
the money was spent in "special pleading"—"in putting a plain
thing so as to perplex and mislead a plain man". "Lord Eldon and the Court of Chancery," as Sydney Smith expressed
it, "sat heavy on mankind." The existence of slavery in our
colonies, strongly supported by a strong aristocratic and parliamentary influence, offended the principles of middle-class
Christianity, and the natural sentiments of simple men. The
cruelty of the penal law—the punishing with death, sheep-
stealing and shop-lifting—jarred the humanity of that second
order of English society, which, from their habits of reading
and non-reading, may be called, *par excellence*, the scriptural
classes. The routine harshness of a not very wise executive
did not mitigate the feeling. The *modus operandi* of Government appeared coarse and oppressive.

We seemed to pay, too, a good deal for what we did not
like. At the close of the war, the ten per cent income tax
was of course heavily oppressive. The public expenditure was
beyond argument lavish; and it was spent in pensions, sinecures (for "them idlers," in the speech of Lancashire), and
a mass of sundries, that an economical man of business will
scarcely admit to be necessary, and that even now, after
countless prunings, produce periodically "financial reform associations," "administrative leagues," and other combinations
which amply testify the enmity of thrifty efficiency to large
figures and muddling management. There had remained from
the eighteenth century a tradition of corruption, an impression that direct pecuniary malversation pervaded the public
offices; an idea true in the days of Rigby or Bubb Dodington,
but which, like many other impressions, continued to exist
many years after the facts in which it originated had passed
away. Government, in the hands of such a man as Lord Liverpool, was very different from government in the hands of Sir
Robert Walpole: respectability was exacted; of actual money-
taking there was hardly any. Still, especially among inferior

officials, there was something to shock modern purity. The
size of jobs was large: if the Treasury of that time could be
revived, it would be depressed at the littleness of whatever
is perpetrated in modern administration. There were petty
abuses too in the country—in municipalities—in charitable
trusts—in all outlying public moneys, which seemed to the
offended man of business, who saw them with his own eyes,
evident instances confirming his notion of the malpractices
of Downing Street. "There are only five little boys in the
school of Richester; they may cost £200, and the income is
£2000, and the trustees don't account for the balance;
which is the way things are done in England: we keeps an
aristocracy," etc. The whole of this feeling was concentrated
into a detestation of rotten boroughs. The very name was
enough: that Lord Dover, with two patent sinecures in the
Exchequer and a good total for assisting in nothing at the
Audit office, should return two members for one house, while
Birmingham, where they made buttons,—"as good buttons as
there are in the world, sir,"—returned no members at all, was
an evident indication that reform was necessary. Mr Canning was an eloquent man; but "even *he* could not say that a
decaying stump was the *people*". Gatton and Old Sarum became unpopular. The source of power seemed absurd, and
the use of power was tainted. Side by side with the incipient
Chartism of the northern operative, there was growing daily
more distinct and clear the Manchester philosophy, which has
since expressed itself in the Anti-Corn Law League, and
which, for good and evil, is now an element so potent in our
national life. Both creeds were forms of discontent. And the
counterpoise was wanting. The English constitution has provided that there shall always be one estate raised above the
storms of passion and controversy, which all parties may respect and honour. The king is to be loved. But this theory
requires, for a real efficiency, that the throne be filled by such
a person as can be loved. In those times it was otherwise. The
nominal possessor of the crown was a very old man, whom
an incurable malady had long sequestered from earthly
things. The actual possessor of the royal authority was a vo-
luptuary of overgrown person, now too old for healthy pleasure, and half sickened himself at the corrupt pursuits in
which, nevertheless, he indulged perpetually. His domestic
vices had become disgracefully public. Whatever might be
the truth about Queen Caroline, no one could say she had

been well treated. There was no royalty on which suffering workers, or an angry middle class, could repose: all through the realm there was a miscellaneous agitation, a vague and wandering discontent.

The official mind of the time was troubled. We have a record of its speculations in the life of Lord Sidmouth, who more than any one perhaps embodied it. He had been Speaker, and was much inclined to remedy the discontent of the middle classes by "naming them to the House". A more conscientious man perhaps has never filled a public position. If the forms of the House of Commons had been intuitively binding, no one could have obeyed them better: the "mace" was a "counsel of perfection" to him; all disorder hateful. In the Home Office it was the same. The Luddites were people who would not obey the Speaker. Constituted authority must be enforced. The claims of a suffering multitude were not so much neglected as unappreciated. A certain illiberality, as we should now speak, pervades the whole kind of thought. The most striking feature is an indisposition, which by long indulgence has become an inability, to comprehend another person's view, to put oneself in another's mental place, to think what he thinks, to conceive what he inevitably is. Lord Sidmouth referred to the file. He found that Mr Pitt had put down disaffection by severe measures. Accordingly, he suspended the Habeas Corpus Act, passed six Acts, commended a Peterloo massacre, not with conscious unfeelingness, but from an absorbed officiality, from a knowledge that this was what "the department" had done before, and an inference that this must be done again. As for the reforming ideas of the middle classes, red tape had never tied up such notions; perhaps it was the French Revolution over again: you could not tolerate *them*.

Between such a dominant mind as this, and such a subject mind as has been described, there was a daily friction. The situation afforded obvious advantages to enterprising men. Its peculiarity did not escape the shrewd eyes of John Lord Eldon. "If," said the Conservative Chancellor, "I were to begin life again, d——n my eyes, but I would begin as an agitator." Henry Brougham did so begin. During the war he had distinguished himself in the exposition of the grievances of the trading interest. Our Government had chosen a mode of carrying it on specially fitted to injure our commerce. "Napoleon had said that no vessel should touch a British port,

and then enter a French one, or one under French control.
The Orders in Council said that no vessel whatever should
enter any such port without having first touched at some
port of Great Britain."[2] The natural results were the annihilation of our trade with the continent and a quarrel with
the United States. The merchants of the country were
alarmed at both consequences. Perhaps until then men
hardly knew how powerful our trading classes had become.
Meetings were held in populous places; petitions in great
numbers—an impressive and important thing in those times
—were presented. Wherever foreign commerce existed, the
discontent expressed itself in murmurs. The forms of the
House of Commons were far more favourable than they are
now to action from without; and this is not unnatural, since
there had been as yet but few actions from without, and it
had not been necessary to have a guard against them. "The
petitions, as has been said, were numerous; and on the presentation of each, there was a speech from the member presenting it, trying to bring on a debate, and suggesting topics which
might irritate the ministry and convince the country." Mr
Brougham was always in his place. "Hardly an hour passed
without detecting some false statement or illogical argument;
hardly a night passed without gaining some convert to the
cause of truth." The result was decisive. "Although opposed
by the whole weight of the Government both in public and
out of doors; although at first vigorously resisted by the energy, the acuteness, the activity, and the expertness which
made Mr Perceval one of the first debaters of his day; although, after his death, the struggle was maintained by the
father of the system[3] with all his fire and with his full knowledge of the subject—nay, although" the Ministry risked their
existence on the question, the victory remained with the pe-
titioners. The Orders in Council were abolished, and the efficacy of agitation proved. "The Session of 1816 offered an example yet more remarkable of the same tactics being attended
with signal success. On the termination of the war, the Government were determined, instead of repealing the whole
income tax, which the law declared to be 'for and during the
continuance of the war, and no longer,' to retain one-half of

[2] This and the following quotations are from the *Speeches of Lord
Brougham and the Introductions to them*, published in 1838. The
latter were written by himself.
[3] Mr. Stephen.

it." "As soon as his intention was announced, several meetings were held." Some petitions were presented. Mr Brougham declared that, if the motion "were pressed on Thursday, he should avail himself of the forms of the House". Of course, the unpopularity of paying money was decisive; the income tax fell. The same faculty of aggression, which had been so successful, in these instances, was immediately so applied as to give voice to the sullenness of the country; to express forms of discontent as real, though not with an object as determinate.

Mr Brougham did not understate his case. "There is one branch of the subject which I shall pass over altogether—I mean the amount of the distresses which are now universally admitted to prevail over almost every part of the empire. Upon this topic all men are agreed; the statements connected with it are as unquestionable as they are afflicting." Nor did he shrink from detail. "I shall suppose," he observed to the House, "a farm of 400 acres of fair, good land, yielding a rent of from £500 to £600 a year." "It will require a four years' course—200 acres being in corn, 100 in fallow, and 100 in hay and grass;" and he seems to prove that at least it *ought* not to answer, "independently of the great rise in lime and all sorts of manure". The commercial mania of the time takes its turn in the description. "After the cramped state in which the enemy's measures and our own retaliation [as we termed it] had kept our trade for some years, when the events of spring 1814 suddenly opened the continent, a rage for exporting goods of every kind burst forth, only to be explained by reflecting on the previous restrictions we had been labouring under, and only to be equalled [though not in extent] by some of the mercantile delusions connected with South American speculations. Everything that could be shipped was sent off; all the capital that could be laid hold of was embarked. The frenzy, I can call it nothing less, after the experience of 1806 and 1810, descended to persons in the humblest circumstances and the farthest removed, by their pursuits, from commercial cares. It may give the committee some idea of this disease, if I state what I know to have happened in one or two places. Not only clerks and labourers, but menial servants, engaged the little sums which they had been laying up for a provision against old age and sickness; persons went round tempting them to adventure in the trade to Holland, and Germany, and the Baltic; they risked their mite in the hopes of boundless profits; it went with the millions of the more regular traders: the bubble soon burst, like its predecessors of the South Sea, the Mississippi, and Buenos Ayres: English goods were selling for much less in Holland and the north of Europe than in London and Manchester; in most places they were lying a dead weight without any sale at all; and either no returns whatever were received, or pounds came back for thousands that had gone forth. The great speculators broke; the middling ones lingered out a precarious existence, deprived of all means of continuing their dealings either at home or abroad; the poorer dupes of the delusion had lost their little hoards, and went upon the parish; but the result of the whole has been much commercial distress—a caution now absolutely necessary in trying new adventures—a prodigious diminution in the demand for manufactures, and indirectly a serious defalcation in the effectual demand for the produce of land."

Next year Mr Brougham described as the worst season ever known. The year 1812, a year before esteemed one of much suffering, rose in comparison to one of actual prosperity. He began with the "clothing, a branch of trade which, from accidental circumstances, is not as depressed as our other great staples"; he passed to the iron trade, etc., etc. He dilated on the distress, the discontent and suffering of the people. Of course, the Government were to blame. He moved that the "unexampled" difficulties of trade and manufactures were "materially increased by the policy pursued with respect to our foreign commerce—that the continuance of these difficulties is in a great degree owing to the severe pressure of taxation under which the country labours and which ought by every practicable means to be lightened—that the system of foreign policy pursued by His Majesty's ministers has not been such as to obtain for the people of this country those commercial advantages which the influence of Great Britain in foreign countries fairly entitled them to expect". As became a pupil of the Edinburgh University, Mr Brougham was not averse to political economy. He was ready to discuss the theory of rent or the corn laws. He made a speech, which he relates as having had a greater success than any other which he made in Parliament, in support of Mr Calcraft's amendment, to "substitute £192,638 4s. 9d. for £385,276 9s. 6d., the estimate for the household troops". Foreign policy was a favourite topic. Almost unsupported, as he said some years

after, he attacked the Holy Alliance. Looking back through
the softening atmosphere of reminiscence, he almost seems to
have a kindness for Lord Castlereagh. He remembers with
pleasure the utter "courage with which he exposed himself
unabashed to the most critical audience in the world, while
incapable of uttering anything but the meanest matter, expressed in the most wretched language"; nor has he "forgotten the kind of pride that mantled on the fronts of the
Tory phalanx when, after being overwhelmed with the fire
of the Whig Opposition, or galled by the fierce denunciations
of the Mountain, or harassed by the splendid displays of Mr
Canning, their chosen leader stood forth, and presenting the
graces of his eminently patrician figure, flung open his coat,
displayed an azure ribbon traversing a snow-white chest, and
declared his high satisfaction that he could now meet the
charges against him face to face, and repel with indignation
all that his adversaries had been bold and rash enough to advance". But the "Mr Brougham" of that time showed no admiration; no denunciations were stronger than his; no sarcasm
impinged more deeply; if the "noble lord in the blue ribbon"
wished any one out of the House, the "man from the Northern Circuit" was probably that one. Kings and emperors met
with little mercy, and later years have shown how little was
merited by the petty absolutism and unthinking narrowness
of that time.

That Mr Brougham indissolubly connected the education
movement with his name everybody knows, but scarcely any
one remembers how unpopular that movement was. Mr
Windham had said, some years before, "that the diffusion of
knowledge was proper, might be supported by many good
arguments; but he confessed he was a sceptic on that point.
It was said, Look at the state of the savages as compared with
ours. A savage among savages was *very well*, and the difference was only perceived when he came to be introduced into
civilised society." "His friend, Dr Johnson, was of opinion
that it was not right to teach reading beyond a certain extent
in society." The same feeling continued. Mr Peel, in his
blandest tones, attacked the education committee. Lord Stowell, not without sagacity, observed, "If you provide a larger
amount of highly cultivated talent than there is a demand
for, the surplus is very likely to turn sour". Such were the
sentiments of some of the best scholars of that era; and so
went all orthodox sentiment. That education was the same

as republicanism, and republicanism as infidelity, half the
curates believed. But, in spite of all this opposition, perhaps
with more relish on account of it, Mr Brougham was ever
ready. He was a kind of prophet of knowledge. His voice was
heard in the streets. He preached the gospel of the alphabet;
he sang the praises of the primer all the day long. "Practical
observations," "discourses," "speeches," exist, terrible to all
men now. To the kind of education then advocated there may
be objections. We may object to the kind of "knowledge"
then most sought after; but there can be no doubt that those
who then laboured in its behalf must be praised for having
inculcated, in the horrid heat of day, as a boring paradox
what is now a boring commonplace.

Our space would fail us if we were to attempt to recount
Brougham's labours on the slavery question, on George IV
and Queen Caroline, or his hundred encounters with the routine statesmen. The series commenced at the Peace, but it
continued for many years. Is not its history written in the
chronicles of Parliament? You must turn the leaves—no unpleasant reading—of those old debates, and observe how often
Mr Brougham's name occurs, and on what cumbrous subjects,
before you can estimate the frequency of his attacks and the
harassing harshness of his labour. One especial subject was
his more than any other man's—law reform. He had Romilly
and Mackintosh as fellow-labourers in the amelioration of
the penal code; he had their support, and that of some others,
in his incessant narrations of the grievances of individuals,
and denunciations of the unfeeling unthinkingness of our
Home administration; but no man grappled so boldly—we
had almost said so coarsely—with the crude complexities of
our civil jurisprudence: for a rougher nature, a more varied
knowledge of action than we can expect of philanthropists
were needed for that task. The subject was most difficult to
deal with. The English commerce and civilisation had grown
up in the meshes of a half-feudal code, further complicated
with the curious narrowness and spirit of chicane which haunt
everywhere the law-courts of early times. The technicality
which produced the evil made the remedy more difficult.
There was no general public opinion on the manner of reform; the public felt the evil, but no one could judge of the
efficacy of a remedy, save persons studious in complicated
learning, who would hardly be expected to show how that
learning could be rendered useless—hardly, indeed, to imag-

ine a world in which it did not exist. The old creed, that
these ingenious abuses were the last "perfection of reason,"
still lingered. It must give Lord Brougham some pride to reflect how many of the improvements which he was the first to
popularise, if not to suggest, have been adopted—how many
old abuses of detail, which he first indicated to Parliament,
exist no longer—how many more are now admitted by everybody to be abuses, though the mode of abolition is contested.
The speech on law reform, which he published in the collected edition of his speeches, is nearly a summary of all that
has been done or suggested in common or civil law reform
for the last thirty years. The effect which so bold an attack
on so many things by a single person produced in that conservative time was prodigious. "There never was such a nuisance as the man is," said an old lawyer whom we knew; and
he expressed the feeling of his profession. If we add, that
beside all these minor reforms and secondary agitations, Mr
Brougham was a bold advocate of Catholic emancipation and
parliamentary reform—the largest heresies of that epoch—we
may begin to understand the sarcasm of Mr Canning: "The
honourable and learned gentleman having in the course of his
parliamentary life supported or proposed *almost every species
of innovation* which could be practised on the constitution,
it was not very easy for ministers to do anything without
seeming to borrow from him. Break away in what direction
they would, whether to the right or to the left, it was all
alike. 'Oh,' said the honourable gentleman, 'I was there before you: you would not have thought of that if I had not
given you a hint.' In the reign of Queen Anne there was a
sage and grave critic of the name of Dennis, who in his old
age got it into his head that he had written all the good plays
which were acted at that time. At last a tragedy came forth
with a most imposing display of hail and thunder. At the
first peal, Dennis exclaimed: 'That is my thunder!' So with
the honourable and learned gentleman; there was no noise
astir for the good of mankind in any part of the world, but
he instantly claimed it for his thunder." We may have wea-
ried our readers with these long references to old conflicts,
but it was necessary. We are familiar with the aberrations
of the ex-Chancellor; we forget how bold, how efficacious,
how varied was the activity of Henry Brougham.

There are several qualities in his genius which make such a
life peculiarly suited to him. The first of these is an aggres-

sive, impulsive disposition. Most people may admit that the
world goes ill; old abuses seem to exist, questionable details
to abound. Hardly any one thinks that anything may not be
made better. But how to improve the world, to repair the
defects, is a difficulty. Immobility is a part of man. A sluggish
conservatism is the basis of our English nature. "*Learn*, my
son," said the satirist, "to bear tranquilly the calamities of
others." We easily learn it. Most men have a line of life, and
it imposes certain duties which they fulfil; but they cannot
be induced to start out of that line. We dwell in "a firm
basis of content". "Let the mad world go its own way, for it
will go its own way." There is no doctrine of the English
Church more agreeable to our instinctive taste than that
which forbids all works of supererogation. "You did a thing
without being obliged," said an eminent statesman: "then
that must be wrong." We travel in the track. Lord Brougham
is the opposite of this. It is not difficult to him to attack
abuses. The more difficult thing for him would be to live in
a world without abuses. An intense excitability is in his nature. He must "go off". He is eager to reform corruption, and
rushes out to refute error. A tolerant placidity is altogether
denied to him.

And not only is this excitability eager, it is many-sided.
The men who have in general exerted themselves in labours
for others, have generally been rather of a brooding nature;
certain ideas, views and feelings have impressed themselves
on them in solitude; they come forth with them among the
crowd, but they have no part in its diversified life. They are
almost irritated by it. They have no conception except of
their cause; they are abstracted in one thought, pained with
the dizziness of a heated idea. There is nothing of this in
Brougham. He is excited by what he sees. The stimulus is
from without. He saw the technicalities of the law-courts;
observed a charitable trustee misusing the charity moneys;
perceived that George IV oppressed Queen Caroline; went
to Old Sarum. He is not absorbed in a creed: he is pricked
by facts. Accordingly, his activity is miscellaneous. The votary
of a doctrine is concentrated, for the logical consequences
of a doctrine are limited. But an open-minded man, who is
aroused by what he sees, quick at discerning abuses, ready to
reform anything which he thinks goes wrong—will never have
done acting. The details of life are endless, and each of them
may go wrong in a hundred ways.

Another faculty of Brougham (in metaphysics it is perhaps but a phase of the same) is the faculty of easy anger. The supine placidity of civilisation is not favourable to animosity. A placid Conservative is perhaps a little pleased that the world is going a *little* ill. Lord Brougham does not feel this. Like an Englishman on the Continent, he is ready to blow up any one. He is a Jonah of detail; he is angry at the dust of life, and wroth at the misfeasances of *employés*. The most reverberating of bastinadoes is the official mind basted by Brougham. You did *this* wrong; why did you omit *that?* Document C ought to be on the third file; paper D is wrongly docketed in the ninth file. Red tape will scarcely succeed when it is questioned; you should take it as Don Quixote did his helmet, without examination, for a most excellent helmet. A vehement, industrous man proposing to untie papers and not proposing to spare errors, is the terror of a respectable administrator. "Such an impracticable man, sir, interfering with the *office*, attacking private character, messing in what cannot concern him." These are the jibes which attend an irritable anxiety for the good of others. They have attended Lord Brougham through life. He has enough of misanthropy to be a philanthropist.

How much of this is temper, and how much public spirit, it is not for any one to attempt to say. That a natural pleasure in wrath is part of his character, no one who has studied the career of Brougham can doubt. But no fair person can doubt either that he showed on many great occasions—and, what is more, on many petty occasions—a rare zeal for the public welfare. He may not be capable of the settled calm by which the world is best administered. There is a want of consistency in his goodness, of concentration in his action. The gusts of passion pass over him, and he is gone for a time you can scarcely say where. But, though he is the creature of impulse, his impulses are often generous and noble ones. No one would do what he has done, no one could have the intense motive power to do what he has done, without a large share of diffused unselfishness. The irritation of the most acute excitability would not suffice. It is almost an axiom in estimates of human nature, that in its larger operations all that nature must concur. Doubtless there is a thread of calculation in the midst of his impulses; no man rises to be lord chancellor without, at least in lulls and intervals of impulse, a most discriminating and careful judgment of men and things and chances. But after every set-off and abatement, and without any softening of unamiable indications, there will yet remain—and a long series of years will continue to admire it—an eager principle of disinterested action.

Lord Brougham's intellectual powers were as fitted for the functions of a miscellaneous agitator as his moral character. The first of these, perhaps, is a singular faculty of conspicuous labour. In general, the work of agitation proceeds in this way: a conspicuous, fascinating popular orator is ever on the surface, ever ready with appropriate argument, making motions, attracting public attention; beneath and out of sight are innumerable workers and students, unfit for the public eye, getting up the facts, elaborating conclusions, supplying the conspicuous orator with the *data* on which he lives. There is a perpetual controversy, when the narrative of the agitation comes to be written, whether the merit of what is achieved belongs to the skilful advocate who makes a subtle use of what is provided for him, or the laborious inferiors and juniors who compose the brief and set in order the evidence. For all that comes before the public, Lord Brougham has a wonderful power: he can make motions, addresses, orations, when you wish and on what you wish. He is like a machine for moving amendments. He can keep at work any number of persons under him. Every agitation has a tendency to have an office; some league, some society, some body of labourers must work regularly at its details. Mr Brougham was able to rush hither and thither through a hundred such kinds of men, and gather up the whole stock of the most recent information, the extreme decimals of the statistics, and diffuse them immediately with eager comment to a listening world. This may not be, indeed is not, the strictest and most straining kind of labour; the anxious, wearing, verifying, self-imposed scrutiny of scattered and complicated details is a far more exhausting task; it is this which makes the eye dim and the face pale and the mind heavy. The excitement of a multifarious agitation will carry the energies through much; the last touches, and it is these which exhaust, need not be put on any one subject. Yet, after all deductions, such a career requires a quantity far surpassing all that most men have of life and *verve* and mind.

Another advantage of Lord Brougham is his extreme readiness; what he can do, he can do at a moment's notice. He has always had this power. Lord Holland, in his Memoirs referring to transactions which took place many years ago, gives an illustration of it. "The management of our press," he is speaking of the question of the general election of 1807, "fell into the hands of Mr Brougham. With that active and able individual I had become acquainted through Mr Allen in 1805. At the formation of Lord Grenville's ministry, he had written, at my suggestion, a pamphlet called *The State of the Nation*. He subsequently accompanied Lord Rosslyn to Lisbon. His early connection with the Abolitionists had familiarised him with the means of circulating political papers, and giving him some weight with those best qualified to co-operate in such an undertaking. His extensive knowledge, his extraordinary readiness, his assiduity and habits of composition, enabled him to correct some articles, and to furnish a prodigious number himself. With partial and scanty assistance from Mr Allen, myself, and one or two more, he in the course of a few days filled every bookseller's shop with pamphlets—most London newspapers, and all country ones without exception, with paragraphs—and supplied a large portion of the boroughs throughout the kingdom with handbills adapted to the local interests of the candidates, and all tending to enforce the conduct, elucidate the measures, or expose the adversaries of the Whigs."

Another power which was early remarked of Brougham, and which is as necessary as any to an important leader in great movements, is a skilful manipulation of men. Sir James Mackintosh noted in his Journal, on 30th January, 1818: "The address and insinuation of Brougham are so great, that nothing but the bad temper which he cannot always hide could hinder him from mastering everybody as he does Romilly. He *leads* others to his opinion; he generally appears at first to concur with theirs, and never more than half opposes it at once. This management is helped by an air of easy frankness that would lay suspicion itself asleep. He will place himself at the head of an opposition among whom he is unpopular; he will conquer the House of Commons, who hate, but now begin to fear him." An observer of faces would fancy he noted in Lord Brougham this pliant astuteness marred by ill-temper. It has marked his career.

Another essential quality in multifarious agitation is an extreme versatility. No one can deny Lord Brougham this. An apparently close observer has described him. "Take the routine of a day, for instance. In his early life he has been known to attend, in his place in court, on circuit, at an early hour in the morning. After having successfully pleaded the cause of his client, he drives off to the hustings, and delivers, at different places, eloquent and spirited speeches to the electors. He then sits down in the retirement of his closet to pen an address to the Glasgow students, perhaps, or an elaborate article in the *Edinburgh Review*. The active labours of the day are closed with preparation for the court business of the following morning; and then, in place of retiring to rest, as ordinary men would after such exertions, he spends the night in abstruse study, or on social intercourse with some friend from whom he has been long separated. Yet he would be seen, as early as eight on the following morning, actively engaged in the court, in defence of some unfortunate object of Government persecution, astonishing the auditory, and his fellow-lawyers no less, with the freshness and power of his eloquence. A fair contrast with this history of a day, in early life, would be that of one at a more advanced period; say, in the year 1832. A watchful observer might see the new Lord Chancellor seated in the court over which he presided, from an early hour in the morning until the afternoon, listening to the arguments of counsel, and mastering the points of cases with a grasp of mind that enabled him to give those speedy and unembarrassed judgments that have so injured him with the profession. If he followed his course, he would see him, soon after the opening of the House of Lords, addressing their lordships on some intricate question of law, with an acuteness that drew down approbation even from his opponents; or, on some all-engrossing political topic, casting firebrands into the camp of the enemy, and awakening them from the complacent repose of conviction to the hot contests with more active and inquiring intellects. Then, in an hour or so, he might follow him to the Mechanics' Institution, and hear an able and stimulating discourse on education, admirably adapted to the peculiar capacity of his auditors; and towards ten, perhaps, at a Literary and Scientific Institution in Marylebone, the same Proteus-like intellect might be found expounding the intricacies of physical science with a never-tiring and elastic power. Yet, during all those multitudinous exertions, time would be found for the composition of a discourse on Natural Theology, that bears no marks of haste or excitement of mind, but presents as calm a face as though it had been the laborious production of a contemplative phi-

losopher." We may differ in our estimate of the *quality* of
these various efforts; but no one can deny to him who was
capable of them a great share in what Adam Smith mentioned as one of the most important facilities to the intellectual labourer—a quickness in "changing his hand".

Nor would any of these powers be sufficient, without that
which is, in some sense, the principle of them all—an enterprising intellect. In the present day this is among the rarest
of gifts. The speciality of pursuits is attended with a timidity
of mind. Each subject is given up to men who cultivate it,
and it only; who are familiar with its niceties and absorbed
in its details. There is no one who dares to look at the whole.
"I have taken *all* knowledge to be my province," said Lord
Bacon. The notion, and still more the expression of it, seems
ridiculous now. The survey of each plot in the world of knowledge is becoming more complete. We shall have a plan of
each soon, on a seven-inch scale; but we are losing the picturesque pictures of the outside and surface of knowledge in
the survey of its whole. We have the petty survey, as we say,
but no chart, no globe of the entire world; no bold sketch of
its obvious phenomena, as they strike the wayfarer and impress themselves on the imagination. The man of the speciality cannot describe the large outlines; he is too close upon
the *minutiæ*; he does not know the relations of other knowledge, and no one else dares to infringe on his province—on
the "study of his life"—for fear of committing errors in detail
which he alone knows, and which he may expose. Lord
Brougham has nothing of this cowardice. He is ready to give,
in their boldest and most general form, the rough outlines of
knowledge as they strike the man of the world, occupied in
its affairs and familiar with its wishes. He is not cooped up
in a single topic, and he has no dread of those who are. He
may fall into error, but he exhibits a subject as it is seen by
those who know other subjects, by a man who knows the
world; he at least attempts an embracing conception of his
topic, he makes you feel its connection with reality and affairs. He has exhibited this virtue at all stages of his career,
but it was most valuable in his earlier time. There is no requisite so important as intellectual courage in one who seeks to
improve all things in all ways.

His oratory also suits the character of the hundred-subject
agitator well. It is rough-and-ready. It abounds in sarcasm,
in vituperation, in aggression. It does not shrink from detail.

It would batter anything at any moment. We may think as we will on its merits as a work of art, but no one can deny its exact adaptation to a versatile and rushing agitator—to a Tribune of detail.

The deficiencies of Brougham's character—in some cases they seem but the unfavourable aspects of its excellences—were also fitted for his earlier career. The first of these, to say it in a sentence, is the want of a thinking intellect. A miscellaneous agitator must be ready to catch at anything, to attack everything, to blame any one. This is not the life for a mind of anxious deliberation. The patient philosopher, who is cautious in his positions, dubious of his data, slow in his conclusions, must fail at once. He would be investigating while he should attack, inquiring while he should speak. He could not act upon a chance; the moment of action would be gone. A sanguine and speedy intellect, ready to acquire, by its very idea all but excludes the examining, scrupulous, hesitating intellect which reflects.

Nor would a man of very sensitive judgment endure such a career. An agitator must err by excess; a delicate nature errs by defects. There is a certain coarseness in the abusive breed. A Cleon should not feel failure. No man has ever praised very highly Lord Brougham's judgment; but to have exceedingly improved it would perhaps have impaired his earlier utility. You might as fitly employ some delicate lady as a rough-rider, as a man of a poising, refining judgment in the task of a grievance-stater.

Harsh nerves, too, are no disadvantage. Perhaps they are essential. Very nice nerves would shrink from a scattered and jangled life. Three days out of six the sensitive frame would be jarred, the agitator would be useless. It is possible, indeed, to imagine that in a single noble cause—a cause that would light up the imagination, that would move the inner soul, a temperament the most delicate, a frame that is most poetic, might well be absorbingly interested. A little of such qualities may be essential. The apostle of a creed must have the nature to comprehend that creed; his fancy must take it in, his feelings realise it, his nature absorb it. To move the finer nature, you need the deeper nature. Perhaps even in a meaner cause, in a cause which should take a hold on the moving mob, sway the masses, rule the popular fancy, rough as the task of the mob-orator is, you require the delicate imagination. One finds some trace of it—still more of what is

its natural accompaniment, a sweet nature—buried in the
huge frame and coarse exterior of O'Connell. No unpoetic
heart could touch the Irish people. Lord Brougham is prose
itself. He was described, many years ago, as excelling all men
in a knowledge of the course of exchange. "He is," continued
the satirist,[4] "apprised of the exact state of our exports and
imports, and scarce a ship clears out its cargo at Liverpool
or Hull but he has the notice of the bill of lading." To explain the grievances of men of business needs no poetic nature. It scarcely needs the highest powers of invective. There
is something nearly ridiculous in being the "Mirabeau of
sums".

There is a last quality which is difficult to describe in the
language of books, but which Lord Brougham excels in, and
which has perhaps been of more value to him than all his
other qualities put together. In the speech of ordinary men it
is called "devil"; persons instructed in the German language
call it "the demonic element". What it is one can hardly express in a single sentence. It is most easily explained by physiognomy. There is a glare in some men's eyes which seems
to say, "Beware, I am dangerous; *noli me tangere*". Lord
Brougham's face has this. A mischievous excitability is the
most obvious expression of it. If he were a horse, nobody
would buy him; with that eye, no one could answer for his
temper. Such men are often not really resolute, but they are
not pleasant to be near in a difficulty. They have an aggressive eagerness which is formidable. They would kick against
the pricks sooner than not kick at all. A little of the demon
is excellent for an agitator.

His peculiar adaptation to his peculiar career raised Mr
Brougham, in a few years, to a position such as few men have
ever obtained in England—such as no other man perhaps has
attained by popular agitation. When he became member
for Yorkshire, in 1830, he was a power in the country. The
cause which he was advocating had grown of itself. The power
of the middle classes, especially of the commercial classes,
had increased. Lord Eldon was retiring. Lord Sidmouth had
retired. What we now call "liberality" was coming into fashion. Men no longer regarded the half-feudal constitution as
a "form of thought". Argument was at least thought fair.
And this seems likely and natural. No one can wonder that

4 Hazlitt.

the influence of men of business grew with the development
of business, and they adopted the plain, straightforward,
cautious creed, which we now know to be congenial to them.
It is much more difficult to explain how reform became a
passion. The state of the public mind during the crisis of the
Reform Bill is one which those who cannot remember it cannot understand. The popular enthusiasm, the intense excitement, the rush of converts, the union of rectors and squires
with those against whom they had respectively so long
preached and sworn, the acclamation for the "whole bill and
nothing but the bill," are become utterly strange. As the first
French Assembly in a single night abolished, with public outcry, the essential abuses of the old *régime*, so our fathers at
once, and with enthusiasm, abolished the close boroughs and
the old representation, the lingering abuses of half-feudal
England. The present Frenchmen are said not to comprehend August 4: we can hardly understand the year '32. An
apathy has fallen upon us. But we can, nevertheless, and without theorising, comprehend what an advantage such an enthusiasm was to the Liberals of that time. Most Whig ministries have been like Low-Church bishops. There is a feeling
that the advocates of liberty ought scarcely to coerce; they
have ruled, but they seem to deny the succession by which
they ruled; they have been distrusted by a vague and half-
conservative sentiment. In the tumult of 1832 all such feelings were carried away. Toryism was abolished with delight.

Mr Brougham was among the first to share the advantage.
There is a legend that in the first Whig ministry Lord
Brougham was offered the post of Attorney-General, and that
he only replied by disdainfully tearing up the letter containing the offer. Whether the anecdote be literally true or not,
we cannot say. The first of the modern Whig ministries is
in the post-historical period. We have not yet enough of contemporary evidence to be sure of its details: years must pass
before the memoir-writers can accumulate. But in spirit the
tale is doubtless accurate. Lord Grey did not wish to make
Mr Brougham Lord Chancellor, and Mr Brougham refused
any inferior place as beneath his merits and his influence. The
first Whig ministry was, indeed, in a position of some difficulty. The notion that a successful Opposition, as such,
should take the reins of administration, has been much de-
rided. "Sir," said a sceptic on this part of constitutional government, "I would as soon choose for a new coachman the

man who shied stones best at my old one!" And, without
going the length of such critics, it must be allowed that the
theory may produce odd results, when the persons summoned
by their victory to assume office have been for many years in
opposition. The party cannot have acquired official habits:
the traditions of business cannot be known to them; their
long course of opposition will have forced into leadership men
hardly fitted for placid government. There is said to have
been much of this feeling when Lord Grey's ministry was in-
stalled; it seemed as if that "old favourite of the public," Mr
Buckstone, were called to license plays. Grave Englishmen
doubted the gravity of the administration. To make Lord
Brougham Chancellor was, therefore, particularly inconvenient. He was too mobile; you could not fancy him droning.
He had attacked Lord Eldon during many years, of course;
but did he know law? He was a most active person; would
he sit *still* upon the woolsack? Of his inattention to his profession men circulated idle tales. "Pity he hadn't known a
little law, and then he would have known a little of everything," was the remark of one who certainly only knows one
thing. A more circumstantial person recounted that, when
Brougham had been a pupil of Sir Nicholas Tindal, in the
Temple, an uncle of his, having high hopes of his ability,
asked the latter: "I hope my nephew is giving himself up,
soul and body, to his profession?" "I do not know anything,"
replied the distinct special-pleader, "as to his *soul*, but his
body is very seldom in my chambers." Putting aside with contempt this surface of tales, it could not be denied that Mr
Brougham's practice at the bar—large and lucrative as it was
—immense as was the energy required to maintain it at the
same time with his other labours—had yet not shown him to
possess the finest discretion, the most delicate tact of the
advocate. Mr Scarlett stole verdicts away from him. "He
strikes hard, sir," said an attorney; "but he strikes wrong."
His appointment as Chancellor scarcely strengthened the
ministry of the time. Mr Brougham was a hero; Lord
Brougham was "a necessity". It was like Mr Disraeli being
Chancellor of the Exchequer.

After the lapse of years, and with the actual facts before
us, it is not difficult to see how far these anticipations have
been falsified, and how far they have been justified, by the
result. All the notions as to Lord Brougham's ignorance of
law may at once be discarded. A man of his general culture

and vigorous faculties, with a great memory and much experience in forensic business, is no more likely to be ignorant of the essential bookwork of law than a tailor to be ignorant of scissors and seams. A man in business must be brought in contact with it; a man of mind cannot help grasping it. No one now questions that Lord Brougham was and is a lawyer of adequate attainments. But, at the same time, the judgments which supply the conclusive proof of this—the complete refutation of earlier cavillers—also would lead us to deny him the praise of an absolutely judicious intellect. Great judges may be divided into two classes—judges for the parties, and judges for the lawyers. The first class of these are men who always decide the particular case before them rightly, who have a nice insight into all that concerns it, are acute discerners of fact, accurate weighers of testimony, just discriminators of argument. Lord Lyndhurst is perhaps as great a judge in this kind as it is easy to fancy. If a wise man had a good cause, he would prefer its being tried before Lyndhurst to its being tried before any one else. For the "parties," if they were to be considered in litigation, no more would be needed. By law-students, however, and for the profession, something more is desired. They like to find, in a judicial decision, not only a correct adjustment of the particular dispute in court, but also an ample exposition of principles applicable to other disputes. The judge who is peculiarly exact in detecting the precise peculiarities of the case before him, will be very apt to decide only what is essential to, absolutely needed by, that case. His delicate discrimination will see that nothing else is necessary; he will not bestow conclusions on after-generations; he will let posterity decide its own controversies. A judge of different kind has a professional interest in what comes before him: it is in his eyes not a pitiful dispute whether A or B is entitled to a miserable field, but a glorious opportunity of deciding some legal controversy on which he has brooded for years, and on which he has a ready-made conclusion. Accordingly, his judgments are in the nature of essays. They are, in one sense, applicable to the matter in hand—they decide it correctly; but they go so much into the antecedents of the controversy—give so much of principle—that the particular facts seem a little lost: the general doctrine fills the attention. No one can read a judgment of the late Lord Cottenham without feeling that it fixed the law on the matter in hand upon a defined basis for future years.

Very likely he finds an authority for the case which has occurred in his practice; he does not stay to inquire whether
the litigants appreciated the learning; perhaps they did not
—possibly they would have preferred that a more exclusive prominence should be given to themselves. Now Lord
Brougham has neither of these qualities; his intellect wants
the piercing precision which distinguishes the judge—the un-
erring judge—of the case then present; and though com-
petently learned, he has never been absorbed in his profession, as a judge of "principle" almost always must be. A man
cannot provide a dogma suiting all the cases of the past, and
deciding all the cases for the future without years of patient
reflection. His mind must be stored with doctrines. No one
can fancy this of Lord Brougham. He is not to be thought
of as giving still attention to technical tenets, years of brooding consideration to an abstract jurisprudence. Accordingly,
though an adequate, and in his time—for his speed cleared
off arrears—a most useful judge, he cannot be said to attain
the first rank in the judicial scale; and such we believe is
the estimation of the world.

Of the political duties of the Chancellor, and Lord
Brougham's performance of them, it is not easy to speak.
Many of them are necessarily secret, and the history of those
times cannot yet be written. That he showed wonderful energy, zeal, and power, no one can doubt; nor that the essential defects of his character soon showed him but little
qualified for an administrator. In the year 1802, Francis
Horner anticipated, that if "an active career were opened to
Brougham, he would show a want of prudence and moderation"; and it is curious to read, as a commentary on it, what
the Duke of Wellington wrote to Sir R. Peel, on the 15th November, 1835. "His Majesty mentioned that Lord Brougham[5]
had threatened he would not put the great seal to a commission to prorogue the parliament;" and afterwards correcting himself: "It appears that Lord Brougham did not make
the threat that he would not prorogue the parliament, but
that Lord Melbourne said he was in such a state of excitement that he might take that course". We must wait for Lord
Brougham's memoirs before we know the exact history of

[5] The editors of Sir R. Peel's *Memoirs* have left this name in
blank; but if they had wished it not to be known, they should have
suppressed the passage. Everybody knows who held the great seal at
that time.

that time; but all the glimpses we get of it show the same picture of wildness and eccentricity.

The times—the most nearly revolutionary times which England has long seen—were indeed likely to try an excitable temperament to the utmost; but at the same time they afforded scope to a brilliant manager of men, which only such critical momentary conjunctures can do. Mr Roebuck gives a curious instance of this:—

"The necessity of a dissolution had long been foreseen and decided on by the ministers; but the king had not yet been persuaded to consent to so bold a measure; and now the two chiefs of the administration were about to intrude themselves into the royal closet, not only to advise and ask for a dissolution, but to request the king on the sudden— on this very day, and within a few hours—to go down and put an end to his parliament in the midst of the session, and with all the ordinary business of the session yet unfinished. The bolder mind of the Chancellor took the lead, and Lord Grey anxiously solicited him to *manage* the king on the occasion. So soon as they were admitted, the Chancellor, with some care and circumlocution, propounded to the king the object of the interview they had sought. The startled monarch no sooner understood the drift of the Chancellor's somewhat periphrastic statement, than he exclaimed in wonder and amazement against the very idea of such a proceeding. 'How is it possible, my lords, that I can after this fashion repay the kindness of parliament to the queen and myself? They have just granted me a most liberal civil list, and to the queen a splendid annuity in case she survives me.' The Chancellor confessed that they had, as regarded his Majesty, been a liberal and wise parliament, but said that nevertheless their further existence was incompatible with the peace and safety of the kingdom. Both he and Lord Grey then strenuously insisted upon the absolute necessity of their request, and gave his Majesty to understand that this advice was by his ministers unanimously resolved on; and that they felt themselves unable to conduct the affairs of the country in the present condition of the parliament. This last statement made the king feel that a general resignation would be the consequence of a further refusal. Of this, in spite of his secret wishes, he was at the moment really afraid; and therefore,

he, by employing petty excuses, and suggesting small and
temporary difficulties, soon began to show that he was
about to yield. 'But, my lords, nothing is prepared; the
great officers of state are not summoned.' 'Pardon me, sir,'
said the Chancellor, bowing with profound apparent humility, 'we have taken the great liberty of giving them to
understand that your Majesty commanded their attendance
at the proper hour.' 'But, my lords, the crown and the
robes, and other things needed are not prepared.' 'Again
I most humbly entreat your Majesty's pardon for my boldness,' said the Chancellor; 'they are all prepared and ready
—the proper officers being desired to attend in proper
form and time.' 'But, my lords,' said the king reiterating
the form in which he put his objection, 'you know the thing
is wholly impossible; the guards, the troops, have had no
orders, and cannot be ready in time.' This objection was
in reality the most formidable one. The orders to the troops
on such occasions emanate always directly from the king,
and no person but the king can in truth command them
for such service; and as the Prime Minister and daring
Chancellor well knew the nature of royal susceptibility on
such matters, they were in no slight degree doubtful and
anxious as to the result. The Chancellor, therefore, with
some real hesitation, began again as before, 'Pardon me,
sir, we know how bold the step is that, presuming on your
great goodness, and your anxious desire for the safety of
your kingdom, and happiness of your people, we have pre-
sumed to take. I have given orders and the troops are ready.'
The king started in serious anger, flamed red in the face,
and burst forth with, 'What, my lords, have you dared
to act thus? Such a thing was never heard of. You, my Lord
Chancellor, ought to know that such an act is treason, high
treason, my lord.' 'Yes, sir,' said the Chancellor, 'I do know
it; and nothing but my thorough knowledge of your Majesty's goodness, of your paternal anxiety for the good of
your people, and my own solemn belief that the safety of
the state depends upon this day's proceedings, could have
emboldened me to the performance of so unusual, and, in
ordinary circumstances, so improper a proceeding. In all
humility I submit myself to your Majesty, and am ready
in my own person to bear all the blame, and receive all
the punishment which your Majesty may deem needful;
but I again entreat your Majesty to listen to us and to

follow our counsel, and as you value the security of your crown and the peace of your realms, to yield to our most earnest solicitations.' After some further expostulations by both his ministers, the king cooled down and consented. Having consented, he became anxious that everything should be done in the proper manner, and gave minute directions respecting the ceremonial. The speech to be spoken by him at the prorogation was ready prepared and in the Chancellor's pocket. To this he agreed, desired that everybody might punctually attend, and dismissed his ministers for the moment with something between a menace and a joke upon the audacity of their proceeding."

With the fall of Lord Melbourne's first administration terminated Lord Brougham's administrative career. As every one knows, on the defeat of Sir Robert Peel and the subsequent return of the Whigs to power, he was not invited to resume office. Since that time—for now more than twenty years—he has had to lead the life, in general the most trying to political reputation, perhaps to real character, and more than any other alien to the character of his mind and the tendencies of his nature. We have had many recent instances how difficult it is to give what is variously termed an "independent support," and a "friendly opposition," to a Government of which you approve the general tendencies, but are inclined to criticise the particular measures. The Peelites and Lord John Russell have for several years been in general in this position, and generally with a want of popular sympathy. As they agree with the Government in principle, they cannot take, by way of objection, what the country considers broad points; their suggestions of detail seem petty and trivial to others—the public hardly think of such things; but men who have long considered a subject, who have definite ideas and organised plans, can scarcely help feeling an eager interest in the smallest *minutiæ* of the mode of dealing with it. Sometimes they discern a real importance undiscerned by those less attentive; more commonly, perhaps, they fancy there is something peculiarly felicitous in contrivances settled by themselves and congenial to their habits or their notions. Lord Brougham was in a position to feel this peculiarly. The various ideas which he had struggled for in earlier life were successful one by one; the hundred reforms he suggested were carried; the hundred abuses he had denounced were abolished. The world which *was*, was changed to the world which *is*; but it was not changed by him. That he should have been favourably disposed to the existing liberal administrations was not likely; the separation was too recent, perhaps too abrupt. An eager and excitable disposition is little likely to excel in the measured sentences, the chosen moments, the polished calm of the *frondeur*. Accordingly, the life of Brougham for many years has not been favourable to his fame. On particular occasions, as on the abolition of Negro apprenticeship, he might attain something of his former power. But, in general, his position has been that of the agitator whose measure is being substantially carried, yet with differences of detail aggravating to his temper and annoying to his imagination. Mr Cobden described Sir Robert Peel's mode of repealing the corn-laws with the microscopic sliding-scale for three years, as seventeen-and-sixpence on the demand of the Anti-corn-law League, and good security for the other half-crown. Yet excitable men at that very moment clamoured for the last half-crown; they could not bear the modification, the minute difference from that on which they had set their hearts. We must remember this in relation to what is now most familiar to us in the life of Lord Brougham. To a man so active, to be put out of action is a pain which few can appreciate; that other men should enter into your labours is not pleasant; that they should be Canningites does not make it any better. We have witnessed many escapades of Lord Brougham; we perhaps hardly know his temptations and his vexations.

Such is the bare outline of the career of Lord Brougham. A life of early, broken, various agitation; a short interval of ordinary administration—occurring, however, at a time singularly extraordinary; a long old age secluded from the actual conduct of affairs, and driven to distinguish itself by miscellaneous objection and diversified sarcasm. Singular stories of eccentricity and excitement, even of something more than either of these, darken these latter years. On these we must not dwell. There are many aspects of Brougham's varied character, a few of which we should notice by themselves.

The most connected with his political life is his career as a law reformer. We have spoken of his early labours on this subject; we have said that few men who have devoted themselves to nothing else have exposed so many abuses, propounded so many remedies; that one of his early motions is a schedule of half, and much more than half, that has been, or will be, done upon a large portion of the subject. But here praise must end. The completed, elaborated reforms by which Lord Brougham will be known to posterity are few, are nothing in comparison with his power, his industry, and his opportunities. There is nothing, perhaps, for which he is so ill qualified. The bold vehement man who exposes an abuse has rarely the skilful, painful, dissecting power which expunges it. Lord Brougham once made a speech on conveyancing. "I should not," said, on the next day, an eminent professor of that art, "like him to draw a deed relating to my property." A law reformer, in order that his work may be perfect, requires the conveyancing abilities. He must be able to bear in mind the whole topic—to draw out what is necessary of it on paper—to see what is necessary—to discriminate the rights of individuals—to distinguish, with even metaphysical nicety, the advantage he would keep from the abuse he would destroy. He must elaborate enacting clauses which will work in the complicated future, repealing clauses which will not interfere with the complicated machinery of the past. His mind must be the mind of a codifier. A rushing man, like Lord Brougham, cannot hope to have this. A still and patient man, in quiet chambers, apt in niceties, anxious by temperament, precise in habit, putting the last extreme of perfection on whatever he may attempt, is the man for the employment. You must not expect this quiet precision from an agitator. There is the same difference as that between the hard-striking pugilist and the delicate amputating operator.

The same want of repose has repaired his excellence in a pursuit to which, at first sight, it seems much less needful— the art of oratory. We are apt to forget that oratory is an imaginative art. From our habits of business, the name of rhetoric has fallen into disrepute: our greatest artists strive anxiously to conceal their perfection in it; they wish their address in statement to be such, that the effect seems to be produced by that which is stated, and not by the manner in which it is stated. But not the less on that account is there a real exercise of the imagination in conceiving of the events of a long history, in putting them forward in skilful narration, each fact seeming by nature to fall into its place, all the details appearing exactly where they should—a group, to borrow a metaphor from another art, collecting itself from straggling and desultory materials. Still more evidently is the imagination requisite in expressing deep emotions, even common emotions, or in describing noble objects. Now, it seems to be a law of the imagination that it only works in a mind of stillness. The noise and crush of life jar it. "No man," it has been said, "can say, I *will* compose poetry": he must wait until—from a brooding, half-desultory inaction—poetry may arise, like a gentle mist, delicately and of itself.

> "I waited for the train at Coventry;
> I hung with grooms and porters on the bridge
> To watch the three tall spires; and there I shaped
> The city's legend into this."[6]

Lord Brougham would not have waited so. He would have rushed up into the town; he would have suggested an improvement, talked the science of the bridge, explained its history to the natives. The quiet race would think twenty people had been there. And, of course, in some ways this is admirable; such life and force are rare; even the "grooms and porters" would not be insensible to such an aggressive intelligence—so much *knocking* mind. But, in the meantime, no lightly-touched picture of old story would have arisen in his imagination. The city's legend would have been thrust out: the "fairy frostwork" of the fancy would have been struck away: there would have been talk on the schooling of the porter's eldest boy. The rarity of great political oratory arises in a great measure from this circumstance. Only those engaged in the jar of life have the material for it; only those withdrawn into a brooding imagination have the faculty for it. M. de Lamartine has drawn a striking picture of one who had the opportunity of action and the dangerous faculty of leisure: "Vergniaud s'enivrait dans cette vie d'artiste, de musique, de déclamation et de plaisirs; il se pressait de jouir de sa jeunesse, comme s'il eût le pressentiment qu'elle serait sitôt cueillie. Ses habitudes étaient méditatives et paresseuses. Il se levait au milieu du jour; il écrivait peu et sur des feuilles éparses: il appuyait le papier sur ses genoux comme un homme pressé qui se dispute le temps; il composait ses discours lentement dans ses rêveries et les retenait à l'aide de notes dans sa mémoire; il polissait son éloquence a loisir, comme le soldat polit son arme au repos."[7] This is not the picture of one who is to attain eminence in stirring and

6 Tennyson, *Godiva*.
7 *Histoire des Girondins*, book xviii, ch. ix, p. 88.

combative time. Harsher men prevailed; a mournful fate
swallowed up Vergniaud's delicate fancies. He died, because
he was idle; but he was great, because he was idle. Idleness
with such minds is only the name for the passive enjoyment
of a justly-moving imagination.

We should only weary our readers with a repetition of
what has been said a hundred times already, if we tried to
explain that Lord Brougham has nothing of this. His merit
is, that he was never idle in his life. He must not complain
if he has the disadvantage of it also. That he was a most
effective speaker in his great time, is of course undoubted.
His power of sarcasm, his amazing readiness, his energetic
vigour of language, made him, if not a very persuasive, at
least a most formidable orator. His endless animation must
tell even to excess upon his audience. But he has not acted
wisely for his fame in publishing his speeches. They have the
most unpardonable of all faults—the fault of dulness. It is
scarcely possible to read them. Doubtless, at the time their
influence was considerable; they may even have been pleasant, as you like to watch the play of a vicious horse; but now,
removed from the hearing of the speaker's voice—out of the
way of the motions of his face and the glare of his eye—even
their evil-speaking loses its attractiveness. The sarcasm seems
blunt—the denunciation heavy. They are crowded with a detail which may have been, though acute observers say it was
not, attractive at the time, but which no one can endure now.
Not only do you feel that you are bored, but you are not sure
that you are instructed. An agitator's detail is scarcely to be
trusted. His facts may be right, but you must turn historian in
order to test them; you must lead a life of State papers and
old letters to know if they are true. It is perhaps possible for
the imagination of man to give an interest to any considerable action of human life. A firmly-drawing hand may
conduct us through the narration—an enhancing touch en-
liven the details; but to achieve this with contested facts in a
combative life, is among the rarest operations of a rare power.
The imagination has few tasks so difficult. To Lord Brougham,
least of all, has it been possible to attract men by the business detail and cumbrous aggressions of the last age. His tone
is too harsh. He has shattered his contemporaries, but he will
not charm posterity.

Lord Brougham has wished to be known, not only as an
orator, but as a writer on oratory. He has written a *Discourse*

on Ancient Oratory, recommending, and very deservedly, its
study to those who would now excel in the art; and there is
no denying that he has rivalled the great Greek orator, at least
in one of his characteristic excellences. There is no more
manly book in the world than Brougham's *Speeches;* he always "calls a spade a spade"; the rough energy strikes; we
have none of the tawdry metaphor or half-real finery of the
inferior orators, there is not a simile which a man of sense
should not own. Nevertheless, we are inclined to question
whether his studies on ancient oratory, especially on the great
public oration of Demosthenes, have been entirely beneficial
to him. These masterly productions were, as every one knows,
the eager expression of an intense mind on questions of the
best interest; they have accordingly the character of vehemence. Speaking on subjects which he thought involved the
very existence of his country, he could not be expected to
speak very temperately; he did not, and could not, admit
that there was fair ground for difference of opinion; that an
equally patriotic person, after proper consideration, could
by possibility arrive at an opposite conclusion. The circumstances of the parliamentary orator in this country are quite
different. A man cannot discuss the dowry of the Princess
Royal, the conditions of the Bank Charter, as if they were
questions of existence—all questions arising now present
masses of fact, antecedents in blue-books, tabulated statistics,
on which it is impossible that there should not be a necessity
for an elaborate inquiry—that there should not be discrepancy
of judgment after that inquiry. The Demosthenic vehemence
is out of place. The calm didactic exposition, almost approaching to that of the lecturer, is more efficacious than the
intense appeal of an eager orator. That "Counsellor Broom
was all in a fume," is a line in one of the best ludicrous poems
of a time rather fertile in such things. On points of detail it
is ridiculous to be in a passion; on matters of business it is
unpersuasive to be enthusiastic; even on topics less technical,
the Greek oratory is scarcely a model to be imitated precisely.
A certain *nonchalant* ease pervades our modern world—we
affect an indifference we scarcely feel; our talk is light, almost
to affectation; our best writing is the same; we suggest rather
than elaborate, hint rather than declaim. The spirit of the
ancient world was very different—the tendency of its conversation probably was to a rhetorical formality, a haranguing energy; certainly it is the tendency of its written style. "With
every allowance," says Colonel Mure, "for the peculiar genius

of the age in which the masterpieces of Attic prose were produced—a consideration which must always have a certain weight in literary judgments—still, the impartial modern critic cannot but discern in this pervading rhetorical tone a defect, perhaps the only serious defect, in the classical Greek style. . . . It certainly is not natural for the historian or the popular essayist to address his readers in the same tone in which the defender of a client or the denouncer of a political opponent addresses a public assembly."[8] So great a change in the general world, in the audience to be spoken to, requires a change in the speaker. The light touch of Lord Palmerston is more effective than the most elaborated sentences of a formal rhetorician. Of old, when conversation and writing were half oratorical, oratory might be very oratorical; now that conversation is very conversational, oratory must be a little conversational. In real life, Lord Brougham has too much of the orator's tact not to be half aware of this; but his teaching forgets it.

That Lord Brougham should have adopted a theory enjoining vehemence in oratory, is an instance to be cited by those who hold that a man's creed is a justification for his inclinations. He is by nature over-vehement; and what is worse, it is not vehemence of the best kind; there is something of a scream about it. People rather laughed at his kneeling to beseech the peers. No one is sure that there is real feeling in what he reads and hears; it seems like a machine going. Lord Cockburn has an odd anecdote. An old judge, who loved dawdling, disliked the "discomposing qualities" of Brougham. His revenge consisted in sneering at Brougham's eloquence, by calling it or him *the Harangue*. "Well, gentlemen, what did *the Harangue* say next? Why it said this (mis-stating it); but, here, gentlemen, *the Harangue* was wrong and not intelligible." We have some feeling for the old judge. If you take a speech of Brougham, and read it apart from his voice, you have half a notion that it is a gong going, eloquence by machinery, an incessant talking *thing*.

It is needless to point out how completely an excitable, ungenial nature, such as we have so much spoken of, incapacitates Lord Brougham for abstract philosophy. His works on that subject are sufficiently numerous, but we are not aware that even his most ardent admirers have considered them as

[8] *History of the Language and Literature of Ancient Greece*, vol. iv, p. 17.

works of really the first class. It would not be difficult to extract from the *Political Philosophy*, which is probably the best of them, singular instances of inconsistency and of confusion. The error was in his writing them; he who runs may *read*, but it does not seem likely he will think. The brooding disposition, and the still, investigating intellect, are necessary for consecutive reasonings on delicate philosophy.

The same qualities, however, fit a man for the acquisition of general information. A man who is always rushing into the street will become familiar with the street. One who is for ever changing from subject to subject will not become *painfully* acquainted with any one, but he will know the outsides of them all, and the road from each to the other. Accordingly, all the descriptions of Lord Brougham, even in his earliest career, speak of his immense information. Mr Wilberforce, in perhaps the earliest printed notice of him, recommended Mr Pitt to employ him in a diplomatic capacity, on account of his familiarity with languages, and the other kinds of necessary knowledge. He began by writing on Porisms; only the other day he read a paper on some absurdities imputed to the Integral Calculus, in French, at Paris. It would be in the highest degree tedious to enumerate all the subjects he knows something of. Of course, an extreme correctness cannot be expected. "The most *mis*informed man in Europe," is a phrase of satire; yet, even in its satire, it conveys a compliment to Brougham's information.

An especial interest in physical science may be remarked in Brougham, as in most men of impressible minds in his generation. He came into life when the great discoveries in our knowledge of the material world were either just made, or were on the eve of being made. The enormous advances which have been actually made in material civilisation were half anticipated. There was a vague hope in science. The boundaries of the universe, it was hoped, would move. Active, ardent minds were drawn with extreme hope to the study of new moving power; a smattering of science was immeasurably less common then than now, but it exercised a stronger dominion, and influenced a higher class of genius. It was new, and men were sanguine. In the present day, younger men are perhaps repelled into the opposite extreme. We live among the marvels of science, but we know how little they change us. The essentials of life are what they were. We go by the train, but we are not improved at our journey's end. We have railways, and canals, and manufactures—excellent things, no doubt, but they do not touch the soul. Somehow, they seem to make life more superficial. With a half-wayward dislike, some in the present generation have turned from physical science and material things. "We have tried these, and they fail," is the feeling. "What is the heart of man the better for galvanic engines and hydraulic presses? Leave us to the old poetry and the old philosophy; there is at least a life and a mind." It is the day after the feast. We do not care for its delicacies; we are rather angry at its profusion; we are cross to hear it praised. Men who came into active life half a century ago were the guests invited to the banquet; they did not know what was coming, but they heard it was something gorgeous and great; they expected it with hope and longing. The influence of this feeling was curiously seen in the Useful Knowledge Society, the first great product of the educational movement in which Lord Brougham was the most ardent leader. No one can deny that their labours were important, their intentions excellent, the collision of mind which they created most beneficial. Still, looking to their well-known publications, beyond question the knowledge they particularly wished to diffuse is, according to the German phrase, *factish*. Hazlitt said "they confounded a knowledge of useful things with useful knowledge". An idea, half unconscious, pervades them, that a knowledge of the detail of material knowledge, even too of the dates and shell of outside history, is extremely important to the mass of men; that all will be well when we have a cosmical ploughboy and a mob that knows hydrostatics. We shall never have it; but even if we could, we should not be much the better. The heart and passions of men are moved by things more within their attainment; the essential nature is stirred by the essential life; by the real actual existence of love, and hope, and character, and by the real literature which takes in its spirit, and which is in some sort its undefecated essence. Thirty years ago the preachers of this now familiar doctrine were unknown, nor was their gospel for a moment the one perhaps most in season. It was good that there should be a more diffused knowledge of the material world; and it was good, therefore, that there should be partisans of matter, believers in particles, zealots for tissue, who were ready to incur any odium and any labour that a few more men might learn a few more things. How a man of incessant activity should pass easily to such a creed is evident. He would see the obvious ignorance. The less obvious argument, which shows that this

ignorance, in great measure inevitable, was of far less importance than would be thought at first sight, would never be
found by one who moved so rapidly.

We have gone through now, in some hasty way, most of
the lights in which Lord Brougham has been regarded by his
contemporaries. There is still another character in which
posterity will especially think of him. He is a great memoirist.
His *Statesmen of George III* contains the best sketches of
the political men of his generation, one with another, which
the world has, or is likely to have. He is a fine painter of the
exterior of human nature. Some portion of its essence requires a deeper character; another portion, more delicate sen-
sations; but of the rough appearance of men, as they struck
him in the lawcourt and in Parliament—of the great debater
struggling with his words—the stealthy advocate gliding into
the confidence of the audience—the great judge unravelling
all controversies, and deciding by a well-weighed word all
complicated doubts—of such men as these, and of men engaged in such tasks as these, there is no greater painter perhaps than Brougham. His eager aggressive disposition brought
him into collision with conspicuous men; his skill in the obvious parts of human nature has made him understand them.
A man who has knocked his head against a wall—if such an
illustration is to be hazarded—will learn the nature of the
wall. Those who have passed fifty years in managing men of
the world will know their external nature, and, if they have
literary power enough, will describe it. In general, Lord
Brougham's excellence as a describer of character is confined
to men whom he had thus personally and keenly encountered.
The sketches of the philosophers of the eighteenth century,
of French statesmen, are poor and meagre. He requires evidently the rough necessities of action to make him observe.
There is, however, a remarkable exception. He preserves a
singularly vivid recollection of the instructors of his youth;
he nowhere appears so amiable as in describing them. He is
over-partial, no doubt; but an old man may be permitted to
reverence, if he can reverence, his schoolmaster.

This is all that our limits will permit us to say of Lord
Brougham. On so varied a life, at least on a life with such
varied pursuits, one might write to any extent. The regular
biographer will come in after years. It is enough for a mere
essayist to sketch, or strive to sketch, in some rude outline,
the nature of the man.

LORD ALTHORP AND THE
REFORM ACT OF 1832[1]*

(1877)

John Charles Spencer, Viscount Althorp and Earl Spencer, was
the eldest son of George John, second Earl Spencer, and of La-
vinia Bingham. He was born at Spencer House, St. James, London, in 1782. In childhood he was left to the care of servants;
in 1790 he went to Harrow, and from 1800–2 was at Trinity
College, Cambridge. He had by this time acquired the passionate enthusiasm for field sports which he retained all his life.
He became M.P. for Okehampton in 1804; M.P. for St. Albans
in 1806, and was M.P. for Northamptonshire 1806–34. For
many years he seldom spoke in Parliament or interested himself
in politics at all, devoting himself to the Pytchley hunt, racing,
and prize fights, but his admiration for Fox eventually drew him
into active politics. He began to study economic history and
working-class grievances, supporting Huskisson and Joseph
Hume, and in 1830 became leader of the Whig opposition in
the Commons. In December of that year he became Chancellor
of the Exchequer and leader of the Lower House under Earl
Grey, after Wellington's resignation. He returned to office with
an increased Whig majority in 1831, and when the Lords rejected the Reform Bill in October, he showed his zeal for the
bill by the energy with which he rallied his followers. He saw the
bill pass the Lords in June, 1832. At the rise of Peel, Spencer
began to lose influence and retained office only very reluctantly
until he succeeded to the Earldom in 1834. He then withdrew
from politics to his country pursuits, reappearing only in 1841
to speak in favour of the repeal of the Corn Laws. Lord Althorp
died at Wiseton Hall, Northamptonshire, in 1845.

---

[1] Memoir of John Charles, Viscount Althorp, third Earl Spencer.
By the late Sir Denis Le Marchant, Bart. London: Richard Bentley
& Son, 1876.

* This essay was first published in the Fortnightly Review for November 1876, Volume XX [N.S.], pages 574–600.

"Althorp carried the Bill," such is the tradition of our
fathers: "the Bill," of course, being the Bill to them—the
great Reform Act of 1832, which was like a little revolution
in that generation—which really changed so much, and which
seemed to change so much more. To have been mainly concerned in passing so great a measure seems to many of the
survivors of that generation, who remember the struggles of
their youth and recall the enthusiasm of that time, almost the
acme of fame. And in sober history such men will always be
respectfully and gravely mentioned; but all romance has died
away. *The* Bill is to us hardly more than other Bills; it is one
of a great many Acts of Parliament which in this day, partly
for good and partly for evil, have altered the ever-varying
Constitution of England. The special charm, the charm
which to the last you may see that Macaulay always felt
about it, is all gone. The very history of it is forgotten. Which
of the younger generation can say what was General Gas-
coigne's amendment, or who were the "waverers," or even
how many Reform "Bills" in those years there were? The
events for which one generation cares most, are often those
of which the next knows least. They are too old to be matters
of personal recollection, and they are too new to be subjects
of study: they have passed out of memory, and they have
not got into the books. Of the well-informed young people
about us, there are very many who scarcely know who Lord
Althorp was.

And in another respect this biography has been unfortunate. It has been kept back too long. The Reform Act of 1867
has shed a painful light on the Reform Act of 1832, and has
exhibited in real life what philosophers said were its characteristic defects. While these lingered in the books they
were matters of dull teaching, and no one cared for them;
but now Mr Disraeli has embodied them, and they are living
among us. The traditional sing-song of mere eulogy is broken
by a sharp question. Those who study that time say, "Althorp,
you tell us, passed the Bill. It was his frankness and his high
character and the rest of his great qualities which did it. But
was it good that he should have passed it? Would it not have
been better if he had not possessed those fine qualities? Was
not some higher solution possible! Knowing this bill by its
fruits, largely good, but also largely evil, might we not have

had a better Bill? At any rate, if it could not be so, show *why*
it could not be so. Prove that the great defects in the Act of
1832 were necessary defects. Explain how it was that Althorp
had no choice, and then we will admire him as you wish us."
But to this biographer—a man of that time, then in the House
of Commons on the Whig side, and almost, as it were, on the
skirts of the Bill—such questions would have seemed impossible. To him, the Act of 1832 is still wonderful and perfect
—the great measure which *we* carried in *my* youth; and as for
explaining defects in it, he would have as soon thought of explaining defects in a revelation.

But if ever Lord Althorp's life is well written, it will, I
think, go far to explain not only why the Reform Bill was
carried, but why that Bill is what it was. He embodies all
the characteristic virtues which enable Englishmen to effect
well and easily great changes in politics: their essential fair-
ness, their "large roundabout common-sense," their courage,
and their disposition rather to give up something than to
take the uttermost farthing. But on the other hand also he
has all the characteristic English defects: their want of intellectual and guiding principle, their even completer want
of the culture which would give that principle, their absorption in the present difficulty, and their hand-to-mouth readiness to take what solves it without thinking of other consequences. And I am afraid the moral of those times is that
these English qualities as a whole—merits and defects together—are better suited to an early age of politics than to a
later. As long as materials are deficient, these qualities are
most successful in hitting off simple expedients in adapting
old things to new uses, and in extending ancient customs;
they are fit for instantaneous little creations, and admirable
at bit-by-bit growth. But when, by the incessant application
of centuries, these qualities have created an accumulated
mass of complex institutions, they are apt to fail, unless aided
by others very different. The instantaneous origination of obvious expedients is of no use when the field is already covered
with the heterogeneous growth of complex past expedients;
bit-by-bit development is out of place unless you are sure
which bit should, and which bit should not, be developed;
the extension of customs may easily mislead when there are
so many customs; no immense and involved subject can be
set right except by faculties which can grasp what is immense
and scrutinise what is involved. But mere common-sense is

here matched with more than it can comprehend, like a
schoolboy in the differential calculus;—and absorption in the
present difficulty is an evil, not a good, for what is wanted is
that you should be able to see many things at once, and take
in their bearing, not fasten yourself on one thing. The characteristic danger of great nations, like the Romans, or the
English, which have a long history of continuous creation, is
that they may at last fail from not comprehending the great
institutions which they have created.

No doubt it would be a great exaggeration to say that
this calamity happened in its fulness in the year 1832, and
it would be most unfair to Lord Althorp to cite him as a
complete example of the characteristics which may cause it;
but there was something in him of those qualities, and some
trace in 1832 of that calamity—enough in those cases to be
a warning. Only a complete history of the time can prove
this; but perhaps in a few pages I may a little explain and
illustrate it.

Let us first get, both as more instructive and as less tedious
than analysis, a picture of a man as he stood in the principal
event of his life. A good painter has thus painted him. Lord
Jeffrey, the great Edinburgh Reviewer, who was an able lawyer and practical man of business in his day, though his
criticism on poetry has not stood the test of time, was Lord
Advocate in the Reform Ministry of 1830, and he is never
tired of describing Lord Althorp. "There is something," he
writes, "to me quite delightful in his calm, clumsy, coura-
geous, immutable probity, and it seems to have a charm for
everybody." "I went to Althorp," he writes, "again, and had a
characteristic scene with that most honest, frank, true, and
stout-hearted of God's creatures. He had not come down-
stairs, and I was led up to his dressing-room, with his arms
(very rough and hairy) bare above the elbows, and his beard
half shaved and half staring through the lather, with a desperate razor in one hand, and a great soap-brush in the other.
He gave me the loose finger of his brush hand, and with the
usual twinkle of his bright eye and radiant smile, he said,
'You need not be anxious about your Scotch Bills to-night, for
we are no longer his Majesty's Ministers'." And soon after
he writes again, at a later stage of the ministerial crisis,
"When they came to summon Lord Althorp to a council on
the Duke's giving in, he was found in a shed with a groom,
busy oiling the locks of his fowling-pieces, and lamenting

the decay into which they had fallen during his Ministry".
And on another occasion he adds what may serve as an intellectual accompaniment to these descriptions: "Althorp,
with his usual frankness, gave us a pretended confession of
his political faith, and a sort of creed of his political morality,
and showed that though it was a very shocking doctrine to
promulgate, he must say that he had never sacrificed his own
inclinations to a sense of duty without repenting it, and always found himself more substantially unhappy for having
employed himself for the public good". And some one else
at the time said, "The Government cannot be going out, for
Althorp looks so very dismal". He was made (as we learn
from this volume) a principal Minister, contrary to his expectation and in opposition to his wish. He was always wanting to resign; he was always uncomfortable, if not wretched;
and the instant he could do so, he abandoned politics, and
would never touch them again, though he lived for many
years. And this, though in appearance he was most successful, and was almost idolised by his followers and friends.

At first this seems an exception to one of Nature's most
usual rules. Almost always, if she gives a great faculty she
gives also an enjoyment in the use of it. But here Nature had
given a remarkable power of ruling and influencing men—
one of the most remarkable (good observers seem to say)
given to any Englishman of that generation; and yet the
possessor did not like, but, on the contrary, much disliked to
use it. The explanation, however, is, that not only had Nature bestowed on Lord Althorp this happy and great gift of
directing and guiding men, but, as if by some subtle compensation, had added what was, under the circumstances, a
great pain to it. She had given him a most sluggish intellect
—only moving with effort, and almost with suffering—generally
moving clumsily, and usually following, not suggesting. If you
put a man with a mind like this—especially a sensitive, conscientious man such as Lord Althorp was—to guide men
quickly through complex problems of legislation and involved
matters of science, no wonder that he will be restive and
wish to give up. No doubt the multitude wish to follow him;
but where is he to tell the multitude to go? His mind suggests
nothing, and there is a pain and puzzle in his brain.

Fortune and education had combined in Lord Althorp's
case to develop his defects. His father and mother were both
persons of great cultivation, but they were also busy people

of the world, and so they left their son to pick up his education as he could. A Swiss footman, who did not know English very well, taught him to read, and "was his sole instructor and most intimate associate till he went to Harrow". His father, too, being a great fox-hunter, the son, as a young boy, clearly cared more for, and was more occupied with, hounds and animals, than anything else; and he lived mainly with servants and people also so occupied, from which, as might be expected, he contracted a shyness and awkwardness which stayed with him through life. When he went to Harrow, the previous deficiencies of his education were, of course, against him, and he seems to have shown no particular disposition to repair them. As far as can now be learnt, he was an ordinary strong-headed and strong-willed English boy, equal to necessary lessons, but not caring for them, and only distinguished from the rest by a certain suppressed sensibility and tenderness, which he also retained in after years, which softened a manliness that would otherwise have been rugged, and which saved him from being unrefined.

At Cambridge his mother, as it appears, suddenly, and for the first time, took an interest in his studies, and told him she should expect him to be high at his first college examination. And this seems to have awakened him to industry. The examination was in mathematics, which suited him much better than the Harrow classics, and he really came out high in it. The second year it was the same, though he had good competitors. But there his studies ended. His being a nobleman at that time excluded him from the university examinations, and he was far too apathetic to work at mathematics, except for something of the sort, and his tutor seems to have discouraged his doing so. Then, as since, the bane of Cambridge has been a certain incomplete and rather mean way of treating great studies, which teaches implicitly, if not plainly, that it is as absurd to learn the differential calculus in and for itself as it would be to keep a ledger for its own sake. On such a mind as Lord Althorp's, which required as much as possible to be awakened and kept awake to the interest of high studies, no external surroundings could have been more fatal. He threw up his reading and took to hounds, betting, and Newmarket, and to all which was then, even if not since, thought to be most natural, if not most proper, in a young nobleman.

As far as classical studies are concerned he probably lost

nothing. He was through life very opaque to literary interests, and in his letters and speeches always used language in the clumsiest way. But he had—perhaps from his childish field-sports—a keen taste for animals and natural history, which nowadays would have been developed into a serious pursuit. And as it was, he had an odd craving for figures, which might have been made something of in mathematics. "He kept," we are told, "an account of every shot he fired in the course of a year, whether he missed or killed, and made up the book periodically." He would not pass the accounts of the Agricultural Society without hunting for a missing threepence; and when Chancellor of the Exchequer, he used, it is said, "to do all his calculations, however complicated, alone in his closet," which his biographer thinks very admirable, and contrasts with the habit of Mr Pitt, "who used to take a Treasury clerk into his confidence," but which was really very absurd. It is not by such mechanical work that great Budgets are framed; and a great Minister ought to know what *not* to do himself, and how to use, for everything possible, the minds of others. Still there is much straightforward strength in this, if also some comic dulness.

If Lord Althorp's relatives did not give him a very good education, they did not make up for it by teaching him light accomplishments. They sent him the "grand tour," as it was then called; but he was shy and awkward, seems to have had no previous preparation for foreign society, would not go into it, and returned boasting that he could not speak French. His mother—a woman of great fashion and high culture—must have sighed very much over so uncourtly and so "English" an eldest son.

Then, in the easy way of those times—it was in 1804—he was brought into Parliament for Okehampton, a nomination borough, some "Mr Strange," a barrister, retiring in his favour, and his interest being strong, he was made a Lord of the Treasury. But the same apathy to intellectual interests which showed itself at college clung to him here also. He showed energy, but it was not the energy of a man of business. He passed, we are told, "the greatest part of his time in the country, and when he attended at the Treasury, which was very rarely, and only on particular occasions to make up a Board, he returned home immediately afterwards. Indeed, he used to have horses posted on the road from London to Althorp, and often rode down at night, as soon as the

House had risen, in order that he might hunt with the Pytchley the next morning." "On these occasions," says another
account, "he had no sleep, and often the hacks which he rode
would fall down on the road." And years afterwards the old
clerks at the office used to tell of the rarity and brevity of his
visits to the department, and of the difficulty of getting him
to stay;—all which shows force and character, but still not the
sort of character which would fit a man to be Chancellor of
the Exchequer. But though he had much of the want of culture, Lord Althorp had none of the unfeelingness which also
the modern world is getting somehow to attach to the character of the systematic sportsman. On the contrary, he was
one of the many instances which prove that this character
may be combined with an extreme sensibility to the suffering
of animals and man. He belonged to the class of men in
whom such feelings are far keener than usual, and his inner
character approached to the "Arnold type," "for to hear of
cruelty or injustice pained him" almost "like a blow".

He, it seems, kept a hunting journal, which tells how his
hounds found a fox at Parson's Hill, and "ran over old Naseby
field to Althorp in fifty minutes, and then, after a slight
check, over the finest part of Leicestershire"; and all that sort
of thing. But probably it does not tell one the very natural
consequence which happened to him from such a life. Being
a somewhat uncouth person, addicted to dogs and horses—a
"man's man," as Thackeray used to call it—he did not probably go much into ladies' society, and was not very aggressive
when he was there. But men who do not make advances to
women are apt to become victims to women who make advances to them; and so it was with Lord Althorp. He married
a Miss Acklom, a "Diana Vernon" sort of person, "rather
stout, and without pretension to regular beauty"; but nevertheless, it is said, "with something prepossessing about her
—clever, well-read, with a quick insight into the character of
others, and with much self-dependence". And this self-dependence and thought she showed to her great advantage in
the principal affair of her life. Lord Althorp's biographer is
sure, but does not say how, that the first declaration of love
was made by the lady; he was, it seems, too shy to think of
such a thing. As a rule, marriages in which a young nobleman
is actively captured by an aggressive lady are not domestically
happy, though they may be socially useful, but in this case
the happiness seems to have been exceptionally great; and

when she died, after a few years, he suffered a very unusual grief. "He went," we are told, "at once to Winton, the place where he had lived with her, and passed several months in complete retirement, finding his chief occupation in reading the Bible," in which he found, at first, many grave difficulties, such as the mention of the constellation "Orion" by the prophet Amos, and the high place (an equality with Job and David) given by Ezekiel to the prophet Daniel when still a young man, "and before he had proved himself to be a man of so great a calibre as he certainly did afterwards". On these questions, he adds, "I have consulted a Mr Shepherd, the clergyman here, but his answers are not satisfactory". Happily, however, such a man is not at the mercy of clergymen's answers, nor dependent on the petty details of ancient prophets. The same sensibility which made him keenly alive to justice and injustice in things of this world, went further, and told him of a moral government in things not of this world. No man of or near the Arnold species was ever a sceptic as to, far less an unbeliever in, ultimate religion. New philosophies are not wanted or appreciated by such men, nor are book-arguments of any real use, though these men often plod over them as if they were; for in truth an inner teaching supersedes everything, and for good or evil closes the controversy; no discussion is of any effect or force; the court of appeal, fixed by nature in such minds, is peremptory in belief, and will not hear of any doubt. And so it was in this case. Through life Lord Althorp continued to be a man strong, though perhaps a little crude, in religious belief; and thus gained at the back of his mind a solid seriousness which went well with all the rest of it. And his grief for his wife was almost equally durable. He gave up not only society, which perhaps was no great trial, but also hunting—not because he believed it to be wrong, but because he did not think it seemly or suitable that a man after such a loss should be so very happy as he knew that hunting would make him.

Soon after his marriage he had begun to take an interest in politics, especially on their moral side, and of course the increased seriousness of his character greatly augmented it. Without this change, though he might have thought himself likely to be occasionally useful in outlying political questions, probably he would have had no grave political career, and his life never would have been written. But the sort of interest which he took in politics requires some explanation, for though his time was not very long ago, the change of feeling since then is vast.

"If any person," said Sir Samuel Romilly, the best of judges, for he lived through the times and was mixed up, heart and soul, in the matters he speaks of, "if any person be desirous of having an adequate idea of the mischievous effects which have been produced in this country by the French Revolution and all its attendant horrors, he should attempt some reforms on humane and liberal principles. He will then find not only what a stupid spirit of conservation, but what a savage spirit, it has infused into the minds of his countrymen." And very naturally, for nothing is so cruel as fear. A whole generation in England, and indeed in Europe, was so frightened by the Reign of Terror, that they thought it could only be prevented by another Reign of Terror. The Holy Alliances, as they were then called, meant this and worked for this. Though we had not in name such an alliance in England, we had a state of opinion which did the work of one without one. Nine-tenths of the English people were above all things determined to put down "French principles"; and unhappily "French principles" included what we should all now consider obvious improvements and rational reforms. They would not allow the most cruel penal code which any nation ever had to be mitigated; they did not wish justice to be questioned; they would not let the mass of the people be educated, or at least only so that it came to nothing; they would not alter anything which came down from their ancestors, for in their terror they did not know but there might be some charmed value even in the most insignificant thing; and after what they had seen happen in France, they feared that if they changed a single iota all else would collapse.

Upon this generation, too, came the war passion. They waged, and in the main—though with many errors—waged with power and spirit, the war with Napoleon; and they connected this with their horror of liberal principles in a way which is now very strange to us, but which was very powerful then. We know now that Napoleon was the head of a conservative reaction, a bitter and unfeeling reaction, just like that of the contemporary English; but the contemporary English did not know this. To the masses of them he was *Robespierre à cheval*, as some one called him—a sort of Jacobin waging war, in some occult way, for liberty and revolution, though he called himself Emperor. Of course, the educated few gradually got more or less to know that Napoleon hated Jacobins and revolution, and liberty too, as much as it is possible to hate them; but the ordinary multitude, up to the end of the struggle never dreamed of it. Thus, in an odd way, the war passion of the time strengthened its conservative feeling; and in a much more usual way it did so too, for it absorbed men's minds in the story of battles and the glory of victories, and left no unoccupied thought for gradual improvement and dull reform at home. A war time, also, is naturally a harsh time; for the tale of conflicts which sometimes raises men from pain, also tends to make men indifferent to it: the familiarity of the idea ennobles but also hardens.

This savageness of spirit was the more important because, from deep and powerful economical agencies, there was an incessant distress running through society, sometimes less and sometimes more, but always, as we should now reckon, very great. The greatest cause of this was that we were carrying on, or trying to carry on, a system of Free Trade under a restrictive tariff: we would not take foreign products, and yet we wished to sell foreigners ours. And our home market was incessantly disordered. First the war, and then the corn-laws, confined us chiefly to our own soil for our food; but that soil was of course liable to fail in particular years, and then the price of food rose rapidly, which threw all other markets into confusion—for people must live first, and can only spend the surplus, after paying the cost of living, upon anything else. The fluctuations in the demand for our manufactures at home were ruinously great, though we were doing all we could to keep them out of foreign markets, and the combined effect was terrible. And the next great cause was that we were daily extending an unprecedented system of credit without providing a basis for it, and without knowing how to manage it. There was no clear notion that credit, being a promise to pay cash, must be supported by proportionate reserves of cash held in store; and that as bullion is the international cash, all international credit must be sustained by a store of bullion. In consequence, all changes for the worse in trade, whether brought on by law or nature, caused a destruction of confidence, and diffused an uneasy moral feeling which made them far worse than they would have been otherwise. The immense fluctuations in our commerce, caused by Protection, were aggravated by immense fluctuations in our credit, and the combined result was unspeakably disastrous.

During the French war these causes were not so much felt. Trade was better, because we were creating a foreign market for ourselves. Just as lately, by lending to a miscellaneous mass of foreign countries, we enabled those countries to buy of us, so in the great war, by large subsidies and huge foreign expenditure, we created a "purchasing power" which was ultimately settled by our manufactures. We had nothing else to settle it with; if we did not send them direct, we must use them to buy the bullion, or whatever else it might be which we did send indirectly. This "war demand," of which so much is said in the economical literature of those years, of course ceased at the peace; and as we declined to take foreign products in exchange for ours, no substitute for it could be found, and trade languished in consequence. Agriculture, too, was worse after the peace, for the natural protection given by the war was far more effective than the artificial protection given by the corn-laws. The war kept out corn almost equally whatever was the price, but the corn-laws were based on the "sliding scale," which let in the corn when it became dear. Our farmers, therefore, were encouraged to grow more corn than was enough for the country in good years, which they could not sell; and they did not get a full price in bad years, for the foreign corn came in more and more as the price rose and rose. Though the protection availed to hurt the manufacturer, it was not effectual in helping the farmer. And the constant adversity of other interests, by a reflex action, also hurt him. Committees on agricultural distress, and motions as to the relief of trading distress, alternate in the Parliamentary debates of those years. Our credit system, too, was in greater momentary danger after the peace than before; for during the war it was aided by a currency of inconvertible paper, which absolved us from the necessity of paying our promises in solid cash, though at very heavy cost in other ways, both at the instant and afterwards.

These fluctuations in trade and agriculture of course told on the condition of the working classes. They were constantly suffering, and then the "savage spirit" of which Sir Samuel has spoken showed itself at its worst. Suffering, as usual, caused complaint, and this complaint was called sedition. The Habeas Corpus Act was suspended, harsh laws were passed, and a harsher administration incited to put it down. It could not be put down. It incessantly smouldered and incessantly broke out, and for years England was filled with the fear of violence, first by the breakers of the law and then by the enforcers of it.

Resistance to such a policy as this was most congenial to a nature half unhinged by misfortune, and always in itself most sensitive and opposed to injustice. Even before his wife's death, Lord Althorp had begun to exert himself against it, and afterwards he threw the whole vigour not only of his mind but of his body into it. So far from running away perpetually to hunt, as in old times, he was so constant in his attendance in Parliament that tradition says hardly any one, except the clerks at the table, was more constantly to be seen there. He opposed all the Acts by which the Tory Government of the day tried to put down disaffection instead of curing it, and his manly energy soon made him a sort of power in Parliament. He was always there, always saying what was clear, strong, and manly; and therefore the loosely-knit Opposition of that day was often guided by him; and the Ministers, though strong in numerical majority, feared him, for he said things that the best of that majority understood in a rugged English way, which changed feelings, even if it did not alter votes. He was a man whom every one in the House respected, and who therefore spoke to prepossessed hearers. No doubt, too, the peculiar tinge which grief had given to his character added to his influence. He took no share in the pleasures of other men. Though a nobleman of the highest place, still young, as we should now reckon (he was only thirty-six when Lady Althorp died), he stood aloof from society, which courted him, and lived for public business only; and therefore he had great weight in it, for the English very much value obviously conscientious service, and the sobered fox-hunter was a somewhat interesting character.

He had not indeed any clear ideas of the cause of the difficulties of the time, or of the remedies for them. He did no doubt attend much to economical questions; and his taste for figures, shown before in calculating the ratio of his good shots to his bad, made statistical tables even pleasing to him. His strong sense, though without culture and without originality, struggled dimly and sluggishly with the necessary problems. But considering that he lived in the days of Huskisson and Ricardo, his commercial ideas are crude and heavy. He got as far as the notion that the substitution of direct taxes for the bad tariff of those days would be "a good measure"; but when he came to apply the principle he failed from inability to work it out. Nor did years of discussion effectually teach him. In his great Budget of 1832—the first which the Whigs had made for many years, and at which therefore every one looked with unusual expectation—he proposed to take off a duty on tobacco and to replace it by a tax on the transfer of real and funded property, together with a tax on the import of raw cotton; and it was the necessity of having to withdraw the larger part of this plan, that more than anything else first gave the Whigs that character for financial incapacity which clung to them so long. A crude good sense goes no way in such problems, and it is useless to apply it to them. The other economical problem of the time, how to lay a satisfactory basis for our credit, Lord Althorp was still less able to solve, and excusably so; for the experience which has since taught us so much did not exist, and the best theories then known were very imperfect. The whole subject was then encumbered with what was called the "currency question," and on this Lord Althorp's views were fairly sensible, but no more.

I have said what may seem too much of the distresses of the country fifty or sixty years ago, not only because the mode in which he dealt with them is the best possible illustration of Lord Althorp's character, but also because some knowledge of them is necessary to an understanding of "Parliamentary reform," as it was in his time, on account of which alone any one now cares for him. The "bill," if I may say so, for these miseries of the country was sent in to the old system of Parliamentary representation; and very naturally. The defenders of that system of necessity conceded that it was anomalous, complex, and such as it would have been impossible to set up *de novo*. But they argued that it was practically successful, worked well, and promoted the happiness of the people better than any other probably would. And to this the inevitable rejoinder at the time was: "The system does not work well; the country is not happy; if your system is as you say to be judged by its fruits, that system is a bad system, for its fruits are bad, and the consequences everywhere to be seen in the misery around us". Upon many English minds which would have cared nothing for an argument of theoretical completeness, this "practical" way of arguing, as it was called, pressed with irresistible strength.

The unpopularity was greater because a new generation was growing up with other "thoughts" and other "minds" than that

which had preceded it. Between 1828 and 1830 a new race
came to influence public affairs, who did not remember the
horrors of the French Revolution, and who had been teased
to death by hearing their parents talk about them. The harsh
and cruel spirit which those horrors had awakened in their
contemporaries became itself, by the natural law of reaction,
an object of disgust and almost of horror to the next generation. When it was said that the old structure of Parliament
worked well, this new race looked not only at the evident
evils amid which they lived, but at the oppressive laws and
administrations by which their fathers had tried to cure those
evils; and they "debited" both to the account of the old Parliament. It was made responsible for the mistaken treatment
as well as for the deep-rooted disease, and so the gravest
clouds hang over it.

The Duke of Wellington, too (the most unsuccessful of
premiers as well as the most successful of generals), broke the
Tory party—the natural party to support this system—into
fragments. With a wise renunciation both of his old principles and of his fixed prejudices, he had granted "Catholic
Emancipation," and so offended the older and stricter part of
his followers. They accused him of treachery, and hated him
with a hatred of which in this quiet age, when political passion is feeble, we can hardly form an idea. And he then quarrelled, also, with the best of the moderate Right—Mr Huskisson and the Canningites. He had disliked Mr Canning
personally when alive, he hated still more the liberal principles which he had begun to introduce into our foreign policy, and he was an eager, despotic man, who disliked difference of opinion; so just when he had broken with the most
irrational section of his party, he broke with its most rational
members too, and left himself very weak. No one so much,
though without meaning it, aided the cause of Parliamentary
change, for he divided and enfeebled the supporters of the
old system; he took away the question of Catholic Emancipation which before filled the public mind; and he intensified
the unpopularity of all he touched by the idea of a "military
premier," for which we should not care now, but which was
odious and terrible then, when men still feared oppression
from the Government.

Upon minds thus predisposed, the French Revolution of
1830 broke with magical power. To the young generation it
seemed like the fulfilment of their dreams,

—*"The meagre, stale, forbidding ways*
Of custom, law, and statute, took at once
The attraction of a country in Romance,"

and there came upon them eager thoughts that they might still be

—*"called upon to exercise their skill*
Not in Utopia, subterranean fields,
Or some secreted island, heaven knows where,
But in the very world, which is the world
Of all of us".[2]

And even to soberer persons this new revolution seemed to prove that change, even great change, was not so mischievous as had been said—that the good of 1789 might be gained without the evil, and that it was absurd not to try reform when the unreformed world contained so much which was miserable and so much which was difficult to bear. Even a strong Tory Ministry might have been overthrown, so great was the force of this sudden sentiment; the feeble Ministry of the Duke of Wellington fell at once before it, and the Whigs were called to power.

Their first act was to frame a plan of Parliamentary reform, and that which they constructed was many times larger than anything which any one expected from them. All those who remember those times say that when they heard what was proposed they could hardly believe their ears. And when it was explained to the House of Commons, the confusion, the perplexity, and the consternation were very great. Reform naturally was much less popular in the assembly to be reformed than it was elsewhere. The general opinion was that if Sir Robert Peel had risen at once and denounced the Bill as destructive and revolutionary he might have prevented its being brought in. Another common opinion in the House was that the "Whigs would go out next morning". But the Bill had been framed by one who, with whatever other shortcomings and defects, has ever had a shrewd eye for the probable course of public opinion. "I told Lord Grey," says Lord Russell, "that none but a large measure would be a safe measure." And accordingly, as soon as its provisions came to be comprehended by the country, there was perhaps the greatest burst of enthusiasm which England has ever seen (certainly the

2 Wordsworth's *Prelude.*

greatest enthusiasm for a law, though that for a favourite person may sometimes have risen as high or higher). A later satirist has spoken of it as the "Great Bill for giving everybody everything," and everybody almost seems to have been as much in favour of it as if they were to gain everything by it. Agricultural counties were as eager as manufacturing towns; men who had always been Tories before were as warm as Liberals. The country would have "the Bill, the whole Bill, and nothing but the Bill".

But this enthusiasm did not of itself secure the passing of the Bill. There were many obstacles in the way which it took months to overcome, and which often made many despair. First, the Bill was not one of which the political world itself strongly approved; on the contrary, if left to itself, that world would probably have altogether rejected it. It was imposed by the uninitiated on the initiated, by the many on the few; and inevitably those who were compelled to take it did not like it. Then, the vast proposals of the Ministry deeply affected many private interests. In 1858 I heard an able politician say, "The best way for a Government to turn itself out is to bring in a Reform Bill; the number of persons whom every such bill must offend is very great, and they are sure to combine together, not on Reform, but on something else, and so turn out the Government". And if there was serious danger to a Ministry which ventured to propose such petty reforms as were thought of in 1858, we can imagine the magnitude of the danger which the Ministry of 1832 incurred from the great measure they then brought in. One member, indeed, rose and said, "I am the proprietor of Ludgershall, I am the member for Ludgershall, I am the constituency of Ludgershall, and in all three capacities I assent to the disfranchisement of Ludgershall". But the number of persons who were so disinterested was small. The Bill of 1832 affected the franchise of every constituency, and, therefore, the seat of every member; it abolished the seats of many, and destroyed the right of nomination to seats also possessed by many; and nothing could be more repugnant to the inclinations of most. A House of Commons with such a Bill before it was inevitably captious, unruly, and difficult to guide. And even if there had been or could have been a House of Commons which at heart liked the Bill, there would still have been the difficulty that many other people then most influential did not much like it. A great many members of the Cabinet which proposed it,

though they believed it to be necessary, did not think it to
be desirable. The country would have some such measure,
and therefore they proposed this. "Lord Palmerston and Mr
Grant," says Lord Russell, "had followed Mr Canning in his
opposition to Parliamentary Reform. Lord Lansdowne and
Lord Holland had never been very eager on the subject." Lord
Brougham did not approve of the disfranchisement of nearly
so many boroughs, and others of the Cabinet were much of
the same mind. Their opinion was always dubious, their action often reluctant, and, according to Mr Greville, some of
the most influential of them, being very sensitive to the public
opinion of select political society, were soon "heartily ashamed
of the whole thing".

The House of Lords, too, was adverse, not only as an assembly of men mostly rich and past middle age is ever adverse to great political change, or as a privileged assembly is
always hostile to any movement which may destroy it, but for
a reason peculiar to itself. The English House of Lords, as
we all know, is not a rigid body of fixed number like the upper
chambers of book constitutions, but an elastic body of unfixed number. The Crown can add to its members when it
pleases and as it pleases. And in various ways which I need not
enumerate now, this elasticity of structure has been of much
use, but in one way it does much harm. The Crown for this
purpose means the Ministry; the Ministry is appointed by a
party, and is the agent of that party, and therefore it makes
peers from its own friends all but exclusively. Under a Tory
Government more than nine-tenths of the new peers will be
Tory; under a Whig Government more than nine-tenths will
be Whig; and if for a long course of years either party has
been continuously, or nearly so, in power, the House of Lords
will be filled with new members belonging to it. And this is
a serious inconvenience, because the longer any party has been
thus in power, the more likely it is to have to go out and lose
power; and the new Ministry which comes in, and the new
mode of thought which that Ministry embodies, finds itself
face to face with a House of Peers embodying an antagonistic
mode of thought, and one formed by its enemies. In 1831
this was so; for the Tories had been in office almost without a
break since 1784, had created peers profusely, who were all
Tories, and added the Irish elective peers, who, from the
mode of election, were all Tories too. In consequence, the
reform movement of 1831 and 1832 found itself obstinately

opposed to a hostile House of Lords, whose antagonism aided the reluctance diffused through the House of Commons, and fostered the faintheartedness common in the Cabinet. The King, too, who had begun by being much in favour of reform, gradually grew frightened. His correspondence with Lord Grey gives a vivid picture of a well-meaning, but irresolute man, who is much in the power of the last speaker, who at last can be securely relied on by no one, and who gives incessant (and as it seems unnecessary) trouble to those about him. The rising republicanism of the day will find in these letters much to serve it; for, however convinced one may be, on general grounds, that English royalty was necessary to English freedom at that time, it is impossible not to be impatient at seeing how, month after month in a great crisis, when there was so much else to cause anxiety and create confusion, one stupid old man should have been able to add so much to both.

And all through the struggle the two effects of the new French Revolution were contending with one another. Just as it aroused in young and sanguine minds (and the majority of the country was just then disposed to be sanguine) the warmest hopes, in minds oppositely predisposed it aroused every kind of fear. Old and timid people thought we should soon have in England "Robespierre and the guillotine". Indeed, in a way that is rather amusing now to consider, the French horrors of 1793 are turned into a kind of intellectual shuttlecock by two disputants. One says, "See what comes of making rash changes, how many crimes they engender, and how many lives they lose!" "No," replies the other; "see what comes of not making changes till too late, for it was delay of change, and resistance to change, which caused those crimes and horrors." Nor were these unreal words of mere rhetoric. They told much on many minds; for what France had done and would do then naturally filled an immense space in men's attention, as for so many years not long since, Europe had been divided into France and anti-France.

With all these obstacles in its way, the Ministry of 1831 had the greatest difficulty in carrying the Reform Bill. I have not space to narrate, even in the briefest way, the troubled history of their doing so. Parliamentary debates are generally dull in the narration; but so great was the excitement, and so many were the relieving circumstances, that an accomplished historian will be able to make posterity take some sort of exceptional interest in these. The credit of the victory, such

as it is, must be divided between many persons. Lord Grey
managed the King, and stood first in the eye of the country;
Lord Russell contributed the first sketch of the Bill, containing all its essential features, both good and bad, and he introduced the first Bill into the House of Commons; the late
Lord Derby then first showed his powers as a great debater.
But the best observers say that Lord Althorp carried the Bill:
he was leader of the House at the time, and the main strain
of ruling one of the most troubled of Parliaments was on
him. His biographer, Sir Denis Le Marchant, who was present
at the debates, says:—

> "Lord Althorp's capacity as a leader had been severely
> tested throughout this tremendous struggle, and it extorted
> the praise even of his political opponents. I recollect Sir
> Henry Hardinge saying, 'It was Althorp carried the Bill.
> His fine temper did it. And in answer to a most able and
> argumentative speech of Crocker, he rose and merely said
> that "he had made some calculations which he considered
> as entirely conclusive in refutation of the right honourable
> gentleman's arguments which he had mislaid, but if the
> House would be guided by his advice they would reject
> the amendment,"—which they accordingly did. There is no
> standing against such influence as this.' The Whigs as-
> cribed Lord Althorp's influence not to his temper alone,
> but to the confidence felt by the House in his integrity
> and sound judgment, an opinion so universal that Lord
> Grey was induced by it to press upon him a peerage, that
> he might take charge of the Bill in the committee of the
> Lords; and the design was abandoned not from any hesi-
> tation or unwillingness on the part of Lord Althorp, but
> from the difficulty of finding a successor to him in the
> Commons."[3]

So bad a speaker, with so slow a mind, has never received
so great a compliment in a scene where quickness and oratory
seem at first sight to be the most absolutely requisite of qualities. But it is no doubt a great mistake to imagine that these
qualities are the true essentials to success of this kind. A very
shrewd living judge says, after careful reflection, that they
are even hurtful. "A man," says Mr Massey in his history,
"who speaks seldom, and who speaks ill, is the best leader
of the House of Commons." And no doubt the slow-speeched

[3] *Memoir*, chap. xix.

English gentleman rather sympathises with slow speech in others. Besides, a quick and brilliant leader is apt to be always speaking, whereas a leader should interfere only when necessary, and be therefore felt as a higher force when he does so. His mind ought to be like a reserve fund—not invested in showy securities, but sure to be come at when wanted, and always of staple value. And this Lord Althorp's mind was; there was not an epigram in the whole of it; everything was solid and ordinary. Men seem to have trusted him much as they trust a faithful animal, entirely believing that he would not deceive if he could, and that he could not if he would.

But what, then, was this great "Bill"—which it was so great an achievement to pass? Unfortunately, this is not an easy question to answer shortly. The "Bill" destroyed many old things and altered many old things, and we cannot understand its effects except in so far as we know what these old things were.

"A variety of rights of suffrage," said Sir James Mackintosh, "is the principle of the English representation." How that variety began is not at all to the present purpose; it grew as all English things grow—by day-by-day alterations from small beginnings; and the final product was very different from the first beginning, as well as from any design which ever at any one time entered any one's mind. There always was a great contrast between the mode of representation in boroughs and in counties, because there was a great contrast in social structure between them. The "knight of the shire" was differently chosen from the "burgess of the town," because the "shire" was a different sort of place from the "town" and the same people could not have chosen for the two—the same people not existing in the two. The borough representations of England, too, "struggled up"—there is hardly any other word to describe it—in a most irregular manner. The number of towns which sent representatives is scarcely ever the same in any two of our oldest Parliaments. The sheriff had a certain discretion, for the writ only told him to convene "de quolibet burgo duos burgenses," and did not name any towns in particular. Most towns then disliked the duty and evaded it, if possible, which seems to have augmented the sheriff's power, for he could permit or prevent the evasion as much as he chose. And at a very early period great differences grew up between the ways of election in the towns which were always represented. There seems to have been a kind of "natural selection"; the most powerful class in each borough chose if it could at each election, and if any class long continued the most powerful, it then acquired customary rights of election which came to be unalterable. Nor was there any good deciding authority to regulate this confusion. The judge of elections was the "House of Commons" itself, and it often decided not according to law or evidence, but as political or personal influence dictated. And rights of election thus capriciously recognised became binding on the borough for ever. As might be expected, the total result was excessively miscellaneous. The following are the franchises of the boroughs in two counties as legislators of 1832 found them.

SOMERSETSHIRE.

BRISTOL	Freeholders of 40s., and free burgesses.
BATH	Mayor, aldermen, and common councilmen only.
WELLS	Mayor, masters, burgesses, and freemen of the seven trading companies of the said city.
TAUNTON	Potwallers not receiving alms or charity.
BRIDGWATER	Mayor, alderman, and twenty-four capital burgesses of the borough paying scot and lot.
ILCHESTER	Alleged to be the inhabitants of the said town paying scot and lot, which the town called potwallers.
MINEHEAD	The parishioners of Dunster and Minehead, being housekeepers in the borough of Minehead, and not receiving alms.
MILBORN PORT	The capital bailiffs and their deputies, the number of bailiffs being nine, and their deputies being two; in the commonalty, stewards, their number being two; and the inhabitants thereof paying scot and lot.

LANCASHIRE.

LANCASHIRE	Freemen only.
WIGAN	Free burgesses.
CLITHEROE	Freeholders resident and non-resident.
LIVERPOOL	Mayor, bailiffs, and freemen not receiving alms.
PRESTON	All the inhabitants.

Nothing could be more certain than that a system which was constructed in this manner must sooner or later need great alteration. Institutions which have grown from the beginning by adaptation may last as long as any, if they continue to possess the power of adaptation. The force which created them still exists to preserve them. But in this case the power of adaptation was gone. A system of representation made without design was fixed as eternal upon a changing nation, and somehow or other it was sure to become unsuitable. Nothing could be more false in essence than the old anti-reform arguments as far as they affected the "wisdom of our ancestors"; for the characteristic method of our ancestors had been departed from. Our ancestors changed what they wanted bit by bit, just when and just as they wanted. But their descendants were forbidden to do so; they were asked to be content not only with old clothes, but with much-patched old clothes, which they were denied the power to patch again. And this sooner or later they were sure to refuse.

In 1832 a grave necessity existed for changing it. The rude principle of natural selection by which it had been made, ensured that, at least approximately, the classes most influential in the nation would have a proportionate power in the legislation; no great class was likely to be denied anything approaching to its just weight. But now that a system framed in one age was to be made to continue unchanged through after ages, there was no such security. On the contrary, the longer the system went on without change the more sure it was to need change. Some new class was sure in course of time to grow up for which the fixed system provided no adequate representatives; and the longer that system continued fixed, the surer was this to happen, and the stronger was it likely that this class would be. In 1832, such a class had arisen of the first magnitude. The trading wealth of the country had created a new world which had no voice in Parliament comparable to that which it had in the country. Not only were some of the greatest towns, like Birmingham and Manchester, left without any members at all, but in most other towns the best of the middle class felt that they had no adequate power: they were either extinguished by a franchise too exclusive, or swamped by one too diffused; either way, they were powerless.

There was equal reason to believe that, by the same inevitable course of events, some class would come to have more power in Parliament than it should. The influence which gave

the various classes their authority at the time in which the
machinery of our representation was framed, would be sure
in time to ebb away, wholly or in part, from some of them.
And in matter of fact they did so. The richer nobility and the
richer commoners had come to have much more power than
they ought. The process of letting the most influential people
in a borough choose its members, amounted in time to letting
the great nobleman or great commoner to whom the property
of the town belonged, choose them. And many counties had
fallen into the direction of the same hands also, so that it
was calculated, if not with truth, at any rate with an approach
to it, that one hundred and seventy-seven lords and gentlemen chose as many as three hundred and fifty-five English
members of Parliament. The Parliamentary power of these
few rich peers and squires was much too great when compared with their share in the life of the nation, just as that
of the trading class was too weak; the excess of the one made
the deficiency of the other additionally difficult to bear; and
the contrast was more than ever galling in the years from
1830 to 1832, because just then the new French Revolution
had revived the feud between the privileged classes and the
non-privileged. The excessive Parliamentary power of these
few persons had before been a yoke daily becoming heavier
and heavier, and now it could be endured no longer.

The "Reform Bill" amended all this. It abolished a multitude of nomination boroughs, gave members to large towns
and cities, and changed the franchise, so that in all boroughs,
at any rate, the middle classes obtained predominant power.
And no one can deny that the good so done was immense;
indeed, no one does now deny it, for the generation of Tories
that did so has passed away. No doubt the Reform Act did
not produce of itself at once the new heaven and new earth
which its more ardent supporters expected of it. It did nothing to remove the worst evils from which the country suffered,
for those evils were not political but economical; and the
classes whom it enfranchised were not more economically instructed than those whom they superseded. The doctrine of
Protection then reigned all through the nation, and while it
did so no real cure for those evils was possible. But this Act,
coming as it did when a new political generation was prepared to make use of it, got rid entirely of the "cruel spirit"
by which our distresses had been repressed before, and which
was as great an evil as those distresses themselves, introduced

many improvements—municipal reform, tithe reform, and
such like—in which the business-like habit of mind due to
the greater power of the working classes mainly helped and
diffused a sweeter and better spirit through society.

But these benefits were purchased at a price of the first
magnitude, though, from the nature of it, its payment was
long deferred. The reformers of 1832 dealt with the evils
of their time, as they would have said, in an English way,
and without much thinking of anything else. And exactly in
that English way, as they had under their hands a most curious political machine which had grown without design, and
which produced many very valuable, though not very visible
effects they, without thought, injured and destroyed some of
the best parts of it.

First, the old system of representation, as we have seen,
was based on a variety of franchises. But, in order to augment
the influence of the middle class, the reformers of 1832 destroyed that variety; they introduced into every borough the
£10 household franchise, and with a slight exception, which
we need not take account of, made that franchise the only
one in all boroughs. They raised the standard in the boroughs
in which it was lower than £10, and lowered it in those where
it was higher; and in this way they changed the cardinal principle of the system which they found established, for uniformity as the rule, instead of variety.

And this worked well enough at first, for there was not for
some years after 1832 much wish for any more change in our
constituencies. But in our own time we have seen the harm
of it. If you establish any uniform franchise in a country,
then it at once becomes a question, What sort of franchise is
it to be? Those under it will say that they are most unjustly
excluded; they will deny that there is any real difference between themselves and those above; they will show without
difficulty that some whom the chosen line leaves out, are even
better than those whom it takes in. And they will raise the
cry so familiar in our ears—the cry of class legislation. They
will say, Who are these ten-pound householders, these arbi-
trarily chosen middle-class men, that they should be sole electors? Why should they be alone enfranchised and all others
practically disfranchised, either by being swamped by their
more numerous votes or by not having votes at all? The case
is the stronger because one of the most ancient functions of
Parliament, and especially the Commons' House of Parlia-

ment, is the reformation of grievances. This suited very well
with the old system of variety; in that miscellaneous collection of constituencies every class was sure to have some members who represented it. There were then working-class constituencies sending members to speak for them—"men," says
Mackintosh, "of popular talents, principles, and feelings;
quick in suspecting oppression, bold in resisting it, not thinking favourably of the powerful; listening almost with credulity
to the complaints of the humble and the feeble, and impelled by ambition when they are not prompted by generosity
to be defenders of the defenceless". And in cases of popular
excitement, especially of erroneous excitement, this plan ensured that it should have adequate expression, and so soon
made it calm. But the legislation of 1832 destroyed these
working men's constituencies; "they put the country," as it
was said afterwards, "under ten-pounders only". And in consequence there are in our boroughs now nothing but working-
class constituencies; there are no longer any ten-pound householders at all. There is throughout our boroughs a uniform
sort of franchise, and that the worst sort—a franchise which
gives the predominance to the most ignorant and the least
competent, if they choose to use it. The middle classes have
as little power as they had before 1832, and the only difference is, that before 1832 they were ruled by those who were
richer than themselves, and now they are ruled by those who
are poorer.

No doubt there is still an inequality in the franchise between counties and boroughs—the sole remnant of the variety
of our ancient system. But that inequality is much more difficult to defend now when it stands alone, than it was in old
times when it was one of many. And the "ugly rush" of the
lower orders, which has effaced the "hard and fast" line established in 1832, threatens to destroy this remnant of variety. In a few years probably there will be but one sort of
franchise throughout all England, and the characteristic work
of 1832 will be completely undone; the middle classes, whose
intelligence Macaulay praised, and to whom he helped to
give so much power, will have had all that power taken away
from them.

No doubt, too, there is still a real inequality of influence,
though there is an even equality of franchise. The difference
of size between different boroughs gives more power to those
in the small boroughs than to those in the large. And this is

very valuable, for elections for large boroughs are costly, and entail much labour that is most disagreeable. But here, again, the vicious precedent of establishing uniformity set in 1832 is becoming excessively dangerous. Being so much used to it people expect to see it everywhere. There is much risk that before long there may be only one sort of vote and only one size of constituency all over England, and then the reign of monotony will be complete.

And, secondly, the reformers of 1832 committed an almost worse error in destroying one kind of select constituency without creating an intellectual equivalent. We are not used nowadays to think of nomination boroughs* as select constituencies, but such, in truth, they were, and such they proved themselves to be at, perhaps, the most critical period of English history. Lord Russell, no favourable judge, tells us "that it enabled Sir Robert Walpole to consolidate the throne of the House of Hanover amid external and internal dangers". No democratic suffrage could then have been relied on for that purpose, for the mass of Englishmen were then more or less attached to their hereditary king, and they might easily have been induced to restore him. They had not, indeed, a fanatical passion of loyalty towards him, nor any sentiment which would make them brave many dangers on his behalf; but there was much sluggish and sullen prejudice which might have been easily aroused to see that he had his rights, and there were many relics of ancient loyal zeal which might have combined with that prejudice and ennobled it. Nor did the people of that day much care for what we should now call Parliamentary government. The educated opinion of that day was strongly in favour of the House of Hanover; but the numerical majority of the nation was not equally so; perhaps it would have preferred the House of Stuart. But the higher nobility and the richer gentry possessed a great power over the opinions of Parliament because many boroughs were subject to their control, and by exerting that power they, in conjunction with the trading classes, who were then much too weak to have moved by themselves, fixed the House of Hanover on the throne, and so settled the freedom of England. These boroughs at that time, for this purpose being select constituencies, were of inestimable

* Nomination boroughs were these in which the nomination was controlled, or virtually owned, by a single person or family. —Ed.

value, because they enabled the most competent opinion in England to rule without dispute, when, under any system of diffused suffrage, that opinion would either have been outvoted or almost so.

And to the last these boroughs retained much of this peculiar merit. They were an organ for what may be called specialised political thought, for trained intelligence busy with public affairs. Not only did they bring into Parliament men of genius and ability, but they kept together a higher political world capable of appreciating that genius and ability when young, and of learning from it when old. The Whig party, such as it was in those days especially, rested on this Parliamentary power. In them was a combination of more or less intelligent noblemen of liberal ideas and aims, who chose such men as Burke, and Brougham, and Hume, and at last Macaulay, to develop those ideas and to help to attain those aims. If they had not possessed this peculiar power, they would have had no such intellectual influence; they would have simply been gentlemen of what we now think good ideas, with no special means of advancing them. And they would not have been so closely combined together as they were; they would have been scattered persons of political intelligence. But having this power they combined together, lived together, thought together; and the society thus formed was enriched and educated by the men of genius whom it selected as instruments, and in whom in fact it found teachers. And there was something like it on the Government side, though the long possession of power, and perhaps the nature of Toryism, somewhat modified its characteristics.

The effect is to be read in the Parliamentary debates of those times. Probably they are absolutely better than our own. They are intrinsically a better discussion of the subjects of their day than ours are of our subjects. But however this may be, they are beyond question relatively better. General knowledge of politics has greatly improved in the last fifty years, and the best political thought of the present day is much superior to any which there was then. So that, even if our present Parliamentary debates retained the level of their former excellence they would still not bear the same relation to the best thought of the present, that the old ones bear to the best thought of the past. And if the debates have really fallen off much (as I am sure they have), this conclusion will be stronger and more certain.

Nor is this to be wondered at. If you lessen the cause you will lessen the effect too. Not only are the men whom these select constituencies brought into Parliament not now to be found there, but the society which formed those constituencies, and which chose those men, no longer exists. The old parties were combinations partly aristocratic, partly intellectual, cemented by the common possession and the common use of political power. But now that the power is gone the combinations are dissolved. The place which once knew them knows them no more. Any one who looks for them in our present London and our present politics will scarcely find much that is like them.

This society sought for those whom it thought would be useful to it in all quarters. There was a regular connection between the "Unions"—the great debating societies of Oxford and Cambridge—and Parliament. Young men who seemed promising had even a chance of being competed for by both parties. We all know the lines which the wit of Brookes's made upon Mr Canning:—

> *"The turning of coats so common is grown,*
> *That no one would think to attack it;*
> *But no case until now was so flagrantly known*
> *Of a schoolboy's turning his jacket."*

This meant that it having been said and believed that Mr Canning, who had just left Oxford, was to be brought into Parliament by the Whig Opposition, he went over to Mr Pitt, and was brought in by the Tory Ministry. The Oxford Liberals of our generation are quite exempt from similar temptations. So far from their support in Parliament being craved by both sides, they cannot enter Parliament at all. When many of these tried to enter Parliament in the autumn of 1867, their egregious failure was one of the most striking events of that remarkable time.

There was a connection, too, then between the two parts of the public service now most completely divided—the permanent and the Parliamentary civil services. Now, as we all know, the chief clerks in the Treasury and permanent heads of departments never think of going into Parliament; they regard the Parliamentary statesmen who are set to rule over them much as the Bengalees regard the English—as persons who are less intelligent and less instructed than themselves, but who nevertheless are to be obeyed. They never think of changing places any more than a Hindoo thinks of becoming an Englishman. But in old times, men like Lord Liverpool, Sir George Rose, and Mr Huskisson were found eminent in the public offices, and in consequence of that eminence, were brought into Parliament. The party in office were then, as now, anxious to obtain competent help in passing measures of finance and detail, and they then obtained it thus, whereas now their successors do not obtain it at all.

There was then, too, a sort of romantic element in the lives of clever young men which is wholly wanting now. Some one said that Macaulay's was like a life in a fairy tale;—he opens a letter which looks like any other letter, and finds that it contains a seat in Parliament. Gibbon says that just as he was destroying an army of barbarians, Sir Gilbert Elliot called and offered him a seat for Liskeard. Great historians will never probably again be similarly interrupted. The effect of all this was to raise the intellectual tone of Parliament. At present the political conversation of members of Parliament —a few of the greatest excepted—is less able and less striking than that of other persons of fair capacity. There is a certain kind of ideas which you hardly ever hear from any other educated person, but which they have to talk to their constituents, and which, if you will let them, they will talk to you too. Some of the middle-aged men of business, the "soapboilers," as the London world disrespectfully calls them, whom local influence raises to Parliament, really do not seem to know any better; they repeat the words of the hustings as if they were parts of their creed. And as for the more intellectual members who know better, no one of good manners likes to press them too closely in argument in politics any more than he likes to press a clergyman too strictly on religion. In both cases the status in the world depends on the belief in certain opinions, and therefore it is thought rather ill-bred, except for some great reason, to try to injure that belief. Intellectual deference used to be paid to members of Parliament, but now, at least in London, where the species is known, the remains of that deference are rare.

The other side of the same phenomenon is the increased power of the provinces, and especially of the constituencies. Any gust of popular excitement runs through them instantly, grows greater and greater as it goes, till it gains such huge influence that for a moment the central educated world is powerless. No doubt, if only time can be gained, the excitement passes away; something new succeeds, and the ordinary authority of trained and practised intelligence revives. But if an election were now to happen at an instant of popular fury, that fury would have little or nothing to withstand it. And, even in ordinary times, the power of the constituencies is too great. They are fast reducing the members, especially the weaker sort of them, to delegates. There is already, in many places, a committee which often telegraphs to London, hoping that their member will vote this way or that, and the member is unwilling not to do so, because at the next election, if offended, the committee may, perchance, turn the scale against him. And this dependence weakens the intellectual influence of Parliament, and of that higher kind of mind of which Parliament ought to be the organ.

We must remember that if now we feel these evils we must expect ere long to feel them much more. The Reform Act of 1867 followed in the main the precedent of 1832; and year by year we shall feel its consequences more and more. The two precedents which have been set will of necessity, in the English world, which is so much guided by precedent, determine the character of future Reform Acts. And if they do, the supremacy of the central group of trained and educated men which our old system of Parliamentary choice created, will be completely destroyed, for it is already half gone.

I know it is thought that we can revive this intellectual influence. Many thoughtful reformers believe that by means of Mr Hare's system of voting, by the cumulative suffrage, the limited suffrage, or by some others like them, we may be able to replace that which the legislation of 1832 began to destroy, and that which those who follow them are destroying. And I do not wish to say a word against this hope. On the contrary, I think that it is one of the most important duties of English politicians to frame these plans into the best form of which they are capable, and to try to obtain the assent of the country to them. But the difficulty is immense. The reformers of 1832 destroyed intellectual constituencies in great numbers without creating any new ones, and without saying, indeed without thinking, that it was desirable to create any. They thus by conspicuous action, which is the most influential mode of political instruction, taught mankind that an increase in the power of numbers was the change most to be desired in England. And of course the mass of mankind are only too ready to think so. They are always prone to believe their own knowledge to be "for all practical purposes" sufficient, and to wish to be emancipated from the authority of the higher culture. What we have now to do, therefore, is to induce this self-satisfied, stupid, inert mass of men to admit its own insufficiency, which is very hard; to understand fine schemes for supplying that insufficiency, which is harder; and to exert itself to get those ideas adopted, which is hardest of all. Such is the duty which the reformers of 1832 have cast upon us.

And this is what of necessity must happen if you set men like Lord Althorp to guide legislative changes in complex institutions. Being without culture, they do not know how these institutions grew; being without insight, they only see one half of their effect; being without foresight, they do not know what will happen if they are enlarged; being without originality, they cannot devise anything new to supply, if necessary, the place of what is old. Common-sense no doubt they have; but common-sense without instruction can no more wisely revise old institutions than it can write the Nautical Almanack. Probably they will do some present palpable good, but they will do so at a heavy cost; years after they have passed away, the bad effects of that which they did, and of the precedents which they set, will be hard to bear and difficult to change. Such men are admirably suited to early and simple times. English history is full of them, and England has been made mainly by them; but they fail in later times, when the work of the past is accumulated, and no question is any longer simple. The simplicity of their one-ideaed minds, which is suited to the common arithmetic and vulgar fractions of early societies, is not suited, indeed rather unfits them, for the involved analysis and complex "problem papers" of later ages.

There is little that in a sketch like this need be said of Lord Althorp's life after the passing of the Reform Act. The other acts of Lord Grey's Ministry have nothing so memorable or so characteristic of Lord Althorp that anything need be said about them. Nor does any one in the least care now as to the once celebrated mistake of Mr Littleton in dealing with O'Connell, or Lord Althorp's connection with it. Parliamentary history is only interesting when it is important constitutional history or when it illustrates something in the character of some interesting man. But the end of Lord Althorp's public life was very curious. In the November of

1834 his father, Lord Spencer, died, and as he was then leader of the House of Commons, a successor for him had to be found. But William IV, whose liberal partialities had long since died away, began by objecting to every one proposed, and ended by turning out the Ministry—another event in his reign which our coming republicans will no doubt make the most of. But I have nothing to do with the King and the constitutional question now. My business is with Lord Althorp. He acted very characteristically—he said that a retirement from office was to him the "cessation of acute pain," and never afterwards would touch it again, though he lived for many years. Nor was this an idle affectation, far less indolence. "You must be aware," he said once before, in a letter to Lord Brougham, "that my being in office is nothing less than a source of misery to me. I am perfectly certain that no man ever disliked it to such a degree as I do; and, indeed, the first thing that usually comes into my head when I wake is how to get rid of it." He retired into the country and occupied himself with the rural pursuits which he loved best, attended at quarter-sessions, and was active as a farmer. "Few persons," said an old shepherd, "could compete with my lord in a knowledge of sheep." He delighted to watch a whole flock pass, and seemed to know them as if he had lived with them. "Of all my former pursuits," he wrote, just after Lady Althorp's death, and in the midst of his grief, "the only one in which I now take any interest is breeding stock; it is the only one in which I can build castles in the air." And as soon as he could, among such castles in the air he lived and died. No doubt, too, much better for himself than for many of his friends, who long wanted to lure him back to politics. He was wise with the solid wisdom of agricultural England; popular and useful; sagacious in usual things; a model in common duties; well able to advise men in the daily difficulties which are the staple of human life. But beyond this he could not go. Having no call to decide on more intellectual questions, he was distressed and pained when he had to do so. He was a man so picturesquely out of place in a great scene, that if a great describer gets hold of him he may be long remembered; and it was the misfortune of his life that the simplicity of his purposes and the trustworthiness of his character raised him at a great conjuncture to a high place for which Nature had not meant him, and for which he felt that she had not meant him.

THE CHARACTER OF
SIR ROBERT PEEL[1]*

(1856)

Robert Peel was born at Chamber Hall, Lancashire, in 1788. He was the eldest son of Robert (afterwards Sir Robert) Peel, politician, and of Ellen Yates. He was educated at Harrow and Christ Church, Oxford. In 1809 his father bought a Tory seat in Parliament for him at Cashel. He was Under-secretary for War and the Colonies from 1810–12, and then Chief Secretary for Ireland until 1818. In 1815 he had successfully opposed Catholic emancipation and had established a constabulary for preservation of the peace. In 1817 he became M.P. for Oxford University. He rejoined Lord Liverpool's ministry as Home Secretary in 1822; about this time he had begun to mistrust rigid Toryism as a political creed. After bringing about important reforms in criminal law, he resigned over Catholic emancipation, but upon Canning's death in 1827 he laboured to reunite the Tory party. He joined Wellington's ministry as Home Secretary and leader of the House of Commons in 1828, and seeing that the country was determined on Catholic emancipation, he introduced a bill in 1829 granting the measure. In 1829 he was M.P. for Westbury, and in 1830 and 1833 for Tamworth. In 1830 he resigned office on the defeat of Wellington's government. He became Premier in 1834, holding the offices of First Lord of the Treasury and Chancellor of the Exchequer, but confronted in the Commons by a hostile majority, he resigned office in 1835. He retired to opposition and gradually built up the party which was to become the Conservative party, its policy being to maintain intact the constitution of the church and state. Peel formed a ministry in 1841, and in 1842 introduced his first

---

[1] *Memoirs*, by the Right Hon. Sir Robert Peel, Bart., M.P., etc. Published by the trustees of his papers, Lord Mahon (now Lord Stanhope) and the Right Hon. Edward Cardwell, M.P. Part I. "The Roman Catholic Question," 1828–9.

* This essay was first published in the *National Review* for July 1856, Volume III, pages 146–74. It was reprinted in *Estimates of Some Englishmen and Scotchmen* (1858).

*budget, which was designed to reduce indirect taxation and make
good the temporary deficiency by imposing an income tax. By
1846 he had repealed or reduced more than a thousand duties,
and by this lightening of imposts on trade had ensured a leading
position in the world for English trade. Until 1845 Peel had
steadily opposed Corn Law repeal, but when the harvest failed
and famine threatened, he introduced a measure for the ultimate
repeal of the Corn Laws. He failed to carry his cabinet with him
and resigned in December, but the same month resumed office
and in January 1846 introduced his bill for the repeal of the
Corn Laws. It was passed the following June, but Peel was now
defeated over his Irish bill. He resigned office, and after a few
years in opposition, during which he considered himself the
guardian of free trade, he died in London in 1850.*

Most people have looked over old letters. They have been
struck with the change of life, with the doubt on things
now certain, the belief in things now incredible, the oblivion
of what now seems most important, the strained attention to
departed detail, which characterise the mouldering leaves.
Something like this is the feeling with which we read Sir
Robert Peel's *Memoirs.* Who now doubts on the Catholic
Question? It is no longer a "question". A younger generation
has come into vigorous, perhaps into insolent, life, who regard
the doubts that were formerly entertained as absurd, pernicious, delusive. To revive the controversy was an error. The
accusations which are brought against a public man in his
own age are rarely those echoed in after times. Posterity sees
less or sees more. A few points stand forth in distinct rigid-
ity; there is no idea of the countless accumulation, the collision of action, the web of human feeling, with which, in
the day of their life, they were encompassed. Time changes
much. The points of controversy seem clear; the assumed
premises uncertain. The difficulty is to comprehend "the
difficulty". Sir Robert Peel will have to answer to posterity
not for having passed Catholic emancipation when he did,
but for having opposed it before; not for having been precipitate, but for having been slow; not for having taken "insufficient securities" for the Irish Protestant Church, but for
having endeavoured to take security for an institution too
unjust to be secured by laws or lawgivers.

This memoir has, however, a deeper aim. Its end is rather
personal than national. It is designed to show, not that Sir

Robert did what was externally expedient—this was probably too plain—but that he himself really believed what he did to be right. The scene is laid not in Ireland, not in the county of Clare, not amid the gross triumphs of O'Connell, or the outrageous bogs of Tipperary; but in the Home Office, among files of papers, among the most correctly docketed memoranda, beside the minute which shows that Justice A should be dismissed, that Malefactor O ought not to be reprieved. It is labelled "My Conscience," and is designed to show that "my conscience" was sincere.

Seriously, and apart from jesting, this is no light matter. Not only does the great space which Sir Robert Peel occupied during many years in the history of the country entitle his character to the anxious attention of historical critics, but the very nature of that character itself, its traits, its deficiencies, its merits, are so congenial to the tendencies of our time and government, that to be unjust to him is to be unjust to all probable statesmen. We design to show concisely how this is.

A constitutional statesman is in general a man of common opinions and uncommon abilities. The reason is obvious. When we speak of a free government, we mean a government in which the sovereign power is divided, in which a single decision is not absolute, where argument has an office. The essence of the *gouvernement des avocats*, as the Emperor Nicholas called it, is that you must persuade so many persons. The appeal is not to the solitary decision of a single statesman; not to Richelieu or Nesselrode alone in his closet; but to the jangled mass of men, with a thousand pursuits, a thousand interests, a thousand various habits. Public opinion, as it is said, rules; and public opinion is the opinion of the average man. Fox used to say of Burke: "Burke is a wise man; but he is wise too soon". The average man will not bear this. He is a cool, common person, with a considerate air,. with figures in his mind, with his own business to attend to, with a set of ordinary opinions arising from and suited to ordinary life. He can't bear novelty or originalities. He says: "Sir, I never heard such a thing *before* in my life"; and he thinks this is a *reductio ad absurdum*. You may see his taste by the reading of which he approves. Is there a more splendid monument of talent and industry than *The Times*? No wonder that the average man—that any one—believes in it. As Carlyle observes: "Let the highest intellect able to write epics try to write such a leader for the morning newspapers, it cannot do it; the highest intellect will fail". But did you ever see anything there you had never seen before? Out of the million articles that everybody has read, can any one person trace a single marked idea to a single article? Where are the deep theories, and the wise axioms, and the everlasting sentiments which the writers of the most influential publication in the world have been the first to communicate to an ignorant species? Such writers are far too shrewd. The two million, or whatever number of copies it may be, they publish, are not purchased because the buyers wish to know new truth. The purchaser desires an article which he can appreciate at sight; which he can lay down and say, "An excellent article, very excellent; exactly my own sentiments". Original theories give trouble; besides, a grave man on the Coal Exchange does not desire to be an apostle of novelties among the contemporaneous dealers in fuel;—he wants to be provided with remarks he can make on the topics of the day which will not be known *not* to be his; that are not too profound; which he can fancy the paper only reminded him of. And just in the same way, precisely as the most popular political paper is not that which is abstractedly the best or most instructive, but that which most exactly takes up the minds of men where it finds them, catches the floating sentiment of society, puts it in such a form as society can fancy would convince another society which did not believe—so the most influential of constitutional statesmen is the one who most felicitously expresses the creed of the moment, who administers it, who embodies it in laws and institutions, who gives it the highest life it is capable of, who induces the average man to think, "I could not have done it any better if I had had time myself".

It might be said, that this is only one of the results of that tyranny of commonplace which seems to accompany civilisation. You may talk of the tyranny of Nero and Tiberius; but the real tyranny is the tyranny of your next-door neighbour. What law is so cruel as the law of doing what he does? What yoke is so galling as the necessity of being like him? What *espionage* of despotism comes to your door so effectually as the eye of the man who lives at your door? Public opinion is a permeating influence, and it exacts obedience to itself; it requires us to think other men's thoughts, to speak other men's words, to follow other men's habits. Of course, if we do not, no formal ban issues, no corporeal pain, no coarse penalty of a barbarous society is inflicted on the offender; but we are called "eccentric"; there is a gentle murmur of "most unfortunate ideas," "singular young man," "well-intentioned, I dare say; but unsafe, sir, quite unsafe". The prudent, of course, conform. The place of nearly everybody depends on the opinion of every one else. There is nothing like Swift's precept to attain the repute of a sensible man, "Be of the opinion of the person with whom, at the time, you are conversing". This world is given to those whom this world can trust. Our very conversation is infected. Where are now the bold humour, the explicit statement, the grasping dogmatism of former days? They have departed, and you read in the orthodox works dreary regrets that the *art* of conversation has passed away. It would be as reasonable to expect the art of walking to pass away. People talk well enough when they know to whom they are speaking. We might even say that the art of conversation was improved by an application to new circumstances. "Secrete your intellect, use common words, say what you are expected to say," and you shall be at peace. The secret of prosperity in common life is to be commonplace on principle.

Whatever truth there may be in these splenetic observations might be expected to show itself more particularly in the world of politics. People dread to be thought unsafe in proportion as they get their living by being thought to be safe. "Literary men," it has been said, "are outcasts"; and they are eminent in a certain way notwithstanding. "They can say strong things of their age; for no one expects they will go out and act on them." They are a kind of ticket-of-leave lunatics, from whom no harm is for the moment expected; who seem quiet, but on whose vagaries a practical public must have its eye. For statesmen it is different—they must be thought men of judgment. The most morbidly agricultural counties were aggrieved when Mr Disraeli was made Chancellor of the Exchequer. They could not believe he was a man of solidity; and they could not comprehend taxes by the author of *Coningsby*, or sums by an adherent of the Caucasus. "There is," said Sir Walter Scott, "a certain hypocrisy of action, which, however it is despised by persons intrinsically excellent, will nevertheless be cultivated by those who desire the good repute of men." Politicians, as has been said, live in the repute of the commonalty. They may appeal to posterity; but of what use is posterity? Years before that tribunal comes into life, your life will be extinct. It is like a moth going into Chancery. Those who desire a public career must look to the views of the living public; an immediate exterior influence is essential to the exertion of their faculties. The confidence of others is your *fulcrum*. You cannot, many people wish you could, go into parliament to represent yourself. You must conform to the opinions of the electors; and they, depend on it, will not be original. In a word, as has been most wisely observed, "under free institutions it is necessary occasionally to defer to the opinions of other people; and as other people are obviously in the wrong, this is a great hindrance to the improvement of our political system and the progress of our species".

Seriously, it is a calamity that this is so. Occasions arise in which a different sort of statesman is required. A year or two ago we had one of these. If any politician had come forward in this country, on the topic of the war, with prepared intelligence, distinct views, strong will, commanding mastery, it would have brought support to anxious intellects, and comfort to a thousand homes. None such came. Our people would have statesmen who thought as they thought, believed as they believed, acted as they would have acted. They had desired to see their own will executed. There came a time when they had no clear will, no definite opinion. They reaped as they had sown. As they had selected an administrative tool, of course it did not turn out a heroic leader.

If we wanted to choose an illustration of these remarks out of all the world, it would be Sir Robert Peel. No man has come so near our definition of a constitutional statesman—the powers of a first-rate man and the creed of a second-rate man. From a certain peculiarity of intellect and fortune, he was never in advance of his time. Of almost all the great measures with which his name is associated, he attained great eminence as an opponent before he attained even greater eminence as their advocate. On the corn-laws, on the currency, on the amelioration of the criminal code, on Catholic emancipation—the subject of the memoir before us—he was not one of the earliest labourers or quickest converts. He did not bear the burden and heat of the day; other men laboured, and he entered into their labours. As long as these questions remained the property of first-class intellects, as long as they were confined to philanthropists or speculators, as long as

they were only advocated by austere, intangible Whigs, Sir
Robert Peel was against them. So soon as these same measures, by the progress of time, the striving of understanding,
the conversion of receptive minds, became the property of
second-class intellects, Sir Robert Peel became possessed of
them also. He was converted at the conversion of the average
man. His creed was, as it had ever been, ordinary; but his
extraordinary abilities never showed themselves so much.
He forthwith wrote his name on each of those questions, so
that it will be remembered as long as they are remembered.

Nor is it merely on these few measures that Sir Robert
Peel's mind must undoubtedly have undergone a change. The
lifetime of few Englishmen has been more exactly commen-
surate with a change of public opinion—a total revolution of
political thought. Hardly any fact in history is so incredible
as that forty and a few years ago England was ruled by Mr
Perceval. It seems almost the same as being ruled by the
Record newspaper. He had the same poorness of thought, the
same petty Conservatism, the same dark and narrow superstition. His quibbling mode of oratory seems to have been
scarcely agreeable to his friends; his impotence in political
speculation moves the wrath—destroys the patience—of the
quietest reader now. Other ministers have had great connections, or great estates, to compensate for the contractedness of
their minds. Mr Perceval was only a poorish *nisi prins* lawyer; and there is no kind of human being so disagreeable, so
teasing, to the gross Tory nature. He is not entitled to any
glory for our warlike successes: on the contrary, he did his
best to obtain failure by starving the Duke of Wellington,
and plaguing him with petty vexations. His views in religion
inclined to that Sabbatarian superstition which is of all
creeds the most alien to the firm and genial English nature.
The mere fact of such a premier being endured shows how
deeply the whole national spirit and interest was absorbed in
the contest with Napoleon, how little we understood the sort
of man who should regulate its conduct—"in the crisis of
Europe," as Sydney Smith said, "he safely brought the Curates' Salaries Improvement Bill to a hearing"—and it still
more shows the horror of all innovation which the recent
events of French history had impressed on our wealthy and
comfortable classes. They were afraid of catching revolution,
as old women of catching cold. Sir Archibald Alison to this
day holds that revolution is an infectious disease, beginning

no one knows how, and going no one knows where. There is but one rule of escape, explains the great historian, "Stay still, don't move; do what you have been accustomed to do, and consult your grandmother on everything". In 1812 the English people were all persuaded of this theory. Mr Perceval was the most narrow-minded and unaltering man they could find: he therefore represented their spirit, and they put him at the head of the state.

Such was the state of political questions. How little of real thoughtfulness was then applied to what we now call social questions cannot be better illustrated than by the proceedings on the occasion of Mr Perceval's death. Bellingham, who killed him, was, whether punishable or not, as clearly insane as a lunatic can be who offends against the laws of his country. He had no idea of killing Mr Perceval particularly. His only idea was, that he had lost some property in Russia; that the English government would never repay him his loss in Russia; and he endeavoured to find some cabinet minister to shoot as a compensation. Lord Eldon lived under the belief that he had nearly been the victim himself, and told some story of a borrowed hat and an assistant's greatcoat to which he ascribed his preservation. The whole affair was a monomaniac's delusion. Bellingham had no ground for expecting any repayment. There was no reason for ascribing his pecuniary ruin to the government of that day, any more than to the government of this day. Indeed, if he had been alive now, it would have been agreed that he was a particularly estimable man. Medical gentlemen would have been examined for days on the doctrine of "irresistible impulse," "moral insanity," "instinctive pistol discharges," and every respectful sympathy would have been shown to so curious an offender. Whether he was punishable or not may be a question; but all will now agree, that it was not a case for the punishment of death. In that day there was no more doubt that he ought to be hanged, than there would now be that he ought on no account to be hanged. The serious reasons, of which the scientific theories above alluded to are but the exaggerated resemblance, which indicate the horrible cruelty of inflicting on those who do not know what they do the extreme penalty of suffering meant for those who perpetrate the worst they can conceive, are in these years so familiar that we can hardly conceive their being unknown. Yet the Tory historian[2]

2 Alison.

has to regret "that the motion, so earnestly insisted on by his
counsel, to have the trial postponed for some days, to obtain
evidence to establish his insanity, was not acceded to; that
a judicial proceeding, requiring beyond all others the most
calm and deliberate consideration, should have been hurried
over with a precipitation which, if not illegal, was at least
unusual, and a noble lord "improved" the moment of the
assassination by exclaiming to the peers in opposition, "You
see, my lords, the consequence of your agitating the question
of *Catholic emancipation*." To those who now know England,
it seems scarcely possible this could have occurred here only
forty-four years since. It was in such a world that Sir Robert
Peel commenced his career. He was under-secretary of state
for the colonies at the time of Mr Perceval's assassination.

We cannot, however, believe that, even if Mr Perceval
had lived, his power would have very long endured. It passed
to milder and quieter men. It passed to such men as Lord
Liverpool and Mr Peel. The ruling power at that time in England, as for many years before, as even in some measure,
though far less, now, was the class of aristocratic gentry; by
which we do not mean to denote the House of Lords exclusively, but to indicate the great class of hereditary landed
proprietors, who are in sympathy with the upper house on
cardinal points, yet breathe a somewhat freer air, are more
readily acted on by the opinion of the community, more
contradictable by the lower herd, less removed from its
prejudices by a refined and regulated education. From the
time of the revolution, more or less, this has been the ruling
class in the community; the close-borough system and the
county system giving them mainly the control of the House
of Commons, and their feelings being in general, as it were,
a mean term between those of the higher nobility and the
trading public of what were then the few large towns. The
rule of the House of Lords was rather mediate than direct.
By the various means of influence and social patronage and
oppression which are familiar to a wealthy and high-bred
aristocracy, the highest members of it, of course, exercised
over all below them a sure and continual influence: it worked
silently and commonly on ordinary questions and in quiet
times; yet it was liable to be overborne by a harsher and
ruder power when stormy passions arose, in the days of wars
and tumults. The largest amount of administrative power has
indeed been rarely in the hands of the highest aristocracy,

and in a great measure for a peculiar reason: that aristocracy will rarely do the work, and can rarely do the work. The enormous pressure of daily-growing business which besets the governors of a busy and complicated community is too much for the refined habits, delicate discrimination, anxious judgment, which the course of their life develops in the highest classes, and with which it nourishes the indolence natural to those who have this world to enjoy. The real strain of the necessary labour has generally been borne by men of a somewhat lower grade, trained by an early ambition, a native aptitude, a hardy competition, to perform its copious tasks. Such men are partakers of two benefits. They are rough and ready enough to accomplish the coarse enormous daily work; they have lived with higher gentlemen enough to know and feel what such persons think and want. Sir Robert Walpole is the type of this class. He was a Norfolk squire, and not a nobleman; he was bred a gentleman, and yet was quite coarse enough for any business: his career was what you would expect. For very many years he administered the government much as the aristocracy wished and desired. *They* were, so to speak, the directors of the company which is called the English nation; they met a little and talked a little: but Sir Robert was the manager, who knew all the facts, came every day, saw every body, and was every thing.

Passing over the time of Lord Liverpool, of whom this is not now the place to speak, some such destiny as this would in his first political life have appeared likely to be that of Sir Robert Peel. If an acute master of the betting art had been asked the "favourite" statesman who was likely to rule in that generation, he would undoubtedly have selected Sir Robert. He was rich, decorous, laborious, and had devoted himself regularly to the task. There was no other such man. It was likely, at least to superficial observers, that his name would descend to posterity as the "Sir Robert" of a new time;—a time changed, indeed, from that of Walpole, but resembling it in its desire to be ruled by a great administrator, skilful in all kinds of business and transactions, yet associated with the aristocracy; by one unremarkable in his opinions, but remarkable in his powers. The fates, however, designed Peel for a very different destiny; and to a really close observer there were signs in his horoscope which should have clearly revealed it. Sir Robert's father and grandfather were two of the men who created Lancashire. No sooner did the requisite ma-

chinery issue from the brain of the inventor than its capabilities were seized on by strong, ready, bold men of business,
who erected it, used it, devised a factory system, combined a
factory population—created, in a word, that black industrial
region, of whose augmenting wealth and horrid labour tales
are daily borne to the genial and lazy south. Of course it
cannot be said that mill-makers invented the middle classes.
The history of England perhaps shows that it has not for centuries been without an unusual number of persons with comfortable and moderate means. But though this class has ever
been found among us, and has ever been more active than in
any other similar country, yet to a great extent it was scattered, headless, motionless. Small rural out-of-the-way towns,
country factories few and far between, concealed and divided
this great and mixed mass of petty means and steady intelligence. The huge heaps of manufacturing wealth were not to
be concealed. They at once placed on a level with the highest
in the land—in matters of expenditure, and in those countless social relations which depend upon expenditure—men
sprung from the body of the people, unmistakably speaking
its language, inevitably thinking its thoughts. It is true that
the first manufacturers were not democratic. Sir Robert Peel,
the statesman's father—a type of the class—was a firm, honest,
domineering Conservative; but, however on such topics they
may so think, however on other topics they may try to catch
the language of the class to which they rise, the grain of the
middle class will surely show itself in those who have risen
from the middle class. If Mr Cobden were to go over to the
enemy, if he were to offer to serve Lord Derby *vice* Disraeli
disconcerted, it would not be possible for him to speak as the
hereditary landowner speaks. It is not that the hereditary
landowner knows more;—indeed, either in book-learning or in
matters of observation, in acquaintance with what has been,
or is going to be, or what now is, the owners of rent are not
superior to the receivers of profits; yet their dialect is different—the one speaks the language of years of toil, and the
other of years of indolence. A harsh laboriousness characterises the one, a pleasant geniality the other. The habit of industry is ingrained in those who have risen by it; it modifies
every word and qualifies every notion. They are the βάναυσοι
of work. Vainly, therefore, did the first manufacturers struggle to be Conservatives, to be baronets, to be peers. The
titles they might obtain, their outward existence they might

change, themselves in a manner they might alter; but a surer force was dragging them and those who resembled them into another region, filling them with other thoughts, making them express what people of the middle classes had always obscurely felt, pushing forward this new industrial order by the side, or even in front, of the old aristocratic order. The new class have not, indeed, shown themselves republican. They have not especially cared to influence the machinery of government. Their peculiarity has been, that they wish to see the government administered according to the notions familiar to them in their business life. They have no belief in mystery or magic; probably they have never appreciated the political influence of the imagination; they wish to see plain sense applied to the most prominent part of practical life. In his later career, the second Sir Robert Peel was the statesman who most completely and thoroughly expressed the sentiments of this new dynasty;—instead of being the nominee of a nobility, he became the representative of a transacting and trading multitude.

Both of these two classes were, however, equally possessed by the vice or tendency we commented on at the outset. They each of them desired to see the government carried on exactly according to their own views. The idea on which seems to rest our only chance of again seeing great statesmen, of placing deep deferential trust in those who have given real proofs of comprehensive sagacity, had scarcely dawned on either. The average man had, so to say, varied; he was no longer of the one order, but of an inferior; but he was not at all less exacting or tyrannical. Perhaps he was even more so; for the indolent gentleman is less absolute and domineering than the active man of business. However that may be, it was the fate of Sir Robert Peel, in the two phases of his career, to take a leading share in carrying out the views, in administering the creed, first of one and then of the other.

Perhaps in our habitual estimate of Peel we hardly enough bear this in mind. We remember him as the guiding chief of the most intelligent Conservative government that this country has ever seen. We remember the great legislative acts which we owe to his trained capacity, every detail of which bears the impress of his practised hand; we know that his name is pronounced with applause in the great marts of trade and seats of industry; that even yet it is muttered with reproach in the obscure abodes of squires and rectors. We forget that his name was once the power of the Protestant interest, the shibboleth by which squires and rectors distinguished those whom they loved from those whom they hated; we forget that he defended the Manchester Massacre, the Six Acts, the Imposition of Tests, the rule of Orangemen. We remember Peel as the proper head of a moderate, intelligent, half-commercial community; we forget that he once was the chosen representative of a gentry untrained to great affairs, absorbed in a great war, only just recovering from the horror of a great revolution.

In truth, the character of Sir Robert Peel happily fitted him both to be the chosen head of a popular community, imperiously bent on its own ideas, and to be the head of that community in shifting and changing times. Sir Robert was at Harrow with Lord Byron, who has left the characteristic reminiscence: "I was always in scrapes, Peel never". And opposed as they were in their fortunes as boys and men, they were at least equally contrasted in the habit and kind of action of their minds. Lord Byron's mind gained everything it was to gain by one intense, striking effort. By a blow of the imagination he elicited a single bright spark of light on every subject; and that was all. And this he never lost. The intensity of the thinking seemed to burn it on the memory, there to remain alone. But he made no second effort; he gained no more. He always avowed his incapability of continuous application: he could not, he said, learn the grammar of any language. In later life he showed considerable talent for action; but those who had to act with him observed that, versatile as were his talents, and mutable as his convictions had always seemed to be, in reality he was the most stubborn of men. He heard what you had to say; assented to all you had to say; and the next morning returned to his original opinion. No amount of ordinary argumentative resistance was so hopeless as that facile acquiescence and instantaneous recurrence. The truth was, that he was—and some others are similarly constituted—unable to retain anything which he did not at any rate *seem* to gain by the unaided single rush of his own mind. The ideas of such minds are often not new, very often they are hardly in the strictest sense original; they really were very much suggested from without, and preserved in some obscure corner of memory, out of the way and unknown; but it remains their characteristic, that they seem to the mind of the thinker to be born from its own depths, to be the product of its latent forces. There is a kind of eruption of ideas from a subter-conscious world. The whole mental action is volcanic; the lava flood glows in *Childe Harold*; all the thoughts are intense, flung forth vivid. The day after the eruption the mind is calm; it seems as if it could not again do the like; the product only remains, distinct, peculiar, indestructible. The mind of Peel was the exact opposite of this. His opinions far more resembled the daily accumulating insensible deposits of a rich alluvial soil. The great stream of time flows on with all things on its surface; and slowly, grain by grain, a mould of wise experience is unconsciously left on the still, extended intellect. You scarcely think of such a mind as acting; it seems always acted upon. There is no trace of gushing, overpowering, spontaneous impulse; everything seems acquired. The thoughts are calm. In Lord Byron, the very style—dashing, free, incisive—shows the bold impulse from which it came. The stealthy accumulating words of Peel seem like the quiet leavings of an outward‧tendency, which brought these, but might as well have brought others. There is no peculiar stamp either in the ideas. They might have been any one's ideas. They belong to the general diffused stock of observations which are to be found in the civilised world. They are not native to the particular mind, nor "to the manner born". Like a science, they are credible or incredible by all men equally. This *secondary* order, as we may call it, of intellect, is evidently most useful to a statesman of the constitutional class, such as we have described him. He insensibly and inevitably takes in and imbibes, by means of it, the ideas of those around him. If he were left in a vacuum, he would have no ideas. The primary class of mind that strikes out its own belief would here be utterly at fault. It would want something which other men had; it would discover something which other men would not understand. Sir Robert Peel was a statesman for forty years; under our constitution, Lord Byron, eminent as was his insight into men, and remarkable as was his power, at least for short periods, of dealing with them, would not have been a statesman for forty days.

It is very likely that many people may not think Sir Robert Peel's mind so interesting as Lord Byron's. They may prefer the self-originating intellect, which invents and retains its own ideas, to the calm receptive intellect which acquires its belief from without. The answer lies in what has been said— a constitutional statesman must sympathise in the ideas of the many. As the many change, it will be his good fortune if he can contrive to change with them. It is to be remembered that statesmen do not live under hermetical seals. Like other men, they are influenced by the opinions of other men. How potent is this influence, those best know who have tried to hold ideas different from the ideas of those around.

In another point of view also Sir Robert Peel's character was exactly fitted to the position we have delineated. He was a great administrator. Civilisation requires this. In a simple age work may be difficult, but it is scarce. There are fewer people, and everybody wants fewer things. The mere tools of civilisation seem in some sort to augment work. In early times, when a despot wishes to govern a distant province, he sends down a satrap on a grand horse, with other people on little horses; and very little is heard of the satrap again unless he send back some of the little people to tell what he has been doing. No great labour of superintendence is possible. Common rumour and casual complaints are the sources of intelligence. If it seems certain that the province is in a bad state, satrap No. 1 is recalled, and satrap No. 2 is sent out in his stead. In civilised countries the whole thing is different. You erect a *bureau* in the province you want to govern; you make it write letters and copy letters; it sends home eight reports per diem to the head *bureau* in St Petersburg. Nobody does a sum in the province without somebody doing the same sum in the capital, to "check him," and see that he does it correctly. The consequence of this is, to throw on the heads of departments an amount of reading and labour which can only be accomplished by the greatest natural aptitude, the most efficient training, the most firm and regular industry. Under a free government it is by no means better, perhaps in some respects it is worse. It is true that many questions which, under the French despotism, are referred to Paris, are settled in England on the very spot where they are to be done, without reference to London at all. But as a set-off, a constitutional administrator has to be always consulting others, finding out what this man or that man chooses to think; learning which form of error is believed by Lord B, which by Lord C; adding up the errors of the alphabet, and seeing what portion of what he thinks he ought to do, they will all of them together allow him to do. Likewise, though the personal freedom and individual discretion which free governments allow to their subjects seem at first likely to diminish the work which those governments have to do, it may be doubted whether it does so really and in the end. Individual discretion strikes out so many more pursuits, and some supervision must be maintained over each of those pursuits. No despotic government would consider the police force of London enough to keep down, watch, and superintend such a population; but then no despotic government would have such a city as London to keep down. The freedom of growth allows the possibility of growth; and though liberal governments take so much less in proportion upon them, yet the scale of operations is so much enlarged by the continual exercise of civil liberty, that the real work is ultimately perhaps as immense. While a despotic government is regulating ten per cent of ten men's actions, a free government has to regulate one per cent of a hundred men's actions. The difficulty, too, increases. Anybody can understand a rough despotic community;—a small buying class of nobles, a small selling class of traders, a large producing class of serfs, are much the same in all quarters of the globe; but a free, intellectual community is a complicated network of ramified relations, interlacing and passing hither and thither, old and new—some of fine city weaving, others of gross agricultural construction. You are never sure what effect any force or any change may produce on a framework so exquisite and so involved. Govern it as you may, it will be a work of great difficulty, labour, and responsibility; and no man who is thus occupied ought ever to go to bed without reflecting that from the difficulty of his employment he may, probably enough, have that day done more evil than good. What view Sir Robert Peel took of these duties he has himself informed us.

"Take the case of the Prime Minister. You must presume that he reads every important despatch from every foreign court. He cannot consult with the Secretary of State for Foreign Affairs, and exercise the influence which he ought to have with respect to the conduct of foreign affairs, unless he be master of everything of real importance passing in that department. It is the same with respect to other departments; India for instance: How can the Prime Minister be able to judge of the course of policy with regard to India, unless he be cognisant of all the current important correspondence? In the case of Ireland and the Home Department it is the same. Then the Prime Minister has the patronage of the Crown to exercise, which you say, and justly say, is of so much im-

portance and of so much value; he has to make inquiries into
the qualifications of the persons who are candidates; he has
to conduct the whole of the communications with the Sovereign, he has to write, probably with his own hand, the letters in reply to all persons of station who address themselves
to him; he has to receive deputations on public business;
during the sitting of parliament he is expected to attend six
or seven hours a day, and for four or five days in the week;
at least, he is blamed if he is absent."

The necessary effect of all this labour is, that those subject
to it have no opinions. It requires a great deal of time to have
opinions. Belief is a slow process. That leisure which the poets say is necessary to be good, or to be wise, is needful
for the humbler task of allowing respectable maxims to take
root respectably. The "wise passiveness" of Mr Wordsworth
is necessary in very ordinary matters. If you chain a man's
head to a ledger, and keep him constantly adding up, and take
a pound off his salary whenever he stops, you can't expect
him to have a sound conviction on Catholic emancipation,
tithes, and original ideas on the Transcaucasian provinces.
Our system, indeed, seems expressly provided to make it unlikely. The most benumbing thing to the intellect is routine;
the most bewildering is distraction: our system is a distracting
routine. You see this in the description just given, which is
not exhaustive. Sir Robert Peel once asked to have a number
of questions carefully written down which they asked him
one day in succession in the House of Commons. They seemed
a list of every thing that could occur in the British empire,
or to the brain of a member of parliament. A premier's whole
life is a series of such transitions. It is rather wonderful that
our public men have any minds left, than that a certain un-
fixity of opinion seems growing upon them.

We may go further on this subject. A great administrator
is not a man likely to desire to have fixed opinions. His natural bent and tendency is to immediate action. The existing
and pressing circumstances of the case fill up his mind. The
letters to be answered, the documents to be filed, the memoranda to be made, engross his attention. He is angry if you
distract him. A bold person who suggests a matter of principle, or a difficulty of thought, or an abstract result that seems
improbable in the case "before the board," will be set down
as a speculator, a theorist, a troubler of practical life. To expect to hear from such men profound views of future policy,

digested plans of distant action, is to mistake their genius entirely. It is like asking the broker of the Stock Exchange what will be the price of the funds this day six months! His whole soul is absorbed in thinking what that price will be in ten minutes. A momentary change of an eighth is more important to him than a distant change of a hundred eighths. So the brain of a great administrator is naturally occupied with the details of the day, the passing dust, the granules of that day's life; and his unforeseeing temperament turns away uninterested from reaching speculations, from vague thought, and from extensive and far-off plans. Of course, it is not meant that a great administrator has absolutely no general views; some indeed he must have. A man cannot conduct the detail of affairs without having some plan which regulates that detail. He cannot help having some idea, vague or accurate, indistinct or distinct, of the direction in which he is going, and the purpose for which he is travelling. But the difference is, that this plan is seldom his own, the offspring of his own brain, the result of his own mental contention; it is the plan of some one else. Providence generally bestows on the working adaptive man a quiet adoptive nature. He receives insensibly the suggestions of others; he hears them with willing ears; he accepts them with placid belief. An acquiescent credulity is a quality of such men's nature; they cannot help being sure that what every one says must be true; the vox *populi* is a part of their natural religion. It has been made a matter of wonder that Peel should have belonged to the creed of Mr Perceval and Lord Sidmouth. Perhaps, indeed, our existing psychology will hardly explain the process by which a decorous young man acquires the creed of his era. He assumes its belief as he assumes its costume. He imitates the respectable classes. He avoids an original opinion, like an *outré* coat; a new idea, like an unknown tie. Especially he does so on matters of real concern to him, on those on which he knows he must act. He acquiesces in the creed of the orthodox agents. He scarcely considers for himself; he acknowledges the apparent authority of dignified experience. He is, he remembers, but the junior partner in the firm; it does not occur to him to doubt that those were right who were occupied in its management years before him. In this way he acquires an experience which more independent and original minds are apt to want. There was a great cry when the Whigs came into office, at the time of the Reform Bill,

that they were not men of business. Of course, after a very
long absence from office, they could not possess a technical
acquaintance with official forms, a trained facility in official
action. This Sir Robert Peel acquired from his apprenticeship
to Mr Perceval. His early connection with the narrow Conservative party has been considered a disadvantage to him;
but it may well be doubted whether his peculiar mind was not
more improved by the administrative training than impaired
by the contact with prejudiced thoughts. He never could have
been a great thinker; he became what nature designed, a great
agent.

In a third respect also Sir Robert Peel conformed to the
type of a constitutional statesman; and that third respect also
seems naturally to lead to a want of defined principle, and to
apparent fluctuation of opinion. He was a great debater; and
of all pursuits ever invented by man for separating the faculty
of argument from the capacity of belief, the art of debating
is probably the most effectual. Macaulay tells us that, in his
opinion, this is "the most serious of the evils which are to be
set off against the many blessings of popular government. The
keenest and most vigorous minds of every generation, minds
often admirably fitted for the investigation of truth, are
habitually employed in producing arguments such as no man
of sense would ever put into a treatise intended for publication—arguments which are just good enough to be used once,
when aided by fluent delivery and pointed language. The
habit of discussing questions in this way necessarily reacts on
the intellects of our ablest men, particularly of those who are
introduced into Parliament at a very early age, before their
minds have expanded to full maturity. The talent for debate
is developed in such men to a degree which, to the multitude,
seems as marvellous as the performances of an Italian *impro-
visatore*. But they are fortunate indeed if they retain unimpaired the faculties which are required for close reasoning, or
for enlarged speculation. Indeed, we should sooner expect a
great original work on political science—such a work, for example, as *The Wealth of Nations*—from an apothecary in a
country town, or from a minister in the Hebrides, than from
a statesman who, ever since he was one and twenty, had been
a distinguished debater in the House of Commons." But it
may well be doubted whether there is not in the same pursuit
a deeper evil, hard to eradicate, and tending to corrupt and
destroy the minds of those who are beneath its influence. Con-

stitutional statesmen are obliged, not only to employ arguments which they do not think conclusive, but likewise to
defend opinions which they do not believe to be true.
Whether we approve it or lament it, there is no question
that our existing political life is deeply marked by the habit
of advocacy. Perhaps fifteen measures may annually, on an
average, be brought in by a cabinet government of fifteen
persons. It is impossible to believe that all members of that
cabinet agree in all those measures. No two people agree in
fifteen things; fifteen clever men never yet agreed in anything;
yet they all defend them, argue for them, are responsible for
them. It is always quite possible that the minister who is
strenuously defending a bill in the House of Commons may
have used in the cabinet the very arguments which the Opposition are using in the House; he may have been overruled
without being convinced; he may still think the conclusions
he opposes better than those which he inculcates. It is idle
to say that he ought to go out; at least, it amounts to saying
that government by means of a cabinet is impossible. The
object of a committee of that kind is to agree on certain
conclusions; if every member after the meeting were to start
off according to the individual bent and bias of his mind,
according to his own individual discretion or indiscretion, the
previous concurrence would have become childish. Of course,
the actual measure proposed by the collective voice of several
persons is very different from what any one of these persons
would of himself wish; it is the result of a compromise between them. Each, perhaps, has obtained some concession;
each has given up something. Every one sees in the actual
proposal something of which he strongly disapproves; every
one regrets the absence of something which he much desires.
Yet, on the whole, perhaps, he thinks the measure better
than no measure; or at least he thinks that if he went out, it
would break up the government; and imagines it to be of
more consequence that the government should be maintained
than that the particular measure should be rejected. He con-
cedes his individual judgment. No one has laid this down with
more distinctness than Sir Robert Peel. "Supposing a person
at a dinner-table to express his private opinion of a measure
originating with a party with whom he is united in public life,
is he, in the event of giving up that private opinion out of
deference to his party, to be exposed to a charge almost
amounting to dishonesty? The idea is absurd.—What is the

everyday conduct of government itself? Is there any one in
this House so ignorant as to suppose that on all questions
cabinet ministers, who yield to the decision of their colleagues, speak and act in parliament in strict conformity with
the opinions they have expressed in the cabinet? If ministers
are to be taunted on every occasion that they hold opinions
in the cabinet different from what they do in this House, and
if parliament is to be made the scene of these taunts, I believe I should not be going too far in saying the House would
have time for little else. It is the uniform practice with all
governments, and I should be sorry to think the practice carries any stain with it, for a member of the administration
who chances to entertain opinions differing from those of the
majority of his colleagues, rather than separate himself from
them, to submit to be overruled, and even though he do not
fully concur in their policy, to give his support to the measures which, as an administration, they promulgate. I will give
the House an instance of this fact. It was very generally reported on a late occasion, that upon the question of sending
troops to Portugal a strong difference of opinion took place in
the cabinet. Now would it, I ask, be either just or fair to call
on those who, in the discussion of the cabinet, had spoken
in favour of sending out troops to aid the cause of Donna
Maria, to come down, and in parliament advocate that measure in opposition to the decision of their colleagues? No one
would think of doing so." It may not carry a stain; but it is a
painful idea.

It is evident, too, that this necessarily leads to great apparent changes of opinion—to the professed belief of a statesman at one moment being utterly different from what it
seems to be at another moment. When a government is
founded, questions A, B, C, D, E, F, are the great questions
of the day—the matters which are obvious, pressing—which
the public mind comprehends. X, Y, Z, are in the background,
little thought of, obscure. According to the received morality,
no statesman would hesitate to sacrifice the last to the first.
He might have a very strong personal opinion on X, but he
would surrender it to a colleague as the price of his co-operation on A or B. A few years afterwards times change. Question A is carried, B settles itself, E and F are forgotten, X
becomes the most important topic of the day. The statesman
who conceded X before, now feels that he no longer can concede it; there is no equivalent. He has never in reality changed

his opinion, yet he has to argue in favour of the very measures which he endeavoured before to argue against. Everybody thinks he has changed, and without going into details, the secrecy of which is esteemed essential to confidential co-operation, it is impossible that he can evince his consistency. It is impossible to doubt that this is a very serious evil, and it is plainly one consequent on, or much exaggerated by, a popular and argumentative government. It is very possible for a conscientious man, under a bureaucratic government, to cooperate with the rest of a council in the elaboration and execution of measures, many of which he thinks inexpedient. Nobody asks him his opinion; he has not to argue, or defend, or persuade. But a free government boasts that it is carried on in the face of day. Its principle is discussion; its habit is debate. The consequence is, that those who conduct it have to defend measures they disapprove, to object to measures they approve, to appear to have an accurate opinion on points on which they really have no opinion. The calling of a constitutional statesman is very much that of a political advocate; he receives a new brief with the changing circumstances of each successive day. It is easy to conceive a cold sardonic intellect, moved with contempt at such a life, casting aside the half-and-half pretences with which others partly deceive themselves, stating anything, preserving an intellectual preference for truth, but regarding any effort at its special advocacy as the weak aim of foolish men, striving for what they cannot attain. Lord Lyndhurst has shown us that it is possible to lead the life of Lord Lyndhurst. One can conceive, too, a cold and somewhat narrow intellect, capable of forming, in any untroubled scene, an accurate plain conviction, but without much power of entering into the varying views of others; little skilled in diversified argument; understanding its own opinion, and not understanding the opinions of others;—one can imagine such a mind pained, and cracked, and shattered, by endeavouring to lead a life of ostentatious argument in favour of others' opinions, of half-concealment of its chill, unaltering essence. It will be for posterity to make due allowance for the variance between the character and the position of Lord John Russell.

Sir Robert Peel was exactly fit for this life. The word which exactly fits his oratory is—specious. He hardly ever said anything which struck you in a moment to be true; he never uttered a sentence which for a moment anybody could deny

to be plausible. Once, when they were opposed on a railway
bill, the keen irascibility of Lord Derby stimulated him to
observe "that *no one* knew like the right honourable baronet
how to *dress up* a case for that House". The art of statement,
the power of detail, the watching for the weak points of an
opponent, an average style adapting itself equally to what the
speaker believed and what he disbelieved, a business air, a
didactic precision for what it was convenient to make clear,
an unctuous disguise of flowing periods, and "a deep sense
of responsibility" for what it was convenient to conceal, an
enormous facility, made Sir Robert Peel a nearly unequalled
master of the art of political advocacy. For his times he was
perhaps quite unequalled. He might have failed in times of
deep, outpouring patriotic excitement; he had not nature
enough to express it. He might have failed in an age when
there was nothing to do, and when elegant personality and the
finesse of artistic expression were of all things most required.
But for an age of important business, when there was an unusual number of great topics to be discussed, but none great
enough to hurry men away from their business habits, or
awaken the most ardent passion or the highest imagination,
there is nothing like the oratory of Peel—able but not aspiring,
firm but not exalted, never great but ever adequate to great
affairs. It is curious to know that he was trained to the trade.

"Soon after Peel was born, his father, the first baronet, finding himself rising daily in wealth and consequence, and believing that money in those peculiar days could always command a seat in Parliament, determined to bring up his son
expressly for the House of Commons. When that son was
quite a child, Sir Robert would frequently set him on the
table and say, 'Now, Robin, make a speech, and I will give
you this cherry'. What few words the little fellow produced
were applauded; and applause stimulating exertion produced
such effects that, before Robin was ten years old, he could
really address the company with some degree of eloquence.
As he grew up, his father constantly took him every Sunday
into his private room and made him repeat, as well as he
could, the sermon which had been preached. Little progress
in effecting this was made, and little was expected *at first*,
but by steady perseverance the habit of attention grew powerful, and the sermon was repeated almost *verbatim*. When at
a very distant day the senator, remembering accurately the
speech of an opponent, answered his arguments in correct

succession, it was little known that the power of so doing was originally acquired in Drayton Church."

A mischievous observer might say, that something else had remained to Sir Robert Peel from these sermons. His tone is a trifle sermonic. He failed where perhaps alone Lord John Russell has succeeded—in the oratory of conviction.

If we bear in mind the whole of these circumstances; if we picture in our minds a nature at once active and facile, easily acquiring its opinions from without, not easily devising them from within, a large placid adaptive intellect, devoid of irritable intense originality, prone to forget the ideas of yesterday, inclined to accept the ideas of to-day—if we imagine a man so formed cast early into absorbing, exhausting industry of detail, with work enough to fill up a life, with action of itself enough to render speculation almost impossible—placed too in a position unsuited to abstract thought, of which the conventions and rules require that a man should feign other men's thoughts, should impugn his own opinions—we shall begin to imagine a conscientious man destitute of convictions on the occupations of his life—to comprehend the character of Sir Robert Peel.

That Sir Robert was a very conscientious man is quite certain. It is even probable that he had a morbid sense of administrative responsibility. We do not say that he was so weighed down as Lord Liverpool, who is alleged never to have opened his letters without a pang of foreboding that something had miscarried somewhere; but every testimony agrees that Sir Robert had an anxious sense of duty in detail. Lord Wellesley, somewhere in this volume,[3] on an occasion when it would have been at least equally natural to speak of administrative capacity and efficient co-operation, mentions only "the real impressions which your kindness and high character have fixed in my mind". The circumstances of his end naturally produced a crowd of tributes to his memory, and hardly any of them omit his deep sense of the obligations of action. The characteristic, too, is written conspicuously on every line of these memoirs. Disappointing and external as in some respects they seem, they all the more evidently bear witness to this trait. They read like the conscientious letters of an ordinary practical man; the great statesman has little other notion than that it is his duty to transact his business well. As

[3] *National Review*, July, 1856.

a conspicuous merit, the Duke of Wellington, oddly enough according to some people's notions at the time, selected Peel's veracity. "In the whole course of my communication with him I have never known an instance in which he did not show the strictest preference for truth. I never had, in the whole course of my life, the slightest reason for suspecting that he stated anything which he did not firmly believe to be the fact. I could not sit down without stating what I believe, after a long acquaintance, to have been his most striking characteristic." Simple people in the country were a little astonished to hear so strong a eulogy on a man for not telling lies. They were under the impression that people in general did not. But those who have considered the tempting nature of a statesman's pursuits, the secrets of office, the inevitable complication of his personal relations, will not be surprised that many statesmen should be without veracity, or that one should be eulogised for possessing it. It is to be remarked, however, in mitigation of so awful an excellence, that Sir Robert was seldom in "scrapes," and that it is on those occasions that the virtue of veracity is apt to be most severely tested. The same remark is applicable to the well-praised truthfulness of the duke himself.

In conjunction with the great soldier, Sir Robert Peel is entitled to the fame of a great act of administrative conscience. He purified the Tory party. There is little doubt that, during the long and secure reign which the Tories enjoyed about the beginning of the century, there was much of the corruption naturally incident to a strong party with many adherents to provide for, uncontrolled by an effective Opposition, unwatched by a great nation. Of course, too, any government remaining over from the last century would inevitably have adhering to it various *remanet* corruptions of that curious epoch. There flourished those mighty sinecures and reversions, a few of which still remain to be the wonder and envy of an unenjoying generation. The House of Commons was not difficult then to manage. There is a legend that a distinguished Treasury official of the last century, a very capable man, used to say of any case which was hopelessly and inevitably bad: "Ah, we must apply our majority to this question"; and no argument is so effectual as the mechanical, calculable suffrage of a strong, unreasoning party. There were doubtless many excellent men in the Tory party, even in its least excellent days; but the two men to whom the party, as such, owes most of purification were the Duke of Wellington and Sir Robert Peel. From the time when they became responsible for the management of a Conservative government, there was no doubt, in office or in the nation, that the public money and patronage were administered by men whom no consideration would induce to use either for their personal benefit; and who would, as far as their whole power lay, discourage and prevent the corrupt use of either by others. The process by which they succeeded in conveying this impression is illustrated by a chapter in the Dean of York's *Memoir of Peel,* in which that well-known dignitary recounts the temptations which he applied to the political purity of his relative.

"While Peel was Secretary for Ireland, I asked him to give a very trifling situation, nominally in his gift, to a worthy person for whom I felt an interest. He wrote me word that he was really anxious to oblige me in this matter, but that a nobleman of much parliamentary interest, who supported the government, insisted upon his right to dispose of all patronage in his own neighbourhood. So anxious was Peel to show his good will towards me, that he prevailed upon the Lord-Lieutenant to ask as a favour from the aforesaid nobleman that the situation might be given to my nominee; but the marquis replied, that the situation was of no value, yet, to prevent a dangerous precedent, he must refuse the application.

In times long after, when Sir Robert Peel became prime minister, I asked him often in the course of many years for situations for my sons, which situations were vacant and in his immediate gift. I subjoin three letters which I received from him on these subjects; they were written after long intervals and at different periods, but they all speak the same language:

'*Whitehall, December* 20 (*no date of year*).
MY DEAR DEAN OF YORK,—I thank you for your consideration of what you deem the unrequited sacrifice which I make in the public service. But I beg to say, that my chief consolation and reward is the *consciousness* that my exertions are disinterested—that I have considered official patronage as a public trust, to be applied to the reward and encouragement of public service, or to the less praiseworthy, but still necessary, purpose of promoting the gen-

eral interests of the government. That patronage is so wholly inadequate to meet the fair claims of a public nature that are daily presented for my consideration, and that constitute the chief torment of office, that I can only overcome the difficulties connected with the distribution by the utmost forbearance as to deriving any personal advantage from it. If I had absolute control over the appointment to which you refer, I should apply it to the satisfaction of one or other of the engagements into which I entered when I formed the government, and which (from the absolute want of means) remain unfulfilled. But I have informed the numerous parties who have applied to me on the subject of that appointment, that I feel it to be my duty, on account of the present condition of the board and the functions they have to perform, to select for it some experienced man of business connected with the naval profession, or some man distinguished in that profession.

Believe me, my dear Dean, affectionately yours,

ROBERT PEEL.'

I applied again for another place of less importance; the answer was much as before.

'Whitehall, April 5, 1843.

MY DEAR DEAN OF YORK,—I must dispose of the appointment to which you refer upon the same principle on which I have uniformly disposed of every appointment of a similar nature.

I do not consider patronage of this kind (and, indeed, I may truly say it of all patronage) as the means of gratifying private wishes of any one. Those who have made locally great sacrifices and great exertions for the maintenance of the political cause which they espouse, have always been considered fairly entitled to be consulted in respect to the disposal of local patronage, and would justly complain if, in order to promote the interests of a relative of my own, I were to disregard their recommendations. It would subject me to great personal embarrassment, and be a complete departure from the rule to which I have always adhered.

All patronage of all descriptions, so far from being of the least advantage personally to a minister, involves him in nothing but embarrassment.

Ever affectionately yours,

ROBERT PEEL.'

I publish one more letter of the same kind, because all these letters exhibit the character of the writer, and contain matters of some public interest. The distributor of stamps died in the very place where my son was resident, and where he and I had exerted considerable interest in assisting the government members. I thought that now, perhaps, an exception might be made to the general rule, and I confidently recommended my eldest son for the vacancy. The following was the answer:

'Whitehall, May 1.

MY DEAR DEAN,—Whatever arrangements may be made with respect to the office of distributor of stamps, lately held by Mr ——, I do not feel myself justified in appropriating to myself any share of the local patronage of a county with which I have not the remotest connection by property, or any other local tie.

There are three members for the county of —— who support the government; and, in addition to the applications which I shall no doubt have from them, I have already received recommendations from the Duke of —— and Earl ——, each having certainly better claims than I have personally for local appointments in the county of ——.

I feel it quite impossible to make so complete a departure from the principles on which I have invariably acted, and which I feel to be nothing more than consistent with common justice, as to take ——shire offices for my own private purposes.

Very faithfully yours,
ROBERT PEEL.'

These letters show the noble principle on which Sir Robert's public life was founded. I am quite sure that he had a great regard for my sons. He invited them to his shooting-quarters, was pleased to find them amusement, and made them many handsome presents; but he steadily refused to enrich them out of the public purse merely because they were his nephews. Many prime ministers have not been so scrupulous."

And clearly *one* divine wishes Sir Robert Peel had not been so.

The changes of opinion which Sir Robert Peel underwent are often cited as indications of a want of conscientiousness. They really are, subject of course to the preceding remarks,

proofs of his conscientiousness. We do not mean in the obvious sense of them being opposed to his visible interest, and
having on two great occasions destroyed the most serviceable
party organisation ever ruled by a statesman in a political
age: but in a more refined sense, the timeliness of his transitions may, without overstraining, be thought a mark of their
bona fides. He could not have changed with such felicitous
exactness, if he had been guided by selfish calculation. The
problems were too great and too wide. There have, of course,
been a few men—Talleyrand and Theramenes are instances
—who have seemed to hit, as if by a political sense, the fitting
moment to leave the side which was about to fall, and to join
the side which was about to rise. But these will commonly
be found to be men of a very different character from that of
Peel. Minds are divided into open and close. Some men are
so sensitive to extrinsic impressions, pass so easily from one
man to another, catch so well the tone of each man's thought,
use so well the opportunities of society for the purposes of
affairs, that they are, as it were, by habit and practice, metri-
cal instruments of public opinion. Sir Robert was by character, both natural and acquired, the very reverse. He was
a reserved, occupied man of business. In the arts of society, in
the easy transition from person to person, from tone to tone,
he was but little skilled. If he had been left to pick up his
rules of conduct by mere social perception and observation,
his life would have been a life of miscalculations; instead of
admiring the timeliness of his conversions, we should wonder
at the perversity of his transitions. The case is not new. In
ancient times, at a remarkable moment, in the persons of two
selfish men of genius, the open mind was contrasted with the
close. By a marvellous combination of successive manœuvres,
Julius Cæsar rose from ruin to empire; the spoiled child of
society—sensitive to each breath of opinion—ever living at
least among the externals of enjoyment—always retaining, by
a genial kindliness of manner, friends from each of the classes
which he variously used. By what the vulgar might be pardoned for thinking a divine infatuation, Pompeius lost the
best of political positions, threw away every recurring chance,
and died a wandering exile. As a reserved, ungenial man, he
never was able to estimate the feeling of the time. "I have
only to stamp with my foot when the occasion requires, to
raise legions from the soil of Italy!" were the words of one
who could not in his utmost need raise a force to strike one

blow for Italy itself. The fate of Pompeius would have been
that of Peel, if he too had played the game of selfish calculation. His changes, as it has been explained, are to be otherwise accounted for. He was always anxious to do right. An
occupied man of business, he was converted when other men
of business in the nation were converted.

It is not, however, to be denied that a calm and bland nature like that of Peel is peculiarly prone to self-illusion. Many
fancy that it is passionate, imaginative men who most deceive
themselves; and of course they are more tempted—a more
vivid fancy and a more powerful impulse hurry them away.
But they know their own weakness. "Do you believe in ghosts,
Mr Coleridge?" asked some lady. "No, ma'am, I have seen
too many," was the answer. A quiet, calm nature, when it is
tempted by its own wishes, is hardly conscious that it is
tempted. These wishes are so gentle, quiet, as it would say,
so "reasonable," that it does not conceive it possible to be
hurried away into error by them. Nor *is* there any hurry.
They operate quietly, gently, and constantly. Such a man will
very much believe what he wishes. Many an imaginative out-
cast, whom no man would trust with sixpence, really forms
his opinions on points which interest him by a much more
intellectual process—at least, has more purely intellectual
opinions beaten and tortured into him—than the eminent
and respected man of business, in whom every one confides,
who is considered a model of dry judgment, of clear and pas-
sionless equanimity. Doubtless Sir Robert Peel went on believing in the corn laws, when no one in the distrusted classes
even fancied that they were credible.

It has been bitterly observed of Sir Robert Peel, that he
was "a Radical at heart"; and, perhaps, with a similar thought
in his mind, Mr Cobden said once, at a League meeting, "I
do not altogether like to give up Peel. You see he is a Lancashire man." And it cannot be questioned that, strongly opposed as Sir Robert Peel was to the Reform Bill, he was
really much more suited to the reformed than to the unreformed House of Commons. The style of debating in the latter was described by one who had much opportunity for observation, Sir James Mackintosh, as "continuous, animated,
after-dinner discussion". The House was composed mainly of
men trained in two great schools, on a peculiar mode of education, with no great real knowledge of the classics, but with
many lines of Virgil and Horace lingering in fading memo-

ries, contrasting oddly with the sums and business with which
they were necessarily brought side by side. These gentlemen
wanted not to be instructed, but to be amused; and hence
arose what, from the circumstance of their calling, may be
called the class of conversationalist statesmen. Mr Canning
was the type of these. He was a man of elegant gifts, of easy
fluency, capable of embellishing anything, with a nice wit,
gliding swiftly over the most delicate topics; passing from
topic to topic like the *raconteur* of the dinner table, touching
easily on them all, letting them all go as easily; confusing
you as to whether he knows nothing or knows everything.
The peculiar irritation which Mr Canning excited through
life was, at least in part, owing to the natural wrath with
which you hear the changing talk of the practised talker running away about all the universe; never saying anything which
indicates real knowledge, never saying anything which at the
very moment can be shown to be a blunder; ever on the surface, and ever ingratiating itself with the superficial. When
Mr Canning was alive, sound men of all political persua-
sions—the Duke of Wellington, Lord Grey—ever disliked him.
You may hear old Liberals to this day declaring he was the
greatest charlatan who ever lived, angry to imagine that his
very ghost exists; and when you read his speeches yourself,
you are at once conscious of a certain dexterous insincerity
which seems to lurk in the very felicities of expression, and
to be made finer with the very refinements of the phraseology.
Like the professional converser, he seems so apt at the *finesse*
of expression, so prone to modulate his words, that you cannot imagine him putting his fine mind to tough thinking,
really working, actually grappling with the rough substance
of a great subject. Of course, if this were the place for an estimate of Mr Canning, there would be some limitation, and
much excuse to be offered for all this. He was early thrown
into what we may call an aristocratic debating society, accustomed to be charmed, delighting in classic gladiatorship.
To expect a great speculator, or a principled statesman, from
such a position, would be expecting German from a Parisian,
or plainness from a diplomatist. He grew on the soil on which
he had been cast; and it is hard, perhaps impossible, to separate the faults which are due to it and to him. He and it have
both passed away. The old delicate parliament is gone, and
the gladiatorship which it loved. The progress of things, and
the Reform Bill which was the result of that progress, have

taken, and are taking, the national representation away from the university classes, and conferring it on the practical classes. Exposition, arithmetic, detail, reforms—these are the staple of our modern eloquence. The old boroughs which introduced the young scholars are passed away; and even if the young scholars were in parliament, the subjects do not need the classic tact of expression. Very plain speaking suits the "passing tolls," "registration of joint-stock companies," finance, the Post-office. The petty regulation of the details of civilisation, which happily is the daily task of our Government, does not need, does not suit, a *recherché* taste or an ornate eloquence. As is the speech, so are the men. Sir Robert Peel was inferior to Canning in the old parliament; he would have been infinitely superior to him in the new. The aristocratic refinement, the nice embellishment, of the old time, were as alien to him as the detail and dryness of the new era were suitable. He was admirably fitted to be where the Reform Bill placed him. He was fitted to work and explain; he was not able to charm or to amuse.

In its exact form this kind of eloquence and statesmanship is peculiar to modern times, and even to this age. In ancient times the existence of slavery forbade the existence of a middle-class eloquence. The Cleon who possessed the tone and the confidence of the people in trade was a man vulgar, coarse, speaking the sentiments of a class whose views were narrow and whose words were mean. So many occupations were confined to slaves, that there was scarcely an opening for the sensible, moderate, rational body whom we now see. It was, of course, always possible to express the sentiments and prejudices of people in trade. It is new to this era, it seems created for Sir Robert Peel to express those sentiments, in a style refined, but not too refined; which will not jar people of high cultivation, which will seem suitable to men of common cares and important transactions.

In another respect Sir Robert Peel was a fortunate man. The principal measures required in his age were "repeals". From changing circumstances, the old legislation would no longer suit a changed community; and there was a clamour, first for the repeal of one important Act, and then of another. This was suitable to the genius of Peel. He could hardly have created anything. His intellect, admirable in administrative routine, endlessly fertile in suggestions of detail, was not of the class which creates, or which readily even believes an ab-

solutely new idea. As has been so often said, he typified the
practical intelligence of his time. He was prone, as has been
explained, to receive the daily deposits of insensibly-changing
opinion; but he could bear nothing startling; nothing bold,
original, single, is to be found in his acts or his words. Nothing could be so suitable to such a mind as a conviction that
an existing law was wrong. The successive gradations of opinion pointed to a clear and absolute result. When it was a
question, as in the case of the Reform Bill, not of simple
abolition, but of extensive and difficult reconstruction, he
"could not see his way". He could be convinced that the
anti-Catholic laws were wrong, that the currency laws were
wrong, that the commercial laws were wrong; especially he
could be convinced that the *laissez-faire* system was right,
and the real thing was to do nothing; but he was incapable of
the larger and higher political construction. A more imaginative genius is necessary to deal with the consequences of new
creations, and the structure of an unseen future.

This remark requires one limitation. A great deal of what
is called legislation is really administrative regulation. It does
not settle what is to be done, but *how* it is to be done; it does
not prescribe what our institutions shall be, but directs in
what manner existing institutions shall work and operate.
Of this portion of legislation Sir Robert Peel was an admirable master. Few men have fitted administrative regulations
with so nice an adjustment to a prescribed end. The Currency Act of 1844 was an instance of this. If you consult the
speeches by which that bill was introduced and explained to
parliament, you certainly will not find any very rigid demon-
strations of political economy, or dry compactness of abstract
principle. Whether the abstract theory of the supporters of
that Act be sound or unsound, no exposition of it ever came
from the lips of Peel. He assumed the results of that theory;
but no man saw more quickly the nature of the administrative machinery which was required. The separation of the
departments of the Bank of England, the limitation of the
country issues, though neither of them original ideas of Sir
Robert's own mind, yet were not, like most of his other important political acts, forced on him from without. There
was a general agreement among the received authorities in
favour of a certain currency theory; the administrative statesman saw a good deal before other men what was the most

judicious and effectual way of setting it at work and regulating its action.

We have only spoken of Sir Robert Peel as a public man; and if you wish to write what is characteristic about him, that is the way to do so. He was a man whom it requires an effort to think of as engaged in anything but political business. Disraeli tells us that some one said that Peel was never happy except in the House of Commons, or doing something which had some relation to something to be done there. In common life, we continually see men scarcely separable as it were from their pursuits; they are as good as others, but their visible nature seems almost all absorbed in a certain visible calling. When we speak of them we are led to speak of it, when we would speak of it we are led insensibly to speak of them. It is so with Sir Robert Peel. So long as constitutional statesmanship is what it is now, so long as its function consists in recording the views of a confused nation, so long as success in it is confined to minds plastic, changeful, administrative—we must hope for no better man. You have excluded the profound thinker; you must be content with what you can obtain—the business gentleman.

LORD PALMERSTON*

(1865)

Henry John Temple, third Viscount Palmerston, was born at
Broadlands, Hampshire, in 1784. He was the elder son of Henry
Temple, second Viscount Palmerston, M.P., by his second wife,
Mary Mee. The third viscount succeeded to the peerage in 1802.
He was educated at Harrow; in Edinburgh, where he was sent to
board with Dugald Stewart and attend his lectures; and at St.
John's College, Cambridge, where he went in 1803. In 1807 he
became Tory M.P. for Newport, Isle of Wight. He was Lord of
the Admiralty in the Portland administration. In 1809 he accepted the secretaryship for war from Perceval, which he retained
throughout successive administrations until 1828. He was elected
M.P. for Cambridge University, 1811–31, when he was rejected
owing to his support of parliamentary reform. After occupying
two other seats, he became M.P. for Tiverton in 1835, which
seat he retained until his death. In 1829 he made his first great
speech on foreign affairs, attacking the government's policy on
Portugal and Greece. He supported Catholic emancipation. In
1830 he became Foreign Secretary in Lord Grey's administration,
and retained this office for eleven years with only a short break
during Peel's administration. In 1830–31 he effected the independence of Belgium, and in the next decade supported Spain
and Portugal against pretenders to those realms; supported Turkey against the encroachments of Russia; and made a treaty with
Russia, Austria, and Prussia to defend Turkish territory against
the Egyptians. In 1840–41 he declared war against China and
annexed Hong Kong. In 1841 he effected the slave-trade convention. In 1846, after five years in opposition, Palmerston again
became Foreign Secretary in Lord John Russell's administration.
In that year he preserved Swiss independence from Austrian and
French interference. In 1849 he supported Turkey, at the risk
of war, in her refusal to give up to Russia and Austria certain
refugees. In 1850 he compelled Greece to accept his terms in

---

* This essay was first published in The Economist for October 21,
1865, Volume XXIII, pages 1265–66.

*the Pacifico affair, and blockaded the Piraeus, on which occasion
he made one of his most famous speeches and defeated both
English and foreign attempts to overthrow him. He had already
earned Queen Victoria's disapproval by his independent action,
and when he expressed his approval of Napoleon's coup d'état
in 1851, he was dismissed by Lord John Russell. In 1852 he became Home Secretary in Lord Aberdeen's ministry. On the outbreak of the Crimean War he proposed a campaign, but the
conduct of the war was refused him by Aberdeen, at which Russell resigned, and the ministry fell in 1855. Palmerston now became Prime Minister at a time of great difficulty and danger.
He agreed to the Treaty of Paris in 1856 under pressure from
France and Austria. He was defeated on the Chinese war question, but at the general election of 1857 was returned to power
with an increased majority. He was defeated in 1858 over the
Conspiracy to Murder Bill, but returned as Prime Minister in
1859. He supported Italy's advance towards independence, and
strengthened the national defences. Palmerston maintained English neutrality during the American Civil War. He died at
Brocket Hall, Hertfordshire in 1865.*

Lord Palmerston only died on Wednesday, and already the
world is full of sketches and biographies of him. It is very
natural that it should be so, for he counted for much in English politics: his personality was a power, and it is natural
that every one should, at his death, seek to analyse what we
used to have, and what we have now lost. We will do so, but,
remembering how often the tale has been told, we will be as
brief as possible.

Lord Derby happily said that he was born in the "pre-
scientific" period, and Lord Palmerston was so born, or even
more. He was, it is true, a boarder at Dugald Stewart's, and
we believe transcribed at least a part of the lectures on political economy of that philosopher, lately published. But the
combined influence of interior nature and the surrounding
situation was too strong. His real culture was that of living
languages and the actual world. He was the best French
scholar among his contemporaries—so much so that when he
went to Paris in 1859, the whole society, which fancied he was
an imperious and ignorant Englishman, was charmed by the
grace of his expression. His English in all his speeches was
sound and pure, and in his greater efforts almost fastidiously
correct. The feeling for language, which is one characteristic

of a great man of the world, was very nice in Lord Palmerston, and very characteristic.

It was from the actual knowledge of men—from close specific contact—that Lord Palmerston derived his data. We have heard grave men say with surprise, "He always has an anecdote to cap his argument. He begins, 'I knew a man once,'" and the anecdotes had no trace of the garrulity of age, they were real illustrations of the matter in hand. They were the chosen instances of a man who thought in instances. Some think, as the philosophers say, by "definition," others by "type". Lord Palmerston, like an animated man used to the animated world, thought in examples, and hardly realised abstract words.

It was because of this that in international matters—the only ones for which in youth he cared—he was a great practical lawyer. He knew what hardly any one knows, the subject-matter. He knew the cases with which during a long life he had to deal. To most men international law is a matter of precedent and words; to him it was a matter of personal adventure and reality. Some people not unqualified to judge have said that his opinion on such matters was as good as any law officer's. He might not have studied Vattel or Wheaton so closely as some, but he had, what is far better, followed with a keen interest the actual and necessary practice of present nations.

It was this sort of worldly sympathy and worldly education which gave Lord Palmerston his intelligibility. He was not a common man, but a common man might have been cut out of him. He had in him all that a common man has, and something more. And he did not at all despise, as some philosophers teach people to do, the common part of his mind. He was profoundly aware that the common mass of plain sense is the great administrative agency of the world; and that if you keep yourself in sympathy with this you win, and if not you fail. Sir George Lewis used to say that as Demosthenes declared action to be the first, second, and third thing in a statesman, so intelligibility is the first, second, and third thing in a constitutional statesman. It is to us certainly the first, second, and third thing in Lord Palmerston. This is not absolutely eulogistic. No one resembled less than Lord Palmerston the fancied portrait of an ideal statesman laying down in his closet plans to be worked out twenty years hence. He was a statesman for the moment. Whatever was not wanted now, whatever was not practicable now, whatever would not take now, he drove quite out of his mind. The prerequisites of a constitutional statesman have been defined as the "powers of a first-rate man, and the creed of a second-rate man". The saying is harsh, but it is expressive. Lord Palmerston's creed was never the creed of the far-seeing philosopher; it was the creed of a sensible and sagacious but still commonplace man. His objects were common objects: what was uncommon was the will with which he pursued them.

No man was better in action, but no man was more free from the pedantry of business. People, he has been heard to say, have different minds. "When I was a young man, the Duke of Wellington made an appointment with me at half-past seven in the morning, and some one asked me, Why, Palmerston, how will you keep that engagement? Oh, I said, of course, the easiest thing in the world. I shall keep it the last thing before I go to bed." He knew that the real essence of work is concentrated energy, and that people who really have that in a superior degree by nature, are independent of the forms and habits and artifices by which less able and active people are kept up to their labours.

Lord Palmerston prided himself on his foreign policy, on which we cannot now pronounce a judgment. But it is not upon this that his fame will rest. He had a great difficulty as a Foreign Minister. He had no real conception of any mode of life except that with which he was familiar. His idea, his fixed idea, was that the Turks were a highly improving and civilised race, and it was impossible to beat into him their essentially barbaric and unindustrial character. He would hear anything patiently, but no corresponding ideas were raised in his mind. A man of the world is not an imaginative animal, and Lord Palmerston was by incurable nature a man of the world: keenly detective in what he could realise by experience—utterly blind, dark, and impervious to what he could not so realise. Even the best part of his foreign policy was alloyed with this defect. The mantle of Canning had descended on him, and the creed and interests of Canning. He was most eager to use the strong influence of England to support free institutions—to aid "the Liberal party" was the phrase in those days—everywhere on the Continent. And no aim could be juster and better—it was the best way in which English strength could be used. But he failed in the instructed imagination and delicate perception necessary to its best attainment. He supported the Liberal party when it was bad, and the country unfit for it, as much as when it was good and the nation eager for it. He did not define the degree of his sympathy, or apportion its amount to the comparative merits of the different claims made on it. According to the notions of the present age, too, foreign policy should be regulated by abstract, or at least comprehensive, principles, but Lord Palmerston had no such principles. He prided himself on his exploits in Europe, but it is by his instincts in England that he will be remembered.

It was made a matter of wonder that Lord Palmerston should begin to rule the House of Commons at seventy, and there is no doubt that he was very awkward at first in so ruling it. Sir James Graham, and other judges of business management, predicted that "the thing would fail," and that a new Government would have to be formed. But the truth is, that though he had been fifty years in the House of Commons, Lord Palmerston had never regularly attended it, and even still less attended to it. His person had not been there very much, and his mind had been there very little. He answered a question on his own policy, or made a speech, and then went away. Debate was not to him, as to Mr Pitt or Mr Gladstone, a matter of life and pleasure. Mr Canning used to complain, "I can't get that three-decker Palmerston to bear down". And when he was made leader of the House, it came out that he hardly knew, if he did know, the forms of the House. But it was a defect of past interest, not a defect of present capacity. He soon mastered the necessary knowledge, and as soon as he had done so the sure sagacity of his masculine instincts secured him an unconquerable strength.

Something we wished to say more on these great gifts, and something, too, might be said as to the defects by which they were alloyed. But it is needless. Brevity is as necessary in a memorial article as in an epitaph. So much is certain, we shall never look upon his like again. We may look on others of newer race, but his race is departed. The merits of the new race were not his merits; their defects are not his. England will never want statesmen, but she will never see in our time such a statesman as Viscount Palmerston.

MR COBDEN*

(1865)

Richard Cobden was born at Heyshott, Sussex, in 1804. He was
the son of William Cobden, a farmer. At the age of fifteen Cobden became a clerk, and then a commercial traveller for his uncle,
who was a London calico merchant. In 1828 he became a partner in a calico firm and in 1831 established a calico factory in
Lancashire. Cobden settled in Manchester in 1832. He now began to repair his neglected education, and although he learned
French and attempted other formal studies, his chief reading was
in newspapers, Hansard, and generally in current affairs. He
began to write on economics in the Manchester Examiner, and
in 1835–36 published the pamphlets which opened his career:
England, Ireland and America and Russia. In these he stated
the theory which was to be his policy all his life, that the only
sound policy for Great Britain lay in free trade and non-interven-
tion. Between 1835–38 he travelled in America, Germany, and
the East. In 1838 he joined the movement with which his name
has ever since been connected; in October a group of Manchester
merchants formed a new association which grew to be the Anti-
Cornlaw League. Cobden gave the League his unsparing devotion; he had considerable talent for organisation and a gift for
presenting difficult ideas to untrained minds. He became M.P.
for Stockport in 1841, and early made his mark in parliamentary debate. His chief labours for the Anti-Cornlaw League, however, were on the platform, and with John Bright he travelled
the country year after year. In 1845 Cobden altered the focus
of his arguments against the corn laws to their agricultural aspect, since the revival of trade in 1844 had weakened his arguments against them on grounds of the duties on corn being an
obstacle to foreign demand for British goods. After Peel's resignation in 1845, Cobden set about persuading any government
of the necessity for total repeal of the Corn Laws, and when the
bill for total repeal of them was passed in 1846 after Peel's return to office, Peel acknowledged Cobden's untiring and dis-

---

* This essay was first published in The Economist for April 8,
1865, Volume XXIII, pages 397–98.

interested concern in the matter. Cobden had been privately financially ruined while he had expended all his energies and attention on the Anti-Cornlaw League. A public subscription was raised for him in commemoration of his services, and £80,-000 was collected. A further £40,000 was collected for him in 1860. In the general election of 1847 he became M.P. for the West Riding of Yorkshire as well as Stockport. During the next decade he advocated international arbitration and disarmament, and with Bright stood out against the Crimean War, which earned him a great public repulse. In 1857 he defeated the government on the question of the Chinese war, but when Palmerston at once appealed to the country, Cobden found that his action during the Crimean War had lost him his chance of retaining his Yorkshire seat, and when he stood for Huddersfield he was defeated. In 1859 he was returned as M.P. for Rochdale. During the next year he negotiated the commercial treaty with France. Palmerston offered him a baronetcy or a privy-councillorship, both of which he refused. Cobden died in London in 1865.

Twenty-three years ago—and it is very strange that it should be so many years—when Mr Cobden first began to hold Free-trade meetings in the agricultural districts, people there were much confused. They could not believe the Mr Cobden they saw to be the "Mr Cobden that was in the papers". They expected a burly demagogue from the North, ignorant of rural matters, absorbed in manufacturing ideas, appealing to class-prejudices—hostile and exciting hostility. They saw "a sensitive and almost slender man, of shrinking nerve, full of rural ideas, who proclaimed himself the son of a farmer, who understood and could state the facts of agricultural life far better than most agriculturists, who was most anxious to convince every one of what he thought the truth, and who was almost more anxious not to offend any one". The tradition is dying out, but Mr Cobden acquired, even in those days of Free-trade agitation, a sort of agricultural popularity. He excited a personal interest, he left what may be called a *sense* of himself among his professed enemies. They were surprised at finding that he was not what they thought; they were charmed to find that he was not what they expected; they were fascinated to find what he was. The same feeling has been evident at his sudden death—a death at least which was to the mass of occupied men sudden. Over political Belgravia —the last part of English society Mr Cobden ever cultivated —there was a sadness. Every one felt that England had lost an

individuality which it could never have again, which was of
the highest value, which was in its own kind altogether unequalled.

What used to strike the agricultural mind, as different
from what they fancied, and most opposite to a Northern
agitator, was a sort of playfulness. They could hardly believe
that the lurking smile, the perfectly magical humour which
they were so much struck by, could be that of a "Manchester man". Mr Cobden used to say, "I have as much right
as any man to call myself the representative of the tenant
farmer, for I am a farmer's son,—I am the son of a Sussex
farmer". But agriculturists keenly felt that this was not the
explanation of the man they saw. Perhaps they could not
have thoroughly explained, but they perfectly knew that they
were hearing a man of singular and most peculiar genius,
fitted as if by "natural selection" for the work he had to do,
and not wasting a word on any other work or anything else,
least of all upon himself.

Mr Cobden was very anomalous in two respects. He was
a sensitive agitator. Generally, an agitator is a rough man of
the O'Connell type, who says anything himself, and lets
others say anything. You "peg into me and I will peg into
you, and let us see which will win," is his motto. But Mr
Cobden's habit and feeling were utterly different. He never
spoke ill of any one. He arraigned principles, but not persons. We fearlessly say that after a career of agitation of
thirty years, not one single individual has—we do not say a
valid charge, but a producible charge—a charge which he
would wish to bring forward against Mr Cobden. You cannot find the man who says, "Mr Cobden said this of me, and
it was not true". This may seem trivial praise, and on paper
it looks easy. But to those who know the great temptations
of actual life it means very much. How would any other
great agitator, O'Connell or Hunt or Cobbett look, if tried
by such a test? Very rarely, if even ever in history, has a
man achieved so much by his words—been victor in what was
thought at the time to be a class-struggle—and yet spoken so
little evil as Mr Cobden. There is hardly a word to be
found, perhaps, even now, which the recording angel would
wish to blot out. We may on other grounds object to an agitator who lacerates no one, but no watchful man of the world
will deny that such an agitator has vanquished one of life's
most imperious and difficult temptations.

Perhaps some of our readers may remember as vividly as we do a curious instance of Mr Cobden's sensitiveness. He said at Drury Lane Theatre, in tones of feeling, almost of passion, curiously contrasting with the ordinary coolness of his nature, "I could not serve with Sir Robert Peel". After more than twenty years, the curiously thrilling tones of that phrase still live in our ears. Mr Cobden alluded to the charge which Sir Robert Peel had made, or half made, that the Anti-Corn-Law League and Mr Cobden had, by their action and agitation, conduced to the actual assassination of Mr Drummond, his secretary, and the intended assassination of himself—Sir Robert Peel. No excuse or palliation could be made for such an assertion except the most important one, that Peel's nerves were as susceptible and sensitive as Mr Cobden's. But the profound feeling with which Mr Cobden spoke of it is certain. He felt it as a man feels an unjust calumny, an unfounded stain on his honour.

Mr Disraeli said on Monday night[1] (and he has made many extraordinary assertions, but this is about the queerest) "Mr Cobden had a profound reverence for tradition". If there is any single quality which Mr Cobden had not, it was traditional reverence. But probably Mr Disraeli meant what was most true, that Mr Cobden had a delicate dislike of offending other men's opinions. He dealt with them tenderly. He did not like to have his own creed coarsely attacked, and he did—he could not help doing—as he would be done by; he never attacked any man's creed coarsely or roughly, or in any way except by what he in his best conscience thought the fairest and justest argument. This sensitive nature is one marked peculiarity in Mr Cobden's career as an agitator, and another is, that he was an agitator for men of business.

Generally speaking, occupied men charged with the responsibilities and laden with the labour of grave affairs are jealous of agitation. They know how much may be said against any one who is responsible for anything. They know how unanswerable such charges nearly always are, and how false they easily may be. A capitalist can hardly help thinking, "Suppose a man was to make a speech against my mode of conducting my own business, how much would he have to say!" Now it is an exact description of Mr Cobden, that by the personal magic of a single-minded practicability he made

[1] The day after Cobden's death.

men of business abandon this objection. He made them
rather like the new form of agitation. He made them say,
"How business-like, how wise, just what it would have been
right to do".

Mr Cobden of course was not the discoverer of the Free-
trade principle. He did not first find out that the Corn-laws
were bad laws. But he was the most effectual of those who
discovered how the Corn-laws were to be repealed, how Free-
trade was to change from a doctrine of *The Wealth of Nations* into a principle of tariffs and a fact of real life. If a
thing was right, to Mr Cobden's mind it ought to be done;
and as Adam Smith's doctrines were admitted on theory, he
could not believe that they ought to lie idle, that they ought
to be "bedridden in the dormitory of the understanding".

Lord Houghton once said, "In my time political economy
books used to begin, 'Suppose a man on an island'". Mr
Cobden's speeches never began so. He was altogether a man
of business speaking to men of business. Some of us may
remember the almost arch smile with which he said "the
House of Commons does not seem quite to understand the
difference between a cotton mill and a print work". It was
almost amusing to him to think that the first assembly of
the first mercantile nation could be, as they were and are,
very dim in their notions of the most material divisions of
their largest industry. It was this evident and first-hand familiarity with real facts and actual life which enabled Mr
Cobden to inspire a curiously diffused confidence in all
matter-of-fact men. He diffused a kind of "economic faith".
People in those days had only to say, "Mr Cobden said so,"
and other people went and "believed it".

Mr Cobden had nothing classical in the received sense
about his oratory; but it is quite certain that Aristotle, the
greatest teacher of the classical art of rhetoric, would very
keenly have appreciated his oratory. This sort of economic
faith is exactly what he would most have valued, what he
most prescribed. He said: "A speaker should convince his audience that he was a likely person to know". This was exactly
what Mr Cobden did. And the matter-of-fact philosopher
would have much liked Mr Cobden's habit of "coming to the
point". It would have been thoroughly agreeable to his positive mind to see so much of clear, obvious argument. He
would not, indeed, have been able to conceive a "League
Meeting". There has never, perhaps, been another time in
the history of the world when excited masses of men and

women hung on the words of one talking political economy. The excitement of these meetings was keener than any political excitement of the last twenty years, keener infinitely than any which there is now. It may be said, and truly, that the interest of the subject was Mr Cobden's felicity, not his mind; but it may be said with equal truth that the excitement was much greater when he was speaking than when any one else was speaking. By a kind of keenness of nerve, he said the exact word most fitted to touch, not the bare abstract understanding, but the quick individual perceptions of his hearers.

We do not wish to make this article a mere panegyric. Mr Cobden was far too manly to like such folly. His mind was very peculiar, and like all peculiar minds had its sharp limits. He had what we may call a supplementary understanding, that is, a bold, original intellect, acting on a special experience, and striking out views and principles not known to or neglected by ordinary men. He did not possess the traditional education of his country, and did not understand it. The solid heritage of transmitted knowledge has more value, we believe, than he would have accorded to it. There was too a defect in business faculty not identical, but perhaps not altogether without analogy. The late Mr James Wilson used to say, "Cobden's administrative power I do not think much of, but he is most valuable in counsel, always original, always shrewd, and not at all extreme". He was not altogether equal to meaner men in some beaten tracks and pathways of life, though he was far their superior in all matters requiring an original stress of speculation, an innate energy of thought.

It may be said, and truly said, that he has been cut off before his time. A youth and manhood so spent as his, well deserved a green old age. But so it was not to be. He has left us, quite independently of his positive works, of the repeal of the Corn-laws, of the French treaty, a rare gift—the gift of a unique character. There has been nothing before Richard Cobden like him in English history, and perhaps there will not be anything like him. And his character is of the simple, emphatic, picturesque sort which most easily, when opportunities are given as they were to him, goes down to posterity. May posterity learn from him! Only last week we hoped to have learned something ourselves:—

> "But what is before us we know not,
> And we know not what shall succeed".

MR BRIGHT'S RETIREMENT*

(1870)

*John Bright was born at Rochdale, Lancashire in 1811. He was
the son of Jacob Bright, owner of a spinning-mill, and of Mar-
tha Wood. In his youth he worked in his father's mill. He made
his first public speech in 1830 in defence of the temperance
movement and gained his reputation as an orator by his steady
opposition to the principle of church rates, between 1834–41.
He also advocated the abolition of capital punishment. His life-
long friendship with Cobden began during this period, probably
in 1835. In 1840 he became treasurer of the Rochdale branch
of the Anti-Cornlaw League, and in 1842 began agitation in
London against the Corn Laws, which was later carried on in
the Midlands and in Scotland. In 1843 he became M.P. for
Durham, and in 1847 and 1852 M.P. for Manchester. In 1848
he advocated disestablishment in Ireland and increased occupation for the peasantry by partition of landed property. In 1849
he joined Cobden in forming "The Commons' League" for parliamentary reform. In 1851 he opposed Russell's excluding Sir
David Salomons from the House as a Jew. In 1853–54 he opposed the Crimean War. He was defeated in the election for
Manchester in 1857, but elected for Birmingham and subsequently re-elected in 1858, 1865, 1868, 1873, 1874, and
1880–85. In 1859 Bright opposed the government Reform Bill
in a speech insisting on the need for redistribution of seats. He
negotiated the preliminary treaty of commerce with France in
1860. He was the president of the Board of Trade in Gladstone's first ministry, 1868–70. He became Chancellor of the
Duchy of Lancaster in 1873, which position he resigned in 1882
on British intervention in Egyptian affairs. In 1885 he became
M.P. for the central division of Birmingham, and in 1887 made
his last parliamentary speech, an attack on Gladstone's Home
Rule Bill of 1886. He and Cobden were the two leading representatives of the manufacturing class as a force in English politics after the Reform Act of 1832. Bright died in Rochdale in
1889.*

* This article was first published in *The Economist* for December
24, 1870, Volume XXVIII, pages 1545–46.

The retirement of Mr Bright from the Cabinet, owing to failing health, will give all the older readers of the ECONOMIST
a peculiar feeling of sadness. A new generation is attaining
life and vigour to whom the "Anti-Corn Law League" is a
matter of history. If you chance to speak of it as *"the
League,"* as we always used to speak of it, they ask *"what
League?"* But the great majority of active men still remember the details of that great agitation, the triumphs of "Drury
Lane and Covent Garden" meetings, and how Mr Bright's
voice rung full and penetrating, second in power only to one,
if second to any, over those great open stages. That Mr Bright
has to abandon active administration will come home to
many as an unwelcome hint that it is time for them to give
up themselves.

If, as has been said, "it is a proud thing to have millions
of opponents and *no* enemy," Mr Bright has a full right to
be proud. Persons at a distance who disapprove of his principles, and who only think of him as an incarnation of them,
undoubtedly hate him with a strong political hatred; but no
one brought close to him does so. There is an evident sincerity and bluff *bona fides* about him, which goes straight
to the hearts of Englishmen. We have been often amused to
see how much, in the depths of Tory districts where "John
Bright" was bitterly execrated, the regular residents were puzzled because their own M.P.'s and the most conservative people who went to London always mentioned him with geniality
and toleration, and if young, would say, in the modern dialect—"Well, after all, he is a great *institution.*"

Perhaps great orators, more than any other men, are liable
to be utterly misconceived. Their power—more penetrative
at the moment than any literature—brings home to thousands
and thousands *some* notion, but it can never be a true notion.
An orator works under severe conditions. He can only express
the sort of thoughts an audience will hear, and the sort of
feelings they will apprehend; and every orator of finer nature
has much sentiment which is too subtle for the multitude,
and many conclusions which will not suit public meetings.
There are many things, too, which can only be said in a still,
small voice, and not in the stentorian tones which alone public meetings can take in. No audience, still less any distant
hearer of a speech, gives an orator credit for that which he

has to leave out in order to speak effectually. They fancy that there is nothing in him but the sort of things which he says, especially if he is continually saying them; but an orator of finer genius feels much which he never says, much which under the inevitable conditions of his art he could not say. It is the pursuing penalty of every great orator that he is, in a sense, *mis*known everywhere; for he is compelled to diffuse among mankind a picture of himself drawn in a deceiving light, with some traits aggravated, with other traits diminished—like him of course in many respects, yet to those who have real knowledge, in nearly as many utterly unreal and unlike.

Mr Bright has had his full share of such misconceptions. In the agricultural districts he is even yet looked upon as an excessively pacific person, who cared little for the honour of England, and who would sacrifice that or anything else for peace at any price; but as Lord Granville said—"There are not many persons who have more of the popular "'John Bull' character" than Mr Bright, and among the many ingredients of that character, a certain pugnacity is not the one for which he is the least remarkable.

Again, Mr Bright is often imagined to be a wild incendiary, who would be glad to pull down every present institution, and who would not much care to inquire with what substitutes these institutions were to be replaced. But in the present Cabinet, unless consistent rumour speaks false, his voice has more usually been a Conservative voice than the contrary. And in fact, though Mr Bright has wanted much to change many things, and still may want to change them, he is much too characteristic an Englishman to like change for change's sake, or not to have a full share of the Conservative instinct which if possible clings to the "tried," and will not without plain and clear reason consent to migrate to the unknown and inexperienced.

If Mr Bright has been somewhat misconceived in his own time, he will probably have the compensation of being—we may risk a prophecy—of all our own contemporary politicians the best known to posterity. His speeches are very amusing reading, and, as a rule, those are best known to posterity who can amuse posterity. Nothing can in general be more fleeting than the fame of an orator. A great Budget speech is heard with the most eager attention, and criticised at the time with vehement interest. But who cares for it a few years after-

wards? Who but a very few economical inquirers has the
slightest remembrance of the financial speeches of Pitt or
Peel? But there is a certain mixture of racy fun and sentiment in Bright's speeches which make them capital reading
even now—reading which you can read when you are tired,
but which yet has something in it; and this is the sort of
literature which travels farthest and lives longest.

We are not now reviewing Mr Bright's career. It is not yet
closed. Though we trust he will never again attempt administrative labours, we hope that his powerful tones may often
be heard again in the great assemblages of his countrymen.
If we had to sketch his life, there would be something to
blame as well as much to praise. But we need not go into that
now. We have only to express our regret at his retirement,
and to wonder at the strange dispensations of Providence,
which mixed a fine, and to some extent incapacitating, thread
of nervous delicacy in a mind so healthy, so vigorous, and on
most points so emphatically robust.

THE CONSERVATIVE VEIN IN
MR BRIGHT*

(1876)

It seems a paradox to say that there are few more typical Conservatives in the House of Commons than Mr Bright; and yet the assertion is in one sense certainly true. Vehemently as he has fought for the cause of popular right, and eloquently as he has, at times, attacked the privileged classes who resisted these reforms, Mr Bright's political notions are,—and this is the characteristic of a Conservative,—probably more strictly prepossessions and traditions, less the result of inner deliberation and intellectual judgment, than those of any Conservative in the House of Commons, immeasurably more so than those of the Conservative leader. We doubt very much whether even Mr Gathorne Hardy has as much right to represent the Conservative whose political mind is the product of deep traditional, and, we may say, hereditary preoccupations, as Mr Bright. Of course it is not merely the accident that a man's traditional feelings on politics represent the tendencies of the future rather than the tendencies of the past, which makes him in this sense a Liberal rather than a Conservative. We are now using the word rather in relation to character than in relation to the progress of events. And in this sense we should say that while the Liberal turn of mind denotes the willingness to admit new ideas, and the perfect impartiality with which those ideas, when admitted, are canvassed and considered, the Conservative turn of mind denotes adhesiveness to the early and probably inherited ideas of childhood, and a very strong and practically effective distrust of the novel intellectual suggestions which come unaccredited by any such influential associations. Now in this sense, it hardly needed Mr Bright's very able speech on

---

* This article was first published in *The Economist* for April 29, 1876, Volume XXXIV, pages 506–7.

Wednesday, against Women's Suffrage, to show that constitutionally, though not in the sense which the accident of
chronology attaches to the word, Mr Bright is a Conservative.
Mr Bright has been throughout his life a very warm friend
of what is called progress on all subjects on which he inherited
from his early traditions the ideas of progress. But it is
not possible to mention a single subject on which he has
abandoned the traditions of his youth in favour of the newer
ideas of his maturity, and of the age in which that maturity
has been cast. Let us cast a glance all round the political
world. In relation to the question of Throne or Republic, it
cannot be doubted that he inherited from his forefathers a
sort of abstract preference for a Republic together with a very
decided disposition to let well alone and acquiesce in a throne
so long as that throne is dignified by high character and personal virtues. And this is precisely the shade of policy which
he has always represented whenever such matters have come
into discussion at all. That Mr Bright has always been the
first to claim a kindly and cordial consideration for the Republic ultimately founded by the descendants of the Pilgrim
fathers in the United States of America, we all know. But
we also all know how, whenever anything like a taunt has
been cast at the institution of royalty in England, Mr Bright
has been foremost to lend the shield of his personal enthusiasm to the present wearer of the British crown. When the
Queen is in question it would be impossible to name a more
cordial Conservative than Mr Bright. His feelings are kindled,
like the feelings of a cavalier of old, at the mere mention of
her name, as Mr Ayrton has had occasion to know. No doubt
it is in great measure the simplicity and worth of the present
monarch which endears her so much to Mr Bright. But that,
again, shows that old associations and emotions, not mere intellectual convictions, are at the root of his feelings. He does
not desire to discriminate between the institution and the
form which the institution takes at the present moment. The
mixed feelings which he has always felt grow stronger with his
years. He is as earnest as ever in his abstract admiration for
republics. He is more earnest than ever in his concrete loyalty
to the throne.

Or take questions of constitutional reform, and consider
his attitude on them. He has always been eager for the en-
largement of the franchise up to the point of a household
franchise. He holds that family life is a sort of guarantee for

English sobriety—a notion very dear to the British middle
class, but not perhaps very adequately sustained by the testing of experience. For that inherited idea he has fought gal-
lantly till he has succeeded in making it part of the British
constitution, at least as regards the boroughs, and he is
pledged of course to extend it to the counties. But while he
is eloquent on behalf of the guarantee given by a householder's responsibility and ties, and would be the last, we
suspect, to ask us to dispense with it, as a condition of the
suffrage, any attempt to take guarantees of another sort, which
were not familiar to his childhood—like that known as cumulative voting, or representation of minorities—he has always
hated with an intensity and inexorability almost amusing.
But some one will say that this only shows that Mr Bright is
really Liberal, and not Conservative,—that he sees these suggestions advanced by those who grudge the democracy its triumphs, and not by those who trust the people. Well then
take this question of the women's franchise. Our readers are
aware that we have advocated that change partly on the
ground that in the working class, at least,—the most numerous class,—the women are often more careful, and intelligent,
and scrupulous, and competent to vote, than the men,—partly
because we have regarded them as likely to be themselves the
better for an extension of their practical interests. But Mr
Bright, after voting once reluctantly for it, has at last been
unable to suppress the disgust with which this proposal to
turn family life and traditions (as they have been transmitted
to him) upside down, affects him, and has broken through
the trammels of personal ties to speak with all the force and
vigour of his character on behalf of traditions so deeply ingrained into it. This metamorphosis, as it seems to him, of
the true functions of women, revolts him far more than it
revolts the bulk of the Conservative party, some of whom,
indeed, may, perhaps have adopted the cry for women's suffrage out of party motives, but most of whom, no doubt,
sympathised far more deeply with Mr Bright than with any of
their own leaders. Indeed, Mr Bright dwelt on the idea that
a revolution rather than a reform was involved in the proposal, with the genuine Conservative horror of revolution.
There was not much evidence in his speech that he had carefully weighed the probable results of the change, and found
them dangerous. On the contrary, the speech went to prove
that the change, if adopted, must be adopted on the ground

of considerations fundamentally different from those which
had recommended the various reforms of the franchise already adopted. And this seemed to be almost enough for him.
Prove that it was a proposal not only new in detail, but new
in principle, and it lost all charm for him. Revolution is as
much a term of reproach to Mr Bright as it is to Mr Gathorne
Hardy, though it means somewhat different things in the two
men's mouths. In each of them alike it represents the antithesis of all the cherished traditions of early years.

In short, Mr Bright's political constitution vehemently re-
pels the new ideas of modern statesmanship. He cannot bear
the agitation for the election of labourers or artisans as members of Parliament—a new idea which seems to him subver-
sive of political traditions. He wisely snubs Home Rule. He
will not listen with patience to any argument for the fair
representation of minorities. He declines all invitations to
join the Alliance League for the diminution of public-houses.
His Liberal sympathies are confined to the causes which he
found popular among his people long before he was a great
personage on the political stage—to Free-trade, economy,
peace, a popular franchise of the old kind, the ballot; and
enthusiasm for these causes is really in him political Conservatism. And the manner of his advocacy is as Conservative
as the matter. He always addresses the political affections
rather than the political reason, and this is no doubt the
great secret of his true popularity. The creed of the Mr Bright
of 1876 is probably far less altered from the creed of the Mr
Bright of 1840 than is the creed of the Duke of Richmond
of 1876 from the creed of the same peer in 1840. The Duke
of Richmond has reluctantly abandoned many articles of his
old creed—Mr Bright has abandoned none.

THE PRINCE CONSORT*

(1861)

Albert Francis Charles Augustus Emmanuel was born at Rosenau near Coburg in 1819. He was the second son of Ernest, duke of Saxe-Coburg-Gotha, and of Louise, daughter of Augustus, duke of Saxe-Gotha-Altenburg. Prince Albert visited England in 1836, when the Princess Victoria expressed her willingness to accept him as consort. After some travelling and continuing of his education, Prince Albert became betrothed to Queen Victoria in 1839, and they were married in 1840. In this year, Prince Albert was appointed Regent in case of the Queen's death. Throughout their married life Prince Albert gave the Queen great assistance in the performance of her political duties. The Prince Consort took an active part in the life of the nation: he projected the idea of the Great Exhibition of 1851; he gave valuable advice throughout the Crimean War, and he showed great sympathy with the condition of the working classes. Prince Albert died in London in 1861.

So much has, ere this, been said upon the life and character of Prince Albert, that scarcely anything now remains except to join very simply and plainly in the regret and sympathy which have been everywhere expressed by all classes of the nation—the low as well as the high. A long narrative of a simple career would now be wholly needless, for our contemporaries have supplied many such; and any protracted eulogy would be unsuitable both to our business-like pages and to the simple character of him whom we have lost.

If our loss is not—as has been extravagantly said—the greatest which the English nation could have sustained, it is among the most irreparable. Our Parliamentary constitution, in some sense, renews itself, or tends to do so. As one old statesman leaves the scene, a younger one comes forward, in the

* This article was first published in *The Economist* for December 21, 1861, Volume XIX, page 1401.

vigour of hope and power, to fill his place. When one great orator dies, another commonly succeeds him. The opportunity of the new aspirant is the departure of his predecessor; on every vacancy some new claimant—many claimants probably —strive with eager emulation to win it and to retain it. Every loss is, in a brief period, easily and fully repaired. Even, too, in the hereditary part of our constitution, most calamities are soon forgotten. One monarch dies, and another succeeds him. A new court, a new family, new hopes and new interests, spring up and supersede those which have passed away. What was, is forgotten; what is, is seen. But now we have the old Court without one of its mainstays and principal supports. The royal family of last week is still (and without change) the royal family of to-day; but the father of that family is removed. For such a loss there is not, in this world, any adequate resource or any complete compensation. In no rank of life can any one else be to the widow and children what the deceased husband and father would have been. In the Court as in the cottage, such loss must not only be grief now, but perplexity, trouble, and perhaps mistake hereafter.

The present generation, at least the younger part of it, have lost the idea that the Court is a serious matter. Everything for twenty years has seemed to go so easily and so well, that it has seemed to go of itself. There is no such thing in this world. Everything requires anxiety, and reflection, and patience. And the function of the Court, though we easily forget it when it is well performed, keeps itself much in our remembrance when it is ill performed. Old observers say that some of the half-revolutionary discontent in the times preceding the Reform Bill was attributable to the selfish apathy and decrepit profligacy of George the Fourth. The Crown is of singular importance in a divided and contentious free State, because it is the sole object of attachment which is elevated above every contention and division. But to maintain that importance, it must create attachment. We know that the Crown now does so fully; but we do not adequately bear in mind how much rectitude of intention, how much judgment in conduct, how much power of doing right, how much power of doing nothing, are requisite to unite the loyalty and to retain the confidence of a free people.

Some cynical observers have contrasted the unlimited encomiums of the last week with the "cold observance" and very measured popularity of Prince Albert during his life.

They remember the public hisses in 1855, and perhaps recall many hints and whispers of politics that have passed away. But the most graphic of our contemporaries have found nothing to record of Prince Albert so truly characteristic as this change.

His circumstances, and perhaps his character, forbade him to attempt the visible achievements and the showy displays which attract momentary popularity. Discretion is a quality seldom appreciated till it is lost; and it was discretion which Prince Albert eminently possessed.

MR GLADSTONE[1]*

(1860)

William Ewart Gladstone was born in 1809 in Liverpool, the third son of John Gladstone, merchant and Tory M.P., and of his second wife, Anne Robertson. He was educated at Eton and Christ Church, Oxford. Largely through the patronage of the Duke of Newcastle, Gladstone was elected to Parliament as a Tory in 1833. He became Junior Lord of the Treasury in 1834, and Under-secretary for War and the Colonies in 1835. At this period he denounced liberal innovation and parliamentary reform. In 1841 Gladstone became Vice-president of the Board of Trade under Sir Robert Peel, and in 1843 he became President of the Board and a member of the cabinet. He resigned in 1845 over the government's proposal to assist Catholic education in Ireland. In 1845 he became Colonial Secretary, but because of his free-trade views lost his seat in the Commons. In 1847 he was elected M.P. for the University of Oxford. Gladstone had seceded from the Tory party when Sir Robert Peel did so, and in the next few years he was moving towards Liberalism. In 1852 he contributed very largely to the fall of the Derby-Disraeli ministry by his attack on Disraeli's budget. In the succeeding Ministry of Lord Aberdeen, Gladstone was Chancellor of the Exchequer, and his great budget of 1853 enhanced his already considerable reputation as financier and orator. He resigned office in 1855, and from then until 1859 devoted most of his attention to attacking Palmerston's policies; nevertheless he joined Palmerston as Chancellor of the Exchequer and so became one of the leaders of the new Liberal party. He introduced a series of budgets leading towards more complete free trade. His moderate parliamentary Reform Bill of 1866 was defeated, but his speeches at that time did much to mould Dis-

---

[1] *Speech of the Chancellor of the Exchequer on the Finance of the Year and the Treaty of Commerce with France.* Delivered in the House of Commons on Friday, 10th February, 1860. Corrected by the Author.

* This essay was first published in the *National Review* for July 1960, Volume II, pages 219–43.

raeli's Reform Bill the following year. At the retirement of Lord John Russell in 1868, Gladstone became leader of the Liberal party and Prime Minister. His first administration from 1868–74 was marked by a series of reform measures. The Anglican Church in Ireland was disestablished, freeing the people from supporting a church to which most of them did not belong; the Irish Land Act of 1870 gave a degree of security to Irish tenant farmers. Religious tests for entry to Oxford and Cambridge were abolished; the secret ballot was introduced in elections; trade unions were legalised; and the judiciary was entirely reorganised. These changes provoked much opposition, and the Liberals were defeated in the election of 1874. In 1875 Gladstone relinquished leadership of the Liberal party, but did not retire from politics. The Near Eastern question and his alarm at Disraeli's adventurous foreign and colonial policy roused him to action, and by 1877 he was embarked on an active political campaign against the government. Gladstone was again Prime Minister from 1880–85, in 1886, and from 1892–94. The landmarks of his various ministries after Bagehot's time were the Land Act of 1881, the third Parliamentary Reform Act of 1884, the Boer War, which ended disastrously for England in 1881, the revolt in Egypt of Arabi Pasha, and the Home Rule bills, which were both rejected and the last of which brought Gladstone's last ministry to defeat. Gladstone died at Hawarden in 1898.

We believe that Quarterly essayists have a peculiar mission in relation to the characters of public men. We believe it is their duty to be personal. This idea may seem ridiculous to some of our readers; but let us consider the circumstances carefully. We allow that personality abounds already, that the names of public men are for ever on our lips, that we never take up a newspaper without seeing them. But this incessant personality is wholly fragmentary; it is composed of chance criticism on special traits, of fugitive remarks on temporary measures, of casual praise and casual blame. We can expect little else from what is written in haste, or is spoken without limitation. Public men must bear this criticism as they can. Those whose names are perpetually in men's mouths must not be pained if singular things are sometimes said of them. Still *some* deliberate truth should be spoken of our statesmen, and if Quarterly essayists do not speak it, who will? We fear it will remain unspoken.

Mr Gladstone is a problem, and it is very remarkable that he should be a problem. We have had more than ordinary

means for judging of him. He has been in public life for
seven and twenty years; he has filled some of the most conspicuous offices in the State; he has been a distinguished
member of the Tory party; he *is* a distinguished member of
the Liberal party; he has brought forward many measures;
he has passed many years in independent Opposition, which
is unquestionably the place most favourable to the display of
personal peculiarities in Parliament; he is the greatest orator
in the House of Commons; he never allows a single important topic to pass by without telling us what he thinks of it;
—and yet, with all these data, we are all of us in doubt about
him. What he will do, and what he will think, still more, why
he will do it, and why he will think it, are *quæstiones vexatæ*
at every political conjuncture. At the very last ministerial
crisis, when the Government of Lord Derby was on the verge
of extinction, when every vote on Lord John's resolution[2]
was of critical importance, no one knew till nearly the last
hour how Mr Gladstone would vote, and in the end he voted
against his present colleagues. The House of Commons gos-
sips are generally wrong about him. Nor is the uncertainty
confined to Parliamentary divisions; it extends to his whole
career. Who can calculate his future course? Who can tell
whether he will be the greatest orator of a great administration; whether he will rule the House of Commons; whether
he will be, as his gifts at first sight mark him out to be, our
greatest statesman? or whether, below the gangway, he will
utter unintelligible discourses; will aid in destroying many
ministries and share in none; will pour forth during many
hopeless years a bitter, a splendid, and a vituperative eloquence?

We do not profess that we can solve all the difficulties
that are suggested even by the superficial consideration of a
character so exceptional. We do not aspire to be prophets.
Mr Gladstone's destiny perplexes us—perhaps as much as it
perplexes our readers. But we think that we can explain much
of his past career; that many of his peculiarities are not so
unaccountable as they seem; that a careful study will show
us the origin of most of them; that we may hope to indicate
some of the material circumstances and conditions on which

[2] On the Parliamentary Reform Bill brought forward by Lord Derby's Government in 1859.

his future course depends, though we should not be so bold
as to venture to foretell it.

During the discussion on the Budget, an old Whig who
did not approve of it, but who had to vote for it, muttered of
its author, "Ah, Oxford on the surface, *but* Liverpool below".
And there is truth in the observation, though not in the
splenetic sense in which it was intended. Mr Gladstone does
combine, in a very curious way, many of the characteristics
which we generally associate with the place of his education
and many of those which we usually connect with the place
of his birth. No one can question the first part of the observation. No man has through life been more markedly an
Oxford man than Mr Gladstone. His *Church and State,* published after he had been several years in public life, was instinct with the very spirit of the Oxford of that time. His
Homer, published the other day, bears nearly equal traces of
the school in which he was educated. Even in his ordinary
style there is a tinge half theological, half classical, which
recalls the studies of his youth. Many Oxford men much
object to the opinions of their distinguished representative;
but none of them would deny, that he remarkably embodies
the peculiar results of the peculiar teaching of the place.

And yet he has something which his collegiate training
never would have given him, which it is rather remarkable
it has not taken away from him. There is much to be said
in favour of the University of Oxford. No one can deny to
it very great and very peculiar merits. But certainly it is not
an exciting place, and its education operates as a narcotic
rather than as a stimulant. Most of its students devote their
lives to a single profession, and we may observe among them
a kind of sacred torpidity. In many rural parsonages there
are men of very great cultivation, who are sedulous in their
routine duties, who attend minutely to the ecclesiastical state
of the souls in their village, but who are perfectly devoid of
general intellectual interests. They have no anxiety to solve
great problems; to busy themselves with the speculations of
their age; to impress their peculiar theology—for peculiar it is
both in its expression and in its substance—on the educated
mind of their time. Oxford, it has been said, "disheartens a
man early". At any rate, since Newmanism lost Father Newman, few indeed of her acknowledged sons attain decided
eminence in our deeper controversies. Jowett she would re-
pudiate, and Mansel is but applying the weapons of scep-

ticism to the service of credulity. The most characteristic of
Oxford men labour quietly, delicately, and let us hope usefully, in a confined sphere; they hope for nothing more, and
wish for nothing more. Even in secular literature we may observe an analogous tone. The *Saturday Review* is remarkable
as an attempt on the part of "university men" to speak on the
political topics and social difficulties of the time. And what
do they teach us? It is something like this: "So-and-so has
written a tolerable book, and we would call attention to the
industry which produces tolerable books. So-and-so has devoted himself to a great subject, and we would observe that
the interest now taken in great subjects is very commendable.
Such-and-such a lady has delicate feelings, which are desirable
in a lady, though we know that they are contrary to the facts
of the world. All common persons are doing as well as they
can, but it does not come to much after all. All statesmen
are doing as ill as they can, and let us be thankful that *that*
does not come to much either." We may search and search
in vain through this repository of the results of "university
teaching" for a single truth which it has established, for a
single high cause which it has advanced, for a single deep
thought which is to sink into the minds of its readers. We
have, indeed, a nearly perfect embodiment of the corrective
scepticism of a sleepy intellect. "A B says he has done something, but he has not done it; C D has made a parade of
demonstrating this or that proposition, but he does not prove
his case; there is one mistake in page 5, and another in page
113; a great history has been written of this or that century,
but the best authorities as to that period have not been consulted, which, however, is not very remarkable, as there is
nothing in them." We could easily find, if it were needful,
many traces of the same indifferent habit, the same apathetic
culture, in the more avowed productions of Oxford men. The
shrewd eye of Mr Emerson, stimulated doubtless by the contrast to America, quickly caught the trait. "After all," says
the languid Oxford gentleman of his story, "there is nothing
true and nothing new, and no matter!"

To this, as to every other species of indifferentism, Mr
Gladstone is the antithesis. Oxford has not disheartened *him*.
Some of his colleagues would say they wished it had. He is
interested in everything he has to do with, and often interested too much. He proposes to put a stamp on contract
notes with an eager earnestness as if the destiny of Europe,

here and hereafter, depended upon its enactment. He cannot let anything alone. "Sir," said an old distributor of stamps in Westmoreland, "my head, sir, is worn out. I must resign. The Chancellor, sir, is imposing of things that I can't understand." The world is not well able to understand them either. The public departments break down under the pressure of the industry of their superior. Mr Gladstone is ready to work as long as his brain will hold together—to make speeches as long as he has utterance (words he is sure to have); but the subordinate officials will not work equally hard. They have none of the excitement of origination; they will not share the credit of success. They do, however, share the discredit of failure. In the high-pressure season of this year's Budget, Acts of Parliament have been passed in which essential provisions were not to be found, in which what was intended to be enacted was omitted or exceeded, in which the marginal notes were widely astray of the text. In his literary works Mr Gladstone is the same. His book on Homer is perhaps the most zealous work which this generation has produced. He has the enthusiasm of a German professor for the scholastic detail, for the exact meaning of word No. 1, for the precise number of times which word No. 2 is used by the poet; he has the enthusiasm of a lover for Helen, the enthusiasm of an orator for the speeches. Of his theological books we need not speak; every reader will recall the curious succession of needless *quæstiunculæ* by which their interest is marred.

Some of this energy Mr Gladstone probably owes to the place of his birth. Lancashire is sometimes called "America-and-water": we suspect it is America and very little water. The excessive energy natural to half-educated men who have but a single pursuit cannot, indeed, in any part of England, produce the monstrous results which it occasionally produces in the United States; it is kept in check by public opinion, by the close vicinity of an educated world. But in its own pursuit, in commerce, we question whether New York itself is more intensely eager than Liverpool—at any rate, it is difficult to conceive how it can be. Like several other remarkable men whose families belong to the place, Mr Gladstone has carried into other pursuits, the eagerness, the industry—we are loth to say the rashness, but the boldness—which Liverpool men apply to the business of Liverpool. Underneath the scholastic polish of his Oxford education, he has the speculative hardihood, the eager industry of a Lancashire merchant.

Such is one of the principal peculiarities which Mr Gladstone's character presents even to a superficial observer. But something more than superficial observation is necessary really to understand a character so complicated and so odd. We will touch upon some of the traits which are among the most important; and if our minute analysis has, or seems to have, some of the painfulness of a vivisection, we would observe that a defect of this kind is in some degree inseparable from the task we have undertaken. We cannot explain the special peculiarities of a singular man of genius without a somewhat elaborate and a half-metaphysical discussion.

It is needless to say that Mr Gladstone is a great orator. Oratory is one of the pursuits as to which there is no error. The criterion is ready. Did the audience feel? were they excited? did they cheer? These questions, and others such as these, can be answered without a mistake. A man who can move the House of Commons—still, after many changes, the most severe audience in the world—must be a great orator. The most sincere admirers and the most eager depreciators of Mr Gladstone are agreed on this point, and it is almost the only point on which they are agreed.

It will be well, however, to pause upon this characteristic of Mr Gladstone's genius, and to examine the nature of it rather anxiously, because it seems to afford the true key to some of his most perplexing peculiarities. Mr Gladstone has, beyond every other man in this generation, what we may call the oratorical *impulse*. We are in the habit of speaking of rhetoric as an art, and also of oratory as a faculty, and in both cases we speak quite truly. No man can speak without a special intellectual gift, and no man can speak well without a special intellectual training. But neither this gift of the intellect nor this education will suffice of themselves. A man must not only know what to say, he must have a vehement longing to get up and say it. Many persons, rather sceptical persons especially, do not feel this in the least. They see before them an audience—a miscellaneous collection of odd-looking men—but they feel no wish to convince them of anything. "Are not they very well as they are? They believe what they have been brought up to believe." "Confirm every man in *his own* manner of conceiving," said one great sage. "A savage among savages is very well," remarked another. You may easily take away one creed and then not be able to implant another. "You may succeed in unfitting men for their own purposes without fitting them for your purposes"—thus thinks the *cui bono* sceptic. Another kind of sceptic is distrustful, and speaks thus: "I know *I can't* convince these people; if I could, perhaps I would, but I can't. Only look at them! they have all kinds of crotchets in their heads. There is a wooden-faced man in spectacles. How can you convince a wooden-faced man in spectacles? And see that other man with a narrow forehead and compressed lips—is it any use talking to him? It is of no use; do not hope that mere arguments will impair the prepossessions of nature and the steady convictions of years." Mr Gladstone would not feel these sceptical arguments. He would get up to speak. He has the *didactic* impulse. He has the "courage of his ideas". He will convince the audience. He knows an argument which will be effective, he has one for one and another for another; he has an enthusiasm which he feels will rouse the apathetic, a demonstration which he thinks must convert the incredulous, an illustration which he hopes will drive his meaning even into the heads of the stolid. At any rate, he will try. He has *a nature*, as Coleridge might have said, towards his audience. He is sure, if they only knew what he knows, they would feel as he feels, and believe as he believes. And by this he conquers. This living faith, this enthusiasm, this confidence, call it as we will, is an extreme power in human affairs. One *croyant*, said the Frenchman, is a greater power than fifty *incrédules*. In the composition of an orator, the hope, the credulous hope, that he will convince his audience, is the *primum mobile*, it is the primitive incentive which is the spring of his influence and the source of his power. Mr Gladstone has this incentive in perhaps an excessive and dangerous measure. Whatever may be right or wrong in pure finance, in abstract political economy, it is certain that no one save Mr Gladstone would have come down with the Budget of 1860 to the Commons of 1860. No other man would have believed that such a proposal would have a chance. Yet after the warning—the disheartening warning of a reluctant Cabinet—Mr Gladstone came down from a depressing sick-bed, with semi-bronchitis hovering about him, entirely prevailed for the moment, and three parts conquered after all. We will not say that *the world* is given to men of this temperament and this energy; on the contrary, there is often a turn in the tide, the

ovation of the spring may be the prelude to unpopularity in
the autumn; but we see that *audiences* are given them; we
see that unimpressible men are deeply moved by them—that
the driest topics of legislation and finance are for the instant
affected by them—that the prolonged effects of that momentary influence may be felt for many years, sometimes for
centuries. The orator has a dominion over the critical instant, and the consequences of the decisions taken during
that instant may last long after the orator and the audience
have both passed away.

Nor is the didactic impulse the only one which is essential
to a great political orator; nor is it the only one which Mr
Gladstone has. We say it with respect; but he has the *contentious* impulse. He illustrates the distinction between the
pacific and the peaceful. On all great questions, on the controversies of states and empires, Mr Gladstone is the most
pacific of mankind. He hates the very rumour of war; he
trusts in moral influences; he detests the bare idea of military
preparations. He will not believe that preparations are necessary till the enemy is palpable. In the early part of 1853 he
did not believe that the Russian war was impending; after
the conversations of the Emperor Nicholas with Sir Hamilton
Seymour, he proposed to Parliament a scheme for converting
some portions of the National Debt, which could only be
successful if peace continued, and which, after the outbreak
of the war, failed ignominiously. In 1860, *mutatis mutandis*,
he has done the same. He staked his financial reputation upon
a fine calculation; he gave us a Budget in which the two ends
scarcely met. The Chinese war came, and they no longer
meet. We believe that Mr Gladstone so much hates the bare
idea of the possibility of war, that after many warnings, after
at least one failure which must have been painful, and which
should have been instructive, he has refused to take even the
contingency of hostilities into his calculations. Some one said
he was not only a Christian, but a morbid Christian. He cannot imagine that anything so coarse as war will occur; when
it does occur, he has a tendency to disapprove of it as soon as
he can. During the Russian war he soon joined, in fact if not
in name, the peace-at-all-price party; he exerted his finest reasonings and his most persuasive eloquence against a war which
was commenced with his consent. At the present moment no
Englishman, not Mr Bright himself, *feels* so little the impulse

to arm. He will not believe in a war till he sees men fighting. He is the most pacific of our statesmen in theory and in policy. When you hear Mr Gladstone, he is about the most combative. He can bear a good deal about the politics of Europe; but let a man question the fees on vatting, or the change in the game certificate, or the stamp on bills of lading—what melodious thunders of loquacious wrath! The world, he hints, is likely to end at such observations, and it is dreadful that they should be made by the honourable member who made them—"by the honourable member who four years ago said so-and-so, and five years before that moved," etc. etc. The number of well-intentioned and tedious persons whom Mr Gladstone annually scolds into a latent dislike of him must be considerable.

But though we may smile at the *minutiæ* in which this contentious impulse sometimes shows itself, we must remember that the impulse itself is essential to a great political orator, everywhere in some degree, but in England especially. To be an influential speaker in the House of Commons, a man must be a great debater. He must excel not only in elaborate set speeches, but likewise in quick occasional repartee. No one but a rather contentious person will ever so excel. Mr Fox, the most genial of men, was asked why he disputed so vehemently about some trifle or other. He said, "I *must* do so; I can't live without discussion". And this is the temperament of a great debater. It must be a positive pain to him to be silent under questionable assertions, to hear others saying that which he cannot agree with. An indifferent sceptic such as we formerly spoke of, endures this very easily. "He thinks, no doubt, that what the speaker is saying is quite wrong; but people do not understand what he is saying; very likely they won't understand the answer: besides, we've a majority; what is the use of arguing when you have a majority? Let us outvote him on the spot, and go to bed." And so, report says, have whips argued to Mr Gladstone, but he is ever ready. He takes up the parable of disputation at a quarter past twelve, and goes on till he has exhausted argument, illustration, ingenuity, and research. To hardly any man have both the impulses of the political orator been given in so great a measure: the didactic orator is usually felicitous in exposition only; the great debater is, like Fox, only great when stung to reply by the *œstrus* of contention. But Mr Gladstone is by nature, by vehement overruling na-

ture, great in both arts; he longs to pour forth his own belief; he cannot rest till he has contradicted every one else.

In addition to this oratorical temperament, Mr Gladstone
has in a high degree the most important intellectual talent
of an orator; he has what we may call an adaptive mind. He
has described this himself better than most people would describe it:—

> "Poets of modern times have composed great works in
> ages that stopped their ears against them. *Paradise Lost*
> does not represent the time of Charles the Second, nor
> the *Excursion* the first decades of the present century. The
> case of the orator is entirely different. His work, from its
> very inception, is inextricably mixed up with practice. It
> is cast in the mould offered to him by the mind of his
> hearers. It is an influence principally received from his
> audience (so to speak) in vapour, which he pours back
> upon them in a flood. The sympathy and concurrence of
> his time, is, with his own mind, joint parent of his work.
> He cannot follow nor frame ideals: his choice is, to be what
> his age will have him, what it requires in order to be moved
> by him, or else not to be at all. And as when we find the
> speeches in *Homer*, we know that there must have been
> men who could speak them, so, from the existence of units
> who could speak them, we know that there must have been
> crowds who could feel them."

We may judge of the House of Commons in the same way
from the great Budget speech. No one, indeed, half guides,
half follows the moods of his audience more quickly, more
easily, than Mr Gladstone. There is a little playfulness in his
manner, which contrasts with the dryness of his favourite
topics, and the intense gravity of his earnest character. He
has the same sort of control over the minds of those he is
addressing that a good driver has over the animals he guides:
he feels the minds of his hearers as the driver the mouths of
his horses.

The species of intellect that is required for this task is pre-
eminently the advocate's intellect. The instrument of oratory,
at least of this kind of oratory, is the *argumentum ad ho-
minem*. It is inextricably mixed up with practice. It argues
from the data furnished to him "by the mind of his hearers".
He receives his premises from them "like a vapour," and

pours out his "conclusions upon them like a flood". Such an orator may believe his conclusions, but he can rarely believe them for the reasons which he assigns for them. He may be an enthusiast in his creed, he may be a zealot in his faith, but not the less will he be an advocate in his practice; not the less will he catch at disputable premises because his audience accepts them; not the less will he draw inferences from them which suit his momentary purpose; not the less will he accept the most startling varieties of assertion, for he will imbibe from one audience a different "vapour" of premises from that which he will receive from another; not the less will he have the chameleon-like character which we associate with a consummate advocate; not the less will he be one thing today, with the colour of one audience upon him; not the less will he be another to-morrow, when he has to address, persuade, and influence some different set of persons.

We scarcely think, with Mr Gladstone, that this style of oratory is the very highest, though it is very natural that he should think so, for it exactly expresses the oratory in which he is the greatest living master. Mr Gladstone's conception of oratory, in theory and in practice, is the oratory of Pitt, not the oratory of Chatham or of Burke: it is the oratory of adaptation. We do not deny that this is the kind of oratory which is most generally useful, the only kind which is commonly permissible, the only one which in general would not be a *bore*; but we must remember that there is an eloquence of great principles which the hearers scarcely heed, and do not accept—such as, in its highest parts, is the eloquence of Burke—we must remember that there is an eloquence of great passions, of high-wrought intense feeling, which is nearly independent of the peculiarities of its audience, because it appeals to our elemental human nature—which is the same, or much the same, in almost every audience, which is everywhere and always susceptible to the union of vivid genius and eager passion. Such as this last was, if we may trust tradition, the eloquence of Chatham, the source of his rare, magical, and occasional power. Mr Gladstone has neither of these. Few speakers equally great have left so few passages which can be quoted—so few which embody great principles in such a manner as to be referred to by coming generations. He has scarcely given us a sentence that lives in the memory; nor is his declamation, facile and effective as it always is, the very highest declamation: it is a

nearly perfect expression of intellectualised sentiment, but it
wants the volcanic power of primitive passion.

The prominence of advocacy in Mr Gladstone's mind is in
appearance, though not in reality, diminished by the purity
and intensity of his zeal. There is an elastic heroism about
him. When he begins to speak, we may know that we are
going to hear what we shall not agree with. We may believe
that the measures he proposes are mischievous; we may smile
at the emphasis with which some of their *minutiæ* are insisted upon; but we inevitably feel that we have left the ordinary earth. We know that high sentiments will be appealed
to by one who feels high sentiments; that strong arguments
will be strongly stated by one who believes that argument
should decide controversy. We know that we are beyond the
realm of the Patronage Secretary; we have left behind us the
doctrine that corruption is the ruling power in popular assemblies, that patronage is the purchase-money of power. We
are not alleging that in the real world in which we live there
is not some truth—more or less of truth—in these lower maxims; but they do not rule in Mr Gladstone's world. He was
not born to be a Secretary of the Treasury. If he tried his
hand at it, he would perplex the borough attorneys out of
their lives. And he *could* not keep the office a month; he
would evince a real disgust at detestable requests, and guide
with odd impulsiveness the delicate and latent machinery.
His natural element is a higher one. He has—and it is one of
the springs of great power—a real faith in the higher parts of
human nature; he believes, with all his heart and soul and
strength, that there *is* such a thing as truth; he has the soul
of a martyr with the intellect of an advocate.

Another of Mr Gladstone's characteristics is an extraordinary love of labour. We have alluded several times to his
taste, we might almost say his whimsical taste, for *minutiæ*.
He is ready with whatever detail may be necessary on any
subject, no matter of what kind. He covers his greatest
schemes with a crowd of irrelevant appendages, till it is difficult to see their outline. The Budget of 1860 was large
enough and complicated enough, one would have thought, in
its essential irremovable features; but its author did not think
so. He had supplementary provisions respecting game certificates, respecting the transmission of newspapers by the post,
respecting "several other minuter changes with which he was
almost ashamed to trouble the committee". The labour nec-

essary to all these accessories must have been enormous. Many
of the alterations may have—must have—been lying ready in
his memory, or in some old note-book, for many years. But
the industry to furbish them up, to get them into a practicable, or even into a proposable shape, would frighten not
only most persons, but most laborious persons. And Mr Gladstone's energy seems to be strictly intellectual. Nothing in his
outward appearance indicates the iron physique that often
carries inferior men through heavy tasks. Whatever he does
that is peculiar, he does by the peculiarity of his mind. He
is carried through his work, or seems to be so, by pure will,
zeal, and effort.

The last characteristic of Mr Gladstone which is very remarkable, or which we shall mention, is his scholastic intellect. We have not much of this in conspicuous men in the
present day, but in former times there was a good deal of it.
Lord Bacon had something like it in his eye when he spoke of
minds which were not "discursive" or skilful in discovering
analogies, but were *discriminative* or skilful in detecting differences. The best scene for training this sort of intellect is
the law-court. Lord Bacon must have seen much of it in the
work of Gray's Inn when he was young, and traces of the
discipline which he then underwent may perhaps be found
even in books which were written by him many years afterwards. When, as in positive law, the first principles are. fixed,
there is no room for the highest originality; the only admissible controversy is whether a particular case comes or does
not come within a particular principle. On this point there
is room for endless distinctions and eternal hair-splitting.
When the principles settled by authority are not entirely consistent, the function of this kind of distinguishing reason is
even greater; it has to suggest nice refinements, which may
reconcile the apparent differences between the principles
themselves, as well as to settle the exact relation of the case,
or the facts, to the doctrine of the authorities. Accordingly,
the scholastic theologians of mediæval times were the most
expert masters of the discriminative ratiocination which the
world has ever seen. They had to reconcile the recognised authorities of the Catholic Church—authorities vast in size, and
scattered over centuries in time—with one another, with good
sense, with the facts of special cases, with the general exigencies of the age. By their labour was formed that acute
logic, that subtle, if unreal philosophy which fell at the Ref-

ormation, when the authorities of the Catholic Church were
no longer conclusive, and the art of arranging them was no
longer important. We have learned to smile at the scholastic
distinctions of former times; the inductive philosophy, which
is now our most conspicuous pursuit, does not need them;
the popular character of our ordinary discussion does not admit of them. In a free country we must use the sort of argument which plain men understand—and plain men certainly do not appreciate or apprehend scholastic refinements.
So at least we should say beforehand. Yet Mr Gladstone is
the statesman whose expositions have, for good or for evil,
more power than those of any other; his voice is a greater
power in the country of plain men than any other man's;
nevertheless, his intellect is of a thoroughly scholastic kind.
He can distinguish between any two propositions; he never
allowed, he could not allow, that any two were identical. If
anyone on either side of the House is bold enough to infer
anything from anything, Mr Gladstone is ready to deny that
the inference is correct—to suggest a distinction which he says
is singularly important—to illustrate an apt subtlety which,
in appearance at least, impairs the validity of the deduction.
No schoolman could be readier at such work. We may find
the same tendency of mind even more strikingly illustrated
in his writings. At the time of the Gorham case, for example,
he wrote a pamphlet on the Royal Supremacy. For the purposes of that case, it was of the last importance to determine the exact position of the Crown with respect to ecclesiastical affairs, and especially to the offence of heresy. The
law at first seems distinct enough on the matter. The 1st of
Elizabeth provides "that such jurisdictions, privileges, superiorities, and pre-eminences, spiritual and ecclesiastical, as
by any spiritual or ecclesiastical power or authority hath here-
tofore been or may lawfully be exercised or used for the visi-
tation of the ecclesiastical state and persons, and for reformation, order and correction of the same, and of all manner of
errors, heresies, schisms, abuses, offences, contempts, and
enormities, shall for ever, by authority of this present Parliament, be united and annexed to the imperial Crown of this
realm". These words would have seemed distinct and clear
to most persons. They would have seemed to give to the
Crown all the power it could wish to exercise—all that any
spiritual authority had ever "theretofore exercised"—all that
any temporal authority could ever use. We should think it

was clear that Queen Elizabeth would have applied a rather
summary method of instruction to any one who attempted to
limit the jurisdiction conferred by this enactment. If Mr
Gladstone had lived in the times about which he was writing,
he might have had to make a choice between being silent
and being punished; but in the times of Queen Victoria he
is not subjected to an alternative so painful. He writes securely:—

"We have now before us the terms of the great statute
which, from the time it was passed, has been the actual
basis of the royal authority in matters ecclesiastical; and
I do not load these pages by reference to declarations of
the Crown, and other public documents less in authority
than this, in order that we may fix our view the more
closely upon the expressions of what may fairly be termed
a fundamental law in relation to the subject-matter before
us.

"The first observation I make is this: there is no evidence in the words which have been quoted that the Sovereign is, according to the intention of the statute, the
source or fountain-head of ecclesiastical jurisdiction. They
have no trace of such a meaning, in so far as it exceeds
(and it does exceed) the proposition, that this jurisdiction
has been by law united or annexed to the Crown.

"I do not now ask what have been the glosses of lawyers—
what are the reproaches of polemical writers—or even what
attributes may be ascribed to prerogative, independent of
statute, and therefore applicable to the Church before as
well as after the Reformation. I must for the purposes of
this argument assume what I shall never cease to believe
until the contrary conclusion is demonstrated by fact,
namely, that, in the case of the Church, justice is to be
administered from the English bench upon the same principles as in all other cases—that our judges, or our judicial
committees, are not to be our legislators—and that the
statutes of the realm, as they are above the sacred majesty
of the Queen, so are likewise above their ministerial in-
terpreters. It was by statute that the changes in the position of the Church at that great epoch were measured—
by statute that the position itself is defined; and the statute, I say, contains no trace of such a meaning as that
the Crown either originally was the source and spring of

ecclesiastical jurisdiction, or was to become such in virtue
of the annexation to it of the powers recited; but simply
bears the meaning, that it was to be master over its administration."

So that which seems a despotism is gradually pruned down
into a vicegerency. "All the superiorities and pre-eminences
spiritual and ecclesiastical," which had ever been lawfully exercised, are restricted to the single function of regulation; and
by a judicious elaboration the Crown becomes scarcely the
head of the Church, but only the *visitor* and corrector of it,
as of several other corporations. We are not now concerned
with the royal supremacy—we have no wish to hint or intimate
an opinion on a vast legal discussion; but we *are* concerned
with Mr Gladstone. And we venture to say that a subtler
gloss, more scholastically expressed, never fell from lawyer in
the present age, or from schoolmen in times of old.

The great faculties we have mentioned give Mr Gladstone,
it is needless to say, an extraordinary influence in English
politics. England is a country governed mainly by labour and
by speech. Mr Gladstone will work and can speak, and the
result is what we see. With a flowing eloquence and a lofty
heroism; with an acute intellect and endless knowledge; with
courage to conceive large schemes, and a voice which will
persuade men to adopt those schemes—it is not singular that
Mr Gladstone is of himself a power in Parliamentary life.
He can do there what no one else living can do.

But the effect of these peculiar faculties is by no means
unmixedly favourable. In almost every one of them some
faulty tendency is latent, which may produce bad effects—in
Mr Gladstone's case has often done so, perhaps does so still.
His greatest characteristic, as we have indicated, is the singular vivacity of his oratorical impulse. But great as is the immediate power which a vehement oratorical propensity, when
accompanied by the requisite faculties, secures to the possessor, the advantage of possessing it, or rather of being subject to it, is by no means without an alloy. We have all heard
that Paley said he knew nothing against some one *but* that
he was a popular preacher. And Paley knew what he was saying. The oratorical impulse is a *disorganising* impulse. The
higher faculties of the mind require a certain calm, and the
excitement of oratory is unfavourable to that calm. We know
that this is so with the hearers of oratory; we know that they

are carried away from their fixed principles, from their habitual tendencies, by a casual and unexpected stimulus. We
speak commonly of the power of the orator. But the orator
is subject himself to much the same calamity. The force
which carries away his hearers must first carry away himself.
He will not persuade any of his hearers unless he has first
succeeded, for the moment at least, in persuading his own
mind. Every exciting speech is conceived, planned, and spoken
with excitement. The orator feels in his own nerves, even in
a greater degree, that electric thrill which he is to communicate to his hearers. The telling ideas take hold of him with a
sort of *seizure*. They fasten close upon his brain. He has a
sort of passionate impulse to tell them. He hungers, as a
Greek would have said, till they are uttered. His mind is full
of them. He has the vision of the audience in his mind. Until he has persuaded these men of these things, life is tame,
and its other stimulants are uninteresting. So much excitement is evidently unfavourable to calm reflection and deliberation. Mr Pitt is said to have thought more of the manner
in which his measures would strike the House than of the
manner in which, when carried, they would work. Of course
he did—every great orator will do so, unless he has a supernatural self-control. An ordinary man sits down—say to make a
Budget: he arranges the accounts; adds up the figures; contrasts the effects of different taxes; works out steadily hour
after hour their probable incidence, first of one, then of another. Nothing disturbs him. With the orator it is different.
During that whole process he is disturbed by the vision of his
hearers. How they will feel, how they will think, how they will
like his proposals—cannot but occur to him. He hears his ideas
rebounding in the cheers of his hearers; he is disheartened, at
fancying that they will fall tamely on an inanimate and list-
less multitude. He is subject to two temptations; he is turned
aside from the conceptions natural to the subject by an
imagination of his audience; his own eager temperament
naturally inclines him to the views which will excite that
audience most effectually. The tranquil deposit of ordinary
ideas is interrupted by the sudden eruption of volcanic forces.
We know that the popular instinct suspects the judgment of
great orators; we know that it does not give them credit for
patient equanimity; and the popular instinct is right.

Nor is cool reflection the only higher state of mind which
the oratorical impulse interferes with; we believe that it is

singularly unfavourable also to the exercise of the higher kind
of imagination. Several great poets have written good dra-
matic harangues; but no great practical orator has ever written
a great poem. The creative imagination requires a singular
calm: it is "the still unravished bride of quietness," as the
poets say, "the foster-child of silence and slow time". No
great work has ever been produced except after a long interval of still and musing meditation. The oratorical impulse
interferes with this. It breaks the exclusive brooding of the
mind upon the topic; it brings in a new set of ideas, the faces
of the audience and the passions of listening men; it *jerks*
the mind, if the expression may be allowed, just when the
delicate poetry of the mind is crystallising into symmetry.
The process is stayed, and the result is marred.

Mr Gladstone has suffered from both these bad effects of
the oratorical temperament. His writings, even on imaginative subjects, even on the poetry of Homer, are singularly devoid of the highest imagination. They abound in acute remarks; they excel in industry of detail; they contain many
animated and some eloquent passages. But there is no central
conception running through them; there is no binding idea in
them; there is nothing to fuse them together; they are elaborate aggregates of varied elements; they are not shaped and
consolidated wholes. Nor, it is remarkable, has his style the
delicate graces which mark the productions of the gentle and
meditative mind; there is something hard in its texture, something dislocated in its connections. In his writings, where he
is removed from the guiding check of the listening audience,
he starts off, just where you least expect it. He hurries from
the main subject to make a passing and petty remark. As he
has not the central idea of his work vividly before him, he
overlays it with tedious, accessory, and sometimes irrelevant
detail.

His intellect has suffered also. He is undeniably defective
in the tenacity of first principle. Probably there is nothing
which he would less like to have said of him, and yet it is
certainly true. We speak, of course, of intellectual consistency,
not of moral probity. And he has not an *adhesive* mind; such
adhesiveness as he has is rather to projects than principles.
We will give—it is all we have space to give—a single remarkable instance of his peculiar mutability. He has adhered
in the year 1860 to his project of reducing the amount levied
in England by indirect taxation. He announced in 1853 that

he would do so, and, what was singular enough, he was able to do it when the time came. But this superficial consistency must not disguise from us the entire inconsistency in abstract principle between the Budget of 1853 and the Budget of 1860. The most important element in English finance at present is the income-tax. In 1853 that tax was, Mr Gladstone explained to us, an occasional, an exceptional, a sacred reserve. It had done much that was wonderful for our fathers in the French war; Sir R. Peel had used it with magical efficiency in our own time; but it was to be kept for first-rate objects. In 1860 the income-tax has become the tax of *all work*. Whatever is to be done, whatever other tax is to be relinquished, it is but a penny more or a penny less of this ever-ready and omnipotent impost. We do not blame Mr Gladstone for changing his opinion. We believe that an income-tax of moderate amount should be a permanent element in our financial system. We think that additions to it from time to time are the best ways of meeting any sudden demand for exceptional expenditure. But we cannot be unaware of the transition which he has made. His opinion as to our most remarkable tax has varied, not only in detail but in essence. It was to be a rare and residuary agency; it is now a permanent and principal force. The inconsistency goes further. He used to think that he would be guilty of a "high political offence" if he altered the present mode of assessing the income-tax, if he equalised the pressure on industrial and permanent incomes. But he is now ready to *consider* any plan with that object—in other words, he is ready to do it if he can. A great change in his fundamental estimate of our greatest tax has made an evident and indisputable change in his mode of viewing proposed reforms and alterations in it.

Mr Gladstone's inclination—his unconscious inclination for the art of advocacy—increases his tendency to suffer from the characteristic temptations of his oratorical temperament. It is scarcely necessary to say that professional advocacy is unfavourable to the philosophical investigation of truth; a more battered commonplace cannot be found anywhere. To catch at whatever turns up in favour of your own case; to be obviously blind to everything which tells in favour of the case of your adversary; to imply doubts as to principles which it is not expedient to deny; to suggest with delicate indirectness the conclusive arguments in favour of principles which it is not wise directly to affirm—these, and such as these, are the arts of the advocate. A political orator has them almost of necessity, and Mr Gladstone is not exempt from them. Indeed, without any fault of his own, he has them, if not to an unusual extent, at least with a very unusual conspicuousness. His vehement temperament, his "intense and glowing mind," drive him into strong statements, into absolute and unlimited assertions. He lays down a principle of tremendous breadth to establish a detail of exceeding minuteness. He is not a "hedging" advocate. He does not understand the art which Hume and Peel—different as were their respective spheres—practised with almost equal effect in those spheres. Mr Gladstone dashes forth to meet his opponents. He will believe easily—he will state strongly whatever may confute them. An incessant use of ingenious and unqualified principles is one of Mr Gladstone's most prominent qualities; it is unfavourable to exact consistency of explicit assertion, and to latent consistency of personal belief. His scholastic intellect makes matters worse. He will show that any two principles are or may be consistent; that if there is an apparent discrepancy, they may still, after the manner of Oxford, "be held together". One of the most remarkable of Father Newman's Oxford Sermons explains how science teaches that the earth goes round the sun, and how Scripture teaches that the sun goes round the earth; and it ends by advising the discreet believer to accept *both*. Both, it is suggested, may be accommodations to our limited intellect—aspects of some higher and less discordant unity. We have often smiled at the recollection of the old Oxford training in watching Mr Gladstone's ingenious "reconcilements". It must be pleasant to have an argumentative acuteness which is quite sure to extricate you, at least in appearance, from any intellectual scrape. But it is a dangerous weapon to use, and particularly dangerous to a very conscientious man. He will not use it unless he believes in its results; but he will try to believe in its results, in order that he may use it. We need not spend further words in proving that a kind of advocacy at once acute, refined, and vehement, is unfavourable both to consistency of statement and to tenacious sluggishness of belief.

In this manner, the disorganising effects of his greatest peculiarities have played a principal part in shaping Mr Gladstone's character and course. They have helped to make him annoy the old Whigs, confound the country gentlemen, and puzzle the nation generally. They have contributed to bring

on him the long array of depreciating adjectives, "extravagant," "inconsistent," "incoherent," and "incalculable".

Mr Gladstone's intellectual history has aggravated the unfavourable influence of his characteristic tendencies. Such a
mind as his required, beyond any man's, the early inculcation
of a steadying creed. It required that the youth, if not the
child, should be father to the man: it required that a set of
fixed and firm principles should be implanted in his mind in
its first intellectual years—that those principles should be precise enough for its guidance, tangible enough to be commonly intelligible, true enough to stand the wear and tear of
ordinary life. The tranquil task of developing coherent principle might have calmed the vehemence of Mr Gladstone's
intellectual impulses—might have steadied the impulsive dis-
cursiveness of his nature. A settled and plain creed, which was
in union with the belief of ordinary men, might have kept
Mr Gladstone in the common path of plain men—might have
made him intelligible and safe. But he has had no such good
fortune. He began the world with a vast religious theory; he
embodied it in a book on Church and State; he defended it,
as was said, mistily—at any rate, he defended it in a manner
which requires much careful pains to appreciate, and much
preliminary information to understand; he puzzled the ordinary mass of English Churchmen; he has been half out of
sympathy with them ever since. The creed which he has chosen, or which his Oxford training stamped upon him, was
one not likely to be popular with common Englishmen. It
had a scholastic appearance and a mystical essence which they
dislike almost equally. But this was not its worst defect. It
was a theory which broke down when it was tried. It was a
theory with definite practical consequences, which no one
in these days will accept—which no one in these days will propose. It was a theory to be shattered by the slightest touch
of real life, for it had a definite teaching which was inconsistent with the facts of that life—which all persons who were
engaged in it were, on some ground or other, unanimous in
rejecting. In Mr Gladstone's case it had been shattered. He
maintained, that a visible Church existed upon earth; that
every State was bound to be directed by that Church; that all
members of that State should, if possible, be members of that
Church; that at any rate none of the members should be utterly out of sympathy with her; that the State ought to aid
her in her characteristic work, and refrain from aiding her an-

tagonists in that work; that within her own sphere the
Church, though thus aided, is substantially independent; that
she has an absolute right to elect her own bishops, to determine her own creed, to make her own definitions of orthodoxy and heresy. This is the high Oxford creed, and, in all
essential points, it was Mr Gladstone's first creed.

But a curious series of instructive events proved that England at least would not adopt it,—that the actual Church of
England is not the Church of which it speaks,—that the actual English State is by no means the State of which it speaks.
The additional endowment of the Maynooth College which
Sir Robert Peel proposed was an express relinquishment of
the principle that the Church of England had an exclusive
right to assistance from the State; it proved that the Conservative party—the special repository of constitutional traditions—was ready to aid a different and antagonistic communion. The removal of the Jewish disabilities struck a still deeper
blow: it proved that persons who could not be said to par-
ticipate in even the rudiments of Anglican doctrine might be
Prime Ministers and rulers in England. The theory of the
exclusive union of a visible Church with a visible State vanished into the air. The real world would not endure it. We
fear it must be said that the theory of the substantial independence of the English Church has vanished too. The case of
Dr Hampden proved conclusively that the intervention of the
English Church in the election of her bishops was an ineffectual ceremony; that it could not be galvanised into effective
life; that it was one of those lingering relics of the past which
the steady English people are so loth to disturb. Undisputed
practice shows that the Prime Minister, who is clearly secular prince, is the dispenser of ecclesiastical dignities. And the
judgment of her Majesty's Council in the Gorham case went
further yet. It touched on the finest and tenderest point of all.
It decided that, on the critical question, heresy or no heresy,
the final appeal was not to an ecclesiastical court, but to a lay
court—to a court, not of saintly theologians, but of tough old
lawyers, to men of the world most worldly. The Oxford dream
of an independent Church, the Oxford dream of an exclusive Church, are both in practice forgotten; their very terms
are strange in our ears; they have no reference to real life.
Mr Gladstone has had to admit this. He has voted for the
endowment of Maynooth; he has voted for the admission of
Jews to the House of Commons; he has acquiesced in the

Hampden case; he sees daily the highest patronage of the
Church distributed by Lord Palmerston, the very man who,
on any high-church theory, ought not to dispense it, to the
very men who, on any high-church theory, ought not to receive
it. He wrote a pamphlet on the Gorham case, but he does
not practically propose to alter the constitution of the Judicial
Committee of the Privy Council; he has never proposed to
bring in a bill for that purpose; he acquiesces in the supreme
decision of the most secular court which can exist over the
most peculiarly ecclesiastical questions that can be thought
of. These successive changes do credit to Mr Gladstone's good
sense; they show that he has a susceptible nature, that he will
not live out of sympathy with his age. But what must be the
effect of such changes upon any mind, especially on a delicate and high-toned mind? They tend, and must tend, to
confuse the first principles of belief; to disturb the best landmarks of consistency; to leave the mind open to attacks of
oratorical impulse; to foster the catching habit of advocacy;
to weaken the guiding element in a disposition which was already defective in that element. The "movement of 1833," as
Father Newman calls it, has wrecked many fine intellects,
has broken many promising careers. It could not do either
for Mr Gladstone, for his circumstances were favourable, and
his mental energy was far too strong; but it has done him
harm, nevertheless: it has left upon his intellect a weakening
strain and a distorting mark.

Mr Gladstone was a likely man to be enraptured with the
first creed with which he was thrown, and to push it too far.
He wants the warning instincts. Some one said of him formerly, "He may be a good Christian, but he is an atrocious
pagan"; and the saying is true. He has not a trace of the protective morality of the old world, of the *modus in rebus*, the
μέσον, the shrinking from an extreme, which are the prominent characteristics of the ethics of the old world, which
are still the guiding creed of the large part of the world
that is,—scarcely altered after two thousand years. And this
much we may concede to the secular moralists—unless a man
have from nature a selective tact which shuns the unlimited,
unless he have a detective instinct which unconsciously but
sensitively shrinks from the extravagant, he will never enjoy
a placid life, he will not pass through a simple and consistent
career. The placid moderation which is necessary to coherent
success cannot be acquired, it must be born.

Perhaps we may seem already to have more than accounted
for the prominence of Mr Gladstone's characteristic defects.
We may seem to have alleged sufficient reasons for his being
changeable and impulsive, a vehement advocate and an audacious financier. But we have other causes to assign which
have aggravated these faults. We shall not, indeed, after what
we have said, venture to dwell on them at length. We will
bear in mind the precept, "If you wish to exhaust your readers, exhaust your subject". But we will very slightly allude to
one of them.

A writer like Mr Gladstone, fond of deriving illustration
from the old theology, might speak of public life in England
as an *economy*. It is a world of its own, far more than most
Englishmen are aware of. It presents the characters of public
men in a disguised form; and by requiring the seeming
adoption of much which is not real, it tends to modify and to
distort much which is real. An English statesman in the
present day lives by following public opinion; he may profess
to guide it a little; he may hope to modify it in detail; he may
help to exaggerate and to develop it; but he hardly hopes for
more. Many seem not willing to venture on so much. And
what does this mean except that such a statesman has to
follow the varying currents of a varying world; to adapt his
public expressions, if not his private belief, to the tendencies
of the hour; to be in no slight measure the slave—the petted
and applauded slave, but still the slave—of the world which
he seems to rule? Nor is this all. A Minister is not simply the
servant of the public, he is likewise the advocate of his colleagues. No one supposes that a Cabinet can ever agree;
when did fifteen able men—fifteen able men, more or less
rivals—ever agree on anything? We are aware that differences of opinion, more or less radical, exist in every Cabinet;
that the decisions of every Cabinet are in nearly every case
modified by concession; that a minority of the Cabinet frequently dissents from them. Yet all this latent discrepancy
of opinion is never hinted at, much less is it ever avowed. A
Cabinet Minister comes down to the House habitually to
vote and occasionally to speak in favour of measures which
he much dislikes, from which he has in vain attempted to
dissuade his colleagues. The life of a great Minister is the
life of a great advocate. No life can be imagined which is
worse for a mind like Mr Gladstone's. He was naturally
changeable, susceptible, prone to unlimited statements—to

vehement arguments. He has followed a career in which it is necessary to follow a changing guide and to obey more or less, but always to some extent, a fluctuating opinion; to argue vehemently for tenets which you dislike; to defend boldly a given law to-day, to propose boldly that the same law should be repealed to-morrow. Accumulated experience shows that the public life of our Parliamentary statesmen is singularly unsteadying, is painfully destructive of coherent principle; and we may easily conceive how dangerous it must be to a mind like Mr Gladstone's—to a mind, by its intrinsic nature, impressible, impetuous, and unfixed.

What, then, is to be the future course of the remarkable statesman whose excellences and whose faults we have ventured to analyse at such length? No wise man would venture to predict. A wise man does not predict much in this complicated world, least of all will he predict the exact course of a perplexing man in perplexing circumstances. But we will hazard three general remarks.

First, Mr Gladstone is essentially a man who cannot impose his creed *on* his time, but must learn his creed *of* his time. Every Parliamentary statesman must, as we have said, do so in some measure; but Mr Gladstone must do so above all men. The vehement orator, the impulsive advocate, the ingenious but somewhat unsettled thinker, is the last man from whom we should expect an original policy, a steady succession of mature and consistent designs. Mr Gladstone may well be the expositor of his time, the advocate of its conclusions, the admired orator in whom it will take pride; but he cannot be more. Parliamentary life rarely admits the autocratic supremacy of an original intellect; the present moment is singularly unfavourable to it; Mr Gladstone is the last man to obtain it.

Secondly, Mr Gladstone will fail if he follow the seductive example of Sir Robert Peel. It is customary to talk of the unfavourable circumstances in which the latter was placed, but in one respect those circumstances were favourable. He had very unusual means of learning the ideas of his time. They were forced upon him by a loud and organised agitation. The repeal of the corn-laws, the repeal of the Catholic disabilities—the two Acts by which he will be remembered— were not chosen by him, but exacted from him. The world around him clamoured for them. But no future statesman can hope to have such an advantage. The age in which Peel

lived was an age of destruction: the measures by which he
will be remembered were abolitions. We have now reached
the term of the destructive period. We cannot abolish all
our laws; we have few remaining with which educated men
find fault. The questions which remain are questions of construction—how the lower classes are to be admitted to a
share of political power without absorbing the whole power;
how the natural union of Church and State is to be adapted
to an age of divided religious opinion, and to the necessary
conditions of a Parliamentary government. These, and such
as these, are the future topics of our home policy. And on
these the voice of the nation will never be very distinct. Destruction is easy, construction is very difficult. A statesman
who will hereafter learn what our real public opinion is, will
not have to regard loud agitators, but to disregard them; will
not have to yield to a loud voice, but to listen for a still small
voice; will have to seek for the opinion which is treasured in
secret rather than for that which is noised abroad. If Mr
Gladstone will accept the conditions of his age; if he will
guide himself by the mature, settled, and cultured reflection
of his time, and not by its loud and noisy organs; if he will
look for that which is thought, rather than for that which is
said—he may leave a great name, be useful to his country,
may steady and balance his own mind. But if not, not. The
coherent efficiency of his career will depend on the guide
which he takes, the index which he obeys, the δαιμων which
he consults.

There are two topics which are especially critical. Mr Gladstone must not object to war because it is war, or to expenditure because it is expenditure. Upon these two points Mr
Gladstone has shown a tendency—not, we hope, an uncontrollable tendency, but still a tendency—to differ from the
best opinion of the age. He has been unfortunately placed.
His humane and Christian feeling are opposed to war; he has
a financial ideal which has been distorted, if not destroyed,
by a growing expenditure. But war is often necessary; finance
is not an end; money is but a means. A statesman who would
lead his age must learn its duties. It may be that the defence
of England, the military defence, is one of our duties. If so,
we must not sit down to count the cost. If so, it is not the
age for arithmetic. If so, it is for our statesmen—it is especially for Mr Gladstone, who is the most splendidly gifted
amongst them—to sacrifice cherished hopes; to forego treas-

ured schemes; to put out of their thoughts the pleasant duties of a pacific time; to face the barbarism of war; to vanquish the instinctive shrinkings of a delicate mind.

Lastly, Mr Gladstone must beware how he again commits himself to a long period of bewildering opposition. Office is a steadying situation. A Minister has means of learning from his colleagues, from his subordinates, from unnumbered persons who are only too ready to give him information, what the truth is, and what public opinion is. Opposition, on the other hand, is an exciting and a misleading situation. The bias of every one who is so placed is to oppose the Ministry. Yet on a hundred questions the Ministry are likely to be right. They have special information, long consultations, skilled public servants to guide them. On most points there is no misleading motive. Every Minister decides, to the best of his ability, upon most of the questions which come before him. A bias to oppose him, therefore, is always dangerous. It is peculiarly dangerous to those in whom the contentious impulse is strong, whose life is in debate. If Mr Gladstone's mind is to be kept in a useful track, it must be by the guiding influence of office, by an exemption from the misguiding influence of opposition.

No one desires more than we do that Mr Gladstone's future course should be enriched, not only with oratorical fame, but with useful power. Such gifts as his are amongst the rarest that are given to men; they are amongst the most valuable; they are singularly suited to our Parliamentary life. England cannot afford to lose such a man. If in the foregoing pages we have seemed often to find fault, it has not been for the sake of finding fault. It is *necessary* that England should comprehend Mr Gladstone. If the country have not a true conception of a great statesman, his popularity will be capricious, his power irregular, and his usefulness insecure.

MR GLADSTONE'S CHAPTER OF
AUTOBIOGRAPHY*

(1868)

Mr Gladstone's account of his change of opinion on the subject of the Irish Church is full of character, both intellectual and moral. The intellectual interest lies in the curious process by which the very substance of his present creed on the relation of Church to State is developed from that minute germ of *exception* to his former creed which he stated incidentally in his letter to Mr (afterwards Lord) Macaulay in 1839. The moral interest lies partly in the delicate and scrupulous honour by which Mr Gladstone guarded himself from the danger of succumbing to mere self-interested motives, and partly in the evidence that his intellect was completely moulded into his present opposite views by causes infinitely more powerful than any self-interested motives could possibly have exerted over his mind—namely, that sympathy with the growing political freedom of the day which compelled him year by year to assign an ever-increasing importance to influences wholly unprovided for in his early creed and yet clamourously demanding recognition in any practical view of the future relations between Church and State.

Mr Gladstone started with a theory of the relation of Church to State, which characteristically enough admitted two exceptions—both of them exceptions which we should have thought of a very alarming kind for the prospects of the theory itself, yet both evincing how utterly *unable* Mr Gladstone was even in his youth, and even in the ardour of youthful theorising, to ignore the results already attained by the movement of public thought in England. His theory of the State in relation to the Church was that the State is not

---

* This article was first published in *The Economist* for November 28, 1868; Volume XXVI, pages 1357–58.

only able to discern moral truth and to act upon it, but that
it is able to discern religious truth and to act upon it; from
which his general inference was that the State should not be
indifferent to the religious faith of its own servants, but
should regard that faith as at least a matter of the first moment in selecting them; and secondly, that it is bound in
general to spread the truth in which it believes, and consequently to refuse assistance to all error in which it does not
believe. The first inference led Lord Macaulay to suppose
that Mr Gladstone lamented the repeal of the Test Act, and
would wish to re-enact it. The second inference would have
led any one to suppose that Mr Gladstone was opposed to
the Maynooth grant, and would repeal that. In both cases
the conclusion was or would have been rash. Mr Gladstone,
though a theorist and a warm theorist, was then as now
acutely sensitive to the limits of practicability in the political
condition of the nation within which he lived. He had an
exception covering each case. He explained to Lord Macaulay
that he did not regret the repeal of the Test Act, and did not
wish it re-enacted. Although he thought that the orthodoxy
of any man, proposed as a servant of the Crown, was not
only not an irrelevant but a really important matter, he would
give range and verge enough for taking into account other
considerations which might be, in the special case, of even
greater moment. He would admit men of other than the
prescribed faith into office if there was sufficient reason for
overruling this very important objection to them; but he
would not admit that it was not an objection. On the other
hand, though his theory would not in any way admit of *future* assistance to error, he admitted the plea of a special
covenant as binding on any Government, and such a covenant
having been given in the case of Maynooth, the moral obliga-
tion to fulfil it necessarily overruled the moral objection to
giving it. By these subtle and yet most characteristic and sincere exceptions, Mr Gladstone just brought his theory abreast
of the moment in which he launched it—1838; that is, he
did not compel himself or any one else who might adopt it,
to agitate for a retrogressive step in the direction of repealing
the Test Act, or withdrawing the grant from Maynooth. But
the theory, clogged with its double exception, was like the
astronomical hypothesis of cycles and epicycles to account for
the movements of the planets before the adoption of the
Copernican theory. It would have been clear to most men of

Mr Gladstone's intellectual force that either the main theory must encroach on and subvert the exceptions, or that the exceptions must, like parasitic plants, destroy the theory to which they clung, but it was not clear to him. His mind reflected most powerfully every actual movement of the day, and he evidently never anticipated for a moment that the theory would subvert the exceptions. But neither did he anticipate *then* that the exceptions would encroach upon and destroy the main structure of his theory. His own religious hopes and wishes were at the bottom of his theory; his clear apprehensions of the condition of public thought were at the bottom of the exceptions he admitted to it; and yet there was at that time so complete an equilibrium between the inner religious current of his own mind and the flowing tide of political thought outside him which met and just balanced the force of that current, that he does not seem to have anticipated that this momentary rationale of the relation of State to Church need be disturbed.

The first shock came in 1844, when Mr Gladstone had just become a member of Sir Robert Peel's Cabinet, in Sir Robert Peel's proposal to extend and remodel the Maynooth grant, as a sort of concession to the Catholic claims in Ireland. Mr Gladstone saw at once that the ground was giving way under him, but he could not trust himself—and most honourable to him was it that he would not trust himself—to form an impartial opinion on the subject with so violent a personal inducement as beset him in his desire to remain with his colleagues in the high post which he had just achieved, and which then seemed very naturally almost the goal of his political ambition. He resigned, not to oppose Sir Robert Peel, but to enable himself to reconsider freely convictions which he had so deliberately formed out of office. In the end he assented as an independent member to the proposal, but he felt very justly that only as an independent member could he even have trusted his own sincerity in retracting his theory. Those who laugh scornfully at his scrupulousness should remember, what they are apt to forget, that very few politicians could ever have conceived and believed so subtle and complex a theory as Mr Gladstone's, and that those who could, are just the very men who would most emphatically need very clear moral guarantees of their own sincerity in afterwards rejecting it. It is the subtle-minded who most need to guard themselves against self-deception. Mr Gladstone—except so far as he is checked by his strong sympathy with popular tendencies—is eminently subtle-minded. No statesman has ever felt more keenly the need of guaranteeing himself by external tests against the fear that he might be deceiving himself as to his political motives. No statesman has ever given stronger and more complete guarantees for the perfect purity and disinterestedness of his public conduct. And he has found a double recompense, in a manly self-confidence, which is the secret of much of his influence, and the ample and enthusiastic trust of the people who confer power upon him.

But though Mr Gladstone assented to the extension of the Maynooth grant, which was in fact giving up his principle that the Government should lend its aid only to the propagation of religious truth, he had already perceived that the *other* exception he had admitted to his theory,—the exception permitting persons out of the communion of the national Church to be admitted, on sufficient grounds, to office and influence in the State,—was already demanding much larger and speedier concessions, making in fact much more rapid encroachments on his ecclesiastical theory than the first. He saw that the admission of absolute political equality between English subjects of different religions—the necessity of ignoring altogether objections founded on dissent or other religious differences—was becoming more and more imminent every day. And he evidently felt that the drift of opinion was rather in the direction of removing all real grievances by abating privilege than in that of removing grievances by multiplying privileges—by "levelling down" rather than "levelling up." He wisely and courageously protested against the silly Ecclesiastical Titles Bill, which proposed to make it penal for Roman Catholic prelates to assume territorial titles in the United Kingdom. But since then the whole current of his opinion has obviously set in the direction of removing Irish grievances, not by granting new privileges to the Catholics, but by taking away those which had long ago been unjustly granted to the Protestants.

It will be noticed as one of the most curious features of this autobiographical chapter that Mr Gladstone has never seemed to feel the need of what we may call an overruling principle—that he began by being satisfied with a principle engrafted with glaring exceptions, and that when the exceptions grew into a theory, as they have at last done, he still

feels no annoyance at being entangled with his original principle, in the form (now) of an exception. It is perhaps one
of his great merits as a practical statesman that he rather
enjoys superimposing a subtle exception on the general theory, if practical conditions require it. But it is curious to note
that the principle with which he started, that a Government
can ascertain religious truth and if so ought to propagate it,
is, though abandoned as a principle, still retained as an exception to his new principle, that the political equality of all
religions must be assumed as the basis of a national life like
ours. He admits emphatically that a self-governing nation
with a great variety of religious creeds cannot possibly agree
upon any single form of religious truth to propagate. But
then he makes, wisely enough for practical purposes, this exception in favour of the English establishment, that as it has
come down from times when the members of the Government were not mere spokesmen of the nation, but were in
some sense guardians of the nation,—as in those times they
were quite warranted in propagating their own faith in the
nation,—and as that faith still remains the basis of a great
institution, which is on the whole very popular with all classes
and which does much good,—it ought still to be sanctioned by
Parliament, even though it may have to be admitted that Parliament itself is wholly incapacitated by its own heterogeneous religious composition from again choosing any special
form of Christian faith as "the truth," or even from adhering
to the present form, and sanctioning it as true. Mr Gladstone
still seems to cling to the idea that the established religion
should be supported, not merely as highly *useful* to the nation, but as in some sense spreading "the truth." But whose
truth? Not Parliament's, for it is admitted that Parliament
contains the most opposite forms of belief; not any existing
political power's view of truth—only the view of truth adopted
by an English Government three hundred years ago. What
possible duty can Parliament have to propagate such a body
of "truth" as neither it holds itself nor any other assignable
organ of the people hold? Surely while the great *usefulness*
of the English Church may readily be conceded, Mr Gladstone can scarcely mean that it *now* rests on any higher political foundation than that of a high moral expediency. It
does great good. But can any statesman say that it spreads, or
is capable of spreading, the view of truth adopted by any existing English Government as its own?

MR GLADSTONE AND THE PEOPLE*

(1871)

Mr Gladstone's speech at Greenwich marks a new era in English politics,—not that it is for him a very great speech, and still less that it is the speech of a statesman as such,—if it *had* been, in that place and delivered to such an audience it would probably have been a great mistake and a sad failure, —but that it marks the coming of the time when it will be one of the most important qualifications of a Prime Minister to exert a direct control over the masses—when the ability to reach them, not as his views may be filtered through an intermediate class of political teachers and writers, but *directly* by the vitality of his own mind, will give a vast advantage in the political race to any statesman. We are not saying that the power of addressing twenty-five thousand people for two hours, and holding their attention and interest in spite of plenty of hostile elements in the great crowd, is one which above all others we delight to see in a leading statesman. As far as our own tastes go, we might prefer the sort of statesman who could only reach the nation through comparatively select audiences like Parliament, whose power is reserved for the higher regions of statesmanship, and who possesses none of the notes of the great popular orator. All we are saying is that the time is evidently approaching when such statesmen will be at a considerable disadvantage, even as heads of an Administration, when a power like that evinced by Mr Gladstone will be of the very first importance even for his position as leader of the House of Commons and first Minister of the Queen. Criticise Mr Gladstone's speech as you will—virulently, contemptuously, patronisingly, compassionately, or from any other point of view, however depreciating,—no politician in his senses will deny that it has added

---

* This article was first published in *The Economist*, Volume XXIX, pages 1330–31 November 4, 1871.

greatly to the strength of the Government's position; that it
has to some extent neutralised much of the political result of
the process of many months' slow decay and demolition of his
power. If Parliament were to meet again to-morrow, Mr Gladstone's position would be quite changed. It would be at once
felt by all his discontented allies as well by his party foes that
Mr Gladstone's direct command over the people is still immense,—that the result of an appeal to the people by him
against a divided and hostile Parliament would very probably
end in his full reinstatement in power, with as large a majority as ever. Mr Gladstone has illustrated most remarkably
his reserve power outside Parliament. No English Minister
probably ever had less of a personal Parliamentary following
than Mr Gladstone. There he has no phalanx like Lord Russell's Whig phalanx, and Lord Palmerston's personal admirers.
In Parliament he has no body-guard. But he has shown once
more how easily he can get the ear of the electors themselves,
and that under circumstances of no little difficulty,—circumstances in which both his policy and his shortcomings as a
local representative combined to make him unpopular with
his audience. Parliament fully appreciates this reserve power
in a Prime Minister, which secures him, as it were, a separate
and private appeal to the people,—an appeal not simply
through the people's representatives, and what the people
may or may not understand of his reported Parliamentary
speeches, but by direct personal influence. Parliament may not
like it,—may think it even a dangerous power,—may echo the
grumblings of three years ago over Mr Gladstone's stumping
tour in Lancashire; but Parliament will recognise and respect
it as a new store of political force, as a guarantee that the
Premier has more direct relations to the people than any
other Premier of our times, and that if he becomes unpopular
with the representatives of the people, he may still be more
popular with the people themselves than even those representatives. Undoubtedly Mr Gladstone's Greenwich speech
will serve as a conspicuous mark for the date when it first
became advisable for a Minister to cultivate the gifts of a
great popular orator,—an orator who can deal with political
topics in the broad, easy, and animated style which touches
the people, and without any of that subtle flavour of Parliamentary skill which only suits the statesman.

Mr Gladstone not only displayed this sort of power in a
very remarkable degree at Greenwich, but what is quite as

remarkable as anything else, it is a late-acquired power. He was from the first no doubt a good Parliamentary speaker. Lord Macaulay, in his review of Mr Gladstone's early book on Church and State, speaks of his Parliamentary promise in high terms. But the constitution of his mind was so complex, and his style of argument so little popular, that no one certainly then thought of him as a popular orator. Sir R. Peel, if we remember his words rightly, says in his political memoranda, that Mr Gladstone brought "his high character and great attainments" to the aid of the Conservative Ministry, but evidently thought little of his oratorical powers. Indeed, it was not till he busied himself with finance,—i.e., with very definitely marked-out subject-matter, in which there was no room for subtleties, though much for explanatory and expository dissertation,—that his remarkable faculty as an orator, his artistic power of planning out his subjects, his ease and vivacity in making them interesting to others, his skill in illustrating principles, his animation in recounting facts, began to be generally understood. And it was far later again that he acquired any of that power of fascinating and influencing a genuine multitude, by which Mr Bright first became noticeable. Mr Gladstone's rhetorical powers, at first as little popular as great fluency and earnestness could well be, have gradually worked themselves out into a real command of popular sympathies and the popular intelligence, and the fact is one that at so critical a moment as this will hardly fail to be of the greatest significance to his but recently tottering Government.

We are quite willing to admit that the speech itself, though a very powerful and lively speech from a Prime Minister to his constituents, was in no sense the speech of the head of a great Administration declaring and expounding his policy. Such a speech could hardly have been made to 25,000 people in the open air under the conditions of time and space under which he spoke. A man who has to exert his voice to its utmost, and to interest a great crowd for a considerable time, cannot by any possibility trace out the fine lines of a national policy, even if he had spare energy enough to concentrate his mind upon them in the face of such physical difficulties. But as the speech of a Prime Minister who is also a representative to his constituents, it is not easy to overestimate its ability and its interest. The historical illustration of the difficulty of keeping together large Parliamentary majorities, as introductory to his

own expression of confidence in his colleagues and himself,
and his complete refusal to admit that this address was his
"last dying speech and confession,"—his bold expression of
continued confidence in his Irish policy,—his reply to the
charge of niggardly economies, which was as far from any
yielding of principle as it was from any unfair attack on those
Conservative predecessors who had yet, as he showed, economised (and quite rightly economised) more labour in the
national dockyards than ever he and his colleagues,—his defence of his military policy,—the moderate and just stand he
took upon his education policy,—and finally, his extremely
lively and true remarks on the fundamental popularity of the
House of Lords, even with the working classes, and the un-
desirability therefore of doing away with the hereditary principle,—were all treated with a lightness and yet energy of
touch, and connected together in so natural and taking a manner, that Mr Gladstone taught the audience, which he was
also amusing, without letting them know that he was teaching
them. And the last part of his speech on the mistake made
by the representatives of skilled labour in their negotiations
with certain peers and baronets, through Mr Scott Russell,
and in venturing to hope that legislation could do for them
what really nothing but individual energy and self-denial
could ever achieve, was more than instructive and lively; it
went thoroughly home to his audience, and made them feel
how thoroughly Mr Gladstone understood their position, and
how steadily he could resist unwise demands, even while
heartily entering into their most urgent wants.

Thus when Mr Gladstone left the Greenwich hustings, his
Government certainly stood in a far stronger position than it
has done for many months back. The nation has again learnt
to realise that its Prime Minister understands both its unwise
wishes and its genuine wants better than almost any other
man in it, and that even if misunderstandings must arise between the Cabinet and Parliament, there will be a very strong
disposition on the part of the masses to believe what the
Prime Minister says of Parliament, more easily than what
Parliament says of the Prime Minister.

MR GLADSTONE ON
HOME RULE FOR IRELAND*

(1871)

The Prime Minister's speech at Aberdeen cannot at any rate be charged with that tendency to intellectual hesitation and finesse which is the favourite taunt of his opponents. In speaking of the Irish cry for Home Rule, Mr Gladstone drew no fine distinctions, and came to no ambiguous conclusion. He asked if the United Parliament was to be broken up because it could not or would not do justice to Ireland, or only to please the Irish fancy. If the former were alleged, the answer was that for the last three years the United Parliament has been eagerly engaged in doing for Ireland what it would hardly have done for either England or Scotland—no doubt because neither England nor Scotland stood in need of the measures granted as Ireland did,—but none the less did this sufficiently demonstrate the perfect willingness and capacity of the United Parliament to redress all real Irish grievances. If the latter were alleged, that the Irish do not *choose* to take even good government from the hands of a United Parliament, then the answer is that on that head the Irish have only the right to vote with the other members of the Union; the whole Union has a right to decide what is in this respect for the common benefit, and unless any party can allege that their individual interests are trampled on by the Union, the whole Union has a right to say whether union or separation will best promote the interests of all. And this in point of fact, as everybody knows, Great Britain has long ago decided. In Mr Gladstone's own vigorous words—"can any sensible man, can any rational man, suppose that at this time of day, in this condition of the world, we are going to disintegrate

---

* This article was first published in *The Economist* for September 30, 1871, Volume XXIX, page 1175.

the great capital institutions of this country for the purpose of making ourselves ridiculous in the sight of all mankind, and crippling any power we possess for bestowing benefits through legislation on the country to which we belong?"

That is clear, forcible language, which may, we hope, have the effect of showing the Home Rule party in Ireland that while Ireland may gain almost anything that is reasonable and just from the Imperial Parliament, she will not gain the repeal of the Union for which that Party is now crying out, and which would be indeed in many respects far more mischievous to British interests, and perhaps even to Irish interests, than absolute independence.

Indeed it is hard to conceive anything more mischievous than the opening of an indefinite, and indefinitely increasable, number of debatable issues between Great Britain and Ireland such as would be not merely suggested but forced on the public by the division of duties between an Irish and British Parliament. It is difficult enough to divide the sphere of properly municipal or country from properly central and Parliamentary powers, and almost impossible to do so beneficially without giving Parliament an absolute overriding power in case of conflict. But this difficulty would not only be enhanced a thousand times by the great importance, unity, and national coherence of an Irish Parliament, but it would be quite impossible to give the Imperial (or as it would then be, Federal) Parliament a power to override the decisions of an Irish Parliament without provoking something like a rebellion on every separate occasion. It may be said perhaps that this difficulty has never been felt in the United States, where the State powers and the Federal powers are divided by a hard and fast line, which neither State nor Federation has the power to overleap. But in point of fact the difficulty has been felt, and felt very keenly, and though not for precisely the same reasons as it would be felt in this case, yet for a similar class of reasons—namely, because the genius and policy of a certain group of the States diverged very widely from the genius and policy of the remainder. The Secession war was in fact a State revolt against the Central power, and though that Secession was due not to race, but to a "domestic institution" of a most potent and mischievous kind, yet difference of race and religion conjointly are certainly quite capable of producing as great a chasm of feeling between the different members of a Federation as is any difference in "domestic institutions".

Only consider for a moment what an Irish Parliament would be disposed to feel if it found itself compelled to impose taxes for a war in which the sympathies of Ireland were directly opposed to the sympathies of Great Britain, or were even hindered from imposing taxes for some purely Irish object by the weight of the taxation for Imperial purposes which it disapproved. Is it even conceivable that such a Parliament could long exist without becoming a centre of the fiercest disloyalty and even treason? Or put aside questions of finance, and look only at ecclesiastical policy. Would not it be very probable that one of the first efforts of Ireland's separate Parliament would be to re-establish a Church in Ireland, but not this time a Protestant but a Catholic Church—an effort which would probably give rise to civil war unless England interfered to thwart the wish of the Catholic party, in which case the danger of a violent disruption would arise again from another cause? It is in fact as plain as common sense can make it to all who look at the condition of Ireland with impartial eyes, that "Home Rule" would be but the first step in a series of virulent disputes as to the political relations of the two islands, which could hardly end except in separation, or re-conquest with all the evils that that would bring in its train. The Home Rule party would certainly be imprudent, but they would be far more logical, if they were to raise a cry at once for an Independent Irish Republic.

MR DISRAELI*

(1859)

Benjamin Disraeli was born in London in 1804, son of Isaac D'Israeli, an Italian Jew who made a fortune as a London merchant, and of Miriam Basevi. He was privately educated and in 1821 was articled to a solicitor; he entered Lincoln's Inn in 1824 and kept nine terms, but left the law for unsuccessful ventures in stocks and in journalism. In 1826 he published his first novel, Vivian Grey, in 1830 The Young Duke, and in 1832 Contarini Fleming. Disraeli stood for Parliament as a Radical in 1832 and 1834, but then changed over to the Tory party. He expounded his contention that it was possible to be both a Conservative and a democrat in three pamphlets published during 1835 and 1836. After two more defeats Disraeli was elected for Maidstone in 1837. Although he was refused a position in Sir Robert Peel's government in 1841, he acquired a position of great influence in Tory circles. He differed from Peel in believing that the interests of wealthy manufacturers were not the interests of England, and Disraeli became the spokesman of a small group of younger Tories, nicknamed "Young England," who defended the landed interests against the proposed repeal of the Corn Laws, and the working classes against exploitation by the factory owners. His novels Coningsby, 1844, and Sybil, 1845, embodied these ideas. When Peel's ministry fell after the repeal of the Corn Laws in 1846, Disraeli became the leader of the Conservative party in the Commons. In 1847 he supported the Liberals in removing Jewish exclusion from Parliament and in the same year published Tancred, his last political novel, which concerned the Jewish tradition. In 1852 Lord Derby took office, with Disraeli as Chancellor of the Exchequer, but the ministry soon fell upon Gladstone's attacks on Disraeli's budget. The second Derby-Disraeli cabinet was from 1858–59. Their third administration was from 1866–68, and was notable for the passage of the second parliamentary Reform Bill in 1867, for which Disraeli was largely responsible. He yielded to the more moderate demands

---

* This article was first published in The Economist for July 2, 1859, Volume XVII, pages 725-26.

of the Liberal opposition, knowing that they would pass the bill if the Conservatives did not. The bill added more than a million voters to the register. Lord Derby retired in 1868, and Disraeli became Prime Minister, but his ministry fell almost immediately over the issue of the disestablishment of the Anglican Church in Ireland, a measure supported by the Liberals. While leader of the opposition, Disraeli published Lothair (1870), *a novel chiefly concerned with religious conflicts. After Gladstone's defeat in 1874, Disraeli again became Prime Minister. Although he carried through some necessary legislation for social reform, his real interest was in his foreign policy, which was characterised by a vigorous imperialism. He purchased shares in the Suez Canal in 1875, from the bankrupt Khedive of Egypt, so securing English interests in the canal. He gained for Queen Victoria the title of Empress of India in 1876, after which he was raised to the peerage as the Earl of Beaconsfield. The Russo-Turkish war of 1877 was precipitated by the open support that Disraeli had given to Turkey; he played a large part at the Congress of Berlin in 1878, which resulted in a treaty depriving Russia of much of the reward of victory. Disraeli retired on the defeat of the Conservatives in the elections of 1880, and completed his retrospective novel,* Endymion. *He died at Hughenden Manor, Buckinghamshire, in 1881.*

"The career of the late Chancellor of the Exchequer," said one of Mr Disraeli's political friends soon after his comparative failure as a Minister in 1852, "is not closed; we believe its brightest portion is in the future. We have invariably observed that whenever Mr Disraeli has received a check, it has only been the herald of a great advance; and that when the world has believed him beaten, he has always been on the eve of his greatest victories." Read by the light of recent events, this was undoubtedly a remarkable prophecy. Mr Disraeli has never held a position so eminent as that which he now holds. He was the life and soul of the late Administration. Without him it could not have lasted a single week. He has resigned without accepting any reward. Lord Derby has taken the blue ribbon. Lord Malmesbury and Sir John Pakington have had the Order of the Bath. Mr Disraeli, who was far more essential to the Government than either of them, whose management of the House of Commons won him on this occasion universal admiration, whose recent speeches have scarcely been rivalled for insight, point, and individual character, by any statesman of our day,—has retired with a dig-

nity that will deservedly increase his influence in entering on
the leadership of the powerful Conservative Opposition. It
is not, therefore, an inappropriate time to make a few remarks on his general capacity and character as a statesman.
He has proved, in the last year, that his great abilities are
matured, and his character weighted, by experience. He has
shown that he can do, what in 1852 at least he had not yet
learned to do,—lead with dignity, and fail with dignity after
personal exertions which, so far as their intellectual character
is concerned, might well have earned ample success. What
are the principal characteristics of his strange and brilliant
career?

Mr Disraeli is chiefly remarkable for the unusual combination which his mind presents of individual tenacity of purpose, with a flexibility and pliancy of intellect rarely found
in men of so much audacity and strength. There never was a
statesman of eminence who, when he entered on public life,
was so strangely in need of the lessons of experience; there
never was one who was so apt a learner; there never was one
who was more resolute to turn that ready faculty to the best
account. From the day of his maiden speech, now more than
twenty-one years ago, when he appealed in vain to the House
of Commons for a cheer, and sat down with the warning, "I
am not at all surprised at the reception I have experienced.
I have begun several times several things, and I have often
succeeded at last. I will sit down now, but the time will come
when you will listen to me," up to the day when, amid the
breathless attention of the House, he delivered his gallant,
eloquent, and adroit defence of the late Government, Mr
Disraeli has never quailed beneath the difficulties of his arduous career, and never failed in that self-possession, which
knows how to turn every error, every false step into the materials of a future success. Beginning without rank, without connection, without wealth,—with every difficulty in his path
which the prejudices of race could conjure up,—without entering into the convictions or understanding the political traditions either of the party he was to defend or of the party
he was to assail,—wholly destitute of the kind of practical
sagacity which most easily inspires Englishmen with confidence,—with an ill-regulated literary ambition and a false
melodramatic taste that were well calculated to increase ten-
fold the existing prejudices against him, it is difficult to conceive a greater marvel than the brilliant success which Mr

Disraeli has achieved, singlehanded, in a sphere of life usually thought singularly exclusive and inaccessible to unassisted adventurers.

The success of this great party-leader is, we believe, traceable to two principal gifts—a very sensitive and impressible, but extremely unoriginal imagination, and a dexterity seldom equalled in working up all the impressions he receives into materials for personal attacks. Had Mr Disraeli been a man of deeper and more original imagination than he is, he could not have surrendered as he has done, at every crisis in his career, to the ascendant influence of the hour. He has never had a political faith,—he probably does not know what it means. No man has invented so many political theories. No living politician's fancy has been half so prolific of suggestions for new bases of political creed. No statesman has ever been so "viewy". But notwithstanding all his strictures on Sir Robert Peel for want of originality and imagination, there probably never was a statesman so unoriginal as himself. His efforts at originality—whether political or literary—have ever been of that excessively theatrical kind which seem, as it were, to be always gasping for breath; and he is never successful except when he desists from such efforts, and simply adopts or delineates what he sees in the actual life around him. Whether as a novelist or as a statesman, his efforts at original construction have always been rhapsodical. Those who knew his early fictions and *Coningsby* well, recognised last session, in India Bill No. 2, unmistakable traces of the same mind. The same unsound imagination which filled Mr Disraeli's novels with the most flimsy and eccentric theories of history, society, and political organisation,—which invented the "Venetian-Doge" theory of the English Constitution,—the doctrine of the absolute ascendancy of the "Caucasian" race,—the gospel of "Young England,"—the historical hypothesis that Charles the First was a martyr to the principle of direct taxation,—the identity of Tory principles with those of Free Trade,—the theory that the "tendency of civilisation is to pure monarchy,"—that "an educated nation recoils from the imperfect vicariat of what it calls a representative Government," and a thousand others,—has been equally visible whenever Mr Disraeli has attempted to win the admiration of the House of Commons by any proposition of a directly constructive nature. No politician has ever shown, in the bad sense of the word, so *romantic* a political imagination,—in other words, a fancy so little imbued with the laws of real life, so ready to revolt against those laws, and put feeble idealities in their place. His ideal measures, like his ideal heroes, have always seemed the inventions of a mind on the rack to produce something grand or startling instead of something true and lifelike; there is no trace in them of the genius which breathes in his criticisms of actual measures, and his delineations of actual men. Nothing has really impeded his progress more than his efforts after originality. His mind was made to receive impressions and to interpret the tendencies of others. When he has limited himself to this he has been marvellously successful. When he has striven to engrave something new upon his age, he has fallen far below the standard of even average English sense.

On the other hand, if there have been no statesmen of eminence so devoid of constructive genius as Mr Disraeli—if, even, he has fallen far below his great adversary Sir Robert Peel in his attempts to create, simply because he has been possessed with the desire to astonish, instead of with the desire to interpret, his age,—there has seldom been a statesman with so great a power for understanding and delineating all that comes within the actual range of his experience, and turning it into a weapon of the most formidable efficiency. Mr Disraeli has made himself a *power* in the House of Commons exactly by this art. Whenever he has lost way, it has been by attempts at original statesmanship; but, when he has confined his efforts to showing how well he understands both the weak and strong points of those around him, he has been terrible and quite unsurpassed. Whether in fiction or in debate, there are few who have drawn so many true and subtle sketches of those whom they have actually seen and known. His power seems limited to direct experience. He has no insight into past history,—no power of giving or restoring life to characters with which he has not come into personal contact. But he is an absolute master of personalities of all kinds, whether purely critical, flattering, or caustic; and it is by the unsparing use of this formidable literary weapon that, in spite of all blunders, he has won his way to the eminence on which he now stands. He has said, in one of his works, "nothing is great but the personal," and for him, at least, it has been so. He has adopted the opinions of parties as he would adopt a national costume. "Tory," "Radical," "Tory-Radical," "Free-Trader," "Protectionist," "Conservative," "Reformer," no creed has come amiss to him, and amidst them all he has maintained the same clear eye for the personal qualities of those around him, and the same determined will to use them for individual or party ends.

In short, Mr Disraeli owes his great success to his very unusual capacity for *applying* a literary genius, in itself limited, to the practical purposes of public life. Had his genius been really deeper than it is, it would have absorbed him, and he would have devoted his life to the exercise of an imagination which, as it is, he has principally valued as a formidable political weapon. While his combative instinct has been strong, and so determined him to seek a fair field for its practical satisfaction, his literary insight has been only of that depth which irritates and fires the intellect without absorbing it. It has not been deep enough to engross his powers; it has been quite deep enough to give him the sense of power. He forms, in this respect, a remarkable contrast to Sir E. B. Lytton, who, with probably greater literary genius, has nothing like the same power of wielding it as a practical instrument,— the same art of turning his literary ploughshares and pruning hooks into swords and spears. Indeed, practical politics is not an attractive field for men who care to delineate life more than they care to influence it. Statesmen must usually be occupied more with measures, social tendencies, public wants, national convictions, than with the niceties of individual character. Mr Disraeli is just enough of a literary man to indicate clearly in all his speeches that these things do not seriously occupy him,—that he compels himself to use them as instruments for ends which interest him far more deeply. When we read his speeches we feel, by a kind of instinct, that there is nothing very real or very deep,—nothing which seems to him of essential importance,—as long as he stays in the field of dry argument and exposition. But when we come to the personal phases of the question, all is changed and living. The telling epithets, the graphic hints, the signs of living insight, are all reserved for those passages in which he addresses himself not to measures but to men, in which he throws off a happy picture of a statesman's career, or delineates with life-like touches the demeanour of the House of Commons. He has nothing of the statesman's power of imaging forth the actual effect and operation of the measures he advocates,—nothing of the statesman's power of penetrating to the heart of a deep national conviction. When he attempts these things, he is apt to produce some romantic failure that brings scorn upon himself; but, though almost all his power is limited to the use of a keen and delicate weapon very susceptible of abuse, he has at least recently shown that the responsibility of a high position can make him generous and dignified,—with here and there even a certain touch of chivalry,—in the wielding of a talent so individual and so pungent as his own.

WHY MR DISRAELI HAS SUCCEEDED*

(1867)

Mr Disraeli once said that those "who went down to posterity were about as rare as planets"; but he will succeed in going down there himself. The Reform Act of 1867 will be remembered as long as the Constitution of England is remembered. Why so great a change was made so silently and with so little national discussion will amaze our children—just as we of this generation cannot comprehend the Reform discussions of 1832, and why so much was hoped from a measure upon its face so prosaic. But Mr Disraeli is identified with it. His name was the first on the back of the Bill of the names of those who brought it in, and his will be the name which posterity will think of with it. And the reward is just. It *is* Mr Disraeli's Bill. Without professing to know what happened in the Cabinet, so much as this is certain. Mr Disraeli all along wished to go down very low, to beat the Whigs—if possible, the Radicals too—by basing the support of the Conservative party upon a lower class than those which they could influence. For this end he induced his party to surrender their creed and their policy; he altered what his followers had to say, even more than the Constitution under which they are going to live. How then did he attain such a singular success?

It is usual to say that he attained it by fraud and deceit. And we certainly are not about to defend his morality. On the contrary, we have attacked it often, and, if need were, would attack it now. But a little study of human affairs is enough to show that fraud alone—fraud by itself—does not succeed; it is too ugly and coarse for man to bear; it is only when disguised in great qualities, and helped on by fine talents, that it prospers. What, then, in this case, were the accompanying aids?

* This article was first published in *The Economist* for September 7, 1867, Volume XXV, pages 1009–10.

Mr Disraeli is one of the most observant students of human life in England. He said many years since of Sir R. Peel, "He was a bad judge of character. The prosperous routine of his youth was not favourable to this talent. He never had to *struggle*." But Mr Disraeli has had to struggle. His career is of his own making; it has no precedent; he is the one literary adventurer, who has led the House of Commons, or who is likely, perhaps to lead it, if wealth is strengthened by the new Bill as much as seems probable. In the course of his aspiring youth he observed all classes of men—not deeply and profoundly perhaps; it is only the very greatest men who do that; but distinctly, and in their plain traits. His early novels are studies of conspicuous life. In them all the obvious momentary part of English society is sketched very vividly and very well.

The whole of this observant faculty, which was trained in social life, has been concentrated on Parliament. For years he has sat almost silent—never raising petty discussions and confusing old people who thought a leader of Opposition ought to be always opposing, but watching day by day the course of events till he has, perhaps, the best and nicest Parliamentary memory of his generation. Probably he required all this culture. He has not—at least experience seems to show that he has not—instinctive tact. There is even at times an inaptitude to comprehend those around him. When he asked last Session, "Why, what opinions have we changed?" there was a roar as much from his own side of the House as from the opposite; and, perhaps, there was hardly a man there who did not understand better than Mr Disraeli why it was *gauche* to say that. He failed egregiously in his first speech, though it would be absurd to press that by itself, as many great speakers have failed at first, and most learn by paining their hearers, but there was a sort of opaque, undiscerning vanity about the performance, which was singularly unpromising. Indeed as for instinctive tact, Mr Disraeli has made stupendous blunders: a Budget which everybody was to like, but which no one would accept; an Indian Bill, at which everybody laughed; speeches in Opposition innumerable, which made men say, till Lord Palmerston died, "That Dizzy was the Whigs' best friend". But now, with the training of years, he has developed a sort of second-hand tact by memory, which serves him well, and is surer than any he has to fight against.

Mr Disraeli is not profound in the least, and perhaps he

would laugh at telling what he thinks his best creed. But he has a fatal facility in suggesting hazy theories which would puzzle an Aristotle. The driest and hardest thinker could never get right if he persisted in tying his words into the pretty puzzles which Mr Disraeli delights in, and which so often take. His language upon abstract subjects, for upon those of this world he can talk plainly enough, is to that of a thinker by profession—to the language, say, of Mr Mill—what discolouring artificial light is to daylight. You never know what he is talking about, or whether it means much or little. But, though not deep, Mr Disraeli's mind is beyond measure quick, and, as far as it penetrates, original. There is nothing routine about him. He got the House of Commons to sit at unheard-of hours—from 2 till 7—and seemed to think nothing of it, though some grave members thought it almost a Reform Bill in itself. It has been said, not very wisely, that the best general is he who best knows how to repair a defeat; and if that were translated, it might be said that Mr Disraeli was the best leader of the House of Commons, for he knows how to glide out of a scrape better than anyone.

To this quickness of a keen man, he joins, by some freak of nature, the imperturbability of an apathetic man. Whether he is quite as impassive as he seems, may indeed be doubted. Very near observers are said to be able to detect shades of wincing. But very impassible he must be; and it is a sort of "double first" in skirmishing talent to be so quick to hit, and so hard to *be* hit. No doubt the opportunities of his career have been favourable—at least, they look so now that he has made a good use of them. He found the Tory party at the death of Lord George Bentinck almost barren of great ability in the House of Commons. The trained official Peelites who before led the party had followed Sir Robert Peel. The grade of gentry who fill the country seats, and mostly compose the Conservative party in the Commons, are perhaps the least able and valuable part of English society. They have neither the responsibilities nor the culture of great noblemen, and they have never felt the painful need of getting on, which sharpens the middle class. They have a moderate sort of wealth which teaches them little, and a steady sort of mind fit for common things, but they have no flexibility and they have no ideas. Almost the worst of the class, too, are often sent to Parliament, and the best left out, because a foolish prejudice requires that the member shall have land within the county. Mr Disraeli found himself with the most ingenious and manipulating intellect of his generation at the head of the "Army of Fogies," and the result is what we see.

What have been the consequences of the slow honesty of the Tory party, and the quick dishonesty of the Tory leader, future years will unfold better than we can understand them now. But it is well for us to see exactly what the forces were; and that it was not fraud itself which won, but fraud in a convenient place, and with singular ability.

MR DISRAELI'S ADMINISTRATION*

(1868)

Mr Disraeli's Administration has lasted nominally only nine months; but, in fact, we may fairly assume that he has had the practical guidance of the Tory policy since the resignation of Lord Russell's Government in 1866. It is impossible now not to cast back a glance at his use of the power which he had gained for himself by his brilliant talents and pertinacity. Has that use of power been worthy or unworthy of the skill and tact and undaunted perseverance which Mr Disraeli displayed in climbing to his high office from that obscure position in which it is said, on good authority, that he deliberately resolved on attaining the eminence he has at last reached?

This is not precisely an easy question to reply to. That Mr Disraeli has shown as Prime Minister precisely the same qualities, without any trace at all of degeneration in their kind, by which he reached the top of the ladder, we entirely believe. There has been, as far as we see, no sign of failing power in his administration. He has acted as Prime Minister, and as virtual Tory leader before he was Prime Minister, very much as any shrewd observer would have been disposed to expect, though perhaps with even more moderation and judgment. But whether the class of abilities which were specially fitted for the great political climbing feat which Mr Disraeli has performed were of the class likely to be particularly useful, or as well adapted to Mr Disraeli's position at the summit as they were adapted to the labour of ascent, is certainly very much more doubtful. When the end is attained, we naturally look for the display of new qualities which would justify the laborious appliance of means. We want to see whether the climber climbed—like Lord Clive in his boy-

---

* This article was first published in *The Economist* for December 12, 1868, Volume XXVI, pages 1414–15.

hood when he ascended the Church steeple—simply for the
sake of the gymnastic feat, simply because he was conscious
of a great climbing power, or because he was conscious of
powers which could not be adequately exerted except at the
highest point of political influence. We may say at once that
we see no trace of power of this kind in Mr Disraeli; that his
abilities seem to us to be much more extraordinary when
we look at the position he has won, than when we attempt
to estimate the use which he has made of it; that he seems to
us to have displayed Herculean powers in reaching a position
wherein he found not very much that he cared to do, except
occupying it, and still less that it was of any great advantage
either to his own party or to the country that he should do.
He has been a shrewd, composed, intelligent, and generally
dignified Prime Minister; but he has not gained fresh credit
for his party; he has not developed any original policy; he has
not inspired as First Minister any fresh confidence in himself.

It has been Mr Disraeli's misfortune throughout his main
political career to lead a party of very strong prejudices and
principles, without feeling himself any cordial sympathy with
either the one or the other. No doubt that is precisely the
fact which has enabled him on most great emergencies to be
of use to his party. His completely external intelligence has
been to them what the elephant driver's—the mahout's—is
to the elephant, comparatively insignificant as a force, but so
familiar with all the habits of the creature which his sagacity
has to guide, and so entirely, if it only knew, at its mercy,
that all his acuteness is displayed in contriving to turn the
creature's habits and instincts to his own end, profit, and
advantage,—which, however, cannot be done without also
carefully preserving the creature itself from great dangers,
and guarding it against the violence of its own passions. In
this way Mr Disraeli has necessarily been of great use to the
Tory party. But something more than this is needed for a
great and successful Tory statesman. There must be at least
some sympathy as well as professional counsel. There must
be some power to inspire enthusiasm as well as to create intellectual respect. There must be some sense of common conviction as well as of common interest. There must be some
identity of sentiment as well as of mutual dependence. Mr
Disraeli when he had reached the summit of his ambition
naturally needed more than ever this community of faith and
purpose, in order to teach him how to use his power both for

his party's benefit and his own. But he had it not. He could
only calculate the chances of success without reference to
their aims and wishes; and the effect of course was to diminish
his influence over them, without even giving the appearance
of individual conviction and personal self-denial to his policy.
It seemed a policy in the air, calculated to succeed, not
calculated for any special object higher and better than success.

If we look at Mr Disraeli's legislative policy, no one can
avoid the criticism that while it was in one great instance at
least *not* a policy favourable to his own party, it affected to be
so, and was forced upon them on the plea that it would prove
so. Mr Disraeli proposed as a Conservative policy, because it
would "dish the Whigs," that which was not really Conservative and which dished the Conservatives if anybody; and
so he had neither the party success of a clever strategic move,
nor the national success of sacrificing party to the people's
welfare. With regard to Reform this was conspicuously the
case. What he proposed in pointed opposition to Mr Gladstone, and in order to deprive the Liberals of that "prætorian
guard" of select artisans, to secure whose aid Lord Russell's
borough franchise was, Mr Disraeli thought, specially
adapted,—namely, household suffrage in boroughs,—proved
specially fatal to his party. Instead of getting at the supposed
Conservatism and Toryism of the most ignorant and most
prejudiced class, it evoked a far stronger Liberalism in the
boroughs than we had ever reached before. On the contrary,
the county franchise, which was not due to any *finesse* of Mr
Disraeli's, which was taken with no practical alteration from
the Liberal Bill, did in fact evoke a certain additional Conservative force on which Mr Disraeli had never counted. His
strategy wholly failed. What he proposed to do for party objects failed of those objects. And, unfortunately, he never professed or proposed to sink party in the welfare of the nation.
In the Reform Act as a strategist he unquestionably outflanked
himself.

And on the Irish Church,—the only other great legislative
conflict which falls within the period of his administration,
and for this indeed he alone, and not in any degree Lord
Derby, is responsible,—he again failed in doing the absolutely
best thing for his party, without succeeding in even the appearance of sacrificing party to country. It was a great mistake to throw out feelers in the direction of endowing the

Roman Church, not only without being prepared to follow
them up by a frank declaration of policy, but even when he
was prepared to disavow them and creep out of them as best
he could. He weakened and disheartened the mere Conservatives, without winning the credit of a generous sacrifice of
power for a policy which many would have thought farseeing
and statesmanlike. In this case as in the last, Mr Disraeli's
difficulty was that he had no personal preferences, no political convictions either in common with his party or diver-
gent from them. He acted as he felt, like a statesman living
from hand to mouth, *using* his party rather than expressing
its feelings or rallying its forces. Against a party that was convinced, led by a statesman whose convictions were deep, he
naturally found himself almost powerless.

But if in strategy and in legislation Mr Disraeli's administration has not been admirable, any fair politician will admit
that on the whole his ministerial use of official power in
selecting the men for the appointments he has had to fill
up has been most shrewdly, even wisely used. In distributing
the offices amongst his own colleagues his choice was always
considerate and acute, though this may be originally due to
Lord Derby. Mr Gathorne Hardy showed himself a very able
administrator both at the Poor Law Board and at the Home
Office. Lord Cranborne was perhaps as good an Indian Secretary as was ever appointed, and Lord Carnarvon was excellent at the Colonial Office. Sir Stafford Northcote has
unquestionably made an able Indian Secretary since Lord
Cranborne's resignation, and if the other officials of Mr Disraeli's Government have been less remarkable for administrative ability, it is less from any fault of their chief than from
the radical poverty of his materials. But it is in the external
appointments, especially since Mr Disraeli became solely
responsible for them, that he has, except in one notable instance, shown the greatest ability and insight, and the greatest freedom from partisan feeling. Lord Mayo's appointment to be Governor-General of India appears to most men
a very remarkable exception to this rule. Mr Disraeli, however, asserts positively that he believes him to be eminently
fitted for the post, and though the public have absolutely
no access to his data for that apparently eccentric view, it is
still quite fair that, considering the spirit shown in his other
appointments, he should have full credit for sincerity. In his
ecclesiastical appointments undoubtedly Mr Disraeli has

shown disinterestedness and the acuteness of an impartial man of the world, judging by the qualities which he hears on all sides ascribed to the most eminent candidates for promotion. And it is remarkable that he has evidently regarded a high and impressive moral energy as a quality of the first importance for his episcopal appointments. The promotion of the Dean of Cork to the Bishopric of Peterborough, and the translation of the Bishop of London to the See of Canterbury, are conspicuous instances of this. Mr Disraeli might have been satisfied with learning and a spotless reputation. He has seen that something more was desirable in a leader of the Church—a certain originality of moral nature as well. On the whole, we must recognise in his use of patronage a very dispassionate and, in some sense, elevated judgment, which even Mr Gladstone may scarcely succeed in rivalling. In statesmanship, Mr Disraeli's administration has been a failure; in the choice of officials, it has been in some sense even a distinguished success.

MR DISRAELI AS A MEMBER OF
THE HOUSE OF COMMONS*

(1876)

Nothing could be more out of place or premature than to review as yet Mr Disraeli's career. That career is not yet ended. But some remarks may be made on him as a member of the House of Commons, in which he has sat for forty years, and where he obtained his political eminence and power. That part of his career is certainly over, for he has chosen to leave its peculiar scene.

During this long period Mr Disraeli has filled four parts. First—that of a political free-lance or outsider. And it was in this that he first obtained fame. The best opportunity for such a man is, when parties are breaking up; when secret feelings are in many minds; when cautious men do not know what to say. The latter part of Sir Robert Peel's Ministry was such a period. From the time when he became conspicuously and obviously a Free Trader, there was always a secret anger in the Conservative ranks which craved for an outlet, but which no "regular man" could express. This Mr Disraeli spoke out. From the time of Mr Milne's sugar amendment, in 1844, till the completion of the disruption of the Tories, in 1846, Mr Disraeli poured epigram upon epigram and innuendo on innuendo on the "organised hypocrisy" of his professed leader; and there is no doubt that Sir Robert Peel suffered exceedingly under the smart. He was, in every way, a most sensitive man, and he was especially sensitive in all that related to the House of Commons, which was the scene of his life, and to his position there. But now he was, for the first time in his life, exposed to a style of attack to which he had not the sort of power to reply, but which was for the moment the most effective style of any; and he was pained accordingly.

* This article was first published in *The Economist* for August 19, 1876, Volume XXXIV, pages 969–70.

No "free-lance," perhaps, has ever achieved so much and so suddenly as Mr Disraeli then did. Upon this part of his career an historical examiner would give him first-rate marks—much greater than he would give to any competitor.

The next, and far the longest, of Mr Disraeli's Parliamentary parts is that of Leader of Opposition. And in this he showed eminent mind—not equal to that of his free-lance period, but still very great. His powers of epigram and amusing nonsense gave infinite aid, year after year, to a party that was to be beaten. And, after his fashion, he showed a high magnanimity and conscience in not opposing or hampering the Ministry on great questions—say of foreign policy, when his so doing would hurt the country. But this praise must end here. On all minor Parliamentary questions, Mr Disraeli has simply no conscience at all. He regards them as a game—as an old special pleader regarded litigation, to be played so as to show your skill, and so as to win, but without any regard to the consequences. Indeed, Mr Disraeli, at bottom, believes that they have no consequence—that all is settled by questions of race, "Caucasian or Semitic," and that it is simple pedantry in such things to be scrupulous. And still worse than this, which is an amusing defect after all, and excusable—(for there *are* many deeper issues and causes than are dreamed of in Parliamentary philosophy)— Mr Disraeli often showed in Opposition a turn for nonsense, which was *not* amusing. He has many gifts, but he has not the gift of thinking out a subject, and when he tries to produce grave thought he only makes platitudes. And some of his "mare's nests," like his difficulty in the Franco-German War, arising out of our guarantee to the Saxon provinces of Prussia, have been almost incredible, and could only have been discovered by a mind which, with many elements of genius, has also an element of hare-brained recklessness. Drearier hearing, or drearier reading, than Mr Disraeli's Opposition harangues, when they were philosophical, can hardly anywhere be found. But still, though with these and other defects, he *did* lead the Tory Opposition through long melancholy years, when one did not know who else *could* have or who *would* have led it.

The next of Mr Disraeli's Parliamentary parts was that of Leader of a Ministry in a minority, where again he was first-rate. He showed sometimes—in 1852, in 1858, and in 1866 —a nimbleness, a tact, and dexterity far surpassing, probably,

anything that Parliament has ever seen of a similar kind. He
"hit the House"—to use a phrase which Burke used of a like
but very inferior person[1]—he "hit the House between the
wind and the water," and cut with a light witticism knots
insoluble by solemn argument. If, by a series of "selections,"
nature had made a man so fit for this kind of work, it would
have been a marvel. But Mr Disraeli drifted into it, as if by
chance, from quite another calling and another sphere.

Lastly, Mr Disraeli has been lately, and was but yesterday,
Leader of a Ministry in a majority. And here there was a
wonderful contrast. So far from being first-rate, he was ninth-
rate. He seemed to resemble those guerilla commanders who,
having achieved great exploits with scanty and ill-trained
troops, nevertheless are utterly at a loss and fail when they
are placed at the head of a first-rate army. In 1867 he made
a minority achieve wonderful things; but in 1876, when he
had the best majority—the most numerous and obedient—
since Mr Pitt, he did nothing with it. So far from being able
to pass great enactments, he could not even despatch ordinary business at decent hours. The gravest and sincerest of
Tory members—men who hardly murmur at anything—have
been heard to complain that it *was* hard that, after voting so
well and doing so little, they should be kept up so very late.
The Session just closed will be known in Parliamentary annals as one of the least effective or memorable on record, and
yet one of the most fatiguing. And this collapse is no accident
in Mr Disraeli's career, but a thing essentially characteristic
of the man, and which might have been predicted by any one
who had analysed the traits which he had shown before. If
we may be pardoned the metaphor—though his chaff is exquisite, his wheat is poor stuff. The solid part of his mind—
the part fit for regulating bills and clauses—is as inferior to
that of an ordinary man of decent ability, as the light and
imaginative part is superior. An incessant and almost avowed
inaccuracy pervades him. And if you ask such a man to regulate the stupendous business of Parliament—to arrange, and
if possible effect, the most complex *agenda* that ever was in
the world—failure is inevitable. It is like entering a light hack
for a ploughing match. In the last Parliamentary situation,
Mr Disraeli has scarcely seemed to be what he used to be,
and this because that situation was the one for which he was

[1] Charles Townshend.

the least suited, and the last in which he should have been placed. As so often happens, having obtained the ambition of his life—to be a Minister with power—he found he had only got where he ought not to be—he found that he could not wield the power.

And two things have been common to Mr Disraeli all through these positions. In them all he has charmed the House, and has given debates in which he took part a kind of nice literary flavour which other debates had not, and which there is no one left to give to them. He was the best representative whom the "Republic of Letters" ever had in Parliament, for he made his way by talents—especially by a fascination of words—essentially literary. And on the other hand, though he charmed Parliament, he never did anything more. He had no influence with the country. Such a vast power over Englishmen as has been possessed by Lord Palmerston and by Mr Gladstone was out of the way altogether. Between Mr Disraeli and common Englishmen there was too broad a gulf —too great a difference. He was simply unintelligible to them. "Ten miles from London," to use the old phrase, there is scarcely any real conception of him. His mode of regarding Parliamentary proceedings as a play and game, is incomprehensible to the simple and earnest English nature. Perhaps he has gained more than he has lost by the English not understanding him. At any rate, the fact remains that the special influence of this great gladiator never passed the walls of the amphitheatre: he has ruled the country by ruling Parliament, but has never had any influence in Parliament reverberating from the nation itself.

PARLIAMENTARY REFORM[1]*

(1859)

*This article was written when the agitation for parliamentary
reform which culminated in Disraeli's Reform Act of 1867 was
gathering momentum. It was intended to hold back the movement towards democracy in England, but this proved too strong
a tide of opinion to dam up or deflect. The Reform Act of 1832
had abolished many boroughs and reduced the representation of
others. It fixed the right to vote in all boroughs, new and old, at
a £10 rating franchise. In the counties the forty-shilling franchise was extended from freeholders to tenant farmers. As the
country passed through the industrial revolution the franchise
qualifications laid down in 1832 became irrelevant, and pressure
for a change steadily increased. The Reform Act of 1867 left
the main provisions for the counties unchanged but reduced the
leasehold qualification from £10 to £5 per annum and created
an occupancy franchise of £12 per annum. In the boroughs it
conferred a household franchise, conditional on the payment of
rates, and a clause inserted in the Act allowed the registration
of those who paid rates through landlords. The electorate which
in 1833 had numbered 652,000 and had risen by 1866 to 1,056,-
000 was doubled, giving an absolute majority to workers and*

---

[1] "On the Electoral Statistics of the Counties and Boroughs in
England and Wales during the Twenty-five Years from the Reform
Act of 1832 to the Present Time." By William Newmarch, one of
the Honorary Secretaries of the Statistical Society. Read before the
Statistical Society, 16th June, 1857, and printed in the *Journal* of
that Society, vol. xx, parts 2 and 3. We cannot speak too highly of
these most admirable statistics. No pains have been spared to make
them complete, and extreme judgment has been shown in the selection. When it is not otherwise stated, all our electoral statistics are
from this source.

* This essay was first published in the *National Review* for January
1859, Volume VIII, pages 228–73, and republished as a pamphlet in
February of the same year. I have omitted a note of some 12 pages,
which Bagehot appended to the article but the inclusion of which is
not necessary to the principal argument.

*artisans. The distribution of seats however was such as to mask
the full democratising effects of the Act. Four million residents
in the large towns were represented by 34 out of the 334 borough
members, and two thirds of the constituencies were situated to
the south of the Wash and the Severn. The last great Victorian
instalment of electoral reform came in 1884 and 1885. The
Third Reform Act of 1884 extended the householder franchise
to the counties. This increased the county electorate from 900,-
000 to 2,500,000. This extension was linked with a redistribution of seats by an Act of 1885. All boroughs of less than
15,000 electors were merged in the counties and boroughs of a
population of 50,000 not previously represented, received one
member each. Seventy-two boroughs disappeared and 36 lost one
member, leaving 142 seats for redistribution. The predominance
of the South over the North, the stationary over the growing
districts, and the overrepresentation of the agricultural districts,
which Bagehot had pointed to as anomalous, were thus remedied.*

We shall not be expected to discuss in a party spirit the subject of parliamentary reform. It has never been objected to
the *National Review* that it is a party organ; and even periodicals which have long been such, scarcely now discuss that
subject in a party spirit. Both Whigs and Conservatives are
pledged to do something, and neither as a party have agreed
what they would do. We would attempt to give an impartial
criticism of the electoral system which now exists, and some
indication of the mode in which we think that its defects
should be amended. It is possible, we fear, that our article
may be long, and that our criticism on existing arrangements
may appear tedious. But a preliminary understanding is requisite; unless we are agreed as to what is to be desired, we
cannot hope to agree as to what is to be done: a clear knowledge of the disease must precede the remedy. In business, no
ingenuity of detail can compensate for indistinctness of design.

There is much that may be said against the Reform Act
of 1832; but, on the whole, it has been successful. It is a
commonplace to speak of the legislative improvements of the
last twenty-five years, and it would be tedious to enumerate
them. Free trade, a new colonial policy, the improved poor-
law, the Encumbered Estate Act in Ireland, the tithe com-
mutation, municipal reform, the tentative but most judicious
support of education, are only some of the results of the re-

form of the House of Commons. Scarcely less important is the improvement which the Reform Bill has introduced into the general tone of our administration; our executive has become purer, more considerate, and more humane, and it would be difficult to show that in its ordinary and beneficial action it is much weaker. Nor is this all. So much of agreement in opinion as we see around us is perhaps unexampled in a political age; and it is the more singular, because the English nation is now considerably less homogeneous in its social structure than it once was. The prodigious growth of manufactures and trade has created a new world in the North of England, which contrasts with the south in social circumstances and social habits: at no former time was there such a difference as there now is between Lancashire and Devonshire. It is impossible not to ascribe this agreement to the habit of national discussion which the Reform Act has fostered. The scattered argument, the imperfect but perpetual influence of the press and society, have made us, perhaps even to an excessive degree, unanimous. Possibly we are all too much disposed to catch the voice which is in the air. Still, a little too much concord is better than a little too much discord. It is a striking result, that our present constitution has educed from such dissimilar elements so much of harmony.

Beneficial, however, as are these incidental results of the Reform Bill, they are not the most important parts of its success. This measure has, to a considerable extent, been successful in its *design*. The object which its framers had in view was, to transfer the predominant influence in the State from certain special classes to the general aggregate of fairly instructed men. It is not perhaps very easy to prove upon paper that this has been, at least in a very great degree, effected. The most difficult thing to establish by argument is an evident fact of observation. There are no statistics of opinion to which we can refer, there is no numerical comparison which will establish the accordance of parliamentary with social opinion. We must trust to our eyes and ears, to the vague but conclusive evidence of events. If, indeed, public opinion had always been as unanimous as it now is, we should have some difficulty in ascertaining the fact. When everybody thinks the same, there is no saying which is the stronger party. But during the last twenty-six years there have been many periods at which public opinion was much divided and

strongly excited. The great legislative changes which have
been mentioned were not effected without long and animated
party dissension. The policy of a great country like this has
continually required the determination of critical questions,
both at home and abroad; its ramified affairs have been a
never-failing source of controverted topics. What would have
been the sign if the expressed opinion of Parliament had
been contrary to the distinct opinion of the country? In the
present state of the country we should not have been long in
learning it. We should have had political meetings, not of
one class but all classes, clouds of petitions from every
quarter, endless articles in newspapers; the cry would only
have died away when the obnoxious decision was reversed,
and the judgment of Parliament submitted itself to the will
of the nation. The inclination of the House of Commons is
evidently not to oppose the country. On the contrary, we all
know the power, the undue power, possessed by that part of
the press whose course is supposed to indicate what is likely
to be the common opinion. So far from our legislators dissenting too often from the expressed judgment of the country,
they are but too much swayed by indications of what it probably will be. The history of our great legislative changes of
itself shows that the opinion of Parliament is, in the main,
coincident with that of the nation. Parliament and the country were converted at the same time. Even the history of the
corn-law agitation, which is often referred to as indicating the
contrary, proves this conspicuously. It succeeded almost at
the moment that impartial people, who had no interests on
either side, were convinced that it ought to succeed. Mr
Cobden liked to relate, that when he first began to dream of
agitating the question, a most experienced nobleman observed to him, "Repeal the corn laws! you will repeal the
monarchy as soon". The noble lord was right in estimating
the tenacity and intensity of the protectionist creed; but he
did not know, and Mr Cobden did, the power of plain argument on the common mass of plain men, and the certainty
that *their* opinion, if really changed, would suffice to change
the course of our legislation, even in opposition to strong
aristocratic influence and very rooted prejudice. It has been
said that Sir Robert Peel owed his success in life to "being
converted at the conversion of the average man"; the same
influences acted on his mind that acted on the minds of
most other people throughout the nation, and in much the

same measure. He was, therefore, converted to new views at
the same time that most other people were converted to
them. The same may be said of the present Parliament. Nobody would call the reformed House of Commons original;
it is never in advance of the higher order of cultivated
thought: but every one would agree that it is pre-eminently
considerate, well-judging, and convincible; and when people
say this, they mean that its opinions commonly coincide with
their own.

   In no respect is the reality of the accordance in opinion between Parliament and the nation so convincingly shown as
in the sympathy of Parliament with the eccentricities of public opinion. We are constantly acknowledging that "the English mind" is exclusively occupied with single questions; sometimes with one, and sometimes with another, but at each
time with one only. If Parliament did not share the same influences as the general body of fairly educated men, there
would every now and then be a remarkable contrast between
the subjects which interested Parliament and that which occupied the nation. The intensity of our peculiar sympathies
make this more likely. Satirists say that the English nation is
liable to intellectual *seizures*; and so exclusive and so restless
is our intellectual absorption, so sudden its coming, so quick
sometimes is its cessation, that there is some significance in
the phrase. We are struck with particular ideas, and for the
time think of nothing else. It will be found that Parliament,
if it be sitting, thinks of the same. No instance of this can
be more remarkable than the parliamentary proceedings on
Mr Roebuck's motion for an inquiry into the conduct of the
Crimean campaign. There was great excitement in the nation
at the moment; it has enabled the present generation to understand what historians did not before understand—the fate
of poor Admiral Byng. The English nation cannot bear failure
in war. If there had been any one to hang at the time Mr
Roebuck made his motion, and he could have been hanged
directly, certainly he would have been hanged. On the other
hand, the authority of statesmanlike opinion in Parliament,
the weight of political connection, the legitimate disinclina-
tion to break up a Government during a dangerous crisis,
and—what is more remarkable—the great preponderance of
sound argument, were united to influence Parliament not to
grant even an inquiry. The result showed that the opinion of
our leading statesmen was right, and that the arguments they

produced were incontrovertible. Few investigations that have
been commenced with so much outcry have ever had so trivial
an effect. Yet, in opposition to all these influences, usually
so omnipotent,—in opposition to the combined force of personal feeling and abstract argument,—the House of Commons
so far accurately represented the sentiment of the country as
to grant, and even to insist on granting, the inquiry. This
Parliamentary episode appears to be an *instantia lucifera* on
the subject; it shows that, even when we could wish it otherwise, the House of Commons will echo the voice of the nation.

After all, there can be no more conclusive evidence of the
substantial agreement between Parliament and the nation
than the slight interest which is taken by the public in all
questions of organic reform. Every one knows how the Reform Act of 1832 was carried; no one doubted that the
public mind was excited then; no fair person could doubt
what the decision of the nation then was. The "insurrection
of the middle classes," as it has been called, insured the success of the "Bill". It was alleged by its most reasonable
opponents "that the measure could not be final; that those
on whom it was proposed to confer the franchise would, even
after the passing of the measure, be but small in comparison
with those from whom it would be still withheld; that in a
few years a similar agitation would recur, and a similar necessity of yielding to agitation; that the storm of 1832 would be
a feeble prelude to that of 1842," etc. These prophecies were
not without a species of probability, but they have not been
realised. No excited multitude clamours for enfranchisement;
the reality is the reverse of the anticipation.

Two defects, however, may be discerned in the general
accordance of Parliamentary with national opinion. The Parliament certainly has an undue bias towards the sentiments
and views of the landed interest. It is not easy to trace this
in immediate results. We have said that we scarcely think
that it is proved by the history of the free-trade agitation;
that agitation was successful, nearly if not quite, as soon as it
should have been. We may, indeed, speculate on the results
which might have occurred if the Irish famine had not happened, and if Sir R. Peel had not formed a statesmanlike
judgment upon its consequences; we may believe that there
would in that case have been an opposition between an educated nation converted by reasoning to the principles of

free trade, and a majority in Parliament wedded by prejudice and interest to protection. Still, as this is but conjecture,
we cannot cite it as conclusive evidence. Nor is the partiality
to real property in matters of taxation which is occasionally
dwelt on, very easy to prove in figures. The account is at best
a complicated one. The exemption of land from probate duty
is partly compensated by the succession duty, by the land-tax,
by the more severe pressure of the income-tax, and still more
by the necessary incidence of much local taxation on this
kind of property. Still, a fair observer, closely comparing the
opinion of the House of Commons with that of the public
out of doors, will certainly observe some signs of a partiality
towards the landed interest among our legislators. We cannot
ascribe this to any obvious preponderance in number of the
county over the borough seats. Taking population as a test,
it is otherwise. There are in England and Wales 159 county
members, more than double that number (viz. 335) of
borough members; the population of the represented
boroughs is 7,500,000, that of the counties 10,500,000, consequently the represented boroughs have not as many inhabitants as the counties, though they elect twice the number
of members. This test is, of course, a most imperfect one;
but may serve to show that in mere arithmetic the counties
are not extravagantly favoured. The real cause is the peculiar
structure of our county society. A county member is almost
of necessity one of the county gentry; he must not only possess land, but it must be land in that place: no one else is
"entitled to stand". On the other hand, boroughs return a
very miscellaneous class of members. Many important landowners sit for them. So great is the variety, that no class is
excluded from them altogether. This contrast must affect the
distribution of parliamentary power. The county members
form a peculiar class in the House of Commons, and exercise
a steady influence there out of proportion to their mere numbers. Besides, so much more of social influence belongs to
the territorial aristocracy than to any other class, that its
weight is indefinitely increased. Not a few men enter Parliament mainly to augment their social importance, and over
these the unquestioned possessors of social rank necessarily
have great power. A third circumstance contributes its effect. The Ministers of the Crown are generally large landowners. By imperious social usage, they must be men of
large property; and all opulence gravitates towards the land.

Political opulence does so particularly. Until recently there was much difficulty in finding other investments not requiring sedulous personal attention, and not liable to be affected by political vicissitudes. It is of essential importance that Ministers of State should be persons *at ease* in their worldly circumstances, and it is quite out of the question that they should have any share in the administration of commercial enterprises; they have enough to do without that. Their wealth, too, should not be in a form that could expose them even to the suspicion of stock-jobbing, or of making an improper use of political information. We have now many kinds of property debentures, canal shares, railway shares, etc., which have these advantages in nearly an equal degree with land itself; but the growth of these is recent. It may hereafter have important consequences, but it has not as yet had time to achieve them. Accordingly the series of Cabinet Ministers presents a nearly unbroken rank of persons who either are themselves large landowners, or are connected closely by birth or intermarriage with large landowners. This combination of circumstances gives to real property an influence in our political system greater than in strict theory we should wish it to have. It is true that the owners of much land are men of much leisure, and the possession of such property has a sedative influence, which in moderation may not be undesirable; but the effective representation of national opinion requires the selection of members of Parliament from men of various occupations, various tendencies, and various sympathies. Public opinion in a composite nation is formed by the action and reaction of many kinds of minds; and abstractedly it seems a defect that the solid mass of county members, on whatever side of the house they sit, should present features so marked and uniform.

The second defect in the accordance of Parliamentary with national opinion is but another phase of the same fact. Too little weight is at present given to the growing parts of the country, too much to the stationary. It appears that the county constituencies in England and Wales have only increased, in the twenty years between 1837 and 1857, from 473,000 to 505,000, that is, at about 6 per cent; the borough constituencies, in the same period, have increased from 321,000 to 439,000, or at the rate of 17 per cent. And it further appears, as we should expect, that the principal increase, both in the case of counties and boroughs, is not in the purely agricultural districts, but in the great scenes of manufacturing industry and in the metropolis. The growth of constituencies, according to the present franchise, is a much better test of relative importance than the mere growth of population; it indicates the increase of property, and therefore of presumable intelligence. These figures plainly indicate, if not an existing defect, yet a source of future defect in our representative system. If there was a just proportion between the two halves of England in 1832, there is not that just proportion now. In the long run, public opinion will be much more influenced by the growing portion of the country than by the stationary. It is an indistinct perception of this fact that stimulates whatever agitation for reform at present exists. The manufacturers of Leeds and Manchester do not give levees and entertainments to Mr Bright from any attraction towards abstract democracy; the rate-paying franchise which Mr Bright desires would place these classes under the irresistible control of their work-people. What our great traders really desire is, their own due weight in the community. They feel that the country squire and the proprietor of a petty borough have an influence in the nation above that which they ought to have, and greater than their own. A system arranged a quarter of a century ago presses with irritating constraint on those who have improved with half-magical rapidity during that quarter of a century,—is unduly favourable to those who have improved much less or not at all.

Subject, however, to these two exceptions, the House of Commons of the present day coincides nearly—or sufficiently nearly—in habitual judgment with the fairly intelligent and reasonably educated part of the community. Almost all persons, except the avowed holders of the democratic theory, would think that this is enough. Most people wish to see embodied in Parliament the *true judgment* of the nation; they wish to see an elected legislature fairly representing—that is, coinciding in opinion with—the thinking part of the community. What more, they would inquire, is wanted? We answer, that though this is by much the most important requisite of a good popular legislature, it is not absolutely the only one.

At present, the most important function of the representative part of our legislature—the House of Commons—is the *ruling* function. By a very well-known progress of events, the popular part of our constitution has grown out of very small beginnings to a practical sovereignty over all the other parts. To possess the confidence of the House of Commons is all that a Minister desires; the power of the Crown is reduced to a kind of social influence; that of the House of Lords is contracted to a suspensive veto. For the exercise of this ruling function, the substantial conformity of the judgment and opinion of the House of Commons with that of the fairly cultivated and fairly influential part of the people at large is the most important of possible conditions—is, in fact, the one condition on which the satisfactory performance of that function appears to depend. No legislature destitute of this qualification, whatever its other merits may be, can create that feeling of diffused satisfaction which is the peculiar happiness of constitutional countries, or can ensure that distinct comprehension of a popular policy which is the greatest source of their strength. Nothing can satisfy which is not comprehended: no policy can be popular which is not understood. This is a truth of every-day observation. We are, nowadays, so familiar with the beneficial results of the ruling action of Parliament, that we are engrossed by it; we fancy that it is the sole duty of a representative assembly: yet so far is this from being the case, that in England it was not even the original one.

The earliest function of a House of Commons was undeniably what we may call an *expressive* function. In its origin it was (matters of taxation excepted) a petitioning body; all the early statutes, as is well known, are in this form: the Petition of Right is an instance of its adoption in times comparatively recent. The function of the popular part of the legislature was then to represent to the king the *wants* of his faithful Commons. They were called to express the feelings of those who sent them and their own. Of course, in its original form, this function is obsolete; and if something analogous to it were not a needful element in the duties of every representative assembly, it would be childish to refer to it. But in every free country it is of the utmost importance —and, in the long run, a pressing necessity—that all opinions extensively entertained, all sentiments widely diffused should be *stated* publicly before the nation. We may attribute the real decision of questions, the actual adoption of policies, to the ordinary and fair intelligence of the community, or to the legislature which represents it. But we must also take

care to bring before that fair intelligence and that legislature
the sentiments, the interests, the opinions, the prejudices,
the wants, of all classes of the nation; we must be sure that
no decision is come to in ignorance of real facts and intimate
wants. The diffused multitude of moderate men, whose opinions, taken in the aggregate, form public opinion, are just as
likely to be tyrannical towards what they do not realise, in-
apprehensive of what is not argued out, thoughtless of what
is not brought before them, as any other class can be. They
will judge well of what they are made to understand; they
will not be harsh to feelings that are brought home to their
imagination; but the materials of a judgment must be given
them, the necessary elements of imagination must be provided, otherwise the result is certain. A free government is
the most stubbornly stupid of all governments to whatever is
unheard by its deciding classes. On this account it is of the
utmost importance that there should be in the House of
Commons some persons able to speak, and authorised to
speak, the wants, sentiments, and opinions of every section
of the community—delegates, one might almost say, of that
section. It is only by argument in the legislature that the
legislature can be impressed; it is by argument in the legislature that the attention of the nation is most easily attracted
and most effectually retained.

If, with the light of this principle, we examine our present
system of representation, it seems unquestionable that it is
defective. We do not provide any mode of expression for the
sentiments of what are vaguely but intelligibly called the
working classes. We ignore them. The Reform Act of 1832
assumed that it was expedient to give a representation to
the wants and feelings of those who live in ten-pound houses,
but that it was not expedient to give any such expression to
the wants and feelings of those who live in houses rated below that sum. If we were called to consider that part of this
subject, we should find much to excuse the framers of that
Act in the state of opinion which then prevailed and the
general circumstances of the time. It was necessary to propose
a simple measure; and this numerical demarcation has a
trenchant simplicity. But if we now considerately review our
electoral organisation, we must concede that, however perfectly it may provide an appropriate regulator for our national
affairs, it omits to provide a befitting organ of *expression* for
the desires and convictions of these particular classes.

The peculiar characteristics of a portion of the working classes render this omission of special importance. The agricultural labourers may have no sentiments on public affairs; but the artisan classes have. Not only are their circumstances peculiar, and their interests sometimes different from those of the high orders of the community—both which circumstances are likely to make them adopt special opinions, and are therefore grounds for a special representation—but the habit of mind which their pursuits and position engender is of itself not unlikely to cause some eccentricity of judgment. Observers tell us that those who live by manual ingenuity are more likely to be remarkable for originality than for modesty. In the present age—and to some extent, we must expect, in every age—such persons must be self-taught; and self-taught men are commonly characterised by a one-sided energy and something of a self-sufficient disposition. The *sensation* of perfection in a mechanical employment is of itself not without an influence tending towards conceit; and however instructed in definite learning energetic men in these classes may become, they are not subjected to the insensible influences of cultivated life, they do not live in the temperate zone of society, which soon chills the fervid ideas of unseasonable originality. Being cooped up within the narrow circle of ideas that their own energy has provided, they are particularly liable to singular opinions. This is especially the case on politics. They are attracted to that subject in a free country of necessity; their active intellects are in search of topics for reflection; and this subject abounds in the very atmosphere of our national life, is diffused in newspapers, obtruded at elections, to be heard at every corner of the street. Energetic minds in this class are therefore particularly likely to entertain eccentric opinions on political topics; and it is peculiarly necessary that such opinions should, by some adequate machinery, be stated and made public. If such singular views be brought into daily collision with ascertained facts and the ordinary belief of cultivated men, their worth can be tested, the weakness of their fallacious part exposed, any new grain of truth they may contain appreciated. On some subjects (possibly, for example, on simple questions of foreign policy) the views of self-taught men may be very valuable, for their moral instincts sometimes have a freshness rarely to be found. At any rate, whatever may be the abstract value of the special sentiments and convictions of the operative classes, their

very speciality is a strong indication that our constitution is
defective in providing no distinct outlet for their expression.

A theorist might likewise be inclined to argue that the
Reform Act of 1832 was defective in not providing an appropriate organ for the expression of opinion of the higher orders
of society. It selects a ten-pound householder for special favour. In large towns, nay to a certain extent in any town, the
more cultivated and refined classes, who live in better houses
than these, are practically disfranchised; the number of their
inferiors renders valueless the suffrage conferred on them. We
remember some years ago hearing a conversation between a
foreigner and a most accomplished Englishman, who lived in
Russell Square. The foreigner was expatiating on the happiness of English people in being governed by a legislature in
which they were represented. The Russell-Square scholar
replied, "I am represented by Mr Wakley and Tom Duncombe". He felt the scorn natural to a cultivated man in a
metropolitan constituency at the supposition that such representatives as these really expressed *his* views and sentiments.
We know how constantly in America, which is something like
a nation of metropolitan constituencies, the taste and temper
of the electors excludes the more accomplished and leisured
classes from the legislature, and how vulgar a stamp the taste
and temper of those elected impresses on the proceedings of
its legislature and the conduct of its administration. Men of
refinement shrink from the House of Representatives as from
a parish vestry. In England, though we feel this in some
measure, we feel it much less. Other parts of our electoral
system now afford a refuge to that refined cultivation which is
hateful to and hates the grosser opinion of the small shopkeepers in cities. Our higher classes still desire to rule the
nation; and so long as this is the case, the inherent tendencies
of human nature secure them the advantage. Manner and
bearing have an influence on the poor; the nameless charm of
refinement tells; personal confidence is almost everywhere
more easily accorded to one of the higher classes than to one
of the lower classes. From this circumstance, there is an inherent tendency in any electoral system which does not
vulgarise the government, to protect the rich and to represent the rich. Though by the letter of the law, a man who
lives in a house assessed at £10 has an equal influence on the
constitution of the legislature with a man whose house is
assessed at £100, yet, in truth, the richer man has the security

that the members of Parliament, and especially the foremost members of Parliament, are much more likely to be taken from this class than from a poorer class.

We may therefore conclude that there is not any ground for altering the electoral system established by the Reform Act of 1832 on account of its not providing for the due representation of the more cultivated classes. Indirectly it does so. But we must narrowly watch any changes in that system which are proposed to us, with the view of seeing whether their operation might not have a tendency to impair the subtle working of this indirect machinery. We must bear in mind that the practical disfranchisement of the best classes is the ascertained result of giving an equal weight to high and low in constituencies like the metropolitan.

These considerations do not affect our previous conclusion as to the lower orders. We ascertained that, however perfectly the House of Commons under the present system of election may coincide in judgment with the fairly educated classes of the country, and however competent it may on that account be to perform the ruling function of a popular legislature, it was nevertheless defective in its provision for the performance of the *expressive* functions of such a legislature; because it provided no organ for informing Parliament and the country of the sentiments and opinions of the working, and especially of the artisan classes.

Another deficiency in the system of representation now existing is of a different nature. It is not only desirable that a popular legislature should be fitted to the discharge of its duties, but also that it should be elected by a process which occasions no unnecessary moral evils. A theorist would be inclined to advance a step further. He would require that a popular assembly should be elected in the mode which would diffuse the instruction given by the habitual possession of the franchise among the greatest number of competent persons, and which would deny it to the greatest number of unfit persons. But every reasonable theorist would hasten to add, that the end must never be sacrificed to the means. The mode of election which is selected must be one which will bring together an assembly of members fitted to discharge the functions of Parliament. *Among* those modes of election, this theoretical principle prescribes the rule of choice; but we must not, under its guidance, attempt to travel beyond the circle of those modes. A practical statesman will be very

cautious how he destroys a machinery which attains its essential object, for the sake of an incidental benefit which
might be expected from a different machinery. If we have a
good legislature, he will say, let us not endanger its goodness
for the sake of a possible diffusion of popular education. All
sensible men would require that the advocates of such a measure should show beyond all reasonable doubt that the extension of the suffrage, which they recommend on this secondary
ground, should not impair the attainment of the primary end
for which *all* suffrage was devised. At the present moment,
there certainly are many persons of substantial property and
good education who do not possess the franchise, and to
whom it would be desirable to give it, if they could be distinguished from others who are not so competent. A man of
the highest education, who does not reside in a borough,
may have large property in the funds, in railway shares, or
any similar investment; but he will have no vote unless his
house is rated above £50. But, as we have said, we must not,
from a theoretical desire to include such persons in our list
of electors, run a risk of admitting also any large number of
persons who would be unfit to vote, and thereby impairing
the practical utility of Parliament. No such hesitation should,
however, hold us back when peculiar moral evils can be
proved to arise from a particular mode of election. If that
be so, we ought on the instant to make the most anxious
search for some other mode of election not liable to the same
objection: we ought to run some risk; if another mode of
election can be suggested, apparently equal in efficiency,
which would not produce the same evils, we should adopt it
at once in place of the other. We must act on the spirit of
faith that what is morally wrong cannot be politically right.

This objection applies in the strongest manner to one portion of our electoral system, namely, the smaller borough
constituencies. We there entrust the franchise to a class of
persons few enough to be bought, and not respectable enough
to refuse to be bought. The disgraceful exposures of some
of these boroughs before election committees make it probable that the same abuses exist in others: doubtless, too, we
do not know the worst. The worst constituencies are slow to
petition, because the local agents of both parties are aware
of what would come to light, and fear the consequent penalties. Enough, however, is in evidence for us to act upon.
Some of these small boroughs are dependent on some great

nobleman or man of fortune; and this state is perhaps preferable to their preserving a vicious independence: but even
this state is liable to very many objections. It is most advantageous that the nominal electors should be the real electors.
Legal fictions have a place in courts of law; it is sometimes
better or more possible to strain venerable maxims beyond
their natural meaning than to limit them by special enactment: but legal fictions are very dangerous in the midst of
popular institutions and a genuine moral excitement. We
speak day by day of "shams"; and the name will be for ever
applied to modes of election which pretend to entrust the
exclusive choice to those who are known by everybody never
to choose. The Reform Act of 1832 was distinctly founded
on the principle that all modes of election should be *real*.

We arrive, therefore, at the result that the system of 1832
is defective, because it established, or rather permitted to
continue, moral evils which it is our duty to remove, if by
possibility they can be removed. However, in that removal
we must be careful to watch exactly what we are doing. It
has been shown that the letter of the Reform Act makes no
provision for the special representation of wealth and cultivation; the representation which they have is attained by
indirect means. The purchasable boroughs are undoubtedly
favourable to wealth; the hereditary boroughs to men of
hereditary cultivation; and we should be careful not to impair unnecessarily the influence of these elements by any
alteration we may resolve upon.

We can now decide on the result which we should try to
attain in a new Reform Bill. If we could obtain a House of
Commons that should be well elected, that should contain
true and adequate exponents of all class interests, that
should coincide in opinion with the fair intelligence of the
country, we shall have all which we ought to desire. We have
satisfied ourselves that we do not possess all these advantages now; we have seen that a part of our system of election
is grossly defective; that our House of Commons contains no
adequate exponents of the views of the working classes; that
though its judgment has, as yet, fairly coincided with public
opinion, yet that its constitution gives a dangerous preponderance to the landed interest, and is likely to fail us hereafter
unless an additional influence be given to the more growing
and energetic classes of society.

We should think it more agreeable (and perhaps it would

be so to most of our readers) if we were able at once to proceed to discuss the practical plan by which these objects
might be effected; but in deference to a party which has some
zealous adherents, and to principles which, in an indistinct
shape, are widely diffused, we must devote a few remarks to
the consideration of the ultra-democratic theory; and as we
have to do so, it will be convenient to discuss in connection
with it one or two of the schemes which the opponents of
that theory have proposed for testing political intelligence.

As is well known, the democratic theory requires that Parliamentary representation should be proportioned to mere
numbers. This is not, indeed, the proposition which is at this
moment put forward. The most important section of democratic reformers now advocate a ratepaying or household
franchise; but this is either avowedly as a step to something
further, or because from considerations of convenience it is
considered better to give the franchise only to those whose
residences can be identified. But it is easy to show that the
ratepaying franchise is almost equally liable with the manhood suffrage to a most important objection. That objection,
of course, is that the adoption of the scheme would give entire superiority to the lower part of the community. Nothing
is easier than to show that a ratepaying franchise would have
that effect. In England and Wales—

The number of houses assessed at £10 and
    above is computed to be   990,000
        "   "   at £6 and under £10   572,000
        "   "   under £6   1,713,000
                                           3,275,000

More than half the persons who would be admitted by the
ratepaying franchise are, therefore, of a very low order, living
in houses under £6 rent, and two-thirds are below £10, the
lowest qualification admitted by the present law. It therefore seems quite certain that the effect of the proposed innovation must be very favourable to ignorance and poverty,
and very unfavourable to cultivation and intelligence.

There used to be much argument in favour of the democratic theory, on the ground of its supposed conformity with
the abstract rights of man. This has passed away; but we
cannot say that the reasons by which it has been replaced
are more distinct: we think that they are less distinct. We

can understand that an enthusiast should maintain, on fancied grounds of immutable morality, or from an imaginary conformity with a supernatural decree, that the ignorant should govern the instructed; but we do not comprehend how any one can maintain the proposition on grounds of expediency. We might believe that it was right to submit to the results of such a polity; but those results, it would seem, must be beyond controversy pernicious. The arguments from expediency, which are supposed to establish the proposition, are never set forth very clearly; and we do not think them worth confuting. We are, indeed, disposed to believe, in spite of much direct assertion to the contrary, that the democratic theory still rests not so much on reason as on a kind of sentiment—on an obscure conception of abstract rights. The animation of its advocates is an indication of it. They think they are contending for the "rights" of the people; and they endeavour to induce the people to believe so too. We hold this opinion the more strongly, because we believe that there *is* such a thing, after all, as abstract right in political organisations. We find it impossible to believe that all the struggles of men for liberty—all the enthusiasm it has called forth, all the passionate emotions it has caused in the very highest minds, all the glow of thought and rustle of obscure feeling which the very name excites in the whole mass of men—have their origin in calculations of advantage and a belief that such and such arrangements would be beneficial. The masses of men are very difficult to excite on bare grounds of self-interest; most easy if a bold orator tells them confidently they are *wronged*. The foundation of government upon simple utility is but the fiction of philosophers; it has never been acceptable to the natural feelings of mankind. There is far greater truth in the formula of the French writers that "*le droit dérive de la capacité*". Some sort of feeling akin to this lurks, we believe, in the minds of our reformers; they think they can show that some classes now unenfranchised are as capable of properly exercising the franchise as some who have possessed it formerly, or some who have it now. The £5 householder of to-day is, they tell us, in education and standing but what the £10 householder was in 1832. The opponents of the theory are pressed with the argument, that every fit person should have the franchise, and that many who are excluded are as fit as some who exercise it, and from whom no one proposes to take it away.

The answer to the argument is plain. Fitness to govern—
for that is the real meaning of exercising the franchise which
which elects a *ruling* assembly—is not an absolute quality of
any individual. That fitness is relative and comparative; it
must depend on the community to be governed, and on the
merits of other persons who may be capable of governing
that community. A savage chief may be capable of governing
a savage tribe; he may have the right of governing it, for he
may be the sole person capable of so doing; but he would
have no right to govern England. We must look likewise to
the competitors for the sovereignty. Whatever may be your
capacity for rule, you have no right to obtain the opportunity
of exercising it by dethroning a person who is *more* capable.
You are wronging the community if you do: for you are depriving it of a better government than that which you can
give to it. You are wronging also the ruler you supersede;
for you are depriving him of the appropriate exercise of his
faculties. Two wrongs are thus committed from a fancied idea
that abstract capacity gives a right to rule irrespective of comparative relations. The true principle is, that every person has
a right to *so much political power as he can exercise without
impeding any other person who would more fitly exercise such
power.* If we apply this to the lower orders of society, we see
the reason why, notwithstanding their numbers, they must
always be subject—always at least be comparatively uninfluential. Whatever their capacity may be, it must be less than
that of the higher classes, whose occupations are more instructive and whose education is more prolonged. Any such
measure for enfranchising the lower orders as would over-
power, and consequently disfranchise, the higher, should be
resisted on the ground of "abstract right"; you are proposing to take power from those who have the superior capacity,
and to vest it in those who have but an inferior capacity, or,
in many cases, no capacity at all. If we probe the subject
to the bottom, we shall find that justice is on the side of a
graduated rule, in which all persons should have an influence
proportioned to their political capacity; and it is at this grad-
uation that the true maxims of representative government
really aim. They wish that the fairly intelligent persons, who
create public opinion, as we call it, in society, should rule in
the State, which is the authorised means of carrying that
opinion into action. This is the body which has the greater
right to rule; this is the *felt intelligence* of the nation, "*la*

*légitime aristocratie, celle qu'acceptent librement les masses,
sur qui elle doit exercer son pouvoir".*[2]

It is impossible to deny that this authority, in matters of
political opinion, belongs by right, and is felt to belong in
fact, to the higher orders of society rather than to the lower.
The advantages of leisure, of education, of more instructive
pursuits, of more instructive society, must and do produce
an effect. A writer of very democratic leanings has observed,
that "there is an unconquerable, and, to a certain extent,
beneficial proneness in man to rely on the judgment and
authority of those who are elevated above himself in rank
and riches, from the irresistible associations of the human
mind; a feeling of respect and deference is entertained for a
superior in station which enhances and exalts all his good
qualities, gives more grace to his thoughts, more wisdom to
his opinions, more weight to his judgment, more excellence to
his virtues. . . . Hence the elevated men of society will always maintain an ascendency which, without any direct exertion of influence, will affect the result of popular elections;
and when to this are added the capabilities which they possess, or ought to possess, from their superior intelligence, of
impressing their own opinions on other classes it will be evident that if any sort of control were justifiable, it would be
superfluous for any good purpose."[3] There are individual exceptions; but in questions of this magnitude we must speak
broadly: and we may say that political intelligence will in
general exist rather in the educated classes than in the less
educated, rather in the rich than the poor; and not only that
it will exist, but that it will, in the absence of misleading
feelings, be *felt* by both parties to exist.

We have quoted the above passage for more reasons than
one. It not only gives an appropriate description of the popular association of superiority in judgment with superiority in
station, but it draws from the fact of that association an inference which would be very important if it were correct.
It says, in substance, that as the higher orders are felt by the
lower to be more capable of governing, they will be chosen
by the lower, if the latter are left free to choose; that, therefore, no matter how democratic the government—in fact, the

[2] M. Guizot, *Essai sur les Origines du Gouvernement réprésentatif.*
[3] Bailey on Representative Government; quoted in Sir G. Lewis's
"Essay on the Influence of Authority on Matters of Opinion," p. 228.

more democratic the government, the surer are the upper
orders to lead. But experience shows that this is an error.
If the acquisition of power is left to the unconscious working of the natural influences of society, the rich and the cultivated will certainly acquire it; they obtain it insensibly,
gradually, and without the poorer orders knowing that they
are obtaining it. But the result is different when, by the operation of a purely democratic constitution, the selection of
rulers is submitted to the direct vote of the populace. The
lower orders are then told that they are perfectly able to
judge; demagogues assert it to them without ceasing: the
constitution itself is appealed to as an incontrovertible witness to the fact; as it has placed the supreme power in the
hands of the lower and more numerous classes, it would be
contravening it to suppose that the real superiority was in
the higher and fewer. Moreover, when men are expressly asked
to acknowledge their superiors, they are by no means always
inclined to do so. They do not object to yield a mute observance, but they refuse a definite act of homage. They
will obey, but they will not *say* that they will obey. In consequence, history teaches that under a democratic government
those who speak the feelings of the majority themselves, have
a greater chance of being chosen to rule, than any of the
higher orders, who, under another form of government, would
be admitted to be the better judges. The natural effect of
such a government is to mislead the poor.

We have no room to notice the specific evils which would
accrue from the adoption of an unmixedly democratic constitution. One, however, which has not been quite appreciated follows naturally from the remarks we have made.
There is a risk of vulgarising the whole tone, method, and
conduct of public business. We see how completely this
has been done in America; a country far more fitted, at least
in the northern States, for the democratic experiment than
any old country can be. Nor must we imagine that this vulgarity of tone is a mere external expression, not affecting the
substance of what is thought, or interfering with the policy
of the nation. No defect really eats away so soon the political
ability of a nation. A vulgar tone of discussion disgusts cultivated minds with the subject of politics; they will not apply
themselves to master a topic which, besides its natural difficulties, is encumbered with disgusting phrases, low arguments, and the undisguised language of coarse selfishness. We

all know how we should like to interfere in ward elections, borough politics, or any public matter over which a constant habit of half-educated discussion has diffused an atmosphere of deterring associations. A high morality, too, shrinks with the inevitable shyness of superiority from intruding itself into the presence of low debates. The inevitable consequence of vulgarising our Parliament would be the deterioration of public opinion, not only in its more refined elements, but in all the tangible benefits we derive from the application to politics of thoroughly cultivated minds.

We can only allude briefly to the refutation of the purely democratic theory with which the facts of English history supply us. It is frequently something like pedantry when reference is made to the origin of the House of Commons as a source of *data* for deciding on the proper constitution for it now. What might have been a proper constitution for it when it was an inconsiderable part of the government, may be a most improper one now that it is the ruling part. Still, one brief remark may be advanced as to the early history of our representative system, which will have an important reference to the topic. "Whilst," writes one of our soundest constitutional antiquaries, "boroughs were thus reluctant to return members, and burgesses disinclined to serve in that capacity, the sheriffs assumed a right of sending or omitting precepts at their pleasure. Where boroughs were unwilling or unable to send representatives, the sheriff, from favour or indulgence, withheld the precept, which in strictness he was bound to issue, and thus acquired a discretionary power of settling what places were to elect, and what places were not to elect, members of Parliament. In his return to the writ of summons, he sometimes reported that he had sent his precept to a borough, but had received no answer to it. Sometimes he asserted without the slightest regard to truth, that there were no more cities or boroughs in his bailiwick than those mentioned in his return. At other times he qualified this assertion by adding that there were none fit to send members to Parliament, or that could be induced to send them. No notice seems ever to have been taken of these proceedings of the sheriffs; nor is there the slightest ground for suspecting that in the exercise of his discretionary power he was directed by any secret instructions from the king and council: "I have never seen or heard," says Brady, "of any

BAGEHOT'S HISTORICAL ESSAYS

particular directions from the king and council or others to
the sheriffs, for sending their precepts to this or that borough
only and not to others". *"Provided there was a sufficient attendance of members for the public business, the government
seem to have been indifferent to the number that came, or
to the number of places from which they were sent."*[4] The
public business of that time was different from the public
business which is now transacted by Parliament; but we may
paraphrase the sentence into one that is applicable to us. Provided we have a House of Commons coinciding in opinion
with the general mass of the public, and containing representatives competent to express the peculiar sentiments of all
peculiar classes, we have provided for our "public business";
we need not trouble ourselves much further, we shall have
attained all reasonable objects of desire, and established a
polity with which we may be content.

The most obvious way of attempting this is, to represent,
or attempt to represent, intelligence directly. The simplest
plan of embodying public opinion in a legislature, is to give
a special representation in that legislature, to the politically
intelligent persons who create that opinion. To attain this
end directly is, however, impossible. There is no test of intelligence which a revising barrister could examine, on which
attorneys could argue before him. The absurdity of the idea
is only rendered more evident by the few proposals which
are made in the hope of realising it. Mr Holyoake proposes
that the franchise should be given to those who could pass a
political examination; an examination, that is, in some standard textbook—Mill's *Principles of Political Economy,* or some
work of equal reputation. But it does not need to be explained that this would enfranchise extremely few people
in a country. Only a few persons give, or can give, a scientific attention to politics; and very many who cannot, are in
every respect competent to give their votes as electors, and
even to serve as representatives. It is probable that the adoption of such an examination suffrage, in addition to the kinds
of suffrage which exist now, would not add one per cent to
the present constituencies; and that if it were made a necessary qualification for the possession of a vote, we should
thereby disfranchise ninety-nine hundredths of the country.

[4] Allen on Parliamentary Reform, 1832.

A second proposal with the same object is, to give votes to all members of "learned societies". But this would be contemptibly futile. There is no security whatever that members of learned societies should be really learned. They are close corporations; and the only check on the admission of improper persons in future is the discretion of those who have been admitted already. At present most members of such societies undoubtedly have an interest in the objects for which they were formed; but create a political motive, and a skilful Parliamentary agent will soon fill the lists with the names of persons not celebrated for scientific learning, but who know how to vote correctly upon occasion. The idea of a direct representation of intelligence wholly fails from the non-existence of a visible criterion of that intelligence. All that can be done in this direction must be effected by a gradual extension of the principle which has given members to our universities. No one can obtain admission to these bodies without a prolonged course of study, or without passing a strict examination in several subjects. This is a kind of franchise not to be manufactured; it is only obtained as a collateral advantage, by persons who are in pursuit of quite different objects. Such bodies, however, are obviously few, and such kinds of franchise are necessarily limited. But they should be extended as far as possible; and as many such bodies as can be found will tend to supply us with an additional mode of giving a representation to cultivation and refinement—an object which we noticed as one of the desirable ends apparently least provided for by the letter of our present system.[5]

[5] In relation to this subject, we must call special attention to the claims of the University of London and of the Scotch Universities to representation in Parliament. The former University had a distinct pledge from the Government which founded it that it should be placed on an equality in every respect with Oxford and Cambridge. And such Universities would not only introduce additional representatives of intellectual culture into the House of Commons, but representatives also of *free* intellectual culture, as distinguished from the representatives of the ecclesiastical culture of the older Universities. Mr. Bright has reproached the members for Oxford and Cambridge Universities with their habitual antagonism to Reform. This is, we fear, a true accusation. At a time when educational questions are engrossing a larger and larger share of public attention, an adequate representation of *liberal* intellectual culture is most desirable in the House of Commons.

The criteria by which a franchise can be determined must
have two characteristics. They must be evident and conspicuous—tests about which there can be no question. Our
registration courts cannot decide metaphysical niceties; our
machinery must be tough, if it is to stand the wear and tear
of eager contests. Secondly, as we have explained, such criteria must be difficult to manufacture for a political object.
Our tests must not be counterfeited, and they must be conspicuous. These two requirements nearly confine us to a property qualification. Property is, indeed, a very imperfect test
of intelligence; but it is some test. If it has been inherited, it
guarantees education; if acquired, it guarantees ability. Either
way it assures us of something. In all countries where anything has prevailed short of manhood suffrage, the principal
limitation has been founded on criteria derived from property. And it is very important to observe that there is a special
appropriateness in the selection. Property has not only a certain connection with general intelligence, but it has a peculiar
connection with *political* intelligence. It is a great guide to
a good judgment to have much to lose by a bad judgment.
Generally speaking, the welfare of a country will be most
dear to those who are well off there. Some considerations, it
is true, may limit this principle: great wealth has an emascu-
lating tendency; the knowledge that they have much at stake
may make men timid in action, and too anxious, for the
successful discharge of high duties: still the broad conclusion is unaffected, that the possession of property is not
only an indication of general mind, but has a peculiar tendency to generate *political mind*.

Similar considerations limit the kinds of property to be
selected. Our property qualification must be conspicuous and
uncreatable. Real property—houses and land—on which our
present qualification is based, possess these elements in a pre-
eminent degree. We think, however, that they are not the
only kinds of property which now in a sufficient degree possess these requirements. They probably were so formerly; but
one of the most important alterations in our social condition
is the change in the nature of much of our wealth. The growth
of what lawyers call personal property has of late years been
enormous. Railway shares, canal shares, public funds, bank
shares, debentures without number, are only instances of what
we mean. Great industrial undertakings are a feature in our

age, and it is fitting that a share in them should give a franchise as much as an estate in land. Two conditions only would be necessary to be observed. First, the property must be substantial, as it is called; that is to say, it should be remunerative. Property which does not yield an income is not sufficiently tangible for the purposes of a qualification: men of business may say it is *about* to yield a dividend; but this is always open to infinite argument. It would be necessary to provide that the business property to be represented should have been for a moderate period—say three years—properly remunerative; no one should register for such property unless it had for that period paid a regular interest. Secondly, such property should have been in the possession of the person wishing to register an account of it for at least an equal previous period. This is necessary to prevent the creation of fictitious votes. Real property is, indeed, exposed to this danger; but the occupancy of houses and lands is a very visible fact, and acts of ownership over the soil are tolerably well known on the spot. It is therefore somewhat difficult to create fictitious tenancies or freeholds. In the case of share-property there is no equal check. The only precaution which can be taken is, to make the pecuniary risk of those who try to create such votes as large as possible. If it be required that the property be registered for a moderate period in the company's books as belonging to the person who claims to vote in respect of it, that person must have during that time the sole right to receive the dividends, and the shares will be liable for all his debts. If a real owner chooses to put a nominal one in this position, he does it at the risk of both principal and income.

We have, then, arrived at the end of another division of our subject. We have shown that the democratic theory is erroneous, and that the consequences of acting upon it would be pernicious. We have discussed the most plausible schemes which have been suggested for testing political intelligence, and we have found reason to think that a property qualification is the best of those modes. It has incidentally appeared that the property qualification which at present exists in England is defective, because it only takes cognisance of a single kind of property. We may now resume the thread of our discussion, which we laid aside to show the errors of the democratic theory. We proceed to indicate how the defects which have been proved to be parts of our existing system of representation can be remedied without impairing its characteristic excellence, without destroying a legislature which is in tolerable conformity with intelligent opinion.

The first defect which we noticed was, that the existing system takes no account of the views and feelings of the working classes, and affords no means for their expression. How, then, can this be supplied? It is evident that this end can only be approached in two ways: we may give to the working classes a *little* influence in all constituencies, or we may give them a good deal of influence in a few constituencies. By the conditions of the problem they are to have some power in the country, but not all the power; and these are the only two modes in which that end can be effected.

The objection to the first plan is in the nature of a dilemma. Either your arrangements give to the working classes a sufficient power to enable them to decide the choice of the member, or they do not. If they do, they make these classes absolute in the State. If the degree of influence which you grant to them in *every* constituency is sufficient to enable them to choose the representative for that constituency, you have conferred on these inferior classes the unlimited control of the nation. On the other hand, if the degree of influence you give to the poorer classes is not sufficient to enable them to control the choice of any members, you have done nothing. There will be no persons in Parliament inclined by nature and empowered by authority to express their sentiments; their voice will be as much unheard in Parliament as it is now. If the poor are to have a diffused influence in all constituencies, it must be either a great one or a small one. A small one will amount only to the right of voting for a candidate who is *not* elected; a great one will, in reality, be the establishment of democracy.

We shall see the truth of this remark more distinctly if we look a little in detail at one or two of the plans which are proposed with this object. Perhaps the most remarkable of these is that which is at present in operation in Prussia. The suffrage there is very diffused; it amounts to something very like manhood suffrage. But the influence of the lower classes is limited in this way: the constituency is divided into classes according to the amount of direct taxation they respectively pay. The names of those voters who pay the highest amount of tax are put together till a third part of the whole amount of direct taxes paid by the electoral district has been reached. These form the first class. Again, as many names are taken as will make up another third of the same total taxation; and these form the second class. The third class is formed of all the rest, and each class has an equal vote. By this expedient a few very rich persons in class 1, and a moderate number of moderately rich persons in class 2, have each of them as much influence as the entire number of the poorer orders in class 3. In Prussia a system of double representation has also been adopted, and for that purpose the constituency is divided into sections. But we need not confuse ourselves with prolix detail; the principle is all which is to the purpose. The effect of the plan is evident; it is equivalent to giving to the working classes *one-third* of the influence in every constituency, and no more than one-third. But it is evident that this arrangement not only gives no security for the return of a satisfactory spokesman for the lower orders, but that it provides that no such spokesman shall be returned. The two superior classes are two-thirds of the constituency, and they will take effectual care that no member animated solely with the views of the other third shall ever be elected. So far as class feeling goes, the power given to the lower orders is only the power of voting in a perpetual minority. Undoubtedly, in case of a division between the two superior classes, the lower orders would hold the balance; they would have the power in all constituencies of deciding who should and who should not be the member. But this is not the kind of influence which we have shown it to be desirable that the lower orders should possess. Nothing can be more remote from their proper sphere than the position of arbitrator between the conflicting views of two classes above them. We wish that they should have a few members to express their feelings; we do not wish that they should decide on the critical controversies of their educated fellow-subjects—that they should determine by a casting and final vote the policy of the nation.

Another plan suggested is, that the lower orders should have a single vote, and that persons possessed of property should have a second vote. But statistics show that the power which this would give to the lower orders would be enormous. For example, if it should be enacted that all persons living in houses rated at less than £10 shall have one vote, and that those living in houses rated at more than £10, two votes, we should have—

990,000 living in houses of £10 ⎫
      and more than £10 ⎬ with 1,980,000 votes,
2,280,000 living in houses under £10 ⎭ with 2,280,000 votes;

giving a clear majority throughout the country to the lowest class of ratepayers; and that majority would of course be much augmented if we conferred (as the advocates of manhood suffrage propose) a vote on every adult male in the country, whether he paid rates or not. The inevitable effect of this plan would be to give an authoritative control to the poorer classes. We might, indeed, try to obviate this by giving a still greater number of votes, say three or four, to the richer class; but then we should reduce the poorer class to an impotent minority throughout the country. In the first case, they would have the power of returning nearly all the members of the legislature; in the second, they would not as a class, or with an irresistible influence, return any.

Another scheme, proposed with this object, at least in part, is the "representation of minorities," as it is commonly called. This is to be attained by the ingenious device of making the number of votes to be possessed by each constituent less than the number of members to be returned by the constituency. The consequence is inevitable: an ascertainable minority of the constituency, by voting for a single candidate only, can effectually secure his election. Thus, if the number of members is three and the number of votes two, any fraction of the constituency greater than two-fifths can be sure of returning a member, if they are in earnest enough on the matter to vote for him only. The proof of this is, that a minority of two-fifths will have exactly as many votes to give to one member as the remaining three-fifths have to give to each of three members. If the constituency be 5000, a minority of two-fifths of the electors, or 2000, would have 2000 votes to give to a single candidate; the remaining 3000 would have only 6000 votes to divide between three candidates, which is only 2000 for each. A minority at all greater than 2000, therefore, would, if it managed properly, be certain to return a member. The objection to this plan is, that it would rather tend to give us a Parliament principally elected by the lower orders, with special members among them to express the sentiments of the wealthier classes, than a Parliament generally agreeing with the wealthier classes, and containing special representatives for the lower: the principal representation is almost by express legislation given to the more numerous classes; a less to the minority. It would not solve the problem of giving a certain power to the lower orders, and yet not giving them a predominant power. In the case which we have supposed of a constituency with three members and two votes, the minority also would be a larger one than the richer classes can permanently hope to constitute in the country. Two-fifths of a great town must necessarily include many of the poorer, less cultivated, and less competent. We must remember, also, that the disproportion in number between rich and poor, even between the decidedly poor and the rather wealthy, tends to augment. Society increases most rapidly at its lower end; the wide base extends faster than the narrower summit. At present persons living in "ten-pound houses," or upwards, are something like 21 per cent of the adult males in the nation, and about 30 per cent of the rate-paying population. But in process of time the inevitable increase of the humbler orders will reduce them to a far more scanty proportion. The operation of the plan might become even more defective if it were combined, as is often proposed, with an increase of the number of members returned by the constituencies to which it is to be applied. If four members were given to a populous constituency, and each elector were to have three votes, it would require that the minority should be more than three-sevenths[6] of the constituency, to enable it to be certain of returning a candidate. The rich and educated cannot expect to remain so large a fraction of the nation as this; they are not so now.

The most plausible way of embodying the minority principle in action would be to give only one vote to each person, and only *two* members to the constituency. In this case, any minority greater than one-third of the constituency would be sure of returning a member; and as this fraction is smaller than those we have mentioned, it would evidently be more suitable to the inevitable fewness of the rich and intelligent. But even this plan would give half the members of the coun-

[6] The rule is, that a minority, to be certain of electing its candidate, must be more than that fraction of the constituency, which may be expressed as follows:—

$$\frac{\text{The number of votes.}}{\text{The number of members + the number of votes.}}$$

try to the least capable class of voters; and it would have the additional disadvantage of establishing a poor-class member and rich-class member side by side in the same constituency, which would evidently be likely to excite keen jealousy and perpetual local bitterness.

We believe, indeed, that it was an after-thought in the advocates of "minority representation," to propose it as a means of giving some, but not too much, representation to the poor. Its name shows that it was originally devised as a means of giving a representation to minorities *as such*. The extreme case used to be suggested of a party which had a very large minority in every constituency, but which had not a majority in any, and had not therefore any share in the representation. It cannot be denied that such a case might occur: but if the constituencies be, as they should be, of varied kinds, it is very unlikely; and in politics, any contingency that is very unlikely ought never to be thought of; the problems of practical government are quite sufficiently complicated, if those who have the responsibility of solving them deal only with difficulties which are imminent and dangers which are probable. But in the actual working of affairs, and irrespectively of any case so extreme as that which is put forward, the elimination of minorities which takes place at general elections is a process highly beneficial. It is decidedly advantageous that every active or intelligent minority should have adequate spokesmen in the legislature; but it is often not desirable that it should be represented there in exact proportion to its national importance. A very considerable number of by no means unimportant persons rather disapproved of the war with Russia; but their views were very inadequately represented in the votes of Parliament, though a few able men adequately expressed their characteristic sentiments. And this was as it should be. The judgment of the Parliament ought always to be coincident with the opinion of the nation; it is extremely important that it should not be less decided. Very frequently it is of less importance which of two courses be selected than that the one which is selected should be consistently adhered to and energetically carried through. If every minority had exactly as much weight in Parliament as it has in the nation, there might be a risk of indecision. Members of Parliament are apt enough to deviate from the plain decisive path, from vanity, from a wish to be original, from a nervous conscientiousness. They are subject to special temptations, which make their decisions less simple and consistent than the nation's. We need a counteracting influence; and it will be no subject for regret if that influence be tolerably strong. It is, therefore, no disadvantage, but the contrary, that a diffused minority in the country is in general rather inadequately represented. A strong conviction in the ruling power will give it strength of volition. The House of Commons should think as the nation thinks; but it should think so rather more strongly, and with somewhat less of wavering.

It was necessary to discuss this aspect of the minority principle, though it may seem a deviation from the investigation into the best mode of giving a due but not an undue influence to the working classes. The advocates of that principle generally consider its giving a proper, and not more than a proper, degree of power to the poor as a subordinate and incidental advantage in a scheme which for other reasons ought to be adopted; it was therefore desirable to prove that no such other reasons exist, as well as that it would very imperfectly, if at all, tend to place the working classes in the position we desire.

Some persons have imagined that the enfranchisement of all the lower orders may be obtained without its attendant consequence, the disfranchisement of other classes, by means of the system of "double representation," which gives to the primary electors only the power of nominating certain choosers, or secondary electors, who are to select the ultimate representative. This proposal was made by Hume many years ago; it formed part of more than one of the earlier French constitutions; and it is now being tried, as we have observed, in Prussia. We have an example of its effects likewise in a part of the constitution of the United States. Although, therefore, we may not have quite so full a trial of the proposed machinery as we could wish, we have some experience of it. The most obvious objection to it is, that it gives to the working classes the theoretical supremacy as much as a scheme of single representation. Whether the working classes choose the member of Parliament, or whether they choose an intermediate body who are to choose the member, their power of selection will be equally uncontrolled, the overwhelming advantage derived from their numbers will be the same. It is alleged that the working classes will be more fit to choose persons who would exercise an intermediate suffrage; that they could choose persons in their own neighbourhood well known to them, and for whom they had a respect; and that the ultimate representative nominated by these local worthies would be a better person than the working classes would have nominated themselves at first. And in quiet times, and before a good machinery of electioneering influence had been organised, we are inclined to believe that such would be the effect. The working classes might, in the absence of excitement and artificial stimulus, choose persons whom they knew to be better judges than themselves; and, in accordance with the theory of the scheme, would give to them a *bonâ fide* power of independent judgment. But in times of excitement this would not be the case. The primary electors can, if they will, require from the secondary a promise that they will choose such and such members; they can exact a distinct pledge on the subject, and give their votes only to those who will take that pledge. This is actually the case in the election of the President in the United States. As a check on the anticipated inconveniences of universal suffrage, the framers of the federal constitution provided that the President should be chosen by an electoral college elected by universal suffrage, and not by the nation at large directly. In practice, however, the electoral college is a "sham". Its members are only chosen because they will vote that Mr Buchanan be President, or that Colonel Fremont be President; no one cares to know anything else about them. There is no debate in the college, no exercise of discretionary judgment: they travel to Washington, and give their vote in a "sealed envelope," and they have no other duty to perform. According to these votes the President is elected. Such, indeed, appears the natural result wherever the lower orders take a strong interest in the selection of the ultimate members for the constituency. They have the power of absolutely determining the choice of those members; and when they care to exercise it, they will exercise it. In Prussia, as it would appear from the newspaper narrative of the recent elections, a real choice has been exercised by the Wahlmänner—the secondary electors. But a few years of experience among a phlegmatic people are not a sufficient trial; there are as yet no parliamentary agents at Berlin. In this country, as in America, an effectual stimulus would soon be applied to the primary electors. If twenty intermediate stages were introduced, the result would be identical: a pledge would be exacted at every stage; the primary body would alone exercise a real choice, and the member would be the direct though disguised nominee of the lower orders. This scheme would everywhere, in critical times, and in *electioneering* countries at all times, give to the democracy an uncontrolled power.

An expedient has, it is true, been proposed for preventing this. It has been suggested that the secondary electors—the electoral college in the American phrase—should have other duties to perform besides that of electing the representative. Suppose, for example, that the electors at large chose a municipal town council, and that the latter elected the representative of the town in the legislature; it is thought that persons with good judgment would be chosen to ensure the due performance of the municipal duties, and that a good member of Parliament would be selected by the *bonâ fide* choice of those persons with good judgment. The scheme would be far too alien to English habits and traditions to be seriously proposed for adoption by this country even if its abstract theory were sound; but there is an obvious objection of principle to it. The local duties of a municipal council are too different from that of selecting a parliamentary representative to be properly combined with them. We should probably have a town council of political partisans, as was the case before the Municipal Reform Act; and the uninteresting local duties would be sacrificed to the more interesting questions of the Empire. In the real operation of the scheme very much would depend on the *time* at which the town council was elected. If it were elected simultaneously with the general election of members of Parliament, nobody would think of anything but the latter. The town councillors would be chosen to vote for the borough member, and with no regard to any other consideration. We should have a fictitious electoral college, with the added inconvenience that it would be expected to perform duties for which it was not selected, and to which it would be entirely ill-suited. On the other hand, if the town council were elected when the Parliamentary election was not thought of, we might, in times of fluctuating opinion, have a marked opposition between the opinion of the town council and the opinion of the constituency. In an excitable country— and every country which takes a regular interest in politics becomes excitable—no such opposition would be endured. It would be monstrous that the member for London at a critical epoch, say when a question of war or peace was pressing for decision, should be nominated by a town council elected some time before, when no such question was even thought of. There used in the ante-Reform Bill times to be occasional riots when the close corporations, with whom the exclusive suffrage in many boroughs then rested, made a choice not approved of by the population of the town. If this was the case when the borough councillors were only exercising an immemorial right, it will be much more likely to be so when they are but recently nominated agents, deriving their whole authority from the dissentients, and making an unpopular choice in the express name of an angry multitude. We may therefore dismiss the proposed expedient of double represen-tation with the remark, that if the intermediate body be elected with little reference to its electoral functions, it will be little fitted for such functions; and if it is elected mainly with reference to them, it will have no independent power of choice, but be bound over to elect the exact person whom its constituents have decided to favour.

A much more plausible proposal is suggested by the rec-ommendation which we made some pages back—that the prin-ciple which assigns the franchise to those who can show a property qualification should not be confined to real estate, but be extended to every kind of property that yielded an income and was owned *bonâ fide*. A considerable number of the working classes possess savings; not large, it is true, when contrasted with middle-class opulence, but still most impor-tant to, and most valued by, those who have hoarded them during a lifetime. The total accumulation is likewise very large when set down in the aggregate. It has been suggested that a suffrage conferred on the owners of moneyed property would of itself enfranchise the most thrifty and careful of the working classes; and that, as these would probably be the best judging of their class, it would be needless to inquire as to the mode in which any others could obtain the franchise. There may be a question whether we do wish simply to find representatives for the best of the working classes. We are not now seeking legislators who will exercise a correct judg-ment, but rather spokesmen who will express popular senti-ments. We need not, however, dwell on this, as there is a more conclusive objection to the plan proposed. Unfortu-nately, the savings of the working classes are not invested in a form which would be suitable for political purposes. The most pressing need of the poor is a provision for failing health and for old age. They most properly endeavour to satisfy this by subscribing to "benefit societies" or other similar clubs, which, in consideration of a certain periodical payment, guarantee support during sickness, or a sum of money in case of decease. Now this life and health insurance wants all the criteria of a good property qualification. There is no test of its *bonâ fides*. Simulated qualifications might be manufactured by any skilful attorney. The periodical payment might be easily repaid on pretence of sickness; and it would be perfectly impossible for any revising barrister to detect the fraud. There would be no security that the periodical premium even belonged to the poor man; it might be lent him, and with little risk, by his richer neighbour. Electioneering has conquered many difficulties. It would be easy to have an understanding that the secretary to the society, the clerk of the electioneering attorney, should see that the premium was soon repaid, in name to the poor subscriber, and in fact to the vote-making capitalist. The finances of some of these societies have never been in the best order; and there would be very great difficulty in tracking even a gross electioneering fraud. Perhaps no practical man will question but that the manipulation of a borough attorney would soon change the character of a "benefit society"; it would cease to be, as now, the repository of the real savings of the best working men; it would become a cheap and sure machinery for creating votes in the name of the most corruptible. So large a portion of the savings of thrifty operatives are most properly laid by in these insurance associations, that it is scarcely likely that a moneyed property qualification would give a vote to a considerable proportion even of the very best of them. A few would be admitted by giving the franchise to those who left a certain sum in a savings bank for a certain time; but, to prevent fraud, that time must be considerable, and careful returns, prepared for Lord John Russell's Reform Bill, are said to show that the number enfranchised would be even fewer than might have been expected. At any rate, it would not be safe to rely on such a franchise for creating a Parliamentary organ for the lower classes. Those enfranchised by it would be scattered through a hundred constituencies. There would be no certainty that even one member in the House would speak their sentiments. Moreover, we have doubts whether a constituency composed only of operatives who had a considerable sum in the savings bank after providing, as in all likelihood they

would have done, for the wants of their families in case of
their death and sickness, would not rather have the feelings
of petty capitalists than of skilled labourers. Those who have
just risen above a class can scarcely be relied on for giving
expression to its characteristic opinions. However, as it would
be scarcely possible to create such a constituency, there is no
reason for prolonging an anticipatory discussion on its tendencies. On the whole, therefore, we must, though rather
against our wishes, discard the idea of creating a working-class
franchise by an extension of the suffrage qualification to all
kinds of property. A careful examination appears to show that
we could not obtain in that way a characteristic expression
for the wants of the masses.

These are the principal schemes which have been proposed
for adding to the legislature some proper spokesmen of the
wants of the lower classes by giving to those classes *some*
influence in every constituency. Our survey of them has confirmed the anticipation with which we set out. The dilemma
remains. Either the influence is great enough to determine
the choice of the member, or it is not: if it is not, no spokesmen for the working classes will be elected; if it is, no one
not thoroughly imbued with the views and sentiments of the
lower orders would be chosen,—we should have a democracy.

As this, the first of the only two possible expedients, has
failed us, we turn with anxiety to the second. Since it does
not seem possible to procure spokesmen for the working
classes by a uniform franchise in all constituencies, is it possible to do so by a varying franchise, which shall give votes
according to one criterion in one town, and to another criterion in another town? It evidently *is* possible. Whether
there are any countervailing objections is a question for discussion, but of the possibility there cannot be a doubt. If
all the adult males in Stafford have votes, then the member
for Stafford will be elected by universal suffrage; he will be
the organ of the lower orders of that place. Supposing that
place to be subject in this respect to no important local
anomaly, the lower orders there will be like the corresponding classes elsewhere. By taking a fair number of such towns,
we may secure ourselves from the mischievous results of local
irregularities; we can secure a fair number of spokesmen for
the lower orders.

The scheme is not only possible, but has been tried, and
in this country. Before the Reform Bill of 1832 there was

a great disparity in the suffrage qualification of different constituencies. "A variety of rights of suffrage," said Sir James Mackintosh, in 1818,[7] "is the principle of the English representation;" and he went on to enumerate the various modes in which it might be obtained—by freehold property, by burgage tenure, by payment of scot and lot, etc. The peculiar circumstances of 1832 made it necessary, or seemingly necessary, to abolish these contrasted qualifications. Great abuses prevailed in them, and it would have been difficult to adjust remedies for the removal of those abuses. The great requirement of the moment was a simple bill. During a semi-revolution there was no time for nice reasonings. Something universally intelligible was to be found. The enthusiasm of the country must be concentrated "on the whole bill and nothing but the bill". We must not judge the tumult of that time by the quietude of our own.

At a calmer moment the more philosophic of liberal statesmen were, however, aware of the advantages of the machinery which they were afterwards compelled to destroy. The essay of Sir James Mackintosh, to which we have referred, appeared in the *Edinburgh Review*, and was considered at the time as an authoritative exposition of liberal doctrine: and almost the whole of it is devoted to a proof that this system of varying qualification is preferable, not only to universal suffrage, but to *any* uniform "right of franchise". On the point we are particularly considering, he says: "For resistance to oppression, it is peculiarly necessary that the lower, and in some places the lowest, classes should possess the right of suffrage. Their rights would otherwise be less protected than those of any other class: for some individuals of every other class would generally find admittance into the legislature; or, at least, there is no other class which is not connected with some of its members. Some sameness of interest, and some fellow-feeling, would therefore protect every other class, even if not directly represented. But in the uneducated classes, none can either sit in a representative assembly, or be connected on an equal footing with its members. The right of suffrage, therefore, is the only means by which they can make their voice heard in its deliberations. They also often send to a representative assembly members whose character

[7] *Edinburgh Review*, No. LXI, article "Universal Suffrage"; an admirable essay, singularly worth reading at present.

is an important element in its composition—men of popular
talents, principles, and feelings; quick in suspecting oppression, bold in resisting it; not thinking favourably of the powerful; listening, almost with credulity, to the complaints of
the humble and the feeble; and impelled by ambition, where
they are not prompted by generosity, to be the champions
of the defenceless. It is nothing to say that such men require
to be checked and restrained by others of a different character; this may be truly said of every other class. It is to no
purpose to observe, that an assembly exclusively composed
of them would be ill fitted for the duties of legislation; for
the same observation would be perfectly applicable to any
other of those bodies which make useful parts of a mixed and
various assembly." Sir James had evidently the words of the
member for Westminster sounding in his ears. His words
are not an expression of merely speculative approbation; they
are a copy from the life.

An authority still more remarkable remains. Lord John
Russell, in 1821, expressed a very decided opinion on the
advantages of having a different scale of property qualification
in different places, and rather boldly grappled with an obvious
objection to it. We quote the passage: "All parts of the country, and all classes of the people, ought to have a share in
elections. If this is not the case, the excluded part or class
of the nation will become of no importance in the eyes of
the rest: its favour will never be courted in the country, and
its interests will never be vigilantly guarded in the legislature.
Consequently, in proportion to the general freedom of the
community will be the discontent excited in the deprived
class by the sentence of nullity and inactivity pronounced
upon them. Every system of uniform suffrage except universal contains this dark blot. And universal suffrage, in pre-
tending to avoid it, gives the whole power to the highest and
the lowest, to money and to multitude; and thus disfranchises
the middle class—the most disinterested, the most independent, and the most unprejudiced of all. It is not necessary,
however, although every class ought to have an influence in
elections, that every member of every class should have a
vote. A butcher at Hackney, who gives his vote perhaps once
in twelve years at an election for the county of Middlesex,
has scarcely any advantage over another butcher at the same
place who has no vote at all. And even if he had, the interest
of the State is in these matters the chief thing to be con-

sulted; and that is as well served by the suffrage of some of each class, as by that of all of each class." The necessary effect of the Act of 1832 has been to make us forget the value of what the authors of it considered a most beneficial part of our representative system. That such great statesmen should have pronounced such panegyrics on the diversity of qualifications in different constituencies, when it was a living reality before their eyes, shows at least that it is practicable and possible.

The plan is, indeed, liable to several objections: it is not to be expected that in a complicated subject any scheme which is absolutely free even from serious inconveniences could be suggested. By far the most popular objection is that which Lord John Russell noticed in the passage we have just cited. There is a sense of unfairness in the project. Why should an artisan in Liverpool have a vote,.and an artisan in Macclesfield no vote? Why should the richer classes in one constituency be disfranchised by the wholesale admission of their poorer neighbours, and the richer classes in another constituency not be so disfranchised? The answer is suggested by a portion of our preceding remarks. No one has a right, as we have seen, to any portion of political power which he cannot exercise without preventing some others from exercising better that or some greater power. If all the operatives in the great towns were enfranchised, they would prevent the higher classes from exercising any power: and this is the reply to the unenfranchised artisan in Macclesfield. If there were no representatives of the working classes in Parliament, its measures might be less beneficial, and its debates would be imperfect; the higher classes in some great towns must have less power than in some other great towns, because a uniform suffrage impedes the beneficial work of Parliament, and prevents the ruling legislature from exercising its nearly omnipotent power well and justly. To have a good Parliament, we must disfranchise some good constituents. Perhaps, indeed, the whole difficulty is overrated. We see every day that, so far as the middle classes are concerned, it is of no perceptible consequence to the individual whether he has a vote or not: it is of great consequence to him that the supreme legislature should accord with the views of his class and himself; but whether he has voted for any particular member of that legislature is a trifle. We never dream in society of asking whether the person we are talking to has a vote or not. Both live, and live equally, in the atmosphere of politics. Similarly, it is of great importance to the lower classes that their feelings should be sufficiently expressed in Parliament; but which of them votes for the person who should express them is of no consequence at all. The non-voter ought to take as much interest in politics as the voter. When *all* of a class cannot exercise power without impeding a more qualified class, we may select, from considerations of convenience, those members of the less qualified class who are to have power. There is no injustice in allowing expediency to adjust the claims of persons similarly entitled.

It may also be objected that this plan of representing the lower classes does not give them the general instruction which the exercise of the suffrage is supposed to bestow. An unenfranchised artisan in Macclesfield is not educated by giving the suffrage to an artisan in Manchester. But it is a mistake to suppose that there is much, if any, instruction in the personal exercise of the franchise. Popular elections have no doubt a didactic influence on the community at large; they diffuse an interest in great affairs through the country; but the elevating effect of giving a vote is always infinitesimally small. Among the lower classes it is a question whether the risk of moral deterioration does not quite balance the hope of moral elevation. Popular institutions educate by the intellectual atmosphere which they constantly create, and not by the occasional decisions which they require. And were it otherwise, intellectual instruction is but a secondary benefit of popular government; and we must not throw away, in the hope of increasing it, the primary advantage of being well governed. We believe too that, in fact, mere existence under a good government is more instructive than the power of now and then contributing to a bad government.

We are more afraid of the objection that this inequality of suffrage in otherwise similar constituencies is an anomaly which may grow up imperceptibly, as it did before the Reform Bill, but cannot now be created *de novo*. We admit the difficulty: we are well aware that this inequality, like every other expedient in politics to which the objections are apparent and the advantages latent, is far easier to preserve than to originate. But when great interests are at stake, we should only give up that which is impossible; what is merely difficult should be done. Moreover, a little examination will, we think, show that the obstacles are far slighter than they might seem at first sight.

From this point of view it is worth remarking, that the inequality of suffrage qualification to a certain extent still exists. The effect of the Reform Act has been to hide and diminish, but not to annihilate, the inequalities which existed before. The constituencies in which these inequalities existed were naturally opposed to their abolition, and a compromise was effected. All persons duly qualified to vote on the 7th June, 1832, were to retain their right for life, subject to certain conditions of residence and registration. In all boroughs, likewise, in which freedom of the borough, whether acquired by birth or servitude prescriptively, gave a vote, that franchise was to a certain extent retained. The freemen of such boroughs have votes now just as before, and freedom can be acquired in the same way: no change on this point was effected in 1832, except that a borough franchise so obtained is forfeited by non-residence in the borough. The number of these anomalous votes is still very considerable. Mr Newmarch has shown that in 1853 it amounted to 60,565, which is more than one-seventh of 400,000, the number (or nearly so) of borough electors at that time. We have therefore a very considerable amount of inequality in our present system; we should scarcely propose to increase it, but to distribute it more usefully.

The freemen of Coventry, Derby, Leicester, are not a class of whom we wish to undertake the defence; and in many towns the existence of those old rights is a recognised nuisance. We are not prepared to approve *all* anomalies in our representation. Our principles are especially opposed to the enfranchisement of favoured individuals in minor towns—few enough to be bought, corruptible enough to wish to be bought; who are not in general the majority of the constituency, but who exercise important influence because they can throw in a purchasable balance of votes on critical occasions; who are in no respect fair representatives of the working classes, who do not return to the House a single fit person willing to be spokesman for them. We argue merely that the effect of the Act of 1832 has only been to diminish the inequality of suffrage qualification before existing; and by no means to establish, even if a single act of Parliament could have so done, the erroneous principle that there is to be no inequality.

But the most effectual way of showing that it is possible to create *de novo* a beneficial variety of property qualifications, is to point out how it can be done. If it be admitted that we should found working-class constituencies, it is clear that we should found them where the working classes live. This is of course in the great seats of industry, where work is plentiful and constant. Those who reside in such towns are likewise the most political part of the class: the agricultural labourers, scattered in rural parishes, with low wages and little knowledge, have no views and no sentiments which admit of Parliamentary expression; they have no political thoughts. If we wish to give due expression, and not more than due expression, to the ideas of the democracy, we must select some few of the very largest towns, where its characteristic elements are most congregated. It would have been more fortunate if these towns had acquired such a franchise prescriptively; but it would have been all but miraculous if such had been the case. Many of our greatest towns are situated in what, in more purely agricultural times, were very uninfluential districts; we must not expect an hereditary franchise for newly-created interests. As it is necessary to have a rule of selection, the best which can be suggested is the rule of population; we would propose, therefore, that in the very largest towns in England[8] there should be what Mr Bright advo-

[8] It may, indeed, be objected that these large constituencies are just the ones in which a rate-paying franchise would have the most conclusively democratic effect; and that if we concede it as to these, it is not worth while to resist it with respect to others in which we might hope, by the influence of wealth and social standing, to counteract more or less its democratic tendency. But facts show that in an immense number of constituencies these influences could not control that tendency effectually. If an Act giving votes to all rate-payers be ever passed, it will probably be accompanied by a readjustment of the electoral districts on a democratic principle, which would augment the influence of mere numbers. But we need not consider this, since the introduction of the rate-paying franchise into our present constituencies would introduce a new element, much too large to be easily managed by indirect influences. It is of course not known exactly how large that new element would be; but very careful tables have been compiled of the number of inhabited houses in our present boroughs; and as the number of women rated in respect of them is no doubt small, all but a minute fraction of such houses would give a qualification to a male voter. Now it appears that in all except ten borough constituencies the number of inhabited houses was in 1852,

cates for all towns, a rate-paying franchise. If this were extended to all towns having more than 75,000 inhabitants, it would include at present London, Liverpool, Manchester, the Tower Hamlets, Marylebone, Finsbury, Bristol, Birmingham, Lambeth, Westminster, Leeds, Sheffield, Wolverhampton, Southwark, Greenwich, Bradford, Newcastle-on-Tyne, and Salford. If there were a *bonâ fide* representation of the working classes in these towns, they could not complain of a class disfranchisement; there would be adequate spokesmen for them. A member speaking the voice of places where such numbers of operatives are congregated, could speak the sentiments of that class with authority. No one could be unaware that the constituency in these large towns was ultra-democratic. The representation of the lower orders would be conspicuous as well as effectual.

Nor would the number of representatives so given to the lower classes be sufficient to deteriorate the general character of the legislature. It would not amount to forty for England and Wales, or to fifty for the United Kingdom; a considerable number, no doubt, but not sufficient to destroy the representative character of a house of 658 members. The House of Commons would still represent the educated classes as a whole; its opinion would still be their opinion; the performance of its ruling function would be unimpaired; and that of its expressive function would be improved.

We have dwelt so long on this part of our subject, that we shall not be able to devote as much space as we could wish to the explanation of the mode in which we think the remaining defects of our representative system should be remedied. We can only state briefly a few of the most important considerations.

The first of those defects, which we specified at the outset, is the existence of small boroughs, which are either in the hands of individual proprietors or have become in the process of time nests of corruption. We need not specify examples; the fact is sufficiently familiar. Indeed, all small boroughs in the course of years must rapidly tend towards one or other of these fates. A great deal of wealth in this

---

and doubtless is still, more than double that of the present electors; and consequently the *new* element which would be introduced would greatly preponderate over, and in fact disfranchise, the old. It is evident that it would be very difficult to manage so many new voters by any indirect influences.

country seeks to invest itself politically. A small borough of
this sort necessarily contains a considerable number of corruptible individuals; year by year skilful Parliamentary agents
ascertain who these individuals are, and buy them. The continual temptation is too much for shop-keeping humanity;
with every election the number of purchasable votes tends
to increase: one would not have yielded, only he wanted a
new shop front; another, who is proof against plate-glass, desires money to put out his son in the world. Gradually an atmosphere of corruption closes over the borough, and men of
the world cease to expect purity from it. The only way in
which this sort of retail purchase can be escaped is by a
wholesale purchase. A rich proprietor may buy a large majority of vote-conferring properties in the borough, and so
become despotic in the town. Each presentation (to borrow
a phrase from the Church) is not in that case sold on the day
of election, because the advowson has been bought before by
some one who has a use for it.

We may escape, then, the necessity of ascertaining the
electoral corruption of particular boroughs, and lay it down as
a general condition of permanent purity that a constituency
should contain a fixed number—five hundred, suppose, electors. It is quite true that this remedy is not certainly effectual: there are many boroughs, where the enfranchised constituency exceeds this number, in which the elections are not
at all what we should wish. But the tendency of such a measure is plain. It prevents the wholesale purchase by the neigh-
bouring proprietors, because it makes the property too large
for ordinary wealth to buy. It *tends* to prevent the retail purchase by increasing the supply of votes—which always lessens
their market value, and in very many cases reduces it below
the price which will tempt ordinary voters to corruption. The
expedient is not a perfectly effectual one, but at least it is a
considerable palliative.

What, then, is to be done with boroughs below the prescribed limits? There are in England and Wales about sixty-
seven members, elected by forty-two of such boroughs. What
course would it be wisest to take with respect to such seats?
The most easy plan in theory is to annihilate them at once,
to have a new schedule A of places disfranchised. But it is
easier to write such a recommendation in an essay than to
carry the enactment in practice. These seats have the protective instincts of property. Money has been spent on many

of them for a course of years: in all of them the present electors would vote nearly as a man against the abolition of
"themselves". The strenuous resistance of the members for
such seats must be expected to any bill which should propose
to abolish them *in toto*. And such resistance would be the
more effectual, because in all likelihood it would be indirect.
The interested members, unless a sinister policy were unusually wanting in its characteristic acuteness, would not risk
a division on the unpleasant question of abolishing or not
abolishing their own seats. They would throw the probably
decisive weight of their votes into the scale most inconvenient
to the Government proposing that abolition; would combine
with every strong opposition to it; in the present state of
parties, would soon reduce it to a minority. A proposal to disfranchise many boroughs would soon issue in the resignation
of the proposing Government.

We must therefore assume that for the present, to some
considerable extent, the influence of such boroughs must continue to exist. In 1832 there was a popular feeling which carried everything before it. Now all we can hope to carry is
a compromise. As a compromise, the best expedient which we
can suggest is to combine such boroughs. The English respect
for vested interests would preclude the popularity of a sweep-
ing Act; but the English liking for a moderate expedient
would be a strong support to any measure that could be so
called. The effect of such a combination would probably be
in great part to set the joint constituency free from the yoke
of great proprietors. If Lord A is supreme in borough *a*, and
Mr B in town *b*, *a* and *b* combined will probably be controlled
by neither. The local feeling of *b* will resist Lord A; that of
a would be rigid to the enticements of Mr B. If one of the
burghs should be "independent," that is to say, purchased
voter by voter at each election, its inhabitants would probably rather be purchased by any one than by the proprietor
of the antagonistic borough. We are aware that these are not
very attractive considerations; but what are we to do? *Ils ont
des canons*. We must make the best terms we can with constituencies which we cannot hope entirely to destroy.

We shall be asked why we group these existing boroughs
with one another, instead of combining them with new towns
not now possessed of the borough franchise, which are therefore at present comparatively uncorrupt. We admit that, in
some individual cases, there may be conclusive reasons for

taking the latter course; but we think that there are political
arguments which should disincline us from adopting it in
general.

We saw reason to believe that the principal defects of
our House of Commons, as a *ruling* assembly, were an excessive bias to the landed interest, and an insufficient sympathy
with the growing interests of the country. On this account it
is desirable not to take from the county constituencies all
the liberalising element which they at present possess; on the
contrary, it would be desirable, if possible, to increase it. We
should, however, weaken that liberal element very materially
if, in our extreme desire to remedy borough corruption, we
extracted from the constituency of the counties the inhabitants of all their larger towns. The effect of Mr Locke King's
proposal to reduce the county franchise from £50 to £10,
if it should be adopted, as it probably will be, will be to augment the county influence of the towns which have no borough member. We must not counteract this tendency. As we
think it desirable to diminish the *sectarian* character of our
county members, we must not adopt the most effectual of all
schemes for preserving it unimpaired—we must not absorb
into the boroughs all other influences save those of the country gentlemen.

Our second reason for preferring to combine the very small
boroughs with one another rather than to unite each of them
with some town at present unenfranchised is, that we wish
to diminish the number of seats for such constituencies. If
we annexed new elements to each of them, there would be
a plausible argument for not diminishing their number. But,
as has been explained, we wish to provide a more ample
representation for the growing districts. of the country; and
there is a very general and well-grounded opinion that the
House of Commons is already quite sufficiently numerous.
In order, therefore, to increase the representation of the progressive parts of England in the proportion which seems desirable, we must take from the decaying or stationary towns
of the less active parts of the country the right of sending
members which they have now. On a great scale, the same
plan was adopted in 1832: it was then necessary to remedy a
great evil; and therefore it was necessary that the number
of seats disfranchised should be great, and the number of
newly enfranchised towns considerable also. As we have
shown, no such enormous evil remains at present to be reme-

died. The judgment of Parliament coincides fairly, if not precisely, with the opinion of the nation. All we have to correct
is, a slight bias in one direction, and a perceptible but not
extreme deficiency of sympathy in another. The changes we
have to make, therefore, may be slight in comparison with
those of 1832; still, so important is it that Parliament should
really coincide in opinion with the nation, that we should
take account of the beginnings of a discrepancy; while the
topic of reform in our electoral system is definitely before
the public, we should take the opportunity of correcting the
undue inclination of the legislature towards the less active,
and its contrast of feeling (which though slight is real) to the
more active part of the community.

We are the more certain that it is advisable to make some
such change as this, because, as we have before observed, we
believe this uneasy consciousness of the less perfect representation of the progressive elements in the nation, as compared
with the unprogressive, to be the secret source of almost all
the slight popular enthusiasm which now exists in favour of
reform. The external form of what is proposed is, indeed,
different; the principal, as well as the most popular, suggestion
is one for the representation of the working classes. We have
no doubt that those who are at the head of that movement,
as well as those who join in it, quite believe that such is their
true object. But it is at least an odd undertaking to be headed
by master manufacturers. Whatever view we may take of the
effects of universal or of rate-paying franchise on other parts
of the nation, there can be little question that its influence
would be detrimental to the power of opulent capitalists. We
must alter the world before there ceases to be some opposition of feeling (there is often a momentary opposition of
interest) between the mill-owner and his work-people. In the
days of the short-time agitation both parties understood this
perfectly. Even now a Parliament of capitalists would probably propose to repeal the ten-hours' bill; a Parliament of
working men would very likely desire to extend its principle.
To say the least, it is strange that the characteristic men of
one class should be so ready to throw all power into the hands
of the other.

A letter from Mr Bright himself to a Manchester association puts the matter in a different light. "On a great occasion," he tells us, "like the one now before the country, there
will be differences of opinion. Some think one extent of fran-

chise better than another. Some are for a £6 rental; some
are for a £5 rental; you are for the extension of the right of
voting to every man. Now I prefer to establish the Parliamentary suffrage on the basis which has been tried for some
centuries in our parishes, and which has been adopted at a
recent period in our poor-law unions and in our municipal
governments; with some needless restriction, with regard to
the municipal franchise, which I would not introduce into
our Parliamentary franchise. The more public opinion is
freely and honestly expressed, the more distinctly will a government, engaged in preparing a Reform Bill, be able to discover which is the point likely to be most satisfactory to the
public. I consider these differences of opinion on the subject
as of trifling importance when compared with the question
of the distribution of seats and members. *This is the vital
point in the coming bill*; and unless it be well watched, you
may get any amount of suffrage, and yet find, after all, that
you have lost the substance, and are playing merely with the
shadow of popular representation."

This at least is an intelligible doctrine. A redistribution of
seats in proportion to population would indisputably be most
advantageous to Mr Bright and his associates. Some of their
school have made a calculation that sixty-three boroughs, returning eighty-five members, have not, taken together, as
many electors as Manchester, which returns but two. And,
independently of extreme cases, it is quite indisputable that
the large towns and crowded populations of Lancashire and
the West Riding would, in any grouping based on electoral
numbers, assume a proportionate magnitude that would be
quite different from that which they have at present. If such
a readjustment could be carried, *and the present franchise
retained*, the followers of Mr Bright would be one of the
most numerous divisions of the House of Commons. It is true
that the advantage of their success must be shared with the
class most antagonistic to them in feeling. The county representation would have to be extended if electoral numbers, or
any mere numbers, were to be taken as the guide to a new
adjustment. But Mr Bright probably does not fear a conflict
with Mr Newdegate. We can well understand that he should
esteem the lowering of the franchise, which would impair his
power, less important than a reapportionment of members,
which must increase it.

We can spare but a few words to show the unsoundness of

the principle on which the proposed readjustment is to be based; and we would hope that only a few words are needed. Mr Bright considers it an obvious absurdity that a constituency of 1000 electors should return a member, and that another constituency with 5000 should return but one member also. Such a variety is nevertheless *primâ facie* beneficial: it would be a probable sign of the complete imperfection of an electoral organisation if every constituency in it were equally numerous. All such systems must tend to give undue preponderance to some classes, and to deny, not only substantial influence, but even bare expression, to the views of other classes. If the nation be homogeneous, equal patches of population will tend to return similar members. The more numerous the constituency, the more likely is this to be the result. Thousand A *may* differ from Thousand B; but Million A will assuredly be identical with Million B. The doctrine of chances forbids us to expect contrasted representatives from constituencies with a family likeness. If, indeed, the nation should not be homogeneous, but should contain two very numerous classes of unlike tendencies, whose harmony is preserved by the continual arbitration of less numerous classes intermediate between them, the result of an equal division of electoral districts would be different, and it would be worse. Each of the intermediate classes would be merged in one of the larger. We may, however, look at the living operation, and not at the bare theory. We have mentioned the contrast between Mr Bright and Mr Newdegate. What is it that prevents the continual disturbance of Parliamentary peace between two classes of men so dissimilar as the members for counties—especially purely agricultural counties—and members for manufacturing cities? Obviously the existence of the intermediate elements, of members sent up by agricultural towns, which contain industrial elements, and by smaller manufacturing towns, which have no notion of being offered in sacrifice to the populace of great cities. An electoral system composed of "population sections" would not give us a representative assembly adapted to the performance of either of its two functions. A House of Commons so elected would not represent the public opinion of the country, and therefore could not rule it as it should be ruled. The impartial and arbitrating element would be deficient. And, as has been explained, this complete deficiency in the qualities necessary to a ruling legislature would not be compen-

sated by any excellence in the qualities necessary to secure a
good expression of the grievances and opinions of all classes.
Old English good sense selected a town to send representatives separately from a county in which it was situated because it saw there the conspicuous focus of separate feelings,
separate interests, possibly separate complaints. Our new reformers would undo this wise arrangement. They would (at
least, such is the logical tendency of their argument) destroy
those bounds and limits to constituencies which secure a
character to the constituency; they would represent the shipping interest by throwing Hull into the county of York and
Grimsby into the county of Lincoln: distinct definition is all
that is necessary to disprove such ideas.

Paradoxical as it may sound, the evident untenableness of
Mr Bright's views gives them a claim on our attention. It is
an indication of social unsoundness that men of ability and
energy sincerely advocate very absurd theories, and are able
to collect considerable audiences to applaud those theories.
We may speak of our national contentment; but the answer
comes, What, then, do these people complain of? We must
not rest satisfied with a mere refutation of the doctrines
which are avowed, or an exposition of the mischievous consequences of the plans proposed. There are certain theories of
political philosophy which supply ready arguments against
almost every state of society which has been able to maintain
a long existence. These heresies float among the most ordinary ideas of mankind, and are ready without the least research to the hand of whoever may believe that he wants
them. Latent discontent with the existing form of government catches hastily at whatever justifies it; it seeks in these
old forms of false doctrine a logical basis for itself. One of
these heresies is the purely democratic theory of government;
it has very rarely indeed been adopted as a guide to action,
but its existence is nearly as old as political speculation. In
every age and country a class which has not as much power
as it thinks it ought to have snatches at the notion that all
classes ought to have equal power. Such an "uneasy class" believes that it ought to have as much power as the class which
is in possession; and not liking to put forward even to itself
a selfish claim of individual merit, it tries to found its pretensions on the "equal rights of all mankind". Mr Burke described the first East Indian nabobs as "Jacobins almost to a
man," because they did not find their social position "pro-

portionate to their new wealth". We cannot fail to observe that the new business wealth of the present day (of which Mr Bright is the orator and mouthpiece) has a tendency to democracy for the same reason. Such a symptom in the body politic is an indication of danger. So energetic a class as the creators of Manchester need to be conciliated; their active intelligence has rights which assuredly it will make heard. The great political want of our day is a *capitalist conservatism*. If we could enlist the intelligent creators of wealth in the ranks of those who would give their due influence to intelligence and property, we should have almost secured the stability of our constitution; we should have pacified its most dangerous assailants; we should count them among our most active allies. If the transfer of a moderate number of seats in Parliament from boroughs, which scarcely profess to exercise an independent choice of representatives, to large and growing towns would only in a subordinate degree conduce to this effect, such a transfer should be made. There would still be enough of smaller constituencies for all purposes that are useful.

We have, therefore, completed our task. We have shown the defects which our present system of representation seems to contain; and we have endeavoured to indicate the mode in which those defects might, we think, be remedied. The subject is one of great complexity and extent, and very difficult to discuss within the limits of an article. To be considered profitably, it must be considered as a whole; and it will be evident from our own pages how much space any attempt to discuss the entire topic necessarily requires. Whatever errors of detail may be found in our opinions, we cannot doubt that our general purpose has been correct. A real statesman at the present day must endeavour to enlarge the influence of the growing parts of the nation, as compared with the stationary; to augment the influence of the capitalist classes, but to withstand the pernicious theories which some of them for the moment advocate; to organise an expression for the desires of the lower orders, but to withstand even the commencement of a democratic revolution.

THE AMERICAN CONSTITUTION
AT THE PRESENT CRISIS[1]*

(1861)

*Bagehot wrote this article some months after the outbreak of the
Civil War. The Civil War began in April 1861, and the article
was published in the* National Review *in October of the same
year. It is of considerable interest as an example of intelligent
English reaction to the Civil War in its early stages. It contains
many seeds of Bagehot's later thought on American institutions
which were expressed in his book* The English Constitution
(1867).

It is not at first easy for an ordinary Englishman to appreciate adequately the favourite arguments which the most cultivated and best American writers use at the present juncture.
It seems to him that they are arguments befitting lawyers,
not arguments befitting statesmen. They appear only to
prove that a certain written document, called the Constitution of the United States, expressly forbids the conduct which
the Southern States are consistently pursuing, and that therefore such conduct is culpable as well as illegal. Very few
Englishmen will deny either the premiss or the conclusion
considered in themselves. It is certain that the Constitution
does forbid what the slave States are doing; it is equally
certain, that their policy is as mean, as unjustifiable, and
every way as discreditable, as was ever pursued by any public
bodies equally powerful and equally cultivated. But nevertheless an argument from the mere letter of a written Constitution will hardly convince any Englishman. He knows that
all written documents must be very meagre; that the best of

---

[1] *Causes of the Civil War in America.* By J. Lothrop Motley. Man-
waring.

* This essay was first published in the *National Review* for October
1861, Volume XIII, pages 465–93.

them must often be unsatisfactory; that most of them contain many errors; that the best of them are remarkable for strange omissions; that all of them will fail utterly when applied to a state of things different from any which its authors ever imagined. The complexity of politics is thoroughly comprehended by every Englishman,—the complexity of our history has engraved it on our mind; the complexity of our polity is a daily memento of it,—and no one in England will be much impressed by any arguments which tacitly assume that the limited clauses of an old State-paper can provide for all coming cases, and for ever regulate the future.

It is worth while, however, to examine the American Constitution at the present juncture. No remarkable aspect of the great events which are occurring among our nearest national kindred and our most important trading connexions in our own times, can be wisely neglected; and it will be easy to show that the Constitution of the United States is now failing from the necessary consequence of an inherent ineradicable defect; that more than one of its thoughtful framers perceived that it must fail under similar circumstances; and that the irremediable results of this latent defect have been aggravated partly by the corruptions which the Constitution has contracted in the progress of time, and yet more by certain elaborate provisions which were believed to be the best attainable safeguards against analogous dangers and difficulties.

Like most of the great products of the Anglo-Saxon race, the American Constitution was the result of a pressing necessity, and was a compromise between two extreme plans for meeting that necessity. It was framed in a time of gloom and confusion. The "revolted colonies," as Englishmen then called them, had been successful in their revolt; but they had been successful in nothing else. They had thrown off the yoke of the English Government; but they had founded no efficient or solid government of their own. They had been united by a temporary common sentiment,—by a common antipathy to the interference of the mother country; but the binding efficacy of that feeling ceased when their independence of the mother country had been definitively recognised. Nor was there any other strong bond of union which could supply its place. The American colonies had been founded by very different kinds of persons, at very different periods of English history. They had respectively taken the impress of the class of Englishmen who had framed them: Virginia had the mark of the aristocratic class; Massachusetts of the Puritan; Pennsylvania of the Quakers. The modern colonies of England are of a single type; they are founded by a single class, from a single motive. Those who now leave England are, with some exceptions, but still for the most part and as a rule, a rough and energetic race, who feel that they cannot earn as much money as they wish in England, and who hope and believe that they will be able to earn that money elsewhere. They are driven from home by the want of a satisfactory subsistence, and that subsistence is all they care or seek to find elsewhere. To every other class but this, England is too pleasant a residence for them to dream of leaving it for the antipodes. With our early colonies it was otherwise. When they were founded, England was a very unpleasant place for very many people. As long as the now-balanced structure of our composite society was in the process of formation, one class obtained a temporary ascendency at one time, and another class at another time. At each period they made England an uncomfortable place of residence for all who did not coincide in their notions of politics, and who would not subscribe to their tenets of religion. At such periods the dissident class threw off a swarm to settle in America; and thus our old colonies were first formed.

No one can be surprised that communities with such a beginning should have acquired strong antipathies to one another. Even at the present day, the antipathy of the inhabitants of South Carolina to the people of Boston, the dislike of Kentuckians to New Yorkers, has surprised attentive observers. But when their independence was first recognised, such feelings were infinitely more intense. The original founders of the colonies had hated one another at home. Those colonies were near neighbours in a rude country, and the occasional collision of petty interests had kept alive the original antipathy of each class to its antagonistic class, of each sect to its antagonistic sect. M. de Tocqueville remarked, that even in his time there was no national patriotism in America, but only a *State* patriotism; and though, in 1833, this remark was perhaps exaggerated, it would have been, fifty years before, only the literal expression of an indisputable fact. The name "American" had scarcely as yet any political signification,—it was a "geographical expression."

Grave practical difficulties of detail, too, oppressed the

new community. The war with England had been commenced by a body calling itself a Congress, but very different from the elaborate and composite body which we now know by that name. It was a simple *committee* of delegates from the different States, which could *recommend* to those States whatever military measures it thought advisable, but had no greater power or function whatever. It was in no sense a government. It had no *coercive* jurisdiction, could compel nothing, and enforce nothing. It was an advising council, which had no resources of its own, and could only rely on its dignified position, and the obvious necessity of united opposition to the common enemy. But, as might be anticipated, so frail an organisation was entirely inadequate to the rough purposes of revolutionary warfare. It could not meet a pressing difficulty; and it did not meet it. It worked well when it was not wanted, —when all the States were unanimous; but it was insufficient when the States began to disagree,—at the very moment for which it was required.

The responsible leaders of the revolutionary struggle felt the necessity of a closer bond; and in March 1781, nearly five years after the Declaration of Independence, the first real American Government was formed. It was called the Confederation, and was very simple in its structure. There was no complicated apparatus of President and Vice-president, such as we are now familiar with; no Supreme Court, no House of Representatives. The Confederation rather resembled what existed previously than what exists at present. There was, as before, a committee of delegates from the different States, and there was nothing else: this was the whole government; but this was *not*, as before, simply a committee with powers of recommendation. It could by its own authority make peace and war, establish armies, contract debts, coin money, issue a paper currency, and send ambassadors to foreign nations. It could in theory, and according to its letter, perform all the ordinary acts and functions of sovereignty. It did, in fact, perform the greatest act of sovereignty, as a lawyer would reckon it, that could be conceived. By signing a peace with England, it secured *its own* existence. Being a loose aggregate of revolted colonies, it obtained a recognition by the mother country against which these colonies had revolted. In the face of Europe, and in the face of England more especially, it maintained the appearance of an organised, regular, and adequate government.

It really was, however, very inadequate. Some one has said that the true way to test the practical operation of any constitution is to ask, "How do you get *money* under it?" This is certainly an American mode of testing a polity, and according to this criterion the "perpetual Confederation" was an egregious failure. "You could not get *dollars* by means of it at all." The national Congress could incur liabilities, but it could not impose taxation. It could, as we have explained, raise an army, contract a debt, issue a credit currency; but it could not of itself, and by its own authority, levy a penny. *The States* had retained in their own hands the exclusive power of imposing taxes. Congress could only *require* the several States to find certain quotas of money, and in the event of their not finding them could go to war with them. As a theorist would anticipate, the simplest alternative happened. The States did not find the money, and the Congress did not go to war with them. The debts of the Union were undischarged; the soldiers, even the French soldiers, who had achieved its independence, were unpaid; and the financial conditions of the Treaty of Independence with England were unfulfilled. Congress could do nothing, and the States would do nothing. Other smaller difficulties, too, were accumulating. The large unoccupied territory of the American continent required care; England was irritated at the non-completion or the infraction of several of the articles of peace; petty quarrels between the States on vexing minutiæ were constantly beginning, and were rarely ending. The impotence of Congress was becoming proverbial, and the entire country was discouraged. In the correspondence of Washington and those around him, it is evident that they asked themselves with doubt and despondency, "After all, will America be a *nation?*"

Two schemes floated in the public mind for remedying these evils. It was the opinion of some of the wisest American statesmen, and especially of Hamilton, the greatest political philosopher among them, that it would be better to establish an *omnipotent* Federal Government, which should be to America what the English Government was to England, which should have the full legislative, the full executive, the full judicial power which a sovereign government possesses in ordinary States.[2]

[2] As Hamilton's plan is not easily accessible in this country, and may have some interest at the present moment, when some persons,

Hamilton proposed that the "supreme legislative power of the United States should be vested in two distinct bodies of men," who should have power to pass *all laws whatever*, subject to a veto in a governor or first magistrate. For the choice

at least, are desirous of attempting a similar experiment, we give it at length.

"The following Paper was read by Col. Hamilton, as containing his ideas of a suitable plan of Government for the United States.

"1. The supreme legislative power of the United States of America to be vested in two distinct bodies of men, the one to be called the assembly, the other the senate, who, together, shall form the legislature of the United States, with power to pass all laws whatsoever, subject to the negative hereafter mentioned.

"2. The assembly to consist of persons elected by the people, to serve for three years.

"3. The senate to consist of persons elected to serve during good behaviour; their election to be made by electors chosen for that purpose by the people. In order to this, the States to be divided into election districts. On the death, removal, or resignation of any senator, his place to be filled out of the district from which he came.

"4. The supreme executive authority of the United States to be vested in a governor, to be elected to serve during good behaviour. His election to be made by electors chosen by electors, chosen by the people, in the election districts aforesaid. His authorities and functions to be as follows:

"To have a negative upon all laws about to be passed, and the execution of all laws passed; to have the entire direction of war, when authorised, or begun; to have, with the advice and approbation of the senate, the power of making all treaties; to have the sole appointment of the heads or chief officers of the departments of finance, war, and foreign affairs; to have the nomination of all other officers (ambassadors to foreign nations included) subject to the approbation or rejection of the senate; to have the power of pardoning all offences, except treason, which he shall not pardon without the approbation of the senate.

"5. On the death, resignation, or removal of the governor, his authorities to be exercised by the president of the senate, until a successor be appointed.

"6. The senate to have the sole power of declaring war; the power of advising and approving all treaties; the power of approving or rejecting all appointments of officers, except the heads or chiefs of the departments of finance, war, and foreign affairs.

"7. The supreme judicial authority of the United States to be vested in judges, to hold their offices during good behaviour, with adequate and permanent salaries. This court to have original jurisdiction in all causes of capture, and an appellative jurisdiction in all of the members of these bodies, he would have divided the country into electoral districts, and no State *as such* would have elected a single representative to the united legislature, or have been capable of any function or voice in the Constitution of the Union. "All laws of the particular States contrary to the Constitution of the Union or *laws of the United States* were to be utterly void." And "the better to prevent such laws being passed, the governor or president of each State" was to be appointed by the general Government, was to have a negative upon all laws "about to be passed therein." No State was to have any forces, land or naval; and the militia of all the States were to be under the exclusive direction of the general Government of the United States, which alone was to appoint and commission their officers. In practice this scheme would have reduced the existing States to the condition of mere municipalities; they would have retained extensive powers of interior regulation, but they would have lost all the higher functions of government, all control over any matters not exclusively their own; they would have continued to be, so to say, County Boards for county matters, but they would have had no share in the sovereign direction of general affairs. They would have been as restricted, as isolated, as the

---

causes in which the revenues of the general government, or the citizens of foreign nations, are concerned.

"8. The legislature of the United States to have power to institute courts in each State, for the determination of all matters of general concern.

"9. The governors, senators, and all officers of the United States to be liable to impeachment for mal and corrupt conduct; and, upon conviction, to be removed from office, and disqualified from holding any place of trust or profit. All impeachments to be tried by a court to consist of the chief, or senior judge of the superior court of law in each State; provided that such judge hold his place during good behaviour, and have a permanent salary.

"10. All laws of the particular States contrary to the constitution or laws of the United States to be utterly void. And the better to prevent such laws being passed, the governor or president of each State shall be appointed by the general government, and shall have a negative upon the laws about to be passed in the State of which he is governor, or president.

"11. No State to have any forces, land or naval; and the militia of all the States to be under the sole and exclusive direction of the United States; the officers of which to be appointed and commissioned by them."

Corporations of Liverpool and Bristol are under the Constitution of England.

A theorist would perhaps be inclined to regret that some such plan as that of Hamilton was not eventually chosen. At the present moment political speculators in England are singularly inclined to schemes of political unity. The striking example of Italy has given a natural stimulus to them. We have seen a great nation which had long been divided combine into what, we hope, will be a permanent State at the bidding of a few able and active men, and, as it seems to the many, by a kind of political enchantment. The change, when regarded from a distance, has appeared so easy, that we underrate its real difficulties, and are inclined to erect one of the most exceptional events in history into an ordinary precedent and example. But the state of America eighty years since may easily show us why such events have been rare in history; why *locality* has been called an instinct in the human mind; why large States have almost always been produced by the constraining vigour of some single conquering power. Each of the States of North America was a little commonwealth, with a vigorous political life. Each one of them had its ministry, its opposition, its elections, its local questions; each had its own political atmosphere, each its peculiar ambitions. Even if the different States had been well disposed to one another, it would have been difficult to induce all of them—especially to induce the smaller among them—to give up this local political animation. The Italian States seem to have relinquished it; but, in truth, they had little to relinquish. They were *despotically* governed. None of them had within their own boundaries that vast accumulation of ideas and sentiments and hopes, of love and hatred, which we call a "political life." The best men in Tuscany were not sacrificing a cherished career or an accustomed existence in favouring the expulsion of the Grand Duke; for so long as he remained they had no influence. After his expulsion the question of national unity or of local division could be considered fairly and impartially. It was not so in America: there were in every one of the States men who must have relinquished evident power, attainable proximate ambition,—the dearest of ambitions, the power of governing the persons whom they had known all their lives, and with whom they had all their lives been in actual political competition,—for the sake of an unknown "general government;" which was an abstraction

which could have excited no living attachment, in which but
a very few could take a prominent or gratifying share. Nor,
as we have explained, were the different States mutually well
disposed. The differences of their origin still embittered, and
long seemed likely to embitter, the local squabbles of years.
The saying of the Swiss Anti-federalist, "My shirt is dearer
to me than my coat," was the animating spirit of nine-tenths
of North America. The little State of Delaware refused even
to *consider* the abolition of the fifth article of the Confederation, which preserved the separate existence and the primitive equality of the separate States by enacting that each
should have one vote only. The plan of Hamilton could not
be carried, and he was too wise a statesman to regard it as
much better than a tempting dream.

The second extreme suggestion for amending the "perpetual Confederation" would have been equivalent in practice to a continuance of that Confederation very much as it
was. Its theoretical letter proposed indeed to give additional
powers to the central Congress, but the States were to be
still the component elements in the Constitution. The Congress was still to have no other power than that of requiring
from these States what money it needed. It would still be
compelled to declare war against them if that money was in
arrear. It would still have been in the condition graphically
delineated by a contemporary statesman: "By this political
compact the United States in Congress have exclusive power
for the following purposes, without being able to execute one
of them. They may make and conclude treaties; but can only
recommend the observance of them. They may appoint ambassadors; but cannot defray even the expenses of their tables.
They may borrow money in their own name on the faith of
the Union; but cannot pay a dollar. They may coin money;
but they cannot purchase an ounce of bullion. They may
make war, and determine what number of troops are necessary; but cannot raise a single soldier. *In short, they may declare every thing, but do nothing.*" Thus the second suggestion
for remedying the pressing evils of America was as inefficient
as the first had been impracticable.

The selected Constitution was a mean between the two.
As the State Governments could not be abolished, and could
not be entirely divested of their sovereign rights, a new Government was created, superior to them in certain specified
matters, and having independent means of action with refer-

ence to those matters, but in all other things leaving their previous functions unrestricted, and their actual authority unimpaired. By the active Constitution the central Congress has the right of imposing certain specified revenues, and the power of collecting them throughout each State by officers of its exclusive appointment. It has, as under the Confederation, the power of making peace and proclaiming war,— of engaging soldiers and contracting debts; but it now has likewise a power of collecting a revenue to remunerate those soldiers, and to pay those debts by its own authority, and without the consent of any subordinate body. It has not now to require obedience from the States in their corporate capacity, but to compel the obedience of individuals throughout those States in their natural isolation, and according to the ordinary custom of Governments.

We can now understand the answer of an American architect who was asked the difference between a Federation and Union. "Why," he said, "a Federation is a Union *with a top to it*." There is in the United States, not simply an assemblage of individual sovereign States, but also a *super*-sovereign State, which has its officers side by side with theirs, its revenue side by side with theirs, its law-courts side by side with theirs, its authority on a limited number of enumerated points superior even to theirs. No political invention has been more praised than this one. It has been truly described as the most valuable addition to the resources of political philosophy ever made by professed constitution-makers. Greater things have grown up among great nations; studious thinkers have speculated on better devices; but nothing so remarkable was perhaps ever struck out on the impulse of the moment by persons actually charged with the practical duty of making a Constitution. American writers are naturally proud of it; and it would be easy to collect from European writers of eminence an imposing series of encomiums upon its excellence.

Yet now that we have before us the pointed illustration of recent events, it is not difficult to see that such an institution is only adapted to circumstances exceptionally favourable, and that under a very probable train of circumstances it must fail from inherent defect. It is essentially a collection of *imperia in imperio*. It rather displays than conceals the grave disadvantages which have made that name so very unpopular. Each State is a subordinate Republic, and yet the entire Union is but a single Republic. Each State is in some sense a centre of *dis*union. Each State attracts to itself a share of political attachment, has separate interests, real or supposed, has a separate set of public men anxious to increase its importance,—upon which their own depends,—anxious to weaken the power of the United Government, by which theirs is overshadowed. At every critical period the sinister influence of the *imperium in imperio* will be felt; at every such period the cry of each subordinate aggregate will be, "Our interests are threatened, our authority diminished, our rights attacked."

A presidential election is the very event of all others to excite these dangerous sentiments. It places the entire policy of the Union upon a single hazard. A particular moment is selected when the ruler for a term of years is to be chosen. That ruler has very substantial power of various kinds; he has immense patronage, a legislative veto, great executive authority, and, what is yet more to the present purpose, he has a supreme position in society, which indefinitely attracts this popular choice, and indefinitely aggravates the intensity of the canvass. A homogeneous and simple State, with no subordinate rivals within its frontiers, might well fear to encounter such a struggle. What, then, must be the certain result in a Federal Union whenever a large minority of the States should consider their rights and their interests to be identified with the election or with the rejection of any one presidential candidate? What can we anticipate when the greatest dividing force, the overt choice of a supreme ruler, after canvass and struggle and controversy,—is applied to the most separable of political communities,—to a disjointed aggregate of States, whose local importance has been legally fostered, whose separate existence has been heedfully cherished, whose political vitality is older and more powerful than the bond of constitutional union? Surely, according to every canon of probability, we must confidently anticipate a separation whenever the sinister interest of a large and unconquerable section of the States shall be attacked, or be conceived to be attacked, by the selection of a supreme head for the whole nation. Independently of matters of detail, independently of the actual power which every supreme magistrate possesses, it is too much to expect that a considerable number of vigorous and active communities will, *if they can help it*, be governed by a person who is the *symbol* of the doctrine that they must hate and fear, and who is just elected by their special foes precisely because he is that symbol.

More than one of the most discerning of the framers of the American Constitution seems not only to have perceived the inherent defects of the work in which he had participated, but to have had a prevision of the real source from which ultimate danger was to be foreboded. Most of the controversies in the Convention which framed the Constitution had turned, in several forms, on the various consequences of the very different magnitude of the States which were about to join. The large States were anxious to be strong; the small States were fearful of being weak. But Mr Madison, one of the most judicious men of that time, clearly perceived that, though this was naturally the principal difficulty in securing the voluntary adoption by the several States of any proposed Constitution, it would not be an equally menacing danger to the continuance of the Union when that Constitution was once established. The small States shrank from binding themselves to a Union, exactly because they felt that they must remain in it if they entered. If they once contracted to combine with stronger countries, the superior power of those countries would enforce an adherence to the bargain. The really formidable danger which threatened the American Union was the possibility of a difference of opinion between classes of States of which no one was immeasurably stronger than the other. This Madison saw. He observed:—

"I would always exclude inconsistent principles in framing a system of government. The difficulty of getting its defects amended are great, and sometimes insurmountable. The Virginia State government was the first which was made, and though its defects are evident to every person, we cannot get it amended. The Dutch have made four several attempts to amend their system without success. The few alterations made in it were by tumult and faction, and for the worse. If there was real danger, I would give the smaller States the defensive weapons; but there is none from that quarter. The great danger to our general government *is the great Southern and Northern interests of the continent being opposed to each other. Look to the votes in Congress, and most of them stand divided by the geography of the country, not according to the size of the States.*"

It was not, indeed, very difficult for the eye of a practised politician to discern the great diversity between the North-

ern and Southern societies. It was even then conspicuous to
the eye of the least gifted observer. An accomplished French
writer, whose essay was written before the perceptions of all
of us were sharpened by recent events, has thus described it:
"Au Sud, le sol appartenait à de grands propriétaires entourés
d'esclaves et de petits cultivateurs. Les substitutions et le
droit d'aînesse perpétuaient les richesses et le pouvoir dans
une aristocratie qui occupait presque toutes les fonctions pu-
bliques. Le culte anglican était celui de l'État. La société et
l'Église étaient constituées d'une façon hiérarchique. Au
Nord, au contraire, l'esprit d'égalité régnait dans la société
comme dans l'Église: 'Je crains beaucoup les effets de cette
diversité de mœurs et d'institutions,' écrivait John Adams à
Joseph Hawley, le 25 novembre 1775; 'elle deviendra fatale
si de part et d'autre on ne met beaucoup de prudence, de
tolérance, de condescendance. Des changements dans les constitutions du Sud seront nécessaires si la guerre continue; ils
pourront seuls rapprocher toutes les parties du continent.'"
Probably, however, no one in those times anticipated the
rapidity with which those differences would develop, for no
one apprehended the practical working of slavery. Many persons unquestionably understood the immediate benefit with
which it buys an insidious admission into uncultivated countries; but perhaps no one understood at how great price of ultimate evil that benefit would probably be purchased. No one
could be expected to perceive that both the temporary benefit
and the ultimate disadvantages resembled one another in
being opposed to the continuance of the newly-formed Union; for even at the present day, and after a very painful experience, it is not steadily perceived by all of us.

Slavery is the one institution which effectually counteracts
the assimilative force to which all new countries are subject,
—that force which makes all men alike there, and which
stamps upon the communities themselves so many common
features. In such countries men are struggling with the wilder-
ness; they are in daily conflict with the rough powers of nature, and from them they acquire a hardness and a roughness
somewhat like their own. They cannot cultivate the luxuries
of leisure, for they have no leisure. They must be mending
their fences, or cooking their victuals, or mending their
clothes. They cannot be expected to excel in the graces of
refinement, for these require fastidious meditation and access to great examples, and neither of these are possible to

hard-worked men at the end of the earth. A certain democracy in such circumstances rises like a natural growth of the soil. An even equality in mind and manners, if not in political institutions, is inevitably forced upon those whose character is pressed upon by the same rude forces, who have substantially the same difficulties, who lead in all material points the same life. All are struggling with the primitive difficulties of uncivilised existence, and all are retarded by that struggle at the same low level of instruction and refinement.

Slavery breaks this dead level, and it is the only available device that does so. The owner of a few slaves, partly employed in the service of his house and partly in the cultivation of his land, has a good deal of leisure, and is not exposed to any very brutalising temptation. It is his interest to treat his slaves well, and in ordinary circumstances he does treat them well. They give him the means of refinement, and the opportunities of culture: they receive from him good clothing, a protective *surveillance*, and some little moral improvement. Washington was such a slave-owner, and it is probable that at Mount Vernon what may be called the temptation of slavery presented itself in its strongest and most attractive form. At all events, it is certain that, by the irresistible influence of superior leisure and superior culture, the Virginian slave-owner acquired a singular preëminence in the revolutionary struggle, moved the bitter jealousy of all his contemporaries, and bestowed an indefinite benefit upon posterity. But even this beneficial effect of slavery, momentary as it was, was not beneficial to the Union as such: it did not strengthen, but weakened the uniting bond; it introduced an element of difference between State and State, which stimulated bitter envy, and suggested constant division. In the correspondence of the first race of Northern statesmen, a dangerous jealousy of the superior political abilities of the South is frequently to be traced.

The immense price, however, which has been paid for the short-lived benefit of slavery has been immeasurably more dangerous to the Union than the benefit itself. As we all perceive, it is tearing it in two. In the progress of time slave-owning becomes an investment of mercantile capital, and slaves are regarded, not as personal dependents, but as impersonal things. The necessities of modern manufacture require an immense production of raw material, and in certain circumstances slaves can be beneficially employed on a large scale to raise that material. The evils of slavery are developed at once. The owner of a few slaves whom he sees every day will commonly treat them kindly enough; but the owner of several gangs, on several different plantations, has no similar motive. His good feelings are not much appealed to in their favour; he does not know them by name, he does not know them by sight; they are to him instruments of production, which he bought at such and such a price, which cost so many dollars, which must be made to yield so many dollars. He is often brutalised by working them cruelly; he is still oftener brutalised in other ways by the infinite temptations which a large mass of subject men and subject women inevitably offer to tyranny and to lust. Nor in such a state of society does slavery monopolise the charm which at first attracted men to it. When large capitals have been accumulated, there will be without it sufficient opportunities for moderate leisure and for reasonable refinement. Slavery buys its admission with the attractions of Mount Vernon; it develops its awful consequences in lonely plantations on the banks of the Mississippi, whose owner wants cotton, and wants only cotton; where he himself, or some manager whom he pays, employs himself in brutalities to black men, and enjoys himself in brutalities to black women. The events of this year exhibit the result. The probable disunion of the South and the North is but the inevitable consequence of the existing moral contrast. It is not possible to retain in voluntary combination such a community as Massachusetts and communities whose ruling element is such a slavery as that we have described.

We see, therefore, from this brief survey, that we have no cause to wonder even at the almost magical consequences of Mr Lincoln's election. It was the sort of event which was most likely to produce such consequences. A Republic of United States, which put up the first magistracy to periodical popular election, was most likely to part asunder when fundamental contrasts in character, ideas, and habits had long been growing rapidly between two very large classes of States, and when one of these classes persisted in electing to the first place in the Republic the very person who embodied the aim and tendencies most odious to the other class. It is evident, too, that the Northern and Southern States cannot hope to continue united under the present Constitution, or to form parts of the same Federal Republic under any Constitution whatever. No free State can rule an unwilling dependency of large size, except by excluding that dependency from all share in its own freedom. If Ireland unanimously wished to withdraw from the government of England, we could not rule it without excluding its representatives from Parliament. We know what the Irish members are now: we know that they are not very convenient; we know that they seem invented to give trouble; but who can imagine a House of Commons in which one hundred eager Irish members were united by a consistent intention to make an English government impossible? who can imagine the Parliamentary consequences of so great a voting power, used not for the purposes of construction, but exclusively for those of destruction? who can suppose that during a series of years we could keep any firm administration at all with so powerful a force ever ready to combine with every one who desired to pull down, and never ready to combine with any one who wished to set up? Yet this is a faint example of what the American Congress would be with a regularly organised Southern opposition retained within the Union by force, but desirous to leave it, anxious to destroy it; never voting for any thing except with this object; never voting against any thing save on that account. And such would be the inevitable result of the victory of the North. The Southern States are sure to preserve an intense local feeling for many years. History shows that they have always had it; the occupations and the habits of such bodies insure their having it. Even if the North were to conquer them now, their whole political force for many years would unquestionably be devoted to the attainment of disunion. Who can doubt that they would eventually obtain it by rendering all government impossible upon any lesser conditions? A free union is essentially voluntary. Sir Creswell Creswell may decree the restitution of matrimonial rights; but even he would not venture to decree the enforcement on an unwilling State of a promise to combine with another into a Parliamentary union.

Some of the framers of the American Constitution, as we have seen, foresaw its principal danger, and they did all which they could to provide against it. They erected a *Supreme Court*, a preëminent judicial tribunal, which is empowered to decide causes between State and State, and between any State and the Federal Government. And on many small, and on some important, matters, this Court has worked very well;

it has given able, if not always satisfactory, judgments on
various points of State controversy; it has provided a tolerably
fair umpire, and has thus prevented many small *quæstiunculæ* from growing into grave questions. It was excellent
upon minor points; it has been useless upon the greatest.
When, as recently, great passions have been aroused, great
interests at stake, great issues clearly drawn out, a reference
to the Supreme Court has not even been contemplated. No
judicial establishment could, indeed, be useful in an extra-
judicial matter; no law decide what is beyond the competence
of law; no supplementary provision, however ingenious, cure
the essential and inseparable defects of a Federal Union.

The steadily augmenting power of the lower orders in
America has naturally augmented the dangers of their Federal
Union. In almost all the States there was, at the time the
Constitution of the Union was originally framed, a property
qualification, in some States a high one, requisite for the
possession of the most popular form of suffrage. Almost all
these qualifications have now been swept away, and a dead
level of universal suffrage runs, more or less, over the whole
length of the United States. The external consequences, as
we all know, have not been beneficial: the foreign policy of
the Union has been a perplexing difficulty to European nations, and especially to England, for many years. Nor have the
internal consequences been better. The most enthusiastic advocates of a democratic government will admit that it is both
an impulsive and a contentious government. Its special characteristic is, that it places the entire control over the political
action of the whole State in the hands of the common labourers, who are of all classes the least instructed—of all the
most aggressive—of all the most likely to be influenced by
local animosity—of all the most likely to exaggerate every
momentary sentiment—of all the least likely to be capable of
a considerable toleration for the constant oppositions of opinion, the not unfrequent differences of interest, and the occasional unreasonableness of other States. In democracies,
local feuds are commonly more lasting and more bitter than
in States of other kinds; and those enmities commonly become more bitter in proportion to the greater nearness of
relation, the greater closeness of political connexion, and the
greater contrast of disposition, temper, and internal circumstances. What intensity of bitterness was then to be anticipated in a so-called Union, in which two distinct sets of

democracies—the Southern and the Northern, the slave-holding and the non-slave-holding—have been for many years augmenting in contrast to, and increasing in antipathy to, one another! The existing crisis is only the natural consequence, the inevitable development, of a long antagonism between these two species of Republics, in both of which the most intolerant members are absolute rulers, and each of which presented characteristics which the hidden instincts of the other, even more than its conscious opinion, regarded first as irritating and then as dangerous. The progress of democracy has affected not only the State Government, but the Federal Government. The House of Representatives in the latter is elected by the same persons who choose the most popular branch of the legislature in the former. As the State Governments have become more democratic, the Federal Government has inevitably become more so likewise. To this gradual corruption of the American democracy it is principally owing that Europe at large, and England especially, have not grieved much at the close proximity of its probable fall, but perhaps rejoiced at the prospect of some marked change from a policy which was so inconvenient to its neighbours, which must be attended to because its range was so wide, and the physical force under its direction was so large, but of which the events were mean, the actors base, and the working inexplicable. A low vulgarity, indefinable but undeniable, has deeply displeased the cultivated mind of Europe; and the American Union will fall, if it does fall, little regretted even by those whose race is akin, whose language is identical, whose weightiest opinions are on most subjects the same as theirs. The unpleasantness of *mob* government has never before been exemplified so conspicuously, for it never before has worked upon so large a scene.

These latter truths are very familiar. The evils of democracy and the dangers of democracy are great commonplaces in our speculation, though also formidable perils in our practice. But it is not commonplace to observe, that the existing crisis in America has been intensified almost as much by the precautions which the original founders of the Constitution took to ward off what they well knew to be the characteristic evils of democracy, as by those evils themselves. We have been so much accustomed to hear the "United States" extolled as the special land of democratic liberty, to hear their Constitution praised as the unmixed embodiment of uncon-

trolled popular power,—that we have forgotten how many restrictive provisions that Constitution contains, and how anxiously its framers endeavoured to provide against the special
defects of a purely popular polity.

It is not too much to say that a valuable addition to the
accumulations of Conservative oratory might be extracted
from the debates of the Convention which framed the American revolution. The two objects which its most intelligent
framers were mainly bent on attaining, were, security against
the momentary caprice of a purely numerical majority, and
some effective provision for the maintenance of a strong executive. What would Mr Bright say to the following speech of
Mr Morris, not by any means the most conservative member
of the Convention?

"The two branches, so equally poised, cannot have their
due weight. It is confessed, on all hands, that the second
branch ought to be a check on the first; for without its having this effect it is perfectly useless. The first branch, originating from the people, will ever be subject to *precipitancy*,
changeability, and *excess*. Experience evinces the truth of
this remark without having recourse to reading. This can only
be checked by *ability* and *virtue* in the second branch. On
your present system, can you suppose that one branch will
possess it more than the other? The second branch ought to
be composed of men of great and established property—*an
aristocracy*; men who from pride will support consistency and
permanency; and to make them completely independent, they
must be chosen *for life*, or they will be a useless body. Such
an aristocratic body will keep down the turbulency of democracy. But if you elect them for a shorter period, they will be
only a name, and we had better be without them. Thus constituted, I hope they will show us the weight of aristocracy.

"History proves, I admit, that the men of large property
will uniformly endeavour to establish tyranny. How, then,
shall we ward off this evil? Give them the second branch,
and you secure their weight for the *public good*. They become responsible for their conduct, and this lust of power will
ever be checked by the democratic branch, and thus form a
stability in your Government. But if we continue changing our
measures by the breath of democracy, who will confide in our
engagements? who will trust us? Ask any person whether he
reposes any confidence in the Government of Congress, or
that of the State of Pennsylvania; he will readily answer you,

no. Ask him the reason; and he will tell you it is because he has no confidence in their stability.

"You intend also that the second branch shall be incapable of holding any office in the general Government. It is a dangerous expedient. They ought to have every inducement to be interested in your Government. Deprive them of this right, and they will become inattentive to your welfare. The wealthy will ever exist; and you never can be safe unless you gratify them as a body, in the pursuit of honour and profit. Prevent them by positive institutions, and they will proceed in some left-handed way. A son may want a place—you mean to prevent him from promotion. They are not to be paid for their services—they will in some way pay themselves; nor is it in your power to prevent it. It is good policy that men of property be collected in one body, to give them one common influence in your Government. Let vacancies be filled up, as they happen, by the executive. Besides, it is of little consequence, on this plan, whether the States are equally represented or not. If the State Governments have the division of many of the loaves and fishes, and the general Government few, it cannot exist. This Senate would be one of the *baubles* of the general Government. If you choose them for *seven* years, whether chosen by the people or the States,— whether by equal suffrage or in any other proportion,—how will they be a check? They will still have local and State prejudices. A government by compact is no government at all. You may as well go back to your Congressional Federal Government, where, in the character of ambassadors, they may form treaties for each State. I avow myself the advocate of a strong Government."

This speech, striking as it is, is only a single specimen, and not, in several respects, the most striking of many which might be cited. The predominant feeling of the predominant party in the Convention is clearly expressed in the singularly complicated provisions of the Constitution which they framed. Almost every clause of it bears witness to the anxiety of its composers for an efficient executive, and for an adequate guard against momentary popular feeling.

Unfortunately they either had not at their disposal, or did not avail themselves of, the only effectual instruments for either purpose. There is but one sufficient expedient against the tyranny of the lower orders, and that is to place the predominant (though not necessarily the exclusive) power in the hands of the higher orders. There must be some effectual *sovereign* authority in every government. In England, for example, the sovereign authority is the diffused respectable higher middle-class, which, on the whole, is predominant in the House of Commons, and in the constituencies which return it. Whatever this class emphatically wills, is immediately enacted. It hears representations from the great mass of the orders which are below, it hears other and better-expressed representations from the higher classes, which are above it. But it uses these only as materials by which to form a better judgment. If the House of Commons distinctly expresses an emphatic opinion, no other body or person or functionary hopes to oppose it, or dreams of doing so. Our security against tyranny is the reasonableness, the respectable cultivation, the business-like moderation of this governing class itself; if that class did not possess those qualities, the rest of the community would be always in danger, and very frequently be oppressed.

The framers of the American Constitution chose a very different expedient. They placed the predominant power in the hands of the numerical majority of the population, and hoped to restrain and balance it by paper checks and constitutional stratagems. At the present time, almost every one of their ingenious devices has aggravated the calamities of their descendants.

The mode in which the President of the United States is chosen is the most complicated which could well be imagined. A reader of the Constitution, uninformed as to the circumstances of its origin and the intentions of its framers, would imagine that complexity had sometimes been chosen as such, and for its own sake. Each, however, of these singular details was introduced with a very definite object.

"Each State," it is provided, "shall appoint, in such manner as the legislature thereof may direct, a number of electors equal to the whole number of senators and representatives to which the State may be entitled in the Congress; but no senator or representative, or person holding an office of trust or profit under the United States, shall be appointed an elector.

"The electors shall meet in their respective States, and vote by ballot for two persons, of whom one at least shall not be an inhabitant of the same State with themselves. And they shall make a list of all the persons voted for, and of the

number of votes for each: which list they shall sign and cer-
tify, and transmit, sealed, to the seat of the Government of
the United States, directed to the President of the Senate.
The President of the Senate shall, in the presence of the
Senate and House of Representatives, open all the certificates; and the votes shall then be counted. The person having the greatest number of votes shall be the President, if
such number be a majority of the whole number of electors
appointed; and if there be more than one who have such
majority, and have an equal number of votes, then the House
of Representatives shall immediately choose by ballot one of
them for President; and if no person have a majority, then,
from the five highest on the list, the said House shall in like
manner choose the President. But in choosing the President
the votes shall be taken by States, the representation from
each State having one vote; a quorum for this purpose shall
consist of a member or members from two-thirds of the States,
and a majority of all the States shall be necessary to a choice.
In every case, after the choice of the President, the person
having the greatest number of votes of the electors shall be
the Vice-president. But if there should remain two or more
who have equal votes, the Senate shall choose from them by
ballot the Vice-president.

"The Congress may determine the time of choosing the
electors, and the day on which they shall give their votes:
which day shall be the same throughout the United States."

"In pursuance of the authority given by the latter clause,"
says Mr Justice Story, "Congress in 1792 passed an act, declaring that the electors shall be appointed in each State
within thirty-four days preceding the first Wednesday in
December, in every fourth year succeeding the last election
of President, according to the apportionment of representatives and senators then existing. The electors chosen are required to meet and give their votes on the first said Wednesday of December, in every fourth year succeeding the last
election of President, according to the apportionment of representatives and senators then existing. The electors chosen
are required to meet and give their votes on the said first
Wednesday of December, at such place in each State as shall
be directed by the legislature thereof. They are then to make
and sign three certificates of all the votes by them given, and
to seal up the same, certifying on each that a list of the votes
of such State for President and Vice-president is contained

therein; and shall appoint a person to take charge of and
deliver one of the same certificates to the President of the
Senate at the seat of Government, before the first Wednesday of January then next ensuing; another of the certificates
is to be forwarded forthwith by the post-office to the President of the Senate at the seat of Government; and the third
is to be delivered to the judge of the district in which the
electors assembled. Other auxiliary provisions are made by
the same act for the due transmission and preservation of
the electoral votes, and authenticating the appointment of
the electors. The President's term of office is also declared to
commence on the fourth day of March next succeeding the
day on which the votes of the electors shall be given."

The details of these arrangements are involved, but their
purpose was simple. The framers wished the President to be
chosen, not by the primary electors, but by a body of secondary electors, whom the primary were to choose, because
they thought that these *chosen choosers* would presumably be
persons especially likely to make a good choice. They likewise
intended that an absolute majority (a majority, that is, of
more than one-half of the total number) should be requisite
for a valid election; and if such majority could not be procured, that the House of Representatives, voting by States,
should make the choice (in which case an absolute majority
of all the *States* were likewise to be necessary); and lastly,
they wished that an interval of many months—from November in one year to March in the next—should be secured for
the safe transaction of the entire election.

Every part of this well-studied arrangement has produced
most unanticipated results, and none more so than the last
part. Nothing could be more reasonable than the regulation
that a long interval should be provided for the whole complicated election; since, if the choice unexpectedly lapsed to
the House of Representatives, much delay and consideration
would obviously be necessary. But the consequences have
been disastrous.

"At the outset of the quarrel," observes a recent writer,
"the Constitution occasioned a needless danger. The South
threatened to secede because Mr Lincoln had been elected
President. Under almost any other free Constitution which
has ever existed, and certainly under every good one, the
executive authority, whose function it was to oppose secession, would have been placed exclusively in the hands of

those who were desirous so to oppose it. At an instant of
violent irritation, the dissentient minority were anxious to
break loose from the control of the majority. The majority
were at that time, whatever may be the case now, by no
means fanatical, or irritated, or overbearing. They wished to
preserve the Union, and under a well-framed Constitution
they would have had the power of using the force of the State
to preserve the State. But not so under the American. An
artificial arrangement prolongs the reign of each President
many months after the election of his successor. In consequence, the executive authority was, during a considerable
and critical interval, in the hands of those who by birth,
habit, and sympathy were leagued with the dissentient minority. Mr Buchanan and his ministers had always been attached
to the party of the South, and were the last persons to act
decisively against it. It is the opinion of many well-informed
persons that there was a sufficient Unionist party in several
of the seceding States to have prevented the present movement there, if the Federal Government had acted with vigour
and celerity. And, whether this be so or not, it remains a
singular defect in the working of the American Constitution,
that it gave power at the decisive moment to those least likely
to use that power well,—that just when a revolt was impending, it placed the whole executive influence and the whole
military force in the unfettered hands of the political associates of the revolters."

It is now known that the Southern officials purposely distributed the fleet of the Union in distant countries, placed
stores of artillery where Southern rebels could easily take
them, purposely disorganised the Federal army. Nothing else
could be anticipated from an arrangement which placed the
preparations for maintaining the Union in the exclusive control of the persons desirous to break the Union.

The scheme, too, of a double election has failed of its intended effect, but has produced grave effects which were not
intended. The same writer observes:

"Nor does the accession of Mr Lincoln place the executive
power precisely where we should wish to see it. At a crisis
such as America has never before seen, and as it is not, perhaps, probable she will see again, the executive authority
should be in the hands of one of the most tried, trusted, and
experienced statesmen of the nation. Mr Lincoln is a nearly
unknown man, who has been but little heard of, who has

had little experience, who may have nerve and judgment, or
may not have them, whose character, both moral and intellectual, is an unknown quantity, who must, from his previous
life and defective education, be wanting in the liberal ac-
quirements and mental training which are principal elements
of an enlarged statesmanship. Nor is it true to say that the
American *people* are to blame for this—that they chose Mr
Lincoln, and must endure the pernicious results. The *Constitution* is as much to blame as the people, probably even
more so. The framers were wisely and warmly attached to
the principles of liberty, and, like all such persons, were extremely anxious to guard against momentary gusts of popular
opinion. They were especially desirous that the President to
whom they were intrusting vast power should be the representative, not of a small section of the community, but of a
really predominant part of it. They not only established a
system of double election, in the hope that the 'electoral
college' (of which the electors were chosen by the primary
electors in each State) would exercise a real discretion in the
choice of President, and be some check on popular ignorance
and low violence, but they likewise provided that an absolute
majority of that 'electoral college' (a majority, that is, greater
than one-half of the whole) should give their votes for the
elected candidate. The effect has been painfully different
from the design. In reality, the 'electoral college' exercises no
choice; every member of it is selected by the primitive constituency *because* he will vote for a certain presidential candidate (for Mr Lincoln or Mr Douglas, and so on), and he
does nothing but vote accordingly. The provision requiring
the consent of an absolute majority has had a still worse effect; it has not been futile, for it has been pernicious. It has
made it very difficult to secure *any* election."[3]

If every candidate stood who wished, and every elector
voted for whom he pleased, there would be no election at all.
Each little faction would vote for its own particular favourite,
and no one would obtain the votes of half the whole nation.
A very complicated apparatus of preliminary meetings, called
caucuses, is therefore resorted to, and the working of these is
singularly disastrous.

Every man of any mark in the whole nation has many
enemies, some private, some public; he is probably the head

[3] Economist, June 1, 1861.

of some section or minor party, and that minor party has its own antagonists, its special opponents, who would dislike more than any thing else that its head should on a sudden become the head of the State. Every statesman who has been long tried in public life must have had to alienate many friends, to irritate many applicants by necessary refusals, to say many things which are rankling in many bosoms. Every great man creates his own opposition; and no great man, therefore, will ever be President of the United States, except in the rarest and most exceptional cases. The object of "President makers" is to find a candidate who will conciliate the greatest number, not the person for whom there is *most* to be said, but the person against whom there is *least* to be said. In the English State, there is no great office filled in at all the same way; but in the English Church there is. "Depend on it," said a shrewd banker, not remarkable for theological zeal or scholastic learning, "I would have been Archbishop of Canterbury, if I had been in the Church. Some quiet, tame sort of man is always chosen; and I never *give offence to any one.*" If he did not, he might have been President of the United States. The mode in which all conspicuous merit is gradually eliminated from the list of candidates was well illustrated at the election of Mr Pierce.

"The candidates on the democratic side were no less than eight: General Cass, Mr Buchanan, Mr Douglas, Mr Marcy, Mr Butler, Mr Houston, Mr Lane, and Mr Dickenson; all men 'prominently known to their party,' and the three first supported with great enthusiasm by large sections of that party throughout the Union.

"The Convention appointed by the democratic party in each State to decide which among these various candidates should be recommended for their votes at the election, assembled at Baltimore for their first meeting on the 1st of June 1852. On that day General Cass obtained the greatest number of votes at the first ballot, namely 116, out of the total of 288; but a number far below the requisite majority. A few specimens of the manner in which the votes fluctuated will not be without interest. On the ninth ballot the votes were—Cass, 112; Buchanan, 87; Douglas, 39; Marcy, 28; Butler, 1; Houston, 8; Lane, 13; Dickenson, 1. On the twenty-second ballot—Cass, 33; Douglas, 80; Butler, 24; Lane, 13; Buchanan, 101; Marcy, 25; Houston, 10; Dickenson, 1. On

the twenty-ninth ballot—Cass, 27. On the thirty-fifth ballot—
Cass, 131; Douglas, 52; Buchanan, 32.

"On this, the sixth day of the meeting (the proceedings
of and the scenes in which were fully and somewhat graphically described by the public press of both parties), a new
name appeared for the first time upon the lists—that of Mr
Pierce, of New Hampshire, a gentleman well known to his
friends as a lawyer of ability; also as having creditably fulfilled the duties of a member of the House of Representatives, and of the Senate of the United States; better known,
however, as having joined the army as a volunteer on the
breaking out of the Mexican War, and as having commanded
with distinction a brigade in that war, with the rank of General. It will, nevertheless, imply no disrespect towards Mr
Pierce, if I repeat what was the universal expression, according to the public prints, throughout the Union, that no individual in the United States could have been more surprised
at Mr Pierce's nomination for the exalted and responsible office of chief magistrate of the Republic than Mr Pierce himself. On the thirty-fifth ballot, the first in which Mr Pierce's
name appeared, he received 15 votes. On the forty-eighth, he
received only 55 votes; but on the forty-ninth, the numbers
voting for him were 283, out of the total of 288,—a vote which
5 more would have made unanimous.

"Mr Pierce was accordingly recommended to the democratic constituencies throughout the Union, and was elected
by a considerable majority over his Whig opponent; the numbers being, for Mr Pierce 1,504,471, and for General Scott
1,283,174."

What worse mode of electing a ruler could by possibility
have been selected? If the wit of man had been set to devise
a system specially calculated to bring to the head of affairs an
incompetent man at a pressing crisis, it could not have devised one more fit; probably it would not have devised one
as fit. It almost secures the rejection of tried and trained
genius, and almost insures the selection of untrained and unknown mediocrity.

Nor is this the only mode, or even the chief mode in which
the carefully considered provisions of the American Constitution have, in fact, deprived the American people of the guidance and government of great statesmen, just when these were
most required. It is not too much to say that, under the American Constitution, there was no *opportunity* for a great states-

man. As we have seen, he had no chance of being chosen President; the artificial clauses of the Constitution, and the natural principles of human nature, have combined to prevent that. Nor is it worth a great man's while to be a President's minister. This is not because such a minister would be in apparent subordination to the President, who would probably be an inferior man to him,—for able men are continually ready to fill subordinate posts under constitutional monarchs, who are usually very inferior men, and even under colonial governors, who are rather inferior men,—but because a President's minister has no parliamentary career. As we know, the first member of the Crown is with us the first man in Parliament, and is the ruler of the English nation. In those English colonies which possess popular constitutions, the first minister is the most powerful man in the State,—far more powerful than the so-called governor. He is so because he is the accepted leader of the colonial Parliament. In consequence, whenever the English nation, or a free English colony, is in peril, the first man in England, or in the colony, at least the most trusted man, is raised at once to the most powerful place in the nation. On the Continent of Europe, the advantage of this insensible machinery is just beginning to be understood. Count Cavour well knew and thoroughly showed how far the power of a parliamentary Premier, supported by a willing and confiding parliament, is superior to all other political powers, whether in despotic governments or in free. The American Constitution, however, expressly prohibits the possibility of such a position. It enacts, "That no person holding any office under the United States shall be a member of either House during his continuance in office." In consequence, the position of a great parliamentary member who is responsible more or less for the due performance of his own high administrative functions, and also of all lesser ones, is in America an illegal one. If a politician has executive authority, he cannot enter Parliament; if he is in Parliament, he cannot possess executive authority. No man of great talents and high ambition has therefore under the Constitution of the United States a proper sphere for those talents, or a suitable vista for that ambition. He cannot hope to be President, for the President is *ex officio* a poor creature; he cannot hope to be, *mutatis mutandis*, an English Premier, to be a Sir R. Peel, or a Count Cavour, for the American law has

declared that in the United States there shall be no similar
person.

It appears that the Constitution-makers of North America
were not unnaturally misled by the political philosophy of
their day. It was laid down first that the legislative authority
and the executive authority *ought* to be perfectly distinct; and
secondly that in the English Constitution those authorities
were so distinct. Both dogmas had slid into accepted axioms,
and no one was bold enough to contest them. At that time no
speculative politician perfectly comprehended that the essence of the English Constitution resided in the English
Cabinet; that so far from the executive power being entirely
distinct from the legislative power, the primary motive force,
the supreme regulator of every thing, was precisely the same
in both. A select committee of the legislature chosen by the
legislature is the highest administrative body, and exercises
all the powers of the sovereign executive that are tolerated by
the law. The advantage of this arrangement, though contrary
to a very old philosophical theory, is very great. The whole
State will never work in harmony and in vigour while by possibility its two great powers—the power of legislating and the
power of acting—can be declared in opposition to one another;
and if they are independent, they will very often be in open
antagonism, and be always in dread of it when they are not so.
No government, it may be safely said, can be so strong as it
should be when the enacting legislature and the acting executive are not subjected to a *single* effectual control.

The framers of the American Constitution did not perceive
this cardinal maxim. The admitted theory of that day was
that the English Constitution was one of "checks and bal-
ances;" and the Americans, who were very willing to take it as
their model (the monarchical part excepted), hoped to balance their strong independent legislature by a strong independent executive. They hoped, too, to prevent the introduction into America of that parliamentary corruption—that
bribery of popular representatives by money and patronage,
which filled so large a space in the thoughts of politicians of
the last century, and so large a space in the lives of some of
them. But though their intentions were excellent and their
reasons plausible, the effect of their regulations has been
pernicious. By keeping the two careers of legislation and of
administration distinct, they have rendered the life of a high
politician, of a great statesman, aspiring to improve the laws

and to regulate the policy of a great country, with them an impossibility. They have divided the greatest department of practical life into two halves, and neither of them is worth a man's having.

We see the effect. There is no body of respected statesmen in America at this moment of their extreme need. It is not a fault that they have no great genius at their head. The few marvellous statesmen of the world are of necessity rare, and are not manufactured to order even by the bidding of an awful crisis. But it *is* a fault that they have not one or more possible parliamentary cabinets—several sets of trained men, with considerable abilities and known character, whose policy is decided, whose worth is tried, who have cast in their lot for years with certain ideas, whose names are respected in every household through Europe. In consequence of the unfortunate caution of their Constitution-makers, America has no such men; and Italy has them, or will soon have them; but after a political experience of seventy years the United States have none. They have existed during two generations as a democracy without ideals; and are likely to die now a democracy without champions.

It is, however, only fair to observe, that the American Constitution has one great excellence at this moment, not, indeed, as compared with the English Constitution, but as compared with that degraded imitation of it which exists, for example, in our Australian Colonies. In those governments the parliament is wholly unfit to choose an executive; it has not patriotism enough to give a decent stability to the government; there are "ministerial crises" once a week, and actual changes of administration once a month. The suffrage has been lowered to such a point among the refuse population of the gold colonies, that representative government is there a very dubious blessing, if not a certain and absolute curse. If such a parliament had met in such a crisis as the American Congress lately had to face, it is both possible and probable that no stable administration would have been formed at all. Every possible ministry would have been tried in succession; and every one would have been rejected in succession. We might have witnessed debates as aimless, as absurd, as unpractical in their tenor, as those of certain French Parliaments, without the culture and refinement which made the latter more tolerable, though it could not make them more wise.

The American Constitution has at least the merit of preventing this last extreme of political degradation. Having placed Mr Lincoln, though certainly an unknown and probably an inferior man, in power, it has at least prevented his being superseded, or its being proposed that he should be superseded, by some other equally unknown and equally inferior man. The American Constitution probably necessitated the choice of some second-rate person for the first position at an awful crisis; but it has at least settled once for all who he should be; it has compelled a conclusive choice, which an Australian Constitution would not have done.

But with this single item the aid which the American Constitution has given to Mr Lincoln in his presidency begins and ends. It has put him there, and it has kept him there; but it has done no more. He has had to carry on the government with new subordinates; for at every change of the American President, all the officials, from the cabinet minister to the petty post-master, are changed. So far from giving him any special powers suitable to a civil war; it authoritatively declares that the right of the people to keep and bear arms shall not be infringed; that it shall be illegal "to abridge the freedom of speech or *of the press*, or the right of the people peaceably to assemble or to petition for a redress of grievance." It does not permit the punishment of any person, or the confiscation of his property, except after satisfactory proof before a civil tribunal. Even now, at this early state of the civil contest, martial law has been declared in Missouri and *habeus corpus* suspended in Baltimore; the property (slave-property, certainly, but still legal property in America) of Secessionists has been confiscated; the liberty of speech is almost at an end; the liberty of the press has ceased to exist. These last are indeed infractions of the law, not by the administration, but by the mob; it is they, and not Mr Lincoln, who have burnt printers' offices and proscribed dissentient individuals. But Mr Lincoln and his ministers have broken, and have been obliged to break, the law on almost innumerable occasions, because that law provided no suitable procedure for the extreme contingency of a great civil war. The framers of the Constitution shrank naturally, and perhaps not unwisely, from providing against such an incalculable peril. They may have not unreasonably feared that they might augment the probability of such a calamity by recognising its possibility, even in order to provide against it. But their omission must have been grievously lamented by those who have had now to violate the law, for it may hereafter expose them to imminent danger. The English Parliament, in such an emergency, could and would condone every well-intentioned and beneficial irregularity by an act of indemnity. But the American Congress cannot do so. Its powers are limited powers, defined by the letter of a document; and in that document there is nothing to authorise a bill of indemnity—nor, indeed, could there be consistently with the very nature of it. By its fundamental conception, the States should relinquish certain special powers to the Federal Government, and *those powers only*; if the Federal Government could pass a bill of indemnity for infractions of the law, it would have absolute power; it would be a generally sovereign body, like the King, Lords, and Commons of England; it would have over the States of America, and over their people, not a defined and limited superiority, but an uncontrolled and unlimited one. Mr Lincoln is, therefore, in peril from the inseparable accidents of the office he holds; he is a President under a Constitution which could give him only defined powers, and he is in a position requiring indefinite powers; he has therefore had to take his life in his hand, and violate the law. At present, popular opinion approves of what he has done; but the Republican party, of which he is the head, has many bitter enemies. If his announced aim should be successful, and he should reëstablish the Union, those enemies will be reinforced by the whole constitutional power of the whole South, bitterly hostile to their vanquisher, bitterly aggrieved at the means by which they have been vanquished. Against such a coalition of enemies it will be difficult to defend the illegal, the arbitrary, the impeachable acts (for such, in the eye of American law, they are) of which Mr Lincoln has been guilty. We doubt much whether he can succeed in compelling the South to return to the Union; but if he should, he will have succeeded *at his peril*.

It is easy to sum up the results of this long discussion. We cannot regard the American Constitution with the deference and the admiration with which all Americans used to regard it, and with which many Northern Americans still regard it. We admit that it has been beneficial to the American Republic as a bond of union; it has prevented war, it has fostered commerce, it has made them a nation to be *counted with*. But it always contained the seeds of disunion. There is no chance of saving such a polity when many States wish to separate from it, for the simple reason that its whole action essentially depends on the voluntary union of all, or of nearly all, the States. So far from its being wonderful that the present rupture has happened now, it is rather wonderful that it did not happen long since. It is rather surprising that a Government, which in practice, though not in theory, is dependent on the precarious consent of many distinct bodies, should have lasted so long, than that it should break asunder now. We see, too, that the American Constitution was, in its very essence, framed upon an erroneous principle. Its wise founders wished to guard against the characteristic evils of democracy; but they relied for this purpose upon ingenious devices and superficial subtilties. They left the essence of the government unchanged; they left the sovereign people, sovereign still. As has been shown in detail, the effect has been calamitous. Their ingenuities have produced painful evils, and aggravated great dangers; but they have failed of their intended purpose,—they have neither refined the polity, nor restrained the people.

LETTERS ON THE FRENCH
COUP D'ÉTAT OF 1851*

(1852)

Charles Louis Napoleon was born in Paris in 1808, the third son of Louis, brother of Napoleon, and of Hortense de Beauharnais. One of his brothers died young, the other died without issue. After the final abdication of Napoleon I, all Bonapartes had been banished from France, and the boy was brought up in Germany by his mother, who was separated from her husband. In 1832, upon the death of the duke of Reichstadt, the only son of Napoleon I, Louis Napoleon became heir to the Napoleonic tradition and had already developed a romantic Napoleonic liberalism. In 1836 he plotted in Strasbourg in an attempt to gain the throne but was arrested and forced onto a ship which took him to New York; in 1840 he was again arrested for an attempted insurrection in Boulogne, sentenced to life imprisonment, and placed in the fortress of Ham. In 1846 he escaped to England. After the revolution of 1848 he was elected to the National Assembly and in December of the same year to the presidency of the Republic. His ultimate goal was the re-establishment of the Napoleonic empire, and he made careful preparations for it during the next few years. Profiting from the growing discredit of parliamentary government, he staged the coup d'état of 1851. On December 2 he ordered the arrest of 20,000 of his opponents, dissolved the Assembly, and appealed to the people for virtually dictatorial powers. After a plebiscite on December 20 he was made autocratic President for the next ten years, and a year later another plebiscite made him Napoleon III, Emperor of the French. (Napoleon's only son, who never reigned, was consid-

* Note on Letters: These letters were addressed to the Editor of the *Inquirer* and were published in that journal during 1852. They all appeared in Volume IX, 1852. Letter I is found on page 19 (January 10); Letter II on pages 34–35 (January 17); Letter III on pages 51–52 (January 24); Letter IV on pages 67–68 (January 31); Letter V on pages 83–84 (February 7); Letter VI on page 99 (February 14); Letter VII on pages 145–47 (March 6). All except Letter V are dated from Paris.

ered to have been Napoleon II.) The new emperor instituted an authoritarian régime: the press was censored; the legislature was deprived of the right to amend or initiate laws. These repressive measures were counterbalanced by the encouragement of economic prosperity and public works. Napoleon III strove to enhance the prestige of France by successes in foreign affairs. France participated in the Crimean War, 1854–56; in 1859 she assisted Piedmont in the war against Austria, which was a decisive step in Italy's struggle for independence, and France was able to annex Nice and Savoy. A treaty with Britain in 1860 provided for free trade. Napoleon's ambitions were growing, and he envisaged a Catholic empire in the New World, guided by the French.

For this reason he pressed the Mexican expedition of 1863–67, but it ended in complete failure, as did his attempt to intervene in the Polish insurrection of 1863. His Italian policy, moreover, had alienated the Catholics in France, and he was soon faced by a strengthened Prussia. There was a growing opposition to his despotism at home; through the growth of industry and commerce the bourgeoisie had become increasingly powerful and the working classes less and less willing to submit to his repressive measures. A third party came into being from the ranks of the government deputies, and Napoleon was obliged to liberalise his régime through parliamentary reform and through concessions with respect to the liberty of the press and public meetings. In 1870 Napoleon gave up most of his power to a ministry under the liberal leader Emile Ollivier but still sought to maintain his rule by an external success and declared war on Prussia in July. On September 2 he was forced to capitulate at Sedan, and the fall of the empire was proclaimed in Paris. Napoleon III was released in March 1871, and settled with his wife and son in England, at Chislehurst, where he died in 1873.

LETTER 1.

THE DICTATORSHIP.

Paris, 8th January, 1852.

Sir,—You have asked me to tell you what I think of French affairs. I shall be pleased to do so; but I ought perhaps to begin by cautioning you against believing, or too much heeding, what I say. However, I do not imagine that I need do so; for with your experience of the public journals, you will be quite aware that it is not difficult to be an "occasional correspondent". Have your boots polished in a blacking-shop, and call the interesting officiator an "intelligent *ouvrier*"; be shaved, and cite the *coiffeur* as "a person in rather a superior station"; call your best acquaintance "a well-informed person," and all others "persons whom I have found to be occasionally not in error," and—abroad, at least—you will soon have matter for a newspaper letter. I should quite deceive you if I professed to have made these profound researches; nor, like Sir Francis Head, "do I no longer know where I am," because the French President has asked me to accompany him in his ride. My perception of personal locality has not as yet been so tried. I only know what a person who is in a foreign country during an important political catastrophe cannot avoid knowing, what he runs against, what is beaten into him, what he can hardly help hearing, seeing, and reflecting.

That Louis Napoleon has gone to Notre-Dame to return thanks to God for the seven millions and odd suffrages of the French people—that he has taken up his abode at the Tuileries, and that he has had new napoleons coined in his name—that he has broken up the trees of liberty for firewood —that he has erased, or is erasing (for they are many), *Liberté, Egalité*, and *Fraternité*, from the National buildings,— all these things are so easy and so un-English, that I am pretty sure, with you, they will be thought signs of pompous impotence, and I suppose many people will be inclined to believe the best comment to be the one which I heard—"*Mon dieu, il a sauvé la France: la rue du Coq s'appelle maintenant la rue de l'Aigle!*"[1]

I am inclined, however, to imagine that this idea would be utterly erroneous; that, on the contrary, the President is just now, at least, really strong and really popular; that the act of 2nd December did succeed and is succeeding; that many, that most, of the inferior people do really and sincerely pray *Domine Salvum fac Napoleonem.*

In what I have seen of the comments of the English press upon recent events here, two things are not quite enough kept apart—I mean the temporary dictatorship of Louis Napoleon to meet and cope with the expected crisis of '52, and the continuance of that dictatorship hereafter,—the new, or as it is called, the *Bas*-Empire—in a word, the coming Constitution and questionable political machinery with which

[1] The general reader may not before have read, that the Rue du Coq l'Honoré is an old and well-known street in Paris, and that notwithstanding the substitution of the eagle for cock as a military emblem, there is no thought of changing its name.

"the nephew of my uncle" is now proposing to endow France. Of course, in reality these two things *are* separate. It is one thing to hold that a military rule is required to meet an urgent and temporary difficulty: another, to advocate the continuance of such a system, when so critical a necessity no longer exists.

It seems to me, or would seem, if I did not know that I was contradicted both by much English writing and opinion, and also by many most competent judges here, that the first point, the temporary dictatorship, is a tolerably clear case; that it is not to be complicated with the perplexing inquiry what form of government will permanently suit the French people; that the President was, under the actual facts of the case, quite justified in assuming the responsibility, though of course I allow that responsibility to be tremendous. My reasons for so believing I shall in this letter endeavour to explain, except that I shall not, I fancy, have room to say much on the moral defensibility or indefensibility of the *coup d'état*; nor do I imagine that you want from me any ethical speculation—that is manufactured in Printing-house Square; but I shall give the best account I can of the matter-of-fact consequences and antecedents of the New Revolution, of which, in some sense, a resident in France may feel without presumption that he knows something hardly so well known to those at home.

The political justification of Louis Napoleon is, as I apprehend, to be found in the state of the public mind which immediately preceded the *coup d'état*. It is very rarely that a country expects a revolution at a given time; indeed, it is perhaps not common for ordinary persons in any country to anticipate a revolution at all; though profound people may speculate, the mass will ever expect to-morrow to be as this day at least, if not more abundant. But once name the day, and all this is quite altered. As a general rule the very people who would be most likely to neglect general anticipation are exactly those most likely to exaggerate the proximate consequences of a certain impending event. At any rate, in France five weeks ago, the tradespeople talked of May, '52, as if it were the end of the world. Civilisation and Socialism might probably endure, but buying and selling would surely come to an end; in fact, they anticipated a worse era than February, '48, when trade was at a standstill so long that it has hardly yet recovered, and when the Government stocks fell 40 per cent. It is hardly to be imagined upon what petty details the dread of political dissolution at a fixed and not distant time will condescend to intrude itself. I was present when a huge *Flamande*, in appearance so intrepid that I respectfully pitied her husband, came to ask the character of a *bonne*. I was amazed to hear her say, "I hope the girl is strong, for when the revolution comes next May, and I have to turn off my helper, she will have enough to do". It seemed to me that a political apprehension must be pretty general, when it affected that most non-speculative of speculations, the *reckoning* of a housewife. With this feeling, everybody saved their money: who would spend in luxuries that which might so soon be necessary and invaluable! This economy made commerce—especially the peculiarly Parisian trade, which is almost wholly in articles that *can* be spared—worse and worse; the more depressed trade became, the more the traders feared, and the more they feared, the worse all trade inevitably grew.

I apprehend that this feeling extended very generally among all the classes who do not find or make a livelihood by literature or by politics. Among the clever people, who understood the subject, very likely the expectation was extremely different; but among the stupid ones who mind their business, and have a business to mind, there was a universal and excessive tremor. The only notion of '52 was "*on se battra dans la rue*". Their dread was especially of Socialism; they expected that the followers of M. Proudhon, who advisedly and expressly maintains "anarchy" to be the best form of Government, would attempt to carry out their theories in action, and that the division between the Legislative and Executive power would so cripple the party of order as to make their means of resistance for the moment feeble and difficult to use. The more sensible did not, I own, expect the annihilation of mankind: civilisation dies hard; the organised sense in all countries is strong; but they expected vaguely and crudely that the party which in '93 ruled for many months, and which in June, '48, fought so fanatically against the infant republic, would certainly make a desperate attack, —*might* for some time obtain the upper hand. Of course, it is now matter of mere argument whether the danger was real or unreal, and it is in some quarters rather the fashion to quiz the past fear, and to deny that any Socialists anywhere exist. In spite of the literary exertions of Proudhon and Louis Blanc, in spite of the prison quarrels of Blanqui and Barbès—

there are certainly found people who question whether anybody buys the books of the two former, or cares for the in-
carcerated dissensions of the two latter. But however this may
be, it is certain that two days after the *coup d'état* a mass of
persons thought it worth while to erect some dozen barricades, and among these, and superintending and directing
their every movement, there certainly were, for I saw them
myself, men whose physiognomy and accoutrements exactly
resembled the traditional Montagnard, sallow, stern, compressed, with much marked features, which expressed but
resisted suffering, and brooding one-ideaed thought, men who
from their youth upward had for ever imagined, like Jonah,
that they did well—immensely well—to be angry, men armed
to the teeth, and ready, like the soldiers of the first Republic,
to use their arms savagely and well in defence of theories
broached by a Robespierre, a Blanqui, or a Barbès, gloomy
fanatics, *over*-principled ruffians. I may perhaps be mistaken
in reading in their features the characters of such men, but I
know that when one of them disturbed my superintendence
of barricade-making with a stern *allez vous-en*, it was not too
slowly that I departed, for I *felt* that he would rather shoot
me than not. Having seen these people, I conceive that they
exist. But supposing that they were all simply fabulous, it
would not less be certain that they were *believed* to be, and
to be active; nor would it impair the fact that the quiet classes
awaited their onslaught in morbid apprehension, with miserable and craven, and I fear we ought to say, *commercial*
disquietude.

You will not be misled by any high-flown speculations
about liberty or equality. You will, I imagine, concede to me
that the first duty of a Government is to ensure the security
of that industry which is the condition of social life and
civilised cultivation; that especially in so excitable a country
as France it is necessary that the dangerous classes should be
saved from the strong temptation of long idleness; and that
no danger could be more formidable than six months' beggary
among the revolutionary *ouvriers*, immediately preceding the
exact period fixed by European as well as French opinion for
an apprehended convulsion. It is from this state of things,
whether by fair means or foul, that Louis Napoleon has delivered France. The effect was magical. Like people who
have nearly died because it was prophesied they would die at
a specified time, and instantly recovered when they found or

thought that the time was gone and past, so France, timorously anticipating the fated revolution, in a moment revived when she found or fancied that it was come and over. Commerce instantly improved; New Year's Day, when all the Boulevards are one continued fair, has not (as I am told) been for some years so gay and splendid; people began to buy, and consequently to sell; for though it is quite possible, or even probable, that new misfortunes and convulsions may be in store for the French people, yet no one can say when they will be, and to wait till revolutions be exhausted is but the best Parisian for our old acquaintance *Rusticus expectat.* Clever people may now prove that the dreaded peril was a simple chimera, but they can't deny that the fear of it was very real and painful, nor can they dispute that in a week after the *coup d'état* it had at once, and apparently for ever, passed away.

I fear it must be said that no legal or constitutional act could have given an equal confidence. What was wanted was the assurance of an audacious Government, which would stop at nothing, scruple at nothing, to secure its own power and the tranquillity of the country. That assurance all now have; a man who will in this manner dare to dissolve an assembly constitutionally his superiors, then prevent their meeting by armed force; so well and so sternly repress the first beginning of an outbreak, with so little misgiving assume and exercise sole power,—may have enormous other defects, but is certainly a bold ruler—most probably an unscrupulous one—little likely to flinch from any inferior trial.

Of Louis Napoleon, whose personal qualities are, for the moment, so important, I cannot now speak at length. But I may say that, with whatever other deficiencies he may have, he has one excellent advantage over other French statesmen —he has never been a professor, nor a journalist, nor a promising barrister, nor, by taste, a *littérateur.* He has not confused himself with history; he does not think in leading articles, in long speeches, or in agreeable essays. But he is capable of observing facts rightly, of reflecting on them simply, and acting on them discreetly. And his motto is Danton's, *De l'audace et toujours de l'audace,* and this you know, according to Bacon, in time of revolution, will carry a man far, perhaps even to ultimate victory, and that ever-future millennium, *"la consolidation de la France".*

But on these distant questions I must not touch. I have

endeavoured to show you what was the crisis, how strong the remedy, and what the need of a dictatorship. I hope to have convinced you that the first was imminent, the second effectual, and the last expedient.

I remain yours,

AMICUS.

LETTER II.

THE MORALITY OF THE COUP D'ÉTAT.

Paris, 15th January, 1852.

Sir,—I know quite well what will be said about, or in answer to, my last letter. It will be alleged that I think everything in France is to be postponed to the Parisian commerce —that a Constitution, Equality, Liberty, a Representative Government, are all to be set aside if they interfere even for a moment with the sale of *étrennes* or the manufacture of gimcracks.

I, as you know, hold no such opinions: it would not be necessary for me to undeceive you, who would, I rather hope, never suspect me of *that* sort of folly. But as St Athanasius aptly observes, "for the sake of the women who may be led astray, I will this very instant explain my sentiments".

Contrary to Sheridan's rule, I commence by a concession. I certainly admit, indeed I would, upon occasion, maintain, *bonbons* and bracelets to be things less important than common law and Constitutional action. A *coup d'état* would, I may allow, be mischievously supererogatory if it only promoted the enjoyment of what a lady in the highest circles is said to call "bigotry and virtue". But the real question is not to be so disposed of. The Parisian trade, the jewellery, the baubles, the silks, the luxuries, which the Exhibition showed us to be the characteristic industry of France, are very dust in the balance if weighed against the hands and arms which their manufacture employs—the industrial habits which their regular sale rewards—the hunger and idle weariness which the certain demand for them prevents. For this is the odd peculiarity of commercial civilisation. The life, the welfare, the existence of thousands depend on their being paid for doing what seems nothing when done. That gorgeous dandies should wear gorgeous studs—that pretty girls should be prettily dressed—that pleasant drawing-rooms should be pleasantly attired—may seem, to people of our age, sad trifling. But grave as we are, we must become graver still when we reflect on the horrid suffering which the sudden cessation of large luxurious consumption would certainly create, if we imagine such a city as Lyons to be, without warning, turned out of work, and the population feelingly told "to cry in the streets when no man regardeth".

The first duty of society is the preservation of society. By the sound work of old-fashioned generations—by the singular painstaking of the slumberers in churchyards—by dull care —by stupid industry, a certain social fabric somehow exists; people contrive to go out to their work, and to find work to employ them actually until the evening, body and soul are kept together, and this is what mankind have to show for their six thousand years of toil and trouble.

To keep up this system we must sacrifice everything. Parliaments, liberty, leading articles, essays, eloquence,—all are good, but they are secondary; at all hazards, and if we can, mankind must be kept alive. And observe, as time goes on, this fabric becomes a tenderer and a tenderer thing. Civilisation can't bivouac; dangers, hardships, sufferings, lightly borne by the coarse muscle of earlier times, are soon fatal to noble and cultivated organisation. Women in early ages are masculine, and, as a return match, the men of late years are becoming women. The strong apprehension of a Napoleonic invasion has, perhaps, just now caused more substantial misery in England than once the wars of the Roses.

To apply this "screed of doctrine" to the condition of France. I do not at all say that, but for the late *coup d'état*, French civilisation would certainly have soon come to a final end. *Some* people might have continued to take their meals. Even Socialism would hardly abolish *eau sucrée*. But I do assert that, according to the common belief of the common people, their common comforts were in considerable danger. The debasing torture of acute apprehension was eating into the crude pleasure of stupid lives. No man liked to take a long bill; no one could imagine to himself what was coming. Fear was paralysing life and labour, and as I said at length, in my last, fear, so intense, whether at first reasonable or unreasonable, will, ere long, invincibly justify itself. May, 1852, would, in all likelihood, have been an evil and bloody time, if

it had been preceded by six months' famine among the starv-
able classes.

At present all is changed. Six weeks ago society was living
from hand to mouth: now she feels sure of her next meal.
And this, in a dozen words, is the real case—the political excuse for Prince Louis Napoleon. You ask me, or I should not
do so, to say a word or two on the moral question and the
oath. You are aware how limited my means of doing so are.
I have forgotten Paley, and have never read the Casuists. But
it certainly does not seem to me proved or clear, that a man
who has sworn, even in the most solemn manner, to see another drown, is therefore quite bound, or even at liberty, to
stand placidly on the bank. What ethical philosopher has
demonstrated this? Coleridge said it was difficult to advance
a new error in morals,—yet this, I think, would be one: and
the keeping of oaths is peculiarly a point of mere science, for
Christianity, in terms at least, only forbids them all. And
supposing I am right, such certainly was the exact position of
Louis Napoleon. He saw society, I will not say dying or per-
ishing—for I hate unnecessarily to overstate my point—in danger of incurring extreme and perhaps lasting calamities,
likely not only to impair the happiness, but moreover to de-
base the character of the French nation, and these calamities
he could prevent. Now who has shown that ethics require of
him to have held his hand?

The severity with which the riot was put down on the first
Thursday in December has, I observe, produced an extreme
effect in England; and with our happy exemption from martial bloodshed, it must, of course, do so. But better one
émeute now than many in May, be it ever remembered.
There are things more demoralising than death, and among
these is the sickly-apprehensive suffering for long months of
an entire people.

Of course you understand that I am not holding up Louis
Napoleon as a complete standard either of ethical scrupulosity
or disinterested devotedness; veracity has never been the family failing—for the great Emperor was a still greater liar. And
Prince Louis has been long playing what, morality apart, is
the greatest political misfortune to any statesman—a visibly
selfish game. Very likely, too, the very high heroes of history—
a Washington, an Aristides, by Carlyle profanely called "favourites of Dryasdust," would have extricated the country
more easily, and perhaps more completely, from its scrape.

Their ennobling rectitude would have kept M. de Girardin consistent, and induced M. Thiers to vote for the Revision of the Constitution; and even though, as of old, the Mountain were deafer than the uncharmed adder, a sufficient number of self-seeking Conservatives might have been induced by perfect confidence in a perfect President, to mend a crotchety performance, that was visibly ruining, what the poet calls, "The ever-ought-to-be-conserved-thing," their country.

I remember reading, several years ago, an article in the *Westminster Review*, on the lamented Armand Carrel, in which the author, well known to be one of our most distinguished philosophers, took occasion to observe that what the French most wanted was "*un homme de caractère*". Everybody is aware—for all except myself know French quite perfectly—that this expression is not by any means equivalent to our common phrase, a "man of character," or "respectable individual," it does not at all refer to mere goodness: it is more like what we sometimes say of an eccentric country gentleman, "He is a character"; for it denotes a singular preponderance of peculiar qualities, an accomplished obstinacy, an inveterate fixedness of resolution and idea that enables him to get done what he undertakes. The Duke of Wellington is, "*par excellence, homme de caractère*"; Lord Palmerston rather so; Mr Cobden a little; Lord John Russell not at all. Now exactly this, beyond the immense majority of educated men, Louis Napoleon is, as a pointed writer describes him: "The President is a superior man, but his superiority is of the sort that is hidden under a dubious exterior: his life is entirely internal; his speech does not betray his inspiration; his gesture does not copy his audacity; his look does not reflect his ardour; his step does not reveal his resolution; his whole mental nature is in some sort repressed by his physical: he thinks and does not discuss; he decides and does not deliberate; he acts without agitation; he speaks, and assigns no reason; his best friends are unacquainted with him; he obtains their confidence, but never asks it". Also his whole nature is, and has been, absorbed in the task which he has undertaken. For many months, his habitual expression has been exactly that of a gambler who is playing for his highest and last stake; in society it is said to be the same—a general and diffusive politeness, but an ever-ready reflection and a constant reserve. His great qualities are rather peculiar. He is not, like his uncle, a creative genius, who will leave behind him social in-

stitutions such as those which nearly alone, in this changeful
country, seem to be always exempt from every change; he
will suggest little; he has hardly an organising mind; but he
will coolly estimate his own position and that of France; he
will observe all dangers and compute all chances. He can act
—he can be idle: he may work what is; he may administer the
country. Anyhow, *il fera son possible*, and you know, in the
nineteenth century, how much and how rare that is.

I see many people are advancing beautiful but untrue ethics about his private character. Thus I may quote as follows
from a very estimable writer: "On the 15th October, he re-
quested his passports and left Aremberg for London. In this
capital he remained from the end of 1838 to the month of
August, 1840. In these twenty months, instead of learning
to command armies and govern empires, his days and nights,
when not given to frivolous pleasures, were passed on the
turf, in the betting-room, or in clubs where high play and
desperate stakes roused the jaded energy of the *blasé* gambler."[2]

The notion of this gentleman clearly is, that a betting man
can't in nature be a good statesman; that horse-racing is prov-
identially opposed to political excellence; that "by an interesting illustration of the argument from design, we notice
an antithesis alike marvellous and inevitable," between turf
and tariffs. But, setting Paley for a moment apart, how is a
man, by circumstances excluded from military and political
life, and by birth from commercial pursuits, really and effectually to learn administration? Mr Kirwan imagines that he
should read all through Burke, common-place Tacitus, col-
late Cicero, and annotate Montesquieu. Yet take an analogous
case. Suppose a man, shut out from trading life, is to qualify
himself for the practical management of a counting-house. Do
you fancy he will do it "by a judicious study of the principles
of political economy," and by elaborately re-reading Adam
Smith and John Mill? He had better be at Newmarket, and
devote his *heures perdues* to the Oaks and the St Leger. He
may learn there what he will never acquire from literary
study—the instinctive habit of applied calculation, which is
essential to a merchant and extremely useful to a statesman.
Where, too, did Sir Robert Walpole learn business, or Charles
Fox, or anybody in the eighteenth century? And after all, M.

[2] A. V. Kirwan, Esq., Barrister-at-Law, in *Fraser's Magazine* of
January, 1852.

Michel de Bourges gave the real solution of the matter. "Louis Napoleon," said the best orator of the Mountain, "may have had rather a stormy youth (laughter). But don't suppose that any one in all France imagines you, you *Messieurs*, of the immaculate majority, to be the least better (sensation). I am not speaking to saints" (uproar). If compared with contemporary French statesmen, and the practical choice is between him and them, the President will not seem what he appears when measured by the notions of a people who exact at least from inferior functionaries *a rigid decorum in the pettiest details of their private morals.*

I have but one last point to make about this *coup d'état,* and then I will release you from my writing. I do not know whether you in England rightly realise the French Socialism. Take, for instance, M. Proudhon, who is perhaps their ideal and perfect type. He was *représentant de la Seine* in the late Assembly, elected, which is not unimportant, after the publication of his books and on account of his opinions. In his *Confessions d'un Révolutionnaire,* a very curious book—for he writes extremely well—after maintaining that our well-known but, as we imagine, advanced friends, Ledru Rollin, and Louis Blanc, and Barbès, and Blanqui, are all *réactionnaires,* and clearly showing, to the grief of mankind, that once the legislator of the Luxembourg wished to preserve "equilibrium," and the author of the provincial circulars to maintain "tranquillity," he gives the following *bonâ fide* and amusing account of his own investigations:—

"I commenced my task of solitary conspiracy by the study of the socialisms of antiquity, necessary, in my judgment, to determine the law, whether practical or theoretical, of progress. These socialisms I found in the Bible. A memoir on the institution of the Sabbath—considered with regard to morals, to health, and in its relation to the family and the city—procured for me a bronze medal from my academy. From the faith in which I had been reared, I had precipitated myself headlong, head-foremost, into pure reason, and already, what was wonderful and a good omen, when I made Moses a philosopher and a socialist, I was greeted with applause. If I am now in error, the fault is not merely mine. Was there ever a similar seduction?

"But I studied, above all, with a view to action. I cared little for academical laurels. I had no leisure to become *savant,* still less a *littérateur* or an archæologist. I began immediately upon political economy.

"I had assumed as the rule of my investigations that every principle which, pushed to its consequences, should end in a contradiction, must be considered false and null; and that if this principle had been developed into an institution, the institution itself must be considered as factitious, as utopian.

"Furnished with this criterion, I chose for the subject of investigation what I found in society the most ancient, the most respectable, the most universal, the least controverted,—property. Everybody knows what happened; after a long, a minute, and, above all, an impartial analysis, I arrived, as an algebraist guided by his equations, to this surprising conclusion. Property, consider it as you will,—refer it to what principle you may, is a contradictory idea; and as the denial of property carries with it of necessity that of authority, I deduced immediately from my first axiom also this corollary, not less paradoxical, the true form of government is *anarchy*. Lastly, finding by a mathematical demonstration that no amelioration in the economy of society could be arrived at by its natural constitution, or without the concurrence and reflective adhesion of its members; observing, also, that there is a definite epoch in the life of societies, in which their progress, at first unreflecting, requires the intervention of the free reason of man, I concluded that this spontaneous and impulsive force (*cette force d'impulsion spontanée*), which we call Providence, is not everything in the affairs of this world: from that moment, without being an Atheist, I ceased to worship God. He'll get on without your so doing, said to me one day the *Constitutionnel*. Well: perhaps he may."

These theories have been expanded into many and weary volumes, and condensed into the famous phrase, "*La Propriété c'est le vol*"; and have procured their author, in his own sect, reputation and authority.

The *Constitutionnel* had another hit against M. Proudhon, a day or two ago. They presented their readers with two decrees in due official form (the walls were at the moment covered with those of the 2nd December), as the last ideal of what the straightest sect of the Socialists particularly desire. It was as follows: "Nothing any longer exists. Nobody is charged with the execution of the aforesaid decree. Signed, Vacuum."

Such is the speculation of the new reformers—what their practices would be I can hardly tell you. My feeble income does not allow me to travel to the Basses Alpes and really investigate the subject; but if one quarter of the stories in circulation are in the least to be believed (we are quite dependent on oral information, for the Government papers deal in asterisks and "details unfit for publication," and the rest are devoted to the state of the navy and say nothing), the atrocities rival the nauseous corruption of what our liberal essayist calls "Jacobin carrion," the old days of Carrier and Barère. This is what people here are afraid of; and that is why I write such things—and not to horrify you, or amuse you, or bore you—anything rather than that; and they think themselves happy in finding a man who, with or without whatever other qualities or defects, will keep them from the vaunted Millennium and much-expected *Jacquerie*. I hope you think so, too—and that I am not, as they say in my native Tipperary, "Whistling jigs to a mile-stone".

I am, sir, yours truly,
AMICUS

P.S.—You will perhaps wish me to say something on the great event of this week, the exile of the more dangerous members of the late Assembly, and the transportation of the Socialists to Cayenne. Both measures were here expected; though I think that both lists are more numerous than was anticipated: but no one really knew what would be done by this silent Government. You will laugh at me when I tell you that both measures have been well received: but properly limited and understood, I am persuaded that the fact is so.

Of course, among the friends of exiled *représentants*, among the *littérateurs* throughout whose ranks these measures are intended to "strike terror and inspire respect," you would hear that there never was such tyranny since the beginning of mankind. But among the mass of the industrious classes—between whom and the politicians there is internecine war—I fancy that on turning the conversation to either of the most recent events, you would hear something of this sort: "*Ça ne m'occupe pas*". "What is that to *me*?" "*Je suis pour la tranquillité, moi.*" "I sold four brooches yesterday." The So-

cialists who have been removed from prison to the colony,
it is agreed were "pestilent fellows perverting the nation,"
and forbidding to pay tribute to M. Bonaparte. Indeed, they
can hardly expect commercial sympathy. "Our national honour rose—our stocks fell," is Louis Blanc's perpetual comment
on his favourite events, and it is difficult to say which of its
two clauses he dwells upon with the intenser relish. It is generally thought by those who think about the matter, that both
the transportation, and in all cases, certainly, the exile will
only be a temporary measure, and that the great mass of
the people in both lists will be allowed to return to their
homes when the present season of extreme excitement has
passed over. Still, I am not prepared to defend the *number*
of transportations. That strong measures of the sort were
necessary, I make no doubt. If Socialism exist, and the fear
of it exist, something must be done to reassure the people.
You will understand that it is not a judicial proceeding either
in essence or in form; it is not to be considered as a punishment for what men have done, but as a perfect precaution
against what they may do. Certainly, it is to be regretted that
the cause of order is so weak as to need such measures; but if
it *is* so weak, the Government must no doubt take them. Of
course, however, "our brethren," who are retained in such
numbers to write down Prince Louis, are quite right to use
without stint or stopping this most un-English proceeding; it
is their case, and you and I from old misdeeds know pretty
well how it is to be managed. There will be no imputation
of reasonable or humane motives to the Government, and no
examination of the existing state of France: let both these
come from the other side—but elegiac eloquence is inexhaus-
tibly exuded—the cruel corners of history are ransacked for
petrifying precedents—and I observe much excellent weeping
on the Cromwellian deportations and the ten years' exile of
Madame de Staël. But after all they have missed the tempting
parallel—I mean the "rather long" proscription list which
Octavius—*"l'ancien neveu de l'ancien oncle"*—concocted with
Mark Antony in the marshes of Bononia, and whereby they
thoroughly purged old Rome of its turbulent and revolutionary elements. I suspect our estimable contemporaries regret to remember of how much good order, long tranquillity,
"beata pleno copia cornu" and other many "little comforts"
to the civilised world that very "strong" proceeding, whether
in ethics justifiable or not, certainly was in fact the beginning
and foundation.

The fate of the African generals is much to be regretted, and the Government will incur much odium if the exile of General Changarnier is prolonged any length of time. He is doubtless "dangerous" for the moment, for his popularity with the army is considerable, and he divides the party of order; he is also a practical man and an unpleasant enemy, but he is much respected and little likely (I fancy) to attempt anything against any settled Government.

As for M. Thiers and M. Emile de Girardin—the ablest of the exiles—I have heard no one pity them; they have played a selfish game—they have encountered a better player—they have been beaten—and this is the whole matter. You will remember that it was the adhesion of these two men that procured for M. Bonaparte a large part of his *first* six millions.*
M. de Girardin, whom General Cavaignac had discreetly imprisoned and indiscreetly set free, wrote up the "opposition candidate" daily, in the *Presse* (he has since often and often tried to write him down), and M. Thiers was his Privy Councillor. "*Mon cher Prince*," they say, said the latter, "your address to the people won't do at all. I'll get one of the *rédacteurs* of the *Constitutionnel* to draw you up something tolerable." You remember the easy patronage with which Cicero speaks in his letter of the "boy" that was outwitting him all the while. But, however, observe I do not at all, notwithstanding my Latin, insinuate or assert that Louis Napoleon, though a considerable man, is exactly equal to keep the footsteps of Augustus. A feeble parody may suffice for an inferior stage and not too gigantic generation. Now I really *have* done.

LETTER III.

ON THE NEW CONSTITUTION OF FRANCE
AND THE APTITUDE OF
THE FRENCH CHARACTER
FOR NATIONAL FREEDOM.

Paris, 20th January, 1852.

Sir,—We have now got our Constitution. The Napoleonic era has commenced; the term of the dictatorship is fixed and the consolidation of France is begun. You will perhaps anticipate from the conclusion of the last letter, that *à propos* of

* Votes—Ed.

this great event, I should gratify you with bright anticipations
of an Augustan age, and a quick revival of Catonic virtue,
with an assurance that the night is surely passed and the day
altogether come, with a solemn invocation to the rising lu-
minary, and an original panegyric on the "golden throned
morning".

I must always regret to disappoint any one; but I feel
obliged to entertain you instead with torpid philosophy, constitutional details, and a dull disquisition on national character.

The details of the new institutions you will have long ago
learnt from the daily papers. I believe they may be fairly
and nearly accurately described as the Constitution of the
Consulate, *minus* the ideas of the man who made it. You will
remember that, besides the First Magistrate, the Senate, the
House of Representatives, the Council of State (which we
may call, in legal language, the "common form" of continental constitution), the ingenious Abbé Sieyès had devised some
four principal peculiarities, which were to be remembered to
all time as masterpieces of political invention. These were
the utter inaction of the First Magistrate, copied, as I believe, from the English Constitution—the subordination to
him of two Consuls, one to administer peace and the other
war, who were intended to be the real hands and arms of the
Government—the silence of the Senate—the double and very
peculiar election of the House of Representatives. Napoleon
the Great, as we are now to speak, struck out the first of
these, being at the moment working some fifteen hours a day
at the reorganisation of France. He said plainly and rather
sternly that he had no intention of doing nothing—the *idéo-
logue* went to the wall—the "excellent idea" put forth in
happy forgetfulness of real facts and real people was instantly
abandoned—for the Grand Elector was substituted a First
Consul, who, so far from being nothing, was very soon the
whole Government. Napoleon the Little, as I fear the Parisian
multitude may learn to call him, has effaced the other three
"strokes of statesmanship". The new Constitution of France
is exactly the "common form" of political conveyancing, *plus*
the *Idée Napoléonienne* of an all-suggesting and all-admin-
istering mind.

I have extremely little to tell you about its reception; it
has made no "sensation," not so much as even the "fortified
camps" which his Grace is said to be devising for the defence

of our own London. Indeed, *"Il a peur"* is a very common remark (conceivable to everybody who knows "the Duke"), and it would seem even a refreshing alleviation of their domestic sorrows. In fact, home politics are now *the* topic; geography and the state of foreign institutions are not, indeed, the true Parisian line—but it has, in fine, been distinctly discovered that there are no *salons* in Cayenne, which, once certain, the logical genius of the nation, with incredible swiftness, deduced the clear conclusion that it was better not to go there. Seriously, I fancy—for I have no data on which to found real knowledge of so delicate a point—the new Constitution is regarded merely as what Father Newman would call a "preservative addition" or a "necessary development," essential to the "chronic continuance" of the Napoleonic system; for the moment the mass of the people wish the President to govern them, but they don't seem to me to care how. The political people, I suppose, hate it, because for some time it will enable him, if not shot, to govern effectually. I say, if not shot—for people are habitually recounting under their breath some new story of an attempt at assassination, which the papers suppress. I am inclined to think that these rumours are pure lies; but they show the feeling. You know, according to the Constitution of 1848, the President would now be a mere outlaw, and whoever finds him may slay him, if he can. It is true that the elaborate masterpiece of M. Marrast is already fallen into utter oblivion (it is no more remembered than yesterday's *Times*, or the political institutions of Saxon Mercia); but nevertheless such, according to the ante-diluvian *régime*, would be the law, and it is possible that a mindful Montagnard may upon occasion recall even so insignificant a circumstance.

I have a word to say on the Prologue of the President. When I first began to talk politics with French people, I was much impressed by the fact to which he has there drawn attention. You know that all such conversation, when one of the interlocutors is a foreigner, speaking slowly and but imperfectly the language of the country in which he is residing, is pretty much in the style of that excellent work which was the terror of our childhood—Joyce's *Scientific Dialogues*—wherein, as you may remember, an accomplished tutor, with a singular gift of scholastic improvisation, instructs a youthful pupil exceedingly given to feeble questions and auscultatory repose. Now, when I began in Parisian society thus to

enact the *rôle* of "George" or "Caroline," I was, I repeat,
much struck with the fact that the Emperor had done everything: to whatever subject my diminutive inquiry related,
the answer was nearly universally the same—an elegy on Napoleon. Nor is this exactly absurd; for whether or not "the
nephew" is right in calling the uncle the greatest of modern
statesmen, he is indisputably the modern statesman who has
founded the greatest number of existing institutions. In the
pride of philosophy and in the madness of an hour, the Constituent Assembly and the Convention swept away not only
the monstrous abuses of the old *régime*, but that *régime* itself—its essence and its mechanism, utterly and entirely. They
destroyed whatever they could lay their hands on. The consequence was certain—when they tried to construct they found
they had no materials. They left a vacuum. No greater benefit
could have been conferred on politicians gifted with the creative genius of Napoleon. It was like the fire of London to Sir
Christopher Wren. With a fertility of invention and an obstinacy in execution, equalling, if not surpassing, those of
Cæsar and Charlemagne, he had before him an open stage,
more clear and more vast than in historical times fortune has
ever offered to any statesman. He was nearly in the position
of the imagined legislator of the Greek legends and the Greek
philosophers—he could enact any law, and rescind any law.
Accordingly, the educational system, the banking system, the
financial system, the municipal system, the administrative
system, the civil legislation, the penal legislation, the commercial legislation (besides all manner of secondary creations
—public buildings and public institutions without number),
all date from the time, and are more or less deeply inscribed
with the genius, the firm will, and unresting energies of Napoleon. And this, which is the great strength of the present
President, is the great difficulty—I fear the insurmountable
difficulty—in the way of Henry the Fifth. The first revolution
is to the French what the deluge is to the rest of mankind;
the whole system then underwent an entire change. A French
politician will no more cite as authority the domestic policy
of Colbert or Louvois than we should think of going for
ethics and æsthetics to the bigamy of Lamech, or the musi-
cal accomplishments of Tubal Cain. If the Comte de Cham-
bord be (as it is quite on the cards that he may be) within a
few years restored, he must govern by the instrumentality of
laws and systems devised by the politicians whom he exe-

crates and denounces, and devised, moreover, often enough, especially to keep out him and his. It is difficult to imagine that a strong Government can be composed of materials so inharmonious. Meanwhile, to the popular imagination, "the Emperor" is the past; the House of Bourbon is as historical as the House of Valois; a peasant is little oftener reminded of the "third dynasty" than of the long-haired kings.

In discussing any Constitution, there are two ideas to be first got rid of. The first is the idea of our barbarous ancestors —now happily banished from all civilised society, but still prevailing in old manor-houses, in rural parsonages, and other curious repositories of mouldering ignorance, and which in such arid solitudes is thus expressed: "Why can't they have Kings, Lords and Commons, *like we have?* What fools foreigners are." The second pernicious mistake is, like the former, seldom now held upon system, but so many hold it in bits and fragments, and without system, that it is still rather formidable. I allude to the old idea which still here creeps out in conversation, and sometimes in writing,—that politics are simply a subdivision of immutable ethics; that there are certain rights of men in all places and all times, which are the sole and sufficient foundation of all government, and that accordingly a single stereotype Government is to make the tour of the world—that you have no more right to deprive a Dyak of his vote in a "possible" Polynesian Parliament, than you have to steal his mat.

Burke first taught the world at large, in opposition to both, and especially to the latter of these notions, that politics are made of time and place—that institutions are shifting things, to be tried by and adjusted to the shifting conditions of a mutable world—that, in fact, politics are but a piece of business—to be determined in every case by the exact exigencies of that case; in plain English—by sense and circumstances.

This was a great step in political philosophy—though it *now* seems the events of 1848 have taught thinking persons (I fancy) further. They have enabled us to say that of all these circumstances so affecting political problems, by far and out of all question the most important is *national character.* In that year the same experiment—the experiment, as its friends say, of Liberal and Constitutional Government—as its enemies say, of Anarchy and Revolution—was tried in every nation of Europe—with what varying futures and differing results! The effect has been to teach men—not only speculatively to know, but practically to feel, that no absurdity is so great as to imagine the same species of institutions suitable or possible for Scotchmen and Sicilians, for Germans and Frenchmen, for the English and the Neapolitans. With a well-balanced national character (we now know) liberty is a stable thing. A really practical people will work in political business, as in private business, almost the absurdest, the feeblest, the most inconsistent set of imaginable regulations. Similarly, or rather reversely, the best institutions will not keep right a nation that *will* go wrong. Paper is but paper, and no virtue is to be discovered in it to retain within due boundaries the undisciplined passions of those who have never set themselves seriously to restrain them. In a word—as people of "large roundabout common-sense" will (as a rule) somehow get on in life—no matter what their circumstances or their fortune—so a nation which applies good judgment, forbearance, a rational and compromising habit to the management of free institutions, will certainly succeed; while the more eminently gifted national character will but be a source and germ of endless and disastrous failure, if, with whatever other eminent qualities, it be deficient in these plain, solid, and essential requisites.

The formation of *this* character is one of the most secret of marvellous mysteries. Why nations have the character we see them to have is, speaking generally, as little explicable to our shallow perspicacity, as why individuals, our friends or our enemies, for good or for evil, have the character which they have; why one man is stupid and another clever—why another volatile and a fourth consistent—this man by instinct generous, and that man by instinct niggardly. I am not speaking of actions, you observe, but of tendencies and temptations. These and other similar problems daily crowd on our observation in millions and millions, and only do not puzzle us because we are too familiar with their difficulty to dream of attempting their solution. Only this much is most certain, —all men and all nations have a character, and that character when once taken, is, I do not say unchangeable—religion modifies it, catastrophe annihilates it—but the least changeable thing in this ever-varying and changeful world. Take the soft mind of the boy, and (strong and exceptional aptitudes and tendencies excepted) you may make him merchant, barrister, butcher, baker, surgeon, or apothecary. But once make him an apothecary, and he will never afterwards bake wholesome bread—make him a butcher, and he will kill too extensively, even for a surgeon—make him a barrister, and he will be dim on double entry, and crass on bills of lading. Once conclusively form him to one thing, and no art and no science will ever twist him to another. Nature, says the philosopher, has no Delphic daggers!—no men or maids of all work—she keeps one being to one pursuit—to each is a single choice afforded, but no more again thereafter for ever. And it is the same with nations. The Jews of to-day are the Jews in face and form of the Egyptian sculptures; in character they are the Jews of Moses—the negro is the negro of a thousand years —the Chinese, by his own account, is the mummy of a million. "Races and their varieties," says the historian, "seem to have been created with an inward *nisus* diminishing with the age of the world." The people of the South are yet the people of the South, fierce and angry as their summer sun—the people of the North are still cold and stubborn like their own north wind—the people of the East "mark not, but are still"—the people of the West "are going through the ends of the earth, and walking up and down in it". The fact is certain, the cause beyond us. The subtle system of obscure causes, whereby sons and daughters resemble not only their fathers and mothers but even their great-great-grandfathers and their great-great-grandmothers, may very likely be destined to be very inscrutable. But as the fact is so, so moreover, in history, nations have one character, one set of talents, one list of temptations, and one duty—to use the one and get the better of the other. There are breeds in the animal man just as in the animal dog. When you hunt with greyhounds and course with beagles, then, and not till then, may you expect the inbred habits of a thousand years to pass away, that Hindoos can be free, or that Englishmen will be slaves.

I need not prove to you that the French *have* a national character. Nor need I try your patience with a likeness of it. I have only to examine whether it be a fit basis for national freedom. I fear you will laugh when I tell you what I conceive to be about the most essential mental quality for a free people, whose liberty is to be progressive, permanent, and on a large scale; it is much *stupidity*. I see you are surprised— you are going to say to me, as Socrates did to Polus, "My young friend, *of course* you are right; but will you explain what you mean?—as yet you are not intelligible". I will do so as well as I can, and endeavour to make good what I say—

not by an *a priori* demonstration of my own, but from the details of the present, and the facts of history. Not to begin by wounding any present susceptibilities, let me take the Roman character—for, with one great exception—I need not say to whom I allude—they are the great political people of history. Now, is not a certain dulness their most visible characteristic? What is the history of their speculative mind?—a blank. What their literature?—a copy. They have left not a single discovery in any abstract science; not a single perfect or well-formed work of high imagination. The Greeks, the perfection of narrow and accomplished genius, bequeathed to mankind the ideal forms of self-idolising art—the Romans imitated and admired; the Greeks explained the laws of Nature—the Romans wondered and despised; the Greeks invented a system of numerals second only to that now in use —the Romans counted to the end of their days with the clumsy apparatus which we still call by their name; the Greeks made a capital and scientific calendar—the Romans began their month when the Pontifex Maximus happened to spy out the new moon. Throughout Latin literature, this is the perpetual puzzle—Why are we free and they slaves? we prætors and they barbers? Why do the stupid people always win, and the clever people always lose? I need not say that, in real sound stupidity, the English are unrivalled. You'll hear more wit, and better wit, in an Irish street-row than would keep Westminster Hall in humour for five weeks. Or take Sir Robert Peel—our last great statesman, the greatest Member of Parliament that ever lived, an absolutely perfect transactor of public business—the type of the nineteenth-century Englishman, as Sir R. Walpole was of the eighteenth. Was there ever such a dull man? Can any one, without horror, foresee the reading of his memoirs? A *clairvoyante*, with the book shut, may get on; but who now, in the flesh, will ever endure the open *vision* of endless recapitulation of interminable Hansard? Or take Mr Tennyson's inimitable description:—

> "No little lily-handed Baronet he,
> A great broad-shouldered genial Englishman,
> A lord of fat prize oxen and of sheep,
> A raiser of huge melons and of pine,
> A patron of some thirty charities,
> A pamphleteer on guano and on grain,
> A quarter sessions chairman, abler none."

Whose company so soporific? His talk is of truisms and bull-
ocks; his head replete with rustic visions of mutton and
turnips, and a cerebral edition of Burn's *Justice!* Notwithstanding, he is the salt of the earth, the best of the English
breed. Who is like him for sound sense? But I must restrain
my enthusiasm. You don't want me to tell you that a Frenchman—a real Frenchman—can't be stupid; *esprit* is his essence,
wit is to him as water, *bons-mots* as *bonbons*. He reads and
he learns by reading; levity and literature are essentially his
line. Observe the consequence. The outbreak of 1848 was
accepted in every province in France; the decrees of the
Parisian mob were received and registered in all the municipalities of a hundred cities; the Revolution ran like the fluid
of the telegraph down the *Chemin de fer du Nord*; it stopped
at the Belgian frontier. Once brought into contact with the
dull phlegm of the stupid Fleming, the poison was powerless. You remember what the Norman butler said to Wilkin
Flammock, of the fulling mills, at the castle of the Garde
Douloureuse: "That draught which will but warm your
Flemish hearts, will put wildfire into Norman brains; and
what may only encourage your countrymen to man the walls,
will make ours fly over the battlements". *Les Braves Belges,* I
make no doubt, were quite pleased to observe what folly was
being exhibited by those very clever French, whose tongue
they want to speak, and whose literature they try to imitate.
In fact, what we opprobriously call stupidity, though not an
enlivening quality in common society, is Nature's favourite
resource for preserving steadiness of conduct and consistency
of opinion. It enforces concentration; people who learn slowly,
learn only what they must. The best security for people's
doing their duty is, that they should not know anything else
to do; the best security for fixedness of opinion is, that people should be incapable of comprehending what is to be said
on the other side. These valuable truths are no discoveries
of mine. They are familiar enough to people whose business
it is to know them. Hear what a dense and aged attorney
says of your peculiarly promising barrister: "Sharp! oh yes,
yes! he's too sharp by half. He is not *safe;* not a minute, isn't
that young man." "What style, sir," asked of an East India
Director some youthful aspirant for literary renown, "is most
to be preferred in the composition of official despatches?"
"My good fellow," responded the ruler of Hindostan, "the
style *as we* like is the Humdrum." I extend this, and ad-

visedly maintain that nations, just as individuals, may be too clever to be practical, and not dull enough to be free.

How far this is true of the French, and how far the gross deficiency I have indicated is modified by their many excellent qualities, I hope at a future time to inquire.

I am, sir, yours truly,

AMICUS.

ON THE APTITUDE OF THE FRENCH CHARACTER FOR NATIONAL SELF-GOVERNMENT.

Paris, 29th January, 1852.

Sir,—There is a simple view of the subject on which I wrote you last week, that I wish to bring under your notice. The experiment (as it is called) of establishing political freedom in France is now sixty years old; and the best that we can say of it is, that it is an experiment still. There have been perhaps half a dozen new beginnings—half a dozen complete failures. I am aware that each of these failures can be excellently explained—each beginning shown to be quite necessary. But there are certain reasonings which, though outwardly irrefragable, the crude human mind is always most unwilling to accept. Among these are different and subtle explications of several apparently similar facts. Thus, to choose an example suited to the dignity of my subject, if a gentleman from town takes a day's shooting in the country, and should chance (as has happened) at first going off, to miss some six times running, how luminously soever he may "explain" each failure as it occurs, however "expanded a view" he may take of the whole series, whatever popular illustrations of projectile philosophy he may propound to the bird-slaying agriculturists— the impression on the crass intelligence of the gamekeeper will quite clearly be, "He beint noo shot homsoever—aint thickeer". Similarly, to compare small things with great, when I myself read in Thiers and the many other philosophic historians of this literary country, various and excellent explanations of their many mischances;—of the failure of the constitution of 1791—of the constitution of the year 3—of the constitution of the year 5—of the *charte*—of the system of

1830—and now we may add, of the Second Republic—the annotated constitution of M. Dupin;—I can't help feeling a suspicion lingering in my crude and uncultivated intellect—that some common principle is at work in all and each of these several cases—that over and above all odd mischances, so many bankruptcies a little suggest an unfitness for the trade; that besides the ingenious reasons of ingenious gentlemen, there is some lurking quality, or want of a quality, in the national character of the French nation which renders them but poorly adapted for the form and freedom and constitution which they have so often, with such zeal and so vainly, attempted to establish.

In my last letter I suggested that this might be what I ventured to call a "want of stupidity". I will now try to describe what I mean in more accurate, though not, perhaps, more intelligible words.

I believe that I am but speaking what is agreed on by competent observers, when I say that the essence of the French character is a certain mobility; that is, as it has been defined, a certain "excessive sensibility to *present* impressions," which is sometimes "levity,"—for it issues in a postponement of seemingly fixed principles to a momentary temptation or a transient whim; sometimes "impatience,"—as leading to an exaggerated sense of existing evils; often "excitement,"—a total absorption in existing emotion; oftener "inconsistency,"—the sacrifice of old habits to present emergencies; and yet other unfavourable qualities. But it has also its favourable side. The same man who is drawn aside from old principles by small pleasures, who can't bear pain, who forgets his old friends when he ceases to see them, who is liable in time of excitement to be a one-idea being, with no conception of anything but the one exciting object, yet who nevertheless is apt to have one idea to-day and quite another to-morrow (and this, and more than this, may, I fancy, be said of the ideal Frenchman), may and will have the subtlest perception of existing niceties, the finest susceptibility to social pleasure, the keenest tact in social politeness, the most consummate skilfulness in the details of action and administration,—may, in short, be the best companion, the neatest man of business, the lightest *homme de salon*, the acutest diplomat of the existing world.

It is curious to observe how this reflects itself in their literature. "I will believe," remarks Montaigne, "in anything rather than in any man's consistency." What observer of Eng-

lish habits—what person inwardly conscious of our dull and
unsusceptible English nature, would ever say so? Rather in
our country obstinacy is the commonest of the vices, and
perseverance the cheapest of the virtues. Again, when they
attempt history, the principal peculiarity (a few exceptions
being allowed for) is an utter incapacity to describe graphically a long-passed state of society. Take, for instance—assuredly no unfavourable example—M. Guizot. His books, I
need not say, are nearly unrivalled for eloquence, for philosophy and knowledge; you read there, how in the middle age
there were many "principles"; the principle of Legitimacy,
the principle of Feudalism, the principle of Democracy; and
you come to know how one grew, and another declined, and a
third crept slowly on; and the mind is immensely edified,
when perhaps at the 315th page a proper name occurs, and
you mutter, "Dear me, why, if there were not *people* in the
time of Charlemagne! Who would have thought that?" But
in return for this utter incapacity to describe the people of
past times, a Frenchman has the gift of perfectly describing
the people of his own. No one knows so well—no one can
tell so well—the facts of his own life. The French memoirs,
the French letters are, and have been, the admiration of
Europe. Is not now Jules Janin unrivalled at pageants and
prima donnas?

It is the same in poetry. As a recent writer excellently remarks: "A French Dante, or Michael Angelo, or Cervantes,
or Murillo, or Goethe, or Shakespeare, or Milton, we at once
perceive to be a mere anomaly; a supposition which may indeed be proposed in terms, but which in reality is inconceiva-
ble and impossible". Yet, in requital as it were of this great
deficiency, they have a wonderful capacity for expressing and
delineating the poetical and voluptuous element of everyday
life. We know the biography of De Béranger. The young
ladies whom he has admired—the wine that he has preferred
—the fly that buzzed on the ceiling, and interrupted his de-
licious and dreaming solitude, are as well known to us as the
recollections of our own lives. As in their common furniture,
so in their best poetry. The materials are nothing; reckon up
what you have been reading, and it seems a *congeries* of stupid trifles; begin to read,—the skill of the workmanship is so
consummate, the art so high and so latent, that while time
flows silently on, our fancies are enchanted and our memories
indelibly impressed. How often, asks Mr Thackeray, have we

read De Béranger—how often Milton? Certainly, since Horace, there has been no such manual of the philosophy of this world.

I will not say that the quality which I have been trying to delineate is exactly the same thing as "cleverness". But I do allege that it is sufficiently near it for the rough purposes of popular writing. For this *quickness* in taking in—so to speak—the present, gives a corresponding celerity of intellectual apprehension, an amazing readiness in catching new ideas and maintaining new theories, a versatility of mind which enters into and comprehends everything as it passes, a concentration in what occurs, so as to use it for every purpose of illustration, and consequently (if it happen to be combined with the least fancy), quick repartee on the subject of the moment, and *bons-mots* also without stint and without end—and these qualities are rather like what we style cleverness. And what I call a proper stupidity keeps a man from all the defects of this character; it chains the gifted possessor mainly to his old ideas; it takes him seven weeks to comprehend an atom of a new one; it keeps him from being led away by new theories—for there is nothing which bores him so much; it restrains him within his old pursuits, his well-known habits, his tried expedients, his verified conclusions, his traditional beliefs. He is not tempted to "levity," or "impatience," for he does not see the joke, and is thick-skinned to present evils. Inconsistency puts him out,—"What I says is this here, as I was saying yesterday," is his notion of historical eloquence and habitual discretion. He is very slow indeed to be "excited,"—his passions, his feelings, and his affections are dull and tardy strong things, falling in a certain known direction, fixing on certain known objects, and for the most part acting in a moderate degree, and at a sluggish pace. You always know where to find his mind.

Now this is exactly what, in politics at least, you do not know about a Frenchman. I like—I have heard a good judge say—to hear a Frenchman talk. He strikes a light, but what light he will strike it is impossible to predict. I think he doesn't know himself. Now, I know you see at once how this would operate on a Parliamentary Government, but I give you a gentle illustration. All England knows Mr Disraeli, the witty orator, the exceedingly clever *littérateur*, the versatile politician; and all England has made up its mind that the stupidest country gentleman would be a better Home Secretary than

the accomplished descendant of the "Caucasian race". Now
suppose, if you only can, a House of Commons all Disraelis,
and do you imagine that Parliament would work? It would be
what M. Proudhon said of some French assemblies, "a box of
matches".

The same quality acts in another way, and produces to
English ideas a most marvellous puzzle, both in the philosophical literature and the political discussion of the French.
I mean their passion for logical deduction. Their inhabitual
mode of argument is to get hold of some large principle; to
begin to deduce immediately; and to reason down from it to
the most trivial details of common action. *Il faut être consé-
quent avec soi-même*—is their fundamental maxim; and in a
world the essence of which is compromise, they could not
well have a worse. I hold, metaphysically perhaps, that this is
a consequence of that same impatience of disposition to which
I have before alluded. Nothing is such a bore as looking for
your principles—nothing so pleasant as working them out.
People who have thought, know that inquiry is suffering. A
child stumbling timidly in the dark is not more different from
the same child playing on a sunny lawn, than is the philosopher groping, hesitating, doubting and blundering about his
primitive postulates, than the same philosopher proudly de-
ducing and commenting on the certain consequences of his
established convictions. On this account Mathematics have
been called the paradise of the mind. In Euclid at least, you
have your principles, and all that is required is acuteness in
working them out. The long annals of science are one continued commentary on this text. Read in Bacon, the beginner
of intellectual philosophy in England, and every page of the
Advancement of Learning is but a continued warning against
the tendency of the human mind to start at once to the last
generalities from a few and imperfectly observed particulars.
Read in the *Méditations* of Descartes, the beginner of intellectual philosophy in France, and in every page (once I
read five) you will find nothing but the strictest, the best,
the most lucid, the most logical deduction of all things actual
and possible, from a few principles obtained without evidence, and retained in defiance of probability. Deduction is
a game, and induction a grievance. Besides, clever impatient
people want not only to learn, but to teach. And instruction
expresses at least the alleged possession of knowledge. The
obvious way is to shorten the painful, the slow, the tedious,

the wearisome process of preliminary inquiry—to assume something pretty—to establish its consequences—discuss their beauty—exemplify their importance—extenuate their absurdities. A little vanity helps all this. Life is short—art is long—truth lies deep—take some side—found your school—open your lecture-rooms—tuition is dignified—learning is low.

I do not know that I can exhibit the way these qualities of the French character operate on their opinions, better than by telling you how the Roman Catholic Church deals with them. I have rather attended to it since I came here; it gives sermons almost an interest, their being in French—and to those curious in intellectual matters it is worth observing. In other times, and even now in out-of-the-way Spain I suppose it may be so, the Catholic Church was opposed to inquiry and reasoning. But it is not so now, and here. Loudly—from the pens of a hundred writers—from the tongues of a thousand pulpits—in every note of thrilling scorn and exulting derision, she proclaims the contrary. Be she Christ's workman, or Anti-Christ's, she knows her work too well.—"Reason, Reason, Reason!"—exclaims she to the philosophers of this world—"Put in practice what you teach, if you would have others believe it; be consistent; do not prate to us of private judgment when you are but yourselves repeating what you heard in the nursery—ill-mumbled remnants of a Catholic tradition. No! exemplify what you command, inquire and make search—seek, though we warn you that ye will never find—yet do as ye will. Shut yourself up in a room—make your mind a blank—go down (as ye speak) into the 'depths of your consciousness'—scrutinise the mental structure—inquire for the elements of belief—spend years, your best years, in the occupation; and at length—when your eyes are dim, and your brain hot, and your hand unsteady—then reckon what you have gained: see if you cannot count on your fingers the certainties you have reached: reflect which of them you doubted yesterday, which you may disbelieve to-morrow; or rather, make haste—assume at random some essential *credenda*—write down your inevitable postulates—enumerate your necessary axioms—toil on, toil on—spin your spider's web—adore your own souls—or, if you prefer it, choose some German nostrum—try the intellectual intuition, or the 'pure reason,' or the 'intelligible' ideas, or the mesmeric *clairvoyance*—and when so or somehow you have attained your results, try them on mankind. Don't go out into the highways and hedges—it's unnecessary. Ring the bell—call in the servants—give them a course of lectures—cite Aristotle—review Descartes—panegyrise Plato—and see if the *bonne* will understand you. It is you that say '*Vox populi—Vox Dei*'; but you see the people reject you. Or, suppose you succeed—what you call succeeding —your books are read; for three weeks, or even a season, you are the idol of the *salons*; your hard words are on the lips of women; then a change comes—a new actress appears at the Théâtre Français or the Opéra—her charms eclipse your theories; or a great catastrophe occurs—political liberty (it is said) is annihilated—*il faut se faire mouchard,* is the observation of scoffers. Anyhow, *you* are forgotten—fifty years may be the gestation of a philosophy, not three its life—before long, before you go to your grave, your six disciples leave you for some newer master, or to set up for themselves. The poorest priest in the remote region of the Basses Alpes has more power over men's souls than human cultivation; his ill-mouthed masses move women's souls—can you? Ye scoff at Jupiter. Yet he at least was believed in—you never have been; idol for idol, the *de*throned is better than the *un*throned. No, if you would reason—if you would teach—if you would speculate, come to us. We have our *premises* ready; years upon years before you were born, intellects whom the best of you delight to magnify, toiled to systematise the creed of ages; years upon years after you are dead, better heads than yours will find new matter there to define, to divide, to arrange. Consider the hundred volumes of Aquinas—which of you desire a higher life than that? To deduce, to subtilise, discriminate, systematise, and decide the highest truth, and to be believed. Yet such was his luck, his enjoyment. He was what you would be. No, no—*Credite, credite.* Ours is the life of speculation—the cloister is the home for the student. Philosophy is stationary—Catholicism progressive. You call—we are heard," etc., etc., etc. So speaks each preacher according to his ability. And when the dust and noise of present controversies have passed away, and in the silence of the night, some grave historian writes out the tale of half-forgotten times, let him not forget to observe that skilfully as the mediæval Church subdued the superstitious cravings of a painful and barbarous age—in after-years she dealt more discerningly still with the feverish excitement, the feeble vanities, and the dogmatic impatience of an over-intellectual generation.

And as in religion—so in politics, we find the same desire to teach rather than to learn—the same morbid appetite for exhaustive and original theories. It is as necessary for a public writer to have a system as it is for him to have a pen. His course is obvious; he assumes some grand principle—the principle of Legitimacy, or the principle of Equality, or the principle of Fraternity—and thence he reasons down without fear or favour to the details of everyday politics. Events are judged of, not by their relation to simple causes, but by their bearing on a remote axiom. Nor are these speculations mere exercises of philosophic ingenuity. Four months ago, hundreds of able writers were debating with the keenest ability and the most ample array of generalities, whether the country should be governed by a Legitimate Monarchy, or an illegitimate; by a Social, or an old-fashioned Republic; by a two-chambered Constitution, or a one-chambered Constitution; on "Revision," or Non-revision; on the claims of Louis Napoleon, or the divine right of the national representation. Can any intellectual food be conceived more dangerous or more stimulating for an over-excitable population? It is the same in Parliament. The description of the Church of Corinth may stand for a description of the late Assembly: every one had a psalm, had a doctrine, had a tongue, had a revelation, had an interpretation. Each member of the Mountain had his scheme for the regeneration of mankind; each member of the vaunted majority had his scheme for newly consolidating the Government; Orleanist hated Legitimist, Legitimist Orleanist; moderate Republican detested undiluted Republican; scheme was set against scheme, and theory against theory. No two Conservatives would agree what to conserve; no Socialist could practically associate with any other. No deliberative assembly can exist with every member wishing to lead, and no one wishing to follow. Not the meanest Act of Parliament could be carried without more compromise than even the best French statesmen were willing to use on the most important and critical affairs of their country. Rigorous reasoning would not manage a parish vestry, much less a great nation. In England, to carry half your own crotchets, you must be always and everywhere willing to carry half another man's. Practical men must submit as well as rule, concede as well as assume. Popular government has many forms, a thousand good modes of procedure; but no one of those modes can be worked, no one of those forms will endure, unless by the continual applica-

tion of sensible heads and pliable judgments to the systematic
criticism of stiff axioms, rigid principles, and incarnated propositions. I am, etc.,

Amicus.

P.S.—I was in hopes that I should have been able to tell
you of the withdrawal of the decree relative to the property
of the Orleans family. The withdrawal was announced in the
Constitutionnel of yesterday; but I regret to add was contradicted in the *Patrie* last evening. I need not observe to you
that it is an act for which there is no defence, moral or political. It has immensely weakened the Government.

The change of Ministry is also a great misfortune to Louis
Napoleon. M. de Morny, said to be a son of Queen Hortense
(if you believe the people in the *salons*, the President is not
the son of his father, and everybody else is the son of his
mother), was a statesman of the class best exemplified in
England by the late Lord Melbourne—an acute, witty, fashionable man, acquainted with Parisian persons and things,
and a consummate judge of public opinion. M. Persigny was
in exile with the President, is said to be much attached to
him, to repeat his sentiments and exaggerate his prejudices.
I need not point out which of the two is just now the sounder
counsellor.

LETTER V.

ON THE CONSTITUTION OF THE
PRINCE-PRESIDENT.

[*Undated*]

Sir,—The many failures of the French in the attempt to
establish a predominantly Parliamentary Government have a
strong family likeness. Speaking a little roughly, I shall be
right in saying that the Constitutions of France have perished,
both lately and formerly, either in a street-row or under the
violence of a military power, aided and abetted by a diffused
dread of impending street-rows, and a painful experience of
the effects of past ones. Thus the Constitution of 1791 (the
first of the old series) perished on 10th August, amid the
exultation of the brewer Santerre. The last of the old series
fell on the 18 Brumaire, under the hands of Napoleon, when

the 5 per cents were at 12, the whole country in disorder, and all ruinable persons ruined. The Monarchy of 1830 began in the riot of the three days, and ended in the riot of 24th February; the Republic of February perished but yesterday, mainly from terror that Paris might again see such days as the "days of June".

I think all sensible Englishmen who review this history (the history of more than sixty years) will not be slow to divine a conclusion peculiarly agreeable to our orderly national habits, *viz.*, that the first want of the French is somebody or something able and willing to keep down street-rows, to repress the frightful elements of revolution and disorder which, every now and then, astonish Europe; capable of maintaining, and desirous to maintain, the order and tranquillity which are (all agree) the essential and primary prerequisites of industry and civilisation. If any one seriously and calmly doubts this, I am afraid nothing that I can further say will go far in convincing him. But let him read the account of any scene in any French revolution, old or new, or, better, let him come here and learn how people look back to the time I have mentioned (to June, 1848), when the Socialists,—not under speculative philosophers like Proudhon or Louis Blanc, but under practical rascals and energetic murderers, like Sobrier and Caussidière—made their last and final stand, and against them, on the other side, the National Guard (mostly solid shopkeepers, three-parts ruined by the events of February) fought (I will not say bravely or valiantly, but) furiously, frantically, savagely, as one reads in old books that half-starved burgesses in beleaguered towns have sometimes fought for the food of their children; let any sceptic hear of the atrocities of the friends of order and the atrocities of the advocates of disorder, and he will, I imagine, no longer be sceptical on two points,—he will hope that if he ever have to fight it will not be with a fanatic Socialist, nor against a demi-bankrupt fighting for "his shop"; and he will admit, that in a country subject to collisions between two such excited and excitable combatants, no earthly blessing is in any degree comparable to a power which will stave off, long delay, or permanently prevent, the actual advent and ever-ready apprehension of such bloodshed. I therefore assume that the first condition of good government in this country is a really strong, a reputedly strong, a continually strong Executive power.

Now, on the face of matters, it is certainly true that such a power is perfectly consistent with the most perfect, the most ideal type of Parliamentary Government. Rather I should say, such and so strong an executive is a certain consequence of the existence of that ideal and rarely found type. If there is among the people, and among their representatives, a strong, a decided, an unflinching preference for particular Ministers, or a particular course of policy, that course of policy can be carried out, and will be carried out, as certainly as by the Czar Nicholas, whose Ministers can do exactly what they will. There was something very like this in the old days of King George III, of Mr Pitt, and Mr Perceval. In those times, I have been told, the great Treasury official of the day, Mr George Rose (still known to the readers of Sydney Smith) had a habit of observing, upon occasion of anything utterly devoid of decent defence: "Well, well, this *is* a little too bad; we must apply our *majority* to this difficulty". The effect is very plain; while Mr George Rose and his betters respected certain prejudices and opinions, then all but universal in Parliament, they in all other matters might do precisely what they would; and in all out-of-the-way matter, in anything that Sir John could not understand, on a point of cotton-spinning or dissent, be as absolute as the Emperor Napoleon. But the case is (as we know by experience of what passes under our daily observation) immensely altered, when there is no longer this strong, compact, irrefragable "following," no distinctly divided, definite faction, no regular opposition to be daily beaten, no regular official party to be always victorious—but, instead, a mere aggregate of "independent members," each thinking for himself, propounding, as the case may be, his own sense or his own nonsense—one, profound ideas applicable to all time; another, something meritorious from the Eton Latin Grammar, and a mangled republication of the morning's newspaper; some exceedingly philosophical, others only crotchety, but, what is my point, each acting on his own head, assuming not Mr Pitt's infallibility, but his own. Again, divide a political assembly into three parties, any two of which are greater than the third, and it will be always possible for an adroit and dexterous intriguer (M. Thiers has his type in most assemblies) to combine, three or four times a fortnight, the two opposition parties into a majority on some interesting question—on some matter of importance. The best government possible under the existing circumstances will be continually and, in a hazardous state of society, even desperately and fatally weakened. We have had in our sensible House of Commons—aye, and among the most stupid and sensible portion of it, the country gentlemen—within these few years a striking example of how far party zeal, the heat of disputation, and a strong desire for a deep revenge, will carry the best-intentioned politicians in destroying the executive efficiency of an obnoxious Government. I mean the division of the House of Commons on the Irish Army Bill which ended in the resignation of Sir Robert Peel. You remember on that occasion the country party, under the guidance of Lord G. Bentinck, in the teeth of the Irish policy which they had been advocating and supporting all their lives, and which they would advocate and support again now, in the teeth of their previous votes, and (I am not exaggerating the history) almost of their avowed present convictions, defeated a Government, not on a question of speculative policy or recondite importance, but upon the precautionary measures necessary (according to every idea that a Tory esquire is capable of entertaining) for preventing a rebellion, the occurrence of which they were told (and as the event proved, told truly) might be speedy, hourly, and immediate. Of course I am not giving any opinion of my own about the merits of the question. The Whigs may be right; it may be good to have shown the world how little terrible is the bluster of Irish agitation. But I cite the event as a striking example of an essential evil in a three-sided Parliamentary system, as practically showing that a generally well-meaning opposition will, in defiance of their own habitual principles, cripple an odious executive, even in a matter of street-rows and rebellions. I won't weary you with tediously pointing the moral. If such things are done in the green tree, what may be done in the dry? If party zeal and disputatious excitement so hurry men away in our own grave business-like experienced country—what may we expect from a vain, a volatile, an ever-changing race?

Nor am I drawing a French Assembly from mere history, or from my own imagination. In the late Chamber, the great subject of the very last *Annual Register*, there are not only three parties but four. There was a perpetually shifting element of 200 members, calling itself the Mountain, which had in its hands the real casting vote between the President's Government and the Constitutional opposition. In the very last days of the Constitution they voted against, and thereby negatived, the proposition of the questors for arming the Assembly; partly because they disliked General Changarnier, and detested General Cavaignac; partly because, being extreme Socialists, they would not arm anybody who was likely to use his arms against their friends on the barricades. The same party was preparing to vote for the Bill on the Responsibility of the President, actually, and according to the design of its promoters, in the nature of a bill of indictment against him, because they feared his rigour and efficiency in repressing the anticipated convulsion. The question, the critical question, *Who* shall prevent a new revolution? was thus actually, and owing to the lamentable divisions of the friends of order, in the hands of the Parliamentary representatives of the very men who wished to affect that revolution, was determined, I may say, ultimately and in the last resort by the party of disorder.

Nor on lesser questions was there any steady majority, any distinctive deciding faction, any administering phalanx, anybody regularly voting with anybody else, often enough, or in number enough, to make the legislative decision regular, consistent, or respectable. Their very debates were unseemly. On anything not pleasing to them, the Mountain (as I said) a yellow and fanatical generation—had (I am told) an engaging knack of rising *en masse* and screaming until they were tired. It will be the same, I do not say in degree (for the Mountain would certainly lose several votes now, and the numbers of the late Chamber were unreasonably and injudiciously large), but, in a measure, you will be always subject to the same disorder—a fluctuating majority, and a minority, often a ruling minority, favourable to rebellion. The cause, as I believe, is to be sought in the peculiarities of the French character, on which I dwelt, prolixly, I fear, and *ad nauseam*, in my last two letters. If you have to deal with a *mobile*, a clever, a versatile, an intellectual, a dogmatic nation, inevitably, and by necessary consequence, you will have conflicting systems—every man speaking his own words, and always giving his own suffrage to what seems good in his own eyes—many holding to-day what they will regret to-morrow—a crowd of crotchety theories and a heavy percentage of philosophical nonsense—a great opportunity for subtle stratagem and intriguing selfishness—a miserable division among the friends of tranquillity, and a great power thrown into the hands of those who, though often with the very best intentions, are practically, and in matter of fact, opposed both to society and civilisation. And, moreover, beside minor inconveniences and lesser hardships, you will indisputably have periodically—say three or four times in fifty years—a great crisis; the public mind much excited, the people in the streets swaying to and fro with the breath of every breeze, the discontented *ouvriers* meeting in a hundred knots, discussing their real sufferings and their imagined grievances, with lean features and angry gesticulations; the Parliament, all the while in permanence, very ably and eloquently expounding the whole subject, one man proposing this scheme, and another that; the Opposition expecting to oust the Ministers, and ride in on the popular commotion; the Ministers fearing to take the odium of severe or adequate repressive measures, lest they should lose their salary, their places and their majority: finally, a great crash, a disgusted people, overwhelmed by revolutionary violence, or seeking a precarious, a pernicious, but after all a precious protection from the bayonets of military despotism. Louis Philippe met these dangers and difficulties in a thoroughly characteristic manner. He bought his majority. Being a practical and not over sentimental public functionary, he went into the market and purchased a sufficient number of constituencies and members. Of course the *convenances* were carefully preserved; grossness of any kind is too jarring for French susceptibility; the purchase money was not mere coin (which indeed the buyers had not to offer), but a more gentlemanly commodity—the patronage of the Government. The electoral colleges were extremely small, the number of public functionaries is enormous; so that a very respectable body of electors could always be expected to have, like a four-year-old barrister (since the County Courts), an immense prejudice for the existing Government. One man hoped to be *Maire,* another wanted his son got into St Cyr or the Polytechnic School, and this could be got, and was daily got (I am writing what is hardly denied), by voting for the Government candidate. In a word, a sufficient proportion of the returns of the electoral colleges resembled the returns from Harwich or Devonport, only that the Government was the only bidder; for there are not, I fancy, in any country but England, people able and willing to spend, election after election, great sums of money for procuring the honour of a seat in a representative assembly. In fact, to copy the well-known phrase, just as in the time of Burke, certain gentlemen had the expressive nickname of the King's friends, so these constituencies may aptly be called the King's constituencies. Of course, on the face of it, this system worked, as far as business went, excellently well. For eighteen years the tranquillity was maintained. France, it may be, has never enjoyed so much calm civilisation, so much private happiness; and yet, after all such and so long blessings, it fell in a mere riot—it fell unregretted. It is a system which no wise man can wish to see restored; it was a system of regulated corruption.

But it does not at all follow, nor I am sure will you be apt so to deduce, that because I imagine that France is unfit for a Government in which a House of Commons is, as with us, the sovereign power in the State, I therefore believe that it is fit for no freedom at all. Our own constitutional history is the completest answer to any such idea. For centuries, the House of Commons was habitually, we know, but a third-rate power in the State. First the Crown, then the House of Lords, enjoyed the ordinary and supreme dominion; and down almost to our own times the Crown and House of Lords, taken together, were much more than a sufficient match for the people's House; but yet we do not cease to proclaim, daily and hourly, in season and out of season, that the English people never have been slaves. It may, therefore, well be that our own country having been free under a Constitution in which the representative element was but third-rate in power and dignity, France and other nations may contrive to enjoy the advantage from institutions in which it is only second-rate.

Now, of this sort is the Constitution of Louis Napoleon. I am not going now, after prefacing so much, to discuss its details; indeed, I do not feel competent to do so. What should we say to a Frenchman's notion of a £5 householder, or the fourth and fifth clauses of the New Reform Bill? and I quite admit that a paper building of this sort can hardly be safely criticised till it is carried out on *terra firma*, till we see not only the theoretic ground-plan, but the actual inhabited structure. The life of a constitution is in the spirit and disposition of those who work it; and we can't yet say in the least what that, in this case, will be; but so far as the constitution shows its meaning on the face of it, it clearly belongs to the class which I have named. The *Corps Législatif* is not the administering body, it is not even what perhaps it might with advantage have been, a petitioning and remonstrating body; but it possesses the Legislative veto, and the power of stopping *en masse* the supplies. It is not a working, a ruling, or an initiative, or supremely decisive, but an immense checking power. It will be unable to change Ministers, or aggravate the course of revolutions; but it could arrest an unpopular war—it could reject an unpopular law—it is, at least in theory, a powerful and important drag-chain. Out of the mouths of its adversaries this system possesses what I have proved, or conjectured, or assumed to be the prime want of the French nation—a strong executive. The objection to it is that the objectors find nothing else in it. We confess there is no doubt now of a power adequate to repress street-rows and revolutions.

At the same time, I guard myself against intimating any opinion on the particular *minutiæ* of this last effort of institutional invention. I do not know enough to form a judgment; I sedulously, at present, confine myself to this one remark, that the new Government of France belongs, in theory at least, to the right class of Constitutions—the class that is most exactly suited to French habits, French nature, French social advantages, French social dangers—the class I mean, in which the representative body has a consultative, a deliberative, a checking and a minatory—not as with us a supreme, nearly an omnipotent, and exclusively initiatory function.

I am, yours, etc.,

AMICUS.

P.S.—You may like five words on a French invasion. I can't myself imagine, and what is more to the point, I do not observe that anybody here has any notion of, any such inroad into England as was contemplated and proposed by General Changarnier. No one in the actual conduct of affairs, with actual responsibility for affairs, not, as the event proved, even Ledru Rollin, could, according to me, encounter the risk and odium of such a hateful and horribly dangerous attempt. But, I regret to add, there is a contingency which sensible people here (so far as I have had the means of judging) do not seem to regard as at all beyond the limits of rational probability, by which a war between England and France would most likely be superinduced; that is, a French invasion of Belgium. I do not mean to assure you that this week or next the Prince-President will make a razzia in Brussels. But I do mean that it is thought not improbable that somehow or other, on some wolf-and-the-lamb pretext, he may pick a quarrel with King

Leopold, and endeavour to restore to the French the "natural limit" of the Rhine. Now, I have never seen the terms of the guarantee which the shrewd and cautious Leopold exacted from England before he would take the throne of Belgium, but as the only real risk was a French aggression upon this tempting territory, I do not make any doubt but that the expressions of that instrument bind us to go to war in defence of the country whose limits and independence we have guaranteed. And in this case, an invasion of England would be as admissible a military movement as an invasion of France. I hope, therefore, you will use your best rhetoric to induce people to put our pleasant country in a state of adequate and tolerable defence.

I see by the invaluable *Galignani*, that some excellent people at Manchester are indulging in a little arithmetic. "Suppose," say they, "all the French got safe, and each took away £50, now how much do you fancy it would come to (40,000 men by £50, nought's nought is nought, nought and carry two)—compared to the *existing* burden of the National Debt? Was there ever such amiable infatuation! It is not what the French could carry off, but what they would leave behind them, which is in the reasonable apprehension of reasonable persons. The funds at 50—broken banks—the *Gazette* telling you who had *not* failed—Downing Street *vide* Wales—destitute families, dishonoured daughters, one-legged fathers—the mourning shops utterly sacked—the customers in tears—a pale widow in a green bonnet—the Exchange in ruins—five notches on St Paul's—and a big hole in the Bank of England;—these, though but a few of the certain consequences of a French visit to London, are quite enough to terrify even an adamantine editor and a rather reckless correspondent.

LETTER VI.

THE FRENCH NEWSPAPER PRESS.

Paris, 10th February.

Sir,—We learn from an Oriental narrative in considerable circulation, that the ancient Athenians were fond of news. Of course they were. It is in the nature of a mass of clever and intellectual people living together to want something to talk about. Old ideas—common ascertained truths—are good things

enough to live by, but are very rare, and soon sufficiently discussed. Something else—true or false, rational or nonsensical
—is quite essential; and, therefore, in the old literary world
men gathered round the travelling sophist, to learn from him
some thought, crotchet, or speculation. And what the vaga-
bond speculators were once, that, pretty exactly, is the newspaper now. To it the people of this intellectual capital look
for that daily mental bread, which is as essential to them
as the less ethereal sustenance of ordinary mortals. With the
spread of education this habit travels downward. Not the literary man only, but the *ouvrier* and the *bourgeois*, live on the
same food. This day's *Siècle* is discussed not only in gorgeous
drawing-rooms, but in humble reading-rooms, and still humbler workshops. According to the printed notions of us journalists, this is a matter of pure rejoicing. The influence of the
Press, if you believe writers and printers, is the one sufficient
condition of social well-being. Yet there are many considerations which make very much against this idea: I can't go into
several of them now, but those that I shall mention are suggested at once by matters before me. First, newspaper people
are the only traders that thrive upon convulsion. In quiet
times, who cares for the paper? In times of tumult, who
does not? Commonly, the *Patrie* (the *Globe* of this country)
sells, I think, for three sous: on the evening of the *coup
d'état*, itinerant ladies were crying under my window, "De-
mandez la Patrie—Journal du soir—trente sous—Journal du
soir"; and I remember witnessing, even in our sober London,
in February, 1848, how bald fathers of families paid large
sums, and encountered bare-headed the unknown inclemen-
cies of the night air, that they might learn the last news of
Louis Philippe, and, if possible, be in at the death of the
revolutionary Parisians. "Happy," says the sage, "are the people whose annals are vacant;" but "woe! woe! woe!" he might
add, "to the wretched journalists that have to compose and
sell leading articles therein."

I am constrained to say that, even in England, this is not
without its unfavourable influence on literary morals. Take
in the *Times*, and you will see it assumed that every year
ought to be an era. "The Government does nothing," is the
indignant cry, and simple people in the country don't know
that this is merely a civilised *façon de parler* for "I have nothing to say". Lord John Russell must alter the suffrage, that
we may have something pleasant in our columns.

I am afraid matters are worse here. The leading French journalist is, as you know, the celebrated Emile de Girardin, and, so far as I can learn anything about him, he is one of the most fickle politicians in existence. Since I have read the *Presse* regularly, it has veered from every point of the compass well-nigh to every other—now for, now against, the revision of the constitution—now lauding Louis Napoleon to the skies—now calling him plain M. Bonaparte, and insinuating that he had not two ideas, and was incapable of moral self-government—now connected with the Red party, now praising the majority; but all and each of these veerings and shiftings determined by one most simple and certain principle—to keep up the popular excitement, to maintain the gifted M. de Girardin at the head of it. Now, a man who spends his life in stimulating excitement and convulsion is really a political incendiary; and however innocent and laudable his brother exiles may be, the old editor and founder of the *Presse* is, as I believe, now only paying the legitimate penalty of systematic political *arson*.

When a foreigner—at least an Englishman—begins to read the French papers, his first idea is, "How well these fellows write! Why, every one of them has a style, and a good style too. Really, how clear, how acute, how clever, how perspicuous; I wish our journalists would learn to write like this;" but a little experience will modify this idea—at least I have found it so. I read for a considerable time these witty periodicals with pleasure and admiration; after a little while I felt somehow that I took them up with an effort, but I fancied, knowing my disposition, that this was laziness; when on a sudden, in the waste of *Galignani*, I came across an article of the *Morning Herald*. Now you'll laugh at me, if I tell you it was a real enjoyment. There was no toil, no sharp theory, no pointed expression, no fatiguing brilliancy, in fact, what the man in Lord Byron desired, "no nothing," but a dull, creeping, satisfactory sensation that now, at least, there was nothing to admire. As long walking in picture galleries makes you appreciate a mere wall, so I felt that I understood for the first time that really dulness had its interest. I found a pure refreshment in coming across what possibly might be latent sense, but was certainly superficial stupidity.

I think there is nothing we English hate like a clever but prolonged controversy. Now this is the life and soul of the Parisian press. Everybody writes against everybody. It is not mere sly hate or solemn invective, nothing like what we occasionally indulge in, about the misdemeanours of a morning contemporary. But they take the other side's article piece by piece, and comment on him, and, as they say in libel cases, *innuendo* him, and satisfactorily show that, according to his arithmetic, two and two make five; useful knowledge that. It is really good for us to know that some fellow (you never heard of him) it rather seems can't add up. But it interests people here;—*c'est logique*, they tell you; and if you are trustful enough to answer "*Mon Dieu, c'est ennuyeux, je n'en sais rien*," they look as if you sneered at the Parthenon.

It is out of these controversies that M. de Girardin has attained his power and his fame. His articles (according to me, at least) have no facts and no sense. He gives one all pure reasoning—little scrappy syllogisms; as some one said most unjustly of old Hazlitt, he "writes pimples". But let an unfortunate writer in the *Assemblée Nationale*, or anywhere else, make a little refreshing blunder in his logic, and next morning small punning sentences (one to each paragraph like an equation) come rattling down on him: it is clear as noonday that somebody said "something followed," and it does *not* follow, and it is so agreed in all the million *cabinets de lecture* after due gesticulation; and, moreover, that M. de Girardin is the man to expose it, and what clever fellows they are to appreciate him; but what the truth is, who cares? The subject is forgotten.

Now all this, to my notion, does great harm. Nothing destroys commonplace like the habit of arguing for arguing's sake; nothing is so bad for public matters as that they should be treated, not as the data for the careful formation of a sound judgment, but as a topic or background for displaying the shining qualities of public writers. It is no light thing this. M. de Girardin for many years has gained more power, more reputation, more money than any of his rivals; not because he shows more knowledge—he shows much less; not because he has a wiser judgment—he has no fixed judgment at all; but because he has a more pointed, sharp way of exposing blunders, intrinsically paltry, obvious to all educated men; and does not care enough for any subject to be diverted from this logical trifling by a serious desire to convince anybody of anything.

Don't think I wish to be hard on this accomplished gentleman. I am not going to require of hack-writers to write only

on what they understand—if that were the law, what a life
for the sub-editor; I should not be writing these letters, and
how seldom and how timidly would the morning journals
creep into the world. Nor do I expect, though I may still, in
sentimental moods, desire, middle-aged journalists to be
buoyed up by chimerical visions of improving mankind.

You know what our eminent *chef* (by Thackeray profanely
called Jupiter Jeames) has been heard to say over his gin
and water, in an easy and voluptuous moment: "Enlighten-
ment be ——, I want the fat fool of a thick-headed reader to
say, 'Just *my own* views,' else he ain't pleased, and may be he
stops the paper". I am not going to require supernatural excellence from writers. Yet there are limits. If I were a chemist,
I should not mind, I suppose, selling now and then, a deleteri-
ous drug on a due affidavit of rats, then and there filed before
me; yet I don't feel as if I could live comfortably on the sale
of mere arsenic. I fancy I should like to sell something wholesome occasionally. So, though one might, upon occasion, egg
on a riot, or excite to a breach of the peace, I should not like
to be every day feeding on revolutionary excitement. Nor
should I like to be exclusively selling diminutive, acute, quibbling leaders (what they call in the Temple special de-
murrers), certain to occupy people with small fallacies, and
lead away their minds from the great questions actually at
issue.

Sometimes I might like to feel as if I understood what I
wrote on, but of course with me this indulgence must be very
rare. You know in France journalism is not only an occupation, it is a career. As in far-off Newcastle a coal-fitter's son
looks wistfully to the bar, in the notion that he too may
emulate the fame and fortune of Lord Eldon or Lord Stowell,
so in fair Provence, a pale young aspirant packs up his little
bundle in the hope of rivalling the luck and fame of M.
Thiers; he comes to Paris—he begins, like the great historian,
by dining for thirty sous in the Palais Royal, in the hope after
long years of labour and jealousy he, too, may end by sleep-
ing amid curtains of white muslin lined with pink damask.
Just consider for a moment what a difference this one fact
shows between France and England. Here a man who begins
life by writing in the newspapers, has an appreciable chance
of arriving to be Minister of Foreign Affairs. The class of
public writers is the class from which the equivalent of Lord
Aberdeen, Lord Palmerston, or Lord Granville will most likely

be chosen. Well, well, under that *régime* you and I might have been important people; we might have handled a red box, we might have known what it was to have a reception, to dine with the Queen, to be respectfully mystified by the *corps diplomatique*. But angry Jove forbade—of course we can hardly deny that he was wrong—and yet if the revolutions of 1848 have clearly brought out any fact, it is the utter failure of newspaper statesmen. Everywhere they have been tried: everywhere they have shown great talents for intrigue, eloquence, and agitation—how rarely have they shown even fair aptitude for ordinary administration; how frequently have they gained a disreputable renown by a laxity of principle surpassing the laxity of their aristocratic and courtly adversaries! Such being my imperfect account of my imperfect notions of the French press, I can't altogether sympathise in the extreme despondency of many excellent persons at its temporary silence since the *coup d'état*. I might even rejoice at it, if I thought that the Parisian public could in any manner be broken of their dependence on the morning's article. But I have no such hope; the taste has got down too deep into the habits of the people; some new thing will still be necessary; and every Government will find some of its most formidable difficulties in their taste for political disputation and controversial excitement. The ban must sooner or later be taken off; the President sooner or later must submit to censure and ridicule, and whatever laws he may propose about the press, there is none which scores of ingenious men —now animated by the keenest hatred, will not try every hazard to evade. What he may do to avoid this is as yet unknown. One thing, however, I suppose is pretty sure, and I fancy quite wise. The press will be restrained from discussing the principles of the Government. Socialists will not be allowed to advocate a Democratic Republic. Legitimists will not be allowed to advocate the cause of Henri Cinq, nor Orleanists the cause of the Comte de Paris. Such indulgence might be tolerable in more temperate countries, but experience shows that it is not safe now and here.

A really sensible press, arguing temperately after a clear and satisfactory exposition of the facts, is a great blessing in any country. It will be still more a blessing in a country where, as I tried to explain formerly, the representative element must play (if the public security is to be maintained) a rather secondary part. It would then be a real stimulus to deliberate inquiry and rational judgment upon public affairs; to the formation of common-sense views upon the great outlines of public business; to the cultivation of sound moral opinions and convictions on the internal and international duties of the State. Even the actual press which we may expect to see here, may not be pernicious. It will doubtless stimulate to many factious proceedings, and many interruptions of the public prosperity; it may very likely conduce to drive the President (contrary, if not to his inclination, at least to his personal interest) into foreign hostilities and international aggression; but it may be, notwithstanding, useful in preventing private tyranny, in exposing wanton oppression, in checking long-suffering revenge; it may prevent acts of spoliation like what they call here *le premier vol de l'aigel* —the seizure of the Orleans property;—in a word, being certain to oppose the executive, where the latter is unjust its enemy will be just.

I had hopes that this letter would be the last with which I should tease you; but I find I must ask you to be so kind as to find room for one, and only for one more.

I am, yours, etc.,
AMICUS.

LETTER VII.

CONCLUDING LETTER.

Paris, 19th February, 1852.

Sir,—There is a story of some Swedish Abbé, in the last century, who wrote an elaborate work to prove the then constitution of his country to be immortal and indestructible. While he was correcting the proof sheets, a friend brought him word that—behold! the King had already destroyed the said polity. "Sir," replied the gratified author, "our Sovereign, the illustrious Gustavus, may certainly overthrow the Constitution, but never *my book*." I beg to parody this sensible remark; for I wish to observe to you, that even though Louis Napoleon should turn out a bad and mischievous ruler, he won't in the least refute these letters.

What I mean is as follows. Above all things, I have designed to prove to you that the French are by character unfit for a solely and predominantly Parliamentary Government;

that so many and so great elements of convulsion exist here, that it will be clearly necessary that a strong, vigorous, anti-barricade executive should, at whatever risk and cost, be established and maintained; that such an Assembly as the last is irreconcilable with this; in a word, that riots and revolutions must, if possible, come to an end, and only such a degree of liberty and democracy be granted to the French nation, as is consistent with the consolidated existence of the order and tranquillity which are equally essential to rational freedom and civilised society.

In order to combine the maintenance of order and tranquillity with the maximum of possible liberty, I hope that it may in the end be found possible to admit into a political system a representative and sufficiently democratic Assembly, without that Assembly assuming and arrogating to itself those nearly omnipotent powers, which in our country it properly and rightfully possesses, but which in the history of the last sixty years, we have, as it seems to me, so many and so cogent illustrations that a French Chamber is, by genius and constitution, radically incapable to hold and exercise. I hope that some checking, consultative, petitioning Assembly—some βουλή, in the real sense of the term—some *Council*, some provision by which all grave and deliberate public opinion (I do not speak more definitely, because an elaborate Constitution, from a foreigner, must be an absurdity) may organise and express itself—yet at the same time, without utterly hampering and directing—and directing amiss—those more simple elements of national polity on which we must, after all, rely for the prompt and steady repression of barricade-making and bloodshed.

I earnestly desire to believe that some such system as this may be found in practice possible; for otherwise, unless I quite misread history, and altogether mistake what is under my eyes, after many more calamities, many more changes, many more great Assemblies abounding in Vergniauds and Berryers, the essential deficiencies of debating Girondin statesmen will become manifest, the uncompact, unpractical, over-volatile, over-logical, indecisive, ineffectual rule of Gallican Parliaments will be unequivocally manifest (it is *now* plain, I imagine, but a truth so humiliating must be written large in letters of blood before those that run will read it), and no medium being held or conceived to be possible, the nation will sink back, not contented but discontented, not

trustfully but distrustfully, under the rule of a military despot; and if they yield to this, it will be from no faith, no
loyalty, no credulity; it will be from a sense—a hated sense
—of unqualified failure, a miserable scepticism in the probable success and the possible advantages of long-tried and ill-
tried rebellion.

Now, whether the Constitution of Louis Napoleon is calculated to realise this ideal and intermediate system, is, till
we see it at work, doubtful and disputable. It is not the question so much of what it may be at this moment, as of what
it may become in a brief period, when things have begun to
assume a more normal state, and the public mind shall be
relaxed from its present and painful tension. However, I
should be deceiving you, if I did not inform you that the
state of men's minds towards the Prince-President is not, so
far as I can make it out, what it was the day after the *coup
d'état*. The measures taken against the Socialists are felt to
have been several degrees too severe; the list of exiles too
numerous; the confiscation of the Orleans property could not
but be attended with the worst effect; the law announced by
the Government organs respecting or rather against the Press,
is justly (though you know from my last letter I have no
partiality for French newspapers) considered to be absurdly
severe, and likely to countenance much tyranny and gross
injustice; above all, instead of maintaining mere calm and
order, the excessive rigour, and sometimes the injustice, of the
President's measures, have produced a breathless pause (if
I may so speak) in public opinion; political conversation is a
whispered question, what will he do next? Firstly, the Government is dull, and the French want to be amused; secondly, it is going to spoil the journals (depreciate newspapers
to a Frenchman, disparage nuts to a monkey); thirdly, it is
producing (I do not say it has yet produced, but it has made
a beginning in producing) a habit of apprehension;—in fact,
I believe the French opinion of the Prince-President is near
about that of the interesting damsel in George Sand's com-
edy, concerning her uninteresting *pretendu:* "*Vous l'aimez?
n'est-ce pas?*" "*Oui, oui, oui, certainement je l'aime. Oui,
oui, mille fois, oui. Je dis que oui. Je vous assure.* AU MOINS
je fais mon possible à l'aimer:" the first attachment is not
extinct, but people have begun—awful symptom—to add the
withering and final saving clause. Yet it is, I imagine, a great
mistake to suppose that the present Constitution, if it work

at all, will permanently work as a despotism, or that the *Corps Législatif* will be without a measure of popular influence; the much more helpless *Tribunal* was not so in the much more troublesome times of the Consulate. And the source of such influence and the manner of its operation may be, I imagine, well enough traced in the nature of the forces whereby Louis Napoleon holds his power.

A truly estimable writer says, I know, "that the Legislative body cannot have, by possibility, any analogy with the consultative and petitioning senate of the Plantagenets," nor can any one deny that the likeness is extremely faint (no illustration ever yet ran on all fours), the practical differences clear and convincing. But yet, according to the light which is given me now, I affirm that for one vital purpose—the resisting and criticising any highly unpopular acts of a highly unpopular Government—the *Corps Législatif* of Louis Napoleon must, and will, inevitably possess a power compared with which the forty-day followers of the feudal *noblesse* seem as impotent as a congregation of Quakers; a force the peculiarity of which is that you can't imprison, can't dissolve, can't annihilate it—I mean, of course, the moral power of civilised opinion. You may put down newspapers, dissolve Parliaments, imprison agitators, almost stop conversation, but you can't stop thought. You can't prevent the silent, slow, creeping, stealthy progress of hatred, and scorn, and shame. You can't attenuate easily the stern justice of a retarded retaliation. These influences affect the great reservoir of physical force—they act on the army. A body of men enlisted daily from the people take to the barracks the notions of the people; in spite of new associations, the first impressions are apt to be retained; you overlay them, but they remain. What is believed elsewhere and out of doors gives them weight. Each soldier has relations, friends, a family—he knows what they think. Much more with the officers. These are men moving in Parisian society, accessible to its influences, responsible to its opinion, apt to imbibe its sentiments. Certainly *esprit de corps*—the habit of obedience, the instinct of discipline, are strong, and will carry men far; but certainly, also, they have natural limits. Men won't stand being cut, being ridiculed, being detested, being despised, daily and for ever, and that for measures which their own understandings disapprove of. Remember there is not here any question of barbarous bands overawing a civilised and imperial city; no question of ugly

Croats keeping down cultivated Italians; it is but a question
of French gentlemen and French peasantry in uniform acting
in opposition to other French gentlemen and other French
peasants without uniform. Already there has been talk (I do
not say well-founded, but still the matter was named) of
breaking two or three hundred officers, for speaking against
the Orleans decrees. Do you fancy that can be done every
day? Do you imagine that a Parliament, whatever its nominal
functions may be (remember those of the old *régime*), speaking the sense of the people about the question of the day, in
a time of convulsion, and in a critical hour, would not be
attended to, or at any rate thought of and considered, by an
army taken from the people—commanded by men selected
from and every day mixing with common society and very
ordinary mankind? The 2nd of December showed how readily
such troops will support a decided and popular President
against an intriguing, divided, impotent Chamber. But such
hard blows won't bear repetition. Soldiers—French soldiers, I
take it especially, from their quickness and intelligence, are
neither deaf nor blind. If there be truth in history or speculation, national forces can't long be used against the nation:
they are unmerciful, and often cruel to feeble minorities;
they are ready now for a terrible onslaught on mere Socialists,
just as of old they turned out cheerfully for awful dragon-
nades on the ill-starred Protestants; but once let them know
and feel that everybody is against them—that they are alone,
that their acts are contemned and their persons despised—
and gradually, or all at once, discipline and habit surely fail,
men murmur or desert, officers hesitate or disobey, one regi-
ment is dismissed to the Cabyles, another relegated to rural
solitudes; at last, most likely in the decisive moment of the
whole history, the rulers, who relied only on their troops, are
afraid to call them out; they hesitate, send spies and commissioners to inquire. "*Vive le Gouvernement Provisoire!*"—
the black and roaring multitude rises and comes on; but two
seconds, and the obnoxious institutions are lost in the flood;
nothing is heard but the cry of the hour, sounding shrill and
angry over the waste of Revolution—"*Vive le Diable!*" With
such a force behind them, a French Parliament, of whatever
nature, with whatever written duties, is, if at the head of the
movement, in the critical hour, apt to be stronger than the
strongest of the Barons.

Nor do I concur with those who censure the President for

"recommending" avowedly the candidates he approves. It is a part of the great question, How is universal suffrage to be worked successfully in such a country as France? The peasant proprietors have but one political idea, that they wish the Prince to govern them;—they wish to vote for the candidate most acceptable to him, and they wish nothing else. Why is he wrong in telling them which candidate that is?

Still, no doubt, the reins are now strained a great deal too tight. It is possible, quite possible, that a majority in this Parliament may be packed, but what I would impress on you is that it can't always be packed. Sooner or later constituencies who wish to oppose the Government will, in spite of *maires* and *préfets*, elect the opposition candidate: it is in the nature of any, even the least vigorous system of popular election, to struggle forwards and progressively attain to some fair and reasonable correspondence with the substantial views and opinions of the constituent people.

I therefore fall back on what I told you before—my essential view or crotchet about the mental aptitudes and deficiencies of the French people. The French, said Napoleon, are *des machines nerveuses*.

The point is, can their excitable, volatile, superficial, over-logical, uncompromising character be managed and manipulated as to fit them for entering on a practically uncontrolled system of Parliamentary Government? Will not any large and omnipotent Assembly resemble the stormy Constituent and the late Chamber, rather than the business-like, formal, ennui-diffusing Parliament to which in our free and dull country we are felicitously accustomed? Can one be so improved as to keep down a riot? I foresee a single and but a single objection. I fancy, indeed I know, that there is a school of political thinkers not yet in possession of any great influence, but, perhaps, a little on the way thereto, which has improved or invented a capital panacea, whereby all nations are, within very moderate limits of time, to be surely and certainly fitted for political freedom; and that no matter how formed—how seemingly stable—how long ago cast and constructed, be the type of popular character to which the said remedy is sought to be applied. This panacea is the foundation or restoration of provincial municipalities. Now, I am myself prepared to go a considerable length with the school in question. I do myself think, that a due and regular consideration of the knotty points of paving and lighting, and the deciding in the

last resort upon them, is a valuable discipline of national
character. It exercises people's minds on points they know, in
things of which there is a test. Very few people are good
judges of a good Constitution; but everybody's eyes are excellent judges of good light; every man's feet are profound
in the theory of agreeable stones. Yet I can't altogether admit,
nevertheless, that municipalities are the sufficient and sole,
though they may be very likely an essential, pre-requisite of
political freedom. There is the great instance of Hindostan to
the contrary. The whole old and national system of that remarkable country—a system in all probability as ancient as the
era of Alexander, is a village system; and one so curious,
elaborate, I fancy I might say so profound, that the best
European observers—Sir Thomas Munro, and that sort of people—are most strenuous for its being retained unimpaired. According to them, the village hardly heard of the Imperial
Government, except for the purpose of Imperial taxation.
The business of life through that whole vast territory has always been practically determined by potails and parish-
vestries, and yet nevertheless and in spite of this capital and
immemorial municipal system, our subjects, the Hindoos,
are still slaves and still likely to be slaves; still essentially
slavish, and likely, I much fear, very long indeed to remain
so. It is therefore quite certain that rural and provincial institutions won't so alter and adapt all national characters, as
to fit all nations for a Parliamentary Constitution; consequently, the *onus probandi* is on those who assert that it will
so alter and mould the French. Again, I assure you that the
French do think of paving and lighting; not enough, perhaps,
but still they have begun. The country is, as you know, divided into departments, arrondissements, and communes; in
each of these there is a council, variously elected, but, in all
cases, popularly and from the district, which has the sole
control over the expenditure of the particular locality for
every special and local purpose, and which, if I am rightly
informed, has, in theory, at least, the sole initiative in every
local improvement. The defect, I fancy, is that in the exercise of these, considerable bodies are hampered and controlled by the veto and supervision of the central authority.
The rural councils discuss and decide what in their judgment
should be then done and what money should be so spent; the
better sort of the agricultural population have much more
voice in the latter than have the corresponding class in Eng-

land, in the determination and imposition of our own county
rate; but it is the central authority which decides whether
such proposals and recommendations shall in fact be carried
out. In a word, the provinces have to *ask leave* of the Parisian
Ministry of the Interior. Now I admit this is an abuse. I
should maintain that elderly gentlemen with bald heads and
local influence ought to feel that they, in the final resort,
settle and determine all truly local matters. Human nature
likes its own road, its own bridge, its own lapidary obstacles,
its own deceptive luminosity. But I ask again, can you fancy
that these luxuries, to whatever degree indulged in, alter and
modify in any essential particular, the levity and volatility of
the French character? How much light to how much logic?
How many paving stones to how much mobility? I can't foresee any such change. And even if so, what in the meantime?

We are left then, I think, to deal with the French character pretty much as we find it. What stealthy, secret, unknown, excellent forces may, in the wisdom of Providence, be
even now modifying this most curious intellectual fabric,
neither you nor I can know or tell. Let us hope that they
may be many. But if we indulge, and from the immense records of revolutionary history, I think, with due distrust, we
may legitimately and even beneficially indulge, in system-
building and speculation, we must take the *data* which we
have, and not those which we desire or imagine. Louis Napoleon has proposed a system: English writers by the thousand (if I was in harness instead of holiday-making I should
be most likely among them) proclaim his system an evil one.
What then? Do you know what Father Newman says to the
religious reformers, rather sharply, but still well: "Make out
first of all where you stand—draw up your creed—write down
your catechism"? So I answer to the English eloquence: "State
first of all what you would have—draw up your novel system
for the French Government—write down your political Constitution". Don't criticise but produce; do not find fault but
propose—and when you have proposed upon theory and have
created upon paper, let us see whether the system be such a
one as will work, in fact, and be accepted by a wilful nation
in reality—otherwise your work is nought.

And mind, too, that the system to be sketched out must
be fit to protect the hearths and homes of men. It is easy to
compose polities if you do but neglect this one essential condition. Four years ago, Europe was in a ferment with the

newest ideas, the best theories, the most elaborate, the most artistic Constitutions. There was the labour, and toil, and trouble of a million intellects, as good, taken on the whole, perhaps, as the world is likely to see,—of old statesmen, and literary gentlemen, and youthful enthusiasts, all over Europe, from the Baltic Sea to the Mediterranean, from the frontiers of Russia to the Atlantic Ocean. Well, what have we gained? A Parliament in Sardinia! Surely this is a lesson against proposing politics which won't work, convening assemblies that can't legislate, constructing executives that aren't able to keep the peace, founding Constitutions inaugurated with tears and eloquence, soon abandoned with tears and shame; beginning a course of fair auguries and liberal hopes, but one from whose real dangers and actual sufferings a frightened and terrified people, in the end, flee for a temporary, or may be a permanent, refuge under a military and absolute ruler.

Mazzini sneers at the selfishness of shopkeepers—I am for the shopkeepers against him. There are people who think because they are Republican there shall be no more "cakes and ale". Aye, verily, but there will though; or else stiffish ginger will be hot in the mouth. Legislative Assemblies, leading articles, essay eloquence—such are good—very good,—useful—very useful. Yet they can be done without. We can want them. Not so with all things. The selling of figs, the cobbling of shoes, the manufacturing of nails,—these are the essence of life. And let whoso frameth a Constitution of his country think on these things.

I conclude, as I ought, with my best thanks for the insertion of these letters; otherwise I was so full of the subject that I might have committed what Disraeli calls "the extreme act of human fatuity," I might have published a pamphlet: from this your kindness has preserved me, and I am proportionally grateful.

I am, yours,
Amicus.

CÆSARISM AS IT EXISTED IN 1865*

(1865)

That the French Emperor should have spare leisure and un-occupied reflection to write a biography, is astonishing, but if he wished to write a biography, his choice of a subject is very natural. Julius Cæsar was the first who tried on an imperial scale the characteristic principles of the French Empire,—as the first Napoleon revived them, as the third Napoleon has consolidated them. The notion of a demagogue ruler, both of a fighting demagogue and a talking demagogue, was indeed familiar to the Greek Republics; but their size was small, and their history unemphatic. On the big page of universal history, Julius Cæsar is the first instance of a democratic despot. He overthrew an aristocracy—a corrupt, and perhaps effete, aristocracy, it is true, but still an aristocracy—by the help of the people, of the unorganised people. He said to the numerical majority of Roman citizens: "I am your advocate and your leader: make me supreme, and I will govern for your good, and in your name". This is exactly the principle of the French Empire. No one will ever make an approach to understanding it, who does not separate it altogether, and on principle, from the despotisms of feudal origin and legitimate pretensions. The old Monarchies claim the obedience of the people upon grounds of duty. They say they have consecrated claims to the loyalty of mankind. They appeal to conscience, even to religion. But Louis Napoleon is a Benthamite despot. He is for the "greatest happiness of the greatest number". He says: "I am where I am, because I know better than any one else what is good for the French people, and they know that I know better". He is not the Lord's anointed; he is the people's agent.

We cannot here discuss what the effect of this system was in ancient times. These columns are not the best place for

---

* This article was first published in *The Economist* for March 4, 1865, Volume XXIII, pages 249–50.

a historical dissertation; but we may set down very briefly the results of some close and recent observation of the system as it now exists, as it is at work in France. Part of its effects are well understood in England, but a part of them are, we think, but mistily seen and imperfectly apprehended.

In the first place, the French Empire is really the *best finished* democracy which the world has ever seen. What the many at the moment desire is embodied with a readiness, and efficiency, and a completeness which has no parallel, either in past history or present experience. An absolute Government with a popular instinct has the unimpeded command of a people renowned for orderly dexterity. A Frenchman will have arranged an administrative organisation really and effectually, while an Englishman is still bungling and a German still reflecting. An American is certainly as rapid, and in some measure as efficient, but his speed is a little headlong, and his execution is very rough; he tumbles through much, but he only tumbles. A Frenchman will not hurry; he has a deliberate perfection in detail, which may always be relied on, for it is never delayed. The French Emperor knows well how to use these powers. His bureaucracy is not only endurable, but pleasant. An idle man who wants his politics done for him, has them done for him. The welfare of the masses—the present good of the present multitude—is felt to be the object of the Government and the law of the polity. The Empire gives to the French the full gratification of their main wishes, and the almost artistic culture of an admirable workmanship, of an administration finished as only Frenchmen can finish it, and as it never was finished before.

It belongs to such a Government to care much for material prosperity, and it does care. It makes the people as comfortable as they will permit. If they are not more comfortable, it is their own fault. The Government would give them free-trade, and consequent diffused comfort, if it could. No former French Government has done as much for free-trade as this Government. No Government has striven to promote railways, and roads, and industry, like this Government. France is much changed in twelve years. Not exactly by the mere merit of the Empire, for it entered into a great inheritance; it succeeded to the silent work of the free monarchy which revolution had destroyed and impeded. There were fruitful and vigorous germs of improvement ready to be elicited— ready to start forth—but under an unintelligent Government they would not have started forth; they would have lain idle and dead, but under the adroit culture of the present Government, they have grown so as to amaze Europe and France itself.

If, indeed, as is often laid down, the *present happiness* of the greatest number was the characteristic object of the Government, it would be difficult to make out that any probable French Government would be better, or indeed nearly so good, as the present. The intelligence of the Emperor on economical subjects—on the bread and meat of the people— is really better than that of the classes opposed to him. He gives the present race of Frenchmen more that is good than any one else would give them, and he gives it them in their own name. They have as much as they like of all that is good for them. But if, not the present happiness of the greatest number, but *their future elevation*, be, as it is, the true aim and end of Government, our estimate of the Empire will be strangely altered. It is an admirable Government for present and coarse purposes, but a detestable Government for future and refined purposes.

In the first place, it stops the *teaching apparatus;* it stops the effectual inculcation of important thought upon the mass of mankind. All other mental effort but this, the Empire not only permits, but encourages. The high intellect of Paris is as active, as well represented, as that of London, and it is even more keen. Intellect still gives there, and has always given, a distinctive position. To be a *Membre de l'Institut* is a recognised place in France; but in London, it is an ambiguous distinction to be a "clever fellow". The higher kinds of thought are better discussed in Parisian society than in London society, and better argued in the *Revue des Deux Mondes* than in any English periodical. The speculative thought of France has not been killed by the Empire; it is as quick, as rigorous, as keen as ever. But though still alive, it is no longer powerful; it cannot teach the mass. The *Revue* is permitted, but newspapers—effectual newspapers—are forbidden. A real course of free lectures on popular subjects would be impossible in Paris. *Agitation* is forbidden, and it is agitation, and agitation alone, which teaches. The crude mass of men bear easily philosophical treatises, refined articles, elegant literature; there are but two instruments penetrative enough to reach their opaque minds—the newspaper article and the popular speech, and both of these are forbidden.

In London the reverse is true. We may say that only the loudest sort of expression is permitted to attain its due effect. The popular organs of literature so fill men's minds with incomplete thoughts that deliberate treatment, that careful inquiry, that quiet thought, have no hearing. People are so deafened with the loud reiteration of many half-truths, that they have neither curiosity nor energy for elaborate investigation. The very word "elaborate" is become a reproach; elaboration produces something which the mass of men do not like, because it is above them,—which is tiresome, because it needs industry,—difficult, because it wants attention,—complicated, because it is true. On the whole, perhaps, English thought has rarely been so unfinished, so piecemeal, so *ragged* as it is now. We have so many little discussions, that we get no full discussion; we eat so many sandwiches, that we spoil our dinner. And on the Continent, accordingly, the speculative thought of England is despised. It is believed to be meagre, uncultivated, and immature. We have only a single compensation. Our thought may be poor and rough and fragmentary, but it is effectual. With our newspapers and our speeches—with our clamorous multitudes of indifferent tongues—we beat the ideas of the few into the minds of the many. The head of France is a better head than ours, but it does not move her limbs. The head of England is in comparison a coarse and crude thing, but rules her various frame and regulates her whole life.

France, *as it is*, may be happier because of the Empire, but France *in the future* will be more ignorant because of the Empire. The daily play of the higher mind upon the lower mind is arrested. The present Government has given an instalment of free-trade, but it could not endure an agitation for free-trade. A democratic despotism is like a theocracy; it assumes its own correctness. It says: "I am the representative of the people; I am here because I know what they wish, because I know what they should have". As Cavaignac once said: "A Government which permits its principles to be questioned is a lost Government". All popular discussion whatever which aspires to *teach* the Government is radically at issue with the hypothesis of the Empire. It says that the Cæsar, the omniscient representative, is a mistaken representative, that he is not fit to be Cæsar.

The deterioration of the future is one inseparable defect of the imperial organisation, but it is not the only one,—for the moment, it is not the greatest. The greatest is the corruption of the present. A greater burden is imposed by it upon human nature than human nature will bear. Everything requires the support, aid, countenance of the central Government, and yet that Government is expected to keep itself pure. Concessions of railways, concessions of the privilege of limited liability,—on a hundred subjects, legal permission, administrative help, are necessary to money-making. You concentrate upon a small body of leading official men the power of making men's fortunes, and it is simple to believe they will not make their own fortunes. The very principle of the system is to concentrate power, and power is money. Sir Robert Walpole used to say, "No honest man could be a 'Minister' "; and in France the temptations would conquer all men's honesty. The system requires angels to work it, and perhaps it has not been so fortunate as to find angels. The nod of a minister on the Bourse is a fortune, and somehow or other ministers make fortunes. The Bourse of Paris is still so small, that a leading capitalist may produce a great impression on it, and a leading capitalist working with a great minister, a vast impression. Accordingly, all that goes with sudden wealth; all that follows from the misuse of the two temptations of civilisation, money and women, is concentrated round the Imperial court. The Emperor would cure much of it if he could, but what can he do? They say he has said that he will not change his men. He will not substitute fleas that are hungry for fleas which at least are partially satisfied. He is right. The defect belongs to the system, not to these men; an enormous concentration of power in an industrial system ensures an accumulation of pecuniary temptation.

These are the two main disadvantages which France suffers from her present Government; the greater part of the price which she has to pay for her present happiness. She endures the daily presence of an efficient immorality; she sacrifices the educating apparatus which would elevate Frenchmen yet to be born. But these two disadvantages are not the only ones.

France gains the material present, but she does not gain the material future. All that secures present industry, her Government confers; in whatever needs confidence in the future she is powerless. *Credit* in France, to an Englishman's eye, has almost to be created. The *country* deposits in the Bank of France are only £1,000,000 sterling; that bank has fifty-nine branches, is immeasurably the greatest country bank in France. All discussions on the currency come back to the *cours forcé*, to the inevitable necessity of making inconvertible notes an irrefusable tender during a revolution. If you propose the simplest operations of credit to a French banker, he says: "You do not remember 1848; I do". And what is the answer? The present Government avowedly depends on, is ostentatiously concentrated in, the existing Cæsar. Its existence depends on the permanent occupation of the Tuileries by an extraordinary man. The democratic despot—the representative despot—must have the sagacity to divine the people's will and the sagacity to execute it. What is the likelihood that these will be hereditary? Can they be expected in the next heirs—a child for Emperor, and a woman for Regent? The present happiness of France is happiness on a short life-lease; it may end with the life of a man who is not young, who has not spared himself, who has always thought, who has always *lived*.

Such are the characteristics of the Empire as it is. Such is the nature of Cæsar's Government as we know it at the present. We scarcely expect that even the singular ability of Napoleon III will be able to modify, by a historical retrospect, the painful impressions left by actual contact with a living reality.

THE EMPEROR NAPOLEON*

(1873)

The death of the Emperor Napoleon throws a flood of light upon his later life. It was in 1868 that he first began perceptibly to lose confidence in himself, to shrink from the responsibility of his own power, and to desire if means might be found to transmute his Cæsarism into Constitutional Monarchy. Observers imagined that he was alarmed by the progress of Prussia, and the foreseen necessity of embarking on a new and a great campaign; and no doubt the success of Prince Bismarck's policy did weigh upon his mind and disturb his judgment, but as is now perceived, there was another cause. He had been attacked by a malady, which, besides threatening the constitution, exerts a singular power over the mind, frequently depriving it of nervous strength, of energy, and of the capacity of resolution. It was as a victim to incipient stone that the Emperor formed the Ollivier Ministry and his new plan of Government, and many of his delays, hesitations, and vacillations, together with the febrile irritability with which he pressed forward his idea of a new plebiscite, may be attributed to the growing, though secret, influence of his malady. Under its influence he ceased to be able to examine into details, lost his confidence in old friends, and began to indulge in the despondency which sent him in 1870 to the field a man beaten in advance. He lost the inclination to take the trouble to select new men who had become indispensable, and to bear with men who had independent opinions, or opinions hostile to his own. When during the campaign his exertions increased his complaint, he had no longer the energy to direct; and when at Sedan a tremendous effort might have saved him, he had not the physical power to

---

* This article was first published in *The Economist* for January 11, 1873, Volume XXXI, pages 31–32.

make it, or even to entertain strongly the idea of making it. His later failures were in fact the results of his physical condition, or at all events so far the results of it, that it is impossible to form a just conception of the degree to which his original powers had been impaired.

In spite of his failure, and of the stream of contemporary thought, which is greatly influenced by the misfortunes that failure brought on France, we believe those powers to have been very considerable. Napoleon the Third, though not a great administrator—a function for which he was too indolent—was perhaps the most reflective and *in*sighted, not far-sighted, of the modern statesmen of France. He perceived years before other men the spell which the name of his uncle threw over the Frenchmen who had forgotten the disasters of 1815. He comprehended years before other men that the peasantry were the governing body, and would, if secured in their properties, adhere firmly to any strong Executive. He understood the latent power existing in the idea of nationalities years before old diplomatists could see in it anything but a dream. He was aware of the resources which might be developed by a Free-trade policy before a single politician in France had realised the first principles of economic finance. Alone among French politicians he contrived to conciliate the Papacy, or rather to master it, without breaking with the Republicans, and alone among Frenchmen he ventured to declare that England was the best ally France could have. Whenever his brain could work freely without necessity for previous labour he was a clear-sighted statesman, and it was only when a subject had to be learned up, like the condition of the Northern States of the Union or the organisation of Prussia, that his mental power became useless or even deceptive. We are by no means convinced that had he not gone to war his new Constitution would have failed, for it would have given France her freedom, and yet allowed, through the plebiscite, of the occasional revolutions which France from time to time will always demand. A new generation of men would have come forward, and would have exercised the power which the Emperor, pressed by pain, by despondency, and by indolence, no longer desired to wield. He had perceived long before his great adherents that Frenchmen were tired of compression, and the violence of the expansion was due in great measure to his decaying energy and resolution. Up to the day of his death he could still be resolved, but it was only in the passive way—the way possible to a man not required to do anything but sit quietly in an arm-chair and weigh advice. The effect of his bodily health is an argument to the discredit not the credit of personal government, but it must be considered in any just estimate of the Emperor's mental power. We do not expect from M. Thiers the pliability of a young man, nor is it fair to expect from a middle-aged Emperor, tortured with the stone, the serene reflectiveness of a political philosopher.

It is too early yet to discuss frankly the character of the Emperor, but as we have indicated the greatest of his mental powers—cool and broad political insight—we may also indicate the greatest of his mental defects as a politician. He had, we think, an incapability, almost beyond precedent, of securing competent agents. He never discovered a great soldier. He never found out a great statesman. He never secured a great financier. Only two of his agents—M. de Morny and M. Pietri —can be pronounced first-rate men of any kind, and the mass of them could hardly be classed as fourth-rate or fifth-rate men. This was the more remarkable because he himself was not unpleasant to his people, not capricious, not exacting, not disposed to change; and as France is full of able men only too anxious to serve, it must have been due to some want in his own mind—a want which it is by no means easy to understand. Mere want of insight into individual character does not explain the failure, for that would leave promotion open to everybody, and consequently leave to the able all their chances unimpaired. Mere indolence does not explain it, for amidst the 500,000 officials employed in France it does not take very much trouble to pick out a few strong men; and mere carelessness does not explain it, for the Emperor was well aware how badly he was sometimes served. It is difficult, considering the wealth of intellect in France, to doubt that the Emperor had the foible of men whose position is slightly uncertain, that he was jealous of very able persons, particularly if they were statesmen; regarded all such as his uncle regarded Moreau—as possible rivals and successors. Such men are usually independent, and he wanted his agents to obey. Such men in France argue well, and the Emperor was not good at debate either in public or private. Such men above all, if Frenchmen, are anxious to make their personality felt, and the Emperor could not bear that any personality should be felt except his own, lest it should attract the

regard of a population accustomed to raise its favourites to
the top. It was this feeling which induced him twice to accompany his armies, though he knew he was no soldier, and
so secure that no general should obtain the suffrages of the
army. It was this feeling which made him close up so many
political careers, till it became nearly impossible for an able
man in France to manifest his ability, and this feeling which
induced him to prefer mere red-tapists in the War Department, where he never but once had a first-rate man, Mar-
shal Niel, who was practically nominated by the army. Above
all it was this feeling, greatly exasperated by disease, which
induced him to underrate his own position, and doubt
whether without victory he could retain his hold on France.
There is not a doubt that, if he had remained quiet, the
peasantry and the army would have remained true to him;
but he could not with his morbid sense of insecurity, irritated
to madness by disease, believe the truth, and therefore he
fell. We shall, as time goes on and memoirs appear, know
much more of Napoleon III than we do now, but we believe, when all is known, the world will decide that his grand
merit as a politician was a certain clearness of insight, and
that his grand defect was self-distrust, leading to jealous impatience of capacities unlike or superior to his own. To declare him a great man may be impossible in the face of his
failures, but to declare him a small one is ridiculous. Small
men dying in exile do not leave wide gaps in the European
political horizon.

WHY AN ENGLISH LIBERAL
MAY LOOK WITHOUT DISAPPROVAL
ON THE PROGRESS OF IMPERIALISM
IN FRANCE*

(1874)

We last week endeavoured to explain why Imperialism was making much progress in France, and why, in our judgment, it was likely to make very much more. We now wish to explain why we think that this progress is by no means the grave misfortune which many Liberals believe it to be, but, on the contrary, is an improvement in the present politics of France, and a thing to be glad of in the present sad state of that country.

The French have a neat mode of explaining this when they say that France is fit for a consultative, but not yet fit for a representative Government. The distinction is this: In a consultative Government the first power is the person at the head of the executive. The English Constitution was in that state in the Tudor times. The monarch was then the predominant authority in the realm. King Henry or Queen Elizabeth convened a Parliament; consulted it; regarded or disregarded its advice, not, of course, entirely, but still very much according to his or her own will and pleasure. There were, doubtless, many things which the King could not do without Parliamentary authority; he could not, as we know, impose new taxes or make new laws; but these were rather additional and extraordinary than common and necessary requirements. The ordinary revenue was enough for ordinary times; the old laws did well enough for an age which would hardly have understood, and would certainly have disliked

* This article was first published in The Economist for June 6, 1874, Volume XXXII, pages 681–83.

the idea of constantly changing them. In the ordinary business and daily *rule* of the country the monarch was supreme.
In a Parliamentary Government, on the other hand, as we
daily see, the case is reversed. The Assembly, which in the
consultative Government is the minor, is here the supreme
authority. It is the Parliament which settles all the policy of
the State, which chooses the ministers, which dismisses them,
which incessantly watches that they do all which it enjoins,
and do nothing which it does not approve. The hereditary
sovereign, though in constitutional monarchies he is still permitted to exist, and is still allowed to be first, exists as a relic,
and is first only in name and dignity; the ruling influence
has passed to other hands.

We are not blind to the defects of Parliamentary Government; we are constantly experiencing them, and it is difficult
at times not to exaggerate them. But, nevertheless, a fair
judge will, we are sure, decide that it is a better Government
than the consultative. A Parliamentary Government is essentially a Government by discussion; by constant speaking and
writing a public opinion is formed which decides on all action
and all policy. This opinion is by no means always right, it is
often very wrong; but on familiar matters it has a great average of correctness; and the effort of forming it at first, and
the habit of watching whether it turns out right at last, have
been, and are, the best modes of training nations not only in
political thought, but in all thought. But in consultative
Governments there is no similar process—discussion can only
suggest, and opinion only advise. It is the supreme, and, perhaps, self-willed monarch, who must determine at last. The
nation feels no responsibility, for it does not take the decision; it will learn little from watching whether it turns out
well or ill, for it will always think that it would have avoided
the error if things go ill, and secured the success if things
go well. As it was not consulted, it will always say, and always believe, that if it had been consulted it would have
been right.

Parliamentary Government also brings to the supremacy
of the State an unrivalled average of continued ability. No
doubt it excludes the most peculiar and original understandings; a Bismarck or Richelieu will not consent to ask leave for
all he does, and often would not get leave if he did ask. Such
dominating wills and far-seeing minds are not to be found
among Parliamentary statesmen; the nature of their trade

forbids it. But, on the other hand, Parliamentary Government keeps out all the fools, for a Parliamentary Premier works in the face of day, and utter incapacity would be dismissed in an instant; and it secures an unbroken series of capable men, now rising to a Pitt or Peel, now descending to a Liverpool or Perceval, always surpassing ordinary men in ability, and always presentable in great affairs. To this constant supply of equable excellence consultative Governments have nothing analogous. The hereditary monarch upon whom all depends is an "accident." He may be a sage, or he may be a simpleton or an idiot. All that can be said is that in a restless nation and in stirring times only a man of considerable ability will be able to keep the lead; on the whole, national selection will maintain a high standard; strong kings only will long reign, because weak ones will be unable to cope with insurrection and civil war. But then this is a very costly process. History shows that you will pretty generally get a good ruler if you choose him by a fair fight, but the evils of the conflict are obvious and endless. And as in no other way can consultative Government secure an able ruler, it is plainly in that respect far inferior to Parliamentary Government, even though Parliamentary Government is not perfect.

It is an excellence which follows from those we have mentioned that a Parliamentary Government can change its policy and can suit itself to times far better than a consultative. If a particular kind of policy is wanted, you choose a Premier suited to that kind. If Lord Aberdeen is too pacific for a war policy, you put in a Palmerston; if a Gladstone Government is too innovating for the temper of the time, you turn it out and substitute our present Government. But in a consultative Government, if the fixed head who at last rules is pacific, the policy of the State is, without appeal, pacific; if his temper is innovating, more or less of innovation there is sure to be. Of the two machines, the Parliamentary is the more delicate and serviceable, for it can shift its power whenever it has to change its work.

If, therefore, a nation has a choice between the two forms of Government, we are satisfied that it would prefer the Parliamentary. But has France really such a choice? We own that we much doubt it. Parliamentary Government is not a thing which always succeeds in the world; on the contrary, the lesson of experience is that it often fails, and seldom answers, and this because the necessary combination of elements is rare and complex.

First, Parliamentary Government requires that a nation should have *nerve* to endure incessant discussion and frequent change of rulers. This discussion is its life, and these changes are its sure result. But much present evidence and much past goes to prove that France does not possess this nerve. She now is, as we showed last week at length, anxious for one thing above all others, and that one is fixity. She wants, above all things, to see *who* is to be her ruler; to see it for certain; and to be able to make sure the rule will last for some time—long enough to support industry and confirm credit. But this is exactly what Parliamentary Government will not give to her. It puts the choice of rulers in an assembly, and assemblies are in all countries unstable and fickle—in France they are particularly so. Part of the good of Parliamentary Government is the easy change of rulers, and exactly for that reason France fears it. She does not want an easy change of rulers; on the contrary, she wants to make such changes difficult. To offer her, therefore, this result of Parliamentary Government—specially good and specially characteristic as it is—is to offer her that which she would, above all things, shun and shrink from.

No doubt in countries where Parliamentary Government has been long established, and where it is prized and understood, a change of Ministry tries no nerve and needs no courage. In England for the most part it does not change consols* an eighth. Especially where, as here, there is a Constitutional Monarch behind the Ministry, to preserve at least an appearance of stability, and to disguise from the many the magnitude of the event, no one need fear its consequences. Human life and industry are sure to continue pretty much unchanged. But in France there is no such tradition of Parliament, and no such fixed royal person. To the mind of a common Frenchman a change of Ministry is a portentous event; it amounts to much and it threatens more. He, more than anything else, wishes for a stable Government, and Parliamentary Government seems to him more than any other unstable.

Unquestionably also there are races to whom this would not matter so much, and among whom it would be, in com-

* Consols are government stock.—Ed.

parison, easy to found *de novo* a Parliamentary Government. But the French are not one of those races; they are naturally excitable, uncontrollable, and sensitive to risk; they have been so used to political misfortune that they now are scared at any shadow. There are generally two simultaneous, but contrary, excitements; one of the revolutionist, who wants to revive the *Commune*; the other of the peasant or the shopkeeper, who fears the Commune. And the passion of each tends to intensify the passion of the other. These frenzies—for on both sides they are often little better—work on the most inflammable and least stoical of national characters. There is no soil so unsuitable to Parliamentary Government.

This difficulty lies in the character of the nation, but there is a second in the character of its Parliaments. They have always been—at least, since there was universal suffrage—unruly and excitable past English belief. The Chamber is split into parties who often will not hear one another, who never heed one another, who unite only to hate those who would mediate between them. Such assemblies cannot choose a good Ministry, and would not keep one if they had chosen it. The Parliaments of Louis Philippe, no doubt, belong to a different type, but they were elected by a suffrage now impossible, and cemented by means which could not be revived. The characteristics of a good Parliament are a disposition to hear, a willingness to compromise, and a tendency to cohere; and any French Parliament in our time is more likely to be remarkable for the absence than for the possession of these qualities.

There is, too, as we last week explained, a third difficulty in the present French circumstances. We have been arguing as if the French had to work a Parliamentary Government; but it has in fact to do besides something much more difficult, it has to make that Government. The first step in the undertaking is the election of a "Constituent" Assembly, and it is a step of which France has great experience. There have been many such since 1789, and none have been successful, for the work of all of them has passed away. For a composite chamber of discordant factions to make a free constitution both strong enough and well adjusted enough for such a country as France, would indeed be close on a political miracle.

Such being the difficulty in France of making a Parliamentary Government, she of necessity falls back on the older modes of governing great nations, in which the Monarchial

executive is the first and the strongest force, and in which the
Parliamentary Government is the weaker and the inferior.
The Empire is plainly the Government of this kind which is
most likely to be popular in France, and most likely to be
strong; perhaps it is the one strong Government of this sort
or of any sort which is now possible; at any rate, it is the
Government which, as far as we can at present see, has by
far the best prospect of strength. And, therefore, it is we
think not unreasonable and not inconsistent with firm allegiance to Parliamentary Government, where Parliamentary
Government is possible, to look on the rapid revival of Imperialism in France without dismay and even with satisfaction.

INDEX